CREDIT MANAGEMENT

CREDIT

MANAGEMENT

By

GEORGE N. CHRISTIE, PH.D.
Senior Vice President and Director of Research
Credit Research Foundation Inc.

and

ALBERT E. BRACUTI, M.B.A.
Associate Director of Research
Credit Research Foundation Inc.

CREDIT RESEARCH FOUNDATION INC.
Lake Success, New York

FOREWORD

An outstanding phenomenon of business growth since the end of World War II is the role business credit has played in our expanding economy. Credit executives, charged with the commitment of corporate resources into accounts receivable, have seen their functions become more complicated as they assume greater responsibility for sales and profit strategies.

Credit provides the underlying financing that makes it possible for business to move materials and provide services to its customers. In rough figures, business credit is nearly twice as large as short-term loans made by banks to their commercial and industrial customers. Without it, the economy would very quickly come to a standstill.

The expanded responsibilities of credit executives have imposed a need on them to utilize the latest management principles and financial techniques in administering their receivables portfolios. While literature on these skills is available in separate sources, the trustees of the Credit Research Foundation felt it was time for this knowledge to be collected in one document, oriented to the goals of credit management. The directors of the National Association of Credit Management gave the Foundation their wholehearted support and cooperation in this undertaking.

The principal authors of this book are both staff members of the Foundation: Dr. George N. Christie is senior vice president and director of research; Albert E. Bracuti is associate director of research. Their task was made much easier by the dedicated efforts of many people, all interested in credit management and all seeking to provide a means for its practitioners to improve their decisionmaking capabilities.

Peter C. Peasley, Ph.D.
Executive Vice President
Credit Research Foundation Inc.

PREFACE

Modern-day credit executives regard accounts receivable as a corporate investment lodged in a portfolio that must be managed efficiently. While still charged with controlling the funds advanced to customers through sales, they have an expanded range of responsibilities that lean heavily upon techniques of asset management. The tradeoff between accepting risk and the opportunity to generate profits has become a central theme in their decisionmaking skill and everyday activity.

This book gives the principles of credit management, then incorporates the more advanced financial and analytical techniques, to present a convenient store of knowledge in the field. It is intended as a detailed reference source for credit executives who have a working acquaintance of finance, accounting, and economics; and can use the book to improve their skills in specific topics without being inundated by extraneous detail. It is also exceptionally well-suited for use as a textbook by those who will be studying credit and financial analysis topics in a classroom atmosphere. With an instructor to aid them on particular points, they can use the book to gain accurate, up-to-date knowledge on credit principles, practices, and advanced analytical techniques.

The material has been arranged into nine parts, each dealing with a broad segment of credit management. The first two cover the responsibilities of the credit executive and the role of the credit department in the business structure. The third elaborates upon the basic aspects of credit decisionmaking. Parts four and five treat the nonfinancial and financial elements that are required in order to make a proper decision. Part six provides a detailed discussion of the various trade and nontrade financing terms used in the credit field. The seventh part covers some major techniques of receivables portfolio management, including evaluation of the status of accounts and reporting to top management. The eighth part is devoted to the handling of distressed debtors. The final one focuses on export transactions.

The parts are not mutually exclusive, since topics covered in one part may be relevant to material covered in others. For example, the impact of financial analysis is touched upon under credit decisionmaking but is discussed at length in the part dealing with financial analysis. The same approach is used in the separate chapters which make up the parts of the book. A topic may be highlighted in a particular chapter but, to minimize redundancy, is treated only briefly in other chapters to give a balanced presentation.

No undertaking of this magnitude can be completed without the unselfish contributions of literally scores of people who are particularly knowledgeable in certain phases of our broad field. Those whose comments and suggestions were particularly helpful are listed on the following pages, and we here take the opportunity to thank them for their time, effort, knowledge, and advice during the preparation of the book.

From that list, we wish to recognize a few whose help was crucial to the completion of the work. Bernard Kopel provided valuable material for Chapters 4 and 5; William M. Stevens submitted a manuscript used to develop a significant portion of Chapter 10; George E. Stanley and Allan J. Donald made available their firm's credit department manual from which Chapter 12 was prepared; Messrs. Dutrow, Giblin, Morse, Simms, and Thomas, as members of the Insurance Advisory Council, wrote Chapter 18; Daniel W. Curtiss prepared a major section of Chapter 36; and Steve L. Chen gave us the material used to write Chapter 37.

Lester Nelson, Esq., reviewed the entire manuscript and made many perceptive and helpful comments that improved the presentation. The reading committee appointed to review the manuscript was made up of William H. Bassett, Jr., C. Wm. Bruder, O. D. Glaus, Jr., J. Robert Howells, and Bryce T. Wilson; their comments helped retain the practical nature of the book.

We owe a debt of thanks to the staff of the Foundation for their earnest cooperation at all stages of this book. Joan Leykum typed the drafts. Mary Casey, Catherine Greene, and Carmen Mesis took on additional duties so this work could be accomplished. Ira Mermer, Peter P. Peasley, Jr., and Eugene T. Waters allowed us to test our ideas and views on them, and were always ready with generous and helpful comments. Most of all, Dr. Peter C. Peasley gave us his strong support and encouragement for our task.

Lake Success, NY   George N. Christie
June 1981   Albert E. Bracuti

CONTRIBUTORS

Alban, J. A., Air Products and Chemicals Inc.
Alexander, A. J., Standard Oil Company of California
Auchterlonie, Thomas A., PPG Industries Inc.
Bassett, William H., Jr., Reynolds Metals Company
Bloodgood, Alan L., Morgan Guaranty Trust Company of New York
Bruder, C. Wm., Steelcase Inc.
Bryan, William H., Alton Box Board Company
Burke, John E., The Nestle Company Inc.
Chen, Steve L., Bank of America NA
Cummins, Victor E., Mead Corporation
Curtiss, Daniel W., Honeywell Inc.
DeForge, Stanley M., Dun & Bradstreet Inc.
Desautels, Marcel A., Creditel of Canada Limited
DeVan, Robert P., Hunt-Wesson Foods Inc.
Dixon, Henry C., Eastman Kodak Company
Donald, Allan J., Aluminum Company of America
Donovan, Charles J., Union Camp Corporation
Dundore, Richard F., Morgan Guaranty Trust Company of New York
Dutrow, Gordon P., Nevamar Corporation
Elkin, Maxine, The Robert Morris Associates
Feeney, Harry I., Union Carbide Corporation
Fulmer, Robert J., Armstrong World Industries Inc.
Giblin, John, Liberty Mutual Insurance Company
Glaus, O. D., Jr., GENESCO Inc.
Gliozza, G. L., Inmont Corporation
Gomling, H. L., Lyon Furniture Mercantile Agency
Goodwin, Robert D., National Association of Credit Management
Howells, J. Robert, PPG Industries Inc.
Hunt, Percy C., Cannon Mills Inc.
Hunt, Walter S., Union Carbide Corporation

Kelly, James J., Lever Brothers Company
Kollath, Frank C., The Sherwin-Williams Company
Kopel, Bernard, The First National Bank of Boston
Landsberg, F. John, Chemical Bank
Minard, Francis J., Lincoln Drug Company
Morey, Robert A., National Association of Credit Management-
  Oregon Inc.
Morrison, John J., Pfizer Inc.
Morse, B. H., Allstate Insurance Company
Nelson, Lester, J. D., LL.M., Miller, Montgomery, Sogi & Brady, P. C.
Oakley, Richard H., Honeywell Inc.
Owens, Norman G., Elesco Factors, a division of Levi Strauss & Co.
Pertain, Jack, Pfizer Inc.
Posner, Richard, Credit Exchange Inc.
Raisbeck, Robert F., Fisher-Price Toys, division of the Quaker Oats
  Company
Redding, Harold T., Dun & Bradstreet Inc.
Simms, J. E., American Credit Indemnity Company of New York
Sinnickson, Lloyd, American Cyanamid Company
Stanley, George E., Aluminum Company of America
Stevens, William M., General Electric Company
Stoll, Donald R., Rohm & Haas Company
Thomas, E. Aubrey, Ford and Thomas Inc.
Thompson, N. A., Procter & Gamble Distributing Company
Wey, Frank W., AMAX Inc.
Wilson, Bryce T., National Association of Credit Management, Western
  Washington-Alaska
Witthoeft, George, National Credit Office

CONTENTS

Illustrations xix

PART I. Fundamental Aspects of Credit Management 1

1. Evolution of Credit 3
Types of Early Credit. Role of the New World. Development of New Credit
Facilities.

2. Role of Credit Associations 8
National Association of Credit Management: *Early History of NACM. Organi-
zation. Activities.* Credit Research Foundation Inc.: *Organization. Activities.*
Robert Morris Associates. Creditel of Canada Limited.

3. Role of Credit in the Business World 15
Components of Credit. Credit Sales Versus Cash Sales. Public Credit. Private
Credit: *Bank Credit. Investment Credit. Agricultural Credit. Consumer Credit.
Business Credit.* Bank Credit Versus Business Credit: *Type of Resource. Amounts
Involved. Length of Terms. Depth of Analysis.*

4. Basis for Dynamic Credit Management 24
Role of Credit in Financial Management. Outline of the Flow of Credit. Man-
agement Responsibilities of the Credit Function: *Setting Objectives. Planning.
Organizing. Controlling.* Goals of Dynamic Credit Management.

5. Overview of the Credit Department 34
General Policymaking and Control: *Place in the Firm. Controlling and Evaluating
the Credit Function.* Day-to-Day Administration: *Credit Approval Process. Account Establishment. Order Processing. Accounts Receivable Administration. Collections and Adjustments. Control and Followthrough.* Counseling Services: *Customer
Counseling. Counseling Within the Company.*

PART II. Organizational Aspects of Credit Management . . . 49

6. Organization of the Credit Department 51
Centralization and Decentralization: *General Observations. Important Considerations.* Types of Credit Organization: *Controlled and Administered at a Principal
Office. Decentralized Offices with Control at a Principal Office. Decentralized Offices
with Staff at Principal Office. General Considerations.*

7. Staffing the Credit Department 61
Importance of the Job Description. Developing a Job Description: *Essential
Elements Defined. Analyzing the Position.* Typical Job Descriptions: *Top-Level
Chief Credit Executive. Middle-Level Chief Credit Executive. Credit Manager. Credit
Analyst.* Importance of the Job Specification: *Relation to Job Description. Relation
to Training Programs. Job Qualifications.* Appraisal of Personnel: *Performance
Evaluation. Timing of Promotions and Pay Increases.*

8. Training for Credit Management   76

Need for Credit Training: *Preparation for Credit Training. Selection of Personnel.*
Considerations in a Sound Program: *Objectives. Basic Requirements. Management
Support. Defining the Responsibilities.* Orientation. On-the-Job Training. In-
House Training: *Credit Conference. Observation Tours. Credit Library. Job Rotation
Program. Employee Enhancement.* Continuing Education: *Local Activities. National
Institute of Credit. Graduate School of Credit and Financial Management. Credit
Management Workshops. Mid-Career School. University Programs. Other Programs.*
Credit Training in the Small Department.

9. Credit Department Systems and Procedures   90

Construction of a Credit File. Credit Control Systems and Procedures: *Single
Order Entry Point. Multiple Order Entry Points.* Credit Filing Systems: *Department Filing System. Coding Information. Manual Filing Systems. EDP Storage Devices.* Followup Systems: *Revision of Credit Files. Identifying Delinquent Accounts.
Collection Followup.* Handling Accounts Receivable: *Loose-Leaf Ledger. Open Invoice File. Machine Bookkeeping. Punched Card Accounting. Adapting the Computer
to Credit and Accounts Receivable.*

10. Automated Credit and Accounts Receivable Systems. . . . 102

On-Line Systems: *On-Line System Within a Batch Mode. On-Line, Real-Time System.* Order Entry and Billing Systems: *System Considerations. Order Credit Approval.* Methods of Gathering Cash: *Lockbox Banks. Courier Pickup System.
Preauthorized Debit System. Hand-Carry Method.* Payment Application: *Applying
Payment Using MICR. Applying Payment Using a Turnaround Document. Applying
Payment Using a CRT Terminal.* Generation of Reports. System Design Considerations: *User Oriented. Objectives. Usefulness to Sales Department. Gathering Information. Cost. Personnel. Other Tradeoffs.*

11. Credit Policy 112

Defining Credit Policy: *Policy and Objectives. Policy and Procedures. Policy and
Practice. Exceptions.* Establishing Credit Policy: *Factors Underlying Credit Policy.
Formulation of Credit Policy. Policy Should Be Written. An Example of Credit Policy.*
Implementing Credit Policy: *Communication of Policy. Assigning Responsibility.
Establishing Procedures. Applying Policy Under Varying Conditions. Factors Influenc-
ing Short-Term Policy Application.* Review of Credit Policy. Types of Credit
Policy: *Strict Analysis of Risk and Strict Collections. Strict Analysis of Risk with
Liberal Collections. Liberal Analysis of Risk and Vigorous Collection Effort. Liberal
Analysis of Risk and Liberal Collections.*

12. Credit Policy and Procedure Manual 128

Format. Maintenance. Indexing. Suggested Content.

PART III. Credit Decisionmaking and Collection Procedures . . 141

13. Credit Decisionmaking 143

Automating Credit Approval. Initial Orders: *Blanket Approval of Small Orders.
Approval Based on Agency Ratings. Nonroutine First Orders. Terms Other Than Open
Account.* Credit Lines: *Underlying Factors. Setting Credit Lines. Credit Lines for
Sales Department Use. Informing Customers of Credit Lines.* Reviewing the Credit
Line: *Periodic Review. Handling Orders Exceeding the Credit Line. Extraordinary
Credit Needs. Extended Terms. Unusual Information.* Decisions Based on Limited
Information. Marginal Business. Review of Credit Decisions: *Treatment of
Overdue Customers. Customer Good Will. Treatment of Improving Accounts. Chang-
ing Business Conditions.*

14. Collection Procedures 162

Principles of Collection: *Collect the Money. Systematic Followup. Get the Customer to Discuss the Situation. Preserve Good Will.* Collection Responsibility: *Credit Department. Special Collection Personnel. Accounts Receivable Department. Sales Personnel. Other Personnel.* Collection Effort: *Statements of Account. Early Stages of Collection. Intermediate Stages of Collection. Final Stages of Collection. Model Collection Letters.* Collection Tools and Techniques: *Postdated Checks. Promissory Notes.* Common Collection Problems: *Unearned Cash Discounts. Customer Deductions. New Orders from Overdue Accounts. N.S.F. Checks.* Special Collection Efforts: *When Special Efforts Begin. Collection by Third Parties.* Legal Aspects of Collection Correspondence: *Methods of Collection Subject to Libel. Extortion.*

PART IV. Credit Investigation 191

15. Credit Information 193

Confidential Nature of Credit Information. Legal Aspects of the Exchange of Credit Information: *Conspiracy. Libel and Slander.* Sales Requests for Credit Information. Customer-Supplied Information: *Regulation B, Equal Credit Opportunity Act. Information Required. Direct Correspondence. Personal Interview. Telephone Contacts.* Bank Information: *Statement of Principles for the Exchange of Credit Information. Ways To Make a Bank Investigation. Bank Check Information. Caveats on Requesting Credit Information from Banks.* Trade Information: *Credit Interchange Bureaus. Industry Credit Groups. Credit Reporting Agencies. Direct Interchange.* Other Sources of Credit Information: *Daily Notification Lists. Attorneys. Government Sources. Miscellaneous Sources.*

16. Agency Sources of Information 224

Types of Agencies. Ordering Agency Reports. Dun & Bradstreet Inc.: *The Dun & Bradstreet Business Information Report. The Dun & Bradstreet Rating. The Dun & Bradstreet Reference Book.* National Credit Office: *Activities. NCO Specialized Credit Report.* Lyon Furniture Mercantile Agency: *Lyon Credit Report. Ratings and Other Codes. Lyon Red Book. National Weekly Interchange of Trade Experience.* Credit Exchange Inc.: *Credit Report. Credit Recommendation Service. Credit Exchange Code.* NACM Business Credit Information System: *NACM Business Credit Report. Credit Interchange Reports.*

17. Legal Forms of Business Organization from a Creditor's Viewpoint 263

Creditor's Interest in Legal Composition. Proprietorship: *Management. Continuity. Capital. Liability.* Partnership: *Continuity. Capital. Liability.* Corporation: *Certificate of Incorporation. Capital Stock. Continuity. Capital. Liability.* Subchapter S (Pseudo) Corporation: *Continuity. Capital. Liability.* Estates: *Continuity. Capital. Liability.* Common Law Trusts: *Continuity. Capital. Liability.* Joint Ventures: *Continuity. Capital. Liability.* Cooperative Societies. Not-for-Profit Organizations. Other Features of Organization: *Affiliated Interests. Changes in Legal Composition. Parent-Subsidiary Relationships. Operating Divisions. Mergers or Consolidations. Purchase of Assets.*

18. Credit and Business Insurance 284

Role of Business Insurance: *Background. Insurance and the Creditor. Mandatory Insurance. Contract and Voluntary Insurance. Prerequisites of Insurance. Principles of Insurance. Insurance Agreements.* Property Insurance: *Fire and Extended Coverage Insurance. Business Interruption Insurance. Burglary and Theft Insurance. Inland Marine Insurance. Ocean Marine Cargo Insurance. Data Processing Policy. Difference in Conditions Policy. Flood Insurance. Plate Glass Insurance.* Crime Insurance: *Fidelity Bonds. Additional Policy Coverage.* General Liability Insurance. Life Insurance. Credit Insurance: *Major Benefits of Credit Insurance. Elements of the Contract. Policy Coverage. Coinsurance. Primary Loss. Table of Ratings and Coverages. Policy Endorsements. Claim Settlement.* Credit Executive's Interest in Insurance Coverage.

19. Nonfinancial Analysis of a Business 302
The Four "Cs" of Credit: *Character. Capacity. Capital. Conditions of the Times.* Application of the Four "Cs" of Credit. *Background of the Principals and the Business. Influence of the Method of Operation and Industry Characteristics. Bank Investigations. Trade Investigations.*

PART V. Financial Analysis 321

20. Financial Statements Used in Credit Analysis 323
Scope of Credit Analysis. Types of Financial Statements: *Annual Statements. Interim Statements. Estimated Statements.* Significance of the Balance Sheet: *Assets. Liabilities. Net Worth.* Importance of the Statement of Income and Retained Earnings: *Sales. Cost of Goods Sold. Gross Profit. Expenses. Net Operating Income. Other Income and Expenses. Extraordinary Items. Federal Income Taxes. Net Income. Retained Earnings.* Statement of Changes in Financial Position: *Source and Application of Funds. Changes in Net Working Capital.* Consolidated Financial Statements. Combined Financial Statements. Pro Forma Financial Statements. Trial Balance. Spreading the Statements: *Balance Sheet Spread Sheet. Income Statement Spread Sheet. Condensed Forms. Adjustment of Items.*

21. Accounting Convention in Relation to Credit Analysis . . . 352
Role of the Auditor: *Types of Audit. Unaudited Statements. The Auditor's Certificate. Customary Schedules in Audit Reports. Notes to the Financial Statements. Responsibility for Financial Reporting.* Appraisal of Audit Reliability: *Specialization by Auditors. Frequency of Audit. Change in Auditor. Auditor-Client-Creditor Relationships.* Use of Financial Forms: *Financial Statement Design. False Financial Statements.*

22. Fundamentals of Financial Analysis 362
Internal Analysis: *Balance Sheet Ratios. Turnover Rates. Profit Ratios. Appraising the Use of Ratios.* Trend Analysis: *Balance Sheet Trends. Income Statement Trends.* Statement of Changes in Financial Position. Industry Standards: *Percentage Statements. Sources of Financial Statements Standards.*

23. Case Analysis 376
Internal Analysis: *Current Ratio. Quick Ratio. Inventory to Net Working Capital. Fixed Assets to Tangible Net Worth. Total Noncurrent Assets to Total Capitalization. Current Debt to Tangible Net Worth. Total Debt to Tangible Net Worth. Funded Debt to Net Working Capital. Net Sales to Tangible Net Worth. Net Sales to Total Assets. Net Sales to Net Working Capital. Net Sales to Inventory. Net Sales to Accounts Receivable. Gross Profit on Net Sales. Net Income on Net Sales. Net Operating Income on Net Sales. Net Income on Net Working Capital. Net Income on Tangible Net Worth.* Trend Analysis: *Accounts Receivable. Accounts Payable. Due Banks. Total Debt-Deferred. Retained Earnings. Balance Sheet Ratios. Turnover Rates. Profit Ratios. Souce and Application of Funds. Changes in Net Working Capital.* Overall Appraisal.

24. Additional Financial Analysis Techniques 387
Trial Balance Analysis: *Trial Balance Worksheet. Interpretation of Trial Balance Figures. Break-Even Inventory Analysis. Methods of Estimating Inventory. Evaluation of Trial Balance Analysis.* Analysis by Sales: *Elements of Sales. Procedure for*

Manufacturers. Procedure for Wholesalers and Retailers. Application of Analysis by Sales. Analysis by Sales Without Operating Statement Details. Evaluation of Analysis by Sales.

PART VI. Trade and Nontrade Financing 401

25. Terms of Sale 403
Role of Terms of Sale. Factors Influencing Terms of Sale: *Competition. Market and Product Characteristics.* Elements of Selling Terms: *Maturity. Cash Discount. Trade Discount. Anticipation. Late-Payment Service Charges.* Classification of Terms of Sale: *Terms Based on Invoice Date. Single Payment or Lumped Order Terms. Special Dating Terms. Cash Terms. Terms Other Than Open Account. Advances. Progress Payments. Contra Accounts. Commitments. Consignment.*

26. Negotiable Instruments 420
Essential Elements of a Negotiable Instrument: *Negotiability. Number of Parties. In Writing. Promise or Order To Pay. Sum Certain. Maturity Should Be Specified. Payment in Money. Consideration. Signature. Payee. Drawee.* Forms of Negotiable Instruments: *Promissory Note. Check. Certified Check. Cashier's or Treasurer's Check. Postdated Check. Draft (Bill of Exchange). Trade Acceptance. Banker's Acceptance. Sight Draft/Bill of Lading (SD/BL).* Transfer: *Negotiation. Assignment.* Holder in Due Course: *Conditions. Defenses. Consumer Credit Limitations.* Liabilities of the Parties: *Liability of the Maker. Liability of the Drawer. Liability of the Drawee. Liability of the Endorser. Liability of the Accommodation Party. Finality of Payment or Acceptance.* Notice of Dishonor. Protest.

27. Outside Financing 440
Factors: *Factoring Procedure. Cost of Factoring. Evidence of a Factoring Agreement. Questions to Ask.* Finance Companies: *Financing Procedure. Cost of Financing. Evidence of a Financing Arrangement. Questions to Ask.* Impact of Liens Under UCC. Term Loans: *Restrictive Covenants. Public and Private Placements.* Leasing: *Operating Leases. Finance Leases. Sale-Leaseback Arrangement.* Government Programs: *Small Business Administration. Small Business Investment Corporations.* Evaluation of Customers: *Liquidity of the Account. Liability. Preference. Dependence on Outside Financing.*

28. Security Devices 461
Guaranties. Subordinations. Real Estate Mortgages and Deeds of Trust. Personal Property Security Devices: *Liens. Pledges. Accounts Receivable Financing. Chattel Mortgages and Conditional Sales Contracts. Consignments. Trust Receipts. Warehouse Receipts and Bills of Lading.* Letters of Credit: *Letters of Credit Defined. Domestic Letters of Credit. Standby Letter of Credit.*

29. Credit Risk Under UCC 480
Secured Transactions Under Article 9: *Security Agreement. Classification of Goods. Perfecting the Security Agreement. Default. Credit Analysis of Secured Debtors.* Remedies Under Law of Sales: *Rejected Merchandise. Reclamation Clause.* Applicability of Bulk Transfer Law: *Notice and Disclosure. Creditor's Action.*

PART VII. Managing the Accounts Receivable Portfolio 491

30. Receivables Portfolio Evaluation 493
Cost of Capital: *Formulas. Component Costs of Capital. Overall Weighted Average Cost of Capital. Importance of Taking Offered Discounts.* Time Value of Funds: *Present Value. Future Value.* Capital Cost of Investment in Receivables: *Present Value of Future Receipts. Cost of Carrying Receivables. Effect of Discount Terms on*

Profit. Data Collection. *Class Sales. Average Receivables. Days Sales Outstanding. Class Proportions of Receivables Portfolio. Credit and Collection Expense and Bad-Debt Loss. Annual Cost of Capital for Receivables by Class. Allocation of Costs. Other Operating Data.* Profitability Analysis: *Total Cost of Receivables. Annual Service Cost Per Dollar of Receivables Carried. Operating Profit Margin$_k$. Return on Receivables. PV Analysis of Receivables Contribution to Profit.* Incremental Profitability. Analysis: *Adjusted Receivables Costs. Other Operating Data. Total Cost of Receivables. Annual Service Cost Per Dollar of Receivables Carried. Operating Profit Margin$_k$. Return on Receivables. Comparison of the Two Methods.* Expanding Sales to Marginal Accounts: *Simplified Analysis of Current Sales. Analyzing Projected Additional Marginal Sales.*

31. Cash Budgets and Other Financial Projections 525

Role of the Cash Budget: *Estimate of Cash Receipts. Estimate of Cash Disbursements.* Preparing a Cash Budget: *Data for Preparation of Cash Budget. Cash Receipts. Cash Disbursements. Bank Loans. Budget Using Collection Ratio Method.* Using the Budget for Control. Projected Statement of Income and Retained Earnings: *Preparing the Statement. Evaluation.* Projected Balance Sheet: *Preparing the Balance Sheet. Evaluation.* Projected Statement of Changes in Financial Position: *Source and Application of Funds. Changes in Net Working Capital.* Recapitulation.

32. Credit Department Reporting System 544

Elements of an Efficient Reporting System: *Responsibility for Preparing Reports. Steps in Planning and Preparation. Forms of Presentation. Report Format and Content. Distribution of Reports. Role of Feedback. Periodic Review and Appraisal of Reports.* Statistical Presentation of Financial Data: *Arithmetic Mean. Median and Quartiles. Mode. Range. Time Series. Ratios and Percentages. Comparing Summary Figures. Index Numbers. Composite Indexes. Moving Averages.* Graphic Analysis: *Use of Graphs in Analysis. Use of Index Numbers.*

33. Credit Management Reports 564

Aging of Accounts Receivable: *Conventional Aging of Accounts. Analysis by Risk Classification. Past-Due Accounts Receivable. Other Variations. Usefulness. Limitations.* Collections: *Collections as a Percentage of Accounts Receivable. Collections Compared to a Cash Forecast.* Days Sales Outstanding: *DSO. Last-In, First-Out Method. Optimum DSO.* Uncollectible Accounts: *Allowance for Uncollectibles. Writeoffs. Bad-Debt Analysis.* Accounts Receivable Management Reports: *Status Report. Acvitity Report.* Other Management Reports: *Accounts in Litigation or Under Court Jurisdiction. Customer Visits. Business Refused and Gained Due to Credit and Collection Reasons. New Business Leads to Sales. Annual Review of Operations.* Operating Criteria for Credit Departments: *Standard Measures. Budgetary Control.*

PART VIII. Handling Distressed Debtors 589

34. Out-of-Court Settlements 591

Symptoms of the Distressed Debtor. Voluntary Settlements: *Initiation of the Voluntary Settlement. Creditors' Committee. Creditors' Investigation. The Settlement Plan. Administration Costs. Execution of the Settlement.* Assignment for the Benefit of Creditors: *Common Law Assignment. Statutory Assignment.* Evaluating Settlement Offers: *One-Time Partial Payment. Present Value of Serial Payments. Overall Evaluation.*

35. Bankruptcy Code Proceedings 608

General Provisions, Administration, and the Estate: *Commencement of a Case. Officers. Administration Powers. Creditors and Claims. Debtor's Duties and Benefits.*

The Estate. Liquidation: *Trustee. Creditors' Committee. Handling the Estate. Discharge.* Reorganization: *Creditors' Committee. Trustee or Examiner. The Plan. Execution of the Plan.* Adjustment of Debts: *Trustee. The Plan. Confirmation of Plan. Claims and Creditors. Discharge.*

PART IX. Export Transactions 633

36. Export Credit 635

Export Credit Risks: *Government. Economic Stability. Laws. Language. Geography. Marine Risk. Convertibility Risk. Exchange Rate Risk.* Trading in Foreign Currencies: *Forward Rate. Swap. Discount and Premium. Hedging. Unhedged Position. Contracts Dealing in Strong Currencies. Contract Dealing in Weak Currencies.* Foreign Credit Information: *Customer. Bank. Exporter's Foreign Sales Representative. Commercial Credit Reporting Agencies. FCIB-NACM Corporation (FCIB). U.S. Department of Commerce.* Terms of Sale: *Export Agencies. Cash with Order. Consignment. Authority to Purchase. Open Account.* Export Collections: *Customer Paying Habits and Policies. Billing Practices. Payment Instructions. Past-Due Accounts. Commercial Arbitration.* U.S. Government Programs: *The Export-Import Bank (Eximbank). Agency for International Development (AID). The International Bank for Reconstruction and Development.*

37. Documentary Credits 659

Export Letter of Credit: *Certainty. Time of Enforcement. Documentary Requirements. Negotiation. Renewal.* Export Drafts: *Types of Drafts. Instructions for the Collecting Bank. Risks.* Selling to Exporters: *Assignment of Proceeds. Transferable Letter of Credit. Back-to-Back Letters of Credit.*

INDEX 681

ILLUSTRATIONS

FIG.

4–1. Relationships That Occur Within a Company as It Manages Its Accounts Receivable   25
4–2. Interaction Between Buyer and Seller   26
6–1. Credit Controlled and Administered from a Principal Office   56
6–2. Decentralized Offices with Credit Controlled at a Principal Office   57
6–3. Decentralized Offices with Staff at Principal Office . .   59
7–1. Job Analysis Form   65
7–2. Job Description of Top-Level Chief Credit Executive .   66–67
7–3. Job Description of Top-Level Chief Credit Executive (Staff)   67–68
7–4. Job Description of Middle-Level Chief Credit Executive .   68–69
7–5. Job Description of Credit Manager   69–70
7–6. Job Description of Credit Analyst   71
11–1. Credit Policy   120
13–1. Table of Credit Lines and Initial Order Limits Based Upon Dun & Bradstreet Ratings   146
14–1. Computer-Generated Collection Letters   174–75
14–2. Account Placement Form   185
14–3. Free Demand Letter   186
14–4. Initial Agency Letter   186
14–5. Final Demand Letter   187
15–1. Sales Request for Credit Information   198
15–2. Sales Representative's Report of Changes in Established Accounts   199
15–3. Letter to New Customer Requesting Information . .   202
15–4. Financial Statement Form   203–04
15–5. Simplified Financial Statement Form   205–06
15–6. Letter to Established Customer Requesting Information .   207
15–7. Request for Financial Statement   209
15–8. Statement of Principles for the Exchange of Credit Information   212
15–9. Request for Bank Credit Information   213
15–10. Request for Bank Credit Information (shorter form) . .   214
15–11. Bank Reference Letter Directed to the Inquirer's Bank .   215
15–12. Inquiry Form Directed to Other Suppliers   221

15–13. Trade Tabulation 222
16–1. The Dun & Bradstreet Business Information Report . . 228
16–2. Key to Ratings 231
16–3. Page from D&B Reference Book 233
16–4. NCO Specialized Credit Report 235–37
16–5. Lyon Credit Report 239–43
16–6. Lyon Red Book—Credit Key 244
16–7. Special Ratings—Lyon 245
16–8. Business Classifications and Abbreviations 246
16–9. Lyon National Weekly Interchange of Trade Experience
(Investigation) 247
16–10. Lyon National Weekly Interchange of Trade Experience
(Result of Investigation) 248
16–11. Credit Exchange Report 249–51
16–12. Credit-graphic Recommendation Service 253
16–13. Credit Exchange Code Card 254
16–14. NACM Business Credit Report 257–59
16–15. Credit Interchange Report 261
18–1. Table of Ratings and Coverage 300
19–1. Sample Trade Checkings 319
20–1. Comparison of Inventory Valuation Under FIFO and
LIFO in Inflationary Times 329
20–2. Comparison of Inventory Valuation Under FIFO and
LIFO in Deflationary Times 329
20–3. Computation of Inventory Using the Retail Method . . 331
20–4. Balance Sheet Spread Sheet 345
20–5. Income Statement Spread Sheet 346
20–6. Condensed Spread Sheet 347
20–7. Guide to Classification of Balance Sheet Items . . . 348–51
23–1. Comparative Balance Sheets 377
23–2. Comparative Statements of Income and Retained
Earnings 378
23–3. Financial Ratios 378
23–4. Source and Application of Funds 384
23–5. Changes in Net Working Capital 385
24–1. Trial Balance as of End of 1st Quarter, Year Four . . 388
24–2. Break-Even Inventory Schedule 392
24–3. Estimating Inventory by Gross Profit Percentage Method 394
24–4. Selected Figures for Analysis by Sales 398
25–1. Table of Equivalent Rates of Various Cash Discount
Terms 408
25–2. Table of Equivalents of Chain Discounts 410
25–3. Anticipation Factors at 6 Per Cent for a 360-Day Year . 412
26–1. Straight Note 426

26–2. Check 428
26–3. Certified Check 428
26–4. Cashier's Check or Treasurer's Check 429
26–5. Sight Draft 429
26–6. Time Draft 430
26–7. Trade Acceptance 430
26–8. Banker's Acceptance 431
26–9. Sight Draft/Bill of Lading 432–33
28–1. Individual Credit Guaranty 463
28–2. Corporate Credit Guaranty 464–65
28–3. Corporate Resolution 465
28–4. Subordination Agreement 467–68
28–5. Letter Given by Bank Covering Irrevocable Revolving
Letter of Credit on Domestic Orders 478
30–1. Abbreviations for Cost of Capital Calculations . . . 495
30–2. Financial Statement Summary 497
30–3. Weighted Average Cost of Capital 499
30–4. Adjusted Weighted Average Cost of Capital 499
30–5. Present Value of Future Receipts 502
30–6. PV of Profit at Different Payment Dates, When Discount
is Offered 505
30–7. Summary Receivables Information by Class of Accounts 507
30–8. Credit and Collection Expense and Bad-Debt Loss . . 508
30–9. Annual Cost of Capital for Receivables by Class . . . 509
30–10. Allocation of Credit and Collection Expense, Bad-Debt
Loss, and Cost of Carrying Receivables 509
30–11. Selected Operating Data 510
30–12. Analysis Sheet 511
30–13. Total Cost of Receivables 512
30–14. Receivables PV Contribution to Profit 515
30–15. Adjusted Allocations of Credit and Collection Expense,
Bad-Debt Loss, and Cost of Carrying Receivables . . 516
30–16. Adjusted Allocations of Warehousing, Selling, and Administrative Expenses 516
30–17. Adjusted Analysis Sheet 517
30–18. Total Cost of Receivables 518
30–19. Data Comparison—Full-Costing and Incremental Profitability Analysis 519
30–20. Simplified Analysis Sheet 520
30–21. Pro Forma Analysis Sheet for Expanded Marginal
Accounts 522
30–22. Receivables PV Contribution to Profit—Expanded Marginal Accounts 523
30–23. Receivables Impact of Expanded Marginal Accounts . . 524

31–1. Cash Budget (Aging of Sales Method) 531
31–2. Cash Budget (Collection Ratio Method) 535
31–3. Comparison of Budget and Actual 536
31–4. Projected Statement of Income and Retained Earnings . 538
31–5. Projected Balance Sheet 540
31–6. Projected Source and Application of Funds 541
31–7. Projected Changes in Net Working Capital 542
32–1. Tabular Report Using Raw Data 553
32–2. Tabular Report Using Calculated Data 554
32–3. Sales Over Time on an Arithmetic Graph 556
32–4. Sales Over Time on a Semilogarithmic Graph . . . 557
32–5. Charting Two Variables on a Semilogarithmic Graph . 558
32–6. Charting Three Variables on a Semilogarithmic Graph . 559
32–7. Charting Three Variables on a Semilogarithmic Graph Using Index Numbers 560
32–8. Charting Absolute Numbers on a Semilogarithmic Graph 562
32–9. Charting Index Numbers on a Semilogarithmic Graph . 563
33–1. Aging of Accounts Receivable 565
33–2. Accounts Receivable Aging in Chart Form 565
33–3. Accounts Receivable Aging by Divisions 566
33–4. Aging of Customer Receivables by Terms 567
33–5. Aging by Risk Classification 568
33–6. Comparative Analysis of Past-Due Accounts 569
33–7. Delinquent Accounts Receivable and Percentage Delinquent 570
33–8. Monthly Report of the Top 10 Accounts in Dollars Owing 571
33–9. Collection Ratio Method 573
33–10. Cash Forecast 574
33–11. Collections Compared to Cash Forecast 574
33–12. Monthly Credit Report 578
33–13. Statement of Allowance for Uncollectibles 581
33–14. Statement of Net Writeoffs 582
33–15. Status Report 583
33–16. Credit Department Activities 583
33–17. Monthly Administrative Expense Analysis 587
34–1. Recoveries Under One-Time Settlement Percentages . 601
34–2. Discounting Half-Year Future Payments at 15 Per Cent . 602
34–3. Recoveries Under Two-Year Payout 603
34–4. Recoveries Under Ten Equal Semiannual Payments . . 605
34–5. Recoveries Under Increasing Payments 606
36–1. Foreign Credit Information Report 648
37–1. Revocable Letter of Credit 661

37–2. Confirmed Irrevocable Export Letter of Credit Issued by
Foreign Bank; Confirmed Irrevocably by American Bank   662
37–3. Irrevocable Export Letter of Credit Issued by American
Bank   663
37–4. Unconfirmed Letter of Credit   664
37–5. Irrevocable Deferred Payment Letter of Credit . . .   666
37–6. Sight Dollar Draft Covering Export Shipment . . .   668
37–7. Time Dollar Draft Covering Export Shipment . . .   668
37–8. Letter of Instructions and Attached Draft   669
37–9. Assignment of Proceeds   673
37–10. Instructions for Transfer of Credit   675
37–11. Assignment of Letter of Credit   677
37–12. Letter Advising Issuing Bank of Credit   678

PART I

FUNDAMENTAL ASPECTS OF CREDIT MANAGEMENT

CHAPTER 1

EVOLUTION OF CREDIT

People have traded with each other from the earliest times. Such trades took the form of exchanging items possessed for items desired. In this manner, grain was exchanged for furs and sheep for oxen. The idea of exchanging goods or services in return for a promise of future payment developed only after centuries of bartering, as money and credit were unknown in the earliest stages of human history. While there have been many advances which have facilitated trade, barter in certain forms is still part of the business world and is a factor in the sale of automobiles and tires when replacements are sought.

However, bartering depends upon products for exchange in order to acquire desired goods, a slow and cumbersome process and very time-consuming. Broadening consumption and necessity demanded new and innovative exchange mediums. Shells were used in the Pacific islands; wampum among the American Indians; salt, hides, and pearls in various other localities. With the growth of civilization, the precious metals—gold and silver in particular—became the preferred medium of exchange.

TYPES OF EARLY CREDIT

There were hazards involved in carrying large amounts of money and other valuables about in the pursuit of trade. Only large, well-armed groups could travel safely by land, and there was always the risk of shipwreck in travel by sea. Credit in limited forms was a means of reducing such risks by avoiding the immediate physical transfer of money in the exchange of goods.

The ancient Romans are frequently said to have given credit practices a systematic form, but credit was known and used in a variety of ways centuries before this. As early as 1300 B.C., loans were made among the Babylonians and Assyrians on the security of mortgages, advance deposits, and even trusts. By 1000 B.C., the Babylonians had already devised a crude form of the bill of exchange, so that a creditor merchant could direct the

3

debtor merchant in a distant place to pay a third party to whom the first merchant was indebted. Installment sales of real estate were being made by the Egyptians in the time of the Pharaohs.

Recourse to credit was also prevalent among the traders in the Mediterranean area, including Phoenicia, Greece, Rome, and Carthage. The far-flung boundaries of the Roman Empire, at the beginning of the Christian era, encouraged widespread trading and the fuller use of credit. In the disorganized period that marked the decline and fall of the Roman Empire, credit bills were widely used to reduce the dangers and difficulties of transferring money through unorganized trading areas.

During the Middle Ages, credit bills were essential to the trading activities of the prosperous Italian city-states. Lending and borrowing, as well as buying and selling on credit, became widespread practices; the debtor-creditor relationship was found in all classes of society from peasants to nobles, even including the Pope and other high dignitaries of the Church. A common form of investment and credit, especially in Italy, was the "sea loan," whereby the capitalist advanced money to the merchant and thus shared the risk. If the voyage was a success, the creditor got the investment back plus a substantial bonus of 20 to 30 per cent; if the ship was lost, the creditor could lose the entire sum.

Another form of credit was the "fair letter," which was developed at the fairs held regularly in the centers of trading areas during the Middle Ages. The fair letter amounted to a promissory note to be paid before the end of the fair or at the time of the next fair. It enabled a merchant who was short of cash to secure goods on credit. This gave the merchant time either to sell the goods brought to the fair or to take home and sell the goods which had been purchased on credit.

ROLE OF THE NEW WORLD

The discovery of America provided fresh opportunities for the growth of capitalism and the expansion of credit. As a result of the exploration and conquest of the New World, large quantities of precious metals were sent back to Europe. This influx encouraged the rise of a money economy, and accumulating stocks of gold became the basis of new capital.

The entrepreneurs of the 16th and 17th centuries not only had more money available but also improved their methods of handling it. Bills of exchange were much more widely used in foreign as well as domestic trade. Endorsing bills and promissory notes made payable to the bearer also became increasingly common after 1550 in France and Italy. The negotiability of these credit instruments made it easier for merchants to do business in distant cities and countries.

The settlement of Plymouth was financed by the merchants of London. The original 7-year loan took 25 years to repay because of the many difficulties the settlers had to overcome. During the colonial period, New England merchants bought goods abroad on credit. Because transportation was slow and economic growth limited, credit terms were usually for one year. The early settlers also traded among themselves and engaged in barter with the Indians. Since there was a shortage of hard money, paper money was issued on a limited scale by the colonial governments. In these early days, however, there was no circulating medium that was really satisfactory.

To finance the American Revolution, the Continental Congress made efforts to borrow money at home and abroad. Property confiscated from colonists remaining loyal to England was sometimes used as security; tobacco crops also served as collateral, providing the basis for borrowing and for the issuance of paper money. But the limited resources of the former colonies made them a doubtful risk. Not only the Continental Congress but also the individual states issued large quantities of irredeemable paper money for war financing. Since this currency rapidly depreciated in value, until it was "not worth a continental," those who accepted and held the notes suffered heavy losses. By 1781, the merchants refused to accept paper currency from the Army Quartermaster Corps or to agree to any kind of credit terms. Fortunately, prominent businessmen were able to arrange for the purchase of needed supplies by making partial payment in hard money.

Moreover, the newly independent nation could draw upon the financial genius of Alexander Hamilton to consolidate the national debt, to develop our monetary system, and to aid in the establishment of the first Bank of the United States, which became the fiscal agent of the government. Local banks, which issued currency and extended credit, were also established in several states. Bank credit during this period was generally in the form of bank notes. The uncontrolled issuance of these notes, which in many localities were not accepted at par, often made for confusion and inflation. But it was not until the time of the Civil War, when prices fluctuated drastically and bad debts multiplied, that Congress established a national banking system through the National Banking Act of 1863. Thereafter, banks were more closely regulated and a uniform currency system was assured. State and private bank notes were taxed out of existence, to be replaced by national bank notes and U.S. currency.

DEVELOPMENT OF NEW CREDIT FACILITIES

The settlement of the West, which continued through the greater part of the 19th century, was an extremely important factor in the economic development of the United States. New credit facilities were needed to accompany this vast westward expansion. Sales on credit to purchasers far removed from the trading centers of the East led to the practice of credit investigation by correspondents of the eastern merchants. In 1841, Lewis Tappan established the first mercantile credit agency in New York and sold credit reports to his subscribers. This agency has continued without interruption for over a century; through a steady process of growth and merger, it has evolved into the modern day firm of Dun & Bradstreet Inc.

Terms of sale, as they developed during the 19th century, reflected the changes in our expanding economy. The 12-month period which had prevailed for the 50 years after the Industrial Revolution showed a definite tendency to become shorter. By the 1830s the average period was about six months, and a survey by the Secretary of the Treasury in 1832 revealed that one-third of the manufacturing plants were using terms of less than six months.

During and immediately following the Civil War, terms of sale again contracted because of unstable conditions. In a period of sharply fluctuating prices, it was natural for commercial traders to offer buyers an incentive to pay cash or to make purchases on short terms, in an effort to reduce bad-debt losses and to avoid interest charges on their own purchases by turning merchandise into cash more promptly. Discounts as high as 30 per cent were granted for payment within a specified number of days, usually before the buyer actually received the goods. It was from such practices that our present system of cash discounts developed.

The half-year and year terms of the early 1800s never returned because the need for them had passed. As transportation and communication improved, mercantile buying changed from an annual or semiannual function to a periodic one, with consequent reduction of inventories and of long-term credit. Moreover, sufficient capital was now available in rural areas to permit distant retailers to carry a large part of their customers' credit themselves. And the rapid development of adequate banking facilities made cash more readily available, so that sellers were relieved of the necessity to finance the purchasers' entire marketing period. As a result, by the late 19th century, terms of sale were generally shortened to 30 or 60 days—the terms that still prevail today in mercantile credit. Shorter payment arrangements diminished the usefulness of trade acceptances and promissory notes, and these credit instruments were generally supplanted by the open-account system in general use today.

The panics of 1873 and 1893, caused by factors such as overexpansion, speculation, and excessive borrowing, provoked much concern among responsible businessmen. An important consequence was the formation in 1896 of the National Association of Credit Management, which has worked for over three-quarters of a century to assure sound business practices and healthy credit development. One of the early measures the Association supported was the National Bankruptcy Law of 1898, which helped to stabilize the creditor-debtor relationship in cases of business failure and insolvency. As amended from time to time, particularly in 1938 by the Chandler Act and by the Bankruptcy Reform Act of 1978, the bankruptcy law is meant to provide relief for honest debtors and to assure a fair settlement for the creditors.

The banking system as it functioned at the turn of the century did not assure equal credit facilities throughout the country and did not allow for sufficient elasticity in the circulation of currency to meet changing economic conditions. The increasing clamor for a central, coordinated banking system finally led Congress to pass the Federal Reserve Act in 1913. The basic purpose of the Federal Reserve System is to regulate the supply, availability, and cost of money, thereby helping to maintain a high level of employment, stable values, and a rising standard of living. The Federal Reserve establishment, including a dozen Federal Reserve banks which cover the entire country and thousands of member banks, provides an elastic credit system, capable of expanding and contracting the reserves of the banking system in proportion to the credit needs of business. Federal Reserve bank credit is made available in all sections of the country at virtually uniform rates. Despite certain weaknesses, the credit system has withstood the severe strains of two world wars and a series of financial readjustments.

The rapid industrial and commercial expansion in the 20th century created a need for increasingly specialized credit facilities. Commercial banks, savings banks, insurance companies, factors, and finance companies all made important contributions by encouraging productive use of accumulated capital. Insurance companies and savings banks became prime sources of mortgage funds, besides investing large sums in federal and local bonds. Consumer credit became increasingly important, since it stimulated the mass production and distribution of automobiles, household appliances, farm equipment, and countless other commodities. A trend toward lower down payments and more liberal terms of sale resulted in many products becoming available to American families of modest income that were still luxuries in other parts of the world.

Moreover, many firms vastly expanded their international operations during the post-World War II era, both by exporting goods and services and by sales through foreign subsidiaries. In order to cope with the ever-changing monetary policies and foreign exchange restrictions, companies were forced to be more flexible in their dealings with customers. During this time events took place that had tremendous impact on international operations, such as the rescinding of the Bretton Woods Agreement, whereby currencies were pegged to each other; the devaluation of the U.S. dollar; and the floating of currencies.

As an essential ingredient in almost all commercial transactions and government financing, well-managed credit is a vital asset to American business. It facilitates the movement of goods from producer to consumer and offers a strong impetus to our ever-growing business activity. Without the bridge of credit, there would be a serious gap between production and consumption. Because our credit system is flexible and strong, the American economy can operate at a high level of efficiency, with maximum production and profitable distribution assured.

CHAPTER **2**

ROLE OF CREDIT ASSOCIATIONS

As the sphere of activity in which credit executives operated became more complex, cooperative associations were formed to serve the mutual interests of credit executives and to provide assistance and guidance in solving common problems.

NATIONAL ASSOCIATION OF CREDIT MANAGEMENT

The largest and oldest national association representing credit and financial executives in the United States is the National Association of Credit Management (NACM), a nonprofit business association incorporated in 1896.

Early History of NACM

At first, credit executives did not think in terms of a national organization; the movement toward a national organization began with independent local associations. By the mid-1890s, a number of local creditmen's organizations had appeared in various cities, such as New York, New Orleans, and Sioux City, Iowa. However, the duplication of effort toward solving problems of national scope and the lack of common direction soon suggested the idea of combining credit executives' efforts into one nationwide association.

The National Association of Credit Management was formally founded on June 23, 1896, at a convention of credit executives in Toledo, Ohio. This meeting marked the first successful effort of credit executives to take national action on problems facing them. These included not only the fraudulent practices of debtors and inadequate commercial laws but also the lack of cooperation between credit executives in exchanging information about mutual debtors. The services of existing mercantile credit reporting agencies were inadequate and unreliable. The accuracy and reliability of financial statements were not mandated by law. As a result, the use of such statements in granting credit was uncommon. There were many loopholes in the commercial laws. It was difficult, often impossible, to prosecute an individual debtor who on the verge of insolvency sold out his goods in bulk and pocketed the proceeds. The growth of interstate commerce made particularly serious the absence of a uniform national bankruptcy law to deal with distressed debtors. Various state laws on bankruptcy were chaotic and conflicting.

It was this difficult credit climate which the NACM set about to improve. Within ten years of its founding, NACM had played a major part in securing the passage of the first permanent national bankruptcy act and had developed the earliest adjustment bureaus to reduce waste in business liquidations. It also had begun to sponsor legislation against various types of credit fraud. Anticipating the later program of national credit interchange, NACM adopted the first confidential trade report at its first convention in 1896.

Organization

The National Association of Credit Management represents manufacturers, wholesalers, service, and financial institutions throughout the United States. The membership is organized on a local basis into independent affiliated associations operating in major trade centers. These local units are coordinated to make up the national system.

NACM is governed by its officers and a board of directors elected by the membership on a geographic basis. Administrative officers and staff members carry on the various activities of the organization, with each area of activity served by a national advisory committee composed of representative members.

Local associations are autonomous. Each is governed by its own board of directors and officers, and employs an executive vice president to administer association activities and services. Each association maintains its own departments for the various services performed for its membership, such as interchange, industry groups, collections, adjustments, and education. While each association operates autonomously, it calls upon NACM for expert advice and assistance in specific fields of interest.

The purposes and objectives of the national organization are:

1. To promote honest and fair dealings in credit transactions.
2. To assure good laws for sound credit.
3. To foster and facilitate the exchange of credit information.
4. To encourage efficient service in the collection of accounts.
5. To promote and expedite sound credit administration in international trade.
6. To encourage training for credit work through colleges, universities, correspondence courses, and other means.
7. To foster and encourage research in the field of credit.
8. To disseminate useful and instructive articles and ideas with respect to credit management techniques.

9. To promote economy and efficiency in the handling of the estates of insolvent, financially embarrassed, or bankrupt debtors.
10. To provide facilities for the investigation and prevention of fraud.
11. To perform such other functions as the advancement and protection of business credit may require.

Activities

In accord with these objectives, the combined facilities of NACM and its affiliates engage in the following major activities:

Business Credit Reports. Knowing how a customer pays its bills is at the base of any sound credit decision. NACM business credit reports have been supplying this information for three-quarters of a century. Historically these confidential reports were produced manually, with information gathered by telephone and by mail. In the fast-paced economy of the 1980s, when credit decisions must be made quickly, NACM turned to automation of its credit reporting system. NACM affiliates now offer their members fast, accurate, and current information within minutes after the request is made.

Collections. Being member-owned, NACM associations are able to provide their members with the lowest cost debt-collection service available. A special feature of NACM collections is a 10-day free demand period—no charge if payment is received within 10 days of the first contact with the debtor. And in case there is no collection, there is no charge.

Adjustments. Many NACM associations provide counseling and rehabilitation assistance to distressed debtors. In bankruptcy cases, economies are realized when the association serves as secretary to creditors' committees.

Credit Groups. There are over 1,300 NACM industry credit groups, including nearly 100 national groups. These groups provide their members with the opportunity for face-to-face exchange about pay experience of customers, general industry credit problems, and experience of other credit and financial executives on management problems. NACM provides definitive legal guidelines for the conduct of credit group meetings.

Legislation. NACM has consistently strived to keep business credit free of state and federal regulation that has come about in other areas. That the needs of business credit were considered in the enactment of the Fair Credit Reporting Act, the Fair Debt Collection Practices Act, the Equal Credit Opportunity Act, as well as the Bankruptcy Reform Act of 1978 is due in large part to the efforts of NACM in Washington.

Publications. Since 1908, the *Credit Manual of Commercial Laws* has headed the list of NACM publications dealing with specific areas of credit responsibility and interest. New titles are added each year to keep NACM members abreast of new thinking and techniques.

Credit and Financial Management. Mailed each month to NACM members, *Credit and Financial Management* magazine offers articles of current interest and value to credit and financial executives. Subject matter covers all aspects of credit management as well as business conditions that affect credit operations.

Credit Congress. The annual convention of NACM provides a forum for the latest ideas in credit management techniques and solutions to current problems facing business credit executives. The Credit Congress is held in a different location each year to provide maximum opportunity for attendance by members in all parts of the country.

Fraud Prevention Department. Continuing the fraud prevention operation started by NACM in 1896, this department conducts investigations to obtain indictments and convictions in cases of business fraud, cooperates with local and federal law enforcement agencies, and keeps subscribers informed of the status of existing and potential fraud cases.

Insurance Advisory Council. This council provides speakers, bulletins, and educational programs to alert credit management to customer needs for proper and adequate insurance.

Cooperating Committees. NACM committees maintain close working relationships with other professional bodies, such as bankers and public accountants, on matters of mutual interest.

Credit Women's Groups. The objectives of NACM credit women's groups are to promote and advance the interests of women credit executives and assistants, to foster credit management as a career for women, and to encourage education of women in credit work. The groups subsidize and award scholarships to NACM educational activities.

FCIB-NACM Corporation. This international arm of NACM serves international credit grantor members, including many located in Europe. It offers credit reports on hundreds of thousands of overseas buyers and weekly bulletins on current market conditions around the world. Monthly Round Table conferences are conducted in the United States. Three membership meetings a year are held in Europe, where FCIB-NACM maintains a permanent representative. In addition, the organization serves the interest of international trade chapters of NACM associations in this country.

International Collections. FCIB-NACM offers its members worldwide collection services through correspondents in nearly 100 countries—making it one of the largest international collection services in the world.

International Credit Executives (ICE). This group serves credit executives who are responsible for credit and collection functions of their companies' overseas affiliates.

Accreditation. Recognition of the credit executive as a key member of the management team is another objective of NACM. An important part of this recognition effort is the Accredited Business Credit Executive (ABCE) program. Qualified members of NACM may sit for the ABCE examination, which recognizes outstanding achievement and competence in credit management.

Education. The NACM has an extensive education program which is conducted for it by the Credit Research Foundation.

CREDIT RESEARCH FOUNDATION INC.

Expanding their original objectives, the NACM membership recognized the importance of education and research, and established specific facilities for their development. This led to the formation of the Credit Research Foundation Inc. (CRF), which was chartered in 1949 under Delaware laws as a nonprofit corporation.

Organization

CRF has its own membership, board of trustees, and committee structure but maintains a close liaison with the NACM. Its membership of business firms and financial institutions recognizes the importance of dynamic credit management, both for corporate profit and general economic well-being. These organizations customarily designate their credit executives or other senior financial executives to take part in Foundation activities.

Activities

The Foundation seeks to identify the characteristics, economic impact, and corporate utilization strategy of investment in accounts receivable. The projects for applied research are aimed toward developing more effective credit practices and techniques. On a broader basis, its inquiries in basic research seek to identify and quantify the impact that business credit exerts upon the firm and the national economy.

In addition to the above research activities, the Foundation administers the education programs of the NACM's National Institute of Credit and the NACM Graduate School of Credit and Financial Management. CRF also conducts Credit Management Workshops and a Mid-Career School. These activities are discussed in more detail in Chapter 8.

ROBERT MORRIS ASSOCIATES

Recognizing the cooperative understanding that was being built among creditmen in NACM, a group of bankers, attending the annual NACM convention in Rochester, New York, met at dinner on June 25, 1914. This group became the nucleus of a new association of bank commercial lending personnel, later to be known as the Robert Morris Associates (RMA).

At first this group functioned as a special group within NACM, but in 1919 a full-time secretary was appointed and a national office was opened in Lansdowne, Pennsylvania. It was named in honor of Robert Morris, the man who was largely responsible for the financing of the War of Independence. In 1937, the RMA national office was moved to Philadelphia.

RMA's original purpose in 1914 was to facilitate the flow and interchange of commercial bank credit information. In 1916, it adopted a Code of Ethics for the exchange of credit information. This purpose has been expanded to include a continuous effort to improve the principles and practices of commercial lending, loan administration, and asset management in commercial banks.

The objectives of RMA are to develop and exchange ideas and experiences as they relate to its purpose, to establish and uphold a high standard of ethics in the banking industry, to develop capable personnel for the many areas of responsibility in the commercial lending function of banks, and to cooperate with related organizations in problem-solving for mutual benefit.

Membership in RMA is open to banks, which are represented in the association by their commercial lending personnel at all levels.

RMA is organized into five divisions: Policy, Domestic Lending, International Lending, Credit, and Chapters. Each has the goal of developing products and services for bankers who most closely identify with its specific area of responsibility. A number of committees operate under each division.

Local chapters have been set up by RMA on a city, state, or regional basis. They operate under rules adopted locally, consistent with the bylaws of national RMA; their ultimate objective is to serve member needs at the local level, primarily in education.

RMA publishes two monthly publications: *The Journal of Commercial Bank Lending* and the *Commercial Lending Newsletter*. Since 1923, it has also published the *Annual Statement Studies*, a book of composite balance sheets, income statements, and ratios for over 300 different lines of business. In addition, RMA produces other materials and conducts educational activities on a wide range of subjects of interest to commercial lending personnel.

CREDITEL OF CANADA LIMITED

Organized credit control and information services came into being in Canada in 1910. Emanating from the pressing needs presented during the expansion in Western Canada, the Canadian Credit Men's Association was born in Winnipeg in April of that year. In 1970, the Association changed its name to Creditel of Canada Limited. It is a member-owned nonprofit organization comprised of manufacturers, wholesalers, and distributors in all provinces of Canada.

Services and activities of Creditel include:

1. Credit Interchange department, which prepares factual computerized ledger information reports on a nationwide basis.
2. A comprehensive collection service, which includes collection stickers, free demand drafts, and efficient collection procedures.
3. Special progress and performance construction industry reports, including financial statements.
4. Some 200 industry credit groups, which meet monthly in all of the main centers of Canada for discussing problem accounts.
5. Daily publication of legal information.

6. Credit women's groups in the larger centers.
7. A three-year course in credit management leading to the M.C.I. designation. This program is administered by The Canadian Credit Institute through the Extension Department of the University of Toronto.
8. An active legislation committee which studies all commercial legislation both at the federal and provincial levels. Creditel has been instrumental in introducing or amending much of the commercial legislation now on the statutes.
9. Regular publication of *Viewpoint*, *Credit Management Review*, *Article of the Month*, and *Resume*, which are specifically designed to bring articles of interest to the attention of credit executives.
10. An extensive program of educational seminars.

CHAPTER 3

ROLE OF CREDIT IN THE BUSINESS WORLD

Credit is the ability of an individual or business enterprise to obtain economic value on faith, in return for an expected payment of economic value in the future. This definition is one of many that have been proposed to describe the institution of credit. It is a word derived from the Latin *credere* which means to believe or to trust. A trust is therefore implied in credit, and it is a mutual trust between the grantor and recipient of the credit. A seller's faith in a buyer's willingness and ability to pay for goods or services within a given time must at least equal the buyer's faith in the value of the goods or service offered. Credit is thus a cooperative function between seller and buyer or between creditor and debtor. Both stand to be ultimately benefited by their mutual trust.

COMPONENTS OF CREDIT

Several essential points are always included in any definition of credit. First, there must be an exchange of values. This sets up the transaction. Goods or services are obtained for a promise to pay and payment is made when it comes due. This introduces the second factor: futurity, and its companion, trust.

Where goods or services are exchanged immediately for cash, there is no futurity, no trust, and no need for the seller to have confidence in the buyer. None of these is needed, since immediate economic payment is made at the time of purchase.

When a payment by check is offered, the seller must decide whether or not to accept it. Many times company policy will guide the vendor's action, while at other times a snap judgment may be necessary. Since the check transaction involves futurity, trust, and confidence, the credit concept is involved. The futurity is short, just long enough for the check to clear. Trust and confidence, however, are just as significant here as they are on

15

longer terms. Once the seller has given up title to the goods, legal steps are necessary to repossess them.

When credit terms are offered, the seller releases title to property in exchange for the promise of the buyer to pay at a future date. This is accomplished only after the seller is convinced that payment will be received—that is, that the buyer can be trusted. In a sale made on 30 or 60 days, for instance, the futurity aspect of credit is important; and as selling terms lengthen, the seller's analysis of the buyer's ability to pay at maturity becomes increasingly important.

Later in this book the separate factors that enter into credit analysis are examined, but for now that analysis can be summarized in one statement: "Credit depends upon ability and willingness to pay." Without that, credit is meaningless. Lack of moral character, shortage of funds, and embezzlement by employees are some reasons why a customer's ability and willingness to pay might be affected. By the same token, those are the very factors which affect the buyer's credit. In brief, credit in its broadest sense is based on the components of trust, risk, economic exchange, and futurity. Thus credit may be appropriately described as the transmittal of economic value now, on faith, in return for an expected economic value in the future.

CREDIT SALES VERSUS CASH SALES

The advantages to the vendor of selling on credit include the following:

1. Credit customers are generally more stable than cash customers. They tend to be repeat buyers from the same sources once their credit line is established.

2. The opportunity to obtain merchandise now in exchange for future payment is a convenience to buyers. Consequently, they may tend to purchase more than they would on a cash basis. Many times they feel there is a good chance to sell their products and earn a profit even before the payables become due.

3. The above factors combine to yield one more advantage: the opportunity to build good will. Regular customers given good service and the convenience of credit terms tend to react favorably. The vendor's confidence in them is matched by buyer's confidence towards the vendor. This feeling is called good will. Thus a two-way relationship is established that is good for business.

Credit selling is not all advantages, however. From the point of view of the financial manager, credit sales include the following disadvantages:

1. The costs of doing business are higher than they are for a corresponding cash business. Extra personnel and facilities are needed for the operation of a credit department.

2. Whenever sales are made on credit terms, there is always the possi-

bility that some customers will not pay. Bad-debt losses should be considered a cost of doing business and be included in the pricing structure. Consequently, item for item, prices should normally be higher when sales are made on credit terms.

3. Accounts receivable represent a tie-up of company funds. If the receivables are current, funds are tied up for the normal selling terms. If collections are slow, the restriction of working funds becomes worse.

4. Financial institutions offer plans by which receivables can be converted into cash to eliminate the tie-up problem. Understandably, this is an additional cost of doing business, as these institutions make a charge for their services.

The ease with which credit purchases may be made is sometimes a disadvantage from the seller's point of view. If customers overbuy and later decide to return the merchandise or defer paying for it, the convenience becomes in fact a detriment. The seller's capital is tied up; customers may look for ways to find fault with the merchandise; and even if payment is finally received, it may be preceded by wrangling which hurts good will.

Business credit—which is our chief concern here—can best be understood when set in perspective beside the other major forms of credit. Credit takes many forms and can be classified in any number of ways. On the basis of use, credit can first be divided into two main categories: public and private credit.

PUBLIC CREDIT

Public credit includes all grants of credit to units of government—to states and municipalities as well as to the federal government. In recent decades, state, local, and federal governments have found it increasingly needful to borrow on their credit to meet the rising costs of public needs, including schools, highways, health and social welfare, and military preparedness. In all cases where financing needs exceed revenue, governments must draw upon their borrowing capacity. This is usually done by the issuance of state, municipal, or federal bonds, or in the case of the federal government through the issuance of the shorter-term Treasury bills and notes. Currency itself may be regarded in a sense as a credit obligation of the federal government, though it is not usually so classified. Analysis of public debt is usually made on the basis of government's powers of future taxation.

On the other side of the equation is the federal and state lending, which often has public policy objectives. Such programs as the disaster loans, loans by the Small Business Administration, and many other programs serve as aids to the business community with less attention to the goodness of the credit risk and more to social aims such as employment, economic opportunity, and housing.

PRIVATE CREDIT

Private credit can—on the basis of its various functions—be subdivided into bank credit, investment credit, agricultural credit, consumer credit, credit cards, and business credit. Of all the forms of private credit in use, the one most closely associated with public credit is bank credit.

Bank Credit

For banking purposes, this is represented chiefly by depositors' checking accounts. As such, it constitutes some three-fourths of all the currency in use in this country.

The principal difference between bank credit and other forms of money lending is that no cash changes hands when a bank loan is made. Rather, a paper amount is set up in the borrower's account, available for its use. This might be called "checking account credit." It is backed by a specified cash reserve required by the Federal Reserve Board.

The paper transaction is in effect money, although no physical currency is printed. It acts as a multiplier to the amount of physical currency in circulation, since only a percentage of actual currency is required as a reserve against "checking account" currency.

This ability of banks to create money is an important aspect of the economic and financial climate in the United States. The Board of Governors of the Federal Reserve System, located in Washington, D.C., can regulate this ability by expanding or contracting cash reserves. There are three ways in which this may be done: through the purchase or sale of government securities (open market operations); by increasing or decreasing the percentage of cash reserves each bank must hold to support checking account credit (setting reserve requirements); and by raising or lowering the price charged to member banks by their regional Federal Reserve Bank for the reserves they temporarily borrow (the discount rate).

Bank credit, as checking account credit, is in effect money—the most important kind of money in circulation. In the final analysis, bank credit is also the ultimate source of all other forms of credit in use today.

Investment Credit

This term refers to the placement of funds in productive assets to earn a profit. It consists primarily of loans made to business for the purchase of capital needs such as buildings, machinery, land, and fixtures. Generally major institutions such as insurance companies, banks, pension funds, and educational and charitable organizations are the principal lenders in this type of loan, although individual investors may also participate.

The loans are usually evidenced by bonds. When only the pledge of the borrower is required, the bonds are called debentures. When additional collateral is required, they are called secured bonds. These loans are generally of a long-term nature, though short-term promissory notes may sometimes be considered investment credit.

Longer-term obligations, including bonds and notes, are often secured by a pledge of real estate or chattels such as equipment and movable machinery. A corporation that raises new funds through the issuance of secured bonds often executes a general mortgage on all property owned or later acquired by it, except materials for resale or other property specifically reserved from the lien of the mortgage.

Agricultural Credit

This type of credit presents more risk to the lender than those already discussed. In addition to the normal hazards, the borrowers are exposed to natural hazards beyond their control, such as drought, flood, frost, wind, and insect damage.

Because of the highly seasonal characteristics and the unusual credit risks involved, regular lending agencies are not always willing to include farmers among their clientele. Consequently, the federal government has taken an active hand in financing farm ventures through such agencies as the Farm Security Administration and Federal Land Banks. In addition, the farmers have banded together to form cooperative lending societies. They spread the risk of individual ventures on an actuarial basis in much the same way as insurance companies do.

Consumer Credit

This form of credit is also known as retail credit (regular and revolving charge accounts) or installment credit. Whereas the other forms are used to facilitate production and distribution, retail credit is used by banks and businesses to encourage consumer purchases. Here are the main forms of consumer credit:

Regular Charge Account.   This type of unsecured, open-account credit is offered by many merchants as a convenience to attract customers. The customers may purchase goods up to the limit set by the store, and full payment is generally required within 30 days. When payment extends beyond the 30 days, the customer is subject to a service charge on the balance owing.

Revolving Charge Account.   This is a variation of the regular charge account. It provides in the credit agreement that if customers do not make full payment within 30 days, they can then make minimum monthly payments on the amount owing. There is also a service charge for the payments extending beyond the 30-day period with this type of account.

Installment Credit.   Generally extending for one year or more, installment credit terms are offered to consumers on the purchase of durable goods or items priced too high to be readily available on a 30-day basis. An installment contract is usually signed by the purchaser, and may be evidenced by a legal instrument with payments subject to an interest charge.

Consumer Loan. Commercial banks and loan companies offer this type of service to individuals for periods up to three years or more. Evidence of debt is usually a signed promissory note. Customers receive a coupon book or payment book indicating a schedule of repayment, or payments are automatically deducted from their checking account at scheduled times.

As an additional security, many lenders require the signatures of more than one person on the promissory note. A spouse or a relative or friend may be asked to cosign the note and each is held equally responsible for its payment.

The customer is often asked to pledge collateral or chattel, such as furniture, automobiles, or other personal belongings, to secure the debt. Or it may be secured by marketable securities.

Service Credit. This type of credit is offered by professional people, such as doctors, dentists, and lawyers, for services rendered. Generally these terms anticipate payment within 30 days, although longer terms may be arranged by mutual agreement.

Consumer Mortgage. Mortgage companies, banks, and other lending institutions offer mortgage credit to consumers for the financing of homes or home improvements. Due to the usual long-term duration of consumer mortgages, this financing can be set apart from the other forms of consumer credit. To the extent that it represents permanent investment credit, it is not in effect "credit for consumption."

However, from the credit executive's point of view—particularly for those in consumer durable industries—consumer mortgages should be considered an integral part of consumer credit. In recent years especially, consumer mortgage credit has consistently taken a larger proportion of total spendable income after taxes than all the other forms of consumer credit combined.

Credit Cards. With ordinary charge accounts, the seller must carry the consumer's receivables until payment is received. Credit cards give the seller the option to convert these receivables into cash. The most widely known are bank credit cards, petroleum credit cards, and those used for travel and entertainment.

The credit card is an adaptation of the principles of factoring to the consumer field. Its use is not limited to consumer credit, however, as many business firms use credit cards for travel and entertainment.

Business Credit

This type of credit is granted by a supplier when selling goods to a buyer for use in manufacturing, processing, or reselling such goods for profit.

In the early part of the century, the term "mercantile credit" was most

widely used because the larger portion of business credit involved merchants and traders. As the economy of the country developed, the term
"commercial credit" became more common in reference to business credit
transactions. Over the years, however, some economists and government
agencies have expanded the definition of commercial credit to make it include other types of credit. Consequently, the business community has
come to use "business credit" when referring to credit transactions at the
manufacturing and wholesale levels. The important characteristics of business credit are:

1. Selling terms are relatively short.
2. Transactions are usually on open account (unsecured basis).
3. Cash discounts may be offered for payment before the net due date.
4. The terms include transactions to manufacturers, wholesalers, and retailers,
   but specifically exclude the consumer.
5. Transactions may be on open account, partially secured, or secured in full.

The fact that business credit finances the intermediate and final stages of
production and distribution distinguishes it from consumer credit granted
to the ultimate consumer. The fact that business credit sales yield a profit
on goods sold rather than interest or investment income distinguishes it
from bank and investment credit. Nevertheless, all forms of credit, be they
business, consumer, bank, or investment, are interdependent and many of
their attributes are shared in common.

This interdependence can be depicted in the following example, which
assumes that consumer credit is the starting point for business credit. The
retailer may grant charge account or installment credit to customers for
their convenience, to induce a larger volume of sales or to meet competition. But to do so, the retailer usually must be given time by suppliers—
the wholesalers—to pay for the merchandise. The wholesalers must therefore request enough time and credit from their suppliers—the manufacturers, processors, or converters—so they may carry their retailer customers.
Thus a chain of credit is established from the retailer all the way back
through the marketing and manufacturing process to the original provider
of materials. These may include food growers, ore diggers, and other producers of raw materials or goods for direct distribution through functional
intermediaries. In many cases, however, these producers are in no position
to finance their customers. Consequently, they turn to banks or other lending institutions for help in carrying their receivables. Thus business credit
is ultimately dependent on financial credit.

The need for such interim financial assistance is not restricted to the
original producers of raw materials alone. All the way down the buying
line, most businesses, large and small alike, depend on a certain amount of
this financing to sustain their credit sales. Situations ranging from minor
emergencies to major crises can make an immediate bank loan or other financial aid necessary to permit continued granting of credit to customers.

The need for interim financing periodically arises where products are highly seasonal. For instance, in the apparel trades, in toys, and for certain consumer durables such as air conditioners, vendors must borrow funds for current operational needs while goods are being produced or processed, and until the retailer makes payment. Thus the manufacturers and wholesalers generally finance their customers' seasonal requirements by giving seasonal datings.

While providing this credit, the sellers also benefit in many ways. Manufacturers produce their goods on a more economic scale by spreading their costs over a longer period of time. By having goods on the buyers' premises, the sellers avoid warehousing expense and gain exposure of their products to the customer.

Should the sellers need funds, they can obtain interim bank loans more readily than their smaller customers. This procedure obviates the need for small businesses to seek their own funds or to obtain bank loans in order to finance their operations. Undoubtedly, many of the small businesses would not meet the lending standards of commercial banks. Moreover, if they did, lending to a great number of small borrowers could add new costs to the banking system, which in turn would be passed on to borrowers.

Secured Business Credit. Security is obtained not only when the buyer's financial condition is weak but in order to guarantee payment if buyer's financial condition changes. It is obtained not to buttress the perceived weakness but, to the contrary, as an added payment. Pledge of assets is rarely used as a form of security; more common is security under Article 9 of the Uniform Commercial Code. In addition, mortgages on real estate are often used in closely held corporations.

It is important to note that drafts, trade acceptances, and promissory notes are not forms of security. Each of those instruments (when accepted in the case of time drafts and trade acceptances) is written evidence of a debt. However, no security attaches to the instrument.

Unsecured Open-Account Credit. This is the most widely used form of domestic business credit. Although funds for inventory purchases can be obtained through direct bank loans, this practice can be costly, time-consuming, and inefficient. It has therefore become common practice in business for manufacturers and other suppliers to make inventories available to their customers on unsecured open-account credit.

The method is relatively simple. The supplier establishes a credit line for the customer, permitting it to purchase amounts totaling up to the assigned sum. Transactions are recorded on invoices and in the supplier's records. Periodically the customer is asked to remit in keeping with the terms. Its simplicity is the system's principal advantage. To function effectively, it requires accurate control over receivables and periodic review of the customer's qualification as a credit risk.

Assuming that the buyer is in sound financial condition, open-account credit provides the most efficient and economical method to make goods available for distribution. It is thereby unnecessary for business to finance inventory through direct bank loans at greater cost and with less efficiency.

BANK CREDIT VERSUS BUSINESS CREDIT

Bank credit differs from business credit in a number of ways, but chiefly in terms of the type of resource in question, the amounts involved, the length of terms, and the depth of the credit analysis.

Type of Resource

The most apparent difference between bank and business credit is the type of resource which changes hands in a transaction. As suppliers of resources, banks and business enterprises hold separate roles: the bank furnishes money, while the business supplier furnishes goods or services. After the transaction is completed, however, both are creditors in the same way. The customer owes money to each.

Amounts Involved

Bank loans generally are made in larger amounts than business credit transactions. Chances are the average business will have one or two banks and at the same time use the services of a good number of suppliers. Merchandise requirements will therefore be spread over many business creditors, while bank loans will come from one or two sources.

Length of Terms

As a rule, trade terms are shorter than the periods of repayment offered by banks. Payment for merchandise requirements normally comes due in 30, 60, 90 days, depending on industry characteristics. Bank loans, on the other hand, are generally taken before the beginning of an active season and repaid as cash inflows are generated from the seasonal sales. The money is outstanding for longer periods of time in contrast to business credit where more rapid turnover of debt is the rule.

Depth of Analysis

Because of the differences noted above, bank credit analysis tends to be more extensive than that of business creditors. The bank must satisfy itself that the loan is safe and collectible, since it has a need for liquidity in its own operation to meet the demands of depositors. The bank therefore must be sure that borrowers will pay on time. Further, its actions are subject to regulation by state and federal authorities. Using depositors' money for commercial loans, the bank must minimize loss risk. As amounts are larger, repayment terms longer, and loss potential greater, the bank must make a more in-depth analysis. Consequently, an account which might be considered satisfactory for business credit might not qualify for an unsecured bank loan. However, where the credit exposure on a business transaction is large, credit executives do undertake the same in-depth analysis as bankers.

CHAPTER 4

BASIS FOR DYNAMIC CREDIT MANAGEMENT

A business organization may be regarded as a combination of functions, people, and materials aimed at procuring goods and services, converting them or changing their characteristics, and selling them to customers. Since the large majority of these transactions are conducted on a credit basis, the department charged with the credit function naturally plays a very important role in business.

ROLE OF CREDIT IN FINANCIAL MANAGEMENT

As its name implies, financial management employs a combination of managerial actions concerned with the finances of the firm. It may be divided into three subsections:

1. Obtaining funds for the operation of the business. This is usually the function of the treasurer of the company. The funds may be obtained either by equity investment or by short- and long-term borrowings.

2. Efficient managment of internal funds, an important part of financial management, is also the job of the treasurer. Here the controller, cost accountant, and industrial engineer play an important role. Value analysis is one way to make sure that the firm gets the most for its expenditures. Control of waste, full utilization of machinery and manpower, and elimination of unnecessary clerical and manufacturing steps are other ways that internal costs can be controlled.

3. A third, and probably the crucial area of financial management, is the control of funds temporarily made available to outside interests. This is a function of credit managment. A sale is in effect a loan made to a customer. The merchandise sold has cost the firm money and the receivable includes an amount for company profit on the sale. During the period that credit is outstanding, that money is not available to the seller.

OUTLINE OF THE FLOW OF CREDIT

Initially, when a buyer and a seller come together, they reach an agreement that broadly outlines the framework of their future relationship. Policy guidelines set by each firm are encompassed in this agreement, and they play an important part in the handling of any transaction between the two companies.

Since business is basically concerned with the sale of goods and services on open account, the guidelines are especially important for efficient management of receivables. For the seller, these should govern the order, credit analysis and risk reduction, shipping and attendant documentation, record accounting of receivables, and collection of funds due. Of course, the people establishing policy need feedback from the various phases of the process to make wise decisions. Figure 4–1 shows the relationships that occur within a company as it manages its accounts receivable.

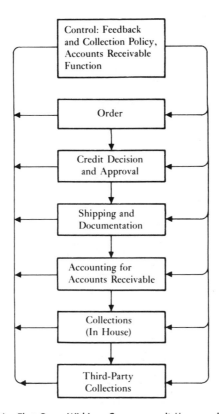

FIG. 4–1.   Relationships That Occur Within a Company as It Manages Its Accounts Receivable.

In Figure 4–2, some of these relationships are expanded to include the actions of the buyer. Together the process may be outlined as follows:

1. The flow of credit begins with the purchase order from the customer. This may come from the customer directly or from the sales department.

2. The order is approved. To be approved without an investigation, the order must meet certain parameters set by the company. If an investigation is required, some of the sources that may be contacted are the customer, sales representatives, banks, credit reporting agencies, credit interchange, and trade suppliers.

3. The approval of an order results in the establishment of an account receivable on the supplier's records. Invoices are issued to itemize the transaction.

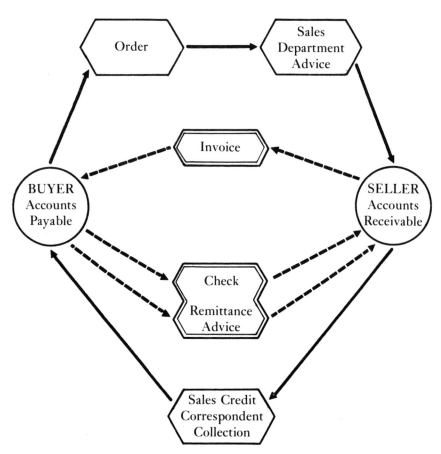

FIG. 4–2.   Interaction Between Buyer and Seller.

4. Upon receipt of the invoice, the customer establishes an account payable on its books. The goods are compared with copies of the purchase order, shipping documents, and invoices.

5. Differences and errors are noted in quantity, quality, prices, terms, delivery dates, and freight. They are adjusted by chargeback or credit memorandum.

6. Trade receivables and payables are usually maintained on an individual item basis. Therefore, when a payment is made, a remittance advice accompanies the check to identify the payer and items being paid.

7. Checks are deposited by the seller and the customer's account is credited. With proper identification, most paid items can be cleared. Short or overpayments may occur for many reasons, including errors, discount violations, duplicate payments or deductions, and purchase order differences. These are usually resolved by direct communication with the customer.

8. Customers that do not pay bills as they mature must be followed with an understanding yet aggressive collection effort. When direct collection is not successful, a third party—a collection agency or attorney—is utilized. If the company is financially distressed, a decision has to be made by the creditors as to whether the business can be salvaged and rehabilitated financially or be liquidated.

9. Credit flow is continuous to most customers paying promptly. It can be continuous to slow-paying customers providing they work with the supplier's credit department. A third-party collection or an insolvency resulting in a bad debt usually terminates the flow of credit.

This description points out that credit systems cannot be designed on internal considerations only. Outside organizations—the customer, credit agencies, banks of the buyer and the seller, carriers, and others—must be included, with a precise identification of each. Furthermore, automation and greater utilization of computers require intimate knowledge of these relationships. The logical flow of credit in business must be charted carefully. The end result will be a communicating system that provides timely and accurate information and reports.

MANAGEMENT RESPONSIBILITIES OF THE CREDIT FUNCTION

In expediting the flow of credit, the credit department plays a critical role and must perform its duties efficiently. Every department therefore needs a philosophy of management that will not only permit full flowering of individual responsibility and strength, but at the same time give cohesive direction of effort, maintain teamwork, and harmonize the goals of the individual and the enterprise. Such a task is not easy; its accomplishment rests squarely on the shoulders of the chief credit executive.

This kind of a management philosophy heightens the spirit of the department. If the objectives are clear, the credit executive and department personnel know what they are supposed to do, and the proper organization of the job enables them to do it. It is the spirit of the department that determines whether they will do it adequately or outstandingly. Good spirit should focus on the strengths of the personnel and should allow full scope for individual creativity.

The functions of management may be divided into four main areas: setting objectives, planning, organizing, and controlling. Each of these will be described in the following pages.

Setting Objectives

The objectives of the credit department may be both short term and long term in nature. One immediate objective may be to operate in such a manner as to maximize company profits by getting the best combination of quality output with minimal costs. Similarly, the automation of routine operations is a long-term objective of many departments.

The department objectives must be broad enough to encourage development of policies and procedures that enhance profits and must conform to overall company objectives. These are the clear responsibility of the top people of the department.

Planning

In bridging the gap between the present and the future, planning serves four distinct and essential purposes:

1. It establishes common objectives so that everyone can know the values which the department hopes to achieve.

2. It establishes what each person must do so that each job is coordinated with others without duplication or omission.

3. It establishes what factors are necessary so that assigned duties can be effectively performed.

4. It establishes a basis of control so that work progresses, and standards are available against which to check results.

Many serious problems of credit management are caused by lack of adequate planning. The chief credit executive must therefore determine the sequence of needed planning steps and the scheduling of activities necessary to accomplish the desired results.

Organizing

Organization increases the effectiveness of people. By clarifying what is to be done and maximizing the opportunity for individual accomplishment, the organizational structure gives freedom of action and reduces limitations. It thus encourages high productivity and creativity.

Organizing for action involves structure, staffing, and training. These elements can be discussed separately, even though the idea of organizing has to include a sensitive balance among the three. A sound organization structure makes effective management possible. It creates the pattern that affects the performance and effectiveness of all members of the department. Lack of a sound organization structure causes many of the problems of management.

Structure. There are certain essential steps in developing an improved organization structure. The first step is to clarify in writing the overall objectives, purposes, and results desired for the credit department as a whole—the summary results of the total money, personnel, and facilities utilized by the department.

The second step is to determine what major activities are necessary in order to accomplish the desired objectives and results.

The third step is to group these activities into closely related functions in conformity with the specialized abilities, interests, and skills of functional teams of personnel whose efforts can be most effectively coordinated, integrated, and controlled. This grouping must be simple; it must be tailor-made for the credit department and accepted by those persons affected. It should contribute to the following objectives:

1. Maximum effectiveness of total department operations.
2. Ease of direction, coordination, and control.
3. Most effective utilization of the total work force.
4. Maximum utilization of each employee's highest abilities, skills, and interests.
5. Future growth and development of the department with a minimum of changes in the basic structure.

The fourth step is to systematically unite designated major functions into an overall framework which constitutes the skeleton of the department structure. Every function and every position in the department should be prescribed in writing—accurately, briefly, and clearly.

The structure as a whole, and each part, should be specifically related to the accomplishment of definite objectives and purposes, and must create a pattern, or climate, which encourages:

1. Maximum performance of the entire department, the functional groups within the department, and the individual persons within each functional team.
2. Ease and continuity of work flow; harmonious relationships.
3. Ease of appraisal and remedial action whenever required.
4. Ease of communications, up and down and across all organizational levels.
5. Optimum productivity, morale, and job satisfaction on the part of every person in the department.

The fifth step is to use practical techniques for putting an ideal organization structure into effect:

1. Develop the ideal departmental structure—in conformity with principles indicated in previous steps.
2. Identify the major problems standing between the ideal structure and the present structure; analyze viewpoints, objectives, vested interests, trends, and personnel.

3. Review the potential utilization of the present staff in conjunction with resources, facilities, markets, services, products, and so on; determine in order of importance what improvements can and should be made immediately. Then prepare a tentative schedule of subsequent changes.
4. Continue to improve the organization structure in conformity with a well-designed overall plan. Do this only as rapidly as appropriate changes can be made with the least possible disturbance of morale and productivity.

Staffing. Since effective managment is "getting results through people," the chief credit executive must establish and maintain basic controls governing the selection, compensation, and development of department employees. As in the case of organization structure, defects in staffing may result from disregarding fundamental principles. Adequate staffing requires the placement of the right person in the right job, at the right time, at the right compensation, and with the right satisfaction to all concerned.

To accomplish this goal there are three steps to consider. First, establish the results required of each position and what criteria are used to measure them. Next, determine what the present occupant of each position has to do (the activities that must be carried out) in order to secure desired results. Finally, ascertain what knowledge (general and specific), skills, and personal qualifications are needed to perform the activities.

Education and experience are the traditional means of acquiring the requisite knowledge and skills, but should not be substituted for definite measurements when determining the required qualifications for each position. Personal history records; psychological, trade, and informational tests; and skillful interpretation of these data can help put the right people in the right jobs.

Effective staffing puts the best possible people in positions so that:

1. Appropriate skills and abilities are provided at points needed and in adequate amounts.

2. Instructions can be given easily and are clearly understood.

3. Everyone knows exactly what must be done and what standards must be met.

4. Everyone has authority equal to responsibility so that the requirements of the job can be fulfilled.

5. Everyone knows what the reporting requirements are when dealing with superiors.

6. Everyone is stimulated to perform well.

7. Teamwork and cooperation are natural and easy.

The proper combination of the above factors provides for effective utilization of personnel and results in a smoothly working organization with high productivity.

Training. It is generally accepted in modern management that every executive is responsible for the selection, performance, training, and development of each employee in the department. Assistance from training specialists may be secured but final responsibility for training in the credit department rests with the department head. Effective training requires:

1. Objectives and standards for the department as a whole, and accepted criteria for performance measurement.

2. Manuals and instructions to foster uniform interpretation of established practices.

3. Appraisals of employee performance, made regularly or for special reasons, to identify gaps between actual performance and desired results, to ascertain specific training needs, and to develop effective ways of meeting those needs.

4. Training programs that help develop good employee performance, with criteria to measure the effectiveness of all training activities.

5. Leadership, motivation, and followthrough by the head of the department to identify opportunities for improvement or need for remedial action, and to point out areas where unfavorable results or trends should receive executive attention.

6. Recognition of improved performance through nonfinancial awards, financial rewards, or both.

Effective organization permits the execution of plans which help attain the department objectives. The primary responsibility for the execution of these plans rests with the chief credit executive who needs to take the following steps:

1. Establish controls to guarantee that the department is working harmoniously and effectively with other departments.

2. See to it that each major unit within the credit department carries out its full responsibility in the accomplishment of the company's credit plans.

3. See to it that credit department results conform with the objectives, policies, and programs for which the department head is accountable.

Controlling

The basis of effective control is a plan for control based upon some realistic set of standards. Perhaps the best statement of the purpose of control is the simple definition: "To assure performance in accordance with plans." The price of performance is everlasting followthrough. One of the skills of leadership is the art of getting desirable responses and results from individuals and groups in conformity with established objectives and goals. Hence, a necessary qualification of a chief credit executive is the ability to review and appraise the operations of the department and the performance of the staff in terms of desired results, and to provide conditions which encourage the staff to produce to the best of their abilities. Toward the achievement of these ends, it is necessary to develop, interpret, and maintain effective controls and standards which will assist all concerned to project desired results more accurately; identify and forecast major trends that affect significant credit activities; determine the need for changes in policies, practice, or both; detect credit problems, insofar as possible, in time to take corrective action before they become critical; and conserve time and effort on the part of all concerned.

A primary challenge in establishing effective controls in the credit department is to determine what is significant. It is equally important to determine what is not essential. Good credit controls are those that give subordinates optimum freedom and opportunity to utilize their resourcefulness, abilities, and potential power to accomplish their assignments. There is no effective substitute, however, for the one-to-one chain of influence from the head of the department downward. A systematic review of all operations should be made by the head of the department to assure conformity with established goals and objectives, and remedial action should be taken through appropriate channels. The appraisal of results can be done most effectively if significant facts are portrayed in graphic charts which are available when needed; eliminate all nonessential data; are easy to compare for conformity with established objectives, goals, and standards; and are easy to understand.

Another factor to note is that the economic climate in which business operates is fluid and complex. It is almost constantly in a state of change, or subject to change. Progress in some fields may be very rapid. Technological changes may have repercussions throughout an entire industry on short notice. This requires that every policy, every control, every record, and every report be periodically appraised and questioned for the purpose of making necessary changes in the light of experience and for planning anew. Definite responsibility should be established for appraising the observance of credit policies, for reporting lack of compliance, and for recommending remedial action wherever indicated. Also, definite responsibility should be placed for a periodic review of all credit techniques, procedures, practices, and standards of performance, and for recommending adoption of changes, additions, and deletions wherever indicated.

GOALS OF DYNAMIC CREDIT MANAGEMENT

In summary, it is the responsibility of the manager of the credit department to plan and direct the activities of the credit function in keeping with company policy and with the following ends in mind:

1. Increased sales and profits, resulting from a better understanding and more skillful handling of all credit functions.
2. Improved quality of work performed within the department, due to greater accuracy, thoroughness, and care exercised by every member of the staff.
3. Increased volume of credit workload handled with less effort and expense, and with greater promptness; the most effective utilization of the abilities, skills, and interests of the individual members of the staff and the total work force.
4. Decreased cost per unit of work performed, resulting from improved planning, direction, and supervision.

5. Greater satisfaction to all concerned, resulting from a clarification of the results that are expected.

Dynamic credit management requires, in addition to expertness in all the technical phases of credit, the ability to:

1. Analyze, plan, and develop objectives, policies, and programs.
2. Build an organization.
3. Assign responsibility, delegate commensurate authority, and maintain accountability for results.
4. Review and appraise operations for conformity with objectives, policies, standards, and practices; take remedial action wherever and whenever required.
5. Inspire confidence, motivate teamwork, and maintain growth.

CHAPTER 5

OVERVIEW OF THE CREDIT DEPARTMENT

To attain the goals and objectives set forth in Chapter 4 and to optimize credit flow, a credit department should be organized in such a manner that the entire company will receive maximum benefits from the varied talents and experiences of its members. The management of credit takes place at three principal levels: general policymaking and control, day-to-day administration of department operations, and counseling services outside the department. The principal functions which must be performed in the management of credit are discussed briefly below.

GENERAL POLICYMAKING AND CONTROL

The credit policy provides a framework for consistent credit decisions directed toward attaining company goals. It is established by the credit department in conjunction with the chief financial officer, with an emphasis on customer relationships and in keeping with overall company policy.

Among policy matters to be considered are the standards as they relate to the assignment of responsibility and the delegation of authority, the terms of sale, and the criteria that customers must meet to obtain credit within the terms. Other considerations include the degree of automated versus personal handling of department activities, the personnel and staffing requirements, the management reporting system adopted for control purposes, and the broad area of receivables portfolio management.

Place in the Firm

Since credit is finance-oriented, the credit department is usually responsible to and reports to the treasurer or chief financial officer. Some of its finance-related functions include cash forecasting, protecting and managing the investment in the accounts receivable portfolio, the timely conversion of receivables to cash, financial analysis, handling of collateral which secures a customer's account, deposit of funds and relationship with banks, and evaluation of economic trends on sales, receivables, and collections.

Coordinating Interdepartmental Relationships. A key function of the chief credit executive is to integrate and coordinate the credit department's defined responsibilities with the treasury department and the other parts of the enterprise. The relationship of one department to another must be understood by all. Since the credit department comes into contact with almost every area of business, the chief credit executive should participate in meetings of other department heads when plans are being considered that impact on credit. Some of the important relationships with the many departments are now briefly discussed:

Marketing or Sales—Dealing with the Customer. Establishing a viable credit-sales relationship is one of the most difficult tasks of the chief credit executive. Credit policy must be clearly defined to reduce misunderstandings between sales and credit. Participation in sales meetings is essential to clarify the role and responsibility of credit, especially in dealings with the customer. It should be stressed that one of the major goals of credit is to help move goods to the customer on a timely basis, but with a reasonable assurance of payment. Additionally, there should be a clear delineation of responsibility for resolving customer disputes and unauthorized deductions.

Thus one of the major contributions of the credit department to the selling function is to work with customers and sales representatives and to seek ways to approve orders. For example, a credit executive may be able to suggest a financing method not previously considered by the customer, or may be helpful in locating sources of capital for a customer's contemplated program. Occasionally, in talks with customers, a credit executive will learn about planned purchases which have not come to the attention of sales. This information should be relayed as quickly as possible.

Finally, what may be termed a marketing risk should be distinguished from a credit risk. For example, to achieve adequate geographic distribution in marketing a name-brand product, it may be necessary to sell to a company that may not be acceptable creditwise. These marginal accounts are taken on for strategic reasons and should be identified as such when receivables investment is being analyzed.

This does not mean that credit and sales files are interchangeable. The credit executive is cautioned that they should be kept separate, particularly with respect to credit information that the credit department may obtain in connection with industry credit group meetings.

Purchasing. Purchasing departments often check the financial responsibility of new supply sources through the credit department to assure that the vendor or subcontractor will be able to deliver as agreed. Besides inquiring into the backgrounds of these potential suppliers, the credit department can also analyze their finances. At times, the credit department is also used to collect or adjust debit memorandums issued to cover claims for defective material or to settle other chargebacks.

In other instances, the credit department is helpful in negotiating with suppliers. For instance, it can arrange for security or protective clauses in contracts with suppliers that do not have strong finances. Or it may suggest bailment or other devices for title retention when company goods are placed with another concern for further processing. Again, the purchasing department may contact the credit department for opinions about terms and conditions of purchase orders. The credit department may also see to it that setoff rights are retained when its company both sells to and buys from another concern; in some instances, these rights may be requested for additional security.

Manufacturing. When overproduction leads to excess inventory, it may be necessary to dispose of the goods through sales to accounts that are not ordinarily creditworthy. Just as with marketing risk sales, these production risk sales are closely followed by the credit department to minimize collection cost and bad debts.

Sometimes orders are put into production subject to recheck with the credit department before shipment. An approval subject to recheck usually means the customer must do something before goods are released: pay an overdue balance, reduce outstandings to an acceptable level, submit an interim or annual financial statement, or the like. This allows the goods to be manufactured for delivery on time to the buyer. While most of these conditional approvals result in a release of goods when they are ready, they do comprise a production risk.

On the other hand, in periods of shortages a customer may order well in excess of actual requirements in the hope that the amount allotted will be near the quantity actually required. A credit executive can usually recognize this practice and prevent the marketing and manufacturing departments from being misled into believing that growing sales potential has made additional production facilities necessary. Further, when a company is considering an increase in plant capacity, the credit executive can estimate whether customers are capable of absorbing the greater volume of production.

Systems and Data Processing. A major function of the credit department is to establish guidelines and parameters to be used by data processing people establishing computer systems and procedures for credit, collection, and accounts receivable.

Other Departments. Determining the status of a customer's account often requires close cooperation with the accounting department. Also, a credit department frequently accounts for payments received and for collateral taken in settlement of customer accounts, credit adjustments, and corrections of sales. Further, legal regulations and requirements as well as the proper use of legal documents have an important bearing on business operations, so the credit department has close contact with the company's legal department.

In other cases, when a customer has difficulty with one of the company's products, it may be necessary for the credit department to consult with engineering groups about corrections or replacements to be made before the account can be collected. Or the traffic department may wish to determine the financial responsibility of carriers and occasionally may require assistance in the collection of claims for shortages or damages.

A close relationship must also exist with the personnel department. It may be necessary to define the characteristics of each credit position and to prepare adequate job descriptions. Recommended salary ranges must be sufficient and competitive. Training programs should be coordinated with the personnel department.

The varied relationships of a credit department have been briefly discussed here in order to emphasize that the credit function goes considerably beyond the appraisal of customers' credit and the collection of accounts receivable. Therefore, in the organization of a credit department as well as the provision of personnel and facilities, allowance should be made for these additional responsibilities. The assistance that a credit department can give the other components of a business can be just as important in establishing the department's value to a company as its performance in connection with accounts receivable.

Organizing the Credit Department. Each function to be performed must be provided for in the organizational structure of the credit department in order to ensure a smooth flow of credit. Two essential functions briefly discussed here are defining responsibility and staffing.

Defining Responsibility. The structure should be flexible and clearly delineate responsibility for each function to be performed and for each customer account. If a company classifies accounts by degree of risk, it may assign the highest-risk accounts to the more experienced and knowledgeable credit executives and the relatively risk-free accounts to those with less experience and ability. This approach is particularly useful where a company has a large number of accounts that vary in size, quality, and quantity.

Staffing. The credit department must have a staff large enough for the current workload. It must have qualified individuals in each position, systematically trained and developed for promotion to greater responsibility. Forecasting staff requirements and budgeting for growth are key functions of the chief credit executive, along with the need to cover each position with an accurate and up-to-date job description.

Controlling and Evaluating the Credit Function

Controls and guidelines must be established to provide for a timely evaluation of key functions. This will ensure prompt and suitable decisions and enable appropriate action to be taken when required. Quantitative and qualitative data should be available for adequate reports to each control point. The goal of the department is to achieve an optimum combination of profitable sales, turnover of accounts receivable investment, bad-debt expense, and credit department operating expense.

DAY-TO-DAY ADMINISTRATION

The major functions performed on a daily basis by the credit department include credit approval process, account establishment, order processing, accounts receivable administration, collections and adjustments, and control and followthrough.

Credit Approval Process

Certain procedures must be followed before a credit decision can be made. The relationship with the customer must be established; essential information about the account must be obtained, analyzed, and stored; and the data must be evaluated so that the processing of future orders may be facilitated.

Establishing a Customer Relationship. Customer relationships are basically established through the sales department by visits, marketing programs, and advertising and solicitation. Customer orders come through the sales department, which furnishes the necessary credit information about the prospective customer.

Credit Investigation. Few companies make shipments on open account to a new customer without some sort of credit investigation. The sales representative's credit advice which identifies the customer should include sources to contact for their experience. They should include banks, other suppliers, and accountants. Credit agency reports can also be utilized, as can direct interviews or correspondence with the prospect.

Communicating with the Customer. The credit department is usually the only group, other than sales, to make substantial and frequent contact with the customer. This happens when the credit investigation fails to provide sufficient data to warrant approval of the amount of credit requested. When additional information is required, letters should be written, phone calls made, or visits arranged to meet the management team and facilities or to discuss financial plans and budgets. Although the sales force is ordinarily not involved in the financial coversations with a customer, they should be kept informed of these matters. Sales has the prime responsibility for dealing with customers, so communication should be a coordinated effort.

Documentation. Special documentation may be necessary. It may require participation of the attorneys for both the company and customer. A security agreement along with filings under the Uniform Commercial Code should be made if collateral is required. A guaranty or subordination if agreed upon should be prepared. A letter of credit and other special documentation may be called for in international dealings.

Credit Files. A credit file is established to store all the gathered data. Documents and collateral obtained to secure a credit appraisal are stored separately, usually in a fireproof cabinet or vault. The credit file is the prime storage place for information on a customer's account, including its history and current status. It must be readily accessible but handled in a confidential manner. Periodic purging of the files will weed out obsolete material and keep them manageable.

Financial Analysis. Financial statements should be spread and analyzed, with appropriate ratios and flows calculated as an aid to the evaluation. Statements received direct from the customer should be promptly acknowledged. Most customers look for and expect comments about their financial condition. There is always the possibility that fraudulent statements may be submitted by mail, so it is good practice to keep the envelopes.

Credit Decision—Setting Lines. All the data help the credit executive to decide whether to approve or decline the request for credit. Determined lines or limits are an aid to processing further orders. A letter should be sent informing the customer of the credit decision and specifying the credit parameters of the relationship. This will minimize questions and future disputes.

Account Establishment

The ultimate responsibility for a customer account status rests with the credit executive. It is essential therefore to set guidelines for performing the necessary component functions. The account must be precisely identified with its correct name and address. Additional identifiers may include an alphanumeric identifier, a D-U-N-S number, bank transit number, or a Social Security or government business identification number. If orders are to be prescreened for credit approval, it may be necessary to spell out credit lines or overdue parameters. Check processors must have guidelines for handling errors, short payments or overpayments, and terms and discount violations. They should know how to communicate with customers and the sales and credit departments to resolve problems. Collectors must be told how to minimize customer slowness and to resolve problems arising from such items as returns, traffic claims covering shortages and damage, pricing disputes, or allowances for advertising and promotion.

Order Processing

Every order that falls within established credit parameters should be processed quickly for shipment to the buyer. If it does not, it should be referred to the credit executive for personal handling.

The reason for the referral—such as order over the limit, new account, balance past due, and the like—is transmitted to the credit executive; also, the account status, the credit files, and any other pertinent information. Wherever possible, orders should be released for shipment quickly. If it is necessary to hold them until a credit deficiency is made up, the sales department and the customer should be notified.

Accounts Receivable Administration

The sum of all customer account ledgers must agree with the accounts receivable control account in the general ledger; this total reflects the company's investment in accounts receivable. As a shipment is made, its invoice is posted to the customer account; manually with a hand-posted system or as a by-product of billing in an automated system. Credits and payments are also posted, so at any time the sum of the open items represents the balance due from the customer.

From a credit point of view, accounts receivable administration reflects the credit parameters established for customers, along with a historical summary of the transactions that have taken place. Thus it may involve customer identifiers, credit lines, credit agency ratings, daily shipping amounts, aging of open items, terms, and a payment summary. Quantitative data for reports include number of invoices, checks, credits, discount or other terms violations, and short payments and overpayments. The ledger should also contain a summary of order activity along with the impact on the balance due of any orders that have been approved or held but not yet been shipped. This will provide a view of the account as it will look when those orders are shipped and billed.

Collections and Adjustments

The collection aspect consists of cash inflows from accounts receivable and rests with the customers' accounts payable departments. Their payables ledgers should mirror the creditor's receivables ledger both in amounts and terms. Most customers pay invoices as they fall due and need no special collection effort. They may send payments to a lockbox bank, some third party such as a factor, or directly to the selling company.

Two major functions of a lockbox bank are to coordinate and speed the flow of good funds into a central or control bank and thus optimize cash availability, and to provide the lockbox customer with manually or semiautomated data about the items being paid. A fully automated payment system will provide not only for funds inflows but also for computer-to-computer order placement, invoicing, and data transmission between buyer and seller to properly maintain both receivables and payables ledgers.

A collection effort is needed when payment is not received for invoices as they mature. It may be only a statement but can include letters, phone calls, telegrams, visits, and third-party collections that lead to meetings of creditors or bankruptcy. The resolution of disputes about how much is due is also a function of the collection effort. The customer may require an invoice copy or proof of delivery; clarification of prices, terms, and discounts; information concerning damaged or undelivered merchandise; or explanation of some other adjustment claim. Usually the sales and other departments are consulted to resolve these items.

Control and Followthrough

This activity seeks to identify and remedy whatever is out of line. For instance, budgets spell out the goals and benchmarks. There are budgets for personnel and workload, expenditures, investment in accounts receivable, days sales outstanding, bad debts, cash inflows, and the many other items that can be forecast with some degree of accuracy. Then controls such as aged trial balances define whether predetermined goals have been met and point to action that is necessary. Cash received is screened daily, either manually or by computer, to make certain that delinquent accounts are in fact paying as they promised; also to see that held orders are processed on time. Necessary reports are prepared for management to understand the status and accomplishments of the credit department.

COUNSELING SERVICES

The emergence of the credit executive as a business counselor has been one of the most dramatic changes in credit management in recent years. This development in the credit executive's role reflects changing concepts which are being applied at all levels of management. No longer is the credit executive adequately fulfilling a function by simply granting or denying credit approvals. Instead, credit is part of a management team, charged with responsibility for increasing both sales and profits. Because of its broad exposure to business situations, the credit staff is in a position to counsel in controlled circumstances with customers and with other departments of the firm.

Customer Counseling

A credit executive's opportunities for discussing financial and operating circumstances with customers are almost unlimited. Small businesses frequently need credit which is large in relation to their financial resources. These small businesses are commonly operated by one or two persons who may be thoroughly competent in their own fields, who may be excellent salespeople, but who have limited experience in financial management and control. The suggestions of the credit executive can often help the small business grow and make it possible for the seller to nurture a more substantial customer.

Legal and Ethical Aspects of Counseling. While it is true that counseling is an accepted part of a credit executive's job, certain legal and ethical considerations must be kept in mind. It is perfectly proper to offer advice and counsel in areas that are familiar to the business executive, provided the advice is sought by the customer and is reasonable. On the other hand, it is easy to overstep the bounds of effective counseling, which could lead to bad feeling on the part of the recipient if the advice is followed and yields poor results. In extreme cases, the customer may even claim legal liability on the part of the firm offering the advice, stating that the advice led to financial difficulty.

Counseling should always be viewed by customers as their choice, and not something they are directed to do. While many will welcome advice and assistance given in the right way, some will resent even a carefully worded suggestion, claiming their problems are not the business of anyone else. For this reason, credit executives must move very carefully in counseling in order to build up relationships with customers. A keen sensitivity to human reactions is of the greatest importance.

Approach to Counseling. Customer counseling can be regarded as a way of describing how a creditor looks at a business. Opportunities to counsel are brought to the credit executive's attention in various ways, but mostly through the analysis of a customer's financial statement. Other means of determining the need for counseling include conversations with other suppliers, discussion with company salespeople, and review of published data. An active file of contacts in the business is a useful tool. Moreover, with the business world so complex and specialized, the astute executive learns to seek sources of specialized knowledge. Some of the popular sources are banks, accountants, lawyers, and the state and federal governments.

By training and experience, credit executives may detect indications of trouble long before they are apparent to the customer. Needless to say, the solution of many problems is much easier when recognized early. Besides helping to correct faulty situations, a credit executive can pass along new ideas or serve as a sounding board of someone else's ideas.

The credit executive becomes aware of opportunities for counseling in many ways. Analysis of customer's financial statements or other reports may indicate the need for suggestions. Sales representative's reports, a change in the manner of payment, newspaper information, and many other sources may bring such situations to the attention of the credit executive. Many credit executives make it a practice to call on their marginal customers regularly; they are on the lookout for situations in which an outsider's suggestions may be helpful.

Purposes. In a counseling situation, it is important for the credit executive to have clearly in mind the purpose of the consultation. In one stance, it may be to save a customer from bankruptcy. In another, it may be to help a small but financially strong customer to achieve sound and well-balanced growth and thus become a better customer. In still another, it may be to alert the customer to an unnoticed problem.

Who Is To Do the Counseling?   This question is closely related to the size and organization of the credit department, and the extent to which this service is part of the creditor's policy approach to customers. Surely the credit executive and qualified assistants should be involved. If the department is organized by region, the counseling may be performed by several individuals locally. Or if a company has several major product divisions, different credit executives may specialize in order to keep fully informed about the specific problems in their fields.

General Counseling.   The broad-based type of general counseling that a company can do is naturally restricted by the viability of generalizations to meet specific situations. Nevertheless, this method is often used to disseminate information that can apply to many customers at the same time.

Books and Pamphlets.   Many books and other sources of information are available for customers having neither the time nor the initiative to seek theoretical solutions to their problems. These sources provide typical information that can be adapted for their own use. Several companies have prepared booklets, manuals, or written material which can be made available to all who are interested. Such matters as financial requirements for a certain type of operation, intelligent use of credit, the use of budgets, the importance of inventory control, how to set up a time-payment plan, and how to use break-even point analysis can be described in a popular style of presentation.

Some companies distribute recommended forms for keeping records, maintaining inventory control, and analyzing or recording other aspects of their customer's business. Other companies point out to their customers certain basic principles or guideposts and suggest ways in which interested customers can investigate further.

Financial Statements.   Credit reporting agencies, trade associations, and other organizations make elaborate composite studies of financial and operating ratios for different lines of business. These can be most useful as a source of general information, but in some cases an analysis of financial statements received from one's own customers may be even more helpful. By drawing averages or composite figures, a credit executive can use such information without divulging the source and hence without betraying any confidence.

When such information is compiled in summary form, the credit executive is able to analyze any individual financial statement more thoroughly and to draw sound conclusions. In addition, sharing this information with customers gives them a management tool not otherwise available.

Credit Opportunities.   There are other ways in which to offer general counseling to customers—for example, information about changes in legislation, new ideas that have been used successfully, or sources of information for specific types of problems.

Counseling with Individual Customers.   The most effective means of counseling is personal consultation. This could take place either in the credit executive's office or if possible at the customer's place of business. Calling on customers is ideal to the extent that time and other factors permit, but a credit executive must make use of other means as well. When the proper rapport has been achieved, it is frequently possible to counsel by mail. For specific problems the telephone can be used to advantage.

There are many ways in which opportunities can be discovered for counseling with individual customers. Among the best are the financial statements received periodically. Careful analysis of each statement, and a comparative study of its relation to prior statements and to statements of similar concerns, frequently indicates opportunities for constructive counseling.

Accounts Receivable. Frequently a customer's accounts receivable may get out of line. The counselor may wish to describe where to secure credit information, how to analyze that information, what are reasonable terms of sale for the types of transactions involved, how to set up a collection procedure, how to calculate cost of carrying receivables, and whether the customer can really afford to sell on credit or to offer a time-payment plan. Too often these topics are well known to the larger concerns, but not the small business.

Merchandise Inventory. An experienced credit executive can tell at a glance whether a customer's investment in inventory is in line with sales volume and net working capital. As a rule, the credit executive cannot set up a stock control system or make decisions for a customer, but can very properly call attention to situations which seem out of line. Too often a small business finds an easy satisfaction in the net profit figure, without realizing that all of the profit may be tied up in slow-moving inventory.

To forestall inventory difficulties, the customer may need a better method of stock control. It may be necessary to analyze the business by products and reduce or discontinue those that are not profitable. If operating capital is limited, an excessive amount may be tied up in high-priced articles.

Payments and Purchases. Unusual increases in accounts payable and purchases, and slowing payments, may be the warning sign to the credit executive that special attention is required. A personal call on a customer can assure the creditor that the situation is satisfactory and help the customer locate the cause of the slowness.

Outside Borrowing. When it becomes necessary for a customer to seek outside financing, a credit executive can assist by compiling and clarifying the actual funding needs, and explaining the available sources that would be most economical and productive. For example, a customer should be encouraged to establish a bank line of credit and use it to take advantage of suppliers' discount terms.

Profits. A declining trend in profits is a serious warning signal. Composite operating figures for other concerns may be helpful in pinpointing the areas of specific shortcomings. For example, if labor costs are the most important factor in a particular industry, detailed analysis of labor costs for a number of customers will give the credit executive composite figures against which to judge individual situations.

Inadequate profits or a declining trend in profits may also lead to an analysis of gross profit in order to determine whether pricing policies are at fault, or to a break-even analysis which would help to identify the specific corrective action.

Other Opportunities for Customer Counseling.   Many other situations lend themselves to counseling. A partial list of specific problems which might come up for discussion include:

1. Cash budgeting and the use of other projections in financial planning.
2. Automation of the accounts receivable system.
3. Unwise investments outside of the business operations which could dissipate management attention and company funds.
4. Excessive withdrawals from the business that could hamper a company's potential growth.
5. Inadequate business insurance coverage.
6. Overly rapid expansion of the business that could cause a financial concentration in plant and equipment at the expense of operating funds.

Counseling Within the Company

When undertaking the role of an internal advisor, the credit executive is simply taking a broad management view. The counseling function is part and parcel of every executive's functions and activities. While no attempt is made here to cover all the situations which may arise, most of them fall within three general areas—marketing, purchasing and procurement, and finance.

Marketing.   There are a great many opportunities for the credit department to help the company do a more effective job of marketing. The more common examples include checking the credit of prospective dealers or distributors to help select good ones, directing the sales department's attention to existing outlets where the financial and credit information indicates additional volume could be used, and furnishing the sales department with the names of prospective customers with credit already checked. For example, the credit executive may learn of a new customer branch or plant to be established. Credit should be checked quickly and, if found satisfactory, the lead should be given to the sales department with a notation as to the size of credit order that would be approved immediately.

When a company is considering a change in its method of distribution or is setting up a distribution system for a new product, the credit executive has another opportunity to be constructive. One specific area where many credit executives have made such a contribution is in devising special terms or financing arrangements to fit the requirements of a particular product. This can involve working out the details for a subsidiary financing corporation, and developing specific terms and other financial arrangements for the type of product and the particular customers. In addition, special protective clauses or controls may be needed in large contracts with the government or with other special customers.

Purchasing and Procurement. There are risks represented on the buying side of the business as well as on the receivables side. The credit executive can thus be of service to the purchasing department and other departments that have a problem of procurement. It is advisable to check periodically on the credit and financial standing of the principal suppliers of the company's requirements, not only to avoid problems in connection with returned merchandise or adjustments but also to assure continued sources of supply. Such checks are most important in the event of sizable or long-term commitments, when the success of the credit executive's company may depend upon the completion of a contract on the part of a supplier. The credit executive may also help with terms offered to the company on special purchase contracts for large quantities of materials or supplies.

At times, the credit department also needs to assist in the collection or adjustment of debit memorandums for defective merchandise or in the settlement of other chargebacks.

Many companies find it desirable to watch closely the financial responsibility of truckers or other carriers used in the procurement and shipment of merchandise. This is important in the ordinary handling of claims and adjustments, and especially in the event of any loss resulting from an accident or disaster. The same point holds true for other service organizations, such as advertising agencies or accountants, where ability to perform as contracted is essential.

Frequently one company must place its own materials with another for processing. The credit department will then want to make appropriate investigation and in some instances may work out special protective measures in the form of contract provisions or security arrangements. If scrap material is to be disposed of, the credit department should check the financial responsibility of the scrap purchaser before terms other than cash are allowed.

Finance. The credit executive should be well informed on current economic conditions and trends, and familiar with the significance of economic indicators. Such understanding is important for carrying out the credit function and in equipping the executive to share in top management decisions.

Certain techniques used with customers may also be used to solve financial problems within the company. Budgets, cash forecasts, and other management and control tools can be demonstrated by the knowledgeable credit executive when they are not being used in the company.

The credit executive is usually in a position to offer sound opinions regarding plant expansion. Past experience with customers can lead to accurate estimates regarding the ability of customers to absorb a greater volume of production from both a financial and a physical standpoint. The validity of sales forecasts can thus be tested, and the method of financing any planned expansion can be probed.

ORGANIZATIONAL ASPECTS OF CREDIT MANAGEMENT

CHAPTER 6

ORGANIZATION OF THE CREDIT DEPARTMENT

The requirements of the specific business enterprise determine the size and type of credit department. In some organizations, a very small staff may successfully perform the credit function. In organizations where the flow of credit is more complicated, a larger staff with a wider variety of skills may be required. It is extremely important that the type of credit department be determined only after a careful analysis of the specific functions and objectives of the credit department within a particular company.

Unlike most other company operations, the credit department tends to remain fairly constant in size and scope of activities during periods of changing business conditions. In fact, a credit department is ordinarily confronted by an even greater number of problems in a depressed economy than during a period of general prosperity. Consequently, the organization of the department is particularly important; a measure of permanence and stability must be achieved which will assure satisfactory performance of the departmental functions under all conditions. This does not mean that the organization should remain static or that a company can afford to disregard the desires of employees for training, promotion, or transfer. It is highly desirable, however, to have a nucleus of experienced and capable employees always available within the department.

CENTRALIZATION AND DECENTRALIZATION

The role of asset management in all business environments has been rapidly gaining in importance and will continue to play a very active part in the overall profitability. With company growth and diversification, management on both the executive and administrative levels of many large multiple-unit companies has become increasingly concerned with the function of credit management. A question often faced by these companies is whether the administration of credit should be centralized or decentralized.

General Observations

It is important to point out that neither centralization nor decentralization are absolutes. Instead, they reflect the amount of authority required in each of the organizational levels. Decentralization identifies itself with dispersion of authority. There is some decentralization of authority in any organizational structure. No business could survive unless some authority is delegated to subordinates. On the other hand, neither could it survive with complete decentralization. While centralization and decentralization are extremes in theory, neither is found in actual practice. The vital concern is the degree to which centralization or decentralization is practiced.

Either organizational structure can be effective if managed properly and staffed with competent personnel. This can be exemplified by the diversity of credit department organizational structures in varied industries—for example, petroleum, chemicals, and leisure. To try to label any industry or any company within an industry as simply centralized or decentralized from a credit organizational point of view would be misleading. The best companies use elements of each to achieve the greatest positive contribution to their overall objectives.

Important Considerations

In the most widely accepted sense, most credit departments are centralized in a structure that provides the proper environment to establish and maintain controls. Under such a structure almost all the day-to-day functions are performed within a central place, with a subordinate hierarchy reporting to the chief credit executive. Consequently, the department head is in a better position to exercise personal influence and experience in day-to-day activities.

The inclusion of credit on a day-to-day, face-to-face basis with other management personnel offers credit management the opportunity to participate in a variety of corporate objectives. These objectives include the achievement of stated profit goals, the establishment of a public image for the company, the meeting of competition, the utilization of funds available, and the direction of the total efforts of the firm toward the satisfaction of a particular segment of the market. Such an organizational structure has its authority and responsibility shared with middle-level chief credit executives. This requires clearly identified levels of authority and responsibility along with periodic reporting requirements.

Customer Service. One of the most important aspects of credit work is the opportunity to create and maintain customer good will. The relative ease with which customers can be contacted enhances a credit executive's relationship with marginal customers and those customers with which a sizable dollar exposure is maintained. A decentralized credit operation may better be able to accomplish this goal by its physical proximity.

Many credit departments may be reluctant to incur the expense of a trip for a personal visit except in cases of utmost urgency. Thus, with the exception of a few major purchasers, a centralized credit group may not be well acquainted with customers and have little knowledge of circumstances peculiar to an individual business.

Further, while there is no formula for determining when sales become too great to give satisfactory customer service from a central point, this type of operation undoubtedly can reach a point of diminishing returns. When customer accounts grow so numerous that a split is required, it is often made on a geographical basis. This gives the individual in charge an opportunity to become a specialist on the problems of a particular area.

The critical factor is for the company to decide which form of organization permits it to readily adjust to prevailing market conditions, harmonize effectively with field sales personnel, and perform the credit functions in a timely manner.

Credit and Sales Relationships. One of the most difficult problems encountered by credit personnel at decentralized locations is the pressure exerted by their local middle management. Often they are asked to disregard sound credit practices for the sake of a sale. Conversely, credit personnel can have a decided influence on the management of a decentralized operation. Sound credit practices can greatly enhance the profit performance of the underlying unit through increased sales and minimal losses.

Sales personnel are a valuable source of credit information and should be readily tapped by local credit executives. This close proximity and frequent contact with sales personnel should promote exchange of information and close coordination of action.

Controlling Credit Exposure. A prime advantage of centralized credit is the ease with which credit policies and procedures can be enforced. The authority is retained to make major decisions at central points within an organization. This is particularly important in controlling overall credit exposure when several units of a company sell to the same customer. In a decentralized operation, the ability to consolidate the orders is limited unless a common customer number is adopted by all the underlying units.

In addition, the day-to-day activities of underlying units and customer credit lines can best be controlled by a centralized credit operation. Allocation of a credit line could be considered in a decentralized operation, but a degree of flexibility must exist since the product requirements of customers vary from time to time.

Delegation of Authority. In order to gain maximum efficiency, sufficient authority must be delegated to the decentralized credit operation. There is always the question of how much authority should be given to credit personnel in the field consistent with retaining proper overall control. While new policies can go into effect immediately in a centralized group, the transmittal of policies and instructions to a field organization may become quite complicated and time-consuming. In many instances, policies cannot be applied uniformly in all branches; valuable time may be lost before the necessary changes are developed and authorized.

Communication.   A centralized system presents no problems of communication. Policies can be determined and placed in effect immediately, without the delay involved in transmitting and interpreting them to a field organization. Moreover, there is less chance of misunderstanding instructions or procedures. No division of authority exists with centralized operations, since the headquarters group has complete responsibility. There is much to commend this feature; all too frequently responsibility is placed in field offices without commensurate authority for execution—a situation that discourages efficient performance and retards initiative.

Training and Management Development.   Training of personnel is simplified under a centralized credit department, since a balanced operating group at headquarters allows careful indoctrination combined with on-the-job instruction. The central location includes a varied group of management personnel who, in addition to performing the daily functions of a credit department, can find and take the necessary time to properly train employees. A training program can be instituted which is best suited for group training. Periodic formal lectures can be held with various members of management who conduct these sessions for the lower echelon members of management. It is generally accepted that with a centralized credit operation and its advantages in training personnel, more competent personnel are available at the low-job classification levels.

The problem of training and transfer of credit and collection personnel is accentuated when credit is administered from decentralized locations. A training program suited to group training at a central point frequently cannot be used in a widely scattered organization because of the time and expense involved. When a person is transferred to a division or branch, it must be determined in advance that the individual has the experience necessary to handle the varied problems of a local credit department without continual reference to headquarters. When a member of a centralized organization is assigned to a different job, on the other hand, the immediate superiors can continue to supervise the individual's training. In making transfers in a decentralized organization, the personal requirements of employees must be considered, and these occasionally cause problems. Thus a particular individual may seem eminently qualified for a specific position, but outside factors may rule out a move to the new location. Furthermore, considerable expense can be incurred in transferring employees from one point to another in a field organization.

Taxes and Regulations.   Both taxes and legal considerations may enter into a decision to decentralize. Since these are technical matters which often require consultation with experts, only one salient point is mentioned here. In those locations where property taxes are levied on accounts receivable balances, this factor should be taken into consideration in establishing branch offices. The advice of a tax expert should be secured on such matters if decentralization is being considered by a company.

Costs Versus Benefits.   In addition to the tangible organizational differences in a centralized versus decentralized credit structure, the factor of applicable costs and benefits is important. It is readily apparent that the centralized credit department has a relatively lower cost of operation than a decentralized one. No duplication of personnel or equipment is required, and practically every other expense associated with centralization is lower, with the possible exception of telephone, telegraph, and traveling costs.

However, the top management's decision to structure a credit department one way or another is usually influenced by the balance between the costs and the supportive marketing and customer service role a credit department is required to play in the overall corporate strategy. An efficient level of consistent customer service requires a credit department not only to sustain a solid customer relationship but also to assure prompt payment of all invoices. In a market place where product technology is very similar and competitive products abundant, the competitive edge can well be the level of customer service and counseling guidance given to an account in the day-to-day working environment.

TYPES OF CREDIT ORGANIZATION

As noted in the prior chapter, management of credit takes place at three principal levels: general policymaking and control, day-to-day administration of department operations, and counseling services outside the department. Although there may be numerous variations in the structure of different companies, it is possible to classify the control and administration functions into three broad types of operations:

1. Credit that is controlled and administered at a principal office.
2. Credit that is controlled at a principal office but is administered from decentralized locations.
3. Credit that is controlled and administered from decentralized locations with a staff office maintained at headquarters.

Controlled and Administered at a Principal Office

Under this type of organization, the credit department functions as a line operation. It is situated entirely at company headquarters where all of its business is transacted. There are no field offices; although the central department may service a number of different business units, its activity is not duplicated in any of the operating units. The chief credit executive and staff approve credit on all orders at headquarters. Contact with customers is largely by telephone or correspondence, although field trips are made when necessary. A centralized credit system may be modified in certain respects. In some companies, for example, most of the credit functions are carried on at headquarters, but collections offices are located in the field to assist in securing payments or making adjustments.

Figure 6–1 illustrates a credit department that is administered and controlled from a principal office. The chief credit executive devotes almost full time to the management of credit and reports to an executive officer (in most manufacturing or trading companies, the credit function reports to the treasurer; this example and the two that follow reflect this consensus). This type of operation not only maintains a close connection with the financial function but also the sales department. It is particularly suitable to small and medium-sized businesses that do not have too much geographical dispersion or product diversification.

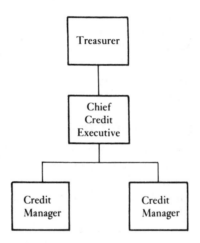

FIG. 6–1.   Credit Controlled and Administered from a Principal Office.

Decentralized Offices with Control at a Principal Office

This is another line form of operation under which a middle-level chief credit executive reports functionally to a top-level chief credit executive at headquarters and also reports to the division head (the principle is the same for subsidiary or branch operations). Authority in credit and collection is received from the top-level chief credit executive, but in all other respects procedures to which the credit executive must conform are established by middle management.

Figure 6–2 illustrates a decentralized operation under which the middle-level chief credit executive has line authority. This type of arrangement requires close cooperation between the top-level chief credit executive and the division general manager regarding the dual reporting of the line credit executive. For the best results, the division general manager should consult with the top-level chief credit executive periodically in regard to administrative and operational problems. The top-level chief credit executive in turn will give considerable weight to the division general manager's view concerning the conduct of credit activities in the division.

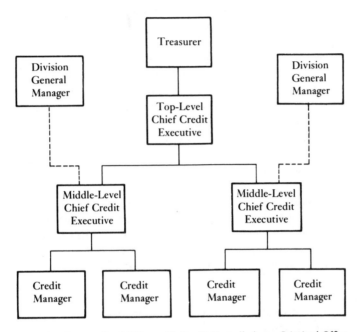

FIG. 6–2.   Decentralized Offices with Credit Controlled at a Principal Office.

Authority of the Middle-Level Chief Credit Executive.   The middle-level chief credit executive is normally authorized by the division general manager to take care of personnel problems, operating expenses, and all other nonfunctional matters within the scope of local policy. In supervising the conduct of local credit and collection activities, the top-level chief credit executive may follow one of several procedures. Generally the middle-level chief credit executive is given authority to give final credit approval on all orders not exceeding a stipulated amount; such final authority probably extends to 80 per cent or more of the orders received by a division, subsidiary, or branch. Orders in larger amounts are referred to headquarters for processing and approval, usually with local recommendation. In some instances, the middle-level chief credit executive may be authorized to give preliminary credit approval so the order may be put into production at the factory, with shipment approval to come from the top-level chief credit executive.

Another method is to designate certain customers as "headquarters accounts" because of special circumstances; all credit matters pertaining to these orders are accordingly processed by the headquarters credit office. When this procedure is followed, the middle-level chief credit executive ordinarily has final approving authority for all other orders, and may be empowered to recommend credit lines for accounts of unquestioned financial resources whose orders normally exceed local authorization.

In the area of miscellaneous adjustments or writeoffs, the middle-level chief credit executive is usually given a blanket authorization to process the great majority of individual cases, only those of major importance being brought to the attention of the top-level chief credit executive. In addition, a middle-level chief credit executive is often asked to recommend the amount of allowance for uncollectibles that will be required for the underlying unit's portfolio of accounts. The top-level chief credit executive then can factor in these local recommendations with overall company expectations and objectives in order to make adequate provision for this contingency.

Authority Retained by the Top-Level Chief Credit Executive. In many firms, the top-level chief credit executive retains the right to establish the credit policy under which the divisions operate. The department head thereby gains a considerable degree of indirect control over operations, regardless of the amount of authority assigned to and properly used by the middle-level chief credit executive. Here the top-level chief credit executive considers approvals in cases that exceed the limits set for an underlying chief credit executive and is completely responsible for all headquarters accounts if such a system is used.

The top-level chief credit executive, in conjunction with the accounting and systems departments, also determines the procedures, techniques, and practices to be followed by the divisions in their credit and collection operations. In the general supervision of the middle-level chief credit executives, close cooperation with all the division managers is necessary and covers the review and approval of budgets and operating expenses, the status of accounts, customer contacts, and the performance of all credit functions. It is important in a decentralized operation that the activities of the various divisions be coordinated so that substantial discrepancies will not exist among them in salaries, facilities, or methods.

Training of credit personnel and the assignment of employees to the divisions—with the agreement of the division manager—are primary responsibilities of the top-level chief credit executive. Programs must be established and administered to assist in the development of credit and collection employees. Since middle-level chief credit executives frequently seek advice and counsel of the top-level chief credit executive in connection with unusual or special situations, the staff in headquarters location must be organized in such a manner that the necessary assistance can be given promptly and expertly.

Decentralized Offices with Staff at Principal Office

Under this type of organization, the top-level chief credit executive is responsible for collecting information and preparing reports for top management, providing advice and counsel to the line credit executives, and participating in major problem-risk analyses. Figure 6–3 illustrates a decentralized operation with a staff office maintained at headquarters. This type of arrangement requires the chief credit executives of the underlying units to be responsible for order approvals and collections, and to control their own unit credit departments.

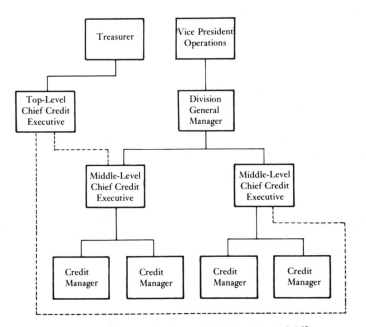

FIG. 6–3. Decentralized Offices with Staff at Principal Office.

Regardless of the delegation of authority and responsibility under this form, the top-level chief credit executive usually determines the overall credit policies. Divisions coordinate their activities and select the best alternative action in the light of prevailing conditions. Compliance with the overall policies is especially important, so periodic field trips and reports on division operations are the basic means for monitoring the activities of the line credit executive.

In those cases where control is completely decentralized, the middle-level chief credit executive reports only to the division general manager and has complete authority in all credit and collection matters without reference to headquarters. The division is required to carry out the general credit policies of the company, but the operation within those policies is the responsibility of the division. Consequently, the line credit executive is responsible to the division general manager both for the performance of the function and for the operation of the division.

General Considerations

In general, the credit department tends to be a line operation managed from a principal office, although in many cases its administration is carried on at decentralized locations. Despite the fact that their major duties are usually line, almost every credit executive performs some staff activity such as appraisal of business conditions and forecast of economic trends. This staff work becomes increasingly important as an organization grows larger, particularly in the manufacturing field, and executive management requires increasing relief from the pressures of accumulated problems. In some large corporations, particularly those whose credit departments are decentralized to the fullest extent, a credit executive will devote principal time to staff functions.

When sufficient work of a staff nature develops, the credit executive should be relieved of operating duties so that full time may be devoted to this important function. Otherwise, there is a danger that staff duties will be neglected under the pressure of line problems. Eventually a full-time staff executive will require the services of additional personnel who have a background in credit work. A group of this kind will provide the necessary training, counseling, planning, and appraising for operating units, and will assist executive management with broad company policies or long-term plans and programs.

CHAPTER 7

STAFFING THE CREDIT DEPARTMENT

Emphasis on the job to be done is the essential consideration in making the proper assignment of personnel to spots on the credit department organization chart. The aim must be to allocate effectively the total functions and responsibilities of the credit department. The basic tools for accomplishing this are the job description and the job specification, each described in the following pages.

IMPORTANCE OF THE JOB DESCRIPTION

The job description is essentially a statement of the duties, responsibilities, and authorities of each position. It helps define the amount and type of training required by qualified personnel for the various credit department jobs. It is also valuable when developing measures of performance.

Although precise job descriptions are essential to the administrator, their limitations must be recognized. It is characteristic of modern business organizations to constantly alter their form, objectives, and procedures. An effective credit department is similarly flexible; therefore, job descriptions, regardless of the care that has gone into their initial development, must be periodically reviewed and brought up to date.

Further, many in personnel management feel that job descriptions work well for the lower positions, but the higher the position being described the more difficult it is to pinpoint the intangible and indefinable aspects of the job. Credit department employees can also assist in the preparation of their own job descriptions. Effective two-way communication—upward, downward, and lateral—is realistically encouraged for both improved performance and benefits to human relations.

DEVELOPING A JOB DESCRIPTION

The four primary elements of the successful job description are position objective; duties and responsibilities of the position; the authority of the position (should be commensurate with the duties and responsibilities); and relationships with other individuals, departments, or functions that the position entails.

Essential Elements Defined

The four primary elements are discussed in more detail in order to show their relative importance in the job description.

Objective. The job description should begin with a succinct statement of the position's objective that will serve as a general introduction to the particular position under consideration. In this section of the job description there should be no detail—not even a partial breakdown of the major duties. The statement should simply describe a general indication of the nature of the position in relation to the department as a whole. For example, the statement of objectives for a chief credit executive might read:

> To establish sound and constructive credit policies and practices, and to administer all credit operations of the company in a manner that will increase distribution and sales volume, contribute to the profit of the company and to customer stability, and provide for the prompt turnover and adequate protection of the company's investment in accounts receivable.

Duties and Responsibilities. The longest section of the job description is usually devoted to the major responsibilities of the job, which should be stated in sufficient detail to guide the individual in the job. This section should also enumerate the special activities, beyond normal business routine, that are involved in fulfilling the position objective or function.

For example, the duties and responsibilities of a chief credit executive can be classified as follows: establishes credit policy, interprets approved credit policy, establishes operating procedures, maintains adequate controls, participates in periodic analyses of business and economic conditions, and keeps management informed on the status of the accounts receivable portfolio.

In the job description, each of these duties is analyzed in specific terms. For example, the chief credit executive *establishes* companywide credit policies and then *interprets* them to the members of the staff, *establishes* and *controls* all operating procedures, *participates* in periodic analyses of business conditions, and *advises* management concerning the status of the accounts receivable investment. It is important that the key words be clearly understood by all who will refer to the job description.

Authority. It is generally agreed that a basic principle of sound administration is to give the individual sufficient authority to do the job—that is, commensurate responsibility and authority. For this reason some job descriptions discuss the two elements of "responsibility" and "authority" in one section. It is extremely important to specify the authority delegated to the position with respect to the major duties and responsibilities for which the individual is to be held accountable. To delegate less authority than is needed to fulfill a stated responsibility is in effect to reduce the degree of responsibility. On the other hand, delegation of authority in excess of the attendant responsibility usually has the effect of increasing the responsibility. It would then be safe to conclude that responsibility and authority are usually commensurate in practice, regardless of what their relative weight may be in theory.

Relationships. The section in the job description devoted to relationships—sometimes omitted in otherwise excellent job descriptions—is particularly important in the case of credit positions because of the many contacts the credit department may have throughout the organization. This section should describe the types, levels, and organizational location of individuals with whom the person in the job will have contact. The specific nature of the relationship (advisory, coordinating, etc.) should be stated in every instance, since these contacts can have a significant bearing upon the accomplishment of the position function.

Analyzing the Position

Various methods of analysis have been used successfully in the process of developing a job description. The method that follows is based upon factors present (though not to the same degree) in all credit department positions.

Fact Finding, Analysis, and Interpretation. The first factor to be considered is the amount of investigation, research, and creative thinking that the position requires. This may include analysis and interpretation of factual material relating to economic, social, and political conditions, as well as legal and technological trends. It may be necessary, in certain positions, to draw inferences and conclusions in the process of formulating policies and objectives. If the position is concerned not only with analysis and interpretation but also the supervision of the information-gathering process, the job description must make clear those responsibilities.

Organization/Planning and Administration. The planning factor entails those requirements of the position related to the formulation and execution of plans for achieving specified objectives. This factor includes establishing and administering organizational functions, positions, responsibilities, and relationships. When a position is analyzed in terms of this factor, the size and complexity of the organization must be considered, as well as the levels of the positions within that organization, and the extent to which all organizational functions (such as staffing, salary administration, and employee relations) are included within the position duties. A further consideration is the extent to which the position is responsible for the direction, supervision, and coordination of subordinates as indicated by the number of persons directly and indirectly supervised.

Planning and Execution of Operations. This factor represents the degree to which the position is involved in achieving established objectives through planning, developing, and executing work programs and maintaining controls. In evaluating a position with respect to this factor, one must consider the extent to which the position requires the translation of overall objectives and policies into work programs that will facilitate the achievement of these objectives. The complexity of the problems and the degree of participation in formulating departmental or companywide plans also are to be weighed.

Interpersonal Contacts. This factor represents the requirements of the position for initiating and maintaining effective contacts with individuals other than subordinates. Internally it refers to consultative and nonsupervisory relationships within the company. Externally it refers to contacts with customers, governmental agencies, suppliers, potential employees, and the community at large. In evaluating a position with respect to interpersonal contacts, the possible effects of successful or unsuccessful relationships should be considered, as well as the complexity of the problems involved. On the basis of this analysis, it may be concluded that diplomacy and salesmanship are necessary qualifications for certain positions.

Influence on Progress of the Organization. This factor represents the influence the position may exert on the general progress of the company. Among the elements to be taken into account are the scope of responsibility and authority, and exposure to opportunities and risks. When evaluating a position with respect to this factor, one should consider the possible effects of undue delay or poor judgment in making decisions and taking action, and the likelihood of finding and correcting errors in time to prevent loss.

Some positions should be evaluated primarily in terms of their potential contribution to the organization through long-range planning—for example, research and development activities. In this area, mistakes may delay the accomplishment of objectives but are not likely to cause large immediate losses.

Weighting the Factors. Particularly for purposes of position grading and salary administration, the above factors may be graded by level on a ten-point scale. In respect to fact finding, analysis, and interpretation, for example, a job in which the subject matter is greatly diversified or requires complex analysis and interpretation might be given a level of eight or nine. If the subject matter is moderately diversified, the factor could be given a rating of six or seven—and if there is no problem of getting or interpreting the information, the rating might be one. Such a system, although mechanical, does give some indication of the quality or work required in a particular job.

After assigning points to every factor, some evaluators consider the sum of the assigned points to be the rating for the job. A further refinement of such a rating system is to weight the factors, one against the other. For example, in a particular organization "influence on the progress of the organization" might be considered the most important factor and therefore weighted to make up 25 per cent of the total rating. Figure 7–1 presents a form which can be used in this type of analysis.

Date_____			
Job Title_____			
Location _____			
Factor	Basis of Evaluation	Level	Point Value
A. Fact Finding, Analysis, and Interpretation			
B. Organization Planning and Administration Part 1—Organization			
Part 2—Number of Subordinates			
C. Planning and Execution of Operations			
D. Interpersonal Contacts			
E. Influence on Progress of the Organization			
		Total Points	
Approved by:_____			

FIG. 7–1.   Job Analysis Form.

TYPICAL JOB DESCRIPTIONS

The job descriptions that follow consider only the executive and supervisory levels of the credit function. They comprise credit personnel who are responsible for a certain, definable accounts receivable portfolio—in some cases, this may be only high-risk accounts. Consequently, job descriptions of credit personnel engaged in routine work—such as clerks, typists, bookkeepers, cash control clerks, cash appliers and processors, and adjusters—are not considered.

The job descriptions are presented as a guide for the development of similar statements within a company. A brief description of each position level is given, which is then followed by a more detailed example.

Top-Level Chief Credit Executive

Generally exercises overall control of a firm's credit function in a line form of organization, may operate at a staff level with the credit function administered and controlled at the underlying units, or may perform at a level which represents a combination of these activities (see Figures 7–2 and 7–3 for detailed descriptions).

TOP-LEVEL CHIEF CREDIT EXECUTIVE

Reports to: Treasurer
Objective: To establish sound and constructive credit policies and practices, and to administer all credit operations of the company in a manner that will increase sales volume, contribute to the profit of the company and enhance customer stability, and provide for the prompt turnover and adequate protection of the company's investment in accounts receivables.

Duties and Responsibilities:

1.0 Formulates companywide credit policies for top management approval and establishes general policies, procedures, and practices governing overall credit operations. Interprets and delegates the approved credit policies to the immediate staff for dissemination and compliance by all concerned.

2.0 *Operating Procedures.* Responsible for the judicious granting of credit and the maintenance of efficient collection practices for the overall company.

   2.1 Exercises prudent control and good judgment to improve the sales potential of the company while protecting its accounts receivable investment. This requires sound dealings with customers and the intelligent minimizing of bad-debt losses, acknowledging the fact that from a marketing viewpoint some bad-debt losses are to be expected and are acceptable. To the extent practicable, visits are made with customers and counseling services are provided so as to establish and build favorable customer-credit-sales relations. At the least, no high-volume marginal account should be restricted or refused credit without a visit, wherever possible.

   2.2 Provides facilities and guidance for the gathering and proper maintenance of sufficient, reasonable up-to-date information on customers upon which to base a decision on an individual order or on an account as a whole. The investigation should be conducted with the view of finding reasons to approve not disapprove credit. This examination enables the customer credit lines to be current and up to date.

   2.3 Periodically reviews all activities of the credit organization and recommends to the treasurer the organizational structure best suited to carry out its objectives. Approves changes recommended by the staff for subordinate elements of the credit organization in accordance with operating requirements and current conditions.

   2.4 Manages cash inflows from credit sales. This requires determining the optimum investment in receivables and the cash to be realized from such receivables over designated periods of time.

   2.5 Manages and controls the receivables portfolio by knowing the status of the accounts receivable investment, thus assuring that the accounts are in reasonably sound condition. This may be accomplished by direct supervision or through reporting by subordinates.

   2.6 Determines staffing requirements for the credit organization, recommends additions or reductions in executive and supervisory positions, and approves staff personnel recommendations.

FIG. 7–2. Job Description of Top-Level Chief Credit Executive.

2.7 Establishes and monitors standards of performance for all credit positions.

2.8 Recommends changes in salary and status, including reclassification, transfers, promotions, and terminations.

2.9 Establishes and updates training and education programs.

3.0 Formulates and applies adequate controls as a means of measuring and regulating credit operations in conformity with standards established by management; takes remedial action as required.

4.0 Participates with the treasurer and others in periodic analyses of the market, economic, industry, and business conditions affecting the company's credit policies.

5.0 Keeps corporate management informed concerning the status of the accounts receivable portfolio, the forecasts of cash inflows, the expenses in administering the department, and any special purpose activities.

Authority: Acts within established company policy on all credit matters. Exercises considerable influence on the business-building and income potentials of the company through the determination of credit policy that is positive and constructive rather than restrictive.

Relationships:

1.0 *Internal.* Maintains staff, liaison, and consultative relationships on the executive level with sales, purchasing, legal, data processing, advertising, personnel, and other departments of the overall organization; coordinates and directs such relationships between credit personnel and other departments at appropriate levels.

2.0 *External.* Initiates, develops, and maintains external relationships with customers, financial institutions, service agencies, the trade, credit organizations, attorneys, accountants, and others as required; establishes such relationships for subordinate credit personnel.

FIG. 7–2 (cont'd.).

TOP-LEVEL CHIEF CREDIT EXECUTIVE (STAFF)

Reports to: Treasurer

Objective: To provide corporate management with essential information and analysis of facts and figures. This involves continuous investigation and research designed to assist in formulating credit objectives, policies, plans, and programs.

To foster the administration of credit operations of the company in a manner that will increase sales volume, contribute to the profit of the company and enhance customer stability, and provide for the prompt turnover and adequate protection of the company's investment in accounts receivable.

Duties and Responsibilities:

1.0 Acts in a staff advisory capacity to all credit executives and supervisors in the determination of working methods and sequences; coordinates the installation of systems and procedures and the flow of work throughout the credit organization.

2.0 Has no direct responsibility for the handling of accounts, other than making special investigations and studies of customers as directed.

3.0 Has no immediate authority for the direction of others, except in those instances where responsibility is assigned for conducting special studies and projects involving others.

4.0 Prepares and compiles all required data on the status of the accounts receivable investment, and assists immediate superior in analyzing the company's standing as a result of current credit policies and actions.

5.0 Collects and analyzes current information on economic, legal, technical, and educational matters pertaining to credit and collections; prepares and reports findings in appropriate form.

6.0 Assists and advises credit executives and supervisors in ascertaining training needs and plans; develops and recommends training materials and programs.

7.0 Maintains responsibility for auditing and coordinating established procedures, systems, and standards, and for referring deviations with recommended remedial action to the executive or supervisor concerned, the treasurer, or both.

FIG. 7–3. Job Description of Top-Level Chief Credit Executive (Staff).

8.0 Prepares organizational charts and job descriptions, participates in training as an instructor, and prepares special material for conference.

Authority: Has the authority to make observations and to conduct studies and audits on those aspects of credit operations that pertain to specialized activities.

Relationships:

1.0 *Internal.* As credit staff consultant, maintains contacts and working relationships with any company personnel requesting information, advice, and assistance on credit matters; acts for the treasurer in developing plans for use in special programs and in making special studies and surveys.

2.0 *External.* Maintains contacts in the industry, credit organizations, government agencies, and with other sources for the purpose of research, investigation, exchanging ideas, and obtaining information pertinent to any studies.

FIG. 7–3 (cont'd.).

Middle-Level Chief Credit Executive

Exercises control of the receivables portfolios of divisions or subsidiaries, and is given wide latitude in performing the duties; usually required to report to the top-level chief credit executive or to an officer of the division or subsidiary (Figure 7–4 gives a more complete description).

MIDDLE-LEVEL CHIEF CREDIT EXECUTIVE

Reports to: Division Controller

Objective: To apply the company's credit and collection policies, practices, and procedures to the administration of the credit requirements of an underlying unit (subsidiary or division) in a manner that will result in maximum sales, sound receivables, and their prompt conversion into cash.

Duties and Responsibilities:

1.0 Assists in the formulation and development of constructive and progressive credit policies and practices; interprets approved policies to all concerned and assures conformity thereto.

2.0 *Operating Procedures.* Responsible for the judicious granting of credit and the maintenance of efficient collection practices for an underlying unit.

2.1 Exercises prudent control and good judgment to improve the sales potential of the subsidiary or division while protecting its accounts receivable investment. This requires sound dealings with customers and the intelligent minimizing of bad-debt losses, acknowledging the fact that from a marketing viewpoint some bad-debt losses are to be expected and are acceptable. To the extent practicable, visits are made with customers and counseling services are provided so as to establish and build favorable customer-credit-sales relations. At the least, no high-volume marginal account should be restricted or refused credit without a visit, wherever possible.

2.2 Provides facilities and guidance for the gathering and proper maintenance of sufficient, reasonable up-to-date information on customers upon which to base a decision on an individual order or on an account as a whole. The investigation should be conducted with the view of finding reasons to approve not disapprove credit. This examination enables the customer credit lines to be current and up to date.

2.3 Periodically reviews all activities of the underlying unit and recommends to the division controller the organization structure best suited to carry out its objectives. Approves changes recommended by the staff for subordinate elements of the credit organization in accordance with operating requirements and current conditions.

2.4 Manages cash inflows from credit sales. This requires determining the optimum investment in receivables and the cash to be realized from such receivables over designated periods of time.

FIG. 7–4.   Job Description of Middle-Level Chief Credit Executive.

2.5 Manages and controls the underlying unit's receivables portfolio by knowing the status of the accounts receivable investment, thus assuring that the accounts are in reasonably sound condition. This may be accomplished by direct supervision or through reporting by subordinates.

2.6 Determines staffing requirements for the credit organization; recommends additions or reductions in executive and supervisory positions; approves staff personnel recommendations.

2.7 Establishes and monitors standards of performance for all credit positions.

2.8 Recommends changes in salary and status, including reclassification, transfers, promotions, and terminations.

2.9 Establishes and maintains training and education programs.

3.0 Formulates and applies adequate controls as a means for measuring and regulating credit operations in conformity with standards established by management; takes remedial action as required.

4.0 Participates with immediate superior and others in periodic analyses of the market, economic, industry, and business conditions affecting the company's credit policies.

5.0 Keeps subsidiary or division management informed concerning the status of the accounts receivable investment, the forecast of cash inflows, the expenses in administering the department, and any special purpose activities.

Authority: Has full authority within defined dollar limits to apply credit and collection policies, procedures, and standard terms to the underlying unit's group of accounts. Deviations are subject to approval by the immediate superior but the line credit executive's judgment frequently influences decisions.

Relationships:

1.0 *Internal.* Maintains operational relationships with line supervisors of other departments concerned with the customers comprising the underlying unit's group of accounts.

2.0 *External.* Initiates, develops, and maintains contact with customers, financial institutions, credit organizations, the trade, attorneys, accountants, and others as required; establishes such relationships for subordinate personnel.

FIG. 7–4 (cont'd.).

Credit Manager

Manages a certain, definable portfolio and generally reports to the top-level or middle-level chief credit executive (Figure 7–5 describes the position more fully). Among the position titles used for this function are regional credit manager, zone credit manager, district credit manager, credit supervisor, field credit manager, product credit manager, and credit sales manager.

CREDIT MANAGER

Reports to: Top-Level or Middle-Level Chief Credit Executive
Objective: To direct all credit and collection activities of a designated major part of the credit organization in accordance with established policies, practices, and procedures in a manner that will result in maximum sales, sound receivables, and their prompt conversion to cash.

Duties and Responsibilities:

1.0 Maintains responsibility for applying the company's credit and collection policies, practices, and procedures to the credit requirements of a designated number of customer accounts within specified dollar limits or normal credit lines.

2.0 *Granting of Credit.* Extends credit to customers in accordance with established company policy and terms.

FIG. 7–5. Job Description of Credit Manager.

2.1 Analyzes requests for credit in order to ascertain what information and security will be required to arrive at a sound decision.

2.2 Plans investigations to be performed personally or by others.

2.3 Assigns assistants to obtain data on present and prospective customers.

2.4 Reviews assembled files and reports, analyzes financial statements and supplementary information, makes any further investigation and contacts required, evaluates the credit risks, and approves or rejects accounts.

2.5 Establishes credit lines for individual accounts and makes all credit arrangements.

2.6 Personally handles credits beyond subordinates' authority, major accounts requiring individual attention, marginal accounts, problem accounts, special credit arrangements, and deviations from standards.

2.7 Consults immediate superior for advice on particularly complex problems and cases requiring policy decision.

2.8 Handles nonroutine credit inquiries and correspondence.

3.0 *Collections:* Plans and maintains a program for the systematic followup and collection of receivables.

3.1 Reviews regularly the status of collections to assure that accounts receivable are in reasonably sound condition.

3.2 Checks monthly balances of customers; when records indicate that customers may be exceeding safe limits, takes appropriate steps to prevent past-due accounts.

3.3 Follows closely the course of aging accounts and determines action to be taken personally or by assistants on delinquent accounts.

3.4 Represents the company at creditors' meetings and bankruptcy proceedings of customers.

3.5 Consults with superior, appropriate sales personnel, or both on particularly complex collection situations requiring unusual action.

3.6 Obtains approval from immediate superior on the acceptance of notes, compromise settlements, partial payments, time extensions, and the writing off of uncollectible accounts.

3.7 Arranges for forced collections and the filing of suits or bankruptcy claims, and furnishes complete information to representatives.

3.8 Represents the company at creditors' meetings and bankruptcy proceedings.

3.9 Supervises the processes and procedures relating to recorded contracts, use of collateral, insurance claims, lien instruments, and the like.

3.10 Takes appropriate action on collection irregularities (such as payment discrepancies and unearned discounts), adjustments (shipment errors, etc.), and customer complaints and inquiries.

3.11 Supervises collection correspondence.

4.0 *Controls.* Carries out the established program for controlling the credit function.

4.1 Prepares and submits periodic operating reports to immediate superior on the status of receivables.

4.2 Appraises the results of assistants; takes or recommends remedial action as required.

5.0 Trains the staff; interprets credit policy and gives instruction in credit communication to new employees.

Authority: Has full authority within approved policies, procedures, standards, and defined limits on credit matters within the designated area of responsibility. Deviations are subject to approval by higher authority but the credit manager's judgment frequently influences decisions.

Relationships:

1.0 *Internal.* Maintains staff and operational relationships on the supervisory and administrative levels with sales, purchasing, legal, advertising, personnel, and other departments concerned with company administration and credit and collection operations; coordinates the internal relationships of subordinates at appropriate levels.

2.0 *External.* Initiates, develops, and maintains relationships with customers, financial institutions, credit sources, and the trade; directs the maintenance of such contacts in the designated area of activity.

FIG. 7–5 (cont'd.).

Credit Analyst

Under direction of the chief credit executive or credit manager, depending upon the organization depth, manages a specified receivables portfolio (see Figure 7–6 for a more detailed description). Other titles for this position may include credit representative, credit administrator, and credit assistant.

CREDIT ANALYST

Reports to:　Credit Manager
Objective:　To approve or decline credit orders in accordance with established policies, practices, and procedures in a manner that will result in maximum sales, sound receivables, and the prompt conversion of receivables into cash with a minimum of past-due accounts.

Duties and Responsibilities
1.0 Applies the company's credit and collection policies, practices, and procedures to the credit requirements of a designated number of customer accounts within specified dollar limits or normal credit lines.
2.0 Generally has no direct subordinates, but exercises immediate day-to-day functional supervision over personnel assigned to the analyst's portfolio of accounts.
3.0 *Extension of Credit.* Extends credit to customers in accordance with established policy and terms.
　3.1 Analyzes requests for credit and plans investigations to be performed personally or by others.
　3.2 Reviews files, reports, and financial statements analyses of prospective customers.
　3.3 Makes field contacts and further investigations when necessary.
　3.4 Evaluates, then approves or rejects, the credit risks.
　3.5 Discusses with superior, when necessary, questionable or special applications for credit.
　3.6 Sets temporary lines on new accounts.
　3.7 Submits credits beyond the position's authority to the credit manager, with all necessary reports, data, and analyses.
4.0 *Collections.* Carries out the established program for the followup and collection of accounts receivable.
　4.1 Reviews regularly the status of collections to assure that accounts receivable are in a relatively sound condition.
　4.2 Checks monthly balances of customers; when records indicate that customers may be exceeding safe limits, takes appropriate steps to prevent past-due accounts.
　4.3 Follows closely the course of aging accounts and determines action to be taken on delinquent accounts.
　4.4 Discusses delinquent accounts with sales personnel.

Authority:　Has full authority within approved policies, procedures, standards, and defined limits on credit matters within the defined area of responsibility. Deviations are subject to approval by the credit analyst's superior.

Relationships:
1.0 *Internal.* Maintains working relationships with operating personnel of other departments concerned with the analyst's accounts, primarily for the purpose of giving and obtaining information and working jointly on customer problems.
2.0 *External.* Initiates contacts and maintains close, harmonious relationships with customers; follows standard operating procedure in other outside contacts concerned primarily with obtaining and furnishing credit information.

FIG. 7–6.　Job Description of Credit Analyst.

IMPORTANCE OF THE JOB SPECIFICATION

The other tool for staffing any organizational activity is the job specification. This is a statement of the qualifications that an individual should have to fill a particular job—usually including educational requirements, experience requirements, and special characteristics and abilities.

Relation to the Job Description

The job specification details "what it takes" to do the job set forth in the job description. Therefore, the job specification should clearly state the qualities, training, and experience required to accomplish the assigned task satisfactorily. Because the job specification is more intimately concerned with people than the job description, it is much more difficult to formulate. The feeling is widespread that the statement of specifications for a particular job should be derived from the job description, rather than being based on the qualifications of the person in the job, however competent the person may be. When the specification is kept impersonal, it becomes a yardstick by which the incumbent can be measured. At the same time, the specification itself can be tested by comparison with the individual in the job.

When the job specification clearly states what the person in the job should be—in the fullest sense—it becomes another effective yardstick by which to measure the individual. Just as the individual's actual record can be set against the job that the person is expected to do (the job description) to measure job performance, the individual's total capabilities (profile) thus can be compared with the job specification to measure the individual's personal development. The latter procedure may be used to determine how the individual is doing in the development phase, as well as to measure the effectiveness of a company's training program.

Relation to Training Programs

Besides helping to determine who should be placed in what position, job specifications can be most useful in establishing training goals for personnel at all levels. Initially, the job specification should be accurate and reflect the current job. It then can be modified or expanded to meet the job requirements as they may be expected to develop in the next few years. If desired, the specifications can be further revised in terms of the expanded requirements of the "job ahead"—the logical next step upward for the current occupant of the job.

The modified job specification can then be set against a comparable profile of the job incumbent. Consequently, management can determine those areas in which a certain individual needs additional experience or training. Removal of these limitations then becomes the development goal or objective for that particular individual. Thus a more meaningful training program can be developed and adapted to individual needs.

Job Qualifications

The qualifications for the position of credit executive are of two types: technical and personal. The technical may be further defined as the education and experience requirements, while the special characteristics and abilities of the individual would comprise the personal.

Education. Most positions require a college degree or equivalent. A degree in business administration is most desirable. The candidate must have basic training in and knowledge of accounting, credits and collections, financial statement analysis, banking and finance, commercial law, marketing, statistics, economics, human behavior, and psychology.

Experience. The length of experience required depends a great deal upon the position level. The chief credit executive, for example, would require eight to ten years of progressive and balanced experience in all branches of credit and collection work. This experience may be developed within the company or while employed with other companies in the same or a similar industry. In addition, the experience may enable the executive to use modern methods of research, analysis, and forecasts; define objectives, plan toward those objectives in terms of profits, and sense operating problems; maintain adequate standards and instructions covering credit policies and procedures; use internal checks and controls; know statistical and financial aspects of management reporting; coordinate credit activities with sales, accounting, orders, shipping, claims, and other related operations; and carry out successful external relations, especially relationships with customers, financial institutions, and credit organizations.

The other credit position levels would generally require experience that is not quite so demanding. In some cases a special type may be needed, such as a statistical background for the preparation of reports or familiarity with electronic data processing in order to process orders smoothly. The position of credit manager, for example, might require three to five years of experience in credit and collections, with at least one year as general assistant in a small credit organization or supervisory head of a segment of a large credit organization. Experience should include investigation, analysis, and establishment of lines of credit; followup for collection of accounts receivable; training of credit personnel; working with the other company departments; and maintenance of customer relations.

The credit analyst, on the other hand, would require the least experience of the position levels discussed. This could include two to three years of credit work, including credit investigations; familiarity with credit sources, analysis of financial statements, preparation of credit reports, credit and collection correspondence; and some exposure to sales, accounting, and order procedures.

Special Characteristics and Abilities. The full qualifications listed below are not likely to be possessed by any one individual. However, the higher the position level the more likely it is that the executive will have most of the attributes.

1. Constructive imagination for determining appropriate methods of observing, organizing, analyzing, and reporting data.
2. Initiative, adaptability, and ingenuity in meeting new situations and changing conditions.
3. Ability to communicate effectively and convincingly through speaking and writing.
4. Resourcefulness in identifying needs, unsatisfactory conditions, and the causes of such conditions.
5. Willingness to take considered risks for profitable company growth and development of the sales potential.
6. Perseverence in eliciting confidential information.
7. Ability to analyze complex problems constructively, and resourcefulness in following up difficult situations to a successful conclusion.
8. Emotional stability in handling unpleasant situations with tact and diplomacy.
9. Ability to handle customer and internal relations diplomatically and firmly when required.
10. Considerate interest and fairness in dealing with people.
11. Pleasing appearance, speech, and personal manner.
12. Uncompromising honesty.

APPRAISAL OF PERSONNEL

Because the human assets of a business are at least as important to its progress as its material resources, it is necessary to establish some method of personnel appraisal. This is essential not only to determine how well individuals have been doing their jobs but also to help them improve their performance. As already indicated, the job description is one of the most effective tools for evaluating personnel. In addition, there are many useful evaluating systems and programs.

Performance Evaluation

A yearly or more frequent review of personnel is a useful means of appraising performance. This review may be accomplished by the immediate superiors of the individual whose performance is being evaluated. The reviewers should also seek to determine individual potentialities and should offer constructive criticism.

The use of job descriptions for each type of position in the credit department, coupled with annual personal performance evaluations, can enable employees to work in an environment which provides clear descriptions of what is expected on the job and a review of how these expectations were fulfilled in the prior period.

Moreover, a policy of joint career development planning can be implemented. Whereas such planning was generally conducted only within the confines of management, procedures can now provide for periodic management reviews of current work interests and career aspirations with each selected employee. Further, management could be required to prepare written one-year individual career development plans appropriately related to those interests and aspirations; that would ensure that such plans would be implemented.

Timing of Promotions and Pay Increases

Those responsible for the credit department operation should recognize that no program will succeed if advancement is slow, if encouragement and criticism are withheld, if the wage scale is below standard, and particularly if pay increases are infrequent. And if, as time progresses, the employee sees no tangible move to provide added responsibilities and authority, the value of the job may soon be questioned. Since the steps to be taken in solving this problem are clearly within the scope of the organizational structure of the company, they become the responsibility of the chief credit executive.

Determining when and to what extent an employee should be advanced is always a difficult matter. A sound promotion policy usually requires some form of systematic appraisal for each member of the company's working force. Such a plan should cover, in addition to performance of office and routine work, relevant personal characteristics, health, emotional stability, analytical ability, initiative, ambition, ability to influence and work with others, ability to make sound decisions, and ability to assume responsibilities and carry out delegated authority. Each of these factors should be carefully weighed so that the appraisal procedure used by the company will be fair and reasonably accurate. No one, not even the chief credit executive, should be left out of such an appraisal, though it may be necessary to modify the criteria as the position changes.

A fair system of appraisal can be most helpful to promotion and reassignment of credit personnel. While this evaluation procedure does not in itself solve the problem of slow advancement, it does put advancement on a businesslike basis.

CHAPTER 8

TRAINING FOR CREDIT MANAGEMENT

Given the increasing complexity of today's business world, management personnel must continue to develop themselves so they can carry out their responsibilities. Credit and finance are increasing in importance, and credit executives must keep themselves equipped to perform these widening functions.

NEED FOR CREDIT TRAINING

Analysis of credit department functions often indicates the need for formalized training, not only to break in new employees but also to enhance the capacities of experienced members of the department. If the credit department is to keep pace with present-day demands, the training program must be adapted to changing, ever-broadening requirements at all levels. The purpose of this chapter is to set forth in some detail the credit training programs and educational activities currently in use, and also to discuss the objectives of such training.

At the executive level, the problem of training successors is a particularly pressing one. Not only the credit department, but other departments as well, may lack a "second team" or even a second individual qualified to assume management of the department should the present head leave the company or move up to a higher position within the company.

Any significant change in company organization may also require an expansion of the present training program. Whenever credit employees face greater responsibilities, some provision must be made for retraining present personnel or for training new personnel.

Preparation for Credit Training

No two companies operate precisely the same. Therefore, a training program used in one company cannot be expected to satisfy all the requirements of another, even when both companies are in the same industry. The point holds equally true for educational activities—particularly when conducted outside the company. Such activities should be carefully evaluated and integrated into an overall company program.

During the training, the advantages of working in and for the company should be emphasized. After the training period is completed, employees should have obtained a broad perspective of their work and its opportunities. If they have decided that they like credit work and plan to stay in the field, then this phase of job training will establish that purpose more firmly. Even if they do not care for credit work, the training may convince them that they would like to remain with the company in some other capacity. Should they decide to leave, they will probably feel that they have been well-treated.

It must be realized that the training process is likely to involve a certain amount of trial and error; there may be false starts and wasted effort before the program is worked out to everyone's satisfaction. No matter how efficient a training program may become, it will continue to be costly in both time and money. Moreover, training implies change, which represents a challenge to the status quo. Whatever the benefits to be expected, it must be recognized that "change hurts." Therefore, it is vital to consider the potential impact of any change—particularly a change which may strike at deep-seated feelings of security and traditional ways of doing things.

In implementing a training program, the credit executive should remember that the new employee is coming into a strange environment and that there are limits to how much new information the trainee can absorb in a given time. The executive must approach this task in an enthusiastic and positive manner, with recognition that it is a very important part of the job. The opportunity is present for the department head to set the tone for effective training, to present credit functions within a broad perspective, and at the same time to get to know new people as they join the staff.

Selection of Personnel

Training begins with careful selection of the personnel to be trained. The aim is to select people with the ambition and capacity to develop into productive workers. It is desirable that they have a career interest in credit and financial management. At the outset, it must be made clear to trainees that the opportunities for advancement are open only to those prepared to accept them and willing to assume the obligations that go with them. They must be made aware that advancement comes as a result of growth and improved capacities. They should also understand that educational preparation is a qualification of major importance, and that the person who is well trained for a job usually stands a better chance of promotion than the one who is not.

There are many factors to look for when selecting personnel for training.

A partial list would include personality, attitudes, abilities, weaknesses, and potential; the facility to follow a planned course of action; ability to make decisions in the light of the facts available and under pressure of time limitations; leadership talent; instinctive acceptance of responsibility; and understanding of the economic, social, and political forces that shape the work environment.

Proper selection of personnel for training also requires clear-cut statements of the objectives of the credit department, so that both the trainee and management clearly understand why the training is being provided. It is important that specifications for the various jobs be clearly established and that job descriptions be specifically set forth. The training program must then be geared to the credit department's functions and objectives on the one hand, and to the needs of the personnel to be trained on the other. Careful planning in these respects helps prevent the misunderstandings which can cause a decline in morale among trainees.

A farsighted chief credit executive will seek to bring to the staff young associates who—with proper training and seasoning—will develop management abilities. In the selection of new personnel, one cannot be sure that these abilities exist. They have their source, however, in basic qualities that may be expressed in school and social activities. They may be revealed by the way in which the individual plans, organizes, and performs daily work; and gets along with associates.

During one's career, improvement of managerial skills is a lifelong process. There are no set rules or formulas by which they are acquired. Experience, education, native abilities, powers of observation, common sense, and creative imagination all play a part in the development of a good manager.

CONSIDERATIONS IN A SOUND PROGRAM

The primary objective of any training program is to provide employees with the opportunity to progress to whatever level of responsibility they can achieve. This requires more than training in specific routine duties under regulated conditions, more than mere adjustment to the company and the departmental working organization, and more than the mastery of details. Rather, it needs programs for developing one's ability to think and to analyze and formulate workable solutions to problems. Personality should be enriched, confidence inspired, and the traits and skills of leadership developed to assure the widest possible use of the available human resources for the company's benefit.

Objectives

A training program that is well-designed should:

1. Help the trainee become more proficient on the job.
2. Provide basic training for another job which the trainee may eventually hold.

3. Develop a higher level of performance.
4. Develop improved skills in handling customer and company relations.
5. Lead to more harmonious working relations with other departments.
6. Provide a broad concept of the company's place in the industry and the department's relation to the whole.

Basic Requirements

The basic requirements of a good training program are as follows:

1. Much of the instruction given by top-level personnel; all of it supervised by them.
2. Adequate time alloted to preparation of instructional materials.
3. Maximum use made of visual and other instructional aids.
4. A quiet environment provided for the instruction, allowing for "give-and-take."
5. Outline of job routines and procedures given to trainees and reviewed with them within a few days. The list should be expanded as the techniques of the job become more familiar.
6. Provision made for testing and followup to determine if the instruction has been effective.
7. Day-to-day office operations described to trainees so they may visualize the work of others on the staff and better understand related responsibilities.
8. Flow of paper work described with which the trainee will be concerned, with emphasis on how important it is to keep the papers moving so that others may not be delayed in their work.
9. Credit forms and credit files explained so trainees may know the importance of the various types of credit information available in the files.
10. Description given of the successive steps in the processing of orders, from the time an order is written by the sales representative until it is ready for shipment. This entails an understanding of the order entry system as it relates to the credit function.
11. Broad understanding given of the work procedures on billing and accounts receivable, especially the payment application function.
12. Full information on collection procedures given, with emphasis on the importance of keeping these receivables current by quick conversion into cash (i.e., time value of money).
13. Importance explained of maintaining friendly working contacts with employees within the credit department and throughout the company. Employees of the credit department should constantly strive for effective relationships in all their working contacts, particularly those with the sales department.

Management Support

However comprehensive a training program may be, it will not succeed if confronted with unfavorable administrative conditions. Conversely, a relatively simple program can be very effective if directed by a sympathetic administration. What then are the administrative and organizational conditions which can contribute to an effective credit training program?

The management of the credit department must believe strongly in the benefits to be derived from credit training, and give unqualified endorsement and active support to it. Known antagonism by superiors frequently causes employees to underestimate the value of their training or enter into it halfheartedly. It also makes it difficult for those in charge of training to retain their zeal. The following policy statements are excellent examples of company support and encouragement of training programs:

> Training is a mutual responsibility. On-the-job training can and will be provided, but good performance and preparation for future opportunities may also cost some of your own time for educational purposes. If you are interested in and qualified for outside training, we will be glad to help you secure it, and, as you know, the company will share the expense.
>
> On the day you begin work in the credit department, you begin training for the future. After you have learned the routine and operations of your first assignment, you will begin your training on another job. This will help qualify you for promotion. In each of the jobs you perform thereafter, as time and your capabilities permit, training will be provided for the next more advanced job.

Defining the Responsibilities

Good training must include provision for the trainee to assume responsibility, no matter how simple or unimportant the area involved. When executives refuse to delegate authority, training is usually ineffective and the development of promising personnel is blocked. The responsibilities of subordinates should be clearly defined to help them develop their capacity for decisionmaking.

It is often difficult for credit executives to determine the extent to which they can entrust credit analysis and credit decision responsibilities to their subordinates. Here are a few recommended procedures to encourage delegation of authority for training purposes:

1. The credit executive and training staff must be ready and willing to support the trainee on those decisions questioned by higher authority. Credit trainees must know that decisions based on reliable information will not result in their being reprimanded simply because someone in the front office has complained.

2. When a trainee makes a mistake, it is the duty of the credit executive or staff not only to correct it but also to prevent its repetition. Under no circumstances, however, should the trainee's freedom of decision be abridged by excessive supervision, for there is no better way to retard the trainee's growth and development. Of course, good supervision will place a limit on the number of times a given mistake can be made. The chronic offender who cannot or will not profit by training must be replaced, and the sooner this is done the better for the morale of all other trainees.

3. Written communications to and from the department should be stated so that misunderstandings are minimized. They should be used mainly for transmitting information and not for making decisions, otherwise trainees may fall into the habit of transferring all problem decisions to their superiors, thus defeating the purpose of the training program.

4. Continually guard against creating a situation where the responsibili-

ties and the work of subordinates is taken over by superiors. The trainee should be given assistance and guidance in solving a problem but the decision should be made by the trainee. Denying a trainee this decisionmaking experience can be a serious deterrent to effective training.

ORIENTATION

Any well-planned training program should provide for introducing employees to a new job by giving them preliminary information and instruction. This initial phase of training is commonly known as orientation. Broadly speaking, it is the attempt to establish in the individual's mind certain basic knowledge about an organization and its operations. The new employee must become acquainted with company rules, regulations, and procedures—as well as opportunities and limitations—in order to make an effective adjustment to the job. The basic requirements of a good orientation program are:

1. A personally delivered message of welcome by the credit executive and a personally written welcome from the president of the company or some other member of top management. Such welcomes to a new employee require little effort from these officials and can mean much to the employee. The purpose is to create a favorable attitude and a sense of belonging.

2. An oral presentation, supplemented by a summary sheet or relevant information about the company—its size, its place in the industry, its services, and its key executive personnel.

3. A carefully prepared, realistic presentation of the job to be filled, its opportunities and challenges, and how it fits into the total pattern of the credit operation.

4. A review of company and departmental rules and regulations, supplemented by an explanation of the reasons for the more important ones.

5. An outline of the conditions of employment, salary and wage policies, Social Security, health and life insurance, and other benefits.

Orientation is generally needed not only by newly employed credit personnel but also by employees transferred from one job to another, for they also need to know the duties of the new position.

ON-THE-JOB TRAINING

Some credit skills and functions, such as the collection of credit information, can only be learned on the job through actual experience. This makes it necessary, in the development of a training program, that instruction materials be related to the day-to-day operations of the credit department.

Achievement of these objectives requires a carefully integrated and well-administered course of study. In addition, each program should be developed to meet the particular needs of the department where it will be used.

Training is best if it is the direct responsibility of one supervisor, although the actual teaching assignment can be delegated to others. After having spent some time reviewing company policies, the new employee should be assigned to meaningful work duties. For example, the first few weeks could be spent studying the training manual, reading sample letters and credit files, setting up financial statements, and responding to credit inquiries. Under supervision, the trainee could gradually work into other responsibilities, such as notifying other interested departments of changes affecting the company's relations with customers. The trainee could then begin to assist in approving orders and handling new account investigations.

The extent of supervision would depend largely on the position level, the employee's past academic background and experience, the speed of training, and the individual's overall progress. Supervision should always be available to provide direction, answer questions, discuss problems, and evaluate the individual. Any periodic progress reports should be discussed with the trainee, along with specific recommendations for improvement.

When on-the-job training is limited only to the opportunity for the trainee to come face-to-face with daily problems, this method of teaching has the following shortcomings:

1. Trial-and-error learning is a slow, costly discouraging process. Because of the complexities of modern business, employees must be equipped with certain basic skills from the beginning and must be given opportunities to develop their skills and abilities to the fullest extent.

2. Experience training often goes hand-in-hand with a tradition-bound department. It thus fails to give the employees that broad perspective toward their job, toward the credit function, and toward management which will encourage fullest development.

3. Training often does not keep pace with promotional opportunities. A trainee, regardless of competence, cannot be considered advanced if only a small part of the training has been completed. The employee should be preparing for the next higher position.

Despite these shortcomings, some facets of every job require practical experience. Trainees on a new job must first learn the current methods of doing their work. When these techniques have been mastered, they can be encouraged to seek improved ways.

IN-HOUSE TRAINING

There is a useful supplement to the day-to-day training that is given to employees while performing their duties—namely, in-house training. It can take many forms and be given either sporadically or on a regular basis.

Credit Conference

A well-conceived program can include weekly conferences devoted to credit problems. In competent hands, they are an effective device for raising the morale and efficiency of the department. Several elements are essential to their success. There must be a fund of common information regarding each employee's functions and responsibilities. There must also be a common desire for coordination of effort and elimination of conflicting work procedures. Moreover, all members of the staff must be willing to exchange ideas freely. The credit problems should be sufficiently challenging to encourage the conferees to take an active part in their solution. This method requires:

1. Advance reading and study to assure intelligent consideration of the problem when the conference takes place.
2. Discussion of the nature and importance of the problem at the conference, with possible solutions to it.
3. After the problem has been discussed and a solution determined, a clear indication of how the employee can apply the solution in practice.

These techniques are adaptable to the training of one employee or a dozen. The credit executive will have to use ingenuity in developing problem materials and in planning the training schedule. In some companies, credit employees are encouraged to suggest topics for discussion. The demands on the credit executive's abilities as a writer of clear and succinct materials for staff study, as a discussion leader, and as a teacher and guide are great; but they are offset by the reward of having given practical assistance to the staff.

A variation of this program would be credit groups to develop self-instructional units. They can consist of selected individuals comprising a cross-section of the entire department. Each group can consist of a specified number of credit analysts, one group leader, and a credit executive to whom they report their progress.

The group theory produces some positive developments. First, there is a greater degree of flexibility, as analysts move from one problem area to another. Second, peer pressure encourages participation by weaker members. Third, instruction is continuous and there is a greater exposure to problems and solutions. Fourth, the group tends to cut down the flow of paperwork from subordinate to management. Last, all members are included in the decisionmaking process, so each person feels more involvement and a greater degree of commitment to the group goals.

Observation Tours

Tours of other departments can help credit employees to understand more fully the working relations between the credit department and other divisions of the company. In addition, visits can be profitably made to credit departments of neighboring companies. By observing how credit work is done in other companies, credit employees may learn ways of improving their own techniques.

Observation tours are a useful supplement to any training, since they give the observer an opportunity to see in operation certain processes that are only read or heard about. This is particularly true in a company with a wide range of product lines and many different industrial classifications of customers. A well-conducted tour will reveal not only how credit operations are performed in another company but also why they are done in a particular way. The observer thus will gain an improved working knowledge and broadened understanding of credit activities.

Credit Library

Some companies have built up credit libraries containing books, articles, case histories, special reports, and other pertinent materials which employees are encouraged to use in the course of their training. In order that these reading materials may be kept in usable order and receive fair distribution, one member of the staff should serve as librarian. A simple charge card can be used to record the whereabouts of materials and to place time limits on their use. It should be the responsibility of the credit executive or a subordinate to keep the library up to date.

Members of the staff should be encouraged to be on the alert for published materials which would be useful additions to the credit library. These might include new books on credit work, economic analyses of the company's industry, and special reports dealing with various phases of credit operations. As new materials are received, group discussions and conferences may be arranged for the purpose of reviewing them and considering their bearing upon the work of the credit department.

From time to time certain significant credit problems are encountered in daily operations. These can easily be written up for inclusion in the credit library. All the correspondence, special reports, and other essential information relating to a problem should be kept together in a single file. The credit executive can make these materials more useful by adding pertinent questions designed to stimulate thinking and to encourage discussion of the problem. The problem may serve as the basis for a group conference, in which applications to problems of a similar nature can be considered. In addition, these reports can be used for orientation training of new credit employees.

Job Rotation Program

It is sometimes desirable to include in the training program some provision for rotating trainees from one job to another within the department, and even from one department to another. Such experience generates a broader credit perspective. The specific plan of rotation depends upon the size, complexity, and organizational setup of the department.

In vertical rotation, the trainee serves under each executive as an observer or assistant for sufficient time to become familiar with the functions and area of responsibility. On a different tack, through an interchange of jobs among lower echelon of employees, an intradepartmental or horizontal rotation can be developed. Both plans must be worked out carefully with full approval of top management. Moreover, all employees in the department should be fully acquainted with the procedures and purposes of the plan.

To prepare for a horizontal job rotation program, each employee should be asked to put together a list of all the duties performed each day, each week, and each month, and how these tasks are performed. The credit executive should go over these descriptions with each employee to be sure that all functions are fully and clearly covered. Duplicate copies are prepared so that each employee in the department will be familiar with the work of every other employee. A conference is then held, at which the job descriptions are reviewed and discussed, and the techniques of the job interchange plan fully explained.

In credit departments where this training technique is skillfully used, the following benefits are likely to be attained with little expense and with only a slight disruption of normal office routines:

1. The overall flexibility of the department and its ability to meet emergencies caused by illness, vacations, and other work interruptions are greatly increased.
2. Employees' enthusiasm for their work is increased.
3. Replacement of lower supervisory personnel is made easier since several persons in the department know several jobs.
4. The discipline of having to think out and describe their jobs often leads credit personnel to better work habits and a better understanding of where their work fits in with that of others.

Employee Enhancement

After the training phase is completed and the employee settles into a normal credit assignment, continuous efforts can be made to involve the employee in assignments of special or nonroutine nature. These can deal with computer applications to credit, internal and external correspondence, word processing procedures, and reappraisal of credit organization and procedures. A growing workload with a more or less fixed number of people requires the department to continually review its system and procedures to maintain an adequate level of control with less human effort. This discloses new and better ways to use the computer; in that respect, both the necessary hardware and technical knowledge would have to be available.

The credit department can hold frequent departmental meetings, usually once a week. These pertain to subjects peculiar to the department's internal structure. Visits by customers, by debtors, and by lecturers who specialize in peripheral credit activities also can be encouraged. In addition, the credit executive can conduct periodic group meetings with the supervisory personnel to ensure a constructive team effort between line and staff people.

In order to help broaden credit understanding and as an additional aid for career planning, an accounting and financial training program can be established. It could consist of a series of seminars held over a period of about six months, where selected new employees are exposed to a detailed review of many activities within the credit department. The topics can cover such diverse fields as taxes, financial analysis, auditing, banking, corporate accounting, foreign exchange, and personnel.

CONTINUING EDUCATION

A continuing education program usually follows a conventional pattern with courses designed to cover a given area of instruction in an orderly manner. Formal education and training is almost a necessity for adults if all the resources of a complex society are to be understood and utilized. The more technical and more advanced the field of learning becomes, the more necessary it is that formal educational training be continued.

The purpose of this program is to offer credit employees educational opportunities not provided by their company and to enable those outside the field to train for credit work. Carefully chosen educational material can introduce the student to new credit practices and encourage the acquisition of new skills, besides providing a broader understanding of credit management and its relationship to business operations as a whole.

There are continuous education programs for credit personnel at every level of experience. In developing this program, the credit executive can ascertain what facilities are available in the community and draw upon the resources of certain national organizations in the credit field. Continuous education is primarily based upon courses offered by local colleges, NACM affiliates, and other groups.

A well-chosen program of continuous education has many advantages. The trainee has the opportunity to exchange viewpoints with business personnel of other companies. By participating with others in the solution of credit problems, the trainee improves the capacity to make decisions and to meet complex situations. By taking part in the discussion of current economic, financial, and managerial problems, the trainee learns to appreciate the outside influences affecting the credit operations.

Local Activities

Local credit associations, affiliated with the National Association of Credit Management, often conduct informal educational activities which can provide desirable supplementary training. Such activities usually take one or more of the following forms:

Problem Clinics. Give members an opportunity to participate in clinical analysis of current credit and financial problems.

Forums. Consist of a series of meetings led by competent authorities who discuss subjects of current interest in the credit field.

Panel Conferences. A panel of competent authorities, guided by a capable moderator, discuss credit and financial management problems. An opportunity is usually given for audience participation through questions and comments from the floor.

Lectures. Outstanding authorities discuss topics of current interest often followed by questions from the floor.

Study Groups. Meet once or twice a month to pursue a planned course of study or to discuss a series of subjects of common interest to members of the group.

National Institute of Credit

The institute, founded in 1918, is one of the educational activities of NACM and is administered by the Credit Research Foundation. The Institute encourages local NACM affiliates to offer courses directly or through local colleges and universities. The courses cover the basic skills in credit and financial management and are presented in an authoritative and realistic manner. The Institute also regulates the Associate and Fellow Awards, which have been earned by thousands of successful applicants since they were first offered more than 60 years ago.

Graduate School of Credit and Financial Management

Founded in 1947, the Graduate School of Credit and Financial Management provides a program of personal development for qualified credit and financial executives who wish to prepare themselves for greater corporate responsibilities, perform their work more effectively, develop their leadership skills, and increase their decisionmaking ability.

The School is conducted each summer for the NACM by the Credit Research Foundation at the Amos Tuck School of Business Administration, Dartmouth College; the Graduate School of Business, Stanford University; and Williams College.

The program consists of an intensive two-week session each year for three years. The curriculum is divided into four general areas: finance, money and credit, policy and procedures, and human resources. Courses include financial management, computer applications to credit and financial decisionmaking, managerial psychology, management of human resources, organizational behavior, management policy, marketing, money and credit, international credit and finance, and management of multinational enterprises. In addition, each participant is required to write a comprehensive Management Study Report on a research project or on some problem directly connected with the participant's firm or on a relevant business subject.

Credit Management Workshops

These are two-day conferences sponsored by the Credit Research Foundation for financial executives in cities throughout the country, in cooperation with affiliated associations of the NACM. Each participant spends a full day in each of two sessions learning the latest concepts and theoretical developments in credit and financial management, and discovering precise applications of these concepts for the advantage of the participant's company.

Mid-Career School

This program is designed for persons who need greater technical knowledge and a deeper understanding of how credit management meshes with other corporate functions. Participants attend classes, study, discuss concepts and cases, exchange views, and learn from the faculty and each other. The formal topics listed in the curriculum are financial aspects of managing accounts receivable, credit management and policy, and management of human resources. Ample time and opportunity are also available for the participants to discuss other problems relating to their work situations.

University Programs

In cooperation with local affiliates of the National Association of Credit Management and the National Institute of Credit, a number of university schools of business offer certificate programs in credit management. Such programs usually require the completion of about 60 semester hours of course work in the fields of business administration and credit management.

Other Programs

Dun & Bradstreet offers well-designed correspondence courses in credit fundamentals. Other correspondence courses in credit are available through the extension divisions of several state universities.

The American Management Association, in its program of workshop seminars, includes meetings devoted to credit. These seminars are held throughout the country. The credit sessions are intended to acquaint general executives with the nature and importance of credit functions in the operation of a business.

CREDIT TRAINING IN THE SMALL DEPARTMENT

Some phases of credit training are necessarily limited to large credit departments. The credit executive of the small centralized department must take into account the more limited resources available for planning a training program. Even though the total expenditure involved may not be large, the management of a small company is likely to question any outlay that will throw the normal budget out of line, unless assurance can be given that the investment will produce savings and profit to the company.

Time limitations may prove even more restrictive. Any large amount of time taken out for training may seriously affect the flow of work through the department. Moreover, the credit executive may have only two or three employees on the staff, and there will be many demands within a limited time frame. Whatever training can be managed is likely to be the credit executive's responsibility, but the problem will be to find adequate time for this important function in the midst of a busy schedule.

In view of these limitations, a small credit department may find it difficult, if not impossible, to adopt an extensive training program. This does not mean, however, that training of the staff should be neglected; in fact, the need for training is probably more urgent here than in larger departments. Assuming that a program would require more time and money than the department can afford, what can the credit executive do to train and develop a staff? First of all, some kind of informal training may be feasible. In addition, supplemental training should be available through local colleges, the National Institute of Credit, Dun & Bradstreet, or a similar source.

In smaller communities where outside educational facilities are limited, a number of small credit departments may well pool their resources for training purposes. Group conferences, study groups, and more formal courses could be arranged at a central location, either on company time or after working hours.

CHAPTER 9

CREDIT DEPARTMENT SYSTEMS AND PROCEDURES

A credit department thrives on information. This holds true whether it is operated manually or is computerized. The department is responsible for obtaining the information stored in various devices, for maintaining a proper balance between the cost and value of the information, and for providing appropriate security for the information. As each department varies in size and scope, the proper method for storing and retrieving the information will be determined by the system requirements. In this chapter, various components of effective credit department systems and procedures are discussed. Where manual operations differ significantly from those that are computerized, the systems are presented under separate sections.

CONSTRUCTION OF A CREDIT FILE

The credit file is an accumulation of credit information in whatever form the department can justify. The information must be gathered promptly and efficiently while mindful of the element of cost. It is generated internally or obtained from outside sources. Information derived from the department's own experience with a customer includes knowledge about the principals, an understanding of how the business operates, and information on the customer's purchasing and paying habits. On a new account, more reliance is placed on outside sources, such as the bank, suppliers, and reporting agencies.

When a credit decision has been made, the record of that decision takes the form of credit instructions placed in the credit file. In their simplest form, the instructions merely state the customer's name and address, the credit line, terms of sale, and billing instructions. These items can be briefly noted inside each file folder. This procedure is commonly used when the credit department handles a large volume of small accounts with relatively few special problems. If credit checking on each individual order is unnecessary, instructions should be plainly marked "No Credit Review," or some such phrase, to avoid duplication of effort. If it is the practice to dispense with credit lines completely on accounts where no credit check is considered necessary, the instructions should be marked "Requirements." Either of the above designations will reduce the credit check to a minimum.

More elaborate credit instructions may be needed in some instances to cover advanced datings for seasonal shipments, to specify cash discount privileges, and to provide for multiple credit lines for the same customer. The instructions may also indicate the amount and kind of collateral that will be accepted for secured amounts, release arrangements for collateral, and the interest rate to be charged.

A credit file should normally also include analysis of financial data, banking arrangements, trade payments, necessary agreements, and the like. These records should be maintained in a uniform manner to permit ready comparison and evaluation over a period of time.

CREDIT CONTROL SYSTEMS AND PROCEDURES

In many companies, the credit department is charged with the responsibility of checking and approving each sales order. While this may be accomplished by an individual review of each order, it is more common and practical to control orders on an exception basis—for example, to review only those accounts that exceed specified credit parameters, those accounts with past-due balances, and those accounts shipped on a bill-to-bill basis. With control by exception, there must be an effective method of control or there can be no assurance that specific credit arrangements and terms of payment will be observed.

A critical factor of any credit control system is the point at which orders enter the order entry system, regardless of the number of locations at which they are entered. These points are established by companies so they may be highly responsive to customer needs. In many companies, a central facility is the most expeditious while others find that multiple order points are the most practical.

Single Order Entry Point

When there is a single order entry point and all orders are routed through the credit department, certain credit procedures are commonly followed. Each customer has an implied or actual credit line and the file shows the balance owing at any particular time. Each order generally contains some form of identification, such as a code number, which appears on invoices and the accounts receivable file. Moreover, notes of approved orders can be made in the file, which then can be compared with the actual postings. Since these marginal notations become a record of unfilled orders, they can provide an effective credit control. Increasingly, the rapid adoption of automated order entry systems has made this record an electronic one, readily accessible by credit personnel.

Under a rudimentary manual system, someone in the credit department should be responsible for checking all orders against the file to see that the amount of the order is within the prescribed limit. (In some companies, the credit department may be assigned the additional task of seeing that the terms shown on the order coincide with the customary terms for the product.) This check is easily made by adding the value of the order to the balance owing and comparing the sum with the credit line in the customer file. If the total exceeds the credit line, the order must be referred to the credit executive who will review the credit data file and determine whether facts justify a temporary or permanent increase in the line. Otherwise a new financial investigation may be necessary. If the order must be refused, the next step becomes a matter of policy. In some organizations, situations of this kind are handled directly by representatives of the credit department; in others, by the sales department.

In some automated systems, the order is matched against the customer file, while in others the order is matched against only those accounts exceeding their credit lines. When matched against the customer file, the order is approved if the order plus the account balance and other orders that have been approved but not yet shipped do not exceed the credit line. If the sum exceeds the credit line, the order is referred to the credit executive. When the order is matched only against customers that have exceeded their credit lines, an approved order may be in excess of the customer's credit line in the one shipment, but this condition will be picked up on the next order. When a system is operating on an exception basis, it approves routine orders and refers major problem orders to the credit executive. In this way it helps the executive to control the receivables portfolio.

Multiple Order Entry Points

With multiple order entry points and centralized administration of credit, sufficient time must elapse between the order and shipment dates for the credit department to conduct its investigation. Fast approval or rejection of an order may be easier when teleprocessing equipment is used.

Some firms write all orders in duplicate, one copy going to the shipping plant or warehouse and another to the credit department. If the order cannot be approved, the shipping point is advised promptly and the shipment is delayed until proper approval can be given. Otherwise all orders may be shipped after a specified waiting period.

Other companies record orders in triplicate; they forward the original to the shipping point, a copy to the credit department, and another copy to the central sales department where prices or other conditions are checked. In that case, the shipment may be delayed by either the sales or the credit department. The rest of the procedure is the same as that described for a single order entry point.

In both automated and manual systems, the initial credit approval may be made by the local credit executive or the customer credit lines may be established by the central office. This speeds up approval of the order. Where a company sells many products at multiple order entry points to any one customer, the ability to control total exposure becomes more complex. It is only by having proper communication links to one central point that such control is maintained.

CREDIT FILING SYSTEMS

Credit departments, whether they operate on a manual or automated basis, employ a wide variety of filing systems. Most effective are those designed specifically for the peculiarities of the company and its customers. Procedures that are well adapted to one situation may be entirely unsuitable to another, so each company should develop a system best suited to its specific needs.

The purpose of any record is to provide information for decisionmaking. Unless this can be accomplished from the records kept in the credit department, the time and money expended on them is wasted. Minimum information that should be provided by credit records includes business history and method of operation of each account; balance owed; what was recently purchased and when; due date; delinquent customers, balance owing, and aged; and payment history.

Department Filing System

For proper access to credit information, the department must establish a system for filing records, memoranda, and other information so it can be found when necessary. Credit records generally fall into three broad categories:

Credit Data File.   This is the principal file of an account. It includes original reference letters; mercantile agency reports; financial statements; memoranda of telephone calls or conversations; bank information; payment history; financial statement; copies of legal documents such as mortgages, guaranties, collateral pledge agreements, and assignment agreements (the originals should be kept under separate cover); analysis work sheets or printouts; and credit instructions or a record of the credit decision.

Correspondence File.   A separate file may be used to hold correspondence concerning a customer's account. As letters become outdated, they are extracted from the credit data file and placed in this secondary file. Those letters considered important enough for evaluating an account are retained as part of the credit data file.

Subject File.   This file includes materials of a general nature, such as industry studies. Files should be confined to a single subject so that they can be a ready reference source.

Coding Information

Unless information for filing is properly coded, it will be difficult to file appropriately. This holds true whether the system is manual or automated. It should be the responsibility of the credit department to devise a coding system that meets the needs of the department and corresponds to the files on each account. Thus, in the above suggested system, Code Number 1 would mean Credit Data File of the account, Code Number 2 would mean Correspondence File, and Code Number 3 would mean Subject File.

To facilitate coding and to prevent extemporaneous filing, it is advisable to use a rubber stamp listing all the filing classifications (in the above example, numbers 1 through 3) with a place for a checkmark and initials of the person coding the information. This will serve as a check on the individual interpretation of document content.

Another helpful device is to include the file coding on the receiving stamp which is placed on all incoming mail, thus reducing the use of a special stamp.

Manual Filing Systems

While many large companies have automated credit files, the majority of firms, particularly the smaller ones, still rely upon manual systems for their credit and accounts receivable records. For this reason, three variations of a manual system are described below.

Central Filing System. Under this system, designated people keep control of all files pertaining to an account. Credit, sales, manufacturing, and purchasing records of each account are kept together, and information received by any department is forwarded to the central section to be filed.

While this system does keep efficient control over the files, it requires each department to keep duplicate files or ticklers because certain information cannot be obtained quickly.

Sectional Filing System. This is an adaptation of the central filing system, which establishes subfiles within a single manila folder for each account. Thus the credit department may index a folder in the following manner: statement; synopsis; statement analysis; memoranda; credit correspondence; inquiries; other correspondence; and agency reports, clippings, and other information. This credit folder is methodical and at the same time permits the credit executive to obtain needed information quickly. It is particularly useful when amounts of credit are large, and frequent and careful analyses are required. It requires careful filing, however, and is probably too exact when orders are relatively small.

Intermediate Filing System. This system fits between the centralized and sectional filing arrangements. The files of the credit department are kept together with those of other departments of the company. They are easily distinguished, however, because they are a different color. For example, all credit department files might be blue; sales department files might be red; purchasing files, yellow; and so on. File copy stationery would follow the same color scheme.

In the above systems, all papers are filed in chronological order, with the latest records on top. Current credit instructions would be placed above all other data. Outdated material should be purged. Information that is not current or applicable can be placed in a second file, appropriately labeled File Number 2 of 2.

Since it is important that the credit department have access to these files, they should be physically close to the department. Any member of the department may remove a file, after having properly signed for it. However, to maintain the files in proper order and to minimize the amount of time required to file data, it is customary to have a central return point for all withdrawn material.

EDP Storage Devices

The rapid advance of electronic data processing system technology offers a number of alternatives to fit a particular credit and accounts receivable environment. From the basic input mechanism through the final output of information, there have been major changes, such as key to magnetic tape, key to disk, and on line. In addition, data may be entered into a computer through optical scanning or magnetic reading devices. Reports may be printed on paper through devices that are part of the computer center, such as impact printers, laser printers, and microfilm; through remote terminals, such as printers or CRT devices; or a combination of these devices. And information can be retrieved almost instantaneously.

The devices used for storing information vary in their capabilities. Most basic is the hard copy, which includes any printed form or document, such as the customer's ledger in a manual system or the printed output in an automated system. Hard copy provides limited storage capacity.

Microfilm/microfiche consists of miniaturized photographic images. Its small size makes fiche capable of storing vast amounts of data. Moreover, computer output microfilm (COM) devices produce fast and cheap film output. Information can be retrieved by using microfilm/microfiche readers or by rapid random access using computers.

Another medium, magnetic tapes, is useful for storing large amounts of data in rows of magnetic fields. It may be used for information that flows in logical sequence, such as in general ledger and some financial reports. While virtually unlimited storage is possible on many tapes, their major limitation is that they are sequential access storage devices—that is, information can be read and stored only in physical sequence.

This shortcoming is overcome by the use of disks, which serve as a random access file. Information stored on disks can be quickly retrieved without a sequential search through unwanted data.

FOLLOWUP SYSTEMS

Every credit department needs an efficient followup system to keep its activities and its records up to date, because the information at its command is the basis on which credit decisions are made. The procedures vary according to the size of the company, the number of accounts handled, the extent of risk, and the extent of automation.

Revision of Credit Files

To determine the status of an account, the credit file must contain up-to-date information. A consistent method of revision must be followed, whether it is done on a regular or on an exception basis.

Chronological Files. Under this system, twelve folders, one for each month, are usually sufficient. Each credit instruction should have an expiration date, after which it will be renewed or cancelled. An extra copy of the credit instruction for each customer is placed in the folder for the month prior to its renewal date. At the proper time, the instruction is matched against the credit data files and a new investigation started on each account.

Chronological files may also consist of twelve folders for the months and thirty-one folders for the days of the month. At the beginning of each month, the extra credit instructions are removed from the monthly folder and distributed among the daily folders to assure that each file is brought to the attention of the proper person at the right time.

Automated Revision Service. The credit interchange bureaus of local affiliates of the National Association of Credit Management offer an automated revision service for marginal customers and high-volume accounts. This option provides for periodic reviews by the bureaus on a scheduled basis to provide the inquirer with current trade payment information.

Where files are computerized, changes in Dun & Bradstreet ratings can be used for updating a company's files. A magnetic tape showing all rating changes can be inputted into the company's system in order to identify those accounts requiring a review of credit lines.

Risk Classes. A more comprehensive approach is to use the computer to identify and print out all accounts on a scheduled basis based upon their risk classification (prime, good, limited, or marginal). For example, marginal customers would be reviewed more frequently than prime or limited accounts. This method places emphasis upon those accounts that need attention. After the customer files have been updated, they are returned to the same cycle if there is no change in the risk class or placed into another cycle if the risk class is changed.

Identifying Delinquent Accounts

As part of the followup, the system must identify delinquent accounts. Four techniques are discussed below.

Open Invoice File. This system is detailed later in this chapter, so comment here is confined to its function in identifying delinquent accounts. Copies of all invoices must be supplied to the credit department for filing by due date. As payments are credited, invoices are removed and balances are aged on a manually prepared analysis report. Computerization is rapidly eliminating the need for such files, since access to invoices is instantaneous and aging is generated quickly either on scheduled dates or on demand.

Customer Ledger Cards. The ledger card shows customer's name and address, credit line, credit rating, date first sold, and a detailed listing of the invoices, payments, and subsequent adjustments. It thus collects in a single unified record the information on all of the company's dealings with a customer. It is used for extending credit, answering credit inquiries, and making adjustments. In addition, if open items are past due, the collection steps taken can be noted on the cards.

Use of ledger cards gives the credit department full control of its own working tools. Since the cards are created specifically for the credit department, their use can be governed entirely by the needs of that department. With computers, however, these also are rapidly giving way to immediate-access cathode-ray tube (CRT) display.

Aged Trial Balance. Another method is to examine the accounts receivable trial balance monthly, note past-due aged items, check accounts receivable ledgers, and start collection activities if the past-due items have not been paid. Aged trial balances are also generated under an automated system.

Since this report is prepared alphabetically by customer, a great amount of manual effort is still required to sort out those accounts requiring immediate attention. Moreover, an analysis is required to review the daily cash received so that the status of the account can be determined before the collection effort begins. This workload requires extended hours and often results in inadequate attention to problem accounts. Fortunately, computerization has once again eliminated the drudgery of compiling such lists and makes it possible to identify problem accounts quickly.

Past-Due Listing. This important report lists all accounts with overdue balances. Ordinarily it is an aged listing. It is used in much the same manner as the aged trial balance but contains a smaller number of accounts. Otherwise, the disadvantages noted for the aged trial balance also apply in the use of this report.

In an automated system, the computer can be programmed to identify those accounts that exceed any of the variable credit parameters and display them on a printer or CRT device. For example, the computer can be programmed to display all of the largest past-due accounts on a particular day; or if the number of accounts is too large, the program can be further refined to show by size the accounts that are 60 days past due.

Collection Followup

After collection activity has begun, some form of followup of delinquent accounts is needed.

Two-Week System. Under one manual method, commonly known as the two-week system, accounts to be followed up are reached automatically every two weeks. Since there are ten working days in each two-week period, ten folders are set aside and numbered one through ten. The letters of the alphabet are distributed in some such manner as follows:

1	2	3	4	5	6	7	8	9	10
a	b	c	d	e	f	g	h	i	j
k	l	m	n	o	p	q	r	s	t
u	v	w	x	y	z				

The file for each account is placed in the proper numbered folder according to its alphabetical listing. This assures a fairly even distribution of the followup workload.

Tickler File. In a manual system, this consists of a file that contains a collection record card on each delinquent account. The cards are filed chronologically, according to the date the collection action is to take place. On that date, the files slated for collection are put on the work list. If a collection is made before the appointed date, the card is removed from the file.

A variation of this is to put a followup date on the file in question, note the date on a calendar, and remove files for review on the date specified. Still another procedure is to use the duplicate system. This requires that an extra copy of all correspondence in the file be made on different colored paper. The files then are returned to the general files. A followup date is placed on the extra copy and it is filed by date; at the specified time, the copy is removed and matched against the followup file.

In an automated system, a review date may be provided in the computer program to indicate the date when future action should be taken on an account. It can also be used to suppress information from appearing on the search list because no action is required until a future date. For example, if a customer promised that a check will be mailed on a certain day, a tickler date entered into the system will call the account to the attention of the credit executive if the expected check is not received on time. Since no action is required until that date, there is no need for the account to appear on work lists generated in the meanwhile. After the tickler date is passed, the account will again appear on the work list if it continues to be past due or if a new tickler date has not been assigned.

HANDLING ACCOUNTS RECEIVABLE

This recordkeeping may be handled on a manual or automated basis, and may use the balance-forward or the open-item method. In any case, a separate account record must be established for each credit customer and include customer's invoices, cash payments, and adjustments.

A manual system uses loose-leaf ledger, open invoice, or machine bookkeeping to record its receivables. With the growing emphasis on automation, however, many companies have adopted punched cards for accounts receivable, and this has led to electronic data processing.

Loose-Leaf Ledger

This is probably the oldest bookkeeping system still in use. New forms for active accounts may be inserted or old forms for inactive accounts may be removed without disarranging any current information. There is a separate form for each customer, with space for dates, descriptive matter, debits, credits, and balance. This system is used by small businesses.

Open Invoice File

This file system, described earlier for identifying delinquent accounts, is much used for processing accounts receivable. The open invoice file is found in various forms and has been identified as the tub system, the tray system, or the simplified unit invoice accounting plan (SUIAP). It consists basically of a folder or pouch for each customer, in which is placed a copy of the invoice or credit advice that is mailed to the customer. When a payment is received, the appropriate invoice is so noted, withdrawn from the folder, and retained in a paid invoice file. When a partial payment is made, the amount of the payment is noted on the copy of the invoice and the balance still owing is recorded in the open file. Thus a quick tabulation of all invoices automatically shows the amount due from the account.

Under this system, no bookkeeping is necessary except basic records on how long a customer has been sold, the highest credit, the amount presently owing, the amount past due, and average number of days to pay an invoice. Since this information is often needed, it can be separately compiled in a continuing or periodic fashion.

Because each invoice is recorded separately, the aging of accounts is a relatively simple matter. Totals of invoices inserted into the folders, invoices removed, and credit memoranda inserted each day are posted to the general ledger account. Therefore, the total of balances remaining in the folders should always be the same as the balance shown in the general ledger.

Machine Bookkeeping

Bookkeeping machines are operated by specially trained personnel and give much the same results as loose-leaf ledgers do, but the saving in time is a vital consideration.

The efficiency of the equipment and the saving of operator's time are influenced by the method of preparing entry data for posting. One popular procedure is to prepare an input form for recording data from invoices, customer remittances, and other adjustment documents. The form may be inserted in a loose-leaf binder or sorting tray, and the operator will automatically post all of the current items when the form is picked up.

Punched Card Accounting

Punched card accounting provides essentially a ledgerless system for accounts receivable. It consists of an open file of punched cards that takes the place of the open invoice file. Each transaction is represented by a punched card. Separate cards are punched for each invoice charge and payment, and for all other debit or credit memo postings. The cards are identified by customer account number. A customer header card, which contains the customer number, name, address, sales district, credit line, and other miscellaneous information, identifies each account in the file. Transaction cards are filed behind each header card in chronological order. By manipulating the cards in the files, an operator can prepare records and reports.

The chief value of this system is the extent to which routine operations are handled by machines. One of the obvious advantages is the saving of clerical time in the preparation of reports and statements, and in filing to the open item file. The speed and flexibility of the machines make it possible to assimilate peak loads.

Closer integration with order-writing, billing, or other functions helps to eliminate duplication of effort. The automated reproduction of accounts receivable cards and the printing of reports directly from the cards also reduce the opportunities for clerical error. However, the human errors that do occur are relatively difficult to locate and correct.

Adapting the Computer to Credit and Accounts Receivable

While punched cards once served as the basic feeder device for entering data into a credit and accounts receivable system, they are being replaced by other devices which are faster and offer more advantages.

Tapes and Disks. Magnetic tapes are convenient for storing a sequence of data items, but the data can only be retrieved by having the computer read the file in sequence from the beginning. A file can also be stored sequentially on disk. This gives the maximum rate of data transfer but only allows retrieval of records in their storage sequence. A file can also be stored on disk on a random access basis, particularly if the anticipated use of the file involves low activity or requires quick response. This permits rapid retrieval of stored data in any sequence, timely updating of files, and prompt response to inquiries.

Database. While these techniques allow economical data processing, they do not provide a large file that permits economical interfile inquiry. This is achieved by the use of a database, which allows for the pooling and processing of a firm's data, and a system for managing such data efficiently. It makes all data potentially available to any application rather than allowing separate applications for separate files.

Under a system called distributed processing, updated inputs and inquiries can be handled locally and still be pooled into a current central database. This often means that users, data, programs, and hardware are located separately and yet are connected. It is a system with both central and decentralized capabilities, and relies on the rapidly improving technology and economics of minicomputers, intelligent terminals, and data communications.

Hardware. Minicomputers are relatively inexpensive and can be used as stand-alone processors or in conjunction with a mainframe computer. Many companies use them for instant processing of invoices and remittances in their credit and accounts receivable systems. Another technological development in hardware is the intelligent terminal. Often described as a minicomputer, it is actually a terminal that can perform limited transactions and also validate them. With it, input is validated before being fed into the mainframe computer. The means for linking computers to other computers and terminals is called data communication, telecommunication, or teleprocessing and consists of sending electronic signals over ordinary telephone lines.

Limitations and tradeoffs on the use of computer equipment still relate to an organization's size and financial position, but are becoming smaller. It is normally not feasible to dedicate a large computer to credit and accounts receivable. Nevertheless, the rapid technology advances in minicomputers and terminals give the innovative credit executive powerful and efficient alternatives to the large mainframe equipment. Hardware computer configuration should be evaluated carefully to be sure that optimum structural makeup is used.

CHAPTER 10

AUTOMATED CREDIT AND ACCOUNTS RECEIVABLE SYSTEMS

A credit executive needs up-to-date information on the status of customer accounts in order to manage the accounts receivable investment. For large volumes of work, this can best be provided by an automated system that provides timely information on those accounts that need attention and avoids wasting time, effort, and money on routine accounts.

Data flows begin with the order. It enters the system as a by-product of the order entry and billing operation and is recorded in the customer account. When the customer payment record is received, the system is required to identify the customer account and to enter the customer payment against outstanding invoices. The check payment is matched against invoice amounts and paid items are removed from the customer's account. Items which cannot be matched are posted without being keyed to a specific invoice amount and are processed later manually. When matched, the invoice amounts then are removed as paid items. These transactions update the customer account in the master file.

The master file also contains other information useful in administering a credit and accounts receivable department: customers' names and addresses, sales and payment history, credit lines, account balances, orders approved but not yet shipped, and other essential data. This information in turn is used to print out those accounts referred to the credit executives and to generate required reports such as the daily balancing report, aged trial balance, and past-due statement.

ON-LINE SYSTEMS

An on-line credit and accounts receivable system has a direct communication line that connects the user's work area with the computer. There are two general classifications of on-line processing, both using an interface device such as a terminal:

1. *Batch processing.* The user enters data to a temporary file on line for later processing against a master file.

2. *Real time.* The user has direct access to current information for inquiry or immediate change.

On-Line System Within a Batch Mode

An on-line system within a batch mode enables nightly updating of the accounts receivable file. Tapes generated by the billing system for product sales are used to update the customer files. Customer payments representing the credits to the customer files are prepared daily off line, using intelligent terminals or subsystems, and are validated before they are released to the central processing unit.

On-line inquiry to the central processing unit is available through cathode-ray tubes (CRTs) and printer-type terminals. Current credit and collection information is thereby available immediately upon request.

A system operating under a batch mode avoids using expensive central processing computer time for time-consuming clerical functions such as payment application. However, it does allow credit and collection personnel to obtain accurate, accessible, and prompt information for decisionmaking.

On-Line, Real-Time System

This system gives a credit executive up-to-the-minute control over accounts. In addition to processing in a batch mode, an on-line, real-time system allows for direct updating of files. New customers may be added, names and addresses changed, credit lines and followup criteria can be adjusted; journal records and chargebacks can be produced on line.

While the on-line, real-time system provides more timely information than the batch mode process, it does cost more. The mainframe computer is more costly to operate than is a buffered subsystem. These higher computing costs, however, may be more than offset by other savings.

ORDER ENTRY AND BILLING SYSTEMS

The receipt of a customer's order starts a long chain of steps involving many departments and functions. After it has been processed and the merchandise shipped, an invoice is prepared (this is postbilling, as opposed to prebilling in which the order set and invoice set are prepared at one writing). Among other things, the invoice identifies the sale and the amount due. A standardized format can help smooth the computer input data, minimize errors, and cut down on customer disputes.

Systems Considerations

A well-designed order entry and billing system should furnish information for updating the seller's accounts receivable; data for adjusting inventory files; records for control over backorders; and statistics for sales representatives' commissions, freight payments, sales taxes, and sales analyses. All of this information must be accurate, detailed, and timely.

The system is usually implemented off line, without the benefit of terminal devices linked to a central computer. Orders are generally batch processed at night or entered through CRTs and fed into the computer in batch mode. Consequently, records are updated and available the following morning, or the data may be buffered and released into the computer on a regular schedule.

Order Credit Approval

Credit approval procedures vary from company to company depending upon the state of automation of both the order processing and credit functions. Some firms have a mechanized review of each order, with exceptions reported to credit executives; others require approval by sales or plant personnel within established dollar lines set by the credit department; still others make a manual review of each order by the credit department before goods are shipped.

There is no single best way. Each organization should look at its internal capabilities and develop an order approval control procedure that considers company exposure and the status of open invoices.

A fully automated system should enable a credit executive to determine whether receivables are being paid within terms. It should also provide a complete record of previously approved but unshipped orders. Where multiple locations are linked into a central computer installation, the credit department should be able to determine the pay status and total exposure to any customer. Remote locations should be able to transmit data to the central unit for immediate update of the central file. Input and output devices should be placed at plants, warehouses, and sales offices, so the computer may serve the entire complex.

An order approval system should be able to react quickly if adverse credit information is received. This becomes doubly important when dealing with high-risk or marginal accounts because in the event of an insolvency the ability to hold orders or stop shipments, even if in transit, may reduce potential loss.

METHODS OF GATHERING CASH

An efficient cash-gathering system begins with systematic collection of customer payments. The best method for a particular company depends upon its nature and diversification. It should reduce float, the time delay on the utilization of funds. Three types of float are:

1. *Mail float.*   Days elapsed from when the customer mails a payment until the check is received by the corporation or its bank.

2. *Processing float.*   The amount of time lost due to sorting and recording

the information after the check has been received and until the check is deposited.

3. *Availability float.* Time elapsed from when the check is deposited until funds are credited to the depositor's account. For example, when a check is deposited into a bank account, the amount of the check is immediately reflected in the daily bank balance. However, these funds cannot be withdrawn, wired out, or invested until the bank converts these funds to available or collected balances.

Lockbox Banks

The lockbox collection system is widely used for gathering cash. The company instructs its customers to remit payments directly to a post office box number. The bank providing the lockbox service collects the mail, processes remittances, and deposits them directly into the company's account.

A properly structured lockbox arrangement reduces float through faster mail time, improved availability, and elimination of processing by corporate employees before checks are deposited.

Certain banks offer manual and automated data capture of lockbox remittance information. In the automated process, the bank captures the MICR (magnetic ink character recognition) information from the checks and transmits it to the company. In the manual process, the bank collects and keypunches certain data required by the customer. This timely information enables the creditor to apply the remittance information directly to the customer's account.

Courier Pickup System

This method, for large remittance customers, uses a courier service which picks up checks from customers and deposits them into the company's bank account. It eliminates mail float completely.

Preauthorized Debit System

This method is used by insurance, finance, leasing, and mortgage companies which receive regular high-volume, fixed payments from the same customers. A preauthorized debit is a commercial demand deposit instrument used to transfer funds from one corporation to another. The corporation that is to receive the funds on the due date will deposit a preauthorized check drawn on the debtor's account and made payable to the depositor. This method, if properly handled, can reduce mail time as well as availability time.

Hand-Carry Method

This collection method, very simple but cost-effective, is used for large remittances only. A company employee is sent to deposit a check at the bank where it is drawn, thus bypassing the normal check gathering system and some of the float.

PAYMENT APPLICATION

Payment application, commonly called cash application, is an essential part of any credit and accounts receivable system. As noted earlier, the check payment cannot be merely posted to an account as in consumer credit (the balance forward system) but must be carefully applied to specific items being paid (open item system). In this case, the check payment serves as the authority for removing all paid items from the customer file.

In computerized systems, the data sources for payment application include the original punched cards, a computer printout of open items, a list of open items displayed in a cathode-ray tube or microfilm reader screen, and a computer to search out and delete the invoices to be paid.

The initial task in payment application is the identification of the payer. This may be accomplished by using a segment of the check containing the MICR line, a turnaround document, or the customer remittance advice. The MICR line contains the serial number, a transit routing number, the customer's account number, and the check amount. There are two types of turnaround documents. One type contains such prepunched information as the account number, account name, invoice number, and gross and net amounts. Another type is an invoice with a tear-off strip that includes the customer number, invoice number, and date, all in precoded form.

Applying Payment Using MICR

Under this method of payment application, customers forward their remittances to designated lockbox banks. These banks capture customer remittance details and prepare input on magnetic tape, using MICR number, check amount, and invoice numbers. Since the lockbox bank's normal procedures require processing of the MICR line, the only additional items needed are the invoice numbers.

At a scheduled period each day, the banks transmit their tape to the client company's open item accounts receivable master file. Under a batch mode this input is buffered to a subsystem, while under real time the data are entered into the mainframe computer.

Batch Mode. After the cash has been inputted, the system extracts from the master customer file the open item data for those accounts making payments. MICR numbers, cross referenced to customer account numbers, are used to identify the accounts and put them into the subsystem for payment application.

The edited data received from the bank passes against the cross-reference file. When a MICR number shown on a remittance matches a MICR number shown in the file, the corresponding accounts receivable number is assigned to the remittance. If a MICR number on a remittance does not find a match, the computer automatically assigns a house account receivable number to the remittance for manual followup and application.

The account number helps the system to find the proper account. Using algorithms, the system initially compares the check amount to the account balance, then the past-due total, invoice amounts, and so on. When a match is made, payment is applied and the open invoice item is cleared. If there is no match, the payment is applied on account. This is later resolved manually by a cash applier using the customer's remittance data.

Real Time.   In a system that operates on a real-time basis, each batch of cash is inputted in the evening batch run. During this processing, the mainframe computer searches for a match on the MICR number. When the computer identifies the account, the check amount and serial number are posted to the customer's account. Using a few simple algorithms, the computer then seeks a combination of invoices that coincides with the check amount. When successful, the computer removes the paid invoices from the customer's open item file.

If the computer cannot identify the account, the amount is placed in an unidentified cash account which is later processed by the operator on line using remittance documents.

Checks identified in either the batch run or on line but not automatically applied against a specific invoice are entered into the customer's account as unapplied. They are later resolved by the operator on line using the customer remittance data. Chargebacks and journal entries also are made on line by the operator.

Applying Payment Using a Turnaround Document

In a payment application system that employs a turnaround document, customers return the documents with their remittances. The prepunched information on these documents enables each lockbox location to process the remittance. When the turnaround document is not returned, the bank prepares a manual form to identify the customer and process the remittance. When a customer cannot be identified, the item is processed, transmitted, and applied to a sundry account for future research and proper application.

With an invoice strip, the lockbox banks may use optical scanning devices which automatically read the visual pattern of recorded data and convert this information to a computer-compatible form such as tape. The data are then transmitted to a central processing unit where a set of algorithms gives the computer the capability to apply these remittances. Any that cannot be applied automatically are later processed manually.

Applying Payment Using a CRT Terminal

Payment application using a cathode-ray tube may include the use of a turnaround document, photocopied checks and remittance details, or "live" checks and remittance details. ("Live" checks are those used for payment application before they are deposited at the bank.) The payment application is performed strictly on an interactive basis between the cash applier and the CRT.

Batch Mode. Under one type of application procedure, the operator requests the customer file from the central processing unit and draws it off onto an intelligent CRT terminal. To apply the payment, the operator looks at the CRT and selects the items that are being paid *one by one*, then makes any necessary journal entries for discount and miscellaneous shortages as required. As payment application is completed for each customer, the operator requests the terminal to balance and validate the application. If the program accepts the operator's input, it releases the operator to the next customer account. These steps are repeated until the entire remittance batch is processed, validated, and balanced. The terminal then saves the input for transmittal back to central processing unit that night.

Real Time. In a faster method of application, the operator receives remittances from a lockbox bank and enters the deposit totals into the system. Each paying customer's name is then entered into the computer. If the computer cannot recognize the customer's account by its name, it displays alternative customer accounts with similar alpha prefixes. The operator selects the proper account from the CRT display and begins keying the customer's remittance advice. Once this information is keyed for all customers within the batch, the operator requests application based on a set of algorithms. Within seconds the computer reports back by customer account only those input items that it cannot locate. The operator then refers to that customer's remittance advice to edit and resolve the differences that will balance and validate the batch.

GENERATION OF REPORTS

An automated system should be designed to prepare reports in three forms: the on-line inquiry, the printed or hard copy report, and microfilm/microfiche. Some reports are intended to appear on a terminal while others are for hard copy only. However, most reports should be designed for both media, so users may have their choice.

Printed reports can be prepared on high-speed printers during the night's batch operation. These include:

1. Reports needed to keep the system in balance—that is, the cash inputted for application to customer accounts should agree with the funds credited to the company by the wire transfers from the lockbox bank.
2. Reports that comprise the credit personnel's working tools, such as the aged trial balance, listing of past-due accounts, exception reports, and the like.
3. Reports needed for evaluating the status of the accounts receivable investment. Reports of this type are discussed in Chapter 33.

Many of these printed reports can be individually requested as needed. When inquiry is made on line, a hard copy of the information on the CRT screen can be produced immediately from a terminal printer located in the credit department.

Exception reports on those payments that cannot be applied to specific invoices should include not only the essential data, such as check number, invoice number, and amount, but also the reason why the remittance could not be applied. This enables the clerk to pinpoint the areas that require particular attention, process the exceptions, and update the file.

SYSTEM DESIGN CONSIDERATIONS

The motivation for a company to adopt an automated credit and accounts receivable system comes from four needs: to bring more operations into the automated data information flow, to provide timely and detailed information for financial planning and control, to reduce systems costs and clerical expenses through more intensive use of the computer, and to accelerate turnover of the receivables investment.

The design of a credit and accounts receivable system involves a series of tradeoffs. The most common is the cost versus benefits decision. These tradeoffs make a system operate effectively within its environment. Cost and system requirements are not inseparable but, finely tuned, will most likely give an optimum design.

User Oriented

The existing system is a key factor in the design of any new system and will give a clue as to its requirements. The logic behind each user's requirements does much to tell the designers why the information is needed and how it is obtained.

Rather than be oriented only to accounts receivable or the credit department, the system should satisfy the needs of all users without producing extraneous, irrelevant information. To accomplish this requires an objective evaluation of requirements and limitations. Billing, credit approval, collections, payment application, and generation of reports must all be considered. The flow-through of these functions provides not only the general concept of a credit and accounts receivable system but also an information system.

The diversification and decentralization of the company organization requires the utmost care in bringing together these diverse functions. The system is fed by various amounts of required input; consequently, the cooperation of the users in supplying, modifying, changing, or increasing volume of input data is fundamental. It is also essential that users of the system feel that they are part of the design team to ensure cooperation, acceptance, and utilization.

Objectives

The initial task is to identify the need for the system. This is determined by the value of the information received from the system and the impact it has on a user's productivity or decisionmaking. Accurate, relevant information must be obtained by the design team establishing the system objectives. If the requirements of each user are not adequately defined, understood, and related to company objectives, the system will not be complete. The design should provide relevant, timely, and accurate information to serve all components of a large company.

After setting the general objectives for the new system, it is time to set the objectives for each user. What does each department want from an automated system? Why does it need this information? How does it want to see it? These are questions that need to be asked of every user. The answers will give the design team a much greater understanding of what the system needs to provide. If the design team understands these needs, innovation and ingenuity may provide even better and more useful information than was thought possible.

Usefulness to Sales Department

Like the credit and accounts receivable department, the sales department is a vital part of the entire system. The objective of a sales department must include optimizing sales. This includes the providing of service to the customer and makes service part of a product's measure. The sales department benefits from an automated accounts receivable system that provides accurate and timely information on sales, receivables, and customer claims and disputes.

An automated system should therefore be an information system for both the credit and sales departments. Since its creditworthiness affects a customer's ability to buy the company's product, this creditworthiness is of prime importance to the sales department. Conversely, the size of a customer's claims and disputes against the company may have an adverse effect on its opinion of the company's product, so the system should report this information to sales as well as to credit.

Gathering Information

Information for decisionmaking, the primary object of a new system, must be evaluated in terms of needs, costs, and tradeoffs that must be made. In this connection, the credit executive should understand that members of a design team may not always understand the relevance and importance of information for a user. This problem is best overcome by including in the team representatives from the various departments that will use the new system. In any event, the team should keep an open mind to these requirements. If the demands of the users seem impossible, they must ask themselves. What?, Why?, and How? A series of compromises and consolidations may give the same result without an enormous price tag.

One of the most effective methods of gathering information for an automated credit and accounts receivable system is to observe existing installations. This approach gives the team an opportunity to discuss common problems with their hosts and to include their observations in their feasibility report. It also gives warning as to potential pitfalls and allows the team to benefit from others' mistakes. Frequently it will point out the direction of attack, control, and restraint in a system design.

Cost

The cost of any system is one of the principal constraints on design. Though certainly important, however, cost should not be the only yardstick. Placing cost in its proper perspective is probably the design team's key task. It should be measured against benefits, needs, speed, and many other criteria that may be unique to each department.

In payment application, for example, one company may use batch mode while another may opt for a real-time computer application. The first system sacrifices speed to avoid the costly on-line, real-time computer usage; while the second system incurs greater running costs to gain the speed required for a larger volume of payment application.

Personnel

The clerical functions of payment application, the handling of claims, disputes, and other jobs associated with accounts receivable are costly and time-consuming. Anything that can be done to relieve personnel of these tasks can be assumed to be beneficial to the organization. Having automated data processing systems take over routine clerical tasks will release skilled people so they can devote their attention to more important work.

Automated systems are designed to assist people and contribute to overall effectiveness. Balancing the workload between an automated system and company personnel leverages the resources of an organization. In planning the system, however, the design team must take into consideration the effect that their design will have on personnel. The cost savings or payroll reductions may offer an enticing rationale for system justification but may have a hidden tradeoff which reduces the productivity of the organization. Will job descriptions and responsibilities change? Will departments have to be reorganized, eliminated, or restructured? If drastic changes are required, will personnel be affected to the same extent? The reallocation of manpower resources with a minimum of disruption does much to maintain the productiveness, stability, and morale of personnel.

Other Tradeoffs

Other tradeoffs will be encountered at every stage of the design: better and more timely information possible at greater cost, department restructuring in order to handle a greater volume of work automatically, and high-cost hardware for faster data handling. Heavy costs will have to be borne at the front end of any new system, and the benefits will be realized only after a longer period of time. The learning costs of the new system will be high at the beginning. All of these will need careful balancing by the design team.

CHAPTER 11

CREDIT POLICY

A policy may be defined as a general course of action developed for recurring situations, designed to achieve established objectives. In business concerns, complementary policies exist at several levels: some apply to the activities of the company as a whole, others to the activities of major division, and still others to a single department. With regard to the credit function, credit policies apply to the credit department's activities for the company as a whole. They establish a framework or guide for consistent credit decisions directed toward attaining the goal established by the company for the credit function.

DEFINING CREDIT POLICY

All companies, whether they sell on credit or for cash, have a credit policy. When a company sells on credit, individual credit decisions follow a pattern consistent with the company's overall aims and policies. On the other hand, a company that makes all its sales for cash has adopted a credit policy to the effect that no credit will be extended. This is just as much a credit policy as any other; one that should be formulated very carefully and only in line with overall corporate objectives. Moreover, a company that has not yet started operations should not be without a credit policy. It is essential that a credit policy be formulated along with other corporate policies in the organizational stages of a business.

Companies vary widely, however, in the extent to which they express a stated policy. In this sense, credit policy is not fully developed in many companies. It is often formulated in very broad terms, such as "to effect maximum sales with minimum losses," and fails to differentiate one customer from another or to provide a useful basis for individual credit decisions. Further difficulties arise from confusion of policy with objectives, procedures, or practices. All of these are interrelated in the process which leads from the statement of goals to the daily operation of a credit department. It is helpful, however, to distinguish among them.

112

Policy and Objectives

Typically, a company has written and defined objectives over stated periods of time. They may involve sales volume, return on capital employed, profit levels, and general recognition of prestige for the company, its products, and its management. To help the company achieve these overall objectives, each functional department, including the credit department, must reach certain specific goals. For the credit department these might be stated in terms of sales volume to customers in various risk classifications, relationship to the sales department, training and development of credit personnel, amount of capital committed to accounts receivable, and measurement of the status of the accounts receivable investment.

These objectives define a position which the department is striving to reach; they answer the question, "What are we trying to accomplish?" Credit policy answers in general terms the question, "What will we do to accomplish these objectives?" Thus policy is established to meet the objectives of the company, which are determined before any other actions can be taken.

Policy and Procedures

Credit policy serves as a guide in determining how to handle given kinds of problems, but it does not offer a definitive solution. It presents a range of solutions within which the credit executive is free to exercise judgment.

In the process of decisionmaking, credit policy is constantly interpreted and applied to concrete situations with the help of specific guides or procedures. These procedures are generally devised by the chief credit executives to standardize the actions of their subordinates in specific situations. They are usually published in procedural manuals as ready references for employees. They allow little discretion since they formalize reactions to particular situations.

Policy and Practice

Credit policy provides wide latitude for the credit executive's judgment. In practice, this range of possible decisions is narrowed for particular personnel, kinds of situations, or time periods. Considerable scope for individual judgment may still be provided, although in some instances company practice imposes stricter constraints on the decisionmaker.

Changes in practice within a given policy provide flexibility in meeting changing conditions. A change in the effective range of decisions which will be made serves to change emphasis within the same policy. In this way, for example, the extension of credit can be made more conservative without any change in the basic policy under which the department operates.

Exceptions

A company's credit policy is intended to be applicable to the majority of credit situations over a long period of time. Even within such a broad context, however, exceptions do arise. The fact that credit policy is explicitly stated does not preclude decisions contrary to the policy, although the authority to make such decisions is usually reserved to the head of the department. In addition, not all of the decisions required of a credit executive will fall within the areas covered by existing credit policy. In most companies, these nonpolicy decisions are also reserved for the head of the department. Like the credit policy itself, they must be consistent with overall company policy and objectives.

ESTABLISHING CREDIT POLICY

Since credit policy concerns the company as a whole, it is usually established officially by top management. Sometimes responsibility for its formulation lies altogether with top management, but more commonly the chief credit executive and associates play an active role in its development. The heads of other interested departments may also be consulted. Credit policy is probably most effectively implemented when all who are directly affected have some voice in its development and it has the endorsement of top management—preferably the board of directors.

While credit policy is the cornerstone of credit administration, there is no single acceptable format. If a credit policy is to have practical value, it must of course be related to a specific company. Every credit executive is entitled to a written policy statement from the officers of the company, one that is fully understood and accepted by sales as well as credit people. An effective credit policy strikes a positive note for credit management. It permits and encourages the fullest development of the opportunities in administering credit. It can be a blueprint for action as well as a training aid for the development of credit personnel. It provides the latitude to plan departmental operations within the scope of the company policy, to create effective procedures and techniques to implement that policy, and to establish adequate controls. Through a well-conceived credit policy there is a climate and an incentive for positive thinking, creativeness, and initiative.

Factors Underlying Credit Policy

When a company is developing a new credit policy or is reviewing an existing one, a number of factors should be considered. Some of these are internal in nature while others are external. Depending on the company, they vary in relative importance. All of them together establish the context within which credit policy must operate.

Objectives. In deciding on a course of action directed toward a goal, it is of first importance to have a clear understanding of the goal. In the development of credit policy, this means an understanding of the company's overall objectives, both for operations such as production and sales and for less tangible areas such as public relations. A progressive and aggressive top management, for example, may tend toward more risk and a greater return opportunity. In terms of this overall program, objectives for the credit department can be formulated. Any statement of policy can then be tested by the question, "Will this help us toward company and department objectives?"

In pursuit of these goals, the following financial considerations may be noted:

1. The amount of capital commitment a company is willing to make toward its receivables investment. This is concerned not only with the protection of this capital but also the return that it will generate.

2. The type of risks acceptable to the company or the basis upon which the company will exchange its products and services for the customer's credit. This can range all the way from credit based on the analysis of factual information through to the area of so-called calculated risk, where credit may be given to anyone willing to buy from the company.

Company and Coordinate Policies. In order that the company as a whole may work most efficiently toward the established objectives, the policies adopted for various areas of interest must function together. In developing a credit policy, its relationship to company policies and the policies of coordinate departments must be carefully considered. This requires credit executives to be familiar with them. Where others have not stated them specifically, it may be necessary to infer objectives and policies from the statements and actions of top management.

In credit administration there are financial, sales, and personnel implications. All should be carefully considered in the wording and content of the policy:

1. What will be the relation of the credit function to the financial management of the company? Will it act primarily to protect the company funds invested in customers, or will it endeavor to increase the turnover of these funds and consequently aid in the generation of profits?

2. What will be the relation of credit to the marketing function of the company? Will it give the selling organization an understandable concept under which credit is to be used as they sell the company's products? Will the policy indicate the manner in which the company wants its customers and potential customers treated in credit dealings?

3. How does the credit policy of the firm fit in with its own personnel policy and programs? Does it present a realistic, acceptable basis upon which credit decisions can be made in an atmosphere of mature consideration?

Legal Restraints. Credit terms are deemed to be an aspect of price. There can be no agreement with competitors with respect to credit policies and no discounts or special credit terms to customers which would violate the Robinson-Patman Act.

Industry Characteristics. Credit practices within the industry also bear upon the credit policy of an individual company. Depending upon the industry, credit varies in importance as a basis for competition. Its role is governed by a number of factors, including tradition, the stability of demand for the industry's products, the rate of technological change, and so on.

Where credit is a fundamental factor in competition within the industry, the credit policy of a company is important for maintaining or improving its competitive position. Even where credit is not generally a competitive tool, an individual company can use it in this way if it is willing to do so. In any case, whether a company chooses to adopt a credit policy which conforms to industry practice or one which varies from it, management should be fully aware of the implications of this decision.

In considering credit policy in relation to competitive conditions within the industry, the credit executive must also evaluate the company's long-range ability to compete. This would include analysis of the company's present position in the industry and its financial strength, as well as a general awareness of such factors as the strength of its marketing organization and its position in product development.

Some of the influential industry practices to be considered when credit policy is being framed include:

1. *Market position of the company.* Within every industry some companies are leaders and others are followers. The relative standing of a company in its industry will in many cases influence the course of action it sets to meet credit problems. If its position is undisputed, a company may demand more from its customers. A company that is just getting started, on the other hand, may find it advantageous to be more lenient in its credit policy. This factor naturally ties in with the marketing aspects of the company.

2. *Competition in the industry.* Most companies find it necessary to establish credit policies with one eye on competition. There the short-term influences can be very strong. Consequently, policy is broad enough to allow considerable variation in action.

3. *Type of customer.* This factor has a direct limiting influence on the credit policies of all companies in an industry. Where the buyers' line of business is characteristically short of capital, it is unrealistic for credit policy to be unduly restrictive. A company which operates on that basis will not maintain its market.

On the other hand, if an industry has many well-capitalized customers, the company that takes additional risk must expect additional return for this added risk. With enough good credit risks available to provide adequate profits, there must be an added incentive to make sales to fair or marginal risks.

4. *Type of merchandise.* This factor always affects the credit policy of the seller. There is a tendency to sell on a more liberal basis if the merchandise can be repossessed in the same condition as it was sold than if the appearance of the merchandise were changed by the buyer. Yard goods in the bolt, for example, can be taken back if they have not been cut by the clothing manufacturer. Once they have been on the pattern table, however, they lose much of their repossession value. Similarly, steel fabricated to specification has less reclamation value than that prepared in an ordinary run.

The merchandising policy of a company often influences credit policy. A company is required, for example, to place machinery in the hands of a limited number of franchised dealers on some basis so as to enable them to sell a maximum volume during a relatively short retail buying season. This might involve long terms of sale to coordinate it with the problems of manufacturing and shipment. Large extensions of credit may be required in relation to the financial responsibility of many dealers. Reliance is placed on the character and capacity of the dealer to a far greater extent than on capital. The essential factors are experience and proven ability in selling competitively, collecting effectively, and operating profitably.

Markup of the merchandise is important. When profit margins are slim, the credit department may be more careful in the selection of its accounts. High-markup goods, on the other hand, entice credit executives to approve sales to fair and marginal accounts. On a percentage basis, they may find it more profitable to check orders and rely on overall profits to cover relatively large bad-debt losses.

Price range of merchandise similarly influences credit policy. It is generally easier to establish a uniform liberal policy which applies to all customers when the unit price of merchandise is relatively low. Even on a wrong decision, the dollar amount of risk is not great. On a big-ticket item, however, credit exposure is greater. Consequently, a more detailed analysis is usually conducted before a customer order is approved.

When merchandise can be obtained readily by the supplier, there is no need to restrict sales to customers unless warranted by financial or credit risks. When a particular item is scarce, however, credit policy may be influenced to the extent that stricter requirements are set for customers needing that item. This situation might occur during shortages of material because of production shutdowns or other restrictions. It is also true in instances where supplies of materials may be scarce.

When goods have been stored in inventory for some time and an opportunity arises to dispose of them, credit policy should be sufficiently flexible to approve the transaction. An extreme example of this is the case of the shoe wholesaler that has stored some out-of-style shoes for a number of years, then receives an offer for the entire lot. Even if the customer wanted extra terms or was not a good credit risk, it is doubtful that the offer would be refused.

5. *Geographical considerations.* The geographical distribution of customers determines credit policy to some degree. Widely separated markets require particular modifications in credit analysis and in collection efforts. A highly concentrated selling and buying area, on the other hand, involves a special type of price competition and services requirement. Credit policies may need to be adjusted to meet these conditions.

6. *Financial strength of the company.* Underfinanced operators generally need every dollar they can muster to assure themselves of sufficient funds for operation. Therefore, they might prefer to establish a restrictive credit policy. However, the capital restriction is usually accompanied by a poor market position, so they cannot insist on prompt payments. Further, their accounts are usually not so numerous that they can readily afford to turn away business.

An industrial giant, on the other hand, normally can afford in terms of operating capital to divert a portion of its funds to carrying customers' receivables. As long as a charge is made for this service (it may be included in the selling price), it can continue to operate with a more liberal credit policy. As it usually turns out, however, the company that can afford to carry overdue accounts can better afford to be selective in its choice of credit customers.

7. *Government regulations.* In the case of particular commodities, such as spirits and liquors, government regulations specify credit policies or procedures which must be followed by the seller. There the overall policy must take the regulations into consideration.

8. *Economic trends.* In a very general way, expected long-range trends in the economy also influence credit policy. Economic or business conditions are of much greater significance, however, in determining how policy is to be applied over a shorter period of time. When times are prosperous, ability of debtors to pay their bills is somewhat improved; however, there is a danger that they may tend to overbuy. During slack business periods, debtors tend to delay payment of their bills and credit requirements may tend to be stricter. Concurrently, as sales drop, the company is faced with the problem of maintaining volume in the face of decreasing sales and more demanding selection of credit customers. While consistency is important to avoid confusion on the part of customers, a sound credit policy requires enough flexibility to be compatible with the wide fluctuations of the economy.

Formulation of Credit Policy

The actual formulation of credit policy can be summarized in three broad steps, although in practice it involves working back and forth among these steps in a continuous process of relating objectives to context to policy. First is the establishment of objectives. What does the company want to accomplish during the period of time for which policy is to be established? If these objectives are to be attained, what should be the role of the credit department?

The second step is a thorough analysis of the context within which the credit policy must operate over this period of time. This includes those factors which, according to a realistic appraisal, will act in some way to define what the credit department will be able to do. They are the established company policies; the objectives and policies of the other departments; and the industry characteristics including credit practices, the role of the credit in competition, the company's position in the industry, the company's financial resources, and so on.

After these steps have been completed, the credit policy can be formulated. Within the given context, it sets a course of action which is expected to lead to the accomplishment of the objectives.

Policy Should Be Written

Careful consideration should be given to writing the credit policy. There are a number of companies that do not have a credit policy; at least they have no written credit policy. Through discussion, unwritten policy may become almost as clearly formulated as written policy, but more often it remains somewhat vague. At the extreme it exists only in the thinking of individual credit executives, in that they attempt to make sound decisions consistent with previous decisions in comparable circumstances. By definition, the understanding of unwritten policy depends on oral communication or on inference from the decisions made by senior credit personnel.

Once established, a credit policy that is written has the following advantages:

1. It is thought through carefully, with the result that any vagueness in the unwritten policy becomes apparent and can be modified. Consideration of a written policy by the executives concerned also helps to reveal differences in their understanding of what the policy is, and areas in which it is inadequate. Thus a written credit policy can result in a more precise, more effective working tool.

2. A written policy is more useful because it can be a source of stability and continuity in the operation, not only of the credit department but of the company as a whole. Individual credit executives and other administrators tend to vary unconsciously in their credit thinking as they interpret and react to the conditions and problems with which they work. Unwritten policy is thus subject to gradual, unnoticed changes. A written policy lessens the possibility of this kind of variability; it requires that changes in policy be conscious and intentional. In this way, policy becomes a more effective vehicle for review of the credit department's total situation. Removing credit policy from dependence on the knowledge and experience of one or a few individuals tends to ensure consistency regardless of changes in department personnel.

3. There is a greater probability of consistent decisions under written policy. This assumes special importance in large and complex credit organizations, where many people are dealing with the same types of problems and where they may be separated organizationally or geographically. Customers, for example, can be shown a copy of the policy statement, so they may know they are not being subject to unusual or discriminatory treatment.

4. A clearly stated credit policy is a valuable aid in the training and development of credit and sales personnel. The trainee in the credit department usually learns by observation, by reading credit files and reviewing past decisions, and by performing certain credit functions under supervision. This learning by doing can be made more meaningful by a written statement of policy, providing orientation to the company's point of view on credit and a frame of reference within which the trainee can proceed. In training sales personnel, they can be made familiar with the credit framework within which they must consummate their sales.

An Example of Credit Policy

The statement of credit policy shown in Figure 11–1 is not presented as a complete or perfect policy statement, but it provides a concrete illustration of some of the concepts discussed.

The credit department shall function under the supervision of the treasurer, and its activities shall be coordinated with overall corporation policy and the activities of the sales department.

It shall be the responsibility of the credit department to help build a broad and durable customer relationship for [the] Corporation. In the performance of this duty, the credit department shall maintain a positive and constructive attitude toward [the] Corporation's customers. Discrimination in customer relationships is to be avoided. Likewise, the credit and sales departments shall maintain a cooperative attitude, with an aim toward promoting sales.

Within the bounds of sound credit practices, the credit department shall endeavor to find a suitable credit basis on which to deal with every customer that the sales department desires to have purchase our products. The decision as to what constitutes a suitable credit basis shall rest with the credit department. From the standpoint of credit, no customer shall be denied the right to purchase our products until every means of selling to that customer on a safe and sound basis has been exhausted.

Standards by which credit risks are accepted or rejected shall be flexible enough to permit the maximum of profitable sales by [the] Corporation. Marginal credit risks are to be dealt with when they are needed to complete operating schedules, and as long as they constitute a source of added net profit to [the] Corporation.

Customer contracts are to be kept on a dignified and friendly basis, conducted so as to promote a wholesome respect for [the] Corporation and its business practices.

Credit department practices shall be designed to permit the maximum number of orders to flow without interruption through the sales department, but to provide for interception when necessary as a means of safeguarding credit extensions.

The credit department shall keep the sales department fully informed regarding the status of a customer's account when the free flow of orders from that customer is in jeopardy.

The credit department has the collection responsibility. Sales department advice or direct help may be sought in exceptional cases.

All credit decisions shall be independently made and shall conform to requirements of law.

Compatible with the foregoing, the credit department shall endeavor to maximize return on investment in receivables while achieving the lowest possible days sales outstanding and bad-debt loss.

FIG. 11–1.   Credit Policy.

Like many policy statements, this one interweaves the department's objectives, such as "to help build a broad and durable customer relationship" and "with an aim toward promoting sales." These lead directly into policy statements: "The credit department shall endeavor to find a suitable credit basis on which to deal with every customer"; "Marginal credit risks are to be dealt with when they are needed to complete operating schedules, and as long as they constitute a source of added net profit to [the] Corporation."

Specific practices are implied in the policy statement; the corporation details them in other documents. The procedures designed to find a credit basis for sales to every customer, for example, cover such matters as obtaining financial information, establishing terms of sale, and setting credit lines.

IMPLEMENTING CREDIT POLICY

To be effective, policy must be directly and explicitly related to action. Credit management should take the steps necessary to translate broad, flexible policy statements into guides which can be used by credit personnel in the daily operation of the department. This usually begins with establishing short-term objectives and determining for the short run what the emphasis is to be within the range of decisions provided by policy.

The implementation of credit policy also involves such actions as assigning duties and responsibilities, delegating authority, establishing procedures and controls, and providing for periodic progress reports and evaluations. Certain aspects of these activities are discussed on the following pages, and many of them are covered in detail in other chapters of this book.

Probably the most significant single step in the implementation of credit policy is the creation by top credit executives of an atmosphere which encourages subordinates to think in terms of policy: to be aware of the effect of their individual credit decisions upon the company's commitment to the accounts receivable investment and to the total department and company operations. To establish this attitude is not easy, but the effort is rewarding in helping different segments of the credit department to work in harmony and in developing the ability of subordinates to take responsibility and to make sound decisions.

Communication of Policy

In creating this atmosphere and in all phases of administration of credit policy, a basic requirement is effective communication of policy to the people concerned, both inside and outside the credit department. Whether policy is disseminated orally or in writing, there must be clear mutual understanding as to what the policy is and how it is to be applied.

Credit policy must be communicated to those who are directly concerned with the credit function. The company may also wish to make its credit policy known to organizations and individuals outside the company, such as its banks, its customers, and its competitors. The extent to which this is done has to be determined in terms of the individual situation, taking into account such considerations as the purpose such publication is expected to serve, the nature and duration of the relationship, and the role of credit in the competitive situation.

Top Management.   First of the groups which must know the credit policy is the top management of the concern. To the extent practical, top management should endorse the credit policy, with that endorsement made known to others. Undoubtedly the financial officers will be familiar with it, but it is just as important to the heads of purchasing, sales, and production to know on what basis credit decisions are made.

Credit Executives and Supervisors of Credit Sections.   They should be fully aware of the implications of the company's credit policy. It is not enough that they be "raised" in the credit department. In a subordinate spot, they may not have had the opportunity to observe company policy in its broader aspects.

Personnel of the Credit Department.   Naturally credit personnel need to know what the company rules have to say about risk analysis and collections. The policy should be explained to all personnel in the department and be made a part of the initial training of all new credit employees.

Sales Personnel.   In most cases, a statement of policy to the sales department should be followed up with information concerning the specific application of the policy as it affects sales personnel. For example, sales representatives should know what information they are expected to furnish with new orders, have some knowledge of the standards by which the credit department decides whether to accept an order on regular credit terms, and so on. Understanding how credit decisions are made improves the sales representatives' knowledge of the business.

Customers.   The customers themselves are better prepared to deal with a supplier if they understand its credit policy. They will better understand the need for current facts, the importance of financial information, and the significance of a good payment record.

The ideal time to describe credit policy to a customer is when the first order is placed. The customer is most receptive then. Time and misunderstandings or disputes have not yet been allowed to build resistance to comprehension. As the business relationship continues, it is wise to remind the customer occasionally of the credit policy of the organization. In that way, the customer's mind can be refreshed on a routine basis rather than at a time when an account is in dispute. This makes reference to terms and policy easier when a misunderstanding does arise.

Assigning Responsibility

While the organization of a credit department is not determined by credit policy, it plays an important part in putting policy into action, particularly through the specific assignment of responsibility and delegation of authority. Credit policy establishes the broad limits within which decisions will be made over a long period of time. In order to make these limits a workable guide to decisionmaking, it is necessary to specify who has the authority to make specified types of decisions or within what range given personnel may exercise their judgment.

Guides of this sort take several forms. As has been pointed out, for example, the authority to make exceptions to basic policy is usually limited to the chief credit executive. The definition of authority for various levels of personnel is often stated in terms of the amount of credit involved. Thus personnel on the lowest organizational level might be authorized to approve extension of credit up to $5,000 per account, those on the next level might be given authority extending to $10,000, and so on. The definition of authority should make clear the channels through which an order must move until it is finally approved.

Establishing Procedures

Closely allied to assignment of responsibility is the development of detailed procedures for day-to-day operation. These carry into detail the more general instructions for the application of policy, elaborating them into clear-cut rules for the handling of specific situations. They cover such matters as order flow, maintenance of credit files, and preparation of periodic reports.

One of the general principles to be followed in delegating authority and in establishing procedures is to include as many situations as possible in the routines administered by lower-level personnel. This frees credit executives who are more highly qualified by training and experience to deal with more complicated situations.

Applying Policy Under Varying Conditions

Credit policy is intended to apply to the great majority of the company's credit activities over a long period of time. To meet specific situations during a given time period, it is often necessary to provide for varying interpretations within the one policy. For example, a company producing two products marketed under widely different competitive circumstances might well develop different interpretations of credit policy for the two products. These varying ways of applying the same policy work toward the same objectives but take cognizance of the difference in the contexts within which they operate.

Similarly, for a given product it may be necessary to shift the emphasis in applying credit policy in different geographic areas, considering the nature of business or the general conditions in each area. This would be true, for example, in industries serving agriculture in various sections of the United States.

Factors Influencing Short-Term Policy Application

The application of policy in the short run can be quite flexible. It may often be desirable to change the emphasis of interpretation, redefine responsibilities, and adjust procedures in order to meet changing conditions under the same policy.

The factors which underlie the credit policy itself also influence the way in which it is applied. Changes in overall company policies or their interpretation, statement of short-range company objectives, and changes in competitive practices all help to determine the specific mode of operation within the broad limits of policy.

Some elements which are of minor or indirect significance in determining the credit policy have a direct bearing on its application. A company's current financial position enters into the establishment of credit policy as one element in the analysis of the company's long-range ability to compete, but in the short term it may be decisive in the application of policy. For example, severely limited operating capital may require emphasis on prompt collections and rapid turnover of accounts receivable.

Business conditions affecting the areas or industries in which the company operates are also of major importance in shaping policy application. Depending upon the scope of the company's operations, the general business conditions which affect it may be those in a particular region, in the United States as a whole, or in areas of foreign trade. Cyclical movements in the economy and changes in the general level of prosperity affect the credit department along with the whole company. During a period of prosperity and expansion, the credit department may be requested to aid in the development of new markets or the introduction of new products, involving decisionmaking in unfamiliar fields. If a recession sets in or is expected, the emphasis may be on greater care in selling to marginal accounts or perhaps on the expansion of customer counseling activities. The same credit policy would be in effect during all phases of the cycle, but its application would change to enable the credit function to be carried out more effectively.

Similarly, business conditions within a given industry affect the interpretation of credit policy in that industry. Not all segments of the economy change at the same rate; some are more stable than others and less subject to sharp fluctuations. Not all change in the same direction; during an extremely prosperous period, certain industries may experience severe difficulty and vice versa. Thus, in evaluating the business conditions within which the company is operating, the credit executive must look at conditions both in that industry and in the economy as a whole.

REVIEW OF CREDIT POLICY

Both the credit policy and the specific arrangements for its application should be reviewed at definite intervals. Both are ordinarily established for stated periods of time, and it is natural that they should be reviewed at the ends of those periods. Reviews at shorter intervals may also be planned or made necessary by unexpected developments of major importance. The frequency of planned reviews depends upon such factors as the difficulty expected in reaching the goals established and the probability of change in the competitive situation.

The policy and its application are evaluated in terms of their effectiveness in reaching the established goals. At the time of review, information must be gathered indicating the present position of the department in relation to the objectives it is attempting to attain. Then this present position must be evaluated to determine whether satisfactory progress has been made. The short-term goals which are established provide convenient benchmarks for evaluating progress toward long-term objectives.

If performance is judged to be satisfactory, the existing policies are reaffirmed. Depending upon the findings of the review, the objectives may be reaffirmed or new objectives established. If, on the other hand, the information indicates that credit performance is less than expected, there should be a critical examination of both the policy and the way it has been applied. The difficulty either may be an inadequate policy or a sound policy inappropriately applied. Once the inadequacy is located, the necessary adjustments can be made in the application or the policy can be changed. In some cases, particularly where the conditions under which the company operates have changed radically, it may be necessary to revise the objectives toward which the credit policy is directed.

When changes are to be made in the credit policy, the responsible executives should proceed in much the same way as in the initial development and application of the policy. Proposed changes should be discussed with the same people as participated in the formulation of the policy. When the changes become definite, they should be carefully communicated to all the individuals and departments concerned so that any necessary adjustments can be made to implement the revised policy.

TYPES OF CREDIT POLICY

Although credit policy has been treated as one subject, it has in fact two distinct components: analysis of risk and degree of collection effort. Policy must provide the answers to these questions:

1. How much risk is the firm willing to take in granting credit to its customers? This question seeks to determine whether the credit analysis of the customer will be strict or liberal. It should also set the basis for analysis, whether it be purely on the financial showing of the customer or include other factors such as the principal's background.

2. How much money and effort is the company willing to spend in collecting amounts owed to it? How will it treat past-due accounts? Will un-

earned discounts be permitted? The answers to these questions will determine the strictness of collection effort.

A number of different credit and collection policies can be set when answers to the two main categories of questions are obtained. Four such policies are listed below. Within these four broad categories there are innumerable shadings of policies, depending upon the particular degree of strictness in credit analysis and in collections. Because of peculiarities in the financial organization, one may work better than another for a particular concern. The credit executive must seek the combination which will yield the greatest results in terms of higher sales, lower costs, and maximum profits.

Strict Analysis of Risk and Strict Collections

Under this policy, only high credit-rated accounts are accepted and very little variation from terms is allowed. The analysis of risk is thorough, collection efforts require a fairly large staff, and the selling effort may be restricted. However, the increased staff costs may pay sizable dividends in the form of improved accounts receivable turnover and minimal bad-debt losses.

Strict Analysis of Risk with Liberal Collections

Somewhat more liberal in its collection procedures, this type of policy concentrates on the selection of good credit risks but does not aggressively press for payment. The assumption is that the good risks will on average pay their bills within terms; any additional time is less expensive to carry than the cost of following up accounts which are only a few days past due.

If a supplier's cost of capital is high, this type of policy may not be wise, especially when customers' orders involve sizable dollars. A more prudent course would be to follow collections closely.

Liberal Analysis of Risk and Vigorous Collection Effort

This policy is the opposite of the one above: emphasis is on collection. The credit analysis is liberal, so nearly all that apply will be accepted. But once the sale is made, close control is kept over collections. This type of policy would normally be followed in lines selling high-markup, low unit-price goods. The cost of credit analysis is relatively low in the firm which has this type of credit policy but collection costs are usually quite high.

Liberal Analysis of Risk and Liberal Collections

Very few lines of business would find it profitable to operate under this sort of credit policy. Its principal advantage might be that credit costs are very low. Undoubtedly, however, the costs of bad debts and of carrying receivables for long periods of time more than offset the savings. The principal concern of the company using this policy is to obtain maximum sales volume. So as not to risk offending its customers, it permits extravagances in the payment of bills. Unless the profit margins can be set so high that the bad-debt losses are counterbalanced effectively, the policy is unwise.

CHAPTER 12

CREDIT POLICY AND PROCEDURAL MANUAL

A credit policy and procedure manual is important as a ready reference; large companies need it as a standard guide for their many department personnel, and even small companies find it useful. The manual should cover rules, regulations, and procedures necessary for consistent department operations. In larger organizations, it should aid in the delegation of authority and in workload control, and give other departments a ready reference to company credit practices. It is also a useful tool in job training programs.

The chief credit executive should have nominal charge of the manual. Actual writing may be done by someone in the credit department or by a special outside group. Whether the final writing is done within the credit department or outside, all other departments should be given the opportunity to approve those sections of the manual pertaining to procedures in which they are directly involved.

FORMAT

The credit policy and procedure manual may be issued as a separate book or as part of the manual of general company instructions. If included in the general manual, a separate section should be set up for credit department instructions.

In companies with highly specialized departments, it is advisable to issue two manuals: a detailed manual for credit department use, and a section in the manual of general company instructions to cover general credit information.

Since credit procedures are characteristically subject to change, it is advisable to issue materials in loose-leaf form to facilitate keeping materials up to date.

Some credit departments that issue instruction letters or memoranda to their staffs compile them into a brochure of credit department policy and procedure. This is not a true manual and is not recommended. The individually addressed memorandum may achieve results with the person to whom it is addressed but will not necessarily influence a successor. With changes in personnel, changes in procedure often take place. Moreover, there is nothing in a memorandum to indicate that an action is definite policy or procedure.

Wherever possible, illustrations, diagrams, flow charts, and sample forms should be included to make content graphic and readily comprehensible.

MAINTENANCE

The credit manual must be kept current. Those responsible for its maintenance must be alert to changes in the credit situation, both inside and outside the company, which would necessitate revision of the manual. Information obtained from banks, customers, credit associations, company attorneys, and the sales department should be carefully reviewed for such possible changes.

Issuing the manual in loose-leaf form simplifies its revision. Obsolete instructions are easily removed and supplementary bulletins inserted. This avoids scrapping the entire manual when sections become outdated.

INDEXING

The method of indexing should be flexible and logical. The index will direct the choice of material, so it is important to begin with an efficient working index. It should be capable of providing for future needs as the manual expands in size and scope, for once an indexing system is established it is difficult to change. A poor index can hinder the usefulness of the manual.

Headings and subheadings should be used freely within the text to permit cross-referencing. It is desirable to identify each heading and subheading with a letter or number. When a decimal indexing system is used, the whole number indicates the general subject area and the first decimal identifies a specific subject within the general area.

SUGGESTED CONTENT

The subjects suggested here for inclusion in a credit policy and procedure manual are of most importance in commercial credit today. Others should be added when required by the company. For the actual writing of the manual, much information can be obtained from other chapters of this book; the *Credit Manual of Commercial Laws*, which is revised annually by the National Association of Credit Management; and company communications such as memoranda, bulletins, and reading materials used in training personnel.

When assembling the manual, a color-coded divider may be used to separate each of the major subjects. For example, a blue tab divider could identify the general subjects while a beige tab divider could identify each of the specific subjects. An index of all specific subjects could be shown on the blue tab divider so that the reader can reference the content matter within the section.

The foreword should point out that the manual is the official reference source on credit department policies and procedures. It should emphasize that the manual outlines only the framework within which credit department personnel should function and does not attempt to provide a specific blueprint for handling each and every credit decision.

The original date of issue of the manual can be shown in the foreword. This eliminates the need to date each page of the manual; only those pages containing revised material would need to show the date that material was revised.

The table of contents is a ready reference of the topics in the manual. Page numbers should not be included since they hamper inserting revised material.

The following outline shows topics ordinarily covered in a department manual. Subjects such as salary ranges, job specifications, and job descriptions, which are common to all departments of the business, are not included. The outline is supplemented by an explanation of the information included in each section and in some cases content matter that might be included.

1.0 DEPARTMENT STRUCTURE

The structure of the credit department should be the first topic covered in the manual. This section should describe the positions held by managerial personnel, the policy under which they must operate, and how they perform their duties under a given form of organizational structure.

1.1 CREDIT DEPARTMENT ORGANIZATION

This subsection lists the titles of key department personnel. It may be shown in chart form indicating the organization structure of the credit department.

1.2 POLICY

Credit policy must be attuned to the changes in the economic environment in which the company operates and must complement the company's objectives. In order to attain these objectives, the credit department must effectively manage its receivables portfolio. This can best be completed when the department assesses credit decisions in terms of account profitability, market conditions, and degree of risk; evaluates the financial condition of a customer, using sound, uniform practices;

pursues collections within approved terms of sale; cooperates with the sales department as required in collections, setting terms, and approving dollar exposure; coordinates with other divisions of the company to meet corporate objectives; and furnishes reports to corporate management and others on the status of the accounts receivable investment.

1.3 OPERATION

This should describe how the credit department functions, whether it is centralized or decentralized, and the chief credit executive's responsibility to senior management for the overall credit function. In addition, it should mention the department head's role in establishing the guidelines for credit executives.

The procedures should also provide the mechanics for the chief credit executive to monitor credit, comments on the handling of account referrals and how they are resolved, and the procedure for handling developments in an account's business activity or financial condition.

2.0 INVESTIGATION

Credit decisions are based on information developed through credit investigation. Every effort must be made to obtain as much accurate information as possible in order to develop a credit profile on new and existing accounts.

2.1 DIRECT INQUIRY

A normal inquiry should be in the form of a written request. The exact language will depend upon the individual circumstances; however, it should include requests for financial statements—both balance sheet and operating statement. Financial statements range from certified audited statements to internally prepared reports. The statements must cover the customer in question, not the parent or an affiliate.

This subsection of the manual could also include the following exhibits: a copy of a letter to a new customer, a balance sheet, an operating statement, a statement of changes in financial position, and a spread sheet for displaying successive financial statements.

Significant financial ratios should be shown, and a brief description of how they are calculated and how they are used.

2.2 AGENCY REPORTS

This subsection covers reports from outside agencies. They state how long a customer has been in operation, review past history of the principals, and give an indication of the customer's trade performance. Widely used sources for this information are Dun & Bradstreet and National Credit Office reports. For current trade information the NACM Business Credit Report is an excellent source. Where an individual's personal financial condition is needed, a report can be obtained from Equifax. Customers that are publicly held corporations will normally be shown in the Moody's Industrial Manuals. Copies of the reports can be used as exhibits.

2.3 BANKS

Bank checks range from a single statement of a customer's average deposit balance to a comprehensive report. Credit executives should develop good contacts with the banking industry to obtain meaningful information, especially when a substantial exposure is involved. A standard request for bank credit information could be shown as an exhibit in this subsection.

2.4 INQUIRIES TO OTHER SUPPLIERS

Every trade inquiry must clearly state the reason for the inquiry—first order for $_____, revising credit file, prospective customer, and so on. If the inquirer has ledger experience, it should be included in the inquiry. A postage-paid envelope is a necessary courtesy.

A trade inquiry normally will incorporate a request for high credit, amount owing, amount past due, terms of sale, and payment performance.

Responses should be reviewed to see if they are reasonable. Reported payment performance should be consistent with the other responses received.

A copy of the company's trade inquiry form should be included in this subsection.

2.5 CUSTOMER VISITATION

The credit executive should visit the customer's facility and talk with the principal officers of the company. This direct exposure will serve the credit executive well for determining whether credit should be established and how the account should be handled after shipments have commenced. Such visits should be made with the sales representative, if at all possible, to reinforce the team approach.

3.0 SECURITY DEVICES

When a complete investigation fails to support the amount of credit in question, it is necessary to obtain security on the sale. The most common method is to obtain this security under the Uniform Commercial Code. Often the investigation will provide a clue to the type of security available. A third party may take responsibility for the customer's obligation (guaranty, letter of credit), or the transaction can be restructured so that exposure and risk are minimized (deposit, sight draft). The risk must not exceed the realizable value of the security. It is important to bear in mind that costs can be involved in obtaining a security position, and certain forms of security lose value if liquidated under distress.

3.1 GUARANTY

A guaranty is an instrument containing a promise by a person, persons, or company to pay an obligation owed in the event the debtor does not pay. It can take the form of a personal or corporate guaranty. Copies of both forms should be made a part of this subsection.

A personal guaranty from one or more of the officers of a corporation who are financially responsible may be acceptable security. The following information is important on personal guaranty: a current financial statement; the names of other companies holding the individual's guaranty; if community property laws are in effect, will the spouse also execute the guaranty; and the costs involved in obtaining a remedy.

Where a prospective corporate customer is an affiliate of another corporation, the guaranty of the latter corporation may be sought. This requires a resolution authorizing the guaranty from the stronger corporation's board of directors; both the guaranty and the resolution should carry the corporate seal. When considering a corporate guaranty, it is important to obtain a current financial statement from the guarantor and to assess the possibility that legal action may be needed to obtain satisfaction.

Where a corporate guaranty is on file with Dun & Bradstreet, it is still preferable to use the selling company's own form because it incorporates the important points as determined by the company's legal department. If this is not possible, a copy of the standing guaranty should be obtained from Dun & Bradstreet.

3.2 IRREVOCABLE LETTER OF CREDIT

In the normal course of business, banks often obtain a major security position with respect to the customer's assets. They can then extend an irrevocable letter of credit. Substituting the bank's credit for that of the customer, letters of credit allow the supplier to initiate a draft against the letter of credit upon delivery of goods. With a standby letter of credit, the supplier invoices normally and does not draw on the letter of credit unless the customer does not pay. Some letters of credit may be worded so that drafts may be drawn if certain contractual arrangements are not satisfied. Copies of all types of letters of credit should be in this subsection.

It should be possible to satisfy the documentation requirements through the company's normal paperwork. If there is insufficient time, say 60 days, between the assigned shipment date and the expiration date, an amendment should be requested and received before proceeding with the order.

Every effort should be made to obtain cancellation protection when such a possibility exists. It is also important to evaluate the bank initiating the letter of credit; if there is a question about the bank's financial responsibility, ask to have a more established bank issue the letter of credit.

3.3 SUBORDINATION AGREEMENT

A subordination agreement can improve a supplier's position by establishing a prior claim to the customer's assets, especially if a significant portion of a customer's debt is owed to officers or stockholders.

Subordination agreements may be general or may apply to an individual account. A general subordination should be reviewed carefully to determine that it in fact covers the supplier. If any questions arise, they should be reviewed with the chief credit executive and the company's legal department. If the subordination is executed specifically for the supplier, the supplier's form should be used. A copy should be shown as an exhibit.

3.4 SECURITY AGREEMENTS AND FINANCING STATEMENTS

The Uniform Commercial Code has been adopted by all states with the exception of Louisiana. Article 9 of the code entitled Secured Transactions deals with the creation of security interests in personal property. Personal property may be tangible, and the most common forms are inventory, accounts receivable, and equipment. A creditor seeking security executes a security agreement, which is a contract intended by the parties to create a security interest in personal property as security for payment of debt. This agreement can be made to give the supplier a security interest in the products of the inventory originally subject to the agreement, and it can be made to cover the proceeds resulting from their sale. The security agreement may be limited to specific types of inventory, accounts receivable, and equipment; or it may be general and cover all of these items.

There is a filing fee for filing of financing statements which varies from state to state. Official forms for financing statements also vary from state to state and can be purchased from local legal stationers.

A security agreement executed by both parties is effective as between the parties, but before it can be effective against third parties (other creditors or trustee in bankruptcy) it must be perfected. The process of perfecting a security interest under the UCC consists of preparing and filing a financing statement with the appropriate state or county office, or both. Filing requirements vary from state to state, and there is often a filing deadline in terms of days after shipment of material. A copy of a financing statement should be in this subsection.

3.5 MECHANICS' LIEN

A mechanics' lien is a statutory lien on a building (and usually the land it occupies) in favor of suppliers of material and contractors to secure their interest on a particular construction project. This type of lien is available in all 50 states, but the statutory requirements, rules, and procedures are so diverse they require a case-by-case review.

Generally a mechanics' lien is available to materialmen for a time period of one to four months (some states permit longer) from the date material is last supplied to a particular job. The material must be identified for use in a particular job or for delivery to a particular job site and must be for consumption on such job; sales to a customer for delivery to a general warehouse are not subject to a mechanics' lien.

Credit approved with anticipated lien remedies should be reviewed with the chief credit executive and the legal department.

3.6 PAYMENT AND PERFORMANCE BONDS

All federal and state agencies and many private interests, seeking to eliminate trouble in getting their project built, require contractors to provide payment and performance surety bonds. Under the payment bond, the bonding company guarantees to the owner that the contractor will properly pay all obligations for labor and material going into the job. Under a performance bond, the bonding company guarantees the completion of the job according to plans and specifications. If the contractor defaults, the bonding company is required to hire another contractor to complete the job.

The fact that a payment bond exists should not be construed to mean that credit can be extended with total assurance of payment. Some factors to be considered are the financial condition of the contractor; the status of the supplier as subcontractor or materialman; accomplishment of the necessary job identification requirements; and acceptability of the bonding company on federal, state, or municipal jobs.

Before relying on a payment bond, the supplier should send a letter to the bonding company to confirm the existence of the bond and learn its coverage with respect to the material. Since the type of project and the notification rules vary substantially, questions should be referred to the legal department through the chief credit executive. A sample letter to the bonding company should be in this subsection.

3.7 FIELD WAREHOUSING

If substantial amounts of money are at stake and a marginal condition exists, a supplier may strengthen the situation by requiring the customer to provide field warehousing. Under this arrangement, goods are stored on the premises of the buyer but are in the custody of the seller. As they are needed for production, they are paid for by the buyer and released by the seller.

Specialized companies can field warehouse on the customer's premises and can structure the agreements, inventory certificates, warehouse receipts, and other requirements to match the circumstances.

Before agreeing to a field warehouse arrangement, credit executives should obtain approval from the chief credit executive and ask legal counsel to review the agreements, filings, and the like.

3.8 DEPOSIT ARRANGEMENTS

Material produced to customer's specifications has very little other use. Consequently, an order for custom production involves credit risk. If a customer's financial condition does not warrant this exposure, the seller should ask for a deposit before starting production. The amount should closely match the termination value (invoice value less scrap allowance) of the order.

3.9 REAL ESTATE MORTGAGES (DEEDS OF TRUST)

Sometimes a customer will offer a first or second real estate mortgage (deed of trust) as security for open-account arrangements. This can be an effective method of securing an account but a number of factors must be considered, such as determining the value of the property, the marketability of the property, and the payoff on the first mortgage. The laws with respect to real estate mortgages vary from state to state, so any arrangements should be cleared with the chief credit executive and legal counsel.

4.0 CREDIT APPROVAL AND ADMINISTRATION

A concise description of credit approval procedures is highly desirable in all types of credit organizations and promotes efficient routing and handling of orders by lower levels. This section includes the procedure to follow when an order exceeds the credit line of the customer or the credit-granting authority of the credit executive.

4.1 TERMS OF SALE

Terms of sale should be sound, practical, competitive, and clearly expressed; the credit period should be spelled out and adhered to as closely as possible. A complete list of the terms offered by the company and a brief explanation of how they are used should be shown in this subsection.

4.2 TERMS CODES

Terms of sale may be coded to facilitate the processing of information into the computer. A terms code should be shown on all sales orders and invoices. An example of a terms code may consist of four digits: the first digit represents a money or currency code, such as U.S. dollars; the second indicates the type of payment, such as open terms or cash against documents; and the third and fourth digits indicate the terms of payment for aging purposes, such as 30 days or 60 days.

The procedure for administering the codes should be described, including the treatment of multiple codes and exceptions. This subsection should include a complete list of terms codes.

4.3 CREDIT INSTRUCTIONS

Instructions refer to those daily routines which guarantee the processing of all orders in accord with prescribed credit lines and terms. This section is addressed to the working force involved in such processing, including members of the sales and accounting staff. Forms should be shown wherever used.

One form, for example, could be used for orders entered before the credit investigation is completed or that require credit supervision of production, shipment, and payment. Another form, a request for release, could be sent by plants to the appropriate sales office. This should be sent in sufficient time for the credit executive to return it without delay in shipment or extra handling of material.

In companies where credit approval is highly automated, forms used in these daily routines have been replaced by cathode-ray screens.

4.4 CREDIT RECOMMENDATIONS

Organizations that recommend credit granting from a lower to a higher level of authority can use this section to show the form of recommendation. Printed forms should be shown properly filled out.

A company that classifies its accounts according to risk would discuss its criteria in this section; also, the more stringent requirements needed for marginal risks compared to prime risks and the more frequent review procedure.

The procedure for reviewing a continuing recommendation could be simplified so that information is not repeated needlessly. If a credit recommendation is not approved from the higher level of authority, a letter should be returned giving the reasons for disapproval. Credit recommendations on marginal accounts should not be approved without current information.

4.5 CREDIT FILES

Certain information must be kept current in the credit files, with the usual minimum requirements of current agency report, a current credit recommendation, and current financial figures.

5.0 COLLECTIONS

Effective collection techniques are important to maintain a satisfactory turnover of accounts receivable. This section can include instructions on commonly used methods of collection.

5.1 NORMAL PROCEDURE

Each account is a separate collection problem. Placing it into a category by size or type assists in determining the intensity of collection effort required.

The several means for collection followup are letter, phone, by personal visit, and through joint credit and sales action.

Collection letters (copies of the series of form letters should be part of this subsection) are useful in specific situations, such as directing attention to an invoice that has been skipped by a customer that normally pays promptly. In general, however, the pressures for immediate attention to past-due invoices have prompted a greater use of telephone contact in lieu of this form letter procedure.

To make an effective collection call by telephone, it is helpful to have a mental game plan worked out before contacting the customer. Check points are sometimes helpful in developing an approach: background of the account, proper person to speak to, future shipments to the customer that would be jeopardized by nonpayment, and an absolute minimum payment proposal.

The effectiveness of telephone collection is increased significantly if the payment date established is reconfirmed to the customer in writing or by mailgram. Where an account fails to pay at any stage of the collection effort, one possible solution is a personal visit to determine if the account is in trouble and to seek the fastest way to settle. On substantial exposures, this action could be warranted in the early stages of delinquency.

Collections can be improved by a joint credit-sales effort. This should be well coordinated, as any disparity between the information supplied the customer by the two departments will quickly erode the effectiveness of this approach.

5.2 COLLECTION SCHEDULE

The collection effort should encompass a definite schedule and should provide the mechanics for a systematic review. Under normal circumstances the initial contact should be made within ten days of delinquency. Shipping embargoes should be considered when the account becomes delinquent a specified number of days, and referral to outside sources for collection should be considered at a later stage of delinquency.

5.3 ACCOUNT REFERRAL

If normal collection procedures fail to net the necessary results, the account should be placed with an attorney or collection agency. When this point is reached, the credit executive should follow established procedures. Ordinarily the customer would be advised of this action and given a final opportunity to pay.

5.4 NOTE ARRANGEMENTS

A note program establishes a future payment date for past-due debt. Before embarking on such a program, it is important to carefully evaluate the customer's overall financial condition and weigh the possibility of action by other creditors. The time frame between acceptance and maturity is critical. If conditions warrant accepting notes, then authorization should be obtained from the chief credit executive.

Copies of the notes used by the company should be included in this subsection. In addition, important points in preparing notes should be commented upon briefly: correct maturity date, correct interest rate, correct signature, and the like.

Note programs commonly ask for additional collateral or endorsement by an individual(s). A note that incorporates security protection can best be drawn up by an attorney. Any individual endorsing the note, whether an officer of the corporation or not, should be asked to sign on the reverse side of the note. If the endorsement is by an outside party, then correspondence should show the endorser's address.

After the notes have been executed and the security agreements completed, they should be forwarded to the proper authority together with appropriate closeout information.

5.5 CREDITORS' EXTENSION AGREEMENTS

As a major creditor, a company may initiate or join in a creditors' extension agreement. This agreement permits a debtor to set aside existing debt under an established plan. It allows the debtor to liquidate this debt and recover if the extension agreement is successfully consummated. Since individual circumstances will dictate whether it is in the best interests of a company to be involved in one of these arrangements, the credit executive should contact the chief credit executive for approval before signing an agreement or serving on a creditors' committee.

5.6 BANKRUPTCY PROCEEDINGS

Normally the notice of a customer's bankruptcy is sent to the main office. Where the notice is directed to a local office, it should be forwarded to the chief credit executive. While proof of claims is not required for a creditor's claim to be properly listed, as a matter of practice creditors should not rely upon the debtor's list but file their own proof of claim. Prior to filing this claim, however, the amount of the claim should be verified and it should be determined if any held material is involved. (A copy of the proof of claim properly completed should be shown as an exhibit in this subsection.) After the necessary filing, the status of a bankruptcy is followed by the credit executive.

Under Chapter 11 proceedings, the supplier may elect to continue to sell an account that is under the jurisdiction of the court. If this occurs, it is imperative that orders be accepted only under the trustee's authority and invoicing should be made in the trustee's name.

5.7 LOCKBOX SYSTEM

In order to improve availability and use of funds, the company may have established a lockbox network to handle customer remittances. Funds received in the lockbox are automatically transferred to the company. The lockbox arrangements call for the banks to forward remittance data to the credit office.

The credit executive should establish a bank contact in case any questions arise.

In the case of a returned item (check), the following procedure will apply: The first time an item is returned, the bank will redeposit the check and notify the credit executive; if an item is returned a second time, the bank will notify the credit executive and return the original of the returned item. The credit executive then should obtain a certified or cashier's check from the customer.

6.0 REPORTS

This section includes procedures and examples for writing reports on past-due accounts, control and inspection reports, forecasts, annual reports to management, and the like as called for by company policy. It is important to include in this section a specific timetable for all credit reports, along with details of approval and distribution.

PART III

CREDIT DECISIONMAKING AND COLLECTION PROCEDURES

CHAPTER 13

CREDIT DECISIONMAKING

The basic approach to credit decisionmaking should be to seek ways to approve orders, with a reasonable expectation that payment will be made in accordance with terms. The credit executive's job is to promote profitable sales; too often reasons are sought for refusing orders without searching hard enough for reasons to approve. The more constructive approach is to try to approve profitable orders, recognizing the dangers and seeking whatever additional protection is available.

A decision to grant credit affects income, sales, profits, production, and procurement. It may take several forms:

1. The order may be approved as submitted for dollar amount and credit terms.

2. The order may be approved for a smaller amount on the same trade terms.

3. The order may be approved for the submitted amount on different terms.

4. The order may be approved for a smaller amount on different terms.

If the account is a good credit risk, the order may be approved as is. Otherwise an alternative must be proposed to the sales department and the customer. This is where diplomacy by the credit department will preserve the good will of the customer.

Too many "yes" decisions (uninvestigated or unchecked) can result in excessive and slow-moving accounts receivable. Too many "no" decisions, on the other hand, can drastically reduce sales volume and cause reduced production, higher unit costs, and lower profit.

Compiling information costs time and money, and a point is eventually reached at which more information is not worth the added cost. Properly interpreted and evaluated, limited information may be adequate for a "yes" or "no" decision, while delay in reaching a decision may cause the seller to lose the order, the customer, or both.

AUTOMATING CREDIT APPROVAL

It is desirable to establish routine procedures for making most credit decisions. Automated credit approval, through the use of order limits or credit lines, for example, causes little work in the credit department. This means minimum delay, improved service to customers, and reduced administrative costs. Equally important, it frees the credit executive to give attention to borderline cases and exceptions.

Routine procedures should define clearly the dollar amount of orders that must be referred to higher-level credit personnel for approval, and to whom they are to go. If order limits are in use, they should govern referrals.

When credit must be refused or when a shipment is to be delayed pending further investigation or payment of an outstanding amount, the customer should be notified immediately. Credit and sales departments should establish who is responsible for this notification. In many ways, credit personnel are in the best position to explain the reasons for refusal or delay, and they should be trained to approach customers diplomatically. Under some circumstances, however, sales personnel can best handle this task.

INITIAL ORDERS

While all orders should be processed quickly, this is particularly important on first orders from new customers. Because proper handling of the initial order often means the difference between a gain or loss from continuing future sales, some system should be adopted whereby initial orders are quickly approved or rejected. The procedures established for handling initial orders from new customers are also applicable to orders from customers that have bought before but considerable time (in many cases, a year) has elapsed since the previous order.

Blanket Approval of Small Orders

If a significant percentage of initial orders are small enough that the expense of a credit investigation is unwarranted, blanket approval may be given to all orders for less than a specified amount. This would save considerable processing time on initial orders.

The maximum amount for blanket approval would be influenced by the exact nature of the company's operations and by overall company and credit policy. It could be changed from time to time according to market conditions, credit terms, loss experience, and other circumstances.

Initial orders below a specified amount are approved automatically on the theory that the time and cost of obtaining credit information on a relatively small order more than offset the normal profit on that order. Experience will show that more initial orders are paid than not. While individual losses will occur, the impact of extra collection expenses on overall results could be reduced by accelerating the collection procedure, writing off slow accounts, or placing them earlier for collection by outside agencies.

Followup work is an important requirement of a blanket approval system. Since the first small order may be a trial shipment which could lead to larger ones, the system should require the sales department to supply an estimate of each customer's credit requirements. This enables the credit department to conduct an investigation so future larger orders can be handled expeditiously.

Approval Based on Agency Ratings

Another method of handling initial and future orders without extensive investigation is to use mercantile agency ratings as a basis for the amount to be approved. This routine method of approving orders provides the following advantages:

1. General understanding as to why certain actions are being taken.
2. Little need for exhaustive investigation for each account when it falls within the criteria set for routine handling.
3. Automated approval of larger orders than would usually be covered by a blanket approval system, providing the sales personnel has access to a mercantile agency ratings key.
4. Time saved for other, more exacting duties when routine cases are handled quickly and efficiently.
5. Exceptions and marginal cases are more easily identified and can be examined carefully by the credit staff.

Many concerns have developed a credit line and an initial order limit key based on Dun & Bradstreet or other agency ratings. Figure 13–1 shows an example of one such key. With an account rated CC2, an initial order up to $2,700 will be approved without investigation. If a firm's rating is EE2, the order size would be limited to $1,000; any amount over that would require a credit investigation.

The system is handy and speedy. It uses agency ratings as the basis for first-order approval. (They may also be used to set credit lines; this technique is discussed later in this chapter.) Since the agency rating is assumed to be up to date, the credit department can be fairly sure of the degree of credit risk. The rating keys of other reporting agencies may similarly be adapted for use by the supplier, although they may be of a more specialized and therefore restricted nature.

Nonroutine First Orders

If a first order fails to meet the requisites for automated approval, the decision to investigate may rest on the answers to the following questions:

1. Is the order large enough to warrant the cost of investigation?
2. Is the potential for future sales large enough that the account should be cultivated?

Dun & Bradstreet Rating	Credit Line	Initial Order Limit
5A1	Requirements	Requirements
5A2	"	"
4A1	"	"
4A2	"	"
3A1	"	"
3A2	"	"
2A1	"	"
2A2	"	"
1A1	"	"
1A2	"	"
BA1	$15,000	$5,000
BA2	"	"
BB1	"	"
BB2	"	"
CB1	"	"
CB2	"	"
1	"	"
CC1	10,000	3,500
DC1	"	"
CC2	8,000	2,700
DC2	"	"
DD1	"	"
2	"	"
DD2	5,000	1,700
EE1	"	"
EE2	3,000	1,000
FF1	2,000	700
FF2	1,500	500
GG1	1,000	300
GG2	800	250
HH1	600	200
HH2	"	"
5A3 thru EE3	300	100
All Others	200	70

FIG. 13–1. Table of Credit Lines and Initial Order Limits Based Upon Dun & Bradstreet Ratings. (The table presented is given only for the purpose of illustrating the construction of Credit Line and Initial Order Limit Keys.)

3. How will the prospect react to a request to do business on other than regular terms?

4. Is it company policy to establish credit terms for all customers for the public relations benefit which might result?

Where present and expected sales potential justifies an investigation, the credit department should seek information regarding the company's history, reputation and ability of principals, and marketability and competitive forces related to products. Naturally the scope of the investigation would be related to the size of expected business from the customer.

Terms Other Than Open Account

If the circumstances do not warrant open-account credit, the sale may be made on some other basis, such as cash in advance, cash on delivery, sight draft, certified check, cashier's check, or standby letter of credit. Of these methods of payment, only a cashier's check and standby letter of credit can guarantee payment, since in these instances the bank's credit is substituted for the customer's. A payment on a certified check technically can be stopped for just cause by the customer. Sight drafts are not a common tool in domestic transactions because they require special consignment instructions which can be cumbersome.

If materials are produced especially for the buyer and are not salable through other outlets, the buyer's refusal to accept delivery could cause loss to the seller. In such cases, if the credit risk is not acceptable, the seller might want to ask for full cash in advance.

Even on goods which are standard in every respect, the terms described above (except for cashier's checks and standby letters of credit) expose the seller to the risk of paying for such expenses as round-trip transportation, repacking, and losses in transit if the buyer refuses to accept delivery. This risk should be considered in evaluating the prospect.

CREDIT LINES

As soon as possible after first-order approval, controls should be established to ensure prompt and appropriate disposition of further orders. The basic means of control is the credit line, indicating the maximum amount of risk to be taken on any customer.

Underlying Factors

There is a growing tendency to use formulas for assigning credit lines, with companies using the factors they consider most meaningful. Such data can be readily adapted to computer use and companies have developed complex programs to do the task. Availability of computer time and the expense of adopting such a system may confine its use to only the largest companies.

A customer's credit line is usually based on two major factors: requirements for the supplier's products and the ability of the customer to pay its debts. In addition, other factors include the company's policy, demand for the company's product, the size and financial condition of the selling company, and the extent of competition. Below are some observations regarding credit lines:

1. In all cases, the ability to pay debts must be evaluated by a thorough analysis of available financial information, agency ratings and reports, bank checks, trade clearances, and similar data.

2. A new customer's requirements can often be estimated by the salespeople at the time the initial order is placed, or the credit executive may be able to determine requirements through direct contact with the customer.

3. A customer that furnishes financial information is usually treated more liberally than one unwilling to do so.

4. Where the seller is the principal supplier, a credit executive may be more liberal on the condition that the buyer furnish detailed financial information.

5. The credit executive must determine what risk categories are acceptable in line with company policy. If the profit margin on the particular product is high, the seller can afford to accept greater credit risks. If the company's credit policy is conservative and profit margins are slim, credit lines are more restrictive.

6. If demand for a company's product is greater than its production capacity or there is an industrywide supply shortage, sales can be made primarily to the most select class of customers, with credit lines to marginal customers minimized.

7. Consideration must always be given to the long-term supply outlook for the product.

8. If a manufacturing operation has high overhead that necessitates a high capacity utilization to show a profit, greater credit risks may be acceptable. Also, greater credit risks may be taken when a company is in a highly competitive market, is introducing a new product, is opening a new manufacturing plant, or is attempting to enter a new market.

9. The size and financial condition of the selling company influences its credit decisions. Can it afford to take the risk of nonpayment or slow payment? Credit lines for a financially weak customer would have to be lower than that of a well-financed concern. A company has to decide what opportunities it wants to pursue and what risks it is willing and able to accept.

10. All classes of trade will produce some bad-debt losses. While it is not possible to foretell which particular customers in the class will be responsible for the losses, certain variables have a casual relationship with failure (e.g., length of time in business, financial ratios, payment patterns, line of business).

11. Outside factors (e.g., external credit pressure, overall health of the company's industry) also determine whether a business will fail.

12. Competition influences credit lines. If, for example, a competitor is extending $25,000 to a customer, the seller may have to meet competition to avoid losing the account.

13. Terms of sale affect lines. The longer the terms, the greater is the financial exposure. A credit line of $10,000 might be adequate for a company purchasing $5,000 per week on terms of net 10 days. But if the terms were net 60 days, a much larger line would be required.

14. The credit line is also influenced by the collection effort that may be

required. Are sufficient personnel, time, and information available to follow a large number of high-risk accounts? If such factors are inadequate, lower lines would have to be set.

15. In the final analysis, profits on the good sales should exceed losses on the bad sales. A high bad-debt record is not necessarily the mark of poor credit judgment. It may be an indication that excellent credit judgment is being used to maximize net profit. On the other hand, low bad-debt losses with a high record of order refusals could be an indication that the credit executive is hurting the company's selling efforts and restricting net profit. A certain amount of bad-debt loss has to be anticipated and should be acceptable to management.

Setting Credit Lines

Credit lines commonly serve as guides for order approval, minimize upward referral of orders, and call immediate attention to any change in a customer's purchasing or paying habits. Any order that does not exceed the line can be approved without further investigation or analysis. An order exceeding the line signals the need for examination of the account by higher-level credit personnel.

Credit lines are sometimes called credit limits and many will define distinctions between the two terms. The credit fraternity does not agree unanimously on definitions, so it is best when discussing lines and limits to determine what the other person's thoughts may be in order to understand the intent of discussion.

Flexible Credit Lines. Because the task of establishing lines of credit is difficult, some concerns will not face the problem. They prefer to use a flexible line, based on previous experience with the account. For example, an initial order for $580 may have been promptly paid. The next order may have been for $600 and again paid on time. The next four orders were for $650, $358, $678, $893, and paid promptly. Without a formal review of the line of credit, the account has been brought from an initial order of $580 to about $900 on the basis of favorable past experience.

Proponents of this system point out that it is a practical way to operate. It requires a review of the file when an order is checked and keeps the credit department aware of the situation. Those who favor a more formal system of establishing lines of credit point out that the account may not be worth a line of $900; that the prompt payments may be a buildup for a later, larger, and unpaid order; or that a formal analysis might have set a credit line high enough to eliminate the need for a review every time a new order was received.

Normal Requirements. Some firms assign a normal requirements line when a customer's financial responsibility and payment performance are particularly good. Such a line authorizes credit for all of a customer's normal purchases, usually with an allowance for some increases—for example,

10 per cent to account for price changes. It emphasizes purchasing patterns, assuming that payment for normal purchases will be made within established terms. The meaning of normal requirements must be clearly understood by the personnel responsible for processing orders, so that orders which exceed normal purchases will be referred to credit personnel for approval.

Requirements. Oftentimes the tendency is to let the credit line become simply a matter of requirements, which means that any order the customer places is approved. Only very substantial and financially sound customers can be sold on a requirements basis.

Order Limit. This specifies the dollar amount that may be released without delay on any single order. It differs from a credit line, which is established without regard to the size of any particular order and is generally set at an amount that can be justified by the available credit information. Some companies place an order limit on every account. This usually serves as a secondary credit check and the customer's file is reviewed when either the credit line or order limit is exceeded. This kind of order limit may be particularly useful in a decentralized credit organization where it is impractical for order processing points to keep complete records of receivables.

Outstanding Balance. One variation of the credit line is based upon the amount that the creditor is willing to have outstanding at any time. For example, several orders may be placed by one concern, and approved if an overall limit is not exceeded. This method requires complete records of unpaid invoices and of orders approved but not yet shipped. When the total outstanding balance exceeds the line, any further orders are referred for approval. To minimize the referral of orders, the dollar credit line should be close to the customer's actual needs.

Specified Time Period. A credit line may also be based on the total amount of orders which can be approved during a given time period. For example, a credit line of $8,000 per month would mean that in any one-month period orders totaling $8,000 could be approved without referral, regardless of the total amount outstanding.

Credit lines stated in this way are particularly useful in companies that process orders at a number of locations but maintain more centralized accounts receivable files. Lines for a specific time period provide control with minimum referral to a central office and little recordkeeping at the order processing point. It should be borne in mind that even prompt payment for all invoices billed during the designated period would not necessarily be received during that period, so total credit exposure will often exceed the credit line. Adequate controls must be established to prevent granting excessive credit to delinquent accounts.

Agency Ratings. A popular method is to assign credit lines based upon agency ratings. The principal advantage of this method is the ease and speed with which lines can be assigned to customers. Dun & Bradstreet ratings, for example, are divided into a capital rating and a composite credit appraisal, so credit lines based upon them take into account the net worth of a customer.

Figure 13–1, used to develop initial order limits, can also be used for credit lines. An account rated CC2, for example, could be given a credit line of $8,000 based on Figure 13–1. A rating of EE2 would qualify for a line of $3,000.

Formulas. The use of formulas for assigning credit lines is increasing. Custom-tailored and easily programmed into computers, they consist of a number of factors selected to suit the individual company: financial ratios, credit agency ratings, bank reports, trade references, paying experience, customer's requirements, profit margin of the product, competition, seasonal requirements, economic conditions, and growth potential of customers. The credit executive can call upon the systems people for help in building a program based upon these factors.

Computers have made it possible to use techniques of statistical and probability analysis for assigning credit lines. These techniques can help predict the outcome of certain credit decisions regarding various classes of customers. This knowledge can be useful in minimizing high-risk exposure where the potential reward is not commensurate with the risk. Moreover, profiles can be developed to help classify customers according to degree of risk and probability of success over both the short and long term. The probability of repayment under various exposure levels can then be related to the customer risk.

A well-designed model could help establish consistent evaluation of customer risk and save time and expense in appraising marginal accounts. The development of a credit rating scale is helpful but poses a major problem in quantifying data of a qualitative nature. By the use of statistical devices, qualitative information can be assigned numerical values that are compared to an established rating scale for a particular industry. A computer programmed in accordance with a firm's credit policy can then accept or reject orders.

Credit Lines for Sales Department Use

Many companies advise their sales department of the credit lines assigned to customers, often expressing the lines in terms of units (300 tons, 20 carloads) or dollars allowed during a given period of time. If, for example, a customer has a credit line of $5,000 on terms of 1/10, n/30 and consistently discounts, this customer could be sold from $10,000 to $15,000 per month; because of discount payments, the highest credit would still be expected to remain within the credit line of $5,000.

Informing Customers of Credit Lines

Credit executives disagree as to the advisability of telling customers their credit lines. Those who favor it say the practice gives them an opportunity to discuss the credit line and to offer suggestions which may help the customer. Furthermore, it informs the customer that there is a credit line and reduces embarrassment and misunderstanding that may result when an order over the line is held.

On the other hand, some credit executives say customers may interpret the credit line as a reflection of their financial responsibility. This may damage good will, and it may also lead the customers to confine their purchases to the original line, even when a larger line has become reasonable. Those who hold this view claim that a credit line should be for internal use only.

REVIEWING THE CREDIT LINE

Lines of credit are based on assumptions, experiences, estimates, and forecasts. Consequently, developments that affect the willingness or ability of a customer to pay are of interest to the credit executives. A review of the file is required when an order exceeds the credit line, when a customer requests extraordinary amounts, when a customer requests extended terms, or when some information concerning a particular customer is deemed significant.

Periodic Review

A well-organized credit procedure should provide for a periodic review of all active files. The frequency and scope of the review will depend upon the type of customer, the quality of risk involved, the amount of credit required, and other circumstances. For normally active customers the review should be made annually, timed if possible to coincide with receipt of the fiscal financial statements or before the customer's active season. For marginal risks the review should occur at more frequent intervals—semiannually, quarterly, or in extreme cases monthly, depending upon the availability of information.

The periodic review can help keep credit lines flexible to fully service the customer and to accommodate the development of business obtained from aggressive and expanding concerns.

The actual process of review will vary with the quality of the account and the amount of credit exposure involved. For top-quality, or prime, accounts it will tend to be very nominal. As the quality of the accounts declines and the risk increases, the scope and intensity of the review will increase. A thorough and complete review should include the following steps, with particular attention to trends:

1. Secure from the sales department an estimate of the customer's current and near-term needs.

2. Request from the sales department an estimate of the customer's potential growth.

3. Review the customer's recent payment record with one's own company.

4. Review the latest agency reports to check for changes in ownership, operation, payment record, rating, and financial information.

5. Review and analyze latest financial statements, whether received directly or contained in the agency report. Obtain current figures if necessary.

6. Review the most recent interchange report and compare it with previous reports.

7. Review the latest direct interchange with other suppliers and obtain new information if necessary.

8. Review the latest information from the customer's bank and obtain new information if necessary.

9. Review notes and memoranda resulting from direct contact with the customer.

10. Make a personal call, if considered advisable, on the customer.

11. Appraise antecedent information on the new principals when important changes in management take place.

12. Decide whether the line of credit and payment terms are reasonable for the customer's financial strength and credit standing, in line with company credit policy, and adequate to supply the customer's needs.

Handling Orders Exceeding the Credit Line

Orders that exceed the customer's credit line require a review to determine answers to "Will the customer pay?" and "If so, when?" The credit executive will need financial and background material that justifies additional credit. Are customer debts in line with trading assets? Are trade payments prompt? What is the experience of other suppliers on the risk? Are other suppliers placing undisputed claims for collection? Is there any evidence of careless or unreliable performance by the customer? Are there any special marketing conditions?

If satisfactory answers to these questions cannot be obtained, it may be possible to work out a collateral security or other special arrangement reducing or eliminating the credit risk. Concurrently, if the available information indicates ability to pay but casts doubts on ability to pay within terms, the question is whether additional cost of the expected delinquency will make the receivable unprofitable.

Extraordinary Credit Needs

Requests for credit not warranted by the customer's financial condition should be examined with an eye to potential sales volume. They may lead to sales and profits which otherwise would not materialize or, on the other hand, to increased credit losses or expanded investment in slow accounts receivable. Thorough investigation and current information should support a decision to extend unusually high credit.

Reasons for Unusual Needs. The common reasons for extraordinary credit needs are:

1. Expanding sales. This is perhaps the most frequent reason.
2. Initial or seasonal buildup of inventory.
3. Special contracts.
4. New or recently established business. In a highly competitive economy, buyers frequently count heavily upon credit from suppliers as the principal source of operating capital.
5. Continuing credit for normal needs when there is a moratorium on previously incurred debts.

Probability of Collection. Once the reasons for unusual needs have been established, the seller must evaluate the probability of collection. Since the amount of credit is excessive by accepted financial standards, the decision must usually be based on nonfinancial factors. These include the personal background and integrity of the principals, business ability, experience with other suppliers, relations with their bank, and willingness to supply financial information.

Legal advice should be sought on special contracts to avoid difficulty in connection with performance, payment specifications, or quality of goods. Payment specifications merit particular attention. Long-term payments carry greater hazard than short-term payments. A general guide is to negotiate for payment schedules that match the customer's cash receipts schedule under the contract.

Considerations of the Seller. It is also important to determine whether the seller's accounts receivable will be adversely affected. If the extension of unusually high credit appears to concentrate the credit risk in one customer, it may be advisable to refuse the request. Accounts should be classed into risk categories and incremental sales should be compared to incremental profits for each category. On this basis, exposure can be controlled and desired relationships among categories maintained.

Overall company policies should also be considered on requests for unusually large amounts of credit. Such factors as profit margins, desirability of the business, distribution needs, competitive situations, marketing of a new product, opening a new sales territory, and efficient utilization of production facilities must be weighed.

Extended Terms

While the element of risk is common to all credit transactions, the degree of risk varies in direct relation to the credit period: the longer the credit period, the greater the risk. Furthermore, when circumstances appear to justify credit terms that extend longer than the usual period, the advice of company legal counsel must be sought before any decision is made.

Terms of sale may be considered a part of the price. Credit executives should be aware that extended payment terms may be regarded as a change in price favoring a particular customer. If extended terms are granted to one customer, they should be available to others under comparable circumstances. In addition, it should be recognized that terms concessions to some customers may be unfair to those that pay on standard terms. Accordingly, the seller should make some provision for penalty or recovery of the added cost of carrying the extended receivables.

Establishing the Necessity for Extended Terms. In any individual case, the need for additional time must be first established. The conditions which bring about this need are similar to those which underlie requests for unusually high credit: expanding sales, seasonal financing of accounts receivable and inventory, special contracts, and so on. Occasionally a customer with limited resources requests longer terms until additional capital may become available.

Current financial information is essential. In a new business, the financial data alone may justify the decision. Where the customer seems to lack operating capital to finance expanding sales, the credit executive should try to determine whether the sales forecasts are realistic. Here the views of the sales representative handling the account can be valuable. If the need stems from a special contract, it should be examined, particularly the payment schedule. When additional time is needed until other capital becomes available, it might be well to seek verification from the source of expected funds.

Terms Offered by Competitors. Another reason for considering extended terms, and an important one in many industries, is often simply a matter of being competitive and not related to actual customer need. This is more of a sales-management problem than one of credit. The credit executive can and should counsel as to the risks involved, but a decision on this point appears to be one for top management, to be reached in the light of overall company policy.

It is appropriate, however, to emphasize the need to verify alleged competitive practices before a decision is reached, for extensive terms competition can have severely demoralizing effects. Requests for lengthened terms to meet competition frequently stem from customers' reports of special arrangements offered by competing suppliers, which may be misleading. Inquiries directed to the sales department can usually determine the accuracy of reports of concessions by competitors. If the reports are verified, a decision mutually acceptable to sales and credit management can be worked out.

Extended terms can have far-ranging effects. For example, rather than reduce prices companies may offer extended terms as nonprice reductions. Sales management may justify them as a business decision. However, competitors or competing customers are affected by this action and it may have serious legal implications to the seller. Extended terms are much harder to deal with than price changes.

Determining Whether Extended Terms Are Realistic. If the customer's need is established, the credit executive must decide whether the proposed extended payment arrangements are a realistic means of meeting this need. Will temporary assistance from the supplier give adequate financing? Does available information, including sales forecasts and cash inflow forecasts, indicate that funds will be available to meet obligations as they mature? Will there be adequate funds to resume normal payments as agreed? Or does close analysis indicate that such aid would serve no long-term purpose and that the actual need is for equity capital or long-term debt?

A manufacturer can help a customer by supplying stock on extended terms. However, this is not realistic if the supplier-customer relationship is of short duration and not profitable to the seller. On the other hand, if a long-time customer fails, the past profit earned by the supplier may more than offset any one-time loss. Hence, in deciding whether to offer extended terms, the determining factor is often the larger picture of the entire relationship between buyer and seller.

If a customer's need is established and if extended terms are considered, the credit executive should give close attention to the amount of credit to be granted under these terms, keeping in mind the increased risk and the legal implications.

Unusual Information

A file is also reviewed upon receipt of information that is deemed significant. This may be a change in the financial condition as reflected by a new financial statement, a change in the accounting method for reporting sales and income, the death of one of the principals, the admission of a new partner or other change in management, a change of banks, the business being incorporated, or a change in payment habits.

DECISION BASED ON LIMITED INFORMATION

Decisions based on limited information involve factors that relate not only to the prospective customer but also to the supplier company. They include the general condition of the economy. If times are prosperous, the risk of financial loss is reduced and the credit executive would be more prone to approve orders; while under depressed conditions, the risk of loss is higher and the credit executive would be more prudent in extending credit to customers.

Competition is also a factor. If it is extremely heavy, it may be necessary to approve orders on limited information in order to obtain business. When there is an overabundance of products or a buyer's market exists, it is common to extend credit on a more liberal basis in order to maintain a reasonable share of the market. Conversely, when products are in short supply and a seller's market exists, credit analysis can be stricter.

Credit information is readily available from so many sources that normal investigation usually produces adequate data for sound and intelligent credit appraisals. Despite this, a credit department is sometimes obliged to act upon limited information. Listed below are some of the reasons for this, together with remedies:

1. A customer refuses to supply customary banking and trade references or financial details. Bank and trade reports can be gathered independently but with delays. When customers refuse to supply information, the reasons should be ascertained. It is often possible to work out a basis on which they will furnish adequate information. For example, financial data are sometimes refused because "We don't want our competition to know what we're doing." Guaranties of confidential handling may satisfy this objection.

2. Time is of the essence and the urgency for credit action does not permit normal investigation. If the credit executive can find no way to obtain adequate information within the time available, the decision must be made on whatever information can be gathered. Unless the business is new, for example, a payment record is almost always available.

3. Full information is not available due to recent formation of the business or inadequate records kept by the customer. Here the principals' past business records may be more important than the financial setup. Without exception, if antecedent information is lacking, credit grantors should proceed with extreme caution.

4. In the minds of the sales organization, competitive circumstances preclude a customer's being asked for information because of possible adverse effects on future sales. This is an internal problem which could be resolved by collaboration between sales and credit. What action to take and how to go about it should be decided after a factual, realistic review of the situation.

The factors that apply to setting credit lines enter into decisions which must be based on limited information. It is helpful to review the situation with immediate superiors and top sales management. Such collaboration creates common understanding of the problem, broadens the perspective of the credit executive, and makes salespeople more aware that it is desirable for them to obtain information from customers.

MARGINAL BUSINESS

Marginal customers fall short of the mark in one or more ways, so a sale to one presents an abnormal risk even when full information is available. Many companies define marginal risks as having one or more of the following characteristics:

1. Management is weak. It is either inexperienced or lacks depth.
2. Finances are inadequate. Companies are either not adequately capitalized for the volume transacted or they are not generating sufficient profits.

3. Payments are slow. Terms of sale are not observed, so extra collection efforts are required.
4. Merchandise is bought in too small quantities and provides low profitability.
5. Orders exceed predetermined credit lines.
6. Rated as third or fourth composite credit appraisal by Dun & Bradstreet.

There is a growing trend to consider marginal customers an important source of business. Those with good growth prospects offer an excellent opportunity for a supplier to make profitable sales despite the fact that credit requests are high in relation to net worth. A sound receivables portfolio includes a percentage of marginal accounts. They satisfy the need for additional business in a specific market. A supplier that has excess production capacity or needs a wider market base is willing to take a greater credit risk. This is especially true when the better customers have absorbed the fixed costs and the marginal accounts are required only to cover the incremental, or out-of-pocket, costs. Of course, when a sold-up condition exists, the supplier can be more selective.

Profit on incremental sales to marginal customers may materially improve the earnings of the business, even allowing for increased credit losses. This can be shown as follows: Assume a company is operating at less than capacity. If all of its fixed costs and an acceptable profit are covered at present levels of production, any increase in output would require expenditure only for the direct, out-of-pocket costs of the additional sales. If they make up 40 per cent of the selling price, the remaining 60 per cent would be profit. Hence any incremental sales that sustained less than 60 per cent bad-debt losses would increase the company's profit. This type of analysis is discussed in more detail in Chapter 30.

A number of factors related to profit margins may influence the decision to sell to marginal accounts. As a rule, a seller with a wider profit margin can afford to sell to greater credit risks. Similarly, the higher the prospective customer's profit, the fewer units it must sell to pay its supplier. Disposition of the customer's profit should also be considered; reinvestment of earnings during good times will not only improve a marginal risk but tend to assure its continued existence during bad times.

Product distribution affects the credit decision on marginal business. When new products are being promoted or when new distribution channels are being developed, marginal risks offer the seller an opportunity to maximize effectiveness. Alternative outlets must also be considered. Selling to one of a few marginal jobbers may be considerably more economical than handling hundreds of direct retailer or manufacturer accounts, for example. On the other hand, it may be constructive to refuse credit to a marginal risk and explore the possibility of selling to alternative outlets which present a more attractive financial picture. Finally, dead or slow-moving inventory may be better sold to a marginal risk than junked. For example, one manufacturing concern was paying a fee to dispose of waste materials. As a result of collaboration between sales and credit, these wastes were sold to a marginal outlet at a profit.

As might be expected, marginal accounts are better risks during prosperous times than they are during recessions, and their industry oftentimes affects their ability to survive. Despite this tendency, there are a number of ways to reduce the risk on marginal accounts. Protective measures such as guaranties or security agreements perfected under the Uniform Commercial Code may serve this purpose. Terms shorter than standard terms, C.O.D., part cash in advance, and cash before delivery may also be considered.

Moreover, the adequacy of fire insurance on property, life insurance on the principals, public liability insurance on hazardous operations, and other types of insurance carried by the buyer may also affect the credit decision. The credit executive should carefully consider the insurable risks and their coverage in evaluating a marginal account.

REVIEW OF CREDIT DECISIONS

As business conditions and the circumstances of individual customers change, it frequently becomes necessary to review credit decisions. In addition to the periodic review, procedures should specify when to review a credit decision because of changes in payment experience, new financial statements or agency reports, and overall credit department experience with days sales outstanding, bad-debt losses, and past-due accounts.

Information from other sources may also cause a review. Local newspapers often publicize changes in ownership and management, the start of legal actions, and information on customers. Industry and trade publications, such as *Women's Wear* and the *Daily News Record* in the textile industry, are useful sources of information both on individual customers and on conditions in the industry. General business conditions are discussed in a wide range of publications, especially financial newspapers and financial sections of leading newspapers, and periodic analyses are issued by prominent banks and a number of government publications.

Credit executives should be alert for surface indications of a customer's financial difficulty: reduced mercantile agency ratings, increasingly irregular or delayed trade payments, reports of contentiousness, protested checks, filing of tax claims, perfected security agreements, and failure to maintain scheduled payments on debentures, mortgages, or other fixed obligations.

On the other hand, there is a great danger in presumptions based on incomplete surface indications. They should always be explored. Thorough investigation is often required to assess their significance. Any decision to curtail credit or to decline a customer's creditworthiness should be delayed until complete information is at hand. Impetuous retrenchment decisions based only on indications of possible financial deterioration can create customer ill will or even lose a customer.

Treatment of Overdue Accounts

Slow payment is probably the factor that most frequently leads to the account review. If slow-paying customers are approached with a frame of mind that seeks knowledge or answers, it may be possible to convert them to prompt and profitable accounts.

As a starting point, credit information should be reviewed and brought up to date. The sales department's appraisal of the risk and potential may also help decide how a past-due account should be handled. If the review indicates that additional credit is too risky, friendly but firm efforts should be initiated to collect the past-due amount. Internal controls can be set up to prevent shipment of new orders until it has been paid. If a new order is received, the credit department may tell the customer that additional credit will be extended after past-due bills are paid.

Some problems of past-due accounts may be solved by amortizing payment of all or a portion of matured balances over a period of time, with a provision for prompt payment of any new credit. Amortization plans may also provide for conversion of extended open-account balances to interest-bearing notes. The objective is to return the accounts to a current basis by liquidating the frozen balances. However, unless such plans are based realistically on ability to meet the schedule of payments out of profits or otherwise, they may serve only to complicate the situation.

Customer Good Will

It is important to retain good will when notifying a customer of reduced credit or when asking for payment of past-due amounts. The approach will depend on established policy. Whether it is undertaken by a credit or sales representative, forthrightness, tact, and sincerity should be exercised.

A telephone call is often the most expeditious means of approaching a customer. Warmer and more flexible than a letter, it is often more effective. Misunderstandings can usually be detected and immediately dispelled during a telephone conversation.

Where feasible, a personal visit may be best. The credit executive has an opportunity to make a direct appraisal of the customer's capacity and to offer on-the-spot advice. Of course, the expense of the visit must be weighed against the amount of credit involved.

Treatment of Improving Accounts

Alertness to improvement in the status of customers is also important. When a customer's financial condition and payment performance improve substantially, it may be possible to extend larger amounts of credit, with fewer orders referred for review. These steps can result in increased sales and profits and in better service to the customer. A compliment to the customer on such improvement can reinforce good will.

Changing Business Conditions

Changing conditions in business, in a particular industry or in a geographic area, generally may warrant review of accounts. Thus a nationwide depression, poor crops in a given section, a prolonged strike, and many less dramatic changes can each have serious consequences for individual concerns. If prolonged or severe enough, they can affect not only the marginal business but the well-financed, well-managed concern as well. Similarly, changing business conditions may improve the position of the supplier or of customers. Reassessment of credit facilities in terms of new situations can be advantageous to both supplier and customer.

CHAPTER 14

COLLECTION PROCEDURES

The statement that a sale is not complete until the cash is in the bank is both familiar and true. A business organization would soon run out of operating capital if it were not continuously replenished through collection of its receivables. Unless receivables are converted to cash on schedule, some of the company assets are unproductively tied up. This situation is encountered by firms that allow customers to become past due. In turn, the financial condition of the seller may become restricted and interfere with its own ability to pay bills on time. This neglect of financial principles could affect a company's reputation in the trade and may even lead to financial embarrassment.

The credit extended beyond regular terms represents capital that cannot be used to meet the seller's own requirements. It may therefore be necessary to compensate for this by borrowing from banks, financing receivables, or paying its own bills in a slow manner. Each of these methods costs money, whether it be interest, financing charges, or loss of cash discount. Unless the selling firm charges for these additional costs in its pricing structure, it is faced with additional and unexpected drains on profits.

When there is a seller's market, the collection of customer accounts becomes almost automatic, stimulated by the desire of customers to stay in the good graces of suppliers. These periods of collection Utopia rapidly disappear, however, when more normal competitive conditions prevail. Since most of the commerce of our Nation today flows from seller to buyer on credit, the ongoing collection of customer accounts is an important consideration in the management of an enterprise.

PRINCIPLES OF COLLECTION

The principles found especially useful by those experienced in the field of collection may be grouped into four areas: collect the money, maintain a systematic followup, get the customer to discuss the account, and preserve good will.

Collect the Money

The prime job of the person responsible for collections is to collect the money as close to the selling terms as possible. There should never be any doubt as to why the individual is engaged in this work. The customer has an obligation to pay invoices within terms. It is the job of the collection representative to make sure that this obligation is met. The tone may be easy at first, but it should be stiffened and accelerated as much as necessary to ensure payment of the delinquent account.

Systematic Followup

After the initial contact with the delinquent account, it is important to keep additional contacts on a strict schedule. If the collection representative is told that a partial payment (not always acceptable) will be mailed in a few days, for instance, that information should be noted. If the check is not received at the promised time, a followup is essential. Otherwise the collection effort may become ineffective.

Systematic followup of accounts, even those which cannot pay immediately, indicates the serious nature of the outstanding debt and emphasizes the importance attached to it by the creditor. That in itself is an important collection advantage.

Get the Customer to Discuss the Situation

Once the collection representative gets the customer to talk about a delinquent account, the collector is well on the way toward receiving payment. That is why emphasis is placed on inviting the customer to talk. The request to respond may be made by mail, by phone, by telegram, or in person.

The object of the discussion is to get the customer's explanation of the delinquency. It may be a question of faulty merchandise; it may be due to a temporary shortage of funds; or the customer may intend to hold off payment so the creditor's money can be used in its own business.

During the discussion, the collection representative may see the debtor's situation more clearly than the customer. If the slow payment seems a temporary thing, toleration of slower payments may be accepted, but it should be emphasized to the customer that the new schedule of payments must be completed.

Preserve Good Will

Even though a customer may be experiencing some difficulty in meeting payments, it does not preclude the account from becoming a good customer in the future. It is therefore important for the collection department to preserve the customer's good will while pressing for collection. This requires not only tact but knowledge of the account. One of the advantages claimed for specialized personnel is that they can develop these techniques to their fullest. On the other hand, the credit representative, in knowing the account, may also be in a very good position to approach it for payment.

Where only one choice has to be made between collecting the money and preserving good will, however, emphasis should be on the former. A customer that does not intend to pay legitimate debts is not a desired client.

COLLECTION RESPONSIBILITY

In a small business operated by one person, it is quite obvious who is responsible for collections. Many proprietors personally attend to the collection of accounts. Their efforts are effective because they are well aware of the need for continual replenishment of operating capital.

However, it is not always true that collection of accounts by principals of small businesses guarantees good collection results. All too often a proprietorship, a partnership, or even a small corporation may be organized by sales personalities who do an exceptional job of selling but devote insufficient talent to collections. Techniques are generally better developed in larger organizations where individuals specialize in the collection process. But it is equally important for the small concern to clearly assign the collection responsibility and make certain that it is properly carried out.

Where the collection responsibility should rest depends on the nature of the company organization. Generally speaking, the larger the company the farther the collection function is removed from the chief executive officer. In medium- or small-sized companies, it is not at all unusual to find one of the officers, most frequently the treasurer, charged with that responsibility. In fact, even in larger organizations where the responsibility for collection is one of the specified functions of the credit department, higher management follows closely the success with which the function is carried out. It cannot be emphasized too strongly that the profitability of a business, in some cases even success or failure, may be determined by the efficiency with which it turns its accounts receivable.

Credit Department

Many medium-sized and larger enterprises assign the responsibility for collections to the department that approves credit sales. This arrangement is based on the theory that credit approval includes assumption of collection effort. Moreover, certain collection techniques are employed at the time the order is processed. An individual engaged exclusively in credit approval and collection becomes a specialist. Properly trained, the person often becomes the best qualified in the organization to perform the collection task.

As a business organization increases in size and trades over a widespread geographic area, it becomes necessary to determine whether a centralized home office credit department should retain the collection function for the entire company, or whether some form of decentralization would be advisable. The relevant considerations include the nature of the company's business, number of customers, size of average account, frequency of orders, costs of decentralization, and many other criteria. Accounts receivable details and the ledgering of the accounts are also important, as are the questions of where invoices are rendered and what system of receivables accounting is employed.

Special Collection Personnel

Certain business organizations generate collection work in such large volume that it becomes advantageous to train and use special collection personnel who do not carry the responsibility of credit approval. Such business organizations may be found in industries where the number of accounts is very high and the average amount of each transaction is rather small and uniform. The advantages of this arrangement include possible savings in salaries, development of expert and adroit collection handling through specialization, and the freeing of other personnel for more complex duties. While this approach is limited to certain types of enterprise, some adaptation of it could benefit many companies with expanding credit and collection activities.

Accounts Receivable Department

Depending again on the size of the business organization, the accounts receivable function may or may not play a role in the collection of accounts. It is not uncommon to include the responsibility for accounts receivable in the area of credit management; in such cases, the personnel handling the accounts receivable work usually do not have true collection responsibility. On the other hand, the accounts receivable function may be placed under the accounting department or may be centralized in a home office location, while the credit and collection functions are located elsewhere in the organization. If delegation of authority seems advisable, the assignment of collection responsibility to accounts receivable personnel deserves consideration.

For example, consider a multiple branch company wherein the financial accounting for receivables is handled at a centralized office, but manufacturing, invoicing, and credit and collections are decentralized. What portion of the collection function might the accounts receivable department carry out? Clerical personnel in accounting could record unpaid accounts which reach a certain age category, or obtain a printout if computerized, and forward the information to central credit personnel or branch credit personnel for collection activity. They might go even one step further and actually send out the initial collection effort, with the specialized credit and collection personnel taking over if further activity is needed.

In some organizations, accounts receivable personnel save the time of credit and collection people by handling the clearance of deductions for discounts, short or damaged merchandise, and traffic matters. In many cases, the efficient clearance of small customer deductions becomes an intracompany problem. Correspondence flows from the collection person to the traffic department, the sales service department, or some other division charged with jurisdiction over these matters. While this type of activity must be handled with intelligence, it need not be treated with the finesse of a customer contact and can be carried out by less experienced, less expensive personnel.

The number of customer accounts, their average size, the number of invoices, the frequency of special deductions, and other factors of this kind need to be analyzed and weighed by management to determine who should have the collection responsibility.

Sales Personnel

There has been much debate on the question of whether sales personnel should be called upon to assist in the collection of accounts. Many business concerns seem to favor cooperation of the salespeople in collection work. Others raise objections to this policy. Since the primary responsibility of sales is to move merchandise, it is often maintained that they must devote their full attention to the techniques and motivations of sales work. If they become too involved in collections, they may develop a negative attitude that makes it more difficult for them to obtain orders. Though such an attitude may not be based on facts, it does point up the importance of educating sales personnel to be credit and collection oriented and to be willing and able to assist the credit department.

A decision to use sales personnel in collection work must be preceded by careful consideration of the nature of the company's business, the caliber of the sales representatives employed by the company, the size of the company's receivables, and the extent of its collection problems. Even if they are not responsible for collections, sales personnel should be aware of the status of their accounts, have an interest in their payment record, understand the need for recovering company capital, and be available for assistance in special cases.

Asked to cooperate on a reasonable basis, salespeople can make a valuable contribution to the collection of accounts. Furthermore, they will gain a new perspective of their customers, which can increase good will. Experienced sales representatives have said they never really knew a major customer until the first collection problem arose with the account. Successful solution of the problem gives sales personnel a much broader basis for their future relationships with the customer.

In certain types of businesses, particularly in the jobber and distributor fields, sales personnel carry out the primary collection job, and in some cases are compensated under a formula that takes into account their ability to collect. The techniques employed by these individuals are probably as varied as the personalities involved. Usually, though, the sales representative-collector is dealing with the retail trade or the individual customer, and the relationship from both sales and collection standpoints becomes a very personal one, with the amounts involved relatively small.

In other types of organizations, though not responsible for collections, sales personnel are kept informed and are expected to participate in an advisory role. Here also the pattern varies from business to business, but one common point is the value of keeping the salespeople informed. An account that is paying its bills is an account in a position to place an order. An account that is delinquent only tends to turn to competitors in placing additional business.

Probably the most common practice is to keep field sales personnel informed through copies of all statements, collection letters, or other correspondence flowing between the collector and the customer. Frequently, in problem cases, the sales department is asked for comments as to the condition of the customer's business, and any unusual circumstances, such as illness, which would affect collections.

Other Personnel

Under some circumstances, other members of the organization may be involved in the collection function. This is frequently true where very large or very difficult collection problems are being faced. For example, the treasurer or perhaps the controller or the chief auditor, may add a note of authority or a greater depth of experience to a difficult problem. Such participation commonly takes the form of advice behind the scenes rather than direct contact with the account. This may lead to periodic management review of collection efforts and problems; a reappraisal of attitude, policy, and techniques; or the contribution of new ideas, a fresh approach, or helpful encouragement.

Other possibilities for wider participation in collection work include preparation of collection correspondence by other personnel and contact by telephone or in person by company officers.

COLLECTION EFFORT

The actual collection procedure begins with the impending maturity of an account. The question then centers upon when the initial collection will be made—that is, how long after the net due date will the collection procedure begin. The time interval may range from one day to a week, 10 days, or in some cases even longer. The basic policy should also specify the timing of the second and subsequent followups if the initial steps do not collect the past-due amount. In considering the timing, it is necessary to consider the distances involved and the time required for an exchange of mail, the total number of followups and the personnel available to handle them, and the practical matter of giving customers a reasonable time to respond to the collection effort; 10 days is average, a more local operation might set a shorter interval, and two weeks or longer might prove most desirable in certain industries.

For proper control, it is important to keep a clear-cut record of accounts which have remained open beyond the regular terms of sale and are past due. There are many systems to do this. One, widely used, is an aging of accounts receivable, generally done on a monthly basis, though it can be carried out at shorter or longer intervals to suit the needs of the particular enterprise. An aging segregates accounts into the following categories: those which are past maturity from 1 to 30 days, 31 to 60 days, 61 to 90 days, and over 90 days. It is widely used to identify the condition of accounts receivable month by month and to determine the scope of the collection job. This report is discussed in more detail in Chapter 33.

The choice of a specific collection system will probably be determined by the basic accounting system used in invoicing customers and ledgering accounts receivable. In many organizations, computers are used to prepare statements and to write collection letters. The net due date of the invoice should be used in preparing the documents rather than a specified number of days past the invoice date. Moreover, each account should have a collection status code that indicates the reminder document to be prepared—past-due statement, collection letter number 1, and so on. And finally, the system of invoicing, ledgering, and collection followup should match the resources, the style, and the objectives of a business organization. A system that is too elaborate might retard growth.

Statements of Account

A simple statement of account, listing the invoices outstanding and due for payment, is widely used as an initial collection effort. Usually it is sent without a message, but sometimes it carries a simple and courteous request for payment. A statement of account should include sufficient basic information, such as a purchase order number, to permit a customer to check it readily against its own records prior to sending a remittance.

A mailing of statements generally results in a substantial number of accounts being paid and reduces the number requiring additional collection effort. But since some accounts will not pay merely on the receipt of a statement, it is a common practice to prepare the statements in more than one copy. The duplicate copy—containing the name, address, and detail of the account—can then be used in followup collection efforts.

Many concerns find it practical to mail no statements except to those customers that request them or to customers that are past due. This practice results in considerable savings in personnel costs, stationery, and postage.

Early Stages of Collection

The essential factor in any collection effort is to use a procedure that is most effective from the standpoint of time and expense. Depending upon customer characteristics, this may be form letters, computer-generated letters, preprogrammed letters using word processing systems, individually prepared letters, copies of invoices, or telephone calls.

Form Letters. Volumes have been written on the subject of form letters and their place in collection work. Those who advocate their use cite the substantial savings of time and expense. Others lean toward specially written communications, claiming that form letters are detectable as such and tend to make the collection effort ineffective. As a general guide, many say that form letters are effective in inverse proportion to the seriousness of the collection problem. After all, a statement of account is a standardized form and yet is effective on newly past-due accounts; on the other hand, a statement of account sent to a customer with indebtedness several months past due would probably be futile.

The important consideration is that form letters must be well-written and properly used. Good form letters, for example, would be efficient on a large number of accounts with small open items where sheer numbers would otherwise prohibit the expense of specially written letters. When the accounts are larger and specific problems more complex, specially written letters become much more important and form letters tend to be ineffective.

Individually Prepared Collection Letters. When the problem is a very specific one and the customer must be made aware of the creditor's concern, the first letter sent to a delinquent account becomes the most important. While simple in detail, it must be carefully devised. It should be as brief as possible and identify the items that have become past due. A first collection letter may be addressed to the company or to an individual, depending on the writer's knowledge of the company organization. Actually, the typical first letter contains little information that would not be shown on a statement of account, but it does command more attention than a statement and is more difficult to brush aside.

Because it is brief, only slight variations are possible, but these can be added as the collector learns about the customer. The first effort lends itself more readily to the use of the form letter than do subsequent collection efforts, but the main point is to get the collection process started properly.

Computer-Generated Letters. Basically these letters list past-due invoices and ask for payment. The message will vary depending upon which letter of a series is being sent, each succeeding letter becoming more urgent.

Using the computer to generate collection letters relieves credit executives of a time-consuming job and permits them to devote more time to managing their accounts receivable portfolio. In addition, the computer is much faster and less costly.

Preprogrammed Letters. These have been made possible by word processing equipment and complement dictated and computer-produced letters. Many exception-type letters or paragraphs can be programmed and thereby eliminate dictation. The new machines are much faster than typewriters and increase productivity, reduce costs, and speed up collection efforts.

This type of letter is often used during the intermediate stages of collection. The first three letters, for example, may be computer-prepared and sent directly to the customer; the fourth would be a customized letter prepared by the credit executive in charge of the account.

Copies of Invoices. Statements and collection letters do not work with a number of large national accounts, mostly because they require more information than is shown on these documents. They need to know the ship-to address, the bill-to address, and other pertinent details regarding the products sold.

In addition, when a shipment is made to a plant site, the invoice normally has to be forwarded to another address where the accounts payable department is located. This can cause the invoices to go astray and lead to a breakdown in the payment process. This situation can best be remedied with a duplicate copy of the invoice.

Telephone. The telephone is the preferred medium on high-risk accounts and where sizable amounts are owing from large companies. With proper use it helps obtain more understanding, collect money, build good will, and possibly increase sales.

Most customers that cannot pay on time are faced with some kind of business problem. The telephone collector should be prepared to listen with sympathy. While it may be possible to obtain the money owed by sheer insistence on immediate payment, it is far better for the collector to be helpful. This approach offers a fine opportunity to improve a relationship and increase the amount of business with the account.

A telephone contact must aim to obtain a definite understanding regarding payment of the past-due items. If the customer cannot pay the entire balance in one payment, a plan should be worked out to receive a partial payment by a certain date and additional checks at one or more future dates until the past-due balance has been paid. The experience and skill of the collector are brought into play in working out the best possible arrangements and at the same time treating customers courteously and considerately.

The cost of a phone call frequently is repaid many times over by additional orders obtained with the settlement of an account. The salient points of the telephone conversation should immediately be confirmed in writing to the customer.

Intermediate Stages of Collection

Customers not responding to early collection efforts represent the real problems and pose a challenge to the collector's ability. The number of intermediate efforts will vary according to the period of time an organization considers its normal collection cycle—usually two to three months, but in some types of business a little longer. They will also be affected by the condition of the customer's account. This makes it imperative that the collector be thoroughly familiar with the credit facts of the account. The followup intervals must be maintained on a regular basis; it is usually considered good business to allow a period of 10 to 15 days between collection efforts.

Intermediate collection efforts are generally handled by correspondence, although there is a very definite place for telephone conversations or personal visits if the expense is justified by the amount involved. At this stage, the collector's full abilities must be applied in writing resourceful, appealing, and tactful letters which induce the customer to clear the obligation without impairing good will.

Intermediate collection letters generated by computer can have the message portion tailor-made. Consequently, they are usually successful, especially when combined with telephone calls that make the customer increasingly aware of the creditor's concern. A variety of psychological appeals may be tried.

Appeals can be made to the customer's spirit of cooperation and fairness. After all, the collection of an account is merely the completion of a business contract usually entered in good faith by both the buyer and seller. The seller's good faith is amply demonstrated by the very granting of credit. Proceeding on the assumption that the buyer also had good intentions, intermediate collection efforts can appeal adroitly to the cooperativeness of the debtor in completing the contract. Appealing to the debtor's fairness is a more delicate area, and care should be taken to avoid the inference that the honesty of the buyer is being questioned.

The intermediate collection letter may stress the idea of maintaining a good credit record. Business concerns which have maintained prompt payment of their obligations over a period of time usually are very proud of this fact. If the customer has an excellent record, it is quite likely that some unusual problem, even some question with reference to the merchandise sold, may be the actual reason the account continues unpaid. The collector should consider carefully the possible situations which might be confronting the debtor and invite feedback as the beginning of a solution.

If the payment record has not been uniformly good, an appeal to the debtor's desire to improve the record has sometimes helped. This approach will depend on the selling organization's importance to the debtor.

Patience and propriety must be maintained at all times. It is desirable to build up the force of the collection approach and increase the concern and urgency in each successive communication. Depending upon the credit information available and the age of the past-due items, it may be necessary to refer to the possibility of special collection action if nonpayment continues.

During this process it is quite common for customers to promise payment, give excuses for nonpayment, or send partial remittances to be applied on their account. Such responses give the collector something to work on. Common sense and good business judgment will assist the collector to set up specific dates and amounts or some type of agreement that will lead to complete payment at the earliest possible date.

The importance of making specific arrangements cannot be emphasized too strongly. Often a debtor responding to the pressure of the collection effort will indicate that payment will be forthcoming "soon." A collector should promptly acknowledge such replies with thanks and suggest a specific date, such as "by the 15th" or "one week from today." If the amount is substantial, it might be advisable to suggest payment of one-half by a specific date with a cleanup remittance after a reasonable interval. A cooperative debtor will normally respond to the reasonableness of these suggestions.

There is always the danger that the collector will tend to lose respect for the customer and let this feeling show in communications with the debtor. It is a paramount rule of all business correspondence, vital as the pressure of collection effort is built up, to maintain an attitude of common business courtesy. Some debtors seeking to take advantage of their suppliers are waiting for an opportunity to embarrass the collector in the eyes of the selling organization and to justify their delay by pointing to some breach of business etiquette in correspondence. It is definitely possible to increase the pressure for payment and reach the final demand for settlement without violating business dignity. Care should always be taken to set forth the facts carefully, so the customer cannot disagree or take offense.

Guided by these basic principles, each individual must develop skills and adeptness through experience. The approach which works with one customer may fail with another, but experience will develop certain techniques that prove repeatedly effective and can be used indefinitely.

Final Stages of Collection

When normal procedures fail to bring in the money and it is concluded that outside assistance or legal action may be necessary, collection activities reach the final stage. The length of time between the intermediate and final stages differs from one business to another. Terms of sale, customs within an industry, and general economic conditions facing a customer must be taken into consideration. Once again the credit file must be reviewed to make certain that the latest information is included before the decision to engage a third party.

In most instances, companies wait two or three months before concluding that the final stage has been reached. If, however, the debtor's credit picture seems to be fading fast, it is advisable to hasten action since the percentage of recovery diminishes quite rapidly as an account ages. If information on the debtor indicates an unfavorable trend in payment habits, with considerable past-due indebtedness showing in trade reports, final action should not be put off.

The customer that has not paid over a long period of time is in one of the following three categories: the debtor has the ability to pay but does not intend to, the debtor is unable to pay all its obligations and so pays those exerting the greatest pressure, or the debtor lacks the ability to pay and will shortly be out of business. The idea of the final collection effort is to motivate the seriously past-due customers to pay their account and thereby avoid the cost of forced settlement through a third-party action.

At the final stage, collection efforts may vary from a single communication to a series of two or three letters. A fairly standard technique is to send what might be considered a semifinal collection letter. This states that unless settlement arrangements are promptly made, it may be necessary to resort to outside agencies. If this approach is ineffective, a so-called final letter is sent, indicating that the account will be placed for collection in a specified number of days. In some cases a final telegram may follow, to give one last opportunity for payment before placement of the account in outside hands for further action.

The approach is limited at this late stage. The most effective letters point out in a businesslike way that further delay can be permitted only if the debtor makes definite and immediate arrangements for settlement, the alternative being a costly legal action. The goal at this point is to get action, to make the debtor pay immediately or stand the expense, involvement, and embarrassment. When the use of third party assistance is indicated, it should be done. In some organizations, a letter signed by a senior officer, the treasurer, or the general attorney has proved effective. Usually at this stage the retention of customer good will becomes secondary; the principal objective is immediate settlement of the amount.

The proper use of telegrams is considered a means of getting action and has its place in collection procedure. Since the telegram is by its very nature a rather stark message, it does not enter the picture until the collection problem has become serious. It unquestionably receives prompt attention. This and the speed with which it reaches a customer are its principal advantages.

Because telegrams are generally used only in the final stages of collection, they do not bolster good will. Care in wording the telegram is required from a legal standpoint. Since the telegraphic message is known to others besides the individuals sending and receiving it, a telegram is not considered a completely private communication. Therefore, it becomes imperative that nothing in a telegraphic message be libelous in any way, so as to give the party receiving it an opportunity to institute legal action. It is highly advisable to prepare a series of telegraphic messages and have them cleared by legal counsel.

Model Collection Letters

Form letters play an important role in collecting past-due amounts. They have been revised many times, so are precise and have better wording. They have the advantage of offering savings in dictation, typing, and employee time, and can be generated by computer.

Figure 14–1 presents a series of computer-generated letters which follow the principles explained in the text. For simplicity, the statement listing the items is omitted and only the message portion is shown. The pressure to pay builds up in each successive letter. The initial letter asks the customer for an explanation of the delinquent items, while the remaining letters stress the urgency of the matter. Each letter is a collection effort by itself, yet forms part of a coordinated, continuing effort.

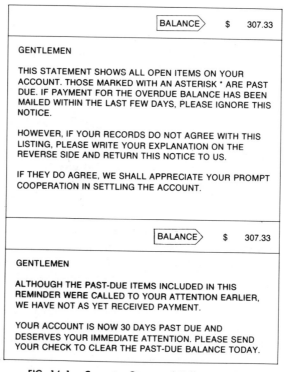

FIG. 14–1.   Computer-Generated Collection Letters.

BALANCE > $ 307.33

GENTLEMEN

THIS IS OUR THIRD REQUEST FOR PAYMENT OF THE PAST-
DUE CHARGES ABOVE. IT IS DISAPPOINTING THAT WE
HAVE RECEIVED NEITHER A REPLY NOR PAYMENT FROM
YOU AND YOUR ACCOUNT IS NOW 60 DAYS PAST DUE.

PLEASE DO NOT DELAY ANY LONGER IN SENDING
PAYMENT. YOUR CHECK TO COVER THE FULL AMOUNT OF
THE OVERDUE BALANCE SHOULD BE MAILED NOW.

BALANCE > $ 307.33

GENTLEMEN

DEFINITE ACTION MUST BE TAKEN NOW ON THE OVERDUE
ACCOUNT LISTED ABOVE. THE AGE OF THIS BALANCE
PRECLUDES ANY FURTHER POSTPONEMENT OF PAYMENT.

THE REMINDERS WE SENT PREVIOUSLY HAVE GONE
UNANSWERED SO THIS MUST BE OUR FINAL NOTICE. IF
YOUR PAYMENT IS NOT RECEIVED WITHIN 10 DAYS OF THE
DATE OF THIS STATEMENT, YOU WILL LEAVE US WITH NO
ALTERNATIVE TO REFERRING YOUR ACCOUNT TO AN
OUTSIDE AGENCY AUTHORIZED TO HANDLE SUCH
COLLECTIONS FOR US.

PLEASE DO NOT MAKE THIS NECESSARY, MAIL YOUR
PAYMENT NOW.

FIG. 14–1 (cont'd.).

COLLECTION TOOLS AND TECHNIQUES

In developing collection procedures, it is helpful to have a working knowledge of collection tools and techniques. A person aware of the methods that have been successful finds it is easier to select the proper combination in particular situations. The procedures that work for one organization will not always do so for another, but knowledge of successful techniques should enable the collector to do a more effective job.

When an open account cannot be paid on time, credit personnel often use promissory notes to strengthen their position. Sometimes postdated checks are obtained if the debt is to be cleared in a short period of time—several weeks or a month. Postdated checks and other negotiable instruments are described briefly here, and in more detail in Chapter 26.

These tools are not used for granting credit before merchandise is shipped but as promises of future payment after credit has been extended. The use of secured debt as a basis for granting credit before the merchandise is shipped is discussed in detail in Chapter 29.

Postdated Checks

Postdated checks as a collection device are used most frequently during difficult economic conditions. Failure to cover the check is not different from any other failure to pay for goods bought on credit. The use of postdated checks to work out settlement of an existing past-due account means that a definite promise of future payment has been put into writing. It does not become an assured payment since the customer may lack sufficient funds in the bank to meet the check at its due date. One caution, however, is that acceptance of a postdated check may prohibit filing a criminal complaint for passing a bad check.

Promissory Notes

Most business organizations have found promissory notes to be a desirable and useful collection tool at one time or another. They differ from postdated checks in that they may be interest bearing. By signing a note, a delinquent debtor acknowledges the existence of the amount owing (often an important point if court action ensues) and promises to pay it by a certain date. If the debtor's position is deteriorating, however, a note may not be desirable, since the note holder cannot press for payment until the note matures. Promissory notes also have their place as a collection tool on past-due accounts for which a predetermined extension has been worked out.

COMMON COLLECTION PROBLEMS

The following section deals with collection situations that occur frequently and is presented as a reference for collectors, who usually are responsible for resolving similar situations in their everyday work. In all of these efforts at collection, the creditor must be constantly aware of problems that may arise because of special state laws and common law that regulate all collection practices. Specific comments dealing with correspondence are outlined later in this chapter. In every instance, it is advisable to consult with legal counsel before amending procedures that have already been approved.

Unearned Cash Discounts

A problem which will remain with business as long as cash discounts are offered is the handling of unearned cash discounts. Every company should review its terms of sale from time to time to satisfy itself that they are fair and reasonable, and that the customer is not expected to make payment at a speed which might be impractical. Once this has been established, most companies look upon their terms of sale as important enough to be maintained equally and fairly to all customers. Overlooking cash discount violations or loosely enforcing the terms of sale tends to increase the problem and makes it far more difficult to solve at a later date.

It has been customary to have a grace period beyond the discount date, varying in length from two to five days. Remittances received within the grace period beyond the discount date have been considered eligible for the discount. This was clearly a price concession given to some customers and penalized those that paid within terms. It should be discouraged as cash management techniques become more sophisticated.

The customers taking unearned discounts can be placed in three groups. First, there are those that take the discount through misunderstanding or carelessness. They can be informed with a courteous letter carefully identifying the payment received late, explaining again the terms of sale, and pointing out the importance of paying within the discount period.

Second, companies attempt to take the discount in the belief that it will not be noticed. Here the most common practice is to deposit the customer's check and then ask for an additional payment covering the unallowed discount. Unless a firm stand is taken at once, a permanent source of trouble will result.

Third are the chronic offenders. In handling them, collectors may return the check and request a new one for the full amount. This is more serious and indicates that the basic relationship between the buyer and the seller is not understood. Having the sales representative go over the matter in person with the customer can be most helpful. If this does not bring results, one might withdraw open-account privileges, notify the top management, or draw a draft on the violator's bank.

Any particular amount taken in unearned cash discount is usually not large. In total, however, they can represent a substantial sum. The collector should not reflect annoyance in any correspondence with the customer. A company must have a reasonable policy and then be consistent and courteous in applying it. It is doubtful that any organization will ever completely overcome the problem of the unearned cash discount, but a consistent policy should keep it from becoming a serious one and will prove well worth the effort and expense involved in administration.

Customer Deductions

Decisions on customer deductions for allowances, returned goods, and complaints about the quality of merchandise are usually based upon policies formulated by top management. Customer deductions are a serious problem. Credit and accounts receivable managers are increasingly aware of the money tied up in these deductions and of the time and effort needed to resolve them. The paperwork has multiplied to a point where it is disproportionate to the allotted clerical-handling facilities. Moreover, these deductions slow up the flow of automated payments.

Most deductions are the result of legitimate customer claims. Significant savings can be realized by resolving them as soon as possible. These include reduced costs of carrying receivables, lower income taxes, and fewer department personnel.

Some reasons for deductions are common to nearly all types of business. These include returns because of incorrect material or quality defects, traffic claims (shortages, damages, and items other than returns), and pricing errors. Allowances in the form of advertising, promotion, and coupons are principally incurred by industries that market products to retail establishments. Certain types of deductions represent a small percentage of customer claims but involve a greater percentage of problems. In those instances, corrective actions can range from improving the present systems to the installation of new equipment. Many solutions are outside the responsibility of the credit department, but better communication among all departments will help. Some of the more frequent reasons are discussed below.

Allowances. Allowances usually arise from advertising contracts, promotional contracts, or coupon redemptions. They are also granted to customers for quality reasons to prevent returns. As noted above, many allowance deductions are incurred by companies marketing goods to retail establishments. The principal way to reduce this problem is to educate customers on company allowance policy. This includes the qualifications for taking the allowances and the procedures for claiming the credit.

The issuance of credits to the customer must be timely: one way is to estimate the allowance ahead of time; another is to deduct the promotional allowance from the face of the invoice and have the customers pay the net amount. In the latter case, however, 100 per cent of the allowances would be honored by the seller, and a system would have to be devised to make certain the customer met the performance requirements.

The number of allowances can be reduced by working with the sales department. If the sales department does not issue the credit or process the promotion information promptly, consideration could be given to transferring promotional and allowance deductions from accounts receivable and charging them to selling expense, thus making the sales department responsible for them. Another solution would be to reduce the incentive or bonus arrangements of uncooperative sales representatives.

Returns. In a quality dispute, material may be sent back for replacement or returned or scrapped for credit. Weight discrepancies or overshipments also require a decision as to whether the customer should pay for the material or return it for credit. The means for reducing this problem are concentrated in the manufacturing end of the business. Quality control and improvement can remedy manufacturing and production problems. Improved inspection procedures will hold down defective goods. Action may be stimulated by a monthly report to manufacturing management which contains claim-loss statistics, analyzes the returns, and provides written corrective action.

Other measures include the elimination of overordering; better warehouse cooperation; and the possibility of scrapping more material in the field, with the sales representative being authorized to pay on the spot for some limited amount of merchandise, the destruction of which was personally witnessed.

Traffic Claims. Traffic claims include shortages, damages, and items other than returns. These are claimed for a discrepancy in the freight bill amount, for freight charges paid by a customer on merchandise shipped back to the seller, or for misroutings in which the seller does not follow the customer's instructions. The use of reputable carriers is the best corrective measure that can be taken to minimize damaged goods and short shipments. Further, the carriers should be required to provide prompt service.

Pricing Errors. Pricing errors usually arise when there are variances between the billed and quoted prices or the billed prices and price lists. They can be minimized by emphasizing pricing discipline and tighter controls. Here the sales department has a key role to play. It should keep customers informed of price changes, especially prior to the shipment of goods. Another remedy would be an audit system to review invoices at random against current pricing and billing information; any errors would be brought to the attention of the department involved. This helps billing department personnel recognize and correct such inaccuracies, and minimizes the chance that they will be repeated.

Order Entry/Editing. Problems in this area can be alleviated by having employees pay more attention to the purchase order detail—checking nonstandard items, determining proper method of transportation, and providing the proper documentation. Moreover, they should check to see if a resale permit is required where the sales and use tax is in question. On the selling end, sales personnel should submit all orders in writing and review them for corrections before submitting them. A purchase order should be mandatory; if there is not sufficient time to obtain a purchase order, the order can be entered into the system but customer confirmation requested. Where the order entry system is computerized, closer supervision of keypunch personnel would be required if keypunch errors are numerous. These recommendations will increase the likelihood that information entered through the order entry system is accurate.

Billing/Invoicing. Periodic audits of random samples of invoices to compare them with pricing and billing information will help detect problem areas in billing and invoicing. Coordination between sales and billing can be improved so that all allowances are reflected in price lists. A built-in expiration date can stop automated billing when sales contracts expire. Late billings should be avoided so customers will get their invoices on time.

Shipping. The customer's purchase order should be checked carefully to make sure that the correct materials are shipped, that the material is shipped to the proper location, and that on-time delivery is possible. If there are any problems, the shipping department should be made aware of them.

Overages/Shortages. This problem, which also affects inventory and stock records, can be alleviated by having the distribution people note any shortages or overages on the invoices, or by installing a system which permits invoicing only of the actual amount of product shipped. Better supervision of shipping and loading personnel is also required when this is a chronic problem.

Warehousing/Loading Practices. Continuous efforts should be made to educate warehouse personnel to the peculiarities of a company's product. For example, the method used to strap palletized shipments should be investigated so that the shifting of ladings can be prevented.

Warranty/Maintenance. In order to minimize the deductions incorrectly taken for repairs, customers should be clearly informed as to which services are being performed under warranty and those for which they will be billed.

New Orders from Overdue Accounts

Most organizations have a rather well-defined policy on handling additional business from overdue customers. This policy should be made known to the sales representatives and in some cases to the slow-paying customers themselves. Many times there are past-due invoices from financially sound customers. The problems arise, however, when dealing with marginal accounts.

When a new order is shipped before past-due items have been paid, it may be advisable to inform the customer that an exception has been made. On the other hand, if the situation is serious, holding orders can sometimes give considerable leverage to collection of an older open item. Under such circumstances, it is important to advise both the sales representative and the customer that the new order will not be shipped until the outstanding items have been paid. Failure to communicate the fact can do more to damage the long-term relationship than the actual holding up of the order. This is another situation which requires tact and a predetermined understanding with the sales organization. It is not easy, but somewhere there is a point at which nonshipment of additional orders is the best course of action.

N.S.F. Checks

When a depository bank advises that a customer's check has failed to clear because of insufficient funds, there are well-defined steps to take. Most simply, the check can be redeposited in the expectation that the funds will now be in the customer's account. Sometimes the customer is asked for a replacement check that is deposited as a new item. In a third, more formal method, the check is endorsed specially for payment to the bank on which it is drawn. This is done by typing on the reverse side of the check "Pay to the order of the (*customer's*) Bank," followed by the signature of the creditor company. The check is next sent to the customer's bank, together with a letter advising that the enclosed check is being sent as a collection item and the reason for such action—for example, notice of default. Usually the bank is instructed to attempt to clear the check, holding it for a week or ten days and forwarding the proceeds to the creditor when collected; or the creditor may request to be advised by collect telegram in a specified number of days if the item remains unpaid.

At the same time that the check is sent directly to the bank as a collection item, the customer is contacted by letter, phone, or wire to stress the urgency of making prompt arrangements for its bank to clear the check when it is received again. If the matter is handled by telephone, a confirming letter should be sent. Serious financial impairment is indicated if the check continues unpaid; it signals the need for legal action by the creditor.

SPECIAL COLLECTION EFFORTS

The vast majority of customers pay their accounts promptly, but a troublesome minority will not pay within terms and will not respond to any ordinary followup. These demand some form of special collection effort.

It is well for the creditor to keep in mind that receipt of payment is the primary objective, but retaining the good will of the customer is also important. Therefore, the request for payment must be firm yet polite. The creditor's attitude may change if the customer's excuses seem unwarranted. At that point, the goal is to salvage the money rather than to continue any sales relationship.

When Special Efforts Begin

While there is no fixed time to begin special efforts, certain types of situations call for them: lack of response to normal collection reminders, special circumstances that occur infrequently, and a customer's request for a time extension.

Lack of Customer Response.   Some customers throw collection letters into the waste basket; others hesitate to write and explain their difficulties; and still others will readily admit their obligation and assert their willingness to settle the amount, but they just do not have the means and cannot promise payment by a particular time. When they do not respond to collection followup, it becomes necessary to take more drastic action.

Special Circumstances.   Information may come to the credit department of a catastrophe, such as a fire, flood, or explosion, which has seriously damaged or destroyed the customer's physical plant. In that case, it is necessary to consider all the circumstances—the past performance of the customer, future possibilities, and the extent of insurance coverage—in order to arrange for extension and orderly liquidation of the account.

Damage caused by flood, for example, is seldom covered by regular insurance, and often a part of the amount is forgiven. The good will generated by this action will usually benefit the creditor company in the long run. This is not merely a credit problem but one which may seriously affect the entire business; therefore, a solution should not be reached without consulting the managers of other functions or departments.

Other special circumstances may affect the condition of the account, all of which require special collection effort: a serious financial loss caused by theft or embezzlement or bad debts; inventory loss due to market decline; unexpected tax liabilities; lease liabilities; cancellation or renegotiation of government contracts; and intangible liabilities such as damage claims or the customer's difficulties with its own customers. All of these situations require individual analysis and possible granting of a time extension for payment.

Another class of delinquent accounts requires fuller investigation than an ordinary past due. Changes adversely affecting the management of the business—some of which may not appear on the surface—require thorough understanding. In a small business, for example, the death of an important customer might not only affect the possibilities of collecting from a past-due account but future business prospects as well. The same point might apply to a change in the personal habits of the owners or members of management (drinking, gambling, or marital troubles). Any of these factors can eventually ruin a business unless corrected. If corrective measures are not taken, the best course is to salvage the past-due account without delay. On the other hand, if there has been a payment delay because of a change in ownership, loss of skilled personnel, or other factors, the long-term effects of such change on the business must be studied before a decision is made. A short extension may convert the account into a good-paying customer.

Request for Time Extension. A customer will sometimes ask for more time to pay a bill. The ordinary inclination is to grant a short extension. If a longer extension is requested and investigation reveals that it is justified, the credit executive should seek to protect the company and yet grant the request.

A sound approach is to devise some type of informal arrangement that will work out the account. For instance, it is practical to add a percentage of the amount owed to each subsequent shipment and to send the shipments on a cash basis; the additional payments reduce the old amount until it is paid in full.

Where there is a temporary reason for the past-due account, it may be useful to ship merchandise equal in value to the amount outstanding, provided that cash payment is made at the time of shipment. The payments are applied to the oldest item, and the account does not become further delinquent.

Losses which are sometimes more serious in nature can be caused by deficiencies in management or poor selling practices. For instance, some customers may sell to too many marginal accounts; others may place too many goods on consignment; still others may give terms that are too long. Before giving an extension of time to an overdue account, the creditor should try to determine whether the weakness has been corrected. If it has not, the customer will continue to have difficulties. The collector might just as well decide that the account is at best a salvage account, and press vigorously and immediately for payment.

In some cases, it may become necessary to operate under a note arrangement or to set aside past-due amounts, and continue to sell on a current basis with current shipments paid for on regular terms. Since more than one creditor is usually involved, this arrangement may cast the customer as a financially distressed debtor. Voluntary settlements of this nature that are geared to rehabilitating debtors or methods designed to put them out of business are discussed in Chapter 34.

Collection by Third Parties

When other efforts have failed, it would be prudent to use outside collection sources. They can be extremely helpful but should be selected with care. Even though the customer has failed to settle the account, the creditor may still desire to keep its good will and to sell to the customer on a cash basis. Therefore, careful consideration should be given to the kind of impression third parties will make on the customer.

Collection Agencies. The creditor should investigate collection agencies carefully before deciding to use the services of any specific one, because they vary in efficiency and responsibility. Some charge a subscription, while others charge only a portion of the amount collected. The services offered to claimants range from simple demand letters and personal contacts to a comprehensive series of collection steps. Some agencies specialize in particular industries; others will accept accounts from every type of manufacturer or wholesaler.

Collection and adjustment bureaus of the National Association of Credit Management locals are extremely effective. As an independent organization, Dun & Bradstreet operates an efficient mercantile claims division which handles the collection of accounts. Some trade associations and credit insurance companies also maintain a collection service. In addition, there are many independent collection agencies located throughout the country.

The collection and adjustment bureaus of the NACM are available to all of its members. When the NACM approves a collection and adjustment bureau, the member can be assured that all its employees are bonded and that remittances will be made promptly on all collected claims. Approved collection bureaus are located in all principal cities, and these together with attorneys skilled in commercial collection work are able to offer nationwide service, often including a free demand period. This is a period of time, usually 10 days, within which no fee is charged if the customer pays. Thoroughly experienced, qualified personnel are used; files of all claims are open for inspection at any time; and all monies collected are placed in special trust accounts. Below is described a typical, comprehensive collection service.

Procedure. When a claimant wishes to turn over an account for collection, an account placement form, similar to that shown in Figure 14–2, is completed. The name and address of the debtor are filled in by the creditor. The contract between the creditor and the collection agency is usually shown on the reverse side of the collection blank, which is the authorization for the collection agency to act in this case. The form provides space for additional instructions and for the creditor's signature. A ledger statement or invoice usually accompanies the collection form.

In making collections, the agency attempts to salvage some of the customer's good will toward the creditor company. This can best be done in the early stages of collection. If the collection procedure has progressed into the final stages, however, there is not much hope to retain good will. By then the important thing is to make the collection. This is a fair procedure for all concerned. If there is little likelihood that the debtor would remain a customer, the best that can be hoped for is that the outstanding amount will be collected.

The services offered by collection agencies can be custom-fitted to the needs of their clients. In most instances, specific combination of services can be requested by the creditor. When a claim is received, most agencies set up a file and make a phone call to the debtor on the first day, regardless of the debtor's location or the amount involved. Letters are used only if the

NACM COLLECTION CONTROL PROGRAM
ACCOUNT PLACEMENT FORM

NATIONAL ASSOCIATION OF CREDIT MANAGEMENT—OREGON, INC.

Affiliated With The National Association of Credit Management

937 S.W. 14th Avenue
Portland, Oregon 97205 • 226-3531

PLEASE COLLECT AMOUNT REPRESENTED BY THE ATTACHED STATEMENT

Debtor ______ Amount ______

Address ______ Telephone ______

City, State, Zip Code ______

Party to Contact ______ Title ______

Banks With ______

☐ SOLE OWNER

☐ CORPORATION

☐ PARTNERSHIP
(List Names of Principals)

Names of Principals ______

Recommendations and Remarks ______

PLEASE CHECK TYPE OF SERVICE DESIRED: ☐ IMMEDIATE ACTION ☐ ATTORNEY SERVICE ☐ FREE DIRECT DEMAND

Creditor ______ Phone ______

Address ______

By ______ Date ______

WE AGREE TO NOTIFY OACM PROMPTLY OF ANY PAYMENTS OR RESPONSES FROM DEBTOR SINCE COMMISSIONS ARE BASED ON THE DATE OACM RECEIVES NOTIFICATION.

CHECK FOR MORE OF: THESE PLACEMENT FORMS; PAST DUE REMINDERS; PRE-COLLECTION LETTER NOTICES; FREE DIRECT DEMAND NOTICES; DIRECT PAYMENT CONFIRMATION NOTICES

FIG. 14–2. Account Placement Form.

agency is unable to contact the debtor by phone after repeated attempts. It is significant to note that collection actions are not a series of steps but a variety of options that can be taken. These are now discussed briefly.

1. *Free demand letter.* This is a tactful request for immediate payment of the obligation, written on the stationery of the collection agency. It stipulates that the creditor *intends* to assign the account for collection. There is

no charge for results obtained within a specified time limit, usually 10 days (see Figure 14–3).

Re: #_____–_____– $____

Your creditor intends to assign this past-due account for collection to this office unless it is paid within TEN DAYS.

This association is mutually owned by the principal manufacturers, wholesalers, distributors, and bankers of this area, and is an affiliate of the National Association of Credit Management. We perform specific functions for member firms which includes the collection of their past-due accounts.

In the absence of any word from you, we will assume the amount is correct and will be paid. Please mail your check in full to this office.

FIG. 14–3.   Free Demand Letter.

2. Initial agency letter.   After the free demand period has expired, a letter indicating that the account *has been referred* to the collection agency is sent, as if it had already accepted the account for collection. Stronger in tone than the free demand letter, it indicates to the debtor that the collection bureau is determined to obtain payment (see Figure 14–4).

Re: _____

THE ABOVE ACCOUNT
HAS BEEN RECEIVED FOR IMMEDIATE COLLECTION

This account is seriously past due and must have your immediate attention. Your creditor has instructed us to take whatever action is necessary to enforce collection.

If you wish to cooperate:

    1. Place a check or money order, payable to your creditor, in the enclosed reply envelope and mail it to us today. . . . . . .

                or

    2. Contact us at once to make arrangements for payment.
Your cooperation will help us to conclude this matter amicably and fairly.

Yours truly,

FIG. 14–4.   Initial Agency Letter.

3. *Final notice letter.*   This demand for payment requires an immediate response from the debtor to avoid possible litigation (see Figure 14–5).

Re: _____

Every opportunity has been given to you to pay this account in a reasonable and businesslike manner.

Unless this account is paid in full within *TEN DAYS*, legal action, with resulting court costs, could be commenced by your creditor without further notice to you.

The enclosed envelope is available for your immediate response if you desire to avoid possible litigation. Make your check payable to your creditor and mail it to this office AT ONCE.

This is our FINAL NOTICE.

Yours truly,

FIG 14–5.   Final Demand Letter.

4. *Telegraphic demand.*   Collection telegrams are used where they are warranted. Usually the account must be of some minimum stated amount ($200, for example) before collection telegrams are sent. This limit is set because the charges of the telegram are assumed by the collection bureau. Although the telegram may be sent immediately, its normal use is as a followup to one or more demand letters.

5. *"One day emergency demand."*   In special circumstances, particularly where the amount involved is sizable, collection bureaus can offer this type of service. A personal presentation is made to the debtor within a very short period, usually one day after receipt of the account. The results are immediately reported to the claimant. The normal followup to this step is attorney service.

6. *Attorney service.*   If the collection efforts of the agency are unsuccessful, it will forward the account to an attorney for legal action upon the approval of such action by the creditor. Should that be done, the agency may continue to act as agent and correspondent of the creditor in channeling information, securing reports, and transmitting the proceeds of collection.

If the client instructs the collection agency to proceed with attorney service, the attorney will first attempt to collect the account amicably and without suit. Should the efforts be unsuccessful and the account is brought to court, the claimant is usually required to advance court costs and the attorney's suit fee. These are in addition to the normal commission.

Collection Bureau Charges.   These are based on the amount placed for collection. For commercial accounts, the charge is based on a percentage of the amount collected by the bureau and on the stage at which it was collected.

Charges normally are contingent upon collection. Accounts which appear uncollectible are returned after collection has been attempted. A full report accompanies the returned accounts.

Collection by Attorneys. Instead of using a collection agency, the creditor can submit a delinquent account to an attorney for appropriate action. The names of lawyers specializing in collection work can be obtained from various "attorney's lists." Usually an attorney can be selected who is located in the customer's community, and therefore may be in a better position to win the customer's confidence and work out some form of settlement. If the delinquent customer does not respond, the attorney has the additional advantage of being able to institute legal action immediately.

At the time a suit is initiated, the creditor can assist the attorney by furnishing the records that will be needed:

1. A sworn affidavit of account, which sets out the state in which the company is incorporated, if it is a corporation; or the names of the partners, if it is a partnership.
2. The original note, if the account is on a note.
3. Copies of each outstanding invoice and an itemized statement of account.

If court action becomes necessary, the company's books of original entry—the first place that a charge appears upon the company's records—will also be needed. These may take the form of the purchase order, shipping list, or invoice upon which the pricing is done. Either the individual who made the entries or the individual in charge of the department should be ready to testify that the charges were made at the time indicated and that the entries are correct. It is also necessary to prove the reasonableness of the charges by establishing that the charge for any particular item was reasonable as compared with charges made for similar items by other concerns. In some instances, it may be necessary to prove delivery. In general, the lawyer's case can be no stronger than the facts presented, and the attorney must depend upon the client to provide all the essential data.

Before a suit comes to trial, the creditor may receive an offer of compromise. The decision to accept or reject the offer requires careful consideration. Obviously the creditor does not wish to give merchandise away to the delinquent debtor. On the other hand, the advantages of a reasonable pretrial settlement should be weighed against the requirements of a trial—the time it will take, the expense of providing witnesses, and the higher legal fees involved. All the facts should be considered before it is decided to continue with the suit.

Even when the case goes to trial and a judgment is obtained, voluntary payment does not necessarily follow. The lawyer may have to order an execution, so that the property can be sold if necessary to satisfy the judgment. To assure prompt action and maximum salvage, the creditor should provide its lawyer with all available information regarding the assets of the debtor.

LEGAL ASPECTS OF COLLECTION CORRESPONDENCE

The legal aspects of the exchange of credit information are discussed in some detail in Chapter 15. Here the main thrust is on collection correspondence.

The credit department letter writer may have good intentions, but the manner in which these intentions are expressed can subject the writer to civil liability, criminal liability, or both. Therefore, it is very important that writers of credit correspondence be aware of legal implications. In the final stages particularly, credit executives must guard against making statements which may subject them or their companies to charges of libel or extortion.

Other areas which can result in the possibility of legal implications are disclosing unfavorable information in regard to a credit inquiry—law of libel, information transmitted by word of mouth—law of slander, and acknowledgment of orders—law of contract.

Outlining the facts in an explicit manner so that no improper inferences can be drawn—and sticking strictly to the facts—will generally be a good safety guide to follow. If any doubt exists, it is best to clear these matters with legal counsel. Common sense and an appreciation of the full impact of what is being written is the best approach to the problems of credit correspondence.

Methods of Collection Subject to Libel

No collection message, letter, telegram, or postal card should contain any libelous material. Simple, true statements of fact without accusations are the only contents that make sense. In every case, it is prudent for the creditor to consult with attorney when setting up collection procedures and form letters.

Extortion

Extortion generally means an attempt by threat, force, or fear, or under the guise of official right, to collect money or property which is not legally due. An attempt to collect money legally due may result in liability, however, if the contents of a letter sent to the debtor are calculated as harassment or coercion for payment of the claim. Generally the following attempts have been considered extortionate:

1. The threat of bankruptcy.
2. The threat of criminal prosecution.
3. The threat to give an unfavorable report to members of an association.
4. The use of any document, letter, or other paper which falsely has the appearance or purports to be a court order or other legal process.

PART IV

CREDIT INVESTIGATION

CHAPTER 15

CREDIT INFORMATION

Sound credit decisions can only be made on the basis of adequate information covering the nature of the customer's business, the character of the principals, its financial condition, and other matters. If a firm previously had done business with an applicant, the information on hand must be brought up to date. If it is a new account, however, the job of collecting facts becomes more difficult. The principal sources of this information are reviewed in the following pages, after a short discussion of the confidential nature and legal aspects of exchanging credit information.

CONFIDENTIAL NATURE OF CREDIT INFORMATION

In the United States almost unlimited sources of credit information are normally available. Over the years, these sources have steadily expanded on the basis of mutual confidence and respect among credit executives themselves, and among credit executives and customers. Of primary importance in the development of these relationships has been the concept of the confidential and privileged nature of credit information. What is the nature of this relationship, and what is its practical meaning? At what point does the term "confidential" bar access to credit information? To whom may a company properly divulge credit information, and to whom should it refuse this information?

Taken in its literal meaning of "secret" or "private," a confidential relationship would prevent a company from giving any credit information about its customer to anyone. Under these conditions the free interchange of credit information could not survive. The average commercial credit user today is quite aware of the interchange of credit information. Therefore, it might be more accurate to say that customer information is held in trust, rather than on a confidential basis, by the credit department. The customer knows that credit departments will only release factual credit information to other creditors that have a legitimate interest. The customer trusts the good judgment of the credit department personnel in knowing to whom they may release information and how much information may be properly divulged. Most customers realize this relationship makes credit easier to obtain, and available in larger amounts and with less delay. They also appreciate that the record of their creditworthiness will follow them wherever they go.

Credit information must not be released to unauthorized companies, agencies, and others; further, it must be kept confidential within the organization itself. A policy should be established as to who may have access to the credit files. This policy must be adapted to the size of the organization, the extent and nature of information contained in the files, and the use to be made of it. It is conceivable that an untrained person could seriously jeopardize the relationship between the customer and the company, and even subject the company to a lawsuit, by unwarranted or unguarded revelations of information which the customer might consider detrimental to its situation, reputation, or character. It is most important therefore that all persons dealing with credit inquiries be properly indoctrinated in credit ethics and principles.

LEGAL ASPECTS OF THE EXCHANGE OF CREDIT INFORMATION

It should be stressed that the exchange of factual credit experience information is legal and proper, but the information exchanged should be restricted to factual information. The courts of the United States have recognized in numerous decisions the legitimate business interest in the exchange of factual credit information among businesses with legitimate interests. As early as 1925 the U.S. Supreme Court held that:

> . . . the gathering and dissemination of information which will enable sellers to prevent a perpetration of fraud upon them, which information they are free to act upon or not as they choose, cannot be held to be an unlawful restraint upon commerce, even though, in the ordinary course of business, most sellers would act upon the information . . . (*Cement Manufacturers Protective Association vs. United States, 268 US 588, 603–604*)

In a 1976 case, the U.S. Court of Appeals for New York commented on the exchange of credit information as follows:

> Unlike exchanges regarding prices which usually serve no purpose other than to suppress competition, and hence fall within the ban of the Sherman Act . . . the dissemination of information concerning the creditworthiness of customers aids sellers in gaining information necessary to protect themselves against fraudulent or insolvent customers . . . Given the legitimate function of such data, it is not a violation of the Sherman Act to exchange such information, provided that any action taken in reliance upon it is the result of each firm's independent judgment, and not of agreement. (*Michelman vs. Clark Schwebel Fibre Glass Corp., 534 F 2nd 1036*)

Conspiracy

While the courts, in these cases and others, have held the exchange of factual credit information to be legal and proper, any agreement between competitors on any action concerning a common customer or class of customers is clearly illegal. Such an illegal agreement, or conspiracy, could be an agreement not to do business with a certain customer or class of customers; or it could be an agreement on terms to be offered to a customer or class of customers. Thus, while exchange of factual information about the credit experience with customers is perfectly proper, care should be taken that no agreements are made for any common action, nor should there be any effort made to influence the credit decision of another credit executive.

Libel and Slander

When exchanging information, credit executives must also be aware of the danger of defamation. Defamation is a communication to a third party or parties which tends to injure reputation in the popular sense: to diminish the esteem, respect, good will, or confidence in which a subject is held; or to cause adverse, derogatory, or unpleasant feelings or opinions against the subject. The form of the communication is not important so long as a defamatory meaning is conveyed.

The broad term defamation includes two types—libel and slander. Libel usually refers to written communications, such as newspapers, magazines, books, or credit reports. Slander usually refers to the spoken word, to statements made in some meeting or public forum or to third parties.

The essential elements for an action in libel are a false, defamatory statement and its publication, causing the person defamed to be shunned, ridiculed, or held in contempt by the community at large. The decision in a particular case can vary from state to state since it is governed by state law. Some statements are libelous *per se*—that is, actionable in themselves or damaging on their face; consequently, in such cases proof of pecuniary loss is not necessary. Other statements may be libelous in some instances but not in others; damages do not necessarily follow from their publication as in statements that are libelous *per se*. In these cases actual damage to the person libeled must be proved.

It is not defamatory to say that a subject is dead, is overly cautious with money, has led an eventful life, is a labor agitator, or owes money. These statements lack the element of personal disgrace necessary for defamation in the eyes of the law. It is defamatory in the legal sense to say that a subject has committed suicide; refuses to pay just debts; or is a scoundrel, crook, liar, oppressive, or dishonorable—because all of these obviously tend to adversely affect the esteem in which the subject is held by neighbors and business associates.

The law has always been very protective of the reputation of businesses and business individuals, and the law of defamation does extend to the protection of the reputation of business firms. Business firms are regarded as having no reputation in any personal sense. Thus firms cannot be defamed by words, such as those imputing unchastity, which would affect the purely personal repute of an individual. But a corporation, partnership, or other business entity has prestige and standing in the business community—and language which casts aspersions upon a firm's honesty, credit, financial standing, efficiency, or other business character may be defamatory. A statement that a business "refuses to pay its bills" or that a firm is "insolvent" (unless it is an established fact) obviously damages that business firm in the business community and may be subject to a charge of defamation.

The question of a standard by which defamation may be determined has been a difficult one. However, legislatures, in passing state laws, and the courts, in applying those laws, have recognized that a person or business firm may suffer real damages by being lowered in the esteem of any substantial and respectable group, especially when that group may represent suppliers.

While it is proper to pass on to another supplier information that is of public record, such as the filing of liens, legal actions, or criminal convictions, such information should not be reported with any malicious intent. Continuous reference to a person's unfavorable past history, for instance, could hinder a person with such a record from being reestablished in society. This is especially pertinent where many years of good conduct have ensued, or where nothing either good or bad is definitely known about the intervening years.

Matter Libelous Per Se. Generally, matter libelous per se is any written words which falsely suggest a criminal act or immorality, or which tend to deprive a person in business of public confidence and esteem. It has been ruled that the following are libelous per se:

1. To charge by letter that a person is a swindler, or knowingly made false representation with intent to deceive, or is lacking of veracity.
2. To publish a false statement imputing insolvency to a merchant or trader.
3. To charge falsely that a person has failed in business or has made an assignment for the benefit of creditors.
4. To publish that a merchant has not succeeded in obtaining the implicit confidence of local people, and is looked on locally as an itinerant trader of small financial responsibility and uncertain prospects.
5. To charge in writing that a business individual is embarrassed, inferring insolvency or lack of creditworthiness.

The charge need not be made in a direct, positive, and open manner. If the words used, taken in their ordinarily accepted sense, convey a degrading imputation—no matter how indirectly—they are libelous. A letter that states a particular debtor has not paid debts which are owing and past due is not libelous, if true. But if the letter imputes insolvency, bankruptcy, or lack of credit on the basis of this fact, it becomes libelous.

Publication. The second element essential to an action in libel is publication, which means communication of the libel to some third person.

Communication to the defamed person alone is not actionable because no third person has learned of the defamatory matter; consequently, there is no possible injury to the defamed party's reputation. If the defamed person, moreover, exhibits the defamatory matter to a third person, there is no publication for which the writer is liable, since the defamed person's own act is the cause of the injury. If the writer reads the defamatory matter to a third party, however, before sending it to the defamed person, there is a publication—that is, a slander.

Defenses to Charges of Libel.   Truth is a complete defense to an action in libel and must be so pleaded. Where several statements are published, however, only some of which are true, the defamer does not escape liability. Despite adhering to the truth, a writer must be wary that a letter does not become libelous through imputation of facts which are not true.

Some defamatory statements are not actionable as libel because they are privileged communications: statements made by one person in pursuance of a duty to another person having a corresponding duty or interest. Such privilege is conditional, however, in that a community of interest must exist and must be exercised in good faith; malicious intent or a wanton and reckless disregard of the defamed person's rights will destroy the privilege. A person bringing suit must prove the existence of malice in order to sustain the action.

The courts have considered the following as privileged communications:

1. Statements made by a former employer whose name has been given as a reference to a prospective employer of an employee.
2. Communications between creditors of the same debtor in reference to their respective claims.
3. Communications by banks, such as a statement as to the financial standing of a person offered as a surety.

SALES REQUESTS FOR CREDIT INFORMATION

Sales representatives, the company's first contact with a new customer and the most frequent contact with an established customer, are an excellent potential source of credit information. While some may not be suited by temperament, interest, or experience, and may feel imposed upon when asked to perform credit or collection functions, they nevertheless must be made aware of how important they can be to the credit department.

Sales representatives should be trained to submit credit applications with all prospective accounts, new accounts, or both (see Figure 15-1). Sales department credit forms vary considerably in their scope. The form shown in Figure 15-1 is prepared in triplicate: the first copy is sent to the credit department, the sales representative keeps the second, and the third goes to the sales-service department. Most firms and individuals are conditioned to the necessity of furnishing credit and financial information to support credit transactions, and generally this will be given freely.

FORM NO. 1-424 (REV. 2/70)

SALES REQUEST FOR CREDIT INFORMATION

Union Camp CORPORATION

DATE _____

NAME _____

STREET ADDRESS _____

CITY _____ STATE _____ ZIP CODE _____

TO: CREDIT DEPARTMENT WAYNE, N.J.

TRADE STYLE (IF DIFFERENT) _____

SALESMAN   No.

SALES OFFICE   SOR No.

HEADQUARTERS ADDRESS (IF DIFFERENT) _____

NAME OF OWNER OR PRINCIPAL _____

DIVISION

ESTIMATE OF CREDIT LINE REQUIRED $ _____   ESTIMATE OF ANNUAL UNION CAMP SALES $ _____

PURPOSE OF INQUIRY

FOR USE OF CREDIT DEPARTMENT

☐ NEW ACCOUNT INITIAL ORDER $ _____

☐ PROSPECT – SHOULD WE SOLICIT

D & B _____

SPECIFIC INFORMATION DESIRED:

☐ PROSPECT – POSSIBLE ORDER $ _____

BANK _____

CR. INT. _____

FILL IN BANK AND THREE TRADE REFERENCES AND ADDRESSES

	NAME	STREET	CITY	STATE	ZIP CODE
BANK					
TRADE					
TRADE					
TRADE					

CREDIT DEPARTMENT REPLY   ONLY CREDIT LINE WILL BE GIVEN UNLESS SPECIFIC INFORMATION IS REQUESTED ABOVE   **CREDIT LINE** _____ **DATE** _____

FIG. 15–1. Sales Request for Credit Information

Some sales personnel are provided with balance sheet forms to be left for the customer to complete and mail direct to the credit department. Frequently, however, it is desirable to have sales representatives bring in the completed form. Also, without asking questions, sales representatives can obtain a great deal of information by keeping their eyes and ears open. They can judge the location and appearance of the place of business and the presence or absence of competition. They can observe the names of other brands and products carried and the personalities of employees and of management. To obtain the full benefit of the sales representatives' observations, a spirit of mutual confidence and cooperation must be developed between the sales and credit departments. Through frequent calls on customers, salespeople may receive early news of changes in sales trends, collections, or movement of inventory. When changes such as those listed in Figure 15–2 are promptly reported, the credit executive can be alerted to investigate further.

```
Dealer _____
Address _____ Town _____
  1.  Sold Out to _____ Date Effective _____
      Address _____
      Has New Owner Submitted Financial Statement?  Yes _____
      No _____
      If Not, When Will It Be Submitted? _____
  2.  Contemplating Selling—To Whom? _____
                                When? _____
  3.  Change in Partnership (List New Partner) _____
  4.  Moving to New Location (Give New Address) _____
  5.  Death of Proprietor or Partner (Remarks) _____
  6.  Neglecting Business (Remarks) _____
  7.  Closed for Sustained Periods (Remarks) _____
  8.  Being Pressed by Collectors (Remarks) _____
  9.  General Remarks, Complaints, etc. _____
      _____
      _____
      _____
      _____

Date _____ Sales Representative _____
```

FIG. 15–2. Sales Representative's Report of Changes in Established Accounts.

CUSTOMER-SUPPLIED INFORMATION

There is no better source of information about a business than the business itself. Direct contact with the principals provides the credit executive with financial details, bank and trade references, and other information of importance. How this information is requested and obtained will depend upon the time available, the location of the customer, the relative importance of the credit exposure, and the degree of cooperation which can be obtained from the customer.

Regulation B, Equal Credit Opportunity Act

In soliciting information direct from customers, the credit executive should be aware of the Equal Credit Opportunity Act. Although this is primarily a federal consumer law, some provisions under Regulation B do apply to business credit. Some of these provisions concern information requested from credit applicants:

1. The business credit grantor may request the marital status (but not the sex) of the applicant (the consumer credit grantor is not allowed to do this).

2. Creditors may not make any oral or written statement, in advertising or otherwise, to applicants or prospective applicants that would discourage on a prohibited basis (sex, marital status, race, color, religion, national origin, or age) a reasonable person from making or pursuing an application for credit.

3. Creditors may not request any information about the spouse or former spouse of the applicant unless that spouse or former spouse will be permitted to use the account or will be contractually liable for the account, and they are restricted from asking whether any income stated in an application is derived from alimony, child support, or separate maintenance.

4. Creditors may not inquire about birth control practices, capability or intent to bear children, race, color, religion, or national origin of any applicant or any other person in connection with a credit application.

Information Required

Direct contact offers many advantages. It can establish a close and friendly working relationship and build mutual confidence and respect. In addition to providing access to information, direct contact can be used to clarify terms of sale and clear the way for a continuing relationship with the customer. Much will depend upon the timing of such contact. If done early, the credit executive will not have to break down a barrier of misunderstanding at a later date.

The facts provided by the customer can be used for further investigation. These would include:

1. *Full, correct, and legal firm name.* This establishes the legal responsibility of the debtor and must be known exactly when the credit executive checks the account with the bank reference or searches state and local records. It prevents mistaking the account for another, perhaps well-known, business. Thus it is important to know the precise legal name of a corporate entity and whether or not it is "Corporation," "Corp." "Incorporated," "Inc.," "Limited," or "Ltd."

2. *Correct address of the business, including branch locations.* When shipments of merchandise are made out-of-town, the credit department can check to see if the ship-to address is bona fide.

3. *Names of all the principals in the company.* This will help the credit executive to determine the business histories of the individuals who control the business. Investigation in the department's own files or in other sources will help to establish the business reputation of the principals.

4. *Distribution of ownership.* This information enables credit personnel to establish who controls the business. It will uncover fronts set up by individuals of unsavory character to avoid having their names associated with the business. A reluctance to disclose this hidden ownership or an evasive answer to a direct question about ownership puts the experienced investigator on guard.

5. *Financial information.* The account may be asked directly for its latest balance sheet and operating statement. Statements should be current, to reflect the financial condition of the firm at the time it is placing its order.

6. *Contemplated changes.* Direct questioning of the principals can elicit information about contemplated changes. They may include changes in ownership, line of business, method of operation, and financial information since the last financial statements.

7. *References.* The principals should not be reluctant to submit business and banking references, since this is a normally accepted part of the credit investigation. The references should be contacted for credit information. At the same time, they could be asked for additional leads.

8. *Auditor.* The name of the auditing firm should be obtained along with permission to discuss the customer's financial condition.

Direct Correspondence

Effective credit department correspondence, like any other form of communication, is the art of impressing and influencing others favorably just as is selling, public speaking, advertising, or any other form of human persuasion. It is the most common basis for contact with all customers, and is used at every stage.

Opening Accounts. This timing in the customer-seller relationship presents an excellent opportunity to set a tone that will keep the customer providing credit information.

1. *Order acknowledgement.* The most economical and convenient means of establishing contact with a new customer may well be a friendly letter which requests information in addition to acknowledging and approving an initial order (see Figure 15–3). A letter of this type, giving honest recognition to the credit standing which the customer has already established in other places, can build mutual respect and good will in the very process of obtaining information.

Even when the seller is not ready to inform the customer that the order has been approved, it may be desirable to acknowledge receipt of the order and to list the seller's terms and other conditions. If the customer is of questionable credit standing, the acknowledgement should be confined to a simple statement that the order has been received; no commitment to accept the order or ship the material on a credit basis should be implied.

Gentlemen:

We certainly appreciate your order No. 756 for approximately 60 tons of continuous weld pipe.

It is a pleasure to inform you that your pipe is being shipped based on the generally favorable information received through commercial agency sources.

Our terms are net 30 days, however, you may elect to earn a discount of 1% if you choose to pay in this manner:

Invoices Dated	Payable
1st to 15th	25th
16th to 31st	10th Prox.

While your first order was approved promptly to avoid causing you delay, we would appreciate your sending us in confidence a copy* of your latest audited balance sheet and operating statement, and any other information you feel may be helpful, for the completion of our credit file.

We hope sincerely that this will be the beginning of a long, most pleasant, and mutually profitable relationship.

                                                    Cordially,

---

*Other options, depending on status of customer, anticipated volume, and credit exposure:
(1) Copy of your latest audit including the supporting schedules.
(2) The attached financial statement form completely filled out. (See Figures 15–4 and 15–5.)

FIG. 15–3.   Letter to New Customer Requesting Information.

2. *Request for financial statements.* The financial statement form published by the National Association of Credit Management, shown in Figure 15–4, can be sent with the letter; when filled out and returned, it will provide the creditor with essential information about the customer. A simplified financial statement form, shown in Figure 15–5, is particularly suited to moderate-sized businesses. When additional information is required at a later date from an established customer, a letter such as the model in Figure 15–6 has proved to be quite effective.

Enclosing a financial statement blank with the order acknowledgement serves several purposes. It reveals to the customer that supplying financial information is indeed a common practice; it makes it easier to comply with the request; and it helps ensure that all information desired by the credit department will be submitted. (The use of a standardized form also makes

(THIS FORM APPROVED AND PUBLISHED BY THE NATIONAL ASSOCIATION OF CREDIT MANAGEMENT)   Form 4

FINANCIAL STATEMENT OF

Date_____19____

FIRM NAME_____

Street _____City_____ State_____Zip _____

At close of business on _____19_____

ISSUED TO_____   [NAME OF FIRM
                                                      [Requesting Statement.

[PLEASE ANSWER ALL QUESTIONS. WHEN NO FIGURES ARE INSERTED, WRITE WORD "NONE"]

BALANCE SHEET

ASSETS	Dollars	Cents	LIABILITIES	Dollars	Cents
Cash in Bank and on hand			Accounts Payable		
Accounts Receivable			Notes Payable — Unsecured:		
Notes and Trade Acceptances Receivable			Banks		
Merchandise Inventory (Do not include Mer-			Partners or Officers		
chandise on Consignment)			Other		
Other Current Assets (Describe)			Notes Payable — Secured:		
			Owing to		
			Taxes Payable or Accrued:		
			Withholding and Payroll		
			Federal and State Income		
			Other		
TOTAL CURRENT ASSETS			Accrued Payroll and Other Expense		
Land and Buildings (Depreciated Value)			Other Current }		
Machinery, Fixtures and Equipment (Depreciated			Liabilities (Describe) }		
Value)			TOTAL CURRENT LIABILITIES		
Due from Others — Not Current (Describe)			Mortgage on Land and Buildings		
			Liens on Merchandise or Equipment		
Other Assets (Describe)			Other Liabilities (Describe)		
			TOTAL LIABILITIES		
			Capital { Capital Stock $ _____ }		
			{ Surplus $		
TOTAL ASSETS			TOTAL LIABILITIES AND CAPITAL		

SUMMARY OF SURPLUS (or of NET WORTH if not Incorporated)

Surplus (or Net Worth at beginning of period) Dated_____19____	$_____
Add — Profit for Period $_____ and Adjustments $_____	$_____
TOTAL ADDITIONS	$_____
Deduct — Loss for Period $_____ and Dividends (or Withdrawals, if not incorporated) $_____	
TOTAL DEDUCTIONS	$_____
SURPLUS (or NET WORTH) in Statement Above	$_____

STATEMENT OF PROFIT AND LOSS FOR PERIOD FROM_____TO_____

			DETAILS OF EXPENSE		
1. NET SALES			Salaries — Officers or Owners		
(Cash $ _____) (Credit $ _____)			Employees		
2. Inventory — Beginning $			Rent		
3. Purchases $			Heat, Light, Other Occupancy Expense		
4. Total (Item 2 plus Item 3) $			Advertising		
5. Deduct Inventory — Close $			Interest		
6. COST OF SALES			Taxes, except Income Taxes		
7. GROSS PROFIT			Depreciation. (Fixtures, Trucks, etc.)		
8. Less Total Expense			All other Expense		
Other Additions and Deductions			TOTAL EXPENSE		
9. Profit Before Income Taxes					
10. Less — Income Taxes					
11. NET PROFIT After Taxes			Continued on Reverse Side ➞		

FIG. 15–4.   Financial Statement Form.

LIST PRINCIPAL SUPPLIERS AND BANKS

NAMES	ADDRESSES

Amount you are liable for as endorser, guarantor, surety
$___

Amount of merchandise held on consignment
$___

Amount of current assets pledged
$___

Amount of Taxes past due
$___

Monthly payment on equipment lease or conditional sale contracts
$___

Latest year income tax examined___

Date of latest physical inventory___

Date of latest audit___

Date business established___

If premises leased state annual rental___

Expiration date of lease___

Are any of your assets subject to a lien under the Uniform Commercial Code? No___ Yes___ (please attach list)

DETAILS OF LAND AND BUILDINGS

DESCRIPTION & LOCATION	TITLE IN NAME OF	Cost	Accumulated Depreciation	Depreciated Cost	Assessed Value	ENCUMBRANCES Amount	To Whom

INSURANCE STATEMENT

1. Do you carry fire insurance (including extended coverage) Yes___ No___ Total Amount $___
2. Do you have periodic insurance appraisals and inventories to determine if coverage is adequate to prevent becoming co-insurer? Yes___ No___ Date of most recent appraisal___ 19___
3. Have your liability insurance limits been reviewed recently? Yes___ No___ Date of most recent review___ 19___
   ☐ If checked, please complete form below for list and description of all insurance policies.

NAME OF INSURANCE COMPANY	POLICY NUMBER	EXPIRATION DATE	DESCRIPTION OF COVERAGE	AMOUNT OR LIMITS	SPECIAL FEATURES

Name and Address of Agent or Broker___

This statement has been carefully read by the undersigned (both the printed and written matter), and is, to my knowledge, in all respects complete, accurate and truthful. It discloses to you the true state of my (our) financial condition on the date indicated. Since that time there has been no material unfavorable change in my (our) financial condition, and if any such change takes place I (we) will give you notice. Until such notice is given, you are to regard this as a continuing statement. You have my (our) permission to disclose this information in confidence to others in order to facilitate the establishment of additional credit lines with them.

Name of Individual or Firm___

If Partnership, Name Partners___

If Corporation, Name Officers___

Signed by___

Title___

FIG. 15—4 (cont'd.).

analysis of information easier for the credit executive.) It is particularly advisable to send a form rather than an individually dictated questionnaire when a followup request for information is necessary to amplify items on a statement already submitted. The followup questionnaire blank may offer a general list of questions of which only those checked are to be filled in by this customer. By revealing that this type of investigation is routine enough

(This form approved and published by The National Association of Credit Management)   **FORM 8**

FINANCIAL STATEMENT OF

DATE_____19____

FIRM NAME_____

Address_____City_____

At close of business on_____19____State_____

ISSUED TO_____ ← ∰ { NAME OF FIRM
                                                                 Requesting Statement

[PLEASE ANSWER ALL QUESTIONS. WHEN NO FIGURES ARE INSERTED, WRITE WORD "NONE"]

ASSETS	Dollars	Cents	LIABILITIES	Dollars	Cents
Cash in Bank	$		Accounts Payable	$	
Cash on Hand			(For Merchandise)		
			Notes and Acceptances Payable		
Accounts Receivable			(For Merchandise)		
(Amounts Pledged $_____)			For Borrowed Money:		
Notes and Trade Acceptances Receivable			Notes Payable—Unsecured		
(Amounts Pledged $_____)					
Merchandise Inventory			Notes Payable—Secured		
(Not on Consignment or Conditional Sale)					
(Amounts Pledged $_____)			Income Taxes Payable or Owing		
Other Current Assets: (Describe)			Other Taxes, including Sales Tax, Owing		
			Rental, Payrolls, Etc., Owing		
			Other Current Liabilities: (Describe)		
TOTAL CURRENT ASSETS			TOTAL CURRENT LIABILITIES		
Land and Buildings (Depreciated Value)			Mortgage on Land and Buildings		
Leasehold Improvements (Amortized Value)			Chattel Mortgage on Merchandise or Equipment		
Machinery, Fixtures and Equipment (Depreciated Value)			Other Liabilities, Unsecured		
Due From Others — Not Customers			Other Liabilities, Secured (Describe)		
Other Assets: (Describe)			TOTAL LIABILITIES		
			Capital { Capital Stock $_____ / Surplus $_____ }		
	$			$	
TOTAL ASSETS			TOTAL LIABILITIES AND NET CAPITAL		

BUY PRINCIPALLY FROM THE FOLLOWING FIRMS:

NAMES	ADDRESSES	AMOUNT OWING
		$

THE REVERSE SIDE OF THIS FORM MUST BE COMPLETED ∰→

FIG. 15–5. Simplified Financial Statement Form.

STATEMENT OF PROFIT AND LOSS FOR PERIOD FROM_____TO_____

			DETAILS OF OPERATING EXPENSES:		$
NET SALES FOR PERIOD	$		Salaries — Officers (or owners) _____		
Cash $					
Credit $			Salaries — Employees		
Inventory at start of Period $			Rent, Heat, Light		
			(Include Amortization of Leasehold)		
Purchases for Period $____			Advertising		
TOTAL $					
Less: Inventory at			Delivery		
Close of Period $____					
			Insurance		
COST OF GOODS SOLD			Taxes, Including Sales Taxes		
GROSS PROFIT					
			Depreciation (Fixtures, Trucks, etc.)		
Less: Operating Expense			Miscellaneous (Other Operating Expenses)		
NET OPERATING PROFIT			TOTAL OPERATING EXPENSE		$
Other Additions and Deductions (net)					
			SUPPLEMENTAL INFORMATION (DETAILED)		$
NET PROFIT BEFORE FEDERAL INCOME TAXES			If Incorporated, Amount of Dividends Paid		
			Interest Paid (Expense)		$
Less: Federal Income Taxes					
NET PROFIT AFTER TAXES	$		Cash Discount Earned (Income)		$

Fire Insurance Carried: On Merchandise $_____On Furniture and Fixtures $_____Other Buildings $_____

Liability Insurance Carried On Premises $_____On Auto and Truck $_____Other Insurance (Type and Am't)_____

Name of Bank_____

Title to Business Premises is in the name of_____

If Premises leased state Annual Rental $_____Lease Expires_____

Name of Individual or Firm_____
If Partnership, name partners_____
If Corporation, name officers_____
How long established_____Previous business experience_____
_____where_____

Date of signing Statement_____ Street_____City_____State_____

Witness_____ Signed by_____
Residence Address
of Witness_____ Title_____

REMARKS: (Attach separate sheet if necessary)

FIG. 15–5 (cont'd.).

to merit a printed form, the followup blank avoids the impression that this buyer has been singled out because there is particular question about its financial strength.

Dear Mr._____:

In reviewing our good customers' credit files, we have found that
your financial statement is more than a year old.

To assist us in a thorough revision of the file and to help us continue
giving you the best possible credit service, we would appreciate your
sending a copy* of your latest audited balance sheet and operating
statement for our confidential use.

We thank you for the fine relationship you have established, and
hope that we may enjoy many more years of close cooperation.

Cordially,

* Other options, depending on status of customer, volume, and credit exposure:
(1) Copy of your latest audit including the supporting schedules,
(2) The attached financial statement form completely filled out. (See Figures 15–4 and
    15–5.)

FIG. 15–6. Letter to Established Customer Requesting Information.

3. *Terms of sale.* Whether in a letter of acknowledgement, a letter requesting additional information, or an individual letter, terms of sale and
expected payment performance should be clearly explained to the customer
early in the establishment of a new account. The letter should state the
firm's credit policy, and describe billing procedures and the terms applicable to the shipment of this order. Discount terms should be unequivocally
stated. Misunderstandings which later result in collection problems often
begin here, due to uncertainty regarding the actual terms of sale. Explicit
statement of terms also earns the respect of the customer by implying careful supervision of credit.

4. *Additional information.* Most companies subscribe to a credit agency
service that will provide a detailed report on a potential customer and a
record of its paying habits with other suppliers. When additional data are
required, the customer may be asked directly. A request for later financial
statements or for names of other suppliers or banks can accompany the
acknowledgement of an order. It should be carefully worded so the customer will desire to give this information freely. If an order will be held up
until the credit investigation has been completed, the customer must be
convinced that the delay is worthwhile.

5. *Refusal of credit.* Even the letter refusing credit to a new customer
can serve a useful purpose. The customer must be encouraged to do busi-

ness on special terms at present, so that open-account terms may be offered at a later date. The reason for the refusal of credit should be explained as specifically as possible without injuring the customer's self-respect or violating the confidential nature of credit information exchange. Negative phrasing should be held to a minimum. The positive aspects should include the favorable factors in the customer situation, and an expression of confidence that the customer will soon improve the factors which prevent open-account credit at this time. Moreover, the customer should be informed that open-account credit must be withheld not only in this case but in the case of any business in a similar situation. In this context, credit executives should be ever mindful of the provisions of Regulation B of the Equal Credit Opportunity Act and transact their business accordingly.

Credit grantors should beware of special terms or conditions printed on any part of a customer's order, particularly when the company is of questionable credit standing. Acceptance of such an order may commit the creditor to fulfilling conditions that are nearly impossible. It would be wise to refer those orders to the sales department for authorization and approval.

Established Accounts. All too frequently a good account is not commended for the fine manner in which it has conducted its affairs. This is a serious shortcoming in all business. Credit correspondence should not be limited to the collection letter but should also include all facets that will build a solid customer relationship.

1. *Acknowledgement letters.* Sometimes routine, these letters play an important part in reaffirming terms of sale, expressing appreciation of an order, or completing a contract by asking for counter signatures.

2. *Periodic requests for financial statements.* Business finances can change greatly from one period to the next, so financial statements covering the year, or even a shorter period, are very important. A normal request made in a standardized letter (see Figure 15–7) can point out that it is routine for all customers and justifies the continuation or expansion of the customer's credit line.

3. *Offer of advice.* The credit executive's knowledge is continually being broadened by contact with different credit and financial situations. Often it can be made available for counseling customers, but only if the legal implications of such counseling are carefully considered. For instance, the claim can always be raised that a customer accepting advice encountered financial problems as a result of following that advice. Some firms minimize this risk by requiring the customer to ask for counseling or assistance in writing, and to sign a form which could be referred to as a letter of release. This establishes a proper relationship between those offering counseling services and those seeking assistance.

4. *Revision of credit line.* If the seller firm makes it a practice to notify customers of their credit lines, the revision of a line offers an opportunity to express the seller's position to the customer.

With a marginal account, particularly, notification may serve a worthwhile purpose. It is always a pleasing task to advise a customer that its line has been increased. Not only does such a letter contain appeal but it also helps build a stronger relationship. To be most effective, it should emphasize that the increased credit line is a direct result of the customer's performance in its payment habits as well as financial growth.

Not so easy is the letter to a customer advising of a revision downward in the credit line. Here it is best to state the facts in a logical, friendly manner, with sufficient explanation so the customer will understand the reasons for the downward revision. If possible, the letter should close on a hopeful note that the circumstances which caused the downward revision will soon be remedied.

Gentlemen:

A routine audit of our confidential files reveals that we do not have a copy of your most recent financial statement. It also appears this information is not available through the usual trade sources.

In order that we might follow the growth of your firm and extend our very best credit consideration to you in the future, please complete the attached financial statement forms and return them to us. The statement, when received, will be placed in our confidential files for our exclusive use.

In the event you do have a statement already prepared, a copy of that statement would be completely satisfactory.

We look forward to your cooperation.

Sincerely yours,

FIG. 15–7.   Request for Financial Statement.

Personal Interview

One of the best occasions for the credit department to promote good will and sales is the personal interview with the customer. While the time and expense involved usually restrict this method of contact, often a personal interview will uncover enough information to permit the granting of credit even though the customer has not submitted financial statements.

A marginal credit risk, judged by the balance sheet alone, may take on a better appearance after a visit and an opportunity to form a personal impression of plant efficiency and the character of the principals. Moreover, a personal call may be the only means to persuade the customer to submit or discuss its financial statement, or to accept cutbacks on terms or order quantities. By developing an open dialogue during a personal visit, the credit executive can go beyond a discussion of financial condition. There is an opportunity to look at records, and to offer carefully considered ideas for improving the customer's operations. Credit contact can be both a sales tool and a chance to establish mutual confidence, respect, and good will.

While it may be highly desirable in many cases to conduct personal interviews at the customer's office, they may also be held in the credit executive's office if the customer prefers this arrangement. After any such interview, a complete memorandum for the credit file should note the date, the occasion, all pertinent points of information, and the credit executive's own impressions.

Telephone Contacts

The experienced credit executive makes effective use of the telephone to communicate with customers. Telephone contacts can be used to supplement financial information on statements submitted to the company or to a credit agency, to obtain references, to bring financial information up to date, and to verify reported contracts. Often the next best thing to a personal call, it is very helpful and has the added advantage of being less costly and time-consuming.

Before making telephone contact, it is wise to prepare a form on which the points to be covered and the information needed are noted. This will be very helpful, particularly for the inexperienced credit executive or when a large number of points are to be discussed. As in the case of the personal interview, a memorandum of the telephone conversation should be written promptly and placed in the credit file.

BANK INFORMATION

The credit executive and business executive generally come into contact with a commercial bank more often than with any other financial institution. Commercial banks provide a variety of services to fulfill the needs of their customers. Among the more common are: they accept deposits and honor checks written against them, accept and pay drafts, issue letters of credit, provide safe deposit boxes for storage of valuables, and lend money. Most of their loans are of a short-term nature, though many banks also make term loans of three years and longer. The loans may be on own paper (unsecured) or secured by collateral.

Commercial banks are also permitted to acquire property and lease it to customers. Because leasing requires a considerable amount of skill and know-how, some banks have joined with existing industrial leasing companies under arrangements which resemble a pooling of the bank's money and the leasing company's expertise. Other banks have established leasing subsidiaries.

A direct way for a bank to finance the long-term requirements of a company is by private arrangement. The borrower deals directly with the bank and a contract is drawn up which specifies the terms of the agreement. The contract negotiated and signed by both parties covers the maturity, method of retirement, interest rate, escalator clause, acceleration clause, endorsements and guaranties, rights of prepayment, security for the loan, and other features. Corporate notes which are placed privately with banks may not be offered by the bank for resale. The notes are excluded from the registration requirements of the Securities and Exchange Commission and are exempted from a number of taxes payable at issuance.

Because of all the services they can provide to their customers, banks are invaluable sources of credit information. Trade creditors can make their own inquiries of the customer's bank, or may ask their own banks to inquire of the customer's bank. In either case, the information is helpful in obtaining a rounded picture of the creditor's financial ability.

Statement of Principles for the Exchange of Credit Information

Recognizing the need to foster and maintain a high level of ethical standards in the exchange of business credit information between banks and business credit grantors, the National Association of Credit Management (NACM) and the Robert Morris Associates (RMA) formed a joint committee in 1955, which ultimately developed a "Statement of Principles for the Exchange of Credit Information Between Banks and Business Credit Grantors." By doing so, these associations also recognized the need for the free and responsible flow of credit information to support the credit-based American economic system.

Through the joint efforts of both associations, the Statement of Principles was revised in 1978 (see Figure 15–8). The respective committees on cooperation with RMA and NACM modified the language of the original statement to reflect current usage. They also developed explanatory comments for each of the seven principles.

The Statement of Principles is designed for commercial transactions, and its use is subject to applicable federal and state laws. Such laws include securities statutes regulating disclosure of inside information and could under particular circumstances include the antitrust laws, credit reporting regulations, and limitations on the use of confidential records and customer information or computerized data.

Both RMA and NACM encourage their members and others with whom credit information is exchanged to become familiar with and respect the Statement of Principles. In addition, each party must understand its obligation to its respective customers and the need for fair, considerate, accurate, and prompt replies in relation to the extension of business credit.

Ways To Make a Bank Investigation

Contact with the customer's bank can be made in four ways: by telephone, by mail, in person, and through the creditor's bank. The name of

STATEMENT OF PRINCIPLES
FOR THE
EXCHANGE OF CREDIT INFORMATION

(1) Confidentiality is the cardinal principle in the exchange of credit information. The identity of inquirers and sources should not be disclosed without their permission.

(2) All parties involved in the exchange of credit information must base inquiries and replies on fact.

(3) The purpose of the inquiry and the amount involved should be clearly stated.

(4) If the purpose of an inquiry involves actual or contemplated litigation, the inquirer should clearly disclose this fact.

(5) The inquirer should make every effort to determine the subject's bank(s) of account before placing an inquiry.

(6) Proper identification should be provided in all credit communications.

(7) Replies should be prompt and contain sufficient facts commensurate with the purpose and amount of the inquiry. If specific questions cannot be answered, the reasons should be clearly stated.

FIG. 15–8.   Statement of Principles for the Exchange of Credit Information.

the customer's bank is generally obtained through direct inquiry or by noting the bank on which a customer's checks are drawn. It is of course desirable to establish some relationship and rapport with the customer's banker, as part of the relationship that exists between the seller and the customer.

Telephone. The telephone has the advantage of speed, and many bankers do not mind telephone calls if they know the individual on the other end of the wire. There is, however, a natural and wise reluctance to talk freely about an account to someone whom they do not know well.

Mail. This type of inquiry is frequently necessary because of distance; the depository bank may be located in another city. In making a mail inquiry with a bank, it is recommended that the inquirer use Form 19, Request for Bank Credit Information, shown in Figure 15–9. (Figure 15–10 is a shorter form of the same request.) The full name and address of the customer is given, along with the full name and address of the inquiring company and the authorized signature and title of the person inquiring. The form also includes the purpose of the request, which indicates the amount of the anticipated credit, and whether this is a first extension of credit or an increase of an existing credit line. A postpaid return envelope should be enclosed to obtain a prompt, complete reply.

Personal Call. The best means of obtaining complete information from a bank, as from any other source, is by personal contact. The credit executive should make a special point of becoming well-acquainted with lending

REQUEST FOR BANK CREDIT INFORMATION

Please provide bank credit information on the account below. This information is requested for use in the extension of credit for business purposes only and will be held in strict confidence. We are providing a summary of our experience with the subject of the inquiry.

TO: _____   _____ (Date)
(Bank Name)

_____   FROM: _____
(Street Address)   (Your Company Name)

_____   _____
(City, State, Zip)   (Street Address)

                                                            _____
                                                            (City, State, Zip)

SUBJECT: _____   _____
(Company on which inquiry is made)   (Inquirer's manual signature)

_____   _____
(Street Address)   (Print or type name of inquirer)

_____   _____
(City, State, Zip)   (Inquirer's title)

INQUIRER TO COMPLETE THIS SECTION

The purpose of the inquiry is:
☐ Initial order $ _____
☐ Anticipated requirements $ _____
☐ Established customer; increased requirements to $ _____
☐ File revision.
☐ Change in payment experience from _____ to _____
☐ Other (describe) _____

We are referring this inquiry to you because:
☐ Your bank was given as a reference (provide branch/account no. if possible) _____
☐ We are checking with other area banks and information from your file only will suffice.
☐ Other (describe) _____

Our experience with the subject has been:
Sold since _____ Amount Owing $ _____
Last Sale _____ Terms _____
High Credit $ _____ Amount Past Due $ _____
Collateral (describe) _____
Are there guarantees, endorsements? _____

Our file contains:
☐ Current trade credit reports.
☐ Financial statement dated _____
   Year end ( )   Interim ( )
The last time we made an inquiry of your bank on the subject was _____
Comments _____

BANK TO COMPLETE THIS SECTION

Our experience with the subject has been:
Depository accounts: Date(s) opened _____ Average Balances _____ If closed, when? _____
Aggregate balances used? ☐ yes ☐ no
Experience and comments _____

Loan Accommodations: Describe, including length of borrowing relationship, high credit, types of loan accommodations (line of credit, term loan, mortgage, installment, etc.), amount outstanding, amount past due (if any), collateral, guarantees and endorsements (if any).

_____
_____
_____
_____
_____

Loan Experience/Comments: _____

Financial Statement: Date _____ Period Covered _____ Audited: ( ) yes ( ) no

_____
(Manual signature of banker)

_____
(Print or type name of banker)

_____
(Banker's title)

_____
(Date)

This form and the "Statement of Principles" (See Reverse Side) have been approved by the Robert Morris Associates and the National Association of Credit Management.

Form 19
Published by NACM
To be submitted in duplicate.
Bank to retain one copy.

FIG. 15–9.   Request for Bank Credit Information.

Form 20

REQUEST FOR BANK CREDIT INFORMATION

(This form approved and published by the National Association of Credit Management)

TO: [   ]   Date _____

RE: [   ]

The above account has given the name of your bank as a reference in applying for credit. Following is our experience:

Sold Since _____   **High Credit** $ _____

Now Owing $ _____   **Days Slow** _____

First Order $ _____

We would greatly appreciate your completing the information below. All information will be held in strict confidence.

Very truly yours,

Company and address: Signed by and title:

[   ]   _____

                                               _____

Date Account Opened _____

| Average | ☐ Low | ☐ Medium | ☐ High |

| Balance | ☐ Four | ☐ Five | ☐ Six Figure |

Deposit Account Relationship Satisfactory? ____ ____
                                            Yes   No

Remarks: _____

Loans	High	Present	**LOAN EXPERIENCE:**
Unsecured	$ _____	$ _____	Satisfactory ☐
Secured	$ _____	$ _____	Unsatisfactory ☐
Mortgage	$ _____	$ _____	Remarks: _____
Instalment	$ _____	$ _____	

Line of Credit Available: ____ ____
                          Yes No

Bank Signature _____

Title: _____

Date _____

FIG. 15–10.   Request for Bank Credit Information (shorter form).

officers in his area, as that is helpful in building confidence and respect between the credit executive and the bank credit officer.

Bank Credit Service. When their own efforts are unsuccessful or when special information is needed, credit executives can call on their own banks for a bank-to-bank check with the customer's bank. A sample letter for this purpose is shown in Figure 15–11. Oftentimes this is a very successful technique, since banks might disclose more information to other banks than they do to trade creditors that are not their depositors. There is usually a fee charged for this service.

Mr. Harold E. Smith, Manager, Credit Department
Fourth National Bank & Trust Company
224 South Fifth Avenue
Salt Lake City, Utah 84101

Subject: Central Denver Manufacturing Co.
1428 South First Avenue
Denver, Colorado 80202

Dear Mr. Smith:

We are considering an order of $2,500 from this new customer for galvanized sheet steel on regular 1%/10 days, Net 15 day terms; however, at peak periods our credit exposure may be as high as $4,000.

Our applicant has referred us to the Third National Bank, Denver, Colorado and we would appreciate your inquiring for us regarding that bank's experience with the company, and obtaining whatever credit and financial information it is free to give.

Thank you for obtaining these details, which it is understood will be held in confidence.

Cordially,

Wayne E. Hodgson
Credit Manager

FIG. 15–11. **Bank Reference Letter Directed to the Inquirer's Bank.**

Bank Check Information

Bank credit departments provide information in proportion to their understanding of the inquirer's need for this information. Accordingly, the credit executive should set forth the scope, nature, and reason for the inquiry. The process of receiving as much information as possible from a bank is based on *quid pro quo*. The depth of response rests on several basic factors: the amount of money involved; being certain that the proper person is contacted at the bank; being well-prepared with precise questions before calling or writing; and being careful not to violate the caveats listed below.

Banks will not usually volunteer unsolicited information. They will, however, answer specific legitimate questions unless the questions invade the area of confidentiality. An inquiry that involves large dollar amounts and is laced with specific data, such as terms of sale and a request for financial details, will receive a more detailed reply than one that refers to a small dollar amount with vague reference to the terms of sale and other factors. Moreover, banks will generally decline comment as to a company's overall responsibility for payment of a stated amount. While all questions might not be answered, the key questions that should be asked include:

1. How long has the bank had the account? If the account was opened recently, who introduced the account?

2. What are the average balances? The banker's reply usually will express the customer's average bank balance in such terms as "medium four figures" or "low six figures." To ensure accuracy and consistency in interpretation, Robert Morris Associates' General Figure Ranges should be used:

> Low 4 figures = $1,000 to 1,999
> Moderate 4 figures = $2,000 to $3,999
> Medium 4 figures = $4,000 to $6,999
> High 4 figures = $7,000 to $9,999

The ranges are adjustable to accommodate all amounts in the following manner:

> Nominal = under $100
> 3 figures = from $100 to $999
> 4 figures = from $1,000 to $9,999
> 5 figures = from $10,000 to $99,999
> 6 figures = from $100,000 to $999,999, and so on.

3. Have any loans been granted? If yes, how high have they been during the past year, and what is owing now? How are cleanups effected—that is, are loans repaid on time with a regular period during which no money is owed?

4. When, why, and how often does the account borrow? "Why" is most important.

5. Are loans made on straight paper? Are they endorsed or guaranteed? If so, by whom? (If endorsements are given by someone not officially connected with the business, this person may be the principal behind the business and a full investigation should then be made to determine personal reputation and financial responsibility.)

6. If borrowings are on a secured basis, what is the collateral—accounts receivable, inventory, real estate, marketable securities, or cash surrender value of life insurance?

7. If loans are secured, has the bank perfected a financing statement under the Uniform Commercial Code. This is normal procedure. If filing notices of a security interest are important to a credit decision, verification of the filing should be obtained either through Dun & Bradstreet or the office of the Secretary of State of the state in which the financing statement was filed.

8. Date of latest financial figures filed with the bank.

9. Highlights on current assets, current liabilities, net working capital, total assets, and net worth.

10. A summary of the customer's latest operating figures, and an indication of profitability.

11. A summary of the latest trade clearance conducted by the bank.

Discussions between a banker and trade creditors should be a two-way street. The credit executive should explain the reason for the inquiry, describing the size and basis of the order, experience with the account, and other available facts. The banker may also ask some pertinent questions:

1. Is the customer a new account? Or is the file being revised? Or is this a delinquent account about which the seller is concerned?

2. On what line of merchandise is credit being extended, and on what terms?

3. What has been the experience of the inquirer, and how much is now owing?

4. How much does the seller know about the account already?

Caveats on Requesting Credit Information from Banks

When a request discloses the nature and scope of the inquiry, the bank normally furnishes whatever data it is free to give. Sometimes, however, it may not answer an inquiry because of previous poor experience with the particular inquirer. Certain practices should be studiously avoided by the credit executive:

1. Disregarding the confidential nature, accuracy, identity, and source of the inquiry and data.

2. Requesting credit information from banks without citing the precise amount of credit involved. When this is not given on the inquiry, banks sometimes ask for it so they may answer properly. The credit executive can avoid delay by providing the information in the first place.

3. Not specifying the spread of the sale. Banks should be informed whether the amount of credit involved (especially when it runs high) is a one-time request or whether the amount is requested for one year.

4. Disguising or hesitating to disclose the reason for an inquiry. Credit executives should be aware that there are situations in which the bank cannot or should not give detailed information to an inquirer. If, for example, the inquirer has a lawsuit pending against a customer and calls the bank for

the purpose of locating the customer's assets, this is not a customary credit inquiry. The bank may understandably object to this type of deception.

Banks also will not handle competitive inquiries, in which the information sought may be used competitively against the subject of inquiry. This is not considered a legitimate trade inquiry. Merger-acquisition inquiries would be considered of a similar nature.

5. Making repeated rush requests. Banks realize that business pressures sometimes need rush information, but will naturally object when rush becomes routine rather than the exception.

6. Making several requests for information on the same company during the same day. This underscores the need to be well-prepared before calling a bank.

7. Using unsigned or rubber-stamped form inquiries, which give the impression that the inquirer is not concerned about receiving credit information. These inquiries draw limited response.

TRADE INFORMATION

Trade information comprises the facts that are obtained from merchandise suppliers of the customer. It can include such facts as the recent high credit, amount owing, amount past due; whether customer payments are discounted, prompt or slow and, if slow, how many days; whether a supplier has referred the account to a collection agency; and other facts about the buying and paying record of the customer. This is vital information. It describes how the customer actually pays bills, regardless of other financial facts.

The payment record should be examined for specifics as well as for the trend of payments, and be reconciled with the condition indicated by the customer's financial statements. Though slow trade payments is a favored signal of trouble, it may also characterize a business that is having growing pains but is substantially healthy; its slowness may be seasonal or due to expansion.

Trade information, like bank information, is an important part of the credit file. It should be complete or at least representative of the customer's pay record. A customer opening a new account is asked for the names of its suppliers. The experienced credit executive will also check with other likely suppliers since references given by the customer almost always will report a good paying record. The payment pattern with all suppliers is needed, including those which the customer may be paying slow.

Depending upon the customer, the industry, location, size of order, and other factors, the credit executive has several places to get this information. The most commonly used include the Credit Interchange Bureaus of the National Association of Credit Management, industry credit groups, credit reporting agencies, and direct interchange with other suppliers.

Credit Interchange Bureaus

The local bureaus of the National Association of Credit Management are a primary source of information about a customer's trade payment habits. This credit reporting service is based upon the idea of collecting trade payment information, maintaining it in computerized files, and having it available to users immediately upon request. The data bank of information is provided by many companies in the United States which submit quarterly computer tapes of their entire accounts receivable files. The databank includes information from national companies and from smaller local or regional companies. As a result, these data are available immediately upon request through local NACM affiliates in one complete trade payments report. Thus this program makes vital, pertinent credit information immediately available to the credit executive.

Industry Credit Groups

Through membership in the National Association of Credit Management, credit executives can participate in industry credit groups. These are special groups of credit executives from particular industries. NACM and its affiliated associations conduct more than 1,000 such groups, with a total membership of over 15,000 credit executives. These groups range in size from small to national, and some international. They represent almost every industry and business—food, electronics, footwear, construction, publishing, and metals manufacturing, to name a few. The purpose of these association-sponsored credit groups is to assist the credit executive in making individual decisions regarding the extension of credit based upon current and accurate information.

All NACM-sponsored credit groups are made up of executives from companies that sell to similar classes of accounts. Consequently, these executives have mutual interests in common customers, and the credit group offers information upon which to base individual analysis of specific credit risks and to make individual credit decisions.

NACM industry credit groups across the country offer a wide variety of credit information services. Written services include delinquent account reports, written credit reports, flash reports with N.S.F. check information, statistical reports, and other items of immediate interest to suppliers. They meet regularly, and these meetings feature educational programs, legal updates affecting credit management, discussions of common customers, and other valuable services. The meetings and services are carefully monitored by executives of NACM and affiliated associations to make sure they are conducted in a fully proper and legal manner.

Credit groups have proven themselves to be an effective credit management tool. They serve the credit executive in the following ways:

1. They provide an opportunity to exchange information on the past-paying experience of common customers.

2. They provide a means of verifying information, reports, and other credit-determining facts.

3. They provide opportunities to exchange the latest information on credit department procedures, equipment, and other credit management functions.

4. They provide an opportunity to discuss the latest legal rulings pertaining to business credit management.

The main caution to all credit executives is that credit groups are not to be used as a vehicle for any noncompetitive agreement, and that all information obtained in credit group meetings is to be used solely for the purpose of making an individual company decision.

Credit Reporting Agencies

Any credit department having more than a limited number of accounts ordinarily uses the services of one or more of the credit reporting agencies. These agencies are discussed in Chapter 16. An important part of every report issued by these agencies is the trade payments section, listing the experience of known suppliers that have recently done business with the account. These trade experiences are updated periodically to reflect recent experience. In unusual circumstances, the agencies will conduct a special trade clearance upon request.

Direct Interchange

Direct exchange of information with other suppliers is costly and time-consuming but can be very useful when there is substantial credit exposure, when agency and bureau reports are inadequate, or when industry group interchange is not practicable. Personal acquaintance, proper identification, and mutual trust and confidence play a large part in these direct exchanges. Also, the credit executives should bear in mind the legal limitations to such an exchange, as noted earlier in this chapter.

Some rules to follow on direct interchange are: always volunteer available pertinent information; provide other suppliers a standardized reply form to be completed, as well as a return postage-paid envelope; stress the importance of a confidential relationship between the two companies; and have the letter signed by a responsible person in the credit department.

Some companies will exchange trade information only when contacted by letter. Figure 15–12 shows a sample request for credit experience. It notes the reason for the inquiry, size of the order, and the inquirer's own credit experience. The form may also be used to record the results of a telephone inquiry.

Union Camp
CORPORATION

1600 VALLEY ROAD, WAYNE, NJ 07470 TELEPHONE (201) 628-9000

TO:

Date________________

Gentlemen:

In order to complete our credit files, we will appreciate your answering the following concerning the account listed below. All information will be treated confidentially and is received without responsibility attaching to the Company or individuals furnishing same.

Re:

REASON FOR INQUIRY	
	We have first order for $
	We are revising our credit file
	Customer refers us to you

CREDIT EXPERIENCE	Our Experience	Your Experience	MANNER OF PAYMENTS	Ours	Yours
Sold Since			Discounts		
Date of last sale			Prompt & Satisfactory		
Highest credit last 12 months	$	$	No. days beyond invoice terms		
Total owing including notes	$	$	Placed for collection		
Amount beyond terms incl. notes	$	$			

COMMENTS (unjust claims-takes unearned discount-pays on account-account secured-account guaranteed-have financial statements, etc.)

FURNISHED BY—________________
(Signed)

A business reply envelope is enclosed for your convenience. Your prompt attention to our request will be appreciated.

Cordially,

ORIGINAL — Return to Us
DUPLICATE — Retain for File

FIG. 15–12. Inquiry Form Directed To Other Supplier.

After the forms are completed, they are usually arranged by high credit and method of payment, then tabulated into a summary of all reported experiences. Figure 15–13 shows a typical trade tabulation.

High Credit	Now Owing	Past Due	Selling Terms	Payments	Sold Since	Remarks
$10,000	$7,500	–0–	2/10, n/30	Discount	Yrs	Good Acct.
8,000	8,000	–0–	2/10, n/30	Discount	1960	Good
9,500	3,000	–0–	net 30	Prompt		—
7,350	4,000	750	2/10, n/30	Usually Ppt	1 yr	Dispute

FIG. 15–13.   Trade Tabulation.

OTHER SOURCES OF CREDIT INFORMATION

The credit department must keep itself well-informed concerning day-to-day activities and developments in the financial community at large, as well as in the specific field in which the business operates. Most effective for this are the financial and business sections of local newspapers, area editions of the *Wall Street Journal,* and trade publications covering the industries in which the company and its customers are active. In addition, if the company has customers whose securities are publicly held, the services of investment fact-finding and reporting agencies, such as Moody's or Standard & Poor's, can be of great assistance. Clippings from the various papers and journals, as well as reports from the investment services, should be made a part of the credit files of customers.

By checking such sources carefully, the alert credit executive can confirm many items of information about which there may be doubt and can obtain much other useful information regarding customers.

Daily Notification Lists

In the principal trading areas, daily lists are published, reporting suits filed, attachments, and other legal notices of interest to the business community. The McCord Company, for example, publishes daily reports of this kind on the Pacific coast. In addition to items concerning litigation, various other legal notices are included, such as filings under the Uniform Commercial Code, filing of tax liens, and the recording of ficticious names or trade styles.

Attorneys

While attorneys' credit reports are no longer used extensively, they have been an important source of credit information, particularly in smaller communities. An attorney located in a county seat can be of help in checking recorded items and determining whether there are any suits pending. Practice has varied as to payments—some attorneys make a flat charge for reports while others furnish the reports free of charge with the understanding that they will also handle any collections and suits in the area at regular fees.

Government Sources

In meeting the legal requirements of state and local governments, business concerns often make credit information available. For example, corporation charters must be filed in most states; corporations with branch offices in some states must file financial statements with the Commissioner of Corporations of that state; and trucking and public utility companies are required to file financial and operating information with state or federal officials.

The Securities and Exchange Commission requires all registered companies, whether or not listed on a securities exchange, to file a form 10-K annually, containing a certified balance sheet and profit and loss statement for the year. Intermediate reports must also be filed, including the 10-Q report, a quarterly balance sheet and profit and loss statement.

When customers are reported to be performing work under government contracts, it is often desirable to contact the interested government agency for verification and for additional information regarding the prime and subcontracts involved. Particular references can be made to progress payment provisions and bond protection.

Miscellaneous Sources

Accountants are another source of information that should not be overlooked. Most businesses that make a financial statement available will also instruct their accountants to answer questions regarding the statement. It should be remembered, however, that the rules for professional conduct of the American Institute of Certified Public Accountants prevent members from giving third parties information, except for reports, unless they have the consent of the client involved.

Other sources of information are the many credit agencies devoted primarily to retail credit, such as Equifax, Hooper-Holmes Bureau, and O'Hanlon Reports. These groups can be particularly valuable for special investigations of various kinds. Their reports may be especially useful in determining the degree of risk or in checking on the value of personal guaranties by officers of corporations for the extension of large credits.

CHAPTER 16

AGENCY SOURCES OF INFORMATION

Ever since they were first established, credit reporting agencies have been a principal help to credit executives seeking information. Some are general in coverage, while others specialize in one or more lines. Geographical coverage of accounts ranges from one's own local area to the broadest international coverage.

The agency report usually attempts to cover all of the major factors involved in the credit decision, from history through operations, including the background of the principals, financial condition, and payment record. Depending upon the location of the office serving the credit executive, reports from agency files can usually be obtained on established companies in several days, with a summary available immediately by telephone. Companies with direct terminal-inquiry capabilities to agencies' files can access their computer-stored information and receive complete written reports immediately. Information secured from agencies may be sufficient to make a credit decision. In other instances, it may provide suggestions and leads for further investigations.

TYPES OF AGENCIES

Briefly, a credit reporting agency may be described as a concern (person or persons) that accumulates credit, financial, and allied information from various sources; consolidates and prepares such information in a simple, readable form; and disseminates such information to clients or subscribers for a monetary fee. They may be classified into three broad categories: general reporting agencies, specialized reporting agencies, and voluntary trade groups.

The largest general reporting agency is Dun & Bradstreet Inc. International in scope, it covers many lines of trade and business, specializing in some while giving a more general treatment to others. The company furnishes information in credit reports and reference books, over the telephone, and through telecommunications.

Specialized reporting agencies usually restrict either their scope of operation or their function. They generally issue reports to only their subscribers and may or may not publish reference books. Within this category, trade reporting agencies restrict their operations to a single line or allied lines of trade. Their coverage may be local or national in scope. They may prepare reports and issue reference books. Examples of this type of agency are the Jewelers' Board of Trade, for the jewelry trade; the Lyon Furniture Mercantile Agency, for the furniture industry, and Proudfoot Reports Inc., for investment houses and financial institutions. This type of agency can be of considerable assistance on accounts in a particular industry. Analysts can maintain a more personal contact with companies and more of the contact work may be done on the phone. News travels fast in these closely knit trades and can be disseminated quickly.

A number of agencies offer credit services in several industries but the scope of their operations is usually smaller than that of the general agencies. They may provide special features which are useful to their subscribers. Examples of this type of agency are National Credit Office, Credit Exchange Inc., and the NACM Business Credit Information System, all discussed later in this chapter.

Voluntary trade groups may be formed within a local credit association or be national in scope to cover a specific trade. As in the case of industry credit groups, an NACM affiliated association services the group by accumulating and compiling pertinent factual trade information for the group. Members generally pay a subscription fee, and the information developed by the group is essentially restricted to its membership.

ORDERING AGENCY REPORTS

The credit executive's need for agency reports is evident when the amount of detailed information required to make a sound credit decision is considered. Sometimes the information is not available directly; at other times the credit executive may not be able to wait until the information can be obtained direct through investigation; and in almost every case it costs less to extract the basic information from an agency report than to develop it personally. After having read the agency report, the credit executive can then decide whether further personal investigation is needed on a particular customer.

Reports may be requested from an agency on first orders, to establish a line of credit, to review lines of credit on a routine basis, or to obtain the details of significant financial or personnel changes. When ordering reports, whether by mail, telephone, telegraph, or data communication lines, the subscriber can contribute to the speed and accuracy with which the request is serviced by observing the following procedures:

1. The name under which the firm does business and its street address should be accurate. This helps the agency to send the correct report.

2. On established accounts, the inquirer's recent ledger experience with the account should be given, and specific points that need investigation should be mentioned.

3. On new accounts, the subscriber can help the agency by· providing the names of the principals and their previous business connections where known, the type of business conducted, trade and bank references submitted by the account, and any other information which would be helpful in a check of agency files and outside records.

Most credit reporting agencies provide the subscriber or member with order forms and a confidential code number which is used to identify the subscriber. The order forms are designed to make it simple for the subscriber to request a report.

DUN & BRADSTREET INC.

Dun & Bradstreet had its beginnings in 1841 when a Boston merchant, Lewis Tappan, founded the Mercantile Agency, the agency for trade. It was Tappan's idea that to best serve the needs of participants in a credit transaction, an impartial third party should be introduced between the buyer and seller. That concept, promoting the free exchange of information for the benefit of all, continues valid to the present day.

In 1859, a former partner in the Mercantile Agency assumed ownership and conducted the activity under his own name as R. G. Dun & Company. At approximately the same time, a competing agency, the Bradstreet Company, came into being. Both firms operated independently until 1933, at which time their operations were merged to form today's Dun & Bradstreet.

Through more than 100 offices, Dun & Bradstreet (D&B) operates around the free world. Its principal activity is that of gathering and maintaining information on commercial enterprises—manufacturers, wholesalers, retailers, and large service organizations—and supplying such data to its legitimately interested subscribers. The information is used primarily for credit-granting purposes but in other formats serves the marketing, sales, and research needs of business.

Dun & Bradstreet provides both dollar recommendations and detailed reports for specialized lines of business through its Credit Clearing House (apparel) and National Credit Office divisions, and operates the Commercial Collection Division to assist businesses in collecting past-due commercial accounts.

Dun & Bradstreet's computerized National Business Information Center—collecting, maintaining, updating, manipulating, and disseminating information on over four million businesses in this country—furnishes fast delivery systems to subscribers. The Duns Dial service, for example, provides almost instant access to partial or total readouts of business information reports via a toll-free telephone call directly to the Duns Dial center.

D&B's Customer Print Terminal service—for subscribers requiring usually large volumes of reports—puts hard copy reports in the hands of subscribers in minutes by means of terminals located on the premises of subscribers. And the Duns-Vue service—utilizing small desk-top video-display terminals—puts summaries of reports before subscribers within seconds through the use of a keyboard.

The information formats are based upon the two traditional forms of the Dun & Bradstreet product—the Business Information Report and the Reference Book. Both are described below.

The Dun & Bradstreet Business Information Report

This document, a detailed yet concisely presented review of an individual enterprise, is developed by D&B reporters, who are men and women trained in commercial reporting. Information is obtained from several sources, starting with a direct interview with the business owner, partner, or corporate officer. In turn, that detail is confirmed and expanded through additional investigations with the business accountant, banks, and supply sources (for payment experiences); by checking public records at federal, state, and county levels; and from a review of D&B's own internal files. Information from all sources is analyzed to determine the strength and desirability of the account as a credit risk. A D&B Rating is then assigned and the data are compiled into the written Business Information Report.

While reports are normally scheduled for updating every six months, revisions are made whenever circumstances warrant. A change in ownership, the physical move of a business headquarters, a recapitalization program, or other equally significant development would trigger new investigations even though the report itself might otherwise be considered in date.

Additionally, other information when uncovered that is of interest to the credit executive is issued in a report form called the Special Notice. These flyers typically contain data on such items as fires, floods, deaths, tax liens, suits, judgments, new products, and branch openings. However, when the information is of such nature as to affect the credit rating—either upward or downward—the entire report is then revised and a new rating assigned.

Information is transmitted from field offices to D&B's National Business Information Center for disk storage. When a subscriber inquires on a particular account, automated systems produce an individually printed Consolidated Report, using a process by which multiple releases on the same business—perhaps with several different dates—are computer-combined into a single report. An added feature of this document is that margin dates identify when the information was first reported. To aid understanding, a sample consolidated report is illustrated in Figure 16–1.

Normally every full D&B report contains at least these principal sec-

---

Dun's Bradstreet Inc.

This report has been prepared for

| BE SURE NAME, BUSINESS AND ADDRESS MATCH YOUR FILE. | ANSWERING INQUIRY | SUBSCRIBER: 008-001042 |

THIS REPORT MAY NOT BE REPRODUCED IN WHOLE OR IN PART IN ANY MANNER WHATEVER

| CONSOLIDATED REPORT | (FULL REVISION) |

```
       DUNS: 06-647-3261          DATE PRINTED             SUMMARY
RETTINGER PAINT CORP               AUG 13, 198-      RATING      CC2
                                   WHOL PAINTS &
727 WHITMAN WAY                    VARNISHES         STARTED     1950
BENSON, MI   48232                                   PAYMENTS    SEE BELOW
        TEL:313 961-0720           SIC NO.            SALES       $424,612
                                   51 98             WORTH   F   $101,867
    CARL RETTINGER, PRES                              EMPLOYS     5
                                                     HISTORY     CLEAR
                                                     CONDITION   GOOD
SPECIAL EVENTS                                       TREND       STEADY
07/10/8-        Business burglarized Jul 3 but $18,000 loss is fully insured.
```

PAYMENTS   (Amounts may be rounded to nearest figure in prescribed ranges)

REPORTED	PAYING RECORD	HIGH CREDIT	NOW OWES	PAST DUE	SELLING TERMS	LAST SALE WITHIN
07/8-	Disc	30000	15000	-0-	2 10 N30	1 Mo
	Disc	30000	15000	-0-	1 10 N30	2-3 Mos
	Disc-Ppt	10000	5000	250	2 10 N30	1 Mo
	Ppt	10000	7500	-0-	30	1 Mo
	Ppt-Slow 30	1000	100	100	2 10 N30	1 Mo
06/8-	Disc	15000	7500	-0-	2 10 N30	2-3 Mos
05/8-	Disc	10000	5000	-0-	2 10 N30	1 Mo
	Ppt	1000	-0-	-0-	30	1 Mo
	Ppt-Slow	500	-0-	-0-	N30	2-3 Mos

```
        Payment experiences reflect how bills are met in relation to the terms granted.
In some instances payment beyond terms can be the result of disputes over merchandise,
skipped invoices etc.
```

FINANCE

06/25/8-

```
        Fiscal statement dated May 31 198-:
        Cash              $     20,623    Accts Pay       $        47,246
        Accts Rec               55,777    Bank Loans               34,000
        Inventory               92,103    Notes Pay
                                          (Trucks)                  7,020
                           ---------------                  ---------------
        Current                168,503    Current                  88,266
        Fixt & Equip            13,630    COMMON STOCK             35,000
        Trucks                   8,000    EARNED SURPLUS           66,867
                           ---------------                  ---------------
        Total Assets           190,133    Total                   190,133
        Annual sales $424,612; Net profit $17,105.  Monthly rent $3,500.  Fire insurance
on mdse & fixt $95,000; Equipment $20,000.
        Prepared from statement(s) by Accountant: Steige Co., CPA's, Detroit, MI.  Extent
of audit, if any, not indicated.
                         --0--
        On Jun 22 198-, John J Lawson defined monthly payments:  $3,000 to bank, $400 on
notes.  Admitted collections slow but losses insignificant.  Said inventory will drop
to $60,000 by December.  Expects 5% sales increase this year.
```

PUBLIC FILINGS

```
03/25/8-        On Mar 17 198-, a suit in the amount of $200 was entered against subject by
Henry Associates, Atlanta, GA (Docket #H27519).  Involves merchandise which Lawson
says was defective.
05/28/8-        On May 21 198-, a financing statement (#H741170) was filed listing subject as
debtor and NCR Corp., Dayton, OH as secured party.  Collateral consists of equipment.
```

BANKING

```
06/25/8-        Account long maintained, carries average balance low to moderate five figures.
Unsecured loans to moderate five extended and now open.
```

HISTORY

```
06/22/8-    CARL RETTINGER, PRES               JOHN J LAWSON, V PRES
            DIRECTOR(S):   THE OFFICER(S)
            Incorporated Michigan Feb 2 1950.  Authorized capital consists of 3,500 shares
common no par value.  Paid in capital $35,000.  Officers own capital stock equally.
            CARL RETTINGER born 1920 married.  Employed by E-Z Paints, Detroit, MI, 12 years;
five as manager until starting subject early 1950.
            JOHN J LAWSON born 1925 married.  Obtained accounting degree 1946 and then
employed by Union Carbide, Chicago, Ill, until joining Rettinger at inception.
```

OPERATION

```
            Wholesales paints and varnishes (85%), wallpaper and supplies.  500 local
accounts include retailers (75%) and contractors.  Terms are 2 10 net 30 days.  Peak
season spring through summer.
            EMPLOYEES:  5, including the officers.
            FACILITIES:  Rents 7,500 sq. ft. one-story block structure, good repair.
```

FIG. 16—1.   The Dun & Bradstreet Business Information Report.

tions: Heading and Summary, Payments, Finance, Banking, History, and Operations. However, in the consolidation process, other captions might include Special Events, Changes, Update, and Public Filings. Two of the latter are illustrated in the sample report, but since the content is self-explanatory, the following paragraphs will concentrate upon the principal report sections. It should be understood, however, that information in any report section might be significant enough in itself to influence the credit decisions. For that reason no caption can be ignored.

Heading and Summary. In the report's heading, starting at the top left, is the DUNS number. D&B assigns every business its own exclusive identification number, which, among other uses, greatly simplifies the computerization of business records. Immediately below the DUNS number appear the business name, full headquarters address, ZIP code, and phone number. The owner's name will also be shown. (On partnerships and corporations only one name will appear in Heading; the other principals are fully identified in History.) In the center portion, the Heading identifies the type of operation being conducted along with the appropriate Standard Industrial Classification (SIC) number, which reflects the type of business activity in numeral terms. SIC classifications are assigned by the U.S. government.

At the top right of the report is the Summary. Starting with the D&B rating, this section provides a capsule view of the entire report and for the most part is understandable at a glance. Some captions, however, require a further word: "Started" represents either the year the business was founded or the date it came under present control; "Sales" is either an exact yearly total or an annualized figure based on partial results; "Worth" is listed net of goodwill, patents, or other intangibles; and "Trend" describes the overall direction of the business after considering profits and net worth as well as sales.

Payments. This section presents the paying habits of the business by reporting the experiences of those sources selling the account on credit terms. Each line is dated and represents the experience of a particular supplier. Reading from left to right: date of recent experience, manner of payment (discount, prompt, or slow), amount of high credit extended, amounts currently owing or past due, selling terms, and an indication of how recently the account was sold.

When there is any slowness reported, this legend appears: "Payment experiences reflect how bills are met in relation to the terms granted. In some instances, payment beyond terms can be the result of disputes over merchandise, skipped invoices, etc."

This points up the fact that it is sometimes difficult, if not impossible, for the creditor to be absolutely certain whether any extenuating circumstances exist. If the amounts of the past-due invoices are in most instances small in relation to the particular amount owing, there is a good chance a legitimate dispute exists. Further, if a relatively small portion of the total experiences reflect some slowness, it may well be that there are satisfactory explanations for that slowness, even though these explanations were not available to Dun & Bradstreet at the time the information was obtained.

Finance. This next portion of the report outlines the financial position of the business as of a specific date. When available, a recent balance sheet will show all assets, all liabilities, and the net worth, together with accompanying figures on sales and profits. These details allow for analysis of financial risk and operating results. Further, when earlier financial statements have been obtained, the report tabulates year-to-year comparisons of figures for an insight into financial trends.

Banking. In this paragraph is found a review of the account's relationship with its bank or banks. Data here cover average balances, present balances, or both (expressed as "middle four figures," "low five figures," etc.); size of credit line or loans outstanding (if any); type of borrowing (secured, unsecured); and manner of repayment. When the account is not a borrower that fact is noted.

History. This section covers both the business entity itself and its principals. The concern's legal name, type of ownership, and starting date is verified; distribution of ownership and control is described; and prior experience and business activities of the owner, partners, or officers is reported. On new businesses (less than three years old), source and amount of starting capital is generally shown.

Operation. To assure that analysis and credit decisions are made with knowledge of activities conducted, this section spells out the concern's function and product line, number and type of accounts sold, selling terms, number of employees, and a description of the physical plant and its location.

The Dun & Bradstreet Rating

Figure 16–2 depicts the Rating Key used by Dun & Bradstreet. Each full rating involves two factors: the first is a double-letter or number-and-letter combination identifying financial strength (net worth); the second is a single-digit number on a scale of one to four, indicating the composite credit appraisal as high, good, fair, or limited. Ratings are a convenient method of measuring accounts in addition to serving as a broad basis for credit insurance classifications.

For example, an account rated DD2 by Dun & Bradstreet means the concern's estimated financial strength (net worth) falls within the $35,000 to $50,000 range and that the composite credit appraisal is good. A business rated DD3, a fair risk, implies a somewhat less desirable account despite its occupying the same net worth bracket. The fair composite credit appraisal would normally reflect a weaker financial or operating position, perhaps some slowness in payments, or both. On the other hand, DD1 identifies a premium risk, a rating reserved for the established business which is financially strong, profitable, and consistently prompt or better in paying habits.

Key to Ratings

ESTIMATED FINANCIAL STRENGTH			COMPOSITE CREDIT APPRAISAL			
			HIGH	GOOD	FAIR	LIMITED
5A	$50,000,000	and over	1	2	3	4
4A	$10,000,000 to	49,999,999	1	2	3	4
3A	1,000,000 to	9,999,999	1	2	3	4
2A	750,000 to	999,999	1	2	3	4
1A	500,000 to	749,999	1	2	3	4
BA	300,000 to	499,999	1	2	3	4
BB	200,000 to	299,999	1	2	3	4
CB	125,000 to	199,999	1	2	3	4
CC	75,000 to	124,999	1	2	3	4
DC	50,000 to	74,999	1	2	3	4
DD	35,000 to	49,999	1	2	3	4
EE	20,000 to	34,999	1	2	3	4
FF	10,000 to	19,999	1	2	3	4
GG	5,000 to	9,999	1	2	3	4
HH	Up to	4,999	1	2	3	4

GENERAL CLASSIFICATION

ESTIMATED FINANCIAL STRENGTH			COMPOSITE CREDIT APPRAISAL		
			GOOD	FAIR	LIMITED
1R	$125,000	and over	2	3	4
2R	$50,000 to	$124,999	2	3	4

EXPLANATION

When the designation "1R" or "2R" appears, followed by a 2, 3 or 4, it is an indication that the Estimated Financial Strength, while not definitely classified, is presumed to be in the range of the ($) figures in the corresponding bracket, and while the Composite Credit Appraisal cannot be judged precisely, it is believed to fall in the general category indicated.

"INV." shown in place of a rating indicates that Dun & Bradstreet is currently conducting an investigation to gather information for a new report. It has no other significance.

"FB" (Foreign Branch). Indicates that the headquarters of this company is located in a foreign country (including Canada). The written report contains the location of the headquarters.

ABSENCE OF A RATING--THE BLANK SYMBOL

A blank symbol (--) should not be interpreted as indicating that credit should be denied. It simply means that the information available to Dun & Bradstreet does not permit us to classify the company within our rating key and that further inquiry should be made before reaching a credit decision.

ABSENCE OF A LISTING

The absence of a listing in the Dun & Bradstreet Business Information File or in the Reference Book is not to be construed as meaning a concern is non-existent, has discontinued business, nor does it have any other meaning. The letters "NQ" on any written report mean "not listed in the Reference Book." The letters "FBN" on any written report also mean that the business is not listed in the Reference Book and that the headquarters is located in a foreign country.

EMPLOYEE RANGE DESIGNATIONS IN REPORTS ON NAMES NOT LISTED IN THE REFERENCE BOOK	KEY TO EMPLOYEE RANGE DESIGNATIONS

Certain businesses do not lend themselves to a Dun & Bradstreet rating and are not listed in the Reference Book. Information on these names, however, continues to be stored and updated in the D&B Business Information File. Reports are available on these businesses but instead of a rating they carry an Employee Range Designation (ER) which is indicative of size in terms of number of employees. No other significance should be attached.

ER 1	1000 or more	Employees
ER 2	500- 999	Employees
ER 3	100 - 499	Employees
ER 4	50 - 99	Employees
ER 5	20 - 49	Employees
ER 6	10 - 19	Employees
ER 7	5 - 9	Employees
ER 8	1 - 4	Employees
ER N		Not Available

Dun & Bradstreet   99 Church Street
a company of   New York, N.Y. 10007   **1981**
The Dun & Bradstreet Corporation

FIG. 16–2.   Key to Ratings.

The Dun & Bradstreet Reference Book

Key information extracted from the Business Information Report forms the basis for listings in the D&B Reference Book. (Figure 16–3 shows a sample page.) These listings include the business name, SIC number, starting date (if active ten years or less), and the D&B ratings. Some listings are prefixed by the letters "A" or "C." The "A" identifies a business listing being added to the Reference Book for the first time. A "C" prefix signals a change in rating since the prior edition.

Containing close to three million listings of commercial enterprises in the United States, Puerto Rico, and the Virgin Islands, entries are arranged alphabetically by cities within states.

Because of the rapid pace of change among business concerns, the Reference Book is updated and republished every 60 days. Among changes necessitating Reference Book revisions are:

1. The voluntary discontinuance or liquidation of an enterprise.
2. Discontinuance by reason of financial difficulty, assignment, failure, bankruptcy, and so on.
3. Merger or consolidation of two or more businesses.
4. Sale of a business to other interests.
5. Addition or withdrawal of a partner.
6. Change in legal form of ownership (partnership to corporation, for example).
7. A change in business name or location.
8. Startup of a new enterprise.
9. Significant new information which may require a change of rating. In such cases an "INV" (investigating) symbol may be assigned for the period of time necessary to develop all details.

NATIONAL CREDIT OFFICE

This specialized agency has its headquarters in New York City, with branch offices in Atlanta, Boston, Camden, Charlotte, Chicago, Cleveland, Los Angeles, Scranton, and Freehold, NJ. It was formed in 1900 to provide credit information on companies in the garment manufacturing trades of New York City. From that beginning it soon branched into other fields of business, though it maintains its specialized character, with each industry covered by a separate department. The agency became a subsidiary of Dun & Bradstreet in 1931 and a division in 1962.

Activities

The reporting activities of National Credit Office (NCO) concentrate on the following lines: apparel, textile, mass merchandisers, department stores, toy and drug wholesalers, supermarkets, metals, electronics, automotive and mobile home, chemicals and coatings, and leather products. This credit service is described below under NCO Specialized Credit Report.

NCO has other related activities that expand its services: credit educa-

8458 BAY—KNI WISCONSIN

53 99 Knievel Fertilizer
    See Knievel Joseph L
51 91 Knievel Joseph L   BB3
51 91 Knievels Store
    See Knievel Joseph L
58 13 Kropp Arthur   FF2
70 11 Mabin Mrs Hallie   EE2
54 11 Munn Ralph J   DC2
51 91 Napier Fertilizer &
    Equipment   DC2
76 99 Noffke Frank Jr   FF2
17 51 Pavel Ed Sr   EE2
14 42 Pollock Sand & Gravel   CB2
17 41 Pruden Robert L   GG2
51 91 Ruroede Donald E   EE3
51x43 Sojkas   GG2
58 12 Two Rivers Inc   5   DD3
58 13 Voss Iva   GG2
42 12 Yelli Edward F Jr   — —

BAYSIDE BAYSIDE 72

54 11 Barkmeiers   8   EE2
55 41 Bender Sinclair Service   FF2
52 11 Charlton Lumber Co Inc   BB1
    Br of Fairmont Wis
50 83 Dawson & Barkmeier Co   DD1
55 41 Dinneen Oil Co   EE2
15 21 Erdkamp Construction   EE2
55 11 Erdkamp Motors   DD2
51 91 Exeter Cooperative Elev
    Co°   BA2
59 12 Exeter Rexall Store   9   EE2
72 61 Farmer Funeral Home   DD2
27 11 Fillmore Country News   GG2
27 11 Fillmore County News   HH2
17 94 Hall Contracting Co Inc   CC1
20 48 Hassler Feed   8   GG2
17 94 Horizontal Boring Co
    Inc   7   CC2
58 12 Johnson Harvey & Teresa   GG2
55 41 Masons Hiway Service   6   EE2
54 11 Norms IGA   0   HH3
55 41 Rasmussen Standard
    Service   HH2
42 13 S & A Trucking Co*   CC3
58 13 Schneider Harold   8   GG2
59 44 Smith Jewelry   HH2
17 81 Styskal Irrigation   CB3

BEAR HILLS 13,118 DODGE 72

58 12 A & W Root Beer   5   — —
56 61 Acker-Gardner Inc   DD2
59 44 Ackerman Jewelry   — —
17 31 Anything Electric   5   GG3
75 38 Arntts Firestone & Auto   8   — —
17 61 Asendorf Tin Shop   FF2
76 22 Austen Wes TV
    Service   EE2
55 41 Backers Service Station   HH2
57 12 Barber Furniture Co Inc   CC1
50 13 Beasleys Automotive   0   FF4
59 41 Bedlans Sporting Goods   DC3
51 91 Bervin Distrg Inc of
    Beatrice   — —
51 91 Bervin Distributing Inc   CC2
15 21 Blackwell Trenching
    Service   DD2
15 21 Boeckner Brothers Inc   DC2
54 11 Boogaarts Fairbury Inc   9
55 41 Bower Fred Motor Service   GG2
C 54 11 Brackles Inc   2R3
15 21 Brown Construction Co   0   HH2
56 61 Browns Shoe Fit Co No 19   1A1
    Br of Shenandoah Iowa
17 31 Cacaks Commercial Service   FF2
42 13 Canning Truck Service   CC3
70 11 Capri Motel The   0   — —
20 21 Central States Dairy Coop   — —

51 81 Fairbury Sales Co   DC1
51 91 Farmers Union Coop Elev
    Assn°   CB1
55 41 Farmers Union Coop Oil
    Assn°   BA1
55 41 Fitzgerald Charles L & Mrs
    C L   CC1
    Br of Jansen Neb
57 22 Flowers TV & Appliance   FF3
54 11 Fuller Thriftway   EE2
76 41 Furniture Fix It Shoppe   2   GG2
32 72 G & M Sand & Gravel   6   — —
53 99 Gamble Skogmo Inc   5A1
    Br of Minneapolis Minn
52 51 Gamble Store 4371   9   FF2
55 71 Garbers Honda Sales   DC2
51 98 Gaugenbaugh Frank   2R3
17 11 Gibson Plumbing & Heating
    Co   DD2
53 99 Gibsons of Fairbury
    Inc   7   — —
59 12 Globe Rexall Drug Store Inc   CC1
17 11 Goeking Plumbing &
    Heating   FF2
C 48 32 Great Plains Broadcasting
    Inc   6   FF3
51 72 Griess Oil Co   FF2
55 41 H & H Sinclair Oil Co   DC2
    Br of Beatrice Wis
59 84 Hess Inc   8   EE3
53 11 Hested Stores of Nebraska°   5A1
    Br of NYC Manhattan N Y
52 11 Howell Lumber Co°   1A2
15 21 Hutson Construction Co   1R2
41 19 Jefferson County Ambulance
    Svc   9   — —
A 56 21 Jerris   1   — —
59 21 Johnnys Liquor   FF2
57 22 Johnson Electric Service &
    Sls   EE2
72 21 Jones Lester Studio   FF2
01 91 Jordening Harlin   EE3
42 22 Junkers Meats Inc   DD3
15 21 K & W Construction   2R2
72 16 Kleen Klose Shop   FF2
59 12 Korbel Drugs Inc   7   EE2
59 21 Kubes Frank   DD2
17 31 L & S Electric Service   EE2
C 59 44 Le Roys Jewelry   DD2
56 11 Livingston & Gates
    See Richardsons
50 83 Lofing Implement Co   2   CC2
50 83 Mannschreck Implement   CB2
51 91 May Seed & Nursery Co Inc   1R2
    Br of Shenandoah Iowa
72 16 Miles Cleaners   FF2
57 12 Modern Furniture   2R3
59 99 Moon & Sun Monument
    Co   2   EE2
54 11 Mr Eds IGA   FF2
55 11 Mulkey Philip   EE2
58 12 My Uncles Place   0   — —
49 24 Natural Gas Distributing
    Co*   — —
55 11 Newton Motor Co Inc   CC2
55 41 Nigh Texaco   GG2
49 11 Norris Public Power
    District   3A2
    Br of Beatrice Wis
55 21 Norton Auto Body Co   CC1
55 31 O K Tire Store   — —
50 93 Paneitz Auto Salvage   EE2
54 11 Pantry Grocery   DD2
17 11 Parks Heating & Sheet
    Metal   — —
55 11 Pilcher Motor Co   CC2
58 12 Pla Mor Cafe   HH2
79 33 Pla-Mor Bowl   EE3
75 38 Porters Repair Shop   GG2
01 89 Prairie Plains Seed Co   1R3
20 41 Preston Milling Industries
    Inc   CB2

FIG. 16-3. Page from D&B Reference Book.

tion, market planning, management services, specialized collections, industry guides and directories, and industry group meetings.

NCO Specialized Credit Report

NCO reports are written by specialists in their fields, who may be called directly by the subscriber with questions on the account. They are reviewed and revised at least twice a year (depending upon the amount of risk involved) or whenever circumstances may require it. Figure 16–4 shows the NCO Specialized Credit Report.

The NCO report is frequently written in three separate sections, each containing a specific type of information. This permits partial updating without the need for rewriting the entire report. These sections are Management & Products, Current Information, and Financial Statement.

Management & Products. The first section contains information of a general nature about the business and its principals, under the following captions:

History. Details of the trade style registration, partnership formation, or incorporation are given in the first paragraph. Other paragraphs provide record information on fires, financial embarrassments, or major litigation.

Personnel. This section covers the background of the principals listing their names, dates of birth, and former employment or business interests.

Method of Operation. The line of business, price ranges of products, type of accounts sold, method and area of distribution, and selling terms are described. Branch office locations, the principal types of machinery used, and the number of employees are also given.

Banks. The names and locations of the banks used by the company are listed.

Current Information. This section contains the new and changing information about the business. Any aspect of the operation may be commented upon. The information is presented under the following headings:

Credit Suggestion. A letter code is assigned to the account, plus a dollar line or comment on its desirability as a credit risk. A line of credit may be suggested, or may not be if available data are insufficient or unsatisfactory. The reasons for the conclusion are stated when a general line is not suggested.

New Information. New developments in the financial trend or operating features of the business are covered. New contracts, changes in operation, litigation, and recent sales and profit trends may be mentioned.

Antecedent Comment. The report comments briefly on the business records of the principals, fire or bankruptcy records of the business or the principals, and an evaluation of the management.

Financial. Statement summaries for the last three fiscal years are given in this section, plus the name of the accountant or auditor. The figures tabulated are cash, accounts receivable, inventory, current assets, current

nco. *specialized credit report*
MANAGEMENT & PRODUCTS

FEMINA FOOTWEAR CO., INC.	MFR. SLIPPERS & PLAYSHOES
123 West Kerry Ave.	Dept. 964 File 704865
Buffalo, N.Y. 14020	Analyst: Jeffrey Jones

JUNE 5, 19--

John W. Sussler, Chairman of Bd.	Edwin W. Delray, Pres.-Treas.
Peter G. Field, Vice-Pres.	Rosanne S. Dooley, Vice-Pres.
F.J. Richman, Secy.	

DIRECTORS: John W. Sussler, Edwin W. Delray, George H. Lee, and
Ronald Lockhart.

HISTORY - Established as partnership 1945 as Adorable Shoe Co. Succeeded
1946 by Femina Footwear Co., N.Y. Corp. 1948 change in control occurred and certain of former interests retired. Charter surrendered
and business re-incorporated under N.Y. laws under present style.
Moved to caption address 1955 from smaller plant at 100 Erie Street.

PERSONNEL - Sussler, born 1914, principal financially, maintains general
supervision over entire operation. Long associated with this line
and officer with subject since 1948. Previously a Partner and
General Manager of Adorable Shoe Co. Originally employed by others
as an auditor. $50,000 insurance carried on his life with company
as beneficiary. Elected Chairman of the Board 1972.

Delray, born 1926, associated with subject since 1948, in charge of
production. Elected Secretary 1965 and assumed the additional office
of Vice-President 1967. Elected President and Treasurer 1972.

Richman, born 1940. Employed by subject since 1960. Elected
Assistant Secretary 1965 and Secretary 1972. In charge of purchasing.

Field, born 1936. Associated since 1964. Sales Vice-Pres. since 1973.

Dooley, born 1939. Employed as stylist and designer since 1966.
Elected Vice-President 1969.

Lee, is a local attorney. Lockhart, is also President of Lockhart
Gear Works, Buffalo, N.Y. and has been associated with that company
throughout his business career.

METHOD OF OPERATION - LINE - Manufacture women's and children's turn
process padded sole and cement process hard sole slippers and playshoes.
Retail price range from $14.95 to $24.95 a pair. Approximately 50%
of production is for in-stock and 50% against orders. DISTRIBUTION -
Direct, nationally, about 75% to department stores and 25% to individual retailers. Terms of sale 3/10EOM. Use trade styles, "Kittens",
and "Play-Cats". EQUIPMENT - Leases 40,000 sq. ft. Output 2,000 pairs
daily. Employs about 125.

BANKS - First Marine Bank, Buffalo, N.Y.
Manufacturers Bank of Buffalo, Buffalo, N.Y.

h1

FIG. 16-4. NCO Specialized Credit Report.

nco® specialized credit report

FEMINA FOOTWEAR CO., INC.
123 West Kerry Ave.
Buffalo, N.Y.　14020
Phone:　716-477-3602

MFR. SLIPPERS & PLAYSHOES
Dept. 964　　File 704865
Analyst:　Jeffrey Jones

JUNE 5, 19--

CREDIT SUGGESTION - (A) - BECAUSE OF FURTHER PROGRESS AND VERY LIQUID
　　CONDITION, REQUIREMENTS ARE SUGGESTED.

NEW INFORMATION - Management recently advised that sales so far this year
　　have shown an increase of about 9% over the corresponding period
　　of last year with profits also ahead of a year ago.

ANTECEDENT COMMENT - Records clear.　Originally formed 1935.　Present
　　management in control since 1938.　Manufacture general line of
　　slippers and playshoes.　Management experienced and well regarded.

FINANCIAL -	12/31/	12/31/	12/31/
Cash	$ 5,000	$ 12,000	$ 20,000
Receivables	126,000	114,000	134,000
Merchandise	181,000	239,000	184,000
Current Assets	312,000	365,000	338,000
Current Debts	68,000	107,000	65,000
Working Capital	244,000	258,000	273,000
Fixed Assets	44,000	34,000	32,000
Net Worth	353,000	369,000	388,000
Sales	1,234,000	1,336,000	1,423,000
Profit	28,000	32,000	38,000
Dividends	14,000	16,000	19,000

Auditor:　Paul D. Hartman & Co., CPA,　Buffalo, N.Y.

TRADE - EXCELLENT

HIGH CREDIT	OWING	PAST DUE	TERMS		PAYMENTS
$ 25,000	10,000	0	2/30		dis
15,000	7,000	0	2/15	prox	dis
11,000	5,000	0	2/30		dis
10,000	6,000	0	2/15	prox	dis
6,000	5,000	0	2/15	prox	dis
5,000	0	0	2/15	prox	dis
2,000	2,000	0	2/15	prox	dis
1,000	0	0	2/30		dis

Union Tanning Co., Boston, Mass.　　　Smith Leather Co., N.Y.C.
Chelsea Heel Corp., Chelsea, Mass.　　Fancy Leather Corp., Boston, Mass.

ANALYSIS - This is a well established business which has shown a con-
　　sistently progressive trend over the years.　Steady increases have
　　been shown in both volume and profits in recent years.　Financial
　　condition has been good for a number of years and was quite liquid on
　　the last statement which featured all indebtedness covered more than
　　twice by the total of cash and receivables.　Financing is assisted
　　by occasional unsecured bank loans but nothing was owing at recent
　　investigation date.

hl

FIG. 16-4 (cont'd.).

FINANCIAL STATEMENT SUBMITTED TO **NATIONAL CREDIT OFFICE**

Name **FEMINA FOOTWEAR CO. INC.**   Business **Mfr. Slippers & Playshoes**

Street and No. **123 West Kerry Avenue**   City **Buffalo**   State **N.Y.**   ZIP **14020**

STATEMENT OF (DATE) DECEMBER 31   19--

ASSETS		LIABILITIES	
CASH IN BANK $ 19,400.00	19,989.81	ACCOUNTS PAYABLE	19,989.81
ON HAND $ 502.51	19,902.51	DUE CONTRACTORS (without offset)	2,222.42
U.S. GOVERNMENT SECURITIES		UNSECURED LOANS PAYABLE	
RECEIVABLES for Mdse. Sold to Customers (Age at Foot of Page)		To Banks	
ACCOUNTS $ 139,363.89		To Partners or Officers	
Less Res. for Discounts $ 2,680.00		To Others	
Less Res. for Doubtful $ 2,800.00	133,883.89	SECURED LOANS PAYABLE	
NOTES & TRADE ACCEPTANCES		Owing to	
(Less $ discounted)		ACCRUED WAGES & EXPENSES	16,190.91
DUE from FACTOR or FINANCE CO.		TAXES—Accrued and Payable a. Withholding & Payroll	13,368.18
		b. Federal & State Income	10,897.02
PHYSICAL INVENTORY OF MDSE. (Valued at lower of Cost or Market)		c. All Other	2,564.88
Raw Materials $ 51,987.11		CURRENT LIABILITIES	65,233.22
In Process $ 61,075.71		RESERVE for Income Taxes since last closing	
Finished Mdse. $ 70,912.10	183,974.92	MORTGAGE—DEFERRED DEBT— Due within 12 mos.	
CURRENT ASSETS	337,761.32	MORTGAGE—DEFERRED DEBT— Due after 12 mos. (date)	
Due from Partners, Officers, or Employees		LOANS Subordinated until (date)	
Due from Affiliated or Assoc. Companies		TOTAL LIABILITIES	65,233.22
LAND & BUILDINGS $		IF CORPORATION	
MCHY., EQUIP., FURN, & FIXT. $ 79,231.58		Capital Stock Pfd. $ 80,000.00	
Less Depreciation $ 46,804.91	32,426.67	Com. $ 80,000.00	
INVESTMENTS (Describe on opp. page)		Capital Surplus $ 308,345.74	388,345.74
PREPAID & DEFERRED	6,000.00	Earned Surplus (Sub-Chapter S) $	
Life Ins. — C.S. Val	77,389.97	Undist. Earnings Deficit (red) $	
Goodwill	1.00	CORPORATE, PARTNERSHIP or INDIVIDUAL NET WORTH	388,345.74
TOTAL ASSETS	$453,578.96	TOTAL LIABILITIES & CAPITAL	$453,578.96

ACCOUNTANT—Was above statement prepared by an outside accountant? Yes ☒ No ☐ Is he CPA? ☒ Registered? ☐ Licensed? ☐
Accountant's Name **Paul D. Hartman & Co.**
Address **Buffalo, N.Y. 12/31**
On what date are your books closed? **Annually**
How often are books audited? **No**
MERCHANDISE—If not valued at Lower of Cost or Market, state basis used
Is original inventory record retained by you ☒ or outside auditor ☐? **No**
Is any merchandise pledged as security for any debt? **No**
If so, state amount so pledged. $
INSURANCE—Fire: Mdse. $ **Full**   Bldg. & Fixt. $ **Full**   Life, Benefit
Use & Occy.: Burglary $ _____ on **John Sussler**
Business $ **30,000**

67

RECEIVABLES
For goods shipped during months of:
a. Dec. $ 85,561.45
b. Nov. $ 45,212.21
c. Oct. $ 3,110.23
d. Prior Months $
Do these include any consigned goods, uncredited returns, or unshipped merchandise? Yes ☐ No ☒
Have all been charged to customers? Yes ☐ No ☐
During the past year were any accounts sold, pledged, assigned, or receivables? Yes ☐ No ☒ If so, describe transaction.

PLEASE LIST SUPPLIERS AND BANKS ON REVERSE SIDE

PROFIT AND LOSS STATEMENT
FOR PERIOD FROM **Jan. 1** 19-- TO **Dec. 31** 19--
GROSS SALES $ 1,471,188
Less RETURNS $ 25,347
Less DISCOUNTS $ 22,734
NET INCOME FROM SALES $ 1,423,107
Inventory—begin'g $ 239,479
Purchases—Net $ 603,105
Labor $ 360,522
Factory Overhead $ 119,370
Total $ 1,322,476
Inventory at end $ 183,975
Cost of Goods Sold $ 1,138,501
GROSS PROFIT ON SALES $ 284,606
Selling & Ship. Exp. $ 90,226
Salaries—Officers or Principals $ 65,200
Bad Debts $ 51,140
Depreciation $ 1,705
Total $ 5,103   213,374
INCOME or (LOSS) ON SALES $ 71,232
Other Income (exclude discount earned) $
Deductions from Income $ Total $ 71,232
NET PROFIT or (LOSS) before Income Taxes $ 71,232
Provision for Fed & State Income Taxes $ 33,179
NET PROFIT or (LOSS) $ 38,053

RECONCILIATION OF SURPLUS OR NET WORTH
Beginning (date) $ 369,293
ADD: Profit for Period $ 38,053
Other Credits to Surplus $
Total $ 407,346
DEDUCT: Loss $
Div & Withdr'ls $ 19,000
Other Charges $
NET WORTH—SURPLUS at end $ 388,346
INVESTMENTS—Describe (if subsidiary or affiliated state % owned)
a.
b.
LIABILITIES—Merchandise received or charged to you but not included in Assets or Liabilities $
Amount of Contingent Liabilities $
Are any liabilities secured in any way? _____ If so, state amount, creditor, and nature of security.
Annual Rent $ _____ Lease Expires.
NET WORTH—Has this been decreased since statement date by withdrawal, retirement of capital, payment of dividends, bonuses, or personal income Taxes?
If so, by what amount? $
TAXES—Have all Federal, State, and Local tax assessments been paid or shown accrued on statement? **YES**
Tax Closing date? **Dec. 31**   Date of latest return examined by Internal Revenue Service?

OWNER—PARTNERS—OFFICERS AND DIRECTORS

Name	Title	% Ownership	In charge of
John Sussler, Ch. of the Bd.		60%	Genl. Superv.
Edwin Delray, Pres.-Treas.		30%	Production
F. J. Richman, Secy.		10%	Purchasing

TO NATIONAL CREDIT OFFICE, a division of Dun & Bradstreet, Inc. The undersigned warrants that the foregoing figures and answers are true and accurate in every respect and orders this statement mailed to you with the intention that it shall be relied upon in the extension of credit or insurance by such concerns, including factors or agents, who may subscribe to your service now or hereafter. My (Our) accountants are authorized to supply you with any supplementary information that may be required

Dated at Buffalo this 20 day of April 19--
Signed in the Presence of:
Name _____
Address _____

Femina Footwear Co., Inc.
(Name of Corporation, Partnership or Proprietorship)
Edwin Delray
By _Edwin Delray_
(Signature of Officer, Partner or Owner)   (Title)

INDEPENDENT ACCOUNTANTS' OPINION (Please use your own Letterhead if additional space is necessary)
We have examined the above balance sheet and profit and loss statement. Our examination was made in accordance with generally accepted auditing standards and included such tests and procedures as we considered necessary. In our opinion the statements present fairly the position of the company in conformity with generally accepted accounting principles applied on a basis consistent with that of the preceding year.

Signature _____   Address Buffalo, N.Y.   Date 4/19/--

FIG. 16—4 (cont'd.).

liabilities, net working capital, net worth, sales, profit, and dividends. They enable the reader to compare key balance sheet and income statement items over a three-year period to determine trends. Certain departments also include key ratios.

Trade. A current trade clearance is tabulated in this section of the report. The analyst makes a short comment about the trend of payments or other significant characteristics of the experience reported.

Suppliers. The names and addresses of principal suppliers are listed in this section.

Analysis. This contains the NCO analysis of the account and is the basis for the credit recommendation. Reasons for changes in operating results and financial condition are provided plus an overall evaluation of the company.

Bulletin. When new information is developed on an account but the report is otherwise in date, the agency may issue a *Bulletin* report. It is a short form report and contains only new information. It is usually consolidated into the Current Information section when that is revised.

Financial Statement. Statements received directly from a company or its accountant, either on its own form or the NCO form, are photographed. Statements not available directly but obtained from outside sources are retyped and the word "Indirect" is placed after the date. Whether received directly or indirectly, the statement is issued as the third section of the report.

LYON FURNITURE MERCANTILE AGENCY

This specialized trade agency began business in 1876. Its present name was taken in 1917 when the older agency combined with the Furniture Commercial Agency Company, a competitor formed in 1890. It has executive offices in New York City and five branches throughout the country. It is regarded as an authority in its own field.

The agency operates in a way similar to that of Dun & Bradstreet, furnishing a variety of services to its subscribers. These services include a reference book, known as the Lyon Red Book, issued every January and July; weekly reports and supplements to the reference book which notify subscribers of changes in ratings, new business formations, liquidations, bankruptcies, fires, litigations, and other news of credit importance; a rating key which classifies accounts as to credit condition, capital strength, and payment record; weekly tabulations of credit experience with the accounts in the industry; credit reports; and collection service.

The services are geared to serve the specialized trade in which the agency operates. The principal points of interest to the credit executive are described below.

Lyon Credit Report

Reports prepared for subscribers to Lyon service provide pertinent data for credit decisions. A sample is shown in Figure 16–5. The sections of the report are:

Heading. The name of the business, the line of business, address, and the name(s) and age(s) of the principal(s) are given in the heading. The date when the report is written is shown after "REV."

Antecedents. The business and personal history of the principals are

---

Form 20 Rev. 11/75

LYON CREDIT REPORT

This report compiled from our records is sent to you confidentially, for your exclusive use, in accordance with the terms of your contract. The Lyon Furniture Mercantile Agency shall not be liable for any loss or injury or that of its agents, in obtaining, compiling or communicating this information; and Agency does not guarantee correctness of same.

(SAMPLE REPORT – NAMES & ADDRESS FICTITIOUS)

DOE, JOHN CORPORATION   FC&APL   NEW YORK.....N.Y. 10016
                                                629 West 34th Street
                                                Tel. 686-7429

Morris Doe, Pres., Age 57, Md.
Frank Blank, Treas., Age 54 Md.
John Smith, Sec., Age 56 Sgle.

Directors: The Officers

REV (md-31) February 1, 19—

ANTECEDENTS
            Incorporated under New York State Laws March 15, 1949, continuing the business of the former John Doe Furniture Co., which had operated at same address as a partnership between Morris Doe and Frank Blank.

            Morris Doe is a son of the late John Doe, who started in the furniture business Feb. 6, 1910 as John Doe Furniture Co., at 1600 Dodge St., New York, N.Y. John Doe died May 5, 1945 at which time a partnership was formed between his son, Morris Doe, and Frank Blank, a son-in-law, as John Doe Furniture Co., to continue the business which at that time moved to 629 W. 34th St. Morris Doe had been assisting his father in the conduct of this business, working part time, while attending school and after graduation, giving full time to the business. Frank Blank had been employed by the late John Doe for about ten years.

            The partnership between Frank Blank and Morris Doe continued until Dec. 1, 1948, when they executed an Assignment for the Benefit of Creditors. On Dec. 5, 1948, an Involuntary Petition in Bankruptcy was filed against them and at the Trustee's sale in Bankruptcy, the assets were purchased by the present corporation. Unsecured creditors of the partnership received a first and final dividend of 50% on Nov. 28, 1949. The partners received their discharge from Bankruptcy Jan. 12, 1950.

            Control of this corporation is divided equally between Morris Doe, Frank Blank and John Smith. John Smith joined with Morris Doe and Frank Blank in forming this corporation to acquire the assets at the sale in Bankruptcy, previous to which time he had been employed for about eight years as a furniture buyer by the New York Department Store, New York, N.Y.

            On December 16, 1954, a fire which occurred here as a result of the faulty operation of an oil burner, caused damage to stock of about $10,000. with insurance adjustment received in that amount.

FIG. 16–5. Lyon Credit Report.

Form 20 Rev. 11/75

LYON CREDIT REPORT

This report compiled from our records is sent to you confidentially, for your exclusive use, in accordance with the terms of your contract. The Lyon Furniture Mercantile Agency shall not be liable for any loss or injury or that of its agents, in obtaining, compiling or communicating this information; and Agency does not guarantee correctness of same.

DOE, JOHN CORPORATION   -2-   NEW YORK.....N.Y.

February 1, 19—

GENERAL INFORMATION

Principals of corporation experienced, although the President and Treasurer have been identified in the past with an unsuccessful venture.

Company occupies a three-story building which it owns in a good shopping center, each floor having about 10,000 sq. ft. of display space, the basement being used for warehouse and storage purposes

Corporation carries a complete line of home furnishings and has a good sized electrical appliance department, handling only major appliances. Deals in medium to low-priced lines, with about 90% of sales made on the installment payment plan. Company has enjoyed a fairly good sales volume during the past few years. However, there appears to have been some falling off in volume during the past several months due to local conditions.

FINANCIAL INFORMATION

Company has an authorized capital of $300,000. in preferred stock, divided into 3,000 shares with a par value of $100. each. The paid-in capital is $150,000., $50,000. each having been contributed by the three principals.

COMPARATIVE SUMMARIZED STATEMENTS

DATE	ASSETS	LIABILITIES	RESERVES	NET WORTH	SALES
Dec. 31, 19—	261,724.	101,827.	2,428.	157,468.	-
Dec. 31, 19—	317,062.	122,674.	7,260.	187,127.	220,647.
Dec. 31, 19—	370,085.	138,864.	14,537.	216,683.	250,128.
Dec. 31, 19—	384,117.	147,824.	17,027.	219,266.	270,877.
Dec. 31, 19—	371,780.	138,473.	18,236.	215,070.	235,608.

The following statement, received by mail, shows condition from books and physical inventory as of Dec. 31, 19—

ASSETS

Current assets:
Cash on hand and in bank	$ 5,096.28	
Accts. rec., install.	220,174.05	
Mdse. inventory	50,650.00	
Total Current Assets		$275,920.33

Fixed Assets:
Real Estate	75,000.00	
Furn., fixt. & signs	15,427.18	
Del. equip.	4,908.76	
Total Fixed Assets		95,335.94

FIG. 16–5 (cont'd.).

shown in this section of the report. Fires and bankruptcies are detailed in a separate paragraph.

General Information. This section begins with a general comment concerning the business. It then describes the premises from which operations are conducted and lists the number of employees. This is followed by a description of the method of operation, including lines carried, types of merchandise, and a volume breakdown of cash and credit sales.

Form 20 Rev. 11/75

LYON CREDIT REPORT

This report compiled from our records is sent to you confidentially, for your exclusive use, in accordance with the terms of your contract. The Lyon Furniture Mercantile Agency shall not be liable for any loss or injury or that of its agents, in obtaining, compiling or communicating this information; and Agency does not guarantee correctness of same.

DOE, JOHN CORPORATION   -3-   NEW YORK.....N.Y.

FINANCIAL INFORMATION (cont'd)
Deferred charges:
Prepaid ins. & interest   524.41
                        TOTAL ASSETS...................   371,780.78

LIABILITIES & CAPITAL

Current Liabilities:		
Accts. Pay.	$89,452.02	
Notes pay. bank, secured by		
endorsement of Pres. & Treas.	15,000.00	
Taxes pay.-Federal & State	1,521.87	
Total Current Liabilities		105,973.89
Fixed Liabilities		
Real estate mtg.		32,500.00
Res. for deprec. of fixed assets		18,236.20
		$156,710.09
Capital:		
100 shares preferred stock		150,000.00
Surplus		65,070.69
TOTAL LIABILITIES & CAPITAL.........		$371,780.78

Sales for year ending Dec. 31, 19— - $235,608.

Ins. on mdse. $45,000; on bldg. $60,000.

                        (SIGNED)   JOHN DOE CORPORATION
                             By: Frank Blank, Treas.

ANALYSIS
        Summarized statements show net worth had been steadily
increasing from 19— to 19— but for year ending Dec. 31, 19—, there
has been some slight reduction in net worth.

        Comparison of current statement with that of Dec. 31, 19—
shows a reduction in cash of about $47,500. with accounts receivable
having increased about $25,000. and inventory expanded about $10,000.
Accounts payable have increased about $28,000. Bank indebtedness has
increased about $5,000. while taxes have been reduced by about $2,400.
and an item of about $40,000. previously shown owing to officers, no
longer appears in the statement. Frank Blank stated upon interview
that this had been paid to officers, which also explained a good part
of the reduction in cash position.

FIG. 16-5 (cont'd.).

Financial Information.   This section of the Lyon Credit Report begins
with a presentation of comparative key figures for several years: assets, liabilities, reserves, net worth, and sales. Then the latest available statement
is photographed and attached, with operating figures and footnotes stated
or information reflected to indicate the source of the statement, the amount
of insurance carried, the name of the accountant, and the person who
signed the statement.

Analysis.   The figures are analyzed in this part of the report. Changes

Form 20 Rev. 11/75

LYON CREDIT REPORT

This report compiled from our records is sent to you confidentially, for your exclusive use, in accordance with the terms of your contract. The Lyon Furniture Mercantile Agency shall not be liable for any loss or injury or that of its agents, in obtaining, compiling or communicating this information; and Agency does not guarantee correctness of same.

DOE, JOHN CORPORATION   -4-   NEW YORK.....N.Y.

February 1, 19—

ANALYSIS (cont'd)
    Current statement shows a liquid ratio of about .57 to 1. and a current ratio of 1.05 to 1. both of which are below accepted standard. Sales compared with receivables indicate average collection period of about 337 days which is slower than accepted standard, indicating that some of the accounts are becoming old. Inventory, compared with sales, indicates a satisfactory turnover of about 3 times a year.

    While the current and liquid positions are below accepted standards, the net worth ratio, which is about 1.4 to 1., is satisfactory and there is indicated some margin of ratable worth placed at slightly better than $60,000. after allowing for adjustments and depreciations.

BANK INFORMATION
    Satisfactory account maintained for several years. Balances previously averaged in moderate five figures, but at present average in moderate four to high four figures. Accommodations extended in high four to low five figures, secured by endorsement of principals and cared for as agreed.

TRADE INVESTIGATION

      NATIONAL INTERCHANGE OF TRADE EXPERIENCE

      Dec. 15, 19— - Results - 18 Houses Reporting

PAYMENTS	OWING	PAST DUE
1- Discount	125.	---
2- Discount	---	---
3- Discount	77	---
4- Medium	340.	---
5- Medium	260.	---
6- Medium	180.	180.
7- Medium	410.	---
8- Medium	---	---
9- Medium	100.	---
10-Slow	600.	320.
11-Slow	390.	175.
12-Slow	740.	650.
13-Slow	367.	367.
14-Slow	239.	140.
15-Very Slow	842.	842.
16-Very Slow	729	560
17-Very Slow	163	163.
18-Very Slow	639.	160.
	6,198.	3,557.

FIG. 16–5 (cont'd.).

in individual items are noted to aid the reader. In addition, the current position and net worth ratios are given.

Bank Information. This section contains the results of either an interview with the subject's bank or a detailed report received by mail in response to an inquiry on the status of the account.

Trade Investigation. The results of the Lyon National Weekly Interchange of Trade Experience are given in this section. Method of payment, amount owing, and amount past due are reported by each participating reference. Additional comments made by suppliers may be included in the

Form 20 Rev. 11/75

LYON CREDIT REPORT

This report compiled from our records is sent to you confidentially, for your exclusive use, in accordance with the terms of your contract. The Lyon Furniture Mercantile Agency shall not be liable for any loss or injury or that of its agents, in obtaining, compiling or communicating this information; and Agency does not guarantee correctness of same.

DOE, JOHN CORPORATION   -5-   NEW YORK.....N.Y.

February 1, 19—

TRADE INVESTIGATION (cont'd)

Inquiry of Jan. 15, 19—

Manner of Payment	Now Owing	Past Due	# Days Slow	High Credit	Period Last Sold
1—Medium	125.	-	-	400.	1/—
2—Medium	680.	110.	-	725.	1/—
3—Slow	319.	284.	30	667.	1/—
4—Slow	723.	416.	30	981.	1/—
5—Slow	1,276.	962.	30-60	1,519.	12/—
6—Slow	693.	487.	60	724.	12/—
7—Very Slow	981	876.	90	1,263.	12/—
8—Very Slow	1,547.	1,029.	90	1,849.	11/—
9—Very Slow	820.	820.	180	1,057.	11/—
10—Very Slow	716.	616.	120	716.	11/—

COLLECTION RECORD

Aug. 7,19— - Claim (H35782) for $420.50 placed with High Point Office
              for inv. 3/6/—. Collected by Agency 10/1/—.
Sept.22,19— - Claim (C-48581) for $232.60 placed with Chicago Office
              for goods sold 4/—. Collected by Agency 10/26/—.
Nov. 15,19— - Claim (H-36784) for $195.80 placed with High Point Office
              for inv. 6/6/—. Collected by Agency 12/2/—.
Dec. 16,19— - Claim (H36787) for $527.00 placed with High Point Office
              for inv. 7/5/—. Collected by Agency 1/8/—.
Dec. 23, 19—- Claim (N-57602) for $947.18 placed with New York Office
              for goods sold May through Sept 19—. Collected by
              Agency 1/23/—.

SUMMARY
        PRINCIPALS EXPERIENCED. PRESIDENT AND TREASURER HAVE BEEN
IDENTIFIED IN THE PAST WITH UNSUCCESSFUL VENTURE. CURRENT STATEMENT
SHOWS SUB STANDARD LIQUID AND CURRENT POSITIONS, MODERATE RATABLE NET
WORTH INDICATED. TRADE PAYMENTS DURING THE PAST FEW MONTHS HAVE BECOME
SLOW WITH CLAIMS PLACED FOR COLLECTION.

N: Rate 13-H-5-116   (s.i.)

FIG. 16–5 (cont'd.).

tabulation. This section might also include the results of a direct inquiry among trade suppliers or other references furnished the agency. Where applicable, it also lists a record of amounts placed with the agency for collection, including disposition of the claim when collected or closed.

Summary. A concise summary of the entire report is given here, highlighting principal points. A rating is assigned to the account on the last line.

Ratings and Other Codes

The Lyon Red Book-Credit Key is similar in theory to those of other agencies, though the details are somewhat different.

Rating Key. Capital ratings are assigned in terms of letters. The letters

F, P, W, and Y are indefinite ratings assigned to estimate the financial worth of a business when data short of an actual balance sheet are furnished. The other letters signify an estimated financial worth based upon a current balance sheet. A rating key is shown in Figure 16–6. The capital rating for a business with an estimated financial worth of $41,000, for example, would be "J."

Indications of the payment habits of the customer are given in terms of numbers, ranging from 1 to 9. Other special conditions are indicated by numbers or by symbols.

NAME_____ Sub. No._____

THIS CREDIT REFERENCE BOOK IS THE PROPERTY OF LYON FURNITURE MERCANTILE AGENCY and is LOANED on Annual Subscription Agreement only. THIS BOOK MUST BE RETURNED upon termination of Subscription Agreement or upon delivery of a new book. (See Page "D" for further conditions).

LYON RED BOOK — CREDIT KEY

CAPITAL RATINGS Estimated Financial Worth	PAY RATINGS Based on suppliers' reports
A ....$1,000,000 or over	1—Discount.
B .... 500,000 to $1,000,000	2—Prompt.
C .... 300,000 to 500,000	3—Medium.
D .... 200,000 to 300,000	
E .... 100,000 to 200,000	4—Variable, prompt to slow.
G .... 75,000 to 100,000	5—Slow.
H .... 50,000 to 75,000	6—Very Slow.
J .... 40,000 to 50,000	7—C. O. D. or C. B. D.
K .... 30,000 to 40,000	8—Pay rating not established, but information favorable.
L .... 20,000 to 30,000	
M .... 15,000 to 20,000	9—Claims to buy always for cash.
N .... 10,000 to 15,000	
O .... 7,000 to 10,000	
Q .... 5,000 to 7,000	
R .... 3,000 to 5,000	SPECIAL CONDITIONS
S .... 2,000 to 3,000	
T .... 1,000 to 2,000	12—Business recently commenced.
U .... 500 to 1,000	13—Inquire for report.
V .... 100 to 500	21—Buys small, usually pays cash.

Z-No financial basis for credit reported.

24—Name listed for convenience only.

29—Rating undetermined.

INDEFINITE RATINGS

31—Financial statement declined, or repeatedly requested and not received.

F—High financial worth indicated.

P—Moderate financial worth indicated.

SYMBOL INTERPRETATION

W—Small financial worth indicated.

● or 12 — Business recently commenced.

Y—Limited financial worth indicated.

✚ or 116 — New Statement recently received.

▲—Indicates information of unusual importance.

The omission of a rating is not unfavorable, but indicates that sufficient information is not at hand on which to base rating.

(?)—Sells from residence, office or catalogue.

CREDIT GRANTORS—NOTE

No system of ratings can ALWAYS convey an accurate summarization of existing conditions. Book ratings reflect conditions believed to exist when assigned, and are based upon information obtained from financial statements, from the trade, special reporters, correspondents, financial institutions and other sources deemed reliable, but the correctness thereof is in no way guaranteed.

Conditions are constantly changing, and changes as made are shown in the "LYON Weekly Supplement and Report", and in Lyon Credit Reports.

Should any error, or inaccuracy in rating be noted, it should be reported immediately to the Agency, in order that correction may be made.

Inquire for Detailed Credit Report on all NEW ACCOUNTS, and make inquiry at least once a year on old accounts or when change in rating is indicated in the "LYON Weekly Supplement and Report."

A

FIG. 16–6. Lyon Red Book—Credit Key.

Special Ratings. These ratings are issued when information regarding an account warrants a change in rating. For example, a business that discontinues operations would be rated 107, discontinued or out of business. Figure 16–7 shows the key numbers interpreting credit items and business conditions. These special ratings are used in the Lyon Weekly Supplement and Report, and the Lyon Special Notification Report.

SPECIAL RATINGS

Key Numbers interpreting Credit Items and
Business Conditions.

12 or ●—Business recently commenced.
13—Inquire for report.
21—Buys small, usually pays cash.
24—Name listed for convenience only.
29—Rating undetermined.
30—Rating in abeyance, pending later information.
31—Financial statement declined, or repeatedly requested and not received.
47—New ownership or change in ownership.
49—Dissolved.
50—Succeeded by —
53—Looting or theft.
54—Rating suspended.
55—Given bill of sale, or notice thereof.
56—Reported selling out, or discontinuing.
57—Have sold out.
58—Sold out at auction.
59—Water damage reported.
60—Flood or storm damage reported.
61—Fire damage reported.
62—Destroyed by fire.
66—No insurance.
67—Will continue.
68—Deceased.
69—Estate continues.
70—Claim placed for collection with Lyon Agency.
78—Attachment proceedings reported.
79—Closed by Sheriff or Marshal.
80—Sold out by Sheriff or Marshal.

81—Chattel mortgage.
82—Chattel mortgage foreclosed.
83—Deed of trust.
85—Real estate mortgage foreclosed.
87—Assignment.
88—Petition for Receiver filed.
89—Temporary Receiver appointed.
90—Receiver appointed.
93—Petition in bankruptcy filed.
94—Petition for arrangement, reorganization extension or composition.
95—In bankruptcy.
96—Inquire for important new report.
98—Trustee appointed.
99—In liquidation.
103—Requesting extension.
104—Called meeting of creditors.
105—Offering to compromise.
106—Unable to locate.
107—Discontinued or out of business.
108—Claims should be given immediate attention.
109—Settled and resumed.
111—Removed to —
114—Name changed to —
115—Cannot report definitely as yet.
116 or ✛—New statement recently received.
119—Not for book listing.
120—Discontinue book listing.

B

FIG. 16–7.   Special Ratings—Lyon

Business Classifications and Abbreviations. Figure 16–8 lists all of the business classifications reported by the agency. This listing is used in the Lyon Red Book, supplements, and reports.

BUSINESS CLASSIFICATIONS AND ABBREVIATIONS
AS USED IN LYON RED BOOK, SUPPLEMENTS AND REPORTS

(?)...............Sells from residence, office or catalogue.

Agt................	Agent	Mach................	Machinery
Alm................	Aluminum	MO................	Mail Order Business
Ant................	Antique	Mfg................	Manufacturing
Apl................	Appliances	Mfr................	Manufacturer
Auc................	Auctioneer	MfrsRep........	Manufacturers
BCgs................	Baby Carriages		Representative
Bdg................	Bedding	Moho................	Mobile Homes
BdRmF............	Bed Room Furniture	Mtrl................	Material
BdSpgs............	Bed Springs	Mtrs................	Mattresses
Bds................	Beds	Mdse................	Merchandise
BkfstRmF........	Breakfast Room	Met................	Metallic
	Furniture	Mir................	Mirrors
Cbts................	Cabinets	Midgs................	Mouldings
CbtHdw..........	Cabinet Hardware	N&2dhd............	New & Second Hand
C or Cpts........	Carpets or Floor	NovF................	Novelty Furniture
	Coverings	Occ................	Occasional
Chrs................	Chairs	OffF................	Office Furniture
ChmF................	Chrome Furniture	OtdrF................	Outdoor Furniture
Col................	Colonial	Pts................	Paints
Contr................	Contractor	ParFr................	Parlor Frames
Conv't............	Converters	Pia................	Pianos
CtnGds............	Cotton Goods	P or Pic..........	Picture Frames
Cur................	Curtains	Pil................	Pillows
DS................	Department Store	Pla................	Plastic
Dsks................	Desks	Plywd............	Plywood
DimSt'k............	Dimension Stock	Prem................	Premium Goods
DngRmF........	Dining Room Furn	Prod................	Products
DinF................	Dinette Furniture	R................	Retail
Distr................	Distributor	Rdo................	Radios
Drap................	Draperies	Ref................	Refrigerators
DG................	Dry Goods	Ren................	Renovate
Equip................	Equipment	Reprod............	Reproductions
Exp................	Exporter	Rtn................	Rattan
F or Furn........	Furniture	Rub................	Rubber
FFr................	Furniture Frames	Rugs................	Rugs
Fab................	Fabric	SchF................	School Furniture
Fea................	Feathers	ShRms................	Show Rooms
Fldg................	Folding	SlipCov............	Slip Covers
FlCov................	Floor Coverings	Spec................	Specialties
Fm................	Foam	Spgs................	Springs
Fr................	Frames	Stge................	Storage
GenMdse........	General Merchandise	S or Sto........	Stoves
GS................	General Store	Sup................	Supplies
Gifts................	Gift Shop	Tbls................	Tables
H or Hdw........	Hardware	TV................	Television
Hdbrds............	Headboards	Tgs................	Trimmings
Hfg................	House Furnishings	U or Und........	Undertaker
Imp................	Importer	Unf'dF............	Unfinished Furn
Inst'l................	Institutional	Uph................	Upholsterer
IntDec............	Interior Decorations	Uph'dF............	Upholstered Furn
IntDesgn........	Interior Design	Uph'g................	Upholstering
Job................	Jobber	Uph'ySup........	Upholstery Supplies
Juv................	Juvenile	VacCln............	Vacuum Cleaners
Kchn................	Kitchen	Var................	Varnish
Lps................	Lamps	Vnrs................	Veneers
LpSha............	Lamp Shade	VenBls............	Venetian Blinds
Lea................	Leather	WP................	Wall Paper
Lib................	Library	WshMch............	Washing Machines
Lin................	Linoleum	Wtbd................	Waterbeds
LivRmF............	Living Room Furn	Wh................	Wholesale
Lbr................	Lumber	Wd................	Wood
		WrIr................	Wrought Iron

C

FIG. 16–8. Business Classifications and Abbreviations.

Lyon Red Book

The Lyon Red Book contains the names, locations, business classification, rating, and other vital information about all the businesses reported by this agency. It is revised and published every six months and kept up to date with the Lyon Weekly Supplement and Report.

National Weekly Interchange of Trade Experience

As part of its regular service, Lyon conducts a weekly interchange of trade experience. A "Tracer" is mailed to Lyon subscribers, listing the names on which ledger experiences are requested. The subscribers complete the form, indicating the method of payment by numbers ranging from 1 to 7 (except number 4) and the amounts owing and past due.

Number 1 indicates payments strictly within discount terms.
Number 2 indicates payments strictly within net terms of sale.
Number 3 indicates payments satisfactory, up to 30 days slow.
Number 5 indicates payments slow, up to 90 days after maturity.
Number 6 indicates payments very slow, over 90 days past due.
Number 7 indicates credit refused, or COD and CBD terms.

The results are collected and tabulated by the agency. Each subscriber responding to the "Tracer" request receives a copy of the tabulation, which is known as a "Result." Sample Tracer and Result forms are shown in Figure 16–9 and 16–10 respectively.

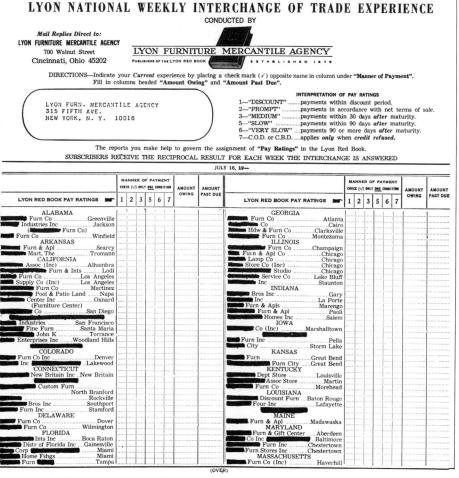

FIG. 16–9.   Lyon National Weekly Interchange of Trade Experience (Investigation).

RESULT OF INVESTIGATION NO. 27

LYON NATIONAL WEEKLY INTERCHANGE OF TRADE EXPERIENCE

CONDUCTED BY

LYON FURNITURE MERCANTILE AGENCY

PUBLISHERS OF THE LYON RED BOOK   ESTABLISHED 1876

EXPLANATION—The numbers in the first column denote the number of suppliers reporting. The 1-2-3-5-6-7 at the head of next column are Lyon Red Book "Pay Ratings",
and numbers under them denote number of suppliers reporting on each condition.
A number in parenthesis in the "Amount Owing" or "Amount Reported Past Due" column indicates the number of suppliers reporting.

Lyon Furniture Mercantile Agency, as your agent, furnishes the information herein under the terms of your subscription agreement. The information is for your exclusive use. It is to be held confidential and not to be revealed, made known or shown to those reported. Any disclosure is a violation of the terms of your contract.

JULY 16, 19—

LYON RED BOOK PAY RATINGS	No. of Suppliers Reporting	1	2	3	5	6	7	AMOUNT REPORTED OWING	AMOUNT REPORTED PAST DUE	LYON RED BOOK PAY RATINGS	No. of Suppliers Reporting	1	2	3	5	6	7	AMOUNT REPORTED OWING	AMOUNT REPORTED PAST DUE
ALABAMA										**IOWA**									
Sales & Service Albertville	2	1	1					(1) $1485		Plaza Inc...... Des Moines	4	4						(1) 40	
Furn Co....... Piedmont	6	1	4	1				(2) 3753		**KANSAS**									
										Ltd... Leawood	7		1	2	2		2	(2) 4770	(2) 1979
ARKANSAS										Furn Inc........... Topeka	2	1					1		
Furn & Apl........... Fordyce	4	3			1					**KENTUCKY**									
County Furn.... Heber Springs	3		1	2				(2) 2615	(2) $859	Furn Outlet.... Evarts	5	1		1	2	1		(2) 6987	(2) 1490
CALIFORNIA										**MAINE**									
Furn.................. Banning	6	1			1	1	3	(1) 204	(1) 204	Hdw Inc........... Auburn	7	1	1	3	1	1		(2) 2426	(2) 1508
Furn & Apl........... Chino	9		1	5	2	1		(6) 3827	(4) 1202	Furn Ints (Inc)..... Bangor	4	1	1	2				(1) 1052	
Furn............... Fresno	9	1	3	3	2			(2) 704		**MARYLAND**									
Los Angeles	12	9	2					(5) 4829		Jewelers Inc... Baltimore	4	1	2		1			(1) 16468	(1) 16021
(Furn)										Inc............. Baltimore	7	4	3					(3) 2834	(1) 664
Furn............ National City	4	1	1	1	1			(3) 2569	(1) 500	**MASSACHUSETTS**									
Inc..... Newport Beach	3		2				1			Inc................. Fitchburg	10	6	4					(1) 666	
& Co)										Inc.. Great Barrington	4		2	2				(3) 1798	(2) 1167
Ints.... Newport Beach	3		2	1				(1) 1636	(1) 640	Furn Co Inc...... Lexington	6	4	2					(2) 798	
Inc........... Rosemead	5		1	3	1			(4) 31535	(2) 3594	Furn Outlet........... Lynn	4	2	1				1	(1) 960	
House ....San Francisco	11	2	4	2	2			(7) 8514	(2) 979	Furn........... Natick	6	1	3	1	1			(3) 1735	(1) 191
Decor Corp...... San Mateo	5	1	4							Furn Co Inc.. New Bedford	7	1	6					(3) 1956	
Furn............ Sonora	3			2		1		(3) 1405	(2) 905	**MICHIGAN**									
COLORADO										Furn Co...... Benton Harbor	6		4	1	1			(3) 5757	(1) 948
Furn ...... Evans	6	4	2					(1) 755		Furn Co........... Detroit	3	1	1		1			(2) 3868	
Furn Inc...... Fort Collins	6		2	2	1	1		(2) 10718	(1) 3275	House Inc....... Detroit	2	2							
CONNECTICUT										Furn............ Fenton	5	1	4					(2) 4004	(1) 268
Interiors Inc.......... Darien	3	2	1							Mancelona....... Mancelona	2						2		
Co (Inc)...... New Haven	10	6	4					(5) 5412	(1) 375	**MINNESOTA**									
DELAWARE										Ints Inc... Bloomington	8			1			7	(1) 666	
Inc........... Wilmington	3	1	1	1				(3) 1749		Ints Inc......... Edina	4			2			2	(1) 457	
FLORIDA										Furn Inc.......... St Cloud	7	4	2	1				(3) 5056	
Furn Co........... Holly Hill	4	1	3					(1) 500		**MISSISSIPPI**									
George C............... Ocala	2	2								Furn & Apl..... Starkville	4	2			1	1		(3) 4081	(2) 1865
Furn. Orlando	5	2	2	1				(3) 1899		**MISSOURI**									
of Orlando Inc.......... Orlando	6	3	3					(3) 2125		Home Fshgs..... Poplar Bluff	3	1	1	1				(2) 1923	
GEORGIA										Furn Co Inc......... St Joseph	2	2						(1) 245	
Furn Co Inc............ Cairo	3	2						(1) 397		**MONTANA**									
Furn Co........... Cartersville	3	1	1					(1) 292		Carpet-Furn...... Great Falls	5	2	3					(1) 1310	
Furn Co............. Jesup	2	1	1					(2) 1871		**NEBRASKA**									
ILLINOIS										of Beatrice........... Beatrice	2	1	1						
Interiors............... Chicago	3									Furn & Apl..... Hastings	4			2		1	1	(1) 2528	(2) 2528
INDIANA										**NEVADA**									
& Furn Co.... Daleville	3		1	2				(1) 1189		Corp............... Las Vegas	3	1	1	1					
Mart Inc.............. Gary	5	3		2				(2) 3094		**NEW HAMPSHIRE**									
Furn Co............. La Porte	3		2		1			(1) 119	(1) 119	Furn Co............. Laconia	4		1	2		1		(2) 1046	(2) 722

(OVER)

FIG. 16–10. Lyon National Weekly Interchange of Trade Experience (Result of Investigation).

CREDIT EXCHANGE INC.

This agency, formed in 1921, has expanded its services and coverage steadily since that time. Its headquarters is in New York City with branch offices located in Philadelphia, Chicago, Los Angeles, and Miami. Credit Exchange conducts its business through several divisions and operating subsidiaries, each providing a specialized service to subscribers. Its principal activities are Credit Recommendations and Reports (apparel and giftware fields), Commercial Collections (all industries), and Sporting Goods Industries Clearing House (golf and tennis industries).

Credit Report

Subscribers to Credit Exchange may elect to receive Recommendation Service only (in which case they receive no detailed report) or may draw reports on their customers (Figure 16–11). The report is an aid to detailed

Credit Exchange, Inc.
461 EIGHTH AVENUE, NEW YORK, N. Y. 10001

DETAILED CREDIT REPORT

Established 1921

TO SUBSCRIBER NO._____DATE_____

The Specialized Agency

APPAREL & ACCESSORIES
GIFT & DECORATIVE
SPORTING GOODS

The Fashion Shop, Inc.
Nelson Building
New Orleans, Louisiana

BRANCH: THE STYLE SHOP, Third Street, Baton Rouge, La.

BUSINESS: RETAIL APPAREL, ACESSORIES AND SPORTSWEAR

OFFICERS: SUSAN A NESSEN, President
MILDRED THOMAS, Secretary and Treasurer

RECORD: CLEAR

HISTORY:

Miss Susan A. Nessen originally established this business in New Orleans,
La., in October of 0000. The initial investment was $10,000. In the
following year she opened four branch units and subsequently discontinued
all but the branch store on Third Street in Baton Rouge, La. In January,
0000, this venture was incorporated under the Laws of Louisiana with
authorized capital of $100,000 of which $85,700 has been paid in.

Miss Nessen has been active in the ladies apparel field for the past
twenty-five years. Prior to this venture she was employed by the Rose
Style Shop as buyer and merchandise manager. She is considered competent
and reliable. Miss Thomas has been employed by this firm since its inception.

Both stores are modern, attractive units situated in good locations in
the main shopping centers of their respective cities. The rentals are
$500.00 per month for the New Orleans store and $400.00 per month for
the store in Baton Rouge.

FINANCIAL:

A photographic copy of the financial statement of August 31,0000 is
attached.

COMPARATIVE DATA:

Date	8/31/00	8/31/00	8/31/00
Current Assets	$97,714.	$108,684.	$122,527.
Current Liabilities	39,788.	38,891.	33.211.
Working Capital	57,926.	69,793.	89,316.
Net Worth	84,741	102,904.	127,967.

NEW YORK • PHILADELPHIA • CHICAGO • LOS ANGELES • MIAMI

FIG. 16–11. Credit Exchange Report.

#2

The Fashion Shop, Inc.
New Orleans, Louisiana

ANALYSIS:

It will be noted that the new financial statement indicates an increase
in Net Worth and Working Capital of approximately $20,000. We have had
occasion to interview the principals at interest who reported to us that
60% of the business is done on a cash basis and 40% on a charge basis.
Collections on Accounts Receivable for the past seven months totaled
$72,836. We have a complete schedule of Accounts Receivable and, as of
statement date, there was no past-due indebtedness. This concern has
sufficient working capital to operate this venture.

BANK:

A local bank advises maintaining a satisfactory account since March 00,00,
with balances averaging in four-figure amounts. They have extended
accommodations on an endorsed basis and payments have always been met
as agreed.

TRADE:

In a recent trade clearance, this account was found to be extended credit
in amounts up to $2,800. The general line of credit ranges from $500.00
to $750.00. Suppliers report that recent payments have been prompt to
occasionally 30 days slow.

CREDIT SUGGESTION:

$2,000.00

FIG. 16–11 (cont'd.).

credit analysis, since it provides the information from which the agency's
credit recommendations are derived. The reports are revised on a regular
basis, as well as whenever unusual circumstances make a review necessary.

Heading. On the first page are listed the name, address, and line of
business; branch locations; names of the principals; and comment on their
business records.

If Credit Exchange is not recommending the account, the first page of
the report is on a red letterhead with the legend, "Not Recommending this
Account," next to the name box.

History. This section contains a description of the business and pertinent information about the principals. Details of its capitalization are given
in the first paragraph. The business records of the principals are given next,
with comment on any financial difficulties they may have encountered.

The bottom paragraphs of this section contain a description of store locations, their state of repair, and the rental paid for them.

Financial. The latest balance sheet and operating details may be shown

STATEMENT MADE TO

CREDIT EXCHANGE, Inc., 461 EIGHTH AVE., NEW YORK, N.Y. 10001

I (We) give you below a statement of my (our) assets and liabilities taken from my (our) books, reflecting the financial condition of my (our) business as of the date appearing below, based upon actual inventory taken and submitted for the purpose of obtaining credit or insurance through your agency for the benefit of all subscribers and future subscribers whom you do or may serve. We hereby authorize our accountants, banks and bankers to supply you, and any business houses to whom you may exhibit or send a copy of this statement, with such information as you or they request. This, or copies of it, may be exhibited, duplicated or photographed without notice to me (us) with the intent and purpose that it can be relied upon by your subscribers, or prospective subscribers, in the extension of credit to my (our) account. Since the date of taking this inventory, there has been no material change in my (our) financial condition, and if such change takes place, the undersigned will give due notice thereof.

Name in Full _The Fashion Shop, Inc._ _____ Trading As _____
Street Address _Nelson Building_ ____ City _New Orleans_ State _LA_ Zip _71234_
Successors To _____ Business Telephone No. (_321_) _543-9876_
Types of Mdse. Carried _Apparel, Accessories, Sportswear_ ☒ Retailer ☐ Jobber ☐ Manufacturer
Branches (Number & Location) _____

FINANCIAL CONDITION AS OF _____ XXX, 00 19 00 _____

ASSETS				LIABILITIES			
Cash on Hand				Accounts Payable, Not Due		14246	13
Cash in _First National_ Bank	6517	43		Accounts Payable, Past Due			
_____ Bank				Notes Payable, Banks ☐ Secured ☐ Unsec.		9541	63
Accounts Receivable (Good and not over six				How Secured			
months old) $ _40818.86_				Due _____ Payable $ _____ per _____			
Less Reserve $ _4081.89_				Notes Payable, Others ☐ Secured ☐ Unsec.			
	36736	97		How Secured			
Notes Receivable _Will Calls_	10025	11		To Whom		1208	63
Merchandise at Cost or Market				Due _____ Payable $ _____ per _____			
(whichever is lower)	67065	66		Accruals		3911	22
Other Current Assets				Due Officers or Partners		4303	84
(specify) _Prepaid Exp._	2182	53		Other Current Liabilities ^Maturity Date^			
CURRENT ASSETS	122527	70		CURRENT LIABILITIES		33211	45
Accounts Receivable Over Six Months Old				Mortgage on Real Estate			
Due from Officers or Members of Firm				Long Term Liabilities		13178	69
Furniture and Fixtures $ _46718.17_				Net Worth ☐ Firm ^Maturity Date^			
Less Depreciation $ _15107.81_	31610	36		☐ Individual			
Investments	20220	00		Capital Stock – Common		85700	00
Other Assets–Specify				– Preferred			
Real Estate				Surplus		42267	92
TOTAL ASSETS	174358	06		TOTAL LIABILITIES & CAPITAL		174358	06

PROFIT AND LOSS STATEMENT		PLEASE ANSWER ALL QUESTIONS
NET SALES–FROM _XX_ TO _XX_ $ _148198.06_		When Started in Business _October XX_
(Do not include Leased Departments)		With What Capital _10000_ Where _____
Inventory–at beginning _____ $ _36990.70_		Under What Name _____
Purchases–(without discounts) $ _123161.48_		Former Connection _____
Total $ _160152.18_		Monthly Rental $ _900_ Lease Expires _XX_
Deduct: Inventory–at end _____ $ _67065.66_		Ever fail or have fire (including all previous business connections)
Cost of Goods Sold (Deduct) $ _93086.52_		Yes ☐ No ☐ Give details _____
$ _55111.54_		Types of Insurance _____
Add: Purchase Discounts $ _7310.26_		Value of Insurance: On Mdse $ _100,000_ Fixtures $ _10,000_
Expenses–(Deduct): Gross Profit $ _62421.80_		Amount of Accts. Rec. Assigned $ _____
Salaries, Officers or Partners $ _8964.99_		To Whom _____
Rent $ _5520.00_		Sales Percent Cash? _60_ % Charge? _40_ % Installment? _____%
Wages & Other Expenses $ _34456.99_		Name of Accountant _Adam Harvey, CPA_
Losses–Bad Debts $ _____		Address of Accountant _New Orleans, LA_
Reserves $ _____		Do You Lease Depts.? Yes ☐ No ☒ How Many? _____
Deprec. on Fixed Assets $ _1216.29_		Incorporated–State of _Louisiana_ on _XX_
Total Deductions $ _55158.27_		Capitalization Authorized Paid In ^Date^
Operating Profit or Loss $ _7263.53_		Preferred $ _____ $ _____
Other Income _____ $ _____		Common $ _100,000_ $ _85,700._
Provision for Taxes _____ $ _2200.00_		

OWNERS OR OFFICERS	HOME ADDRESS AND TELEPHONE NO.	DATE OF BIRTH
Susan A. Nessen	_55 Royale, New Orleans_ _514-1357_	_00/00/00_

776   The above full and correct statement of ^my^/~~our~~ financial condition is made to form a basis for credit with subscribers of CREDIT EXCHANGE, Inc.

SIGN HERE _Susan A. Nessen_

Dated _00/00/00_

Title _President_

New York Representative _____

References (over)

FIG. 16–11 (cont'd.).

in this section, or they may be photographed and attached to the report. The figures are presented without agency comment, although explanatory footnotes and other remarks submitted by the business or its auditors are included. The figures are analyzed in another part of the report.

Comparative Data. Whenever they are available, summary figures for three successive years are shown in this section. Current assets, current liabilities, net working capital, and net worth are shown so the reader may note the trend of those data.

Analysis. In this section the figures of the company are analyzed, and information pertinent to the understanding of the financial condition is presented. Principals' comments are noted, explanations of significant developments are made, and an overall appraisal of the financial condition is given.

Bank. During the course of the investigation, the subject's bank is contacted and the results are given in this section. Average balances, basis and amount of borrowings, amount now owing, and method of retirement are described.

Trade. While Credit Exchange does not show a trade tabulation, it summarizes the results of its latest current trade clearance in this section. High credits, amounts owing and past due, and general lines of credit are noted. Method of debt retirement is also reported.

Credit Suggestion. This is the final section of the report and crystallizes the credit opinion of the account by assigning a suggested line of credit to it. This amount is intended to be adequate for representative suppliers, though individual circumstances may cause subscribers to vary from the agency's suggestions.

Credit Recommendation Service

This service is set up in three divisions, each operating semiautonomously: Apparel and Accessories, Giftware and Decorative Goods, and Sporting Goods. A subscriber may request information on an account by telephone or by mail. To answer these inquiries, Credit Exchange uses its electronic credit inquiry service, "CREDI-graphic." Key information is imprinted on IBM cards and mailed to the subscriber. A different colored card is used for each type of decision (Figure 16–12). The color code is:

Green: the credit is approved.
Pink: the account is not approved.
White and Blue: the account is under revision because of new information.
Salmon: there is a change of recommendation.
Yellow: a special notice has been published concerning the account.
Blue: the account is being investigated and further information follows.

The information coded on the IBM cards is obtained from the detailed credit report. The boxes show:

Date of the Inquiry. This is recorded so the subscriber will continue to receive information for one year following inquiry.

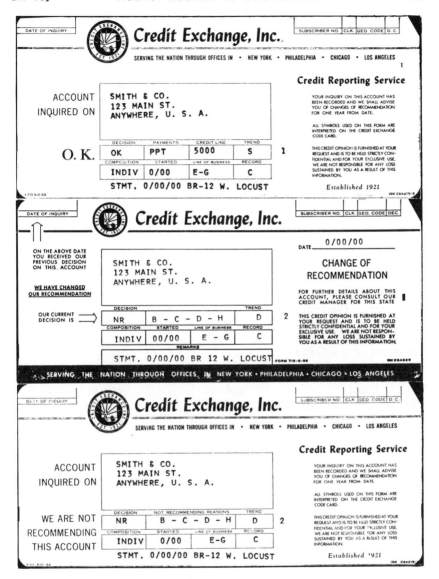

FIG. 16–12.   Credit-graphic Recommendation Service.

Complete Name and Address of the Account. The names of the principals are also given so subscribers can check their information against that which is on record with Credit Exchange. This is an aid to verifying ownership and financial responsibility.

Subscriber's Number. To provide automatic followthrough on the inquiry, this is transcribed to the master control card on the subject of inquiry.

Credit Decision.   When the account is approved, this box contains an "OK" and another box contains the suggested dollar amount of high credit. The pink card carries the notation, "NR," meaning not recommended; in another box the reasons for the decision are coded.

Payment Record.   This is a general comment on the recent trade payments of the account.

Trend.   The trend of the account over the past few years is shown in this box.

Composition.   The legal form of organization is given as individual, partnership, corporation, or estate. This helps to establish the continuity, capital resource, and liability from a creditor's viewpoint.

Started.   This is the starting date of the business. It helps to establish the length of time the business has been operating.

Line of Business.   Products and lines of the business are given in coded abbreviations.

Record.   This box contains the information about the business records of the principals. "C" means a clear record. Financial embarrassments are noted under "Remarks."

Remarks.   The date of the last financial statement, number of branches, and other important information is given in this box.

Credit Exchange Code

The agency uses a letter code on its "CREDI-graphic" Recommendation Service. This code is shown as Figure 16–13. To illustrate, in the top credit approval card in Figure 16–12, Smith & Co. has a steady trend (S); the line of business is women's specialties and accessories (E) and general merchandise (G); and the record of the principal is clear (C).

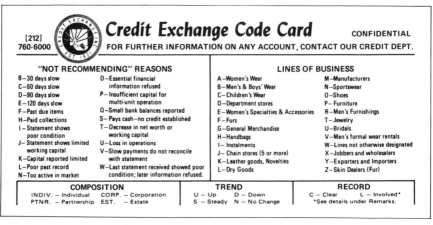

FIG. 16–13.   Credit Exchange Code Card.

NACM BUSINESS CREDIT INFORMATION SYSTEM

In contrast to the agencies described earlier, the NACM Business Credit Information System of the National Association of Credit Management specializes in the collection and dissemination of ledger experience information, bank information, and some public record information. Through the credit interchange departments of NACM affiliated associations, NACM members may obtain both NACM Business Credit Reports and Credit Interchange Reports.

NACM Business Credit Report

This fully automated credit reporting service was developed by the National Association of Credit Management, Credit Research Foundation Inc., and TRW Inc. as a fast way to secure credit information and prepare credit interchange reports. It was made available in 1976. TRW also provides this report to firms outside the NACM structure, in which case the report is called TRW Business Profile.

Major business firms in the United States supply computer tapes of their accounts receivable on a quarterly basis. When they are entered into the databank, the individual payment information is separated by customer accounts, and this up-to-date trade experience is available to NACM members immediately upon request. The requests may come via teleprinter terminals located in NACM participating association offices, or NACM members may install teleprinters in their own offices for direct access to the file. High-speed data transmission lines carry the requests to the central file. They are processed by computer immediately; the information is compiled and sent back within minutes over the communication network to the requesting terminal. The report has been designed so as to best display the information (see Figure 16–14).

Heading. The identification, which generally includes a code number to generate the report, is shown at the top of the report. When a code number is not shown, the name and address of the company being inquired upon is used to generate the reports and is shown below the identification. The report next indicates certain administrative information, including page numbers, date, time, report time, and so on.

Payment Experience. This section indicates how the firm is paying its bills to other suppliers. The ledger-type information displayed includes date reported, date of last sale, terms, recent high credit, and account balances in current and aged categories.

Business Category. Contributors of information are identified only by the business category they select, based on SIC codes.

Date Reported. This indicates the month and year the data were extracted from the contributor's accounts receivable system.

Date Last Sale/Activity. This notes when the most recent sale or other activity was reported.

Payment Terms. Reported terms of sale are displayed for each trade line.

Recent High Credit. This refers to the highest credit extended in the past 12 months or lesser period, rounded to the nearest hundred dollars.

Account Status. Under this heading the report lists Account Balance, the sum of all current and past-due amounts on the date reported; Current, the percentage of the account balance not yet due; and Days Beyond Terms, the percentage of the account balance beyond terms in categories of 1–30, 31–60, 61–90, and 91+ days.

Comments. In this column are displayed any additional remarks provided by contributors.

Payment Trends. This section displays the current reported totals and provides a unique trend analysis of those totals for each of the previous 180 days.

Current Totals. This indicates the number of contributors of trade experience information, the total account balances for all trade lines, and an aging of the account balances calculated as a percentage of total account balances.

Prior Totals. This section lists the same information for total account balances for each of the previous 180 days. It enables the credit executive to quickly and easily determine if the firm's payment performance has improved, remained at the same level, or deteriorated over the past 180 days.

Bank Information. This section notes the names and addresses of banks that do business with the subject firm. This information is obtained only from banks with automated systems that contribute to the databank.

Summary Business Data. This section provides key facts that allow a credit executive to quickly evaluate a company, such as type of product or service offered, estimated annual sales, market share, number of employees at that location, parent company affiliation, and ownership.

Inquiries. All inquiries on this name made within the previous 90 days are listed in this section. The business category of the inquirer may appear, or "Assoc" when an NACM association makes an inquiry for a member. New Customer indicates the subject is a new customer for the subscriber. An unusually large number of inquiries may indicate that the firm is looking for new trade credit sources or that its present suppliers are concerned for some reason.

Standard & Poor's Business and Financial Data. An option is available on reports which supply pertinent business and financial data on thousands of publicly and privately held U.S. companies. The information available is:

1. Three years of comparative balance sheets, operating statements, and critical ratios on 6,000 public companies.
2. In-depth analysis of the operations of the 3,500 largest U.S. corporations.

NATIONAL ASSOCIATION OF CREDIT MANAGEMENT

BUSINESS CREDIT REPORT

NCIS704946HEARTHR-R;K-05574

IN COOPERATION WITH

NACIS

A SERVICE OF TRW INC.

2/26/-	13:02:32	R023	ADMIN.	
PAGE	REPORT DATE	TIME	PORT	TYPE	MEMBER NUMBER

FOR DEMONSTRATION ONLY
THIS REPORT NOT TO BE SOLD

ATLANTA GA 30318

BUSINESS CATEGORY	DATE REPORTED	DATE LAST SALE/ ACTIVITY	PAYMENT TERMS	RECENT HIGH CREDIT	ACCOUNT STATUS					COMMENTS
					ACCOUNT BALANCE	CUR-RENT	DAYS BEYOND TERMS				
							1-30	31-60	61-90	91 +	
				$	$	%	%	%	%	%	
AIR TRANS	12 /-	12 /-	NET 30		200	66	12		22		DDWA 54
AIR TRANS	8 /-	8 /-	NET 30		<100	100					
AIR TRANS	12 /-	10 /-	NET 30		<100		100				DDWA 15
AIR TRANS	8 /-	8 /-	NET 30		200	100					
AUTO EQUIP	12 /-	11 /-	N10/25I	2800	<100	100					
AUTO PARTS	12 /-	11 /-			1700		53	47			SOLD 1 YRS
BUS SERVCS	7 /-	6 /-			<100	100					
BUS SERVCS	1 /-	12 /-			3800	100					
CHEMICALS	1 /-	11 /-	DISC		0						SOLD 1 YRS
CHEMICALS	12 /-	12 /-			400	54	46				SOLD> 1 YRS
CONSTRUCTN	12 /-										
CONTRL DEV	11 /-		DISC		2800	100					
DP SERVCS	5 /-	4 /-	NET 30		2700		100				
EQUIPMENT	12 /-	9 /-	1-10N30	4100	0						ADS 30
FABRICATNG	1 /-	9 /-	NET 30	300	0						ADS 15
INDUS MACH	12 /-				<100	100					
INDUS MACH	11 /-	10 /-	301/210		15000	100					
INDUS SUPL	12 /-	11 /-	VARIED	27800	9200	24	69			7	
INDUS SUPL	10 /-	9 /-	DISC		2900	68	32				
INDUS SUPL	8 /-	8 /-	VARIED		42600	83	17				SOLD 7 YRS
MACHINERY	5 /-	4 /-	0000		<100	100					
METAL DIST	1 /-	1 /-	301/210	44700	44800	49	50	1			
MISC MANUF	12 /-			300	1700	100					ADS 17
MISC MANUF	7 /-	6 /-	NET 30		8400	86	14				
MISC MANUF	12 /-	11 /-		1500	0						
MISC MANUF	4 /-				4300	100					
MISC MANUF	4 /-				0						
MOTR TRANS	4 /-	3 /-			100	100					
PAINTS	10 /_	8 /-	NET 30	3300	3300	100					
CONTINUED											

CONFIDENTIAL

FIG. 16-14. NACM Business Credit Report.

NATIONAL ASSOCIATION OF CREDIT MANAGEMENT

BUSINESS CREDIT REPORT

IN COOPERATION WITH

NACIS

A SERVICE OF TRW INC.

PAGE	REPORT DATE	TIME	PORT	TYPE	MEMBER NUMBER
2	2/26/-	13:02:32	R023	ADMIN.	

FOR DEMONSTRATION ONLY
THIS REPORT NOT TO BE SOLD

ATLANTA GA 30318

BUSINESS CATEGORY	DATE REPORTED	DATE LAST SALE/ ACTIVITY	PAYMENT TERMS	RECENT HIGH CREDIT	ACCOUNT STATUS						COMMENTS
					ACCOUNT BALANCE	CUR-RENT	DAYS BEYOND TERMS				
							1-30	31-60	61-90	91 +	
				$	$	%	%	%	%	%	
PRNTG&PUBL	1 /-				200	100					
PRNTG&PUBL	1 /-		NET 30		0						
PRNTG&PUBL	1 /-		NET 30		0						
RUBR&PLAST	1 /-	12 /-	VARIED	87400	53600	1	27	64		8	
SERVICES	3 /-	2 /-	NET		300	49	51				DBWA 15
SERVICES	1 /-	12 /-	NET		5300	52	48				SOLD> 4 YRS
SERVICES	3 /-	2 /-	NET		<100	100					SOLD> 3 YRS
TIRES	11 /-	11 /-	VARIED		5200	100					
TRANSPORTN	10 /-	5 /-			700					100	
TRUCK EQP	11 /-	11 /-	N10PROX		1200	56	44				DBWA 15
ALL TRADE LINE TOTAL:			39 ACCOUNTS		210900	50	30	17		3	
CURRENT TRADE LINE TOTAL:			25 ACCOUNTS		145800	39	33	24		4	
30 DAYS AGO TOTALS WERE:			26 ACCOUNTS		109100	74	24	1	1		
60 DAYS AGO			23		106600	68	30	1	1		
90 DAYS AGO			22		66200	56	42	1	1		
120 DAYS AGO			16		56900	52	47	1			
150 DAYS AGO			16		48700	55	14	23		8	
180 DAYS AGO			15		45700	57	9	25	1	8	

BANK-TRUST COMPANY BANK,P.O. BOX 4418,ATLANTA,GA
(404)588-7711

PRODUCT/SERVICE: MACHINERY, EXCEPT ELECTRICAL, SIC NO. 35
SALES(EST.): $19-26 MIL   MARKET SHR(EST.): ....   EMPLOYMENT: 490-500
TEL: 404-894-7900
OWNERSHIP: PRIVATE
CONTINUED

CONFIDENTIAL

FIG. 16-14 (cont'd.).

NATIONAL ASSOCIATION OF CREDIT MANAGEMENT

BUSINESS CREDIT REPORT

IN COOPERATION WITH

NACIS

A SERVICE OF TRW INC.

3	2/26/-	13:02:32	R023	ADMIN.	
PAGE	REPORT DATE	TIME	PORT	TYPE	MEMBER NUMBER

FOR DEMONSTRATION ONLY
THIS REPORT NOT TO BE SOLD

ATLANTA GA 30318

BUSINESS CATEGORY	DATE REPORTED	DATE LAST SALE/ ACTIVITY	PAYMENT TERMS	RECENT HIGH CREDIT	ACCOUNT STATUS						COMMENTS
					ACCOUNT BALANCE	CUR-RENT	DAYS BEYOND TERMS				
							1-30	31-60	61-90	91 +	
				$	$	%	%	%	%	%	
AGRI CHEM	12 /-	INQUIRY									
FINCL SVCS	12 /-	INQUIRY									
TIRES	12 /-	INQUIRY									
PAINTS	1 /-	INQUIRY									
GENERAL	2 /-	INQUIRY									

THE INFORMATION HEREIN IS FURNISHED IN CONFIDENCE FOR YOUR EXCLUSIVE USE
FOR LEGITIMATE BUSINESS PURPOSES AND SHALL NOT BE REPRODUCED. NEITHER
TRW INC., NOR ITS SOURCES OR DISTRIBUTORS WARRANT SUCH INFORMATION NOR
SHALL THEY BE LIABLE FOR YOUR USE OR RELIANCE UPON IT.

END - ADMINISTRATIVE REPORT - THIS REPORT NOT TO BE SOLD

CONFIDENTIAL

FIG. 16–14 (cont'd.).

3. Key business facts on more than 30,000 publicly and privately held companies.

Credit Interchange Reports

Since its beginning in 1896, the National Association of Credit Management has supplied economical, thorough Credit Interchange Reports to members through its Credit Interchange Bureaus. Requests for information on individual customers are sent to members, subscribers, and other references which complete the request forms and return them to the bureau or credit reporting agency. The agency then compiles all of the information into a credit report.

Automated Reports. The traditional method of collecting and compiling credit information has become increasingly costly and time-consuming, particularly when the customer is located in a distant city. Consequently, NACM Credit Interchange Bureaus are more and more using automation. Similar to the automated system, this program is designed to collect credit information, maintain it on file, and make it instantly available to inquirers upon request. NACM members with automated accounts receivable supply quarterly computer tapes of their accounts receivable. Nonautomated members prepare scanable forms manually, also on a quarterly basis, for inclusion in the databank. Thus the complete credit information is available to inquirers.

Traditional Credit Interchange Reports. Until the automation process is complete, traditional Credit Interchange Reports will continue to be supplied by NACM Credit Interchange Bureaus. A member inquiring about an account from its local Credit Interchange Bureau is sent any recent report on that account which is in file. If the report is over 120 days old but less than one year old, it is sent to the member with a notation calling attention to the date of the report. At the same time, a new clearance is started. As soon as local information is available to the bureau, the member receives a preliminary report. If subsequent information from nearby markets indicates a change in the payment trend from that reported in the preliminary report, a second preliminary report is issued. When all the returns have been received, a full report is issued to the member.

This method of information exchange assures the members of a representative trade clearance on their accounts. When making a request for a credit report, the member is asked to submit any known references on the customer. The Credit Interchange Bureau also obtains other references from members and from the customer. When a clearance is started, each reference receives an inquiry slip requesting its credit ledger experience with the account. This procedure reduces the likelihood of a biased report, based only upon references submitted by the customer.

Moreover, members are regularly canvassed concerning accounts in which they have expressed credit interest; banks and nonmember firms are also asked for their experience; and the results of these investigations are compiled into Credit Interchange Reports.

Reading A Credit Interchange Report. A sample Credit Interchange Report is shown in Figure 16–15. The information is listed by column with appropriate headings.

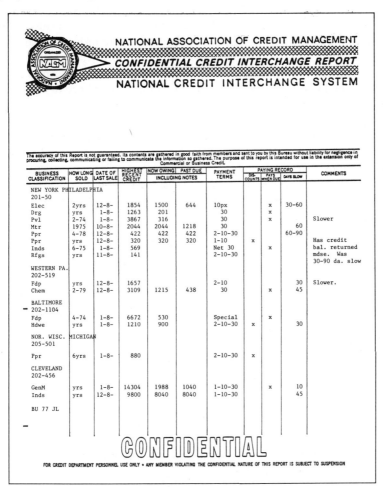

FIG. 16–15.   Credit Interchange Report.

Business Classification. This column indicates the markets in which the account is buying, the business classification of each contributor, and the coded date when the members in that market were canvassed for information. In Figure 16–15, for example, suppliers in the New York-Philadelphia area received requests from the Bureau and supplied the information on or after February 1.

How Long Sold. The buying habits of the account are reflected in this column. Many first orders reported on an account which has been in business for some time might indicate lack of confidence on the part of the former suppliers or preparation for a fraudulent "overbuy."

Date of Last Sale. This gives a picture of the timeliness of the ledger information reported, as well as an indication of the buying habits of the customer and the seasonal aspects of the business.

Highest Recent Credit. This tells the reader where the principal purchases of the customer are being made and how the order compares with the high credits approved by other suppliers. High credit amounts should be examined in conjunction with the manner of payment, terms, and the past-due amounts, since they may indicate either confidence or slow collection by the supplier.

Now Owing and Past Due. These figures should be checked against the highest recent credit. A clearance conducted during the active buying season of the account would probably show current credit and high credit running quite close. If the figures remain close after the manufacturing season had passed, however, there may be some trouble in the collection or receivables from the account. This can be verified by a check of the past-due column.

It is important in the interpretation of trade data to gather additional information before reaching a final conclusion. For instance, one supplier may be having a dispute with the account and report slow payments. In another instance past-due items may be shown, but comment may be included which indicates the reason for this. In fact, the trend of payment may be improving, although some amounts are still past due. On the other hand, a downward trend in the manner of payments may be a symptom of pending financial embarrassment.

Paying Record. This column gives the actual payment experience of the supplier with the account. Room is provided to record discount, prompt, or slow payments. If the account is slow, the number of days slowness is usually included.

Comments. Information that cannot be fitted into the standard headings of the other columns is placed here. Suppliers' comments regarding trend of payment, disputed items, notation of first orders, and accounts placed for collection may be found here.

CHAPTER 17

LEGAL FORMS OF BUSINESS ORGANIZATION FROM A CREDITOR'S VIEWPOINT

A portion of the total risk taken by the creditor arises from the legal composition of the debtor. Consequently, credit decisions are influenced by the form of organization used by the business prospect. The risk is fixed in each state by commercial laws which specify the right and obligations of business owners, corporate officers, and creditors. When questions arise concerning particular applications of state laws, the best source to consult is the *Credit Manual of Commercial Laws,* which is issued annually by the National Association of Credit Management.

The presentation in this chapter has been designed to acquaint the reader with the significance of the legal form of organization as a factor in credit analysis. More detailed treatment may be found in texts which specialize in corporate finance and business.

CREDITOR'S INTEREST IN LEGAL COMPOSITION

The credit executive must consider the form of business organization used by the debtor from the following standpoints:

1. *The continuity of the business.* It is essential to know the likelihood that a business will continue to function in the event of the sickness or death of one or more of the principals.

2. *The capital-raising potential.* Certain forms of organization can raise additional funds more easily than others. The potential of the debtor to raise these funds should the need arise is an important factor in the analysis of a firm.

3. *The liability of the principals.* In some forms of business, additional assets outside the business are sometimes available to support its debts, while in others this is not the case. The implications from the liability

standpoint of the several forms of organization are important in the analysis of a customer.

PROPRIETORSHIP

This form of enterprise is the easiest to organize and probably requires a minimum of technical skills, financial resources, and legal restrictions. The owner must comply with local health and safety regulations, and pay registration or qualification fees required by the community. The owner may then begin operations. Within legal limits, the proprietor can operate the business in an enterprising way.

Management

The freedom of formation and of operation enjoyed by the owner may be favorable from the creditor's viewpoint, if convinced that the principal has sound business judgment. The owner directs the entire business: marketing, production, and financial management. This enables the principal to take advantage of situations that require quick action. More realistic, however, is the fact that one person often may not possess all the skills required to operate a business. Consequently, the principal must seek some of these skills outside the business or chance neglecting a critical phase of operations. This means that the proprietor does not have the freedom to decide all the major business questions but must delegate those jobs which cannot be handled individually. In many instances, the freedom of formation and operation turns out to be a freedom to make business mistakes. The judgment of the proprietor may be required to stretch into unfamilar areas. For example, a good production manager may not know the intricacies of finance, a good sales manager may not be able to supervise manufacture of the product, and so on. Thus two heads often are better than one.

Continuity

The business usually ceases when the owner dies. In some cases it might be continued by the family or estate, providing the proper management skills can be furnished.

In the event of a proprietor's death, the creditors will probably not receive payment until the will is probated and the estate is settled. This may not mean a loss of money (except insofar as time is money), but it may tie up some of the creditor's capital for an unusual period of time.

The creditor is also interested in the proprietor's health and the amount of life insurance carried. As the driving force in the business, the owner must be in good physical and mental condition. Generally the strain of running a business is great, particularly when it rests on the shoulders of one person.

Capital

The proprietorship form can rely only on the assets of the business and those of the owner. There is no other way to increase those assets without allowing outside interests in the business. As soon as someone else invests money in the firm, the proprietorship has changed to another form. Consequently, the total amount of assets available to a proprietorship is limited.

The limited capital of the proprietorship form may be a significant factor in credit analysis. In some cases it is a controlling influence; but in many others the capital invested is sufficient for the scope of operations. Then the point becomes insignificant. The credit executive is primarily interested in seeing that the capitalization is sufficient for the business, not in determining the more theoretical needs of the business should it start a major program of expansion.

Moreover, since the sole owner receives the full benefit of a successful operation, there is no need to share profits with others. This influences the credit executive to observe what the owner does with the profits. Does the owner leave them in the business to strengthen its financial position, or does the owner withdraw them and continue to rely on creditor financing for operating funds? The answer will certainly point out areas needing further investigation.

Liability

The owner has a personal, unlimited liability for the debts of the business. This makes the proprietor vulnerable to creditors. With certain exceptions, the personal assets may be claimed for the payment of business debts.

The owner's personal liability for the debts of the business usually strengthens its credit position. The credit executive should be satisfied, however, that the personal liability means something in terms of assets. If the owner has no personal assets, this obligation would be largely theoretical.

It should also be verified that the owner does in fact own the assets claimed. If they are owned jointly with the spouse, the creditor may have difficulty in acting against them. The analysis should also establish that the owner of record is in fact the dominant principal in the business and not a dummy owner.

PARTNERSHIP

Today, many states have adopted the Uniform Partnership Act, which defines a partnership to be "an association of two or more persons to carry on as coowners of a business for profit." While no particular form of contract is necessary to create a partnership, a partnership contract usually provides what the partners' rights and duties are, and the extent of liability. It formalizes the conditions of the business partnership and is the basis for solving any questions which may come up during the life of the partnership. The following points are usually covered: the type of business to be conducted, the amount to be invested by each partner, the division of profit and losses, the power and duties of each partner, the compensation to be paid to each partner, provision for salaries and drawings of partners, the duration of the partnership and how it is to be dissolved, the division of assets in case of dissolution, provisions for withdrawal or admission of partners, how differences of opinion are to be settled, provision for continuation in the event of one partner's death or incompetence, and anything else of importance.

In addition, the partners should know each other and be willing to cooperate in their common interest. This may be called compatibility. It implies that they can get along, and resolve differences in a manner which will be for the best interests of all concerned.

Partnerships are of two types: the general partnership and limited partnership.

1. *General partnership.* Under the Act, all general partners are entitled to take an active part in the affairs of management. In this role each partner is considered an agent for the firm; as such, each can commit the firm for business obligations. Because there is a broader background of business experience usually available, there is less freedom of decision for partners than that exercised by a proprietor. With more than one principal in the business, it is logical to assume there will be a more equitable distribution of the production, marketing, and financial management skills required to operate successfully.

2. *Limited partnership.* This form differs from the general partnership in that it is composed of one or more general partners and one or more limited partners. It must file a partnership agreement in every state in which it does business; otherwise it will be regarded as a general partnership.

The rights and obligations of the general partners are the same as those in a general partnership. They control the management, have unlimited liability, and participate actively in the day-to-day operation of the firm. Limited partners, however, risk only the amount of their investment. In exchange for this limited liability, they relinquish their voice in the management of the firm.

This type of partnership attracts people who are primarily interested in investment. They are not partners in the usual sense, in that they depend upon return from investment much like those who invest their money in the stock market. The attraction is the higher rate of return or the feeling that they are helping a relative or friend by providing financial backing.

Continuity

The partnership dissolves automatically upon the death of a general partner, although it may continue long enough to enable the surviving partners to wind up the affairs of the business. This may be modified if the partners agree beforehand that the interest of the deceased partner will be purchased by the remaining partners and a new partnership formed simultaneously. Unless some such provision has been made in the partnership agreement, there is a strong likelihood that the business will not survive. In any case, the skills possessed by the deceased partner must be replaced. This makes it particularly important for the credit executive to review the account periodically to be sure there has been no change in its composition.

The death of a limited partner does not usually terminate the partnership. It may be necessary, however, for the remaining partners to purchase the interest held by the estate of the deceased partner.

The impact of ill health is not so great as it is in a proprietorship. One partner may become sick, yet the business may continue to operate in a satisfactory manner. On another tack, disagreements among the partners may have a detrimental effect on the business. If they do not have the personal funds to buy each other's interests, they may be forced to remain together despite personal disagreements.

Capital

Compared to a proprietorship, the partnership can command a higher level of invested capital. The general partnership is made up of more than one general partner; consequently, more funds are available. A limited partnership has at least one general partner, in addition to the individuals who make limited contributions.

The limited partnership is especially attractive to large numbers of investors, since shares can be sold on a pro rata basis in much the same way as a corporation sells shares of ownership. They invest stated amounts in the partnership, which is the extent of their obligation for the debts of the business. They may not usually be held liable for any amounts over their investment.

With regard to benefits, profits are shared equally by the general partners, unless another agreement has been specifically reached and set down in writing by the partners. There is, however, no restriction as to what agreement may be reached.

One of the attractions to the partnership form is that it does not pay federal income taxes as a business entity; the partners pay individual income taxes on their proportionate shares of partnership income. Therefore, there is no double taxation on business profits, a tax advantage that the partnership has over the corporate form. If tax savings are retained in the business, the firm may be able to grow more rapidly than a corporation of comparable size.

Liability

All general partners are jointly and severally liable for the debts of the business. This means that every partner has unlimited liability for the debts of the business. Each may also be required to pay the debts even though they were incurred by other members of the firm. Under the laws of most states, creditors may sue any one partner, as well as the partnership for the amount owed to them. In turn, the partner is legally entitled to recover proportionate shares of this amount from the other partners.

There is a procedure, known as *Marshalling of the Assets*, which is followed to determine the priority in which personal and business debts are paid by the partners if their business encounters financial difficulty:

1. Personal assets are applied to pay the personal debts of the partners.
2. Partnership assets are applied to pay partnership debts.
3. The balance of personal assets are used to pay the deficiency of partnership liabilities.

From the viewpoint of the creditor, the above procedure gives personal creditors first claim on personal assets and business creditors first claim on business assets. If a business creditor has the personal endorsement of a partner, however, this tends to make it both a business and personal creditor.

CORPORATION

The classic definition of a corporation was made by Chief Justice Marshall. He termed it ". . . an artificial being, invisible, and existing only in contemplation of law." A corporation may also be defined as a voluntary association of persons, natural or legal (other corporations); organized under state or federal law and recognized by the law as being a person, fictitious in character, having a corporate name, and being entirely separate and distinct from the people who own it; having continuous life; and set up for some specified purpose or purposes.

A corporation, being a creature of the state, has no inherent rights and powers except within the framework of the law of its creation. Thus the corporation must be organized in strict accordance with the legal requirements of the state of its domicile. While it is afforded protection as a "person" by our Federal Constitution, including its right to engage in interstate commerce, it cannot step beyond the bounds of its domicile into another state without having that state confer upon it the right to exist within its borders. (A corporation is known as a domestic corporation only within the state in which it is organized; as to all other states it is a foreign corporation.) Its powers and purposes are fixed by charter and cannot be changed at will as in the case of an individual or partnership. Such a change as entering into a new type of business or increasing its capitalization, in fact any variation from the rights or powers conferred by its charter, can be effected only by amending that charter in accordance with the laws of the state which issued the charter.

For purposes of credit analysis, this means the financial responsibility is with the corporation, but the business backgrounds of the principals are still an important deciding factor.

Certificate of Incorporation

This legal document is in essence an agreement between the state, the corporation, and shareholders. After it has been completed and filed with the state, it gives the corporation legal life. It can be revoked by the state if the conditions of the agreement are breached, or dissolved by the owners upon application to the state.

The laws of each state specify the procedure to be followed when a corporate charter is sought. Originally, each corporation had to be given "life" by special act of the state legislature. With the growth of the corporate form, the states enacted corporation laws which specify the steps to be taken. If the proper procedure is followed, the corporate charter is issued quite as a matter of course.

The certificate of incorporation, in some states called a charter, includes a full description of the powers which the corporation will expect to exercise. These are called the expressed powers of the corporation.

Some powers which are necessary for the proper performance of the business may have been omitted from the certificate. If that is the case, the corporation may still exercise them as implied powers. Examples of implied powers are the right to buy and sell real estate when used as physical plant location, the right to borrow, the right to have a bank account, and the right to have a corporate seal.

In addition to these, the corporation may have certain other powers, incidental to the conduct of the business. They are called incidental powers.

The corporation is required to comply with the conditions of its charter. In granting the charter, the state agrees that the expressed, implied, and incidental powers may be exercised, but ultra vires acts—those outside the powers of the corporation—are forbidden. The officers and directors of the corporation may be held responsible personally for the ultra vires acts of a corporation. For example, if corporate dividends are paid out of invested capital and not from retained earnings, the directors and officers may be required to replenish capital from their personal assets.

Capital Stock

Issued in the form of certificates, stock is evidence of corporate ownership. Stockholders may own one or more shares in a company and their equity interests would be proportional to the number of shares held in comparison with the total number of shares outstanding. Capital stock is assigned a par value in some instances in which case a specific dollar amount is shown on the face of the stock certificate. This purports to represent the minimum original investment in cash, property, and services behind each share. In many cases the capital stock is authorized with no par value. In this event a stated value is assigned, which establishes the amount that is entered in a corporation's books as capital. Any funds received in excess of the par or stated value are shown on the books as additional paid in capital. The presence or lack of par value has little credit significance other than in the extremely rare case when shares that are accessible and have a par value are sold for a consideration of less than par value. In such an instance, it might be possible for a creditor to realize a sum from the holder of these shares.

Common Stock. This represents the basic form of ownership in a business, and by virtue of this ownership common stockholders have certain rights: usually to vote and thus participate in the selection of management, share in the profits of the business by receiving dividends if and when declared by the directors, and share in the distribution of assets in accordance with the terms of the charter when a company is dissolved. In addition, state laws, the charter, or both can give another right, called the preemptive right, which prevents dilution of stockholders equity without their consent—that is, the right to purchase new stock in proportion to stockholder holdings at the time of new issue.

This ownership is in effect a residual interest, as common stockholders are not entitled to any distribution of earnings or assets until the respective prior claims of preferred stockholders, if any, have been satisfied. If there is no preferred or other special class of stock, common stock and capital stock are synonymous. Since this class of stock has the concentration of voting power, the credit executive should be interested in determining who controls the common stock.

Occasionally an organization may establish more than one class of common stock, maintaining voting rights in only one class, but permitting equal participation by both classes in dividends and giving each class equal rights in liquidation.

A measure of the financial operation of the business is its earnings on the common stock. Regular high earnings enhance the market value of the stock, for dividends are paid out of accumulated earnings. Dividends, or yield, are expressed as a percentage of the market price of the stock. Thus a yield of 5 per cent would mean a $5 dividend payment on a share which has a market value of $100.

The portion of earnings available to common stockholders in the form of dividends is known as the payout ratio. Accordingly, a company is deemed to have a 50 per cent payout ratio if it earns $5 per share and pays a dividend of $2.50 per share. The lower the payout ratio, the greater is the amount of earnings a company retains in the business to improve its financial condition and finance the growth of its operations.

Preferred Stock. As implied in the title, holders of such shares enjoy one or more preferences over holders of other capital shares called common stock. These generally are expressed in the form of dividends, assets in liquidation, voting, convertibility, and redemption. Due to its characteristics, some analysts look at preferred stock as a form of fixed, subordinated debt.

Dividends.   Preferred stock generally is entitled to a fixed dividend (either in terms of dollars per share or as a percentage of par value of the stock) before a distribution is made to common stockholders. This is not an automatic dividend as it does require declaration by directors. Dividend preference may be cumulative or noncumulative, and participating or nonparticipating.

Under cumulative preferred, dividends not paid when due become cumulative and must be paid in full before any common stock dividend is paid. Under noncumulative preferred, the preferred dividend is lost if not paid. This is less desirable from the viewpoint of the preferred stockholder. Participating preferred stock is entitled to dividends in excess of those stipulated in the charter. The most popular form is to permit the preferred to share further dividend distributions with the common after both have received their stipulated rate. Where the stock is nonparticipating, or straight preferred, no additional dividend over the contract rate is received by the holders.

Assets in Liquidation.   After claims of all creditors have been settled, preferred stockholders generally receive a fixed amount per share before distribution is made to common stockholders. Preferred stockholders may also be participating as to assets when the corporation is liquidated.

Voting.   Unless the charter provides otherwise, preferred stockholders have the same voting rights as common stockholders. In actual practice, the charter usually deprives such voting power or limits it so long as the affairs of the company are conducted on a satisfactory basis.

Convertibility.   Preferred stock sometimes has the right to convert (usually into common stock) at the option of the holder.

Redemption.   Preferred stock usually is redeemable after a certain period at the option of the corporation.

Continuity

The business has perpetual life, though a shorter time may be specified. Consequently, it continues to exist despite the death of any principal. New talents and new financing may be necessary, but the surviving management generally has time to find them. The credit executive must follow up on the situation, but does not have the additional problems which arise during a forced liquidation of a proprietorship or partnership.

Management is vested in a board of directors. The stockholders elect the board at the annual meeting, and the management of the corporation is then left in its hands. The board selects the officers, decides policy, and is responsible for the conduct of the business. This procedure together with larger available capital resources enables the corporation to hire expert help in marketing, production, and financial management and thus attain a balanced distribution of management skills and broaden the scope of the operation.

Moreover, even though shares of ownership may change hands, the creditor has an amount owing from the same debtor, the corporation. The company is a legal entity which does its own buying and selling, so there is less problem in following up an account after a change of principals.

Despite the fact that a corporation is an entity, the creditor must remember that it is run by individuals. If a person cannot stand the searching inquiry of a credit investigation as a proprietor or as a partner, chances are that a corporation controlled by this individual would not be a favorable credit risk, either.

Capital

Because a corporation can sell shares of stock, it has a larger potential source of capital for operation and expansion than the other forms of organization. In addition, shares of stock in a corporation can be bought and sold by shareholders without any effect on its capital structure. This permits a continuity of operation and financial strength. A radical change in the management or ownership, however, would require an investigation.

The corporation, being a legal entity, is required to pay taxes on its earnings in addition to those paid by its stockholders on the corporate dividend payments.

Liability

The stockholders have limited liability for the debts of the corporation. This liability is restricted to the amount each stockholder has invested. When the amount invested is equal to the par value of the stock, it is designated as fully paid and nonassessable. Most states prohibit a corporation from issuing shares for less than par value (not fully paid for). In this case, the stockholder is liable for the unpaid balance if the corporation becomes insolvent and the money is needed to pay creditors.

Despite the fact that stockholders may limit the amount of assets they put at the risk of the business, the credit executive is in position to ask the dominant principals to guarantee or endorse the business obligations. Thus the capital funds available for creditor protection are larger than would appear to the casual observer. Before a principal is asked for a guaranty or endorsement, however, it should be ascertained whether it will mean something in terms of tangible assets or just bind the principal in a moral or psychological sense. Unless tangible assets support the extra signature, a creditor realizes little material gain or protection from it.

The legal procedure for forming a corporation is more detailed and complicated than that required for a partnership or proprietorship. In addition, the corporation is subject to more and stricter control by state and federal governments. Certain information, not normally obtainable from the partnership and the proprietorship, is often filed by corporations with regulatory bodies. As such, it is public information and can be obtained readily.

This enables the credit executive to obtain more information about customer accounts.

Special care should be exercised when goods are shipped to another state. Since the laws vary, the rights of a creditor are not the same in every state. For a full description of those rights reference is made to the *Credit Manual of Commercial Laws*, which provides guidance on many of the daily credit problems which come up in this connection.

SUBCHAPTER S (PSEUDO) CORPORATION

In 1958, the relative tax advantages of many partnerships over corporations were eliminated. This came about with the passage of the Technical Amendments Act, which amended the federal income tax laws to permit some corporations to be taxed as partnerships. The Tax Reform Act of 1976 gave shareholders of pseudo corporations a variety of new benefits, and the Revenue Act of 1978 increased to 15 the allowed number of stockholders.

Continuity

The lifespan of a subchapter S corporation is the same as for all other corporations provided it meets certain requirements. It must have been organized in the United States and not be a member of an affiliated group of corporations responsible to a common parent. It must also meet these additional requirements.:

1. The corporation has a limited number of stockholders.

2. Stockholders must be individuals, estates, or certain allowable trusts. The allowable trusts are a revocable trust (one treated as owned by the grantor); a voting trust, with each beneficiary counted as a separate shareholder in computing the maximum number allowed; and a testamentary trust that holds the pseudo corporation stock for not more than 60 days.

3. The individuals must be U.S. citizens or resident aliens.

4. Every coowner, tenant by the entirety, tenant in common, and joint tenant is considered a shareholder for determining the total number of shareholders.

5. If husband and wife are treated as one stockholder while living, depending upon the type of ownership, death of either husband or wife or both will not result in adding a new stockholder, providing the stock continues to be held by their estates in the same proportion as before death.

6. The corporation must earn 80 per cent or more of its gross income from its normal business function. Rent, interest, royalties, dividends, or capital gains are excluded.

7. At the inception of the pseudo corporation, every stockholder must agree and accept the option that the corporation be taxed as a partnership. When a new shareholder is added, however, this consent is not needed.

Capital

The net income of a subchapter S corporation is divided into two general classes: that distributed among stockholders, and that retained in the business and not distributed to the stockholders. The distributed income from the corporation is taxed to the stockholders based on the amount of the distribution each stockholder receives.

Undistributed income is taxed to the stockholders based on the percentage of ownership. Undistributed income from prior years' earnings, for which the owners have previously paid personal income tax, can be distributed in later years to the stockholders without any tax liability.

The credit executive can determine the amount of the available undistributed income by reviewing the capital section of the balance sheet. Where a corporation previously operated as a taxable corporation and had retained earnings not previously taxed to the stockholders, the balance sheet will distinguish between retained earnings and undistributed income.

Since the basic purpose of a subchapter S corporation is to withdraw the profits of each year, the net worth of the company will remain the same but the cash funds will be depleted. These funds are used by the stockholders to pay their personal income taxes on the distributed earnings or their share of undistributed earnings. In some cases, however, the stockholders will use only the cash needed to pay their personal income taxes on the distributed earnings and return the remaining cash to the business in the form of stockholder loans. In the event this procedure continues, stockholder loans will grow and the debt to worth ratio will deteriorate.

Liability

A subchapter S corporation is a corporation in all respects, except for the treatment stockholders are given for federal income taxes. It is exempt from all federal income taxes, and thus treated more like a partnership in that the earnings are considered ordinary income to the shareholders of the corporation.

Moreover, any losses sustained by a subchapter S corporation can pass to the shareholders as business deductions from their personal income tax obligations. These losses are based on the percentage of stockholders' ownership and are limited to the total sum of the stockholders' investment in and loans made to the corporation.

From the creditor's point of view, shareholders of a subchapter S corporation are protected against corporate creditors. If their loans to the corporation become inordinately high, creditors should consider obtaining a subordination or an assignment of the stockholders' loans payable. Personal guaranties from the stockholders should also be considered. Of course, an alternative would be for shareholders to reinvest the profits.

ESTATES

When an owner dies leaving a will and it is admitted to probate, the court issues letters testamentary to the executor named in the will. If the decedent left no will, the court will appoint an administrator rather than an executor and will issue letters of administration.

Continuity

By its nature, the operation of a business by an estate is of short duration. It is the duty of the executor to take possession of the assets of the decedent, pay the expenses of administration and the claims of creditors, and dispose of the balance of the estate in accordance with the decedent's will.

If there be no will, the administrator will do the same in accordance with the statutes governing the distribution of the decedent's estate. In such a case, it is also possible for a creditor, or a group of creditors, to apply for and receive letters of administration. Of course, a creditor that becomes the representative of the estate must administer not only for its own benefit but for the benefit of all interested parties. A creditor so proceeding is entitled to receive, in addition to its claim, the ordinary commissions and fees which the law allows.

Capital

In every case, the creditor should determine what property is at the risk of the business and should verify that assets are not withdrawn prematurely. The creditor should be satisfied that the executor or administrator has qualified to manage the estate. Unless the decedent's will provides that the executor shall not be required to file a bond, the executor must qualify by filing a bond in the amount the court may direct; in the case of an administrator a bond is always required.

Liability

Under the laws of most states, the representative, who may be either the executor or administrator, is required either to advertise for claims or to notify creditors to present their claims on or before a specified date. In some states, no such notice is required although creditors must file their claims within a time prescribed by law after the appointment of the representative.

The credit executive should contact the representative immediately to determine the intended disposition of the estate. Except for possible procedural difficulties and delay, the death of a debtor generally does not affect the validity or collectibility of a debt.

Where a debt has been reduced to judgment prior to death and has become a lien on real or personal property, the lien of the judgment generally continues as if death had not intervened. Nor does death usually shorten the applicable statute of limitations with respect to unsecured claims; in most cases, the period within which an action to enforce collection may be brought is extended for a short period of time to enable creditors to assert their claims against the estate. Mere written notice by the creditor to the representative of the estate generally suffices to stop the running of the statute of limitations without the necessity of instituting legal proceedings.

Where written notice is given to the representative and the claim is admitted to be due, the creditor need do nothing further, since the claim will generally be paid after the account filed by the representative has been audited or confirmed by the court. If after the passage of a statutory period of time (from six months to one year in most states) the representative has not filed an account for audit or confirmation by the court, a creditor may institute proceedings to compel the filing of the account.

If a creditor has given written notice of its claim and it is denied or disputed by the representative, the creditor must submit the claim directly to the court. Unless the creditor is prepared to prove the claim at the time of audit or institute legal proceedings against the representative, the claim will be barred.

COMMON LAW TRUSTS

This form of organization, also referred to as Massachusetts trust or business trust, has been used in England for centuries. It was first used extensively in Massachusetts and has since been recognized and used throughout the United States. In some, notably Texas, it has been regarded more as a partnership than a common law trust.

Unlike the corporation, the powers of the common law trust are not generally derived from statutory law. They come rather from the trust agreement, subject to the rules which govern trusts generally. It is formed by agreement between owners of property (or a business) and a trustee or group of trustees. The terms and powers of each party are set down in a trust agreement, signed by the trustee(s) and the owners of the trust, who are in most instances also the beneficiaries. The beneficiaries are issued trust certificates proportionate to their interests. The trustees hold legal title to all the property of the business, and manage its affairs. Some of their powers may at times be delegated to one of their number, though the trustees normally function as a unit. The certificate holders, or shareholders of beneficial interest as they are sometimes called, participate proportionately in the income from the trust. They also share proportionately in the proceeds when the trust is dissolved.

Continuity

Depending upon the agreement creating it, a trust may continue for a fixed duration of time or may have perpetual existence. The death of a certificate holder does not effect a dissolution of the common law trust. The share passes through the estate of the deceased in much the same way as a share of corporate stock.

Capital

The capital of the common law trust is fairly well-established. It is equal to the value of the property transferred to the trustees. Profits are generally distributed at the end of the fiscal period. For purposes of credit appraisal, the credit executive should be able to determine, quite accurately, what assets are available to the business.

The common law trust was not at first required to pay income taxes; the beneficiaries instead paid personal income taxes on their proportionate earnings distributions. This advantage has been reduced over the years, and the common law trust has increasingly been taxed as a corporation.

Liability

Primarily, the creditor is interested in determining the liability of the principals for the debts of the business. In most cases where a trust has been organized, the certificate holders are protected from claims over and above the extent of their investments. The principal exception occurs when the beneficiary is shown to have a voice in the affairs of management.

In those states where the common law trust is treated as a partnership, the certificate holders are not exempt from personal liability for debts. The creditor can then act as it normally would against a partnership form of business.

Trustees are held accountable for the fiduciary affairs of the common law trust. They are accountable to the certificate holders for the property entrusted to them and for any loss due to misconduct or mismanagement. However, they have no authority to bind the beneficiaries personally. In acting with third parties, the trustees are liable personally for their commitments unless they have been absolved from this responsibility by agreement with the party with which they contract.

In every instance, it is important for the creditor to know how the common law trust is viewed by the courts in the states where merchandise is to be shipped, as well as the state where the headquarters of the trust is located.

JOINT VENTURES

A joint venture (also called syndicate) is a combination of two or more persons (including corporations) formed to perform a specific contract or business transaction. Usually the contract or business transaction is too large in scope to be completed by one of the coadventurers alone. A large construction job or a public offering of securities or a large real estate transaction would normally be undertaken by a joint venture. Some of the reasons for this may be lack of technical knowledge or capital, inability to negotiate for the business with the proper persons, difficulty in placing competent personnel on the contract site, and possible inability to supply materials which meet the contract specifications.

The nature of the contract binding the coadventurers is important for credit analysis. Since the document describes the agreement among the parties that have combined forces, the credit executive should be aware of its provisions. The creditor thereby knows just what protections may be available. In any case, the creditor should deal directly with the elected manager of the venture rather than with the coadventurers separately.

Continuity

The continuity of the joint venture is fairly well established by the length of time it will take to complete the transaction as specified in the contract. A contract drawn properly will bind the coadventurers to meet the obligations of the joint venture, either together or individually, if one or the other fails to perform.

Capital

The capital available to the joint venture includes all resources of the coadventurers, in a technical sense. However, it is normal to expect that the coadventurers will have other interests operating at the same time, for which part of their total capital will be committed. Consequently, it is important to know what funds and equipment will be allocated to the job under consideration. This can be readily determined since it is usual for the venture to keep a separate set of books. In that way, the assets committed to the contract are segregated. Similarly, the creditor should set up a separate account for sales to the joint venture.

Liability

The theory of partnership law is applied more and more in joint ventures. That is, the coadventurers are usually held jointly and severally liable for the debts of the joint venture. Although the words "jointly and severally" or "we, either of us" mean just that in most states, there are some states where the same interpretation is not given. There the creditor may encounter difficulty in establishing that the coadventurers are individually liable for all debts of the joint venture. Consequently, some additional words of explanation may be useful in specifying the obligations of the coadventurers.

In addition, one coadventurer cannot bind the others in dealings with other persons because the joint venture is conducted by an elected manager. Another difference lies in the fact that the joint venture is formed for one particular transaction or contract while the partnership continues in business until dissolved.

Where the liability of the coadventurers is established, it is important to know the significance of that liability in terms of assets. A coadventurer that is not a good credit risk in other business transactions would hardly be a better risk in a joint venture. In such an instance, the credit position of the other coadventurer would weigh heavily in the overall analysis of the combination.

COOPERATIVE SOCIETIES

This form of organization is not usually encountered in the credit department, except in such industries as lumber, groceries, and dairy products. Cooperative societies are organizations of mutual help and betterment, formed when individuals or corporate businesses combine their financial, capital, and other resources to operate in trade or industry.

By this combination, they seek to obtain operating economies and advantages. Savings are distributed to the membership periodically in the form of a patronage dividend, dependent upon each member's participation during the dividend period.

Permissible methods by which cooperative societies obtain funds for operation may vary from one state to another, or may be specified in the charter or bylaws of the society if not restricted by state law. Similarly, the liabilities of the officers, directors, and membership of the society may vary, as may the circumstances which affect its legal life. In all instances, the determination of these points from the viewpoint of credit analysis is made on an individual basis.

NOT-FOR-PROFIT ORGANIZATIONS

This designation of some organizations is permitted by the Internal Revenue Service. They can be either corporations or associations; as corporations they can be membership corporations or stock corporations depending on state law. The term or life of a corporation is established by its certificate of incorporation or its charter. Capital for operation may come from dues and from charges for goods and services furnished to the members or to outsiders.

OTHER FEATURES OF ORGANIZATION

In addition to knowing the implications of the legal composition of customer accounts, the credit executive is often asked to appraise credit significance of organizational changes. Some of the more frequent situations are:

1. The principals of one business are also principals of another.
2. Changes are made in legal composition.
3. One company may have its operations split into more than one unit.
4. Two or more businesses may merge or consolidate.
5. One corporation may purchase the assets of another.

In each instance, these actions may affect the analysis. It will be necessary to determine the effects of these changes on the financial strength and credit position of the accounts. Generally, if no additional borrowing is required for these changes, the financial condition will not suffer. Should outside borrowing be necessary, however, another look at the credit position is in order. Though an exhaustive treatment is outside the scope of this text, a short comment will be made on the credit significance of each of the above situations.

Affiliated Interests

A person is said to have affiliated interests when identified as a principal in more than one business. If these businesses are incorporated they are separate entities even though they may provide similar goods and services to their customers. Thus a person may control any number of corporations in the same line of business, yet not have the assets of one available for payment of others' debts. Further, the individual's personal assets would be insulated from the debts of every corporation.

The credit executive should determine the exact assets and liabilities of each corporation, particularly the one undergoing analysis. A technique used with affiliated interests is to ask the financially strong corporation to guarantee the debts of another.

Affiliated interests are also important because they provide a complete picture of the principal's character and capability. An unfavorable business record can often be uncovered by investigating the affiliates of a new concern.

Changes in Legal Composition

One of the more complex problems faced in credit analysis is a change in the legal composition of an account. A business usually progresses from a proprietorship through the partnership to the corporate form. As the advantages of the various legal forms become better known, changes are made to meet the specific needs of the individuals.

In a business succession, the exact details of the change should be determined. The following examples point out why further questioning is necessary when a partnership is succeeded by a corporation.

1. A corporation is formed. It then purchases the assets of the partnership and assumes its liabilities. In exchange for their proportionate holdings in the old partnership, the partners receive shares of stock in the new corporation.

2. The corporation is formed. The partnership is then liquidated and the partners receive a pro rata distribution of the proceeds of liquidation. They then invest their funds in the new corporation for shares of stock.

3. The corporation is formed. After the partnership is dissolved, the partners invest only a portion of the proceeds of liquidation in exchange for shares of stock in the new corporation.

From the viewpoint of credit analysis, three different situations are described above. In the first, there is no change in the net worth of the business. The change from the creditor's point of view is that a new customer has come into being, the legal entity created by state law. The former partners have also insulated their personal assets from the claims of business creditors.

In the second situation, the new business is formed independently of the old partnership's liquidation. There the partnership would pay all outstanding obligations before it could dissolve. Although there is now limited liability on the part of the principals, there has been no change in net worth of financial strength of the business.

The third situation reflects a complete change in the form of organization, in the liability of the principals, and in the financial strength of the business. By deciding to invest only a portion of the assets in the new corporation, the principals have kept out some of their interest in the old partnership.

It is not unusual for a business to be incorporated under the circumstances of the third illustration. The details are often left to the accountant and attorney. Consequently, the principals may not be fully aware of the specific change nor of its effect on the financial picture of the concern.

When a succession takes place, a typical incident that often confronts a credit executive is the following: In answer to a question on the ownership change, the principal may reply, "Yes, we have incorporated, but there is no other change in the business." This information can be misleading and may cause the credit executive to make an unjustified favorable appraisal of the account. The bank, other suppliers, and the account's attorney or auditor may be in a much better position to describe the true financial structure of the new corporation.

Parent-Subsidiary Relationships

A corporation which owns more than 50 per cent of the stock of another corporation is said to be the parent of its subsidiary. Subsidiaries may be partly owned or wholly owned.

In the eyes of the law, the parent and its subsidiary are generally considered as separate entities, with no intercompany liability for debts. It is therefore important to find out if any debts of the subsidiary have been guaranteed by its parent. Should that be the case, they represent a contingent liability claim on the parent's assets.

Under special circumstances, the parent and its subsidiary have been ruled by the courts to be one organization. These cases have been decided on their individual merits, however, and do not fit in with the usual understanding of parent-subsidiary relationships. They have to be proved in court with the burden of proof on the creditor to show that in effect the subsidiary was an instrumentality of the parent.

The safer approach is to regard the subsidiary as a separate entity and to rely upon analysis of its financial condition for appraisal of credit risk. Naturally if the parent will guarantee the obligations of the subsidiary, the credit task is diminished (assuming, of course, that the financial condition of the parent makes its guaranty meaningful).

Operating Divisions

A credit executive who approves sales to a division of a customer company need not analyze the division as a separate entity. A division is an internal arrangement of a corporation made for the convenience of its management. It does not affect the legal status of the corporation. Thus there is no separation of credit liability.

Mergers or Consolidations

Mergers and consolidations are statutory procedures regulated by state law. They involve the complete corporate entities, not only their assets and liabilities.

In a merger of two corporations, the shares of stock in one company are exchanged by their holders for shares in the other, which will be the survivor corporation. The absorbed corporation files a certificate of succession and its files are absorbed by the survivor corporation. The liabilities of the absorbed corporation are in effect taken over by the survivor.

A consolidation is a somewhat different procedure. A new corporation is formed; the shares of the corporations which are to be consolidated are exchanged for shares in the newly formed corporation; certificates of succession are filed by the corporations which will discontinue; and their files are absorbed by the brand new corporation. Here the liabilities of the old corporations are also taken over by the new one.

The credit executive must determine what factors have been brought into the credit situation by the consolidation or merger of the two or more companies. New capital resources may be available; new or different principals may be in control; there is a new legal responsibility in the consolidation; the creditor must look to the reorganized corporation for payment of debts existing before the change took place; and the combination of facilities in the new organization may broaden the potential for expanded operations.

Purchase of Assets

This type of transaction between two corporations does not affect their positions as separate and unrelated concerns. Any assets may be purchased, though usually it will be inventory, fixed assets, or intangibles such as methods, processes, or customer lists. Purchase of assets is a private contract. Its terms may be specified by the buyer and the seller.

If assets are sold subject to liabilities, the purchaser assumes the debts on the assets bought. Assets may also be sold net, in which case the seller pays any obligations from the proceeds of the sale.

From the creditors' viewpoint, there is no change in the legal form of either corporation. The sale or purchase may affect their financial conditions, but the two companies remain separate and unrelated.

Creditors of the selling company have these further protections:

1. Under law, the selling company must be solvent in order to dispose of its assets. If securities of the purchaser corporation are taken instead of cash, the purchaser is held liable to creditors of the selling company up to the value of the purchased assets.

2. Assets of a bankrupt company may be sold by the trustee with the approval of the court.

3. If the assets are purchased subject to any outstanding obligations on them, the new owner is responsible to the creditors of the original owner.

4. Any purchaser of all or a substantial part of a firm's assets is subject to Article 6 of the Uniform Commercial Code—Bulk Transfers, and must notify creditors that the purchase is being made. This includes transfer of a major part of inventory not in the ordinary course of business. A transfer of a substantial part of equipment is also a bulk transfer if it is made in conjunction with a bulk transfer of inventory, but not otherwise.

CHAPTER 18

CREDIT AND BUSINESS INSURANCE

A credit decision is based on the assumption that the customer is a going concern; that its assets retain their values and its liabilities arise chiefly from the purchase of assets to be used in the conduct of the business. Further, it is expected that the company will continue under the same management, with the principals contributing their talents as in the past.

The position of the going concern may change radically, however, if something unforeseen happens to its earning power and financial strength. Fire, death of a principal, embezzlement, robbery, business interruption, and extraordinary bad-debt losses can change the financial condition of a business overnight. Concurrently, these circumstances can change its creditors' position. It is important therefore for creditors to know the types and amounts of insurance carried by their customers.

ROLE OF BUSINESS INSURANCE

There is no way to foretell many of the misfortunes that can befall a business. The competent manager, however, can provide adequate insurance coverage against these contingencies and thereby protect company assets and earning power, and creditors' interest. The creditor should be satisfied that major risks are covered.

Background

People have insured themselves against disaster for centuries. Even when there was no formal agreement, people banded together to help someone who had suffered a misfortune. For example, if a farmer's barn or crops or personal belongings were destroyed by fire, neighbors would contribute some of their own labor, seed, or personal belongings to set him back on his feet. More formal, insurance was described this way in 1825 by a Select Committee of the British House of Commons:

> Whenever there is a contingency, the cheapest way of providing against it is by uniting with others so that each man may subject himself to a small depriva-

tion in order that no man may be subjected to a great loss. He upon whom the loss does not fall, does not get his money back again, nor does he get for it any visible or tangible benefit; but he obtains security against ruin and consequent peace of mind. He upon whom the contingency does fall gets all that those whom fortune has exempted from it have lost in hard money, and is thus enabled to sustain an event which would otherwise overwhelm him.

Numerous other descriptions of insurance have been made since that time. Though they differ in detail, all have these points in common: people join together to protect the value of their lives and property, and each participant contributes a relatively small amount in exchange for protection against a disastrous personal loss. The ultimate purpose of insurance is self-protection, but each participant cooperates with all others to carry common risk. Payments for this protection can be budgeted and paid in an orderly manner.

Besides providing self-protection to individuals, insurance has a broader, more social, function in the economy. If businesses are also members of society, it follows that each business contributes in some measure to the aggregate wealth of its particular community and to the nation at large. A loss by any business affects this aggregate wealth. By the same token, a method to replenish individual loss of value or earning power helps to stabilize the economic atmosphere of the broader economy.

Insurance and the Creditor

While the social aspects of insurance are important to a general understanding of the subject, the creditor is more directly concerned with the insurance protection carried by the business. This is to be expected, since creditors must be primarily concerned with their customers' ability to operate successfully. In those terms, therefore, are noted some of the advantages of insurance to business.

1. Adequate insurance coverage offers security to the business and to its creditors. It enables the manager to plan for the future, knowing that the financial strength of the business is protected from disaster.

2. Insurance reduces the need for financial reserves. A company that does not carry insurance would necessarily have some of its assets set aside to provide for unforeseen emergency cash needs. By carrying insurance against these contingencies, the firm releases additional assets for business operation. This strengthens its credit position.

3. The manager can devote more time to efficient operations. Relieved of worry about the consequences of events which cannot be predicted or controlled, the firm can plan for the coming year with greater certainty that it is protected against unforeseen loss. Costing procedures can be based on more realistic appraisals of expenses.

4. Creditors are likewise protected. Credit analysis is based largely upon business assets and assumes they will maintain their values. Since these

assets are liable to dissipation or destruction, the creditor assumes an additional risk when customers do not protect business assets with insurance. It therefore follows that the insured account is a better credit risk. The publications department of the National Association of Credit Management carries a stock form that credit grantors can use to assist in their appraisal of their debtor's insurance programs.

The greatest advantage to a creditor lies in having a good knowledge of the customer's line of business. That makes it easier to determine the adequacy of the customer's insurance coverage. In this respect, however, the cost of overprotection can be as harmful as losses due to underprotection.

Mandatory Insurance

While most insurance coverage is optional, the business is faced with certain coverage that is mandatory because of state or federal laws: Old Age and Survivor's Insurance (Social Security), Unemployment Insurance, and Workers' Compensation.

Social Security.   A federal law makes payments for Social Security mandatory. While the employee is the insured, under the law the employer must also contribute a part of the premium and is responsible for the part contributed by the employee. Since this liability is a prior claim, the credit executive needs to be assured that all Social Security payments have been made.

Unemployment Insurance.   This protection for employees is subject to state laws. They impose upon the employer the duty of paying the premium, which is a certain percentage of the employee's wage. In some states the employer is responsible for the entire contribution, while in other states the employee must contribute a portion of the premium.

Workers' Compensation.   Every state and the District of Columbia have enacted a Workers' Compensation law. Under such laws, the employer must provide employee insurance that will pay certain medical expenses and provide weekly indemnity in the event an employee is injured while on the job or in the course of employment. An employer can incur severe penalties if such protection is not in force.

Contract and Voluntary Insurance

Other insurance coverages are brought about by contract requirements or choice. These may be designed to meet union negotiated commitments, such as life insurance, health benefits, and retirement plans. Or there may exist contract requirements protecting the security of lenders and financiers.

Large exposures often exist on intangibles, such as product recall, malpractice suits, bad-debt writeoffs, employee dishonesty, theft and burglary, and so on. No law other than that of good business dictates which of these options should be carried.

Prerequisites of Insurance

Since the purpose of insurance is to protect owners and creditors, it should not be considered a means by which property owners can realize a profit. This makes it necessary to examine the requirements and circumstances surrounding the use of insurance.

Real Risk. An insurance contract should be based upon an actual possibility that the insured party may sustain a financial loss from a hazard to which it is exposed, and which cannot be eliminated. The threat may be to life, physical property, or intangible interests.

Insurance against real risk must be clearly distinguished from risk which can be eliminated completely. For instance, the possibility of a fire loss is always present. That is a real risk. It is different from the risk of financial loss by gambling. There the risk is self-created and should not rightfully be considered insurable.

Necessity of Insurance. Normally a business is not expected to carry insurance on values which are negligible. Premiums are a cost of doing business. If premium payments exceeded the value of the insured property over a short period of time, they would represent a foolish expenditure. The business should have saved those premiums.

From the viewpoint of the insurance company, too, the costs of writing and servicing contacts on negligible values are greater than the value of the protection furnished. It therefore is customary to fix a minimum premium on insurance contracts. In fact, most business insurance programs are designed with layers of protection, wherein the insured and insurer share the responsibility. The insured may pay numerous small claims of, say, up to $500. The insurer may pay the claims from $500 to $500,000, beyond which the insured may pay any infrequent amount over $500,000. This type of insurance program is fairly common in industry. The credit executive's knowledge of the industry should be self-satisfying as to the reasonableness of a particular customer's program.

Cost Must Be Reasonable. As previously mentioned, insurance is based upon the banding together of many people against financial loss from real risk. In order to attract the necessary numbers of people, costs of insurance must be relatively low for the protection offered. The insured must initially be convinced that the premium is reasonable. In addition, the business must be able to afford the payment or it will take a chance without adequate coverage.

Large Number of Individual Risks. It is necessary from the insurer's point of view to have a large number of individual risks for safe operation. Generally, as the number of insured parties increases, individual losses can be absorbed more readily by the insurer company.

Extent of Hazard Calculable. Finally, the insurer should be able to estimate the risk to which each insured party is exposed. This estimate should be close enough to permit adequate and equitable premium rates to be established.

In this way, the insurance company is able to operate effectively and can meet its obligations when an insured sustains a loss. At the same time, an equitable premium structure pro rates contributions according to the extent of risk in each case.

Principles of Insurance

Over the years, a body of knowledge has been built up which clarifies the use of insurance. Many claims are settled quickly and without disagreement between the insured and the insurer. Others are brought to court and decisions obtained. These decisions help in subsequent interpretations of insurance cases and thus refine the principles which guide insurance practice.

Indemnity. Ideally, insurance should restore to each member of the group the exact amount of financial loss sustained from disaster. This prospect is the chief attraction to the insured, and the need to join with others for protection is only incidental. The essence of indemnity is compensation in event of loss. It is not intended that the insured realize a profit from a disaster but only that any financial loss be reimbursed.

Occasionally a situation may be encountered in which insurance coverage exceeds the value of the property insured. Usually this overinsurance provides no additional protection to the owner, since indemnity can be no more than the actual financial loss suffered. Exceptions are found in some states, under what is called a valued policy law. Under this legislation, additional compensation is allowed when a total loss is suffered.

Insurable Interest. A number of different interests may be represented by the same assets. This can be illustrated by a shipment of merchandise from a supplier to a wholesaler. Before the merchandise has been sold, the supplier has an insurable interest in it. As soon as title changes hands, the new owner has an insurable interest in the merchandise. While the merchandise is being shipped to the wholesaler, the carrier transporting the merchandise has an insurable interest in it. Furthermore, if the inventory is pledged as collateral for a loan, the lender also has an insurable interest in it. Thus the same merchandise may represent an insurable interest to one or more parties. Title to the goods is not the chief consideration. Rather, it is the risk of loss which determines insurable interest.

There is another point which should be clarified in this connection. A person cannot obtain an insurance policy on property, but only on an interest in property. It is the risk of financial loss which prompts an insured to purchase a policy, not the opportunity to guarantee that a property will not be destroyed. For example, to assure that business premises do not burn down, the owner makes them as fireproof as possible, using fireproof construction and adequate protection measures. To protect against financial loss resulting from a fire, however, it would be necessary to carry a fire insurance policy.

Mutuality. This principle has developed from the original joining together of people to protect themselves against a common risk. It expresses the method in which funds are obtained to pay losses of insured individuals. The members (subscribers or policyholders) furnish these funds by means of their premiums. This pool of money is used to pay insured losses on operating expenses of the insurance company and to set up certain reserves.

Theory of Probability and Law of Large Numbers. Certain statistical principles form the bases for insurance operation. The first of these is known as the theory of probability. It says that if certain events have taken place repeatedly in the past or certain results have been obtained again and again, there is equal likelihood the event or result will be repeated in the future, so long as the conditions do not change.

The second is called law of large numbers or the law of averages. It complements the theory of probability, saying that as the number of past occurances becomes greater, the likelihood increases that the event will happen again. Consequently, the averages or forecasts drawn from past experience become more reliable. The law further states that forecasts based on past events are more reliable when they are drawn from many experiences than when they are drawn from few experiences.

The classical example to describe these principles is that of the penny thrown in the air and landing either "heads" or "tails." For any one case, the probability of its landing heads is 50 per cent. If count is kept on a small number of tosses, though, it is not certain that exactly half of them would be heads and the other half tails. As the number of tosses increases, however, there is a tendency for the two totals to even out; theoretically, heads and tails are equal on an infinite number of tosses.

In applying these principles, insurance companies collect accurate records of losses and examine them carefully for statistical significance. The information developed from these studies aid the companies to make forecasts of future events. Naturally no forecast can be considered completely accurate. But those based on statistical treatment of comprehensive information give good working results for the insurers. On this basis they can set rates and establish insurance limits.

Uniformity and Distribution of Lines. In order to make the laws of probability and large numbers effective in practice, insurance companies reduce the chance of extraordinary losses to a single insurer from one or several related disasters. They do this in two ways:

1. The unit amounts at risk are kept fairly uniform; otherwise a disproportionately large loss would upset the averages. The insurer will often limit the amount of coverage for any single risk and transfer any amount which exceeds that limit to another company. This is called reinsurance.

2. The various units of risk are, insofar as is practical, separated geographically or physically. This is done to reduce the likelihood that any one disaster will affect a large number of units.

Equity Among Policyholders. This technically is not a principle of insurance, but it is mentioned because it has a great effect on insurance operations. Part of the responsibility carried by the management of insurance companies is to distribute the costs of insurance equitably among policyholders.

The establishment of fair and uniform rates for similar and equal risks, together with the elimination of the usual forms of discrimination, can be accomplished by the insurance companies quite easily. The problem facing them is that all policies do not bear the same proportion of insurance to value.

Further, all disasters do not result in total loss; in many instances the loss is only partial. Consequently, it becomes difficult to establish equitable rates in terms of percentage coverage and degree of risk. The practical rule used by many companies is that they reimburse for partial loss in the same ratio as the insurance coverage bears to the value of the property covered (the coinsurance clause).

Insurance Agreements

The agreement between insured and insurer is known as an insurance contract. It falls under the law of contracts, and court actions arising from insurance agreements are normally tried under this category. In order for the contract to be valid and enforceable, it must meet the following conditions: the parties to the contract must agree to its conditions; both parties must be competent to enter into a contract; there must be a legal object; and there must be some consideration.

Agreement (Offer and Acceptance). The legal interpretation of an offer and acceptance in an insurance contract is somewhat different from the ordinary contract. The person who requests protection from the insurer is, according to law, making the offer. The acceptance is made when the insurance company agrees to the offer and puts the insurance in force. The courts have declared that the activity of insurance representatives soliciting business does not constitute an offer. The offer must be more specific and detail the terms of agreement. Technically, these specific terms cannot be known until the prospect makes the offer.

Competent Parties. While both parties must be legally competent to enter into an insurance contract, contracts signed by minors are enforceable in behalf of the minor and cannot be dissolved by the insurer. (In some states, automobile and life insurance have been declared exceptions to this rule.) Similarly, a person who is officially declared insane does not lose the protection of any policy already purchased.

Legal Object. Insurance contracts that do not have a legal objective in the public interest are not enforceable. By the same token, goods or merchandise illegally held cannot be made the subject of an enforceable contract. Certain drugs and other contraband fit this category of goods.

Consideration. In an insurance contract, consideration on the part of the insurer company consists of its promise to make payment if certain events occur. The insured party's consideration is payment of, or promise to pay, the stipulated premium. By its nature, an insurance contract differs from other contracts in that the values exchanged are not equal. The premium is small when compared to the potential reimbursement in case of loss. By the same token, there is no reimbursement unless a loss is suffered.

The terms of other contracts may be changed to suit the needs of either party. In insurance, the forms of contracts are prepared by the companies and by state regulatory bodies. When a change is desired by the insured, it is made by using a standard rider or endorsement.

PROPERTY INSURANCE

Most business firms begin fulfilling their insurance needs by purchasing protection for the assets of the business; both tangible and intangible assets can be and often are insured. Tangible assets include buildings, merchandise, accounts receivable, rolling equipment, and the like. Intangible assets relate to business interruption forms such as earnings insurance, extra expense insurance, rental value protection, tuition fees coverage, and consequential damage.

While it is possible for a customer to insure itself against almost every possible risk, a sound program will not necessarily include all available types. Some customers may prefer the more costly "all risk" form of coverage with certain specified situations of loss unprotected. On the other hand, others may be completely satisfied by a "named peril" policy with protection for only those perils named, such as fire or windstorm. Then there is also the extent of the risk that the insured is willing to assume. For lesser cost, one may elect not to cover minor exposure, or for a premium savings may select a larger-than-normal deductible.

There are generally two parties to the property insurance contract: the owner of the property to be insured (or some entity charged with responsibility for the property to be insured) and the insurance company. There may be a mortgagee or a loss payee also named whose interest in the property must be settled by the insurance company prior to any settlement with the owner.

Fire and Extended Coverage Insurance

A debtor insuring a building or its contents against fire, lightning, and removal coverage is affording a direct loss coverage. The insurance normally applies only to the location described, and the property covered is stationary and not on the move. In the area of fire losses, there must be a form of unfriendly conflagration in order for a damage claim to be payable.

Basically, a fire insurance policy provides for loss by fire, lightning, and removal. To these perils most often are added the extended coverage perils of windstorm, hail, explosion, riot and civil commotion, aircraft damage, vehicle damage, and smoke damage. Often vandalism and malicious mischief coverage is made a part of the fire insurance policy. Dealing with buildings only, a special extended coverage endorsement may be afforded which causes the fire insurance policy to become an all risk protection to the building. However, this type of policy does not insure accounts, bills, deeds, money, or securities. There are other forms of insurance designed specifically to protect those items.

War risk is never covered nor are losses covered which take place under any ordinance or law regulating the use of property. Power failures that take place away from the insured's premises are not covered. Earthquake, flood, and water backup are not insured.

There are many items excluded from the protection of windstorm and hail insurance. Some of these may be insured for extra premiums, while others may not be insured at all. Among the extra premium items are windmills and their towers, crop silos, metal smokestacks, awnings or canopies, signs, radio or television antennas, sprinkler leakage insurance, and sonic shock waves.

Even the addition of the special extended coverage endorsement fails to remove many of the limitations on coverage involving buildings. A purchaser should be aware of the policy limitations on freezing and what must be done to have coverage for the explosion of a steam boiler or electrical short circuit, to name a few.

Fire insurance forms dealing with business property involve coinsurance requirements. The normal requirement is 80 per cent of the true value of the property covered. The purchaser becomes a coinsurer or a contributor to a partial loss when it fails to maintain the required level of insurance.

There are also two bases of insurance. These are the actual cash value basis and the replacement cost basis. The real difference is that the replacement cost basis envisions no depreciation in the adjustment of losses. Obviously the replacement cost provides better coverage, but it also entails a higher premium expense to the purchaser because of the amount of insurance.

Most businesses qualify for some type of "package" insurance. If such a type of policy is to be used to insure a business, the direct fire and allied peril coverages are an essential part of any package insurance policy.

Business Interruption Insurance

In order to maintain the financial position of a business, business interruption coverage may be essential to protect profits and pay key employees during an insurable shutdown. The amount of the coverage is dependent on the length of time that it takes to get the damaged property operating again. The loss of profits can be referred to as insuring an intangible, since profits are not necessarily guaranteed.

Business interruption insurance is available under package policies at premium discounts. It is nearly always advisable to package insurance where possible because of lower costs to the customer.

Burglary and Theft Insurance

There are three types of insurance available for this type of risk, two of which offer limited protection while the other offers a package of protection.

Mercantile Open Stock Insurance. This is available for almost any type of business that manufactures products or has merchandise for sale or storage. It insures against loss of merchandise, furniture, fixtures, and equipment, and pays for damage to the premises described in the policy if the insured is the owner or is liable for the damage. The coverage is effective while the premises are not open for business. Generally there are discounts for first-class alarm systems and some reduction allowed for deductible insurance. This type of protection is available in one form which is totally devoid of theft; the other form covers both theft and burglary. (Burglary means abstraction from within the premises by someone making an entry therein by force or violence with visible marks having been left as evidence. Theft is a broader protection term than that of burglary.)

This form of insurance is also provided for those that purchase package policies. On the other hand, it is generally less expensive to buy the all risk program under a package policy if open stock insurance is to be a part of the protection. Those package insurance forms dealing with all risk for contents of a building include the perils of open stock.

Mercantile Robbery and Safe Burglary. This is another form of limited coverage in a crime area. The robbery portion is nothing more than holdup insurance and may be the least expensive form of crime insurance that deals with money. It provides protection for both money and merchandise taken through force or threat of force from a business premises or from a messenger of a business. The burglary portion protects both money and merchandise locked up in a safe on the business premises. Both of these forms exclude mysterious disappearance as well as infidelity of employees, and should not be purchased unless one of the broader crime coverage policies is too expensive.

Storekeepers Burglary and Robbery Insurance. This is a package of protection in itself which covers the loss of money and merchandise through safe burglary on the premises, holdup of night watchman or messenger, or imposition of duress upon an insured or an employee to open the premises or the safe within the premises. The latter is called kidnapping. All of these coverages in the burglary area are available for incorporation in package policies at premium discounts.

Inland Marine Insurance

This type of insurance deals with a number of situations requiring broad insurance coverage. The objects covered may not be stationary or they may be excluded directly from fire and allied peril insurance. Coverage generally includes accounts receivable, camera and musical instrument dealers, cargo insurance, equipment dealers, contractors' equipment, garment contractors, jewelers, physicians' and surgeons' equipment, agricultural equipment and livestock, signs, and valuable papers.

The appropriate inland marine coverage needed by a business may be purchased on either all risk or named peril basis. There is generally a deductible amount involved. Because the coverage often involves expensive materials or equipment, it is more often written on an all risk basis.

Most of the coverage outlined above is available for incorporation in a package policy. While some companies discount the coverage when packaging them, others refuse to do so because of the breadth of the protection.

Ocean Marine Cargo Insurance

All exported goods (whether they are initially transported by railroads, trucks, or air) that are waterborne during any time of their shipment can be insured by this policy. The open cargo type covers all shipments made by a business. The shipper (the insured) reports the shipments made and protection is automatic once the report of a shipment is filed. The protection can be tailored to meet special requirements; it may provide all risk protection or be on a named peril basis. The policy contains a valuation clause that states the amount of insurance per shipment is equal to the amount of the invoice and all contingency charges. Many special clauses can be added to make this into exactly the type of protection a shipping business desires.

Data Processing Policy

This covers electronic data processing equipment that a business may own, plus component parts and data processing media which are owned or leased by a business. Insurance is on an all risk basis subject to certain exclusions. The policy may be extended to include extra expense incurred as a result of damage to equipment or media. Business interruption loss attributable to total or partial suspension of operations can be purchased. The policy can be extended to cover valuable papers and records of accounts receivable if so desired.

Difference in Conditions Policy

This is a form of property insurance designed to provide all risk insurance for perils not normally available through fire and extended coverage insurance plans. Its intent is to cover catastrophic perils such as flood and water damage, earthquake, collapse, burglary, and transit exposure, and is subject to a sizable deductible amount.

This can be purchased as a supplement to fire, extended coverage, vandalism, and sprinkler leakage insurance. It is simply supposed to repay the purchaser for the difference in condition of the property insured after a loss has occurred. It is about the only source of coverage that provides flood insurance outside the federal program.

No standard policy is available and many insurance companies offer varying clauses dealing with protection and exclusions. Therefore, protection of this type should be examined thoroughly by a customer before purchase.

Flood Insurance

This is made available and partially subsidized by the federal government through the Flood Disaster Protection Act of 1973. It protects against both flood and mudslide (mudflow) for all types of buildings and their contents, subject to a deductible. The condition causing the flooding or inundation must be of a general nature; coverage is not provided when damage results solely from causes on the insured property or from causes within control of the insured.

Plate Glass Insurance

This is generally a replacement insurance. It provides protection on scheduled glass and (if separately described) lettering and ornamentation. In addition, the insuring company will also pay for repair or replacement of frames, installation of temporary plates, and boarding up of openings necessitated by glass breakage from almost any cause except fire. There may be a limitation on damage to frames, temporary plates, and boarding-up requirements.

CRIME INSURANCE

Dishonesty, both from within and without the business, can cause serious financial loss to a customer. Insurance coverage to protect against these losses is known by two names, fidelity bonds and policies.

Fidelity Bonds

A fidelity bond is a contract between the parties: the insurer (also known as the surety), the insured (employer or obligee), and the principal (employee). In the contract, the surety agrees to reimburse the employer for any loss caused by the dishonest act of an employee.

Name Schedule Bond.   Employees selected by the employer are covered by this bond. They are listed by name, and the amount of desired coverage on each is shown. Names may be added or removed and coverage increased or decreased. The insured is covered against loss caused through the fraud or dishonesty of the employee. This means the insurer is liable for dishonest omissions and dishonest acts of the employee.

Position Schedule Bond.   Almost similar to the name schedule bond, this type lists the positions in the organization but does not list names of employees. The coverage is extended to the positions rather than to the individuals holding the positions.

Blanket Bond.   This type of contract covers all officers and employees and therefore broadens the protection. Its two main forms are the blanket position bond and the primary commercial blanket bond.

The blanket position bond reimburses the insured for loss due to the dishonesty of an employee up to the amount specified in the bond; the primary commercial blanket bond differs from it in that the amount covered applies to each loss rather than to each employee.

Additional Policy Coverage

In addition to insurance against losses from dishonest employees, some businesses obtain coverage against such actions as counterfeit currency, depositors forgery, and commercial forgery.

Comprehensive Dishonesty, Disappearance, and Destruction Policy.   This policy combines several features of other policies. It provides coverage for fidelity, on-premises loss, off-premises loss, money orders and counterfeit paper currency, and depositors forgery.

Depositors Forgery Policy.   Usually written in connection with fidelity bonds, depositors forgery policies also cover forgery by employees and others. Personal signatures and facsimile signatures applied by check-signing machines are included in this coverage.

Commercial Forgery Policy.   Protection is given against loss caused by accepting a draft or check that has been forged or altered in payment for personal property or services. Checks cashed in full are not covered.

Blanket Crime Policy.   This comprehensive policy covers all employees, locations, and messengers, and comprises five insuring agreements: employee dishonesty coverage, loss inside the premises coverage, loss outside the premises coverage, money orders and counterfeit paper currency coverage, and depositors forgery coverage. The policy is designed to provide single amount insurance coverage rather than the varying amounts available through the purchase of separate policies.

GENERAL LIABILITY INSURANCE

Every business may sustain a financial loss caused by injury to the person or property of an individual or another business entity. The general liability policy transfers the legal liability for such injury from the insured to the insurance company.

The major sources of potential injury may include premises, operations, contractual agreements, products liability, completed operations, or work done by independent contractors. Historically, coverage was provided by narrow contracts that addressed the insured's primary exposure—that is, an Owners, Landlords, and Tenants policy for a premises exposure or a Manufacturers and Contractors policy for operations coverage. While many of these policies are still written and provide the necessary coverage for the particular circumstances, protection now is usually provided by a Comprehensive General Liability policy, which addresses itself to all of the policyholder's liability exposures.

The Comprehensive General Liability policy is broad and can protect the policyholder for most liability exposure. Often it is broadened further by the addition of special endorsements to provide coverage excluded in the basic contract. Very briefly, the following hazards are covered:

1. The ownership, maintenance or use of premises, and all operations.
2. The ownership, maintenance, or use of any elevator designated in the declarations.
3. Operations performed by independent contractors for the insured, if the accident occurs during operations (with certain exceptions).
4. Goods or products manufactured or sold—and title has passed—that cause an accident away from the premises.
5. Completed or abandoned operations, if the accident occurs away from the premises.
6. Other coverages that may have been separately endorsed into the policy, such as when an insured has entered into a written contract assuming certain liabilities of others.
7. Property damage, known as coverage B. This coverage can be excluded by the insured.
8. Medical Payments, known as coverage C. This coverage is usually endorsed into the policy.

In the early 1960s, the commercial insurance industry followed the personal lines insurance industry in including property insurance and liability insurance in one policy. These multiperil or package policies have become widely accepted, but the liability coverage provided is the same as that provided by a separate liability policy.

LIFE INSURANCE

Creditors must be concerned with the effect that the death of a principal or a key employee will have on the earning power and financial condition of a customer. For instance, the death of a proprietor dissolves the business. It may continue to be operated by an estate, but the valuable contribution of the owner is no longer available. The earning power of the business will be radically affected; it should be protected for the good of the estate and of the creditors.

In another case, a partnership may suffer when a principal dies. Again, the deceased partner's talents are no longer available to the business. Just as important, however, the heirs of the deceased may wish to withdraw their interest from the business. This can cause a serious drain on the finances of the company.

Similarly, a corporation may suffer a loss of earning power when an officer or key employee dies. In addition, it may be forced to buy back a deceased officer's interest and thus decrease its own capitalization.

Insurance on the lives of the principals and key employees relieves some of the financial loss caused by their deaths. A number of different policies are written to cover this contingency. Usually premiums are paid by the business and the firm is named beneficiary. This protects the earning power of the business and enables the company to buy back the interest of a deceased principal without decreasing its usual financial resources.

CREDIT INSURANCE

As previously noted, insurance coverage is protection against loss from disastrous and, by implication, infrequent occurrences. In buying credit insurance, the business purchases protection against disastrous bad-debt losses while retaining the risk of ordinary losses.

Credit insurance is not a substitute for competent credit analysis but does relieve some of the pressure on the credit department. It is different from a factoring agreement in that receivables are not sold by the client to the insurer. It also differs from a financing arrangement because receivables are not pledged as collateral for secured loans. Both of these methods are used to increase the cash available for company operation. The chief benefit of credit insurance, however, serves chiefly to protect the company investment in receivables.

Major Benefits of Credit Insurance

A credit insurance policy provides a number of valuable features. It protects against excessive bad-debt losses, promotes safe sales expansion, provides effective collection assistance, strengthens borrowing and purchasing power, improves planning and budgeting accuracy, and provides loss prevention guidance on key risks.

Elements of the Contract

In order for a contract of credit insurance to apply, there must be a sale, shipment, and delivery; or a service must be provided for which there is a legally sustainable claim against the debtor or the debtor's estate. Generally, coverage is limited to sales on regular terms of not more than one year.

Policy Coverage

Credit insurance is available only to firms engaged in manufacturing, wholesaling, and certain service businesses. It is written with a deductible provision, primary loss provision, and may provide for coinsurance.

In every policy, the insured and the insurer agree on a maximum amount of coverage, which is the policy amount. It is the maximum amount the insured can recover for all covered losses sustained during the one-year term of the policy.

Coinsurance

The insured company participates in 10 or 20 per cent of the bad-debt loss sustained on a debtor. This coinsurance feature causes the insured to participate in each loss. A higher premium is charged if the insured wants a policy without coinsurance.

Primary Loss

Since credit insurance is not intended to eliminate all credit risk, the policy covers losses over and above an agreed-upon annual deductible. This deductible is based on the normal expected loss for the business and the overall risk to be insured. This initial deductible loss is termed the primary loss and is not reimbursed to the insured. It is set as a percentage of sales, but in no case less than a stated dollar amount.

Table of Ratings and Coverages

Figure 18-1 shows a table of ratings and coverage based on Dun & Bradstreet ratings. Column one contains high credit ratings and column two, good credit ratings. The corresponding coverage is shown next to each rating. For example, a sale to an account rated BB1 would be covered up to $50,000; one rated CC2 would have $15,000 coverage; and one rated GG1 would be covered up to $2,500. All of these coverages are subject to the policy amount set in the contract.

A loss against a covered debtor may be a provable claim under the policy because of an insolvency of the debtor, or by the insured filing a claim against a past-due debtor within a required period as stated in the policy.

The insurance company provides a collection service and there is an extra charge for the collection of amounts from debtors against which a claim has been filed.

Policy Endorsements

A number of endorsements can be made to the credit insurance policy to cover particular situations. Some are as follows:

Column 1		Column 2	
Rating	Gross Amount Covered	Rating	Gross Amount Covered
5A 1	$100,000.	5A 2	$25,000.
4A 1	100,000.	4A 2	25,000.
3A 1	100,000.	3A 2	25,000.
2A 1	50,000.	2A 2	25,000.
1A 1	50,000.	1A 2	25,000.
BA 1	50,000.	BA 2	25,000.
BB 1	50,000.	BB 2	25,000.
CB 1	50,000.	CB 2	25,000.
1R 2	25,000.	2R 2	15,000.
CC 1	30,000.	CC 2	15,000.
DC 1	25,000.	DC 2	12,500.
DD 1	20,000.	DD 2	10,000.
EE 1	10,000.	EE 2	5,000.
FF 1	5,000.	FF 2	3,000.
GG 1	2,500.	GG 2	1,500.
HH 1	1,500.	HH 2	750.

FIG. 18–1. Table of Ratings and Coverage.

Bank Endorsement. This endorsement is used when an account uses its receivables as collateral for bank borrowing. It gives the lending bank the right to file accounts in the same way as the insured does.

Construed Coverage. In case a customer's credit agency rating is changed downward between the time an order is accepted and the merchandise is shipped, this endorsement provides coverage at the higher rating for up to 120 days after the order is accepted.

Interim Claim Settlement. This endorsement allows the insured to request three interim settlements within 60 days after filing a claim rather than waiting until the end of the policy term.

Claim Settlement

Within one month after the expiration of the insolvency period of the policy, the insured submits a Final Statement of Claims listing all claims to be included in the loss settlement. A settlement date is made with the insured within two months after receipt by the insurer of the Final Statement of Claims, at which time the amount ascertained to be due the insured will be paid.

CREDIT EXECUTIVE'S INTEREST IN INSURANCE COVERAGE

Creditors are interested in the ability of a company to recover from financial loss and to stay in business. The types and amounts of insurance carried affect this ability and should be known in every detailed credit analysis.

Emphasis up to this point has been on the protection of tangible and intangible assets of the debtor, but there are other related points that a credit executive should know. First, a company's insurance program should be kept under continuous review by knowledgeable persons, either directly employed or retained on contract. A growing company adds new products, expands its territory, purchases new equipment, adds new employees, enters into new contracts, and so on. Each of these represents a consideration that needs attention.

Second, business insurance is seldom a fixed cost item; the larger the cost the more likely this will be true. Business insurance contracts usually involve an estimated premium charge at inception, to be followed by an adjustment at the end of the period based on a physical audit conducted by the insurer that determines the actual premium. A business that has grown or changed substantially during the period could owe a sizable additional amount to its insurer. Many times this has not been anticipated and provided for, and may result in a financial strain.

Third, a financial statement issued by a customer may not reflect the contingency or added obligations to its insurer. The best safeguard is to inquire whether the financial statements have been audited and through what date. In this respect, insurance is similar to federal income taxes and should be approached on the same basis. An insurer's audit privilege may extend beyond one year, and many go to two or even three years. This contingency can be missed in audited reports.

Finally, there is one more area of business insurance that usually relates to the larger firms. It is referred to as retrospective. In this case, the insured buys a contract with a built-in fee to compensate the insurer for servicing the firm's claims. This can become an important consideration due to the amount of dollars and time element involved. Many claims involve litigation that can extend up to and beyond 10 to 15 years. Until the claims have been settled, the costs between the insured and the insurer cannot be fully determined.

CHAPTER 19

NONFINANCIAL ANALYSIS OF A BUSINESS

Character and experience were recognized as important nonfinancial factors in evaluating creditworthiness as far back as colonial times. Mercantile credits were granted for periods ranging from eight months to several years. It was not unusual for accounts to run months and even years past due, but invariably the debtor paid a charge for interest on the overdue amount. As we became a Nation, credit was customarily extended for periods of from six to twelve months. Business corporations were few in number. The proprietorship and partnership were the common business structures of that day, so the outside means of the owner or owners could be attached by creditors.

In these early days, two practices were customarily followed to place credit information in the hands of mercantile creditors. By one, the buyer would forward letters of reference and recommendation obtained from friends, the local minister, a neighboring lawyer, or locally established fellow merchants. By the other, the seller would write to customers or to friends located in the buyer's neighborhood, requesting what is today called credit information, as well as personal opinions regarding the subject's honesty, ingenuity, and local reputation.

Inquiries were occasionally made regarding the financial condition of a debtor, but very quietly, to avoid arousing any general suspicion. Rarely did a creditor obtain exact information regarding the financial responsibility of the potential buyer. There was no such thing as bank credit in our present-day sense of the term until the Bank of North America was organized in Philadelphia in 1781 and the Bank of New York in New York City in 1784. The most important nonfinancial factor in credit analysis was then as now, management—the experience, background, knowledge, aggressiveness, honesty, and ingenuity of the individuals who actively operate a business. Today, this and other nonfinancial and financial factors in credit analysis are incorporated into the four "Cs" of credit.

THE FOUR "Cs" OF CREDIT

It is the primary role of the credit department to decide whether to approve or reject every customer as a credit risk. The policy of the company will naturally affect the final decision, but preliminary credit investigation procedure is fairly standard. By standardizing the steps taken to investigate a risk and determine its desirability, the credit department minimizes the possibility of oversight in the investigation.

The factors examined in a credit analysis are known as the "Four Cs of Credit": character, capacity, capital, and conditions of the times. Understandably each factor may be more important in one specific case than in another, but in every case the credit executive must determine how the account measures against all four "Cs" before giving a final opinion about the account.

Character

This factor inquires into the willingness of the debtor to pay obligations. To properly develop an idea of the business character of an individual, the credit executive must know as much as possible about previous business habits.

For individuals who have previously been in business on their own account or who have been members of the management staff of a corporation, the record of their success, the capacities in which they were employed, and how they performed would provide information on their character. For example, a long-standing record of operation without litigation or financial embarrassments is a prima facie indicator of this factor. On the other hand, an individual who has a record of bankruptcies, litigation, or both is generally a questionable risk insofar as this one factor is concerned.

Where information is detrimental to an individual, full details regarding the surrounding circumstances are essential. If an individual has been involved in failures, it should be determined how much on the dollar was paid in settlement to unsecured creditors in each case. Accurate, comprehensive information on these points is essential background for practical credit analysis. There is no system which will provide this information automatically. It is obtained by bankers, credit executives, and the trained reporters of mercantile credit agencies in their searches for comprehensive antecedent information. In many cases, background and personal history may be obtained by a sales representative at the time the first order is set up.

For individuals who have set up a business for the first time, judgment of their ability, conscientiousness, integrity, and aggressiveness depends on their record as employees. Therefore, it is essential to secure the name of all business concerns with which they have been employed and to obtain information regarding them from responsible persons in these concerns. When they do not have a long business history, it is more difficult to make this judgment. Intangibles such as family background, employment record, and personal credit history can be judiciously used to form a tentative opinion.

Capacity

This aspect deals with the ability of the business to operate successfully. A business may be regarded as an operation of three separate, specialized, and interlocking functions: marketing, production, and finance. To be successful the principals must be able to provide these specialties to the business. Otherwise the lacking ingredient will retard successful operation.

In a very small business, the three functions are undertaken by one person. An expanding business makes it necessary to split the functions and to assign them to experts, or at least to people who will devote most of their time to them. If the principals cannot provide the specialized knowledge or abilities, those services must be purchased from the outside. For instance, a small business formed by a production manager and a sales manager will need the firm's accountant to provide the financial supervision for the concern. Another firm may be forced to use sales agents because none of the principals has sufficient sales experience to perform that function effectively. Still another business may require outside labor contractors to produce its goods. The principals may be competent in sales, finance, and design but be lacking in the practical know-how of volume production.

Previous business experience is again a valid indicator of the capacity of a firm. Particularly when large volume orders, exacting specifications, or tight delivery schedules are involved, the credit executive is interested in knowing whether the concern has actual prior experience in that type of operation. In the building contracting industry, for example, a job may be let on the basis of previous performance and capacity, as well as on the basis of low bid.

Capital

In this phase, the credit executive seeks to determine whether the account will be able to pay its obligations. This approach is different from that of the first "C," which seeks to judge if the account will be willing to pay.

This factor highlights the financial condition and trend of operations. Each case is judged on its own merits, since many factors affect the financial condition of a business. In some lines of business a large investment is needed in fixed assets. Others require only a minimum investment in machinery and fixtures. This affects the financial picture of the concern. Similarly, some lines of business must have large amounts of ready cash and liquid assets to meet seasonal operating expenses, while others can rely on regular cash inflow to meet maturing debts.

The trend of business is significant and weighs heavily in the overall judgment of the account. The credit executive looks more favorably on a business that shows increasing sales, profits, and net worth.

Conditions of the Times

General economic conditions in the nation, in the community, and in the industry will exert a modifying influence on the final analysis of the account. At any particular time, certain industries will be on the uptrend, while others will be stagnant or on the downswing. The likelihood of a satisfactory credit experience is greater when the subject is in an industry that is in a period of dynamic growth.

Likewise, during prosperous times risk of credit loss is generally less than it is during a depressed period. Community conditions also affect the likelihood that merchants will pay their bills on time, since they must rely upon receipts from their own customers.

APPLICATION OF THE FOUR "Cs" OF CREDIT

The four "Cs" of credit are a handy reference against which to judge a business credit applicant and, more recently, other "Cs" such as collateral and computers have been added by some analysts. More modern analytical procedure groups the information into background of the principals and the business, influence of the method of operation and industry characteristics, bank and trade investigations, and financial information and analysis. A detailed discussion of financial analysis techniques is reserved for Chapters 20 through 24, although it is noted at this point that financial statements are precise indicators of success.

Background of the Principals and the Business

It is true that no business situation is completely stable. The possibility always exists that a debtor company may encounter financial difficulty. But when a company has a good business record and is operated by capable people who are good moral risks, the likelihood of this kind of trouble is decreased. Business reputation takes a long time to build. It includes the ability, integrity, and experience of the principals, and is a valuable indicator of a firm's future actions.

To develop the information needed for understanding the personal and business background of an account, the credit executive follows a prescribed method of investigation, inquiring into a number of key points.

Names of the Principals. This is the normal starting point of this phase of the investigation. The people who have invested money in the business should be identified and their backgrounds checked.

This may not be practical when companies are widely or publicly held;

in those instances, background investigations of the chief stockholders, officers, and members of the board of directors are usually enough. More usually, however, companies are closely held, with a handful of people owning control. Then the background of each person should be investigated.

It is especially important to uncover hidden ownership, for in that case the business may be controlled by people who have unfavorable backgrounds. Credit judgments based on the integrity and ability of the principals cannot be realistic when facts regarding the true ownership are kept from creditors.

For example, it is important to know the business record of the husband when the wife is listed as an officer or principal. It is entirely possible that she has active control over the firm, in which case her record would govern. But if she is a "front" for her husband whose business record may not be able to stand scrutiny, then his business record becomes an important part of the total picture.

A similar situation is sometimes encountered when a relatively young person starts business with an abnormal initial investment from supposed "savings." The credit executive should be able to gauge the amount of money a young person would have normally saved, and ask for a detailed explanation about the source of larger amounts.

Aliases are sometimes uncovered during a credit investigation. The simplest way to proceed in that case is to turn the information over to a credit agency, and ask for a detailed record search.

Ages of the Principals.   While the age of any one principal in the business may not be a critical factor, a spread of top management ages provides for continuous operation in case an officer dies or retires.

Age plays another role in the day-to-day management of a firm. Generally, young managers are aggressive and ambitious. At the same time, these desirable qualities may not be tempered with experience and judicious action, and they may lead the firm into difficult situations.

Older managers, usually having more experience than their younger counterparts, tend to be conservative. Consequently, they may be expected to make fewer decisions without considering the consequences. By the same token, however, this conservative attitude may lead to less willingness to take a chance.

Perhaps the ideal combination is to be found in companies where an aggressive young management is tempered by the addition of several experienced older persons who advise on long-range projects and planning for the future. The benefits of youth are then combined with the advantages of advanced years. It is important to be sure, however, that the combination is made in the right way. It would be calamitous to have youth's recklessness place the business in a difficult situation, then have that difficulty compounded by the older members' conservative approach in seeking solutions to their problems.

Business Experience.   To say that principals have business experience is not enough. It must be ascertained that the experience is in the same line of business. An electronics manufacturer, for example, who enters the textile field may be experienced in one industry yet be totally unprepared for the problems of the new endeavor. Only after being exposed to the textile field could the principal be considered experienced.

Size of previous ventures and type of work done are also important points in the experience of principals. For instance, an individual seasoned in a relatively small venture may not be prepared for entry into big business. This person would not be able to run the new undertaking individually but would need to learn administrative techniques and financial management before being considered experienced.

Financial Worth of the Principals.   By law, the personal assets of partners and proprietors are available for the payment of business debts; this may also be true for corporations. Though a corporation protects its principals' personal assets from the debts of the business, the individuals may be asked by creditors to endorse or guarantee business debts. Thus principals who are wealthy in their own right are able to reinforce the credit position of their companies.

Relatives.   This feature of a business background is not important in many cases, but it arises often enough to make some mention of it worthwhile. When a rather young or inexperienced management is being appraised, it is proper for the credit executive to inquire into the principals' family connections. It may be discovered that a relative has lent financial support to the company, either as a loan or as an investment. Significant family relationships may suggest additional methods of approving an account on a secured basis or with endorsement or guaranty.

Integrity.   The ultimate decision in any credit analysis is based on the creditor's confidence that the debtor will pay its obligation. Ability to pay is important in this determination, but more important perhaps is the debtor's willingness to pay. This makes the debtor's integrity a key point in the analysis of credit risk.

Record Information.   Generally it is assumed that a person has good moral character unless there are specific facts to the contrary. To uncover unfavorable information, it is usually necessary to check agency reports and local records. Any facts concerning fire, failure, or fraud should be examined carefully. The circumstances surrounding the particular situation should be ascertained by direct investigation or through an agency, and should be clearly understood before a decision is made.

When a fire has occurred, it is important to know if the account carried insurance coverage. Where this is so, it should be determined if payment was made without question or if the fire was criticized. The number of fires may also be significant, though they are more common in industries working with inflammable materials.

Failures may have been caused by actions of the principals or may have resulted from the incompetent actions of others. A person who has been in a bankrupt concern at an early age, for instance, was probably not in a position to influence its actions. If, on the other hand, the individual was a dominant principal, this information becomes more important in the overall analysis of the person's capabilities. The credit executive must also be aware of the circumstances under which the difficulty occurred. For instance, a person who filed bankruptcy during a time of serious business recession would not be viewed in the same perspective as one who found it necessary to file a petition during a prosperous period. Similarly, as events recede into the years they may become relatively less important than are current events. The number and frequency of failures are likewise significant, since they indicate inability to operate successfully.

Fraud is a difficult thing to prove and requires court proceedings. This aspect of one's business history can be uncovered by a check of court records in the locales where the principal has conducted business. In this connection, it is important to obtain a complete listing of the individual's prior business interests, since those which did not meet with success might be omitted by the principal. An effective way to do this is to go over a chronological listing of prior affiliations and obtain explanations for any years not covered. It goes without saying that when the procedure is followed, it is necessary to check the listing against agency and public records.

Ability of the Principals.   The ability of principals is largely determined by their past records. In starting a new business, one who has had a successful business for many years would normally be considered a better risk than one who is beginning a first venture.

That comment holds true on a general basis but needs refinement in terms of the specific management skills required to operate a business— namely, production, marketing, and finance. Some of these skills may be furnished by employees or consultants, but the management of a company must still be responsible for them. Thus, when a company is analyzed, the credit executive must be satisfied that the necessary skills are provided in adequate proportions to ensure successful operation.

Distribution of Functions.   Individual control of a complicated business venture is usually inadequate, since the demands are too great for any one person to meet. Preferably, the managerial functions should be divided among the principals. This not only allows each to specialize in a particular phase of operations but also spreads the danger of serious business loss if one principal becomes ill or incapacitated. In addition, it is wise for a company to provide management in depth, with subordinates trained to take over the next higher job should it become vacated for any reason.

Outside Interests.   Principals having several interests must be expected to divide their time among them. As a result, they do not give full attention to the affairs of any one business. This may not be unfavorable in many cases where a company has made adequate provision for the day-to-day operation, but it becomes a serious matter when one individual takes on too many responsibilities.

The extent of intercompany relations between commonly owned companies must also be examined. Where a principal operates and controls a number of separate entities, there may be a tendency to consider them as one group. Consequently, their affairs may be directed to the mutual benefit of all, but particularly for personal gain. While this is not undesirable in itself, it may create some problems for creditors of any one company. They must understand these intercompany relations and how they affect their own positions as creditors.

Personal Habits.   The personal habits of the principals are of natural concern to creditors. Undesirable traits when carried to excess can influence business operation and take the principal's time and attention away from business. This jeopardizes the creditor's position.

Business Name.   A proprietor or a partnership using a trade style should register that name and keep a bank account under it. Orders should be placed and payments made in the legal name of the business. If that is not done, it may confuse creditors when they invoice the company.

A check with the firm's bank will disclose the name under which its account is maintained. When it is convenient, court records may also be searched for details of trade style registration.

Charter details of a corporation may be obtained from the Secretary of State in which the company is organized. These list the date of incorporation, the state of incorporation, the number and type of shares authorized, and their par value. During the personal investigation, it can be determined how many shares are outstanding, and who holds them. This identifies the control of the business.

Age and Reputation of the Business.   Businesses have their own personalities in much the same way as the principals who operate them. Thus it is important to determine how long a concern has been in existence, the extent of its success, and its public image. It is generally acknowledged that the first five years of business operation are the most trying. During that time, the concern must become established in its industry or community, must develop a following of customers, and must demonstrate its ability to compete effectively for a share of the market.

During the same period, the business is slowly establishing its reputation in the trade. Some are known as price cutters, others stress quality and service, while still others are able to develop a reputation for effective performance on schedule. Credit executives are interested in these aspects of their accounts, since they reflect their stability of operations.

Legal Form of Organization.   The legal form of organization, which is discussed in detail in Chapter 17, influences the capital, continuity, and liability of the business and of its principals. In reviewing a case which is up for credit decision, the credit executive should be satisfied that the seller's position will be protected if it becomes necessary to press for collection.

Influence of the Method of Operation and Industry Characteristics

This phase of the analysis requires a careful look into the line of business to analyze the industry in which the business operates, and to examine other facets such as selling terms, buying terms, distribution, seasons, time lags, and location. All of these factors affect a debtor's ability to pay.

Function. It is important for the understanding of an account to know whether it retails, wholesales, or manufactures merchandise. This may seem relatively simple to do, but the lines are not clearly drawn in practice. For instance, one company may manufacture and sell directly to customers; another may purchase some products ranging from semifinished to ready made, while others purchase raw materials for their own manufacture.

To determine the function of a company, a percentage breakdown is needed in terms of retailing, wholesaling, and manufacturing done by the account. It is likely that the different functions will have different buying and selling terms, which in turn will influence the financial requirements of the company. In addition, the function breakdown may indicate the amount of dependence the company places on local business, as well as the stability of its share of the total market.

Industry. The industry in which a company operates is extremely important for evaluating a given company. Every line of business has characteristics that apply to it alone and distinguish it from other industries. These should be known by the credit executive, since they vitally affect its financial operation. For example, a company selling to a growth industry plays an active part in a dynamic sector of the economy that is growing more rapidly then the economy as a whole. Continued growth is characterized by companies whose sales and profits rise rapidly and are usually not subject to business downturns. However, companies in this group are vulnerable to technological changes and to the transition from rapid growth to slower growth. This could then lead to a period of stabilization which may ultimately develop into a decline. Since cash needs are relatively high and capital turns rapidly in growth industries, creditors occasionally may be required to carry their customers. By the same token, suppliers selling to companies in growth industries can expect a more satisfactory profit.

A firm's customers also exert an influence on liquidity. If a company sells to customers in a strong industry, the likelihood is greater that it will have little trouble with collections. By the same reasoning, if a company sells in an industry that is cyclical, collection problems are more likely. Also, since a cyclical industry moves up and down more rapidly than business in general, purchase of its product can be readily postponed in times of adverse economic conditions.

Many companies in cyclical industries are prone to leverage their operations. This means that a prime source of their funds is long-term debt, used to finance plant expansion when the prospects for business are good. Companies in this type of industry are vulnerable to business downturns, however. With high fixed costs, a sharp reduction in sales volume paves the way for losses. These drains cause a sharp reduction in their liquid assets and their ability to meet trade obligations when they become due.

On the other hand, a company selling in a relatively stable industry would normally expect its customers to show a more consistent financial condition with sales and profits holding or rising. Those customers sell goods that are consumed or used immediately and their replenishment cannot be postponed.

While there are basically three patterns of industrial progress—growth, cyclical, stable—not all companies within a given industry will always follow the industry pattern. Moreover, the categories are not mutually exclusive. For example, the sales and profits for an industry may fluctuate during a business cycle but have better than average growth from one business cycle to the next. Such an industry would have both cyclical and growth characteristics.

Credit executives can obtain a fair picture of their customers' business outlooks by knowing the trends in their industries. While there is a spread between good, marginal, and poor accounts within every industry, the general characteristic within an industry will influence all companies. It is conceivable that marginal companies in slow-growth industries would be less desirable risks than marginal companies in fast-growth industries. When prospects are good, it is naturally easier to look favorably upon a credit risk; when the trend is downward, more careful examination of the facts is required.

Some industries are characterized by concerns that forego customer service and rely upon price competition as a chief attraction. If that is the case, their operating costs should be lower and their profit margins carefully shaved. At the same time, the companies should have vigorous collection procedures. Operations are so delicately balanced that the slightest slowdown of collections will have a major influence on the liquidity position of the seller. This type of operation relies upon smooth functioning of the entire buying-selling-collection-payment cycle.

Other companies that enjoy higher profit margins have a built-in buffer in their accounts receivables. Consequently, the companies may be able to carry accounts for longer periods of time. The creditor helps to finance the customer but charges for the service in the form of higher profit margins.

Products. The actual products sold by a company do, in the final analysis, reflect company success. Pricing, quality, and service are related to each other. Usually when quality and service are good, prices tend to rise. By the same token, prices are sometimes less important to buyers when a supplier can deliver good quality merchandise and provide adequate service. In every instance, the acid test of this combination is reflected in the profit and loss statement.

The number and types of accounts sold also bear directly on the vulnerability of a company. For instance, a company selling to a few large accounts can expect a good volume of business and fair success in projecting its cash needs. Profit margins can be predicted with close accuracy. Should the same account lose a single customer, however, the impact of this loss would be much greater than the loss of an account by a company having many customers placing relatively small orders.

Conversely, a company that sells to many accounts could normally expect larger selling and administration expenses. The choice between the two methods of operation must be made by the company after weighing the advantages of each method against its disadvantages.

Selling and Buying Terms. It has already been noted that a supplier helps to finance customers by providing goods or services on credit. To obtain a clearer picture of the relative importance of this feature, the buying and selling terms of customer accounts can be compared. For instance, a company that buys material on 30-day terms and sells its products on 30-day terms is in effect obtaining one month's financing from its suppliers and furnishing one month's financing to its customer. Meanwhile, a second company buying on 60-day terms and selling on 30-day terms has an advantage over the first company. Its suppliers are furnishing material on terms that are long enough to allow the company to fabricate it, sell the finished merchandise, and make its collections before the original invoices for raw materials are due. On the other hand, a third company buying on 30-day terms and selling on 60-day terms is in the worst position of the three. It is expected to pay for raw materials purchases before its own receivables have been collected. This third position is critical and will eventually lead to financial distress, unless additional funds are constantly pumped into the business.

The spread between buying terms and selling terms is naturally of concern, since it is a potent indicator of the long-range cash demands on a customer's business. Seasonal datings also fall into this category and must be compared in terms of buying and selling datings. Ideally, a company wishes to purchase on longer terms than it requires to manufacture, sell its products, and collect the resulting receivables. This is hardly ever permitted by a company's suppliers, since they realize the dangers of totally financing the customer's operations.

Distribution. Geographical separation of market areas has become less distinct with the development of rail, air, water, and truck transportation. Consequently, a company may have customers in all parts of the United States and in many parts of the world. This broadened market is generally favorable, as it spreads the base of company operations. Firms having a purely local distribution are more vulnerable to community economic fluctuations, since they have no way in which to spread their credit risk geographically.

The influence of local economic conditions on collections from any particular area pursues a distinct pattern. Usually a slowdown begins at the retail level, when consumers are laid off from their jobs and cannot pay charge accounts and installment purchases. As the retailers' collections slow down, they look to their suppliers for cooperation in carrying these slow receivables; they pay their own obligations slow. By that time, wholesalers have felt the deteriorating local economic conditions and may seek to pay their own accounts slow to manufacturers. Now the local influence has extended to areas many miles away.

If the economic conditions are very serious, their effects may be felt throughout the country. In most instances, however, large manufacturers and suppliers spread their markets to more than one geographical location. Consequently, drastic curtailment of collections from any one area has been offset by good collections in other areas serviced by the company.

Seasons. Most industries operate on a seasonal basis. During some part of the year, sales activity is high; during other months it is low. For purposes of credit analysis, this means that an account would normally require high trade and bank credit at particular times during the year. Once its season had passed, merchandise would normally have been manufactured and sold. Immediately following a heavy selling season, an account would be expected to have large accounts receivable, relatively low cash, and low inventories. At that same time, chances are high that payables had not yet been paid so its balance sheet would show heavy accounts payable and bank debt.

After the normal selling terms period had passed, the company should have collected its receivables. This would change the balance sheet: cash would be high, accounts receivables would be relatively low, and inventory would still be relatively small. When debts were paid, cash would decrease and payables would decline.

Following this period, the account would start to buy for the next season. Inventories would rise, accounts payable would start to get heavy, and bank loans would start to appear on the balance sheet. As manufacuring progresses, cash balances would tend to decline because of the daily cash needs of the business. Receivables should be in relatively low proportions, but bank loans would increase. As sales are made in the next active season, receivables start to rise and inventory declines, but payables and bank loans are still at seasonally high peak. This cycle is repeated for each season.

The credit executive takes the seasonal aspects of business into account when analyzing a risk. Not only are the balance sheet and profit and loss figures important, but the frequency of seasonal activity also influences a firm's earning power and ability to recover from a poor season. Thus a company that relies principally on Christmas trade is affected more seriously by a poor Christmas season than one that can count on Christmas, Easter, June graduation, and September back-to-school flurries of activity. In the first case, nine or more months must pass before strong prospects for earnings again become evident. The second firm has another chance at earnings in a much shorter period of time.

Time Lags. This feature of manufacturing and wholesale operations has received much attention during recent years. It affects inventory positions, collections of receivables, and predictions of cash needs. It determines in large part the established buying and selling terms in an industry. Two examples illustrate this feature:

1. The infants wear industry specializes in hand-embroidered baby garments. Much of this hand detail is done in foreign countries. In terms of time requirements, this means the manufacturer must purchase the raw materials, ship them abroad by boat, and have the hand work done and the dresses shipped back to the United States. This may take up to six months. In the meanwhile, the merchandise has been purchased but is not in condition to be sold. The time lag involved in manufacturing plays an important role in the capital requirements of this line of business.

2. Automobile designs for the next models have already been developed and tooling up has started, while current models are being sold. Planning for cash and materials requirements in this industry is detailed and exacting. Cash resources are projected up to five and ten years in advance. This time lag is a critical factor in the planning and placement of orders for component parts.

Other industries do not need long periods of manufacture. When high style is an important consideration, time lags are cut as short as possible. Industry terms usually follow this trend and are likewise shortened. The reason for this is obvious: styles are volatile and vulnerable; consequently, long selling terms restrict the supplier's ability to press for collection and threaten the value of merchandise sold.

Changes in Operation. A business that has been established for a long time may occasionally find it necessary to adapt its method of operation to meet changing conditions. Technology, market locations, labor markets, and economic conditions may change and influence the market position of a concern. Consequently, the credit executive is interested in finding out what changes have taken place in the operations of customer accounts, and what has caused these changes. As an added step, the investigation should be pursued to determine the success of these changes.

Location. The location of a business affects costs of operation and nearness to buying and selling markets. Physical facilities should be large enough for efficient operations, yet not so large that space is wasted.

Rent or Own. Many well-established concerns own the buildings in which they operate. There are, however, just as many that prefer to rent physical facilities, claiming it gives them more financial flexibility.

On the balance sheet, a company that rents its plant and equipment may show a relatively small investment in fixed assets. This increased liquidity improves the apparent financial condition of the company. On the other hand, a company which owns its own property must show a much larger investment in fixed assets. This results in a diminishing of current assets and less liquidity in the firm.

The idea of leasing equipment, rather than owning it outright, gained acceptance during the years following World War II. At first, there was a simple interpretation of the balance sheet to indicate improved liquidity when assets were sold and then leased back. As analysts gained experience with this type of situation, however, they became more sophisticated. They now recognize that a lease to pay specified rentals is a constant drain on the earnings of the company. Obligations must be met, whether facilities are used or not. In addition, the charges for rental are usually calculated to provide a yield to the owners.

The credit executive must be concerned with the gross charges for plant and equipment. This is true whether the physical facilities are owned or rented. When buildings and machinery are owned, the charges are in the form of depreciation which do not require cash to be paid out. Leased equipment charges show up as a rental or lease expense and require cash outlay. Leasing is discussed in more detail in Chapter 27.

Size of Premises.   A company that does its own manufacturing would naturally be expected to have larger premises than one that uses outside contractors. Similarly, a company that uses public warehouses for the storage of its merchandise will need smaller premises than a comparable one that maintains its own warehouse at different locations throughout the country.

Companies requiring small machinery for manufacturing may be able to operate on smaller premises than those needing large capital equipment. By the same token, a company located in a metropolitan area can be expected to build up, while one situated in an urban area can take advantage of low land values and build long structures one or two stories high.

These illustrations have been given in order to point out that the size of premises occupied by a firm must be related to the type of activity performed and the geographical locations of the premises.

Size of Building.   When a company's physical facilities are located in a metropolitan area, the firm often occupies a portion of a multistoried loft building. In addition to knowing the number of square feet occupied, the credit executive should have an idea of the size of the building and the number of floors it has. This influences some of the production and materials-handling methods and consequently affects the costs of operation.

Type of Construction.   Floor loads and type of equipment which can be placed in the building are determined by the type of construction. This also protects the company's materials from damage. A fireproof building, arranged so the spread of fire can be effectively prevented, provides maximum assurance to creditors that the danger of fire loss is minimized. Conversely, a frame building without adequate fire protection equipment increases the possibility of a fire that will interrupt operations or destroy the business.

Surrounding Area. This also affects the fire hazard of a particular location. Located in an area where inflammable materials are stored or processed, a company is more vulnerable to fire loss. The type of construction used in the adjoining buildings also affects the fire hazard.

A retail company must pay particular attention to its location, which must be accessible to its customers. There is more flexibility in the operation of a wholesale or manufacturing concern, since its products can be shipped directly to customers.

Transportation Facilities. The ability of a manufacturing company to receive raw materials economically and to ship out finished products affects its overall costs of operation. Locations near main roads or on railroad spurs are ideal.

Retail stores should provide adequate parking facilities for their customers. Suburban shopping centers apportion a large amount of their total space for parking cars. In downtown areas, retailers may make arrangements with nearby garages and parking lots for customer parking. Additionally, locations near bus stops make it easy for customers to reach the store.

Bank Investigations

A significant factor in the background of a business is its relationship with its bank. The procedures followed in making a bank check and the information available are discussed in Chapter 15. The comments below are confined to the significance of the information contained in a bank check.

The bank check helps provide the credit executive with a more complete understanding of an account. There are basically two ways a bank lends money: unsecured and secured. An unsecured loan relies only upon the customer's promise to pay. Consequently, this form of loan is made only to customers having a good credit standing and the financial ability to repay the loan.

A loan granted on a secured basis is generally backed by a personal guaranty or by collateral such as marketable securities or other pledged assets. When a personal guaranty is given, the financial strength of the names backing the notes determines the ability to pay the loan. When collateral is given, the lender usually looks in whole or in part to liquidation of the pledged property in the event that the loan is not regularly paid.

A credit executive may on occasion come across an account that is considered a prime credit risk, eligible for an unsecured loan, but borrowing on a secured basis. To properly evaluate the credit risk, the executive should discuss the account with the bank to determine the quality of the loan and collateral. It may be that the customer requested such an arrangement in order to obtain a lower interest rate, and thus reduce the cost of carrying the loan.

Trade Investigations

Part of the background of a business also consists of the way in which it has conducted its affairs with trade creditors. If the integrity of management and its business acumen is examined, the credit executive should, and generally does, learn how the company pays its bills. Thus a company with a record of honest dealings and principals who have demonstrated their skill and experience generally wants to discount or pay its obligations promptly, and is able to do so because it knows how to buy, how to sell, and how to manage its finances.

Interpretation of Trade Clearances. The payment record of an account is actual evidence of how it pays its bills. It is therefore natural for a credit executive to examine paying records when evaluating a company's credit risk.

The specific information contained in a trade clearance presents a clear and current picture of the firm's paying habits, and covers:

> How Long Sold
> Date of Last Sale
> Highest Recent Trade
> Now Owing
> Past Due
> Payment Terms
> Paying Record
> Comments

Trend of Payments: A comparison of one trade report with an earlier one establishes the trend of company payments. A trend towards slower payments indicates the need to learn the reasons for this slowness. An account may be expanding sales and relying upon trade creditors to finance this expansion. On the other hand, an account may be experiencing difficulty in the collection of its own receivables. Knowing these two alternatives, the credit executive can proceed with the investigation to determine the actual cause of the slowing trend. On the other hand, an improving payments trend is favorably regarded; the account may be improving its own collections or may have obtained additional financing (either equity or borrowings) in order to pay its bills more promptly.

Age of the Business. If all respondents report the account as new or if a large number of first orders appear on the clearance, it is reasonable to assume that the firm has recently begun operations. There is of course the possibility that the company has recently changed all of its suppliers, but that is not likely.

Size of the Business. By examining the dollar amounts of individual and total high credits, it is possible to estimate the scope of business conducted by the buyer. Large orders from many suppliers indicate a large operation; smaller orders characterize a smaller business.

Confidence of Suppliers. A report on the actual dealings with suppliers reveals their degree of confidence in the account. This is shown by the actual terms of credit which they extend.

Selling Terms. These should be noted for every reply from suppliers and can be compared to find out if special terms are being received by the account. Seasonal datings or extra time or discount allowances put the credit executive on notice that further investigation is required.

Seasonal Clearance. When a trade clearance shows amounts owing very close to the high credits approved, it is likely that the clearance has been taken at the height of the season. This type of clearance is useful in that it gives an idea of how heavy a payable position the company is willing to accept. Cleanup position shows relatively small amounts owing when contrasted to recent high credits. Past-due amounts after cleanup time point to the possibility of a poor season.

Concentration of Purchases. A thorough trade clearance that shows three or four major suppliers and a number of smaller ones indicates that the company concentrates its purchases. If a supplier is asked to become a new source, it should determine its risk position in the overall debt picture of the account.

Changes Indicated. In a comprehensive trade investigation, the respondents are asked to furnish any additional information they may have concerning recent personnel or operational changes in an account. These serve as leads to further investigation. For example, a retailer of drugs which had discounted all invoices consistently for four years began to allow the discount period to pass by. An investigation disclosed that the retailer was not successfully meeting the competition of a new supermarket. The trade report spotted a change brought about by the competitive situation.

Personal Quirks. Trade investigations reveal what might be called personal quirks that affect payments. For example, a manufacturer looked at a poor trade report on a potential customer. It showed that some of the suppliers were being paid promptly while other suppliers were forced to collect their money through attorneys. After checking with a substantial number of the suppliers, the manufacturer learned that the concern paid sales personnel of suppliers promptly when they made calls for their money but was delinquent in mailing out checks. Having learned the peculiarity of this customer, the manufacturer was able to open an account and handle profitable business while others were shutting down on the account.

Special Financial Arrangements. Unpublicized arrangements, guaranties, requests for special terms, and extensions can be discovered during a trade check. They are of considerable importance in analyzing a business.

Analysis of Sample Trade Checkings. In Figure 19-1, six sample trade

High Credit	Now Owing	Past Due	Terms	Payments and Comments
(1) 1,000	1,000	0	30	new account
800	800	0	2/10 n/30	first transaction
600	600	0	10 EOM	ppt on samples
450	450	0	30	just opened
400	400	0	10 EOM	new-know owner from previous
250	250	0	net cash	OK
(2) 50,000+	50,000+	0	70	ppt
35,000+	35,000+	0	60	as agreed
25,000+	25,000+	0	60	ppt—occasionally antic.
20,000+	20,000+	0	2/10/60x	ppt
5,000	5,000	0	60 plus 60	new account
(3) 28,000	1,000	0	30 plus 30	ran slow—sold for years
25,000	25,000	15,000	2/10 n/30	30 slow—sold for years
20,000	20,000	18,000	2/10 n/30	45 slow
20,000	16,000	16,000	2/10 n/30	30–45 slow
18,000	18,000	18,000	net 30	first deal
15,000	13,000	8,000	net 30	55 slow—good account
13,000	12,000	3,000	net 30	30–50 slow
12,500	12,500	12,500	regular	10 days past due
5,000	1,500	0	EOM	ppt
1,000	—	0	net 30	ppt—new account
(4) 25,000	15,000	5,000	60	fmly 60 slow; now averages 30 slow
20,000	20,000	5,000	60	fmly 45 slow; now 20 days slow
18,000	15,000	1,000	60	about cleaned up; pay improved
15,000	13,000	5,000	60	improving; now 15 days p d
8,000	6,000	5,300	60	working along; friendly account
6,000	3,000	1,500	30	recently 60+ p d; now 45 p d
(5) 22,000	5,000	0	2/10 EOM	sold for years—antic & disc.
25,000	3,000	0	2/10 n/30	discount for years
18,000	6,000	0	n/30	sold years—pays prompt
15,000	6,000	0	2/10 EOM	mostly ppt—some discount
13,000	3,500	0	n/30	good discount
12,000	—	0	regular	ppt
30,000	1,500	1,500	2/10 EOM	ppt except one bill 45 days p d
(6) 12,000	12,000	12,000	n/30	placed for collection
10,000	10,000	1,000	n/30	in hands of attorney
8,000	8,000	8,000	2/10 EOM	wants to return first shipment

FIG. 19–1. Sample Trade Checkings.

clearances are shown to illustrate the kinds of information that can be obtained by a careful interpretation of these results.

The first trade checking shows a relatively new business with no payment experience reported. Initial orders have been approved by at least six suppliers in moderate amounts. The owner has some previous business experience, according to one supplier, and that has apparently been satisfactory. The clearance is made at the peak of the buying season, ready for manufacturing or selling, since high credits equal amounts now owing. Terms are regular for the line of business.

The second account is better established than the first. Purchases are fairly concentrated and in larger amounts. Payments are good on terms characteristic of the garment industry. This is a seasonal clearance, with amounts owing equal to recent high credits. There is one new supplier reporting; this may be a company which is trying to get this account as a customer, since it has offered terms of "60 plus 60," or it may carry merchandise needed by the account for a new line.

The third account has spread its purchases more than the first two. It has been buying from at least eight large suppliers, with two smaller ones starting to show some activity. The clearance is taken past the peak season, with most of the amounts already past due. Apparently the account has had some trouble with its own collections or is expanding sales without sufficient equity financing. The first supplier seems to have foreseen this difficulty and restricted its credit exposure; the supplier reporting "first deal" may be replacing the one that is withdrawing.

The fourth trade clearance was evidently conducted on a company which is working itself out of difficulty. The trend of payments is consistently better. Regular suppliers have cooperated with the account and now note some improvements. The clearance seems to have been made just after season, since high credits and amounts owing are fairly close.

The fifth clearance shows a very satisfactory experience with a well-regarded account. It is taken at cleanup time, with outstanding debts low in relation to high credits. With nothing past due, except the obviously disputed $1,500, the company shows an excellent record. Purchases are spread quite evenly among the seven suppliers who reported.

The sixth clearance speaks for itself. It has all the earmarks of a distressed debtor.

There should be enough information on hand to give a clear picture of the account. Basic facts are learned through investigation of the business and its principals, then supplemented by a thorough financial analysis. In addition, the final decision to approve an order is influenced by the credit executive's interpretation of other suppliers' payment experience with the account. In practice, many decisions are made without benefit of full balance sheet and profit and loss information. This may be justified by the other facts concerning the account. It is rare, however, that an order can logically be approved without information concerning the background of the business.

PART V

FINANCIAL ANALYSIS

CHAPTER 20

FINANCIAL STATEMENTS USED IN CREDIT ANALYSIS

Credit granting depends to a large extent on financial analysis of a credit seeker's condition. Such an analysis involves an examination of the balance sheet, statement of income and retained earnings, statement of changes in financial position (funds flow), and a review of the notes to the financial statements. Under certain circumstances, an analysis of trial balance figures is essential. In all cases, though, consideration should be given to general economic conditions, the industry in which the customer is engaged, and the relative position of the customer within a given industry.

SCOPE OF CREDIT ANALYSIS

It has been said that the credit executive's analysis of financial data begins where the auditor's presentation ends. This analysis is generally undertaken to determine the liquidity and debt-paying ability of a firm. It differs from the analysis of the investor or the owner, but is similar to that of a banker considering a short-term loan. The extent of the analysis is generally determined by the size of the credit, the potential sales size of the account, the availability of guaranties or security agreements, and the ongoing relationship with the customer. In practice, there are wide extremes in the scope and intensity of financial analysis. Depending on the credit policies of the firm and the scope of activity, it may be superficial, purely mathematical, or sufficiently detailed to give a full understanding of the conditions and trends. It is the task of the credit executive to conduct the investigation and analysis against the background of company policy and the company's position as a supplier of the client, and to reach a conclusion regarding the acceptability of the prospect as a credit customer.

TYPES OF FINANCIAL STATEMENTS

Financial statements and schedules may cover an annual period or any interim period.

Annual Statements

The annual statement may be prepared for a calendar year, a natural year, or the fiscal year peculiar to the enterprise. The calendar year extends from January 1 to December 31 in a given year; the natural year is the 12-month period that ends when the activities of a business have reached the lowest point in its annual cycle. The fiscal year covers any regular 12-month period after which the books of a firm are closed and an annual statement is issued.

For purposes of credit analysis, the date of the annual financial statement is important in order to relate the figures to the stage or level of seasonal operations, to the condition of the industry itself, and to the state of the overall economy. Moreover, the date of the statement is particularly important when more than one statement is being compared to determine the trend of operations.

Despite the fact that the natural year represents a point in time when business operations are at a low point—that is, its financial position is the most liquid—most businesses have adopted calendar year closings. Since this may be in the midst of the busy season, the customer's financial statement is likely to reflect larger inventories and short-term debt than would be expected at a closing. Conversely, a statement drawn off at the end of a natural year discloses the customer's ability to liquidate short-term indebtedness. A credit executive would do well to assume that the financial statement being reviewed represents the most liquid financial condition possible as of that date. The task then is to determine if the condition becomes more imbalanced or more liquid at any point during the balance of the year.

Interim Statements

The main purpose of interim statements is to give creditors a more up-to-date view of a firm's finances than can be gotten from the fiscal figures. In some seasonal lines, statements are drawn off after the principal selling season, when inventories are at their lowest. Many small concerns are asked by their suppliers to work up midyear balance sheets and trial balances covering operations for one month, quarter, or longer periods. Trial balance figures differ from interim figures in that the latter contain an ending inventory while trial balance figures only have a beginning inventory. Thus the interim figures will reflect the profit for the period.

On a larger scale, publicly held companies are required to file a 10-Q report with the Securities and Exchange Commission (SEC). This quarterly report contains a balance sheet, profit and loss statement, source and application of funds statement, and a narrative analysis which points out any exceptional changes over the previous quarter. Many of these concerns issue interim statements for the benefit of investors and potential subscribers to their securities.

Estimated Statements

Unaudited statements or estimates can be erroneous and misleading, usually by accident but sometimes by deliberate intent of the principals. Where credit exposure is substantial or the risk is sufficiently large, efforts should be made to obtain an audited statement (see Chapter 21). Small concerns tend to resist the use of an auditor, frequently citing the high cost of such services. But it can be argued that an audit will provide assurance of fair and complete reports to all partners or principals and creditors. It will also make certain that tax returns are accurate, thus avoiding costly and time-consuming audits by tax collectors, disputes over taxes due, and possible penalties. Despite these strong arguments, many credit decisions are based on financial estimates. In fact, even an auditor's certificate reading "Prepared from the Company's books without audit" is notice to the prospective creditor that no independent analysis of the company's financial status was made.

If an audited statement cannot be obtained, efforts should be made to verify the assets and liabilities as shown in the estimates. Previous statements should be reconciled with current estimates via application of the profit and loss information submitted. Cash estimates can be compared with the average balance quoted by the bank; if there is great variation, the bank can be asked to verify the figures shown in the statement. Notes payable to banks can also be verified. Sales or service personnel calling at the customer's place of business can observe the inventory on hand and the degree of activity in the business. Accounts payable can be checked against a credit interchange or agency report. Ownership of land and buildings, as well as mortgages, can be verified through public records or a real estate search.

SIGNIFICANCE OF THE BALANCE SHEET

A balance sheet and operating statement contain specific details concerning the major financial items of a company. The amount of detail depends on the auditor and possibly restrictions imposed by the client. Companies that are publicly held are required by SEC regulations to file form 10-K, which presents detailed information regarding the business and its operations, including financial statements for the two most recent years.

Financial details are signposts that specify certain aspects of a company's operation. Without appropriate interpretation, however, they cannot provide the information needed for credit analysis. In the discussion that follows are covered many important points that should come to mind when financial statements are being examined.

Assets

Assets are resources owned by a company. They may take several forms, such as cash, accounts receivable, or physical property. They may be fully paid, in which case they are held free and clear, or they might be owned subject to outstanding debt. In any case, title to the assets is in the company's name. When ownership is acquired by lease, the lease rights are shown as an asset and the lease obligations as a liability.

Current assets are trading assets—the resources of a company that are constantly changing form or being turned over in the normal course of business. These normally are cash, accounts receivable, and merchandise. Added to these items are temporary investments in high-grade securities that might be termed cash reserves or the equivalent of cash—U.S. government securities; those of federal agencies, states, and municipalities; and stocks and bonds, readily marketable and held at the lower of cost or market.

With the exception of inventory, all of the current assets mentioned above may also be called quick or liquid assets. It is easy to convert them to cash. The relationship of these liquid assets to current liabilities (liquid or quick ratio) is an important consideration for the credit executive when examining the current ratio (current assets to current liabilities) and other balance sheet ratios, since it shows the extent of liquid resources available to meet current liabilities.

Cash.   Money on deposit or on hand comprises cash. This includes currency, personal and bank checks, drafts and money orders. The cash shown on a balance sheet is assumed to be available for general business purposes, unless otherwise identified by the auditor. Adjustment of the amount is necessary when funds are earmarked for specific projects, represent compensating balances in connection with a bank loan, or are not immediately available for withdrawals. Deposits under restrictions in foreign countries or funds set aside to retire funded debt, capital stock, or the like are classified as miscellaneous assets.

Marketable Securities.   Obligations of the federal, state, and municipal governments are normally considered current assets, as are stocks and bonds traded on the major exchanges. When they represent a large portion of current assets, marketable securities should be examined carefully to determine their basis of valuation and their value upon liquidation.

Accounts Receivable.   Amounts owed to a company for goods or services sold on credit should be segregated from those arising from other transactions, and the open accounts should be listed separately from those evidenced by notes.

Receivables pledged as collateral for secured borrowing should be identified in the balance sheet and explained in a footnote. Receivables due from affiliated concerns should be listed separately and included among the current accounts only when representing merchandise sold on regular terms. Advances to affiliates or amounts due from officers, directors, and employees should not be listed with current assets.

The balance sheet should show both the gross (invoice) amount outstanding and the amounts deducted for uncollectible accounts. (Other deductions applicable under special circumstances include those for discounts, returns and allowances, and freight.) The amounts deducted are shown as an allowance for uncollectibles, the purpose of which is to reduce the accounts receivables to its estimated realizable value and to provide a buffer against which uncollectible accounts may ultimately be charged.

Some auditors age the receivables on the balance sheet by listing them according to the month billed. This breakdown should be required whenever the receivables are under close scrutiny.

Notes Receivables. When normal selling terms are on a note basis, it is necessary to verify that notes receivable shown as current assets result from sales to customers. In other industries where sales are customarily on open account, the appearance of notes in the current section signals the need for additional investigation. They may represent past-due accounts for which the company has accepted notes, or may indicate activities not related to the normal course of business. It could be significant to determine if the notes are payable in monthly amounts or by a single payment.

Merchandise Inventory. Inventory is intended for sale to customers. Supplies used by a company should not be included in the inventory figure. It is essential to know whether the inventory figure represents an actual physical stock taking, is derived from perpetual inventory records, or is only an estimated figure.

In manufacturing, the merchandise inventory is usually in three stages: raw material, goods in process, and finished goods. It is important to have this breakdown shown on the balance sheet or to obtain it from the auditor.

Raw material has flexibility in use and can also be used by others in a similar line of manufacturing. Consequently, its wholesale value is usually well-established and the resale market for it is relatively broad. Under these circumstances, losses through emergency liquidation of raw material will be proportionately lower than for the other classes of the inventory, and its value as collateral is higher.

Finished goods, as completed products, are in an immediately salable state. The extent of loss in an emergency sale depends on the urgency of the situation, the type and quality of the product, and the demand for the goods being sold.

Both raw materials and finished goods have relatively high values as loan collateral, and borrowing on this basis is facilitated because these inventory segments can be earmarked by segregation or warehousing. Goods in process, however, have already been committed, yet are not ready for sale. They need additional work before they can be sold and therefore represent a poorer salvage value.

The proportion of goods in each stage has significance that goes beyond forced liquidation. Finished goods on hand at the beginning of a selling season can support a heavy debt position because their sale is imminent. If a disproportionate part of the inventory were in raw materials, it would mean added costs and, more important, poor timing and inability to deliver on time.

While knowing the stages of the inventory is important to the analysis of this important asset, it is also essential to determine the bases and methods used in its evaluation.

Basis of Inventory Valuation.   Inventory may be valued at cost, at market, at the lower of cost or market, or by any other recognized basis generally accepted in a given industry. No two give identical values for the same amount of physical goods. Since inventory is such an important component of financial statements, the value finally assigned to it will influence the financial showing of the firm.

The basis most commonly used is the lower of cost or market value. Conservatively, it assigns the lowest reasonable value to inventory on hand. It devalues raw materials which had been purchased at a price higher than is now in effect but does not permit it to be revalued upward if its price rises after purchase. This basis always tends to understate earnings.

LIFO And FIFO Valuation.   In determining cost, any one of a number of methods may be used: average cost; standard cost; book cost as reflected in the perpetual inventory records; estimated costs as applied to long-term contracts in process; and two commonly used methods, last-in, first-out (LIFO) and first-in, first-out (FIFO). The accounting in these two methods, which are described below, refers only to the costing of materials and does not necessarily relate directly to the utilization of the physical units.

The LIFO method assumes that the last material acquired will be the first used. Consequently, the inventory valuation on the balance sheet is based on earlier prices paid for material. The use of LIFO, in a period of rising prices, reports lower earnings, reduces taxes, and thereby increases cash availability. The combination of reduced taxes and increased cash availability takes on added significance during inflationary times, when it is difficult to obtain fresh money and the cost of obtaining it is high.

The FIFO method works opposite to LIFO: the earliest prices of goods are charged against production, and remaining inventory is valued at the more recent prices paid. In a period of rising prices, the FIFO method will report greater profits, result in higher taxes, and yield less cash available than the LIFO method. Figure 20–1 illustrates the operating results of a company under both the LIFO and FIFO methods of inventory evaluation in a period of rising prices.

The composition of inventory at the beginning of the year under both methods is 1,000,000 units at a unit cost of $1. Purchases during the year were made at the following prices:

1st quarter—2,000,000 units @	$1.25 =	$	2,500,000
2nd quarter—2,000,000 units @	1.50 =		3,000,000
3rd quarter—2,000,000 units @	1.75 =		3,500,000
4th quarter—2,000,000 units @	2.00 =		4,000,000
Total purchases			$13,000,000

	FIFO		LIFO	
		FIFO		LIFO
Sales		$16,500,000		$16,500,000
Cost of Goods Sold:				
Inventory at Beginning of Year	$ 1,000,000		$ 1,000,000	
Purchases	13,000,000		13,000,000	
Cost of Goods Available for Sales	14,000,000		14,000,000	
Less Inventory at End of Year	2,000,000	12,000,000	1,000,000	13,000,000
Gross Profit		4,500,000		3,500,000
Expenses		2,000,000		2,000,000
Income before Income Taxes		2,500,000		1,500,000
Income Taxes (at 50% rate)		1,250,000		750,000
Net Income		$ 1,250,000		$ 750,000

FIG. 20–1.   Comparison of Inventory Valuation Under FIFO and LIFO in Inflationary Times.

During the year 8,000,000 units were sold, leaving 1,000,000 units of inventory on hand at the end of the year. Under the FIFO method, the value of the yearend inventory would be $2,000,000 (1,000,000 units @ $2.00, the actual price paid in the fourth quarter); the LIFO method would value inventory at $1,000,000 (1,000,000 units @ $1.00, the price of inventory at the beginning of the year.

The reported net income would be lower under LIFO than under FIFO; income taxes would likewise be lower, while cash availability would be greater by $500,000.

A period of declining prices would produce opposite results. This is illustrated in Figure 20–2. After a few years of inflationary times, deteriorating business conditions set in and actual purchase prices declined from $3.00 to $2.00.

Inventory at the beginning of the year consists of 1,000,000 units at a cost of $3,000,000 for the firm using FIFO; the one using LIFO still had inventory of 1,000,000 units on hand and valued it at $1 each, or $1,000,000. Purchases were made during the year at the following prices by each firm:

1st quarter—2,000,000 units @ $2.75 =	$ 5,500,000
2nd quarter—2,000,000 units @ 2.50 =	5,000,000
3rd quarter—2,000,000 units @ 2.25 =	4,500,000
4th quarter—2,000,000 units @ 2.00 =	4,000,000
Total purchases	$19,000,000

During the year 8,000,000 units were sold, again leaving 1,000,000 units of inventory on hand at the end of the year. Under FIFO the inventory is valued at $2,000,000 (1,000,000 units at the last price paid), while under LIFO the inventory is valued at $1,000,000.

Thus, in a period of declining prices, the net income under LIFO is

		FIFO		LIFO
Sales		$23,000,000		$23,000,000
Cost of Goods Sold:				
Inventory at Beginning of Year	$ 3,000,000		$ 1,000,000	
Purchases	19,000,000		19,000,000	
Cost of Goods Available for Sale	22,000,000		20,000,000	
Less Inventory at End of Year	2,000,000	20,000,000	1,000,000	19,000,000
Gross Profit		3,000,000		4,000,000
Expenses		2,000,000		2,000,000
Income Before Income Taxes		1,000,000		2,000,000
Income Taxes (at a 50% rate)		500,000		1,000,000
Net Income		$ 500,000		$ 1,000,000

FIG. 20–2. Comparison of Inventory Valuation Under FIFO and LIFO in Deflationary Times.

higher than under FIFO, with resulting greater income taxes and consequent decrease in cash availability of $500,000.

The two methods of inventory valuation can have a decided impact on
the balance sheet. In a rising market, the LIFO method of inventory valuation would give a lower valuation than the FIFO method. Conversely,
the net working capital under the LIFO method would compare unfavorably with the FIFO method, although the inventory turnover under the
LIFO method would appear to be more attractive. The opposite would
generally hold true in a period of declining prices.

Whatever the basis or method of valuation, it should be applied consistently year after year and throughout the entire period under review. Failure
to do this would distort any trend analysis. Any major changes in the basis
or method of evaluation should be fully explained and its impact on profits
determined.

Retail Method.   On financial statements of retail stores, the retail method
of valuing inventories is in general use. Under this method the retailer enters the cost of each purchase item in a merchandise record, and against the
entry posts a predetermined selling price. The difference between the totals
of these two values at the end of the accounting period represents the anticipated markup or gross profit. The ratio of cost to retail is then calculated
and this percentage is applied against the aggregate selling price of the unsold inventory to arrive at a computed cost of the merchandise stock. Figure
20–3 illustrates the procedure.

The balance sheet inventory is often taken from the merchandise ledger
or stock record but should be verified periodically by actual stock taking.
The credit grantor should be informed when such physical inventory was
last taken.

Prepaid Expenses.   These are payments that have already been made for
services or benefits not yet received, such as rent and insurance. While

	Cost	Retail
Inventory at Beginning of Year	$ 2,100,000	$ 3,500,000
Purchases	24,000,000	40,000,000
Total	$26,100,000	43,500,000
Ratio of Cost to Retail—60%		
Sales		39,000,000
Inventory at Retail Price		$ 4,500,000
Inventory Computation To Arrive at Cost: 60% of $4,500,000 = $2,700,000		

FIG. 20–3. Computation of Inventory Using the Retail Method.

these payments do not represent assets that can be converted into cash, they do depict funds that have been expended during the period which will be charged to future operations. Most auditors list these items with current assets, as do such agencies as Dun & Bradstreet and Robert Morris Associates in the preparation of their industry averages.

Fixed Assets.   These are permanent or semipermanent investments in tangible properties required for the conduct of the business and not subject to periodic purchases and sale. They include land, buildings, machinery, tools and equipment, furniture and fixtures, trucks and automobiles, and leasehold improvements when the facility is not owned.

In many instances, firms own properties not used in their regular business operations. These items are considered investments, even though they may appear as fixed assets on the balance sheet and are listed separately under miscellaneous assets.

Encumbrances on fixed assets should be listed among the liabilities and never shown as an offset on the asset side of the balance sheet. When only the net values are shown, the credit executive should insist on a full description of the properties, their value, mortgages or liens, and depreciation schedules.

Fixed assets are subject to depreciation, which is an amount regularly charged against operations to recover the cost of those assets. Fixed assets are usually shown at cost in the balance sheet, the amount of depreciation accumulated over the years listed as a deduction, and the net figure posted into the main assets column.

Occasionally a company may engage a firm of appraisers to place a current value on property which has been held for a long time. This is done to obtain a more realistic valuation of the asset, particularly if it had been purchased during a period when building prices were low. The new value is assigned to the assets side of the balance sheet and is offset by an equity item, unrealized capital increment per appraisal, equal to the difference between the old and new valuations.

Leases. Where ownership is transferred through a lease, the lessor is required to show the receivable from the lease as an asset, while the lessee is required to show the lease rights as an asset and the lease obligations as a liability. This balance sheet treatment tends to show larger investment in property and greater liabilities than when the leasing arrangements are covered by a footnote. However, capitalization of the asset is not required when the lease payments are less than 90 per cent of the property value. There are other ways of circumventing the capitalization of leases, such as sale of receivables with recourse to a third party or to a captive finance company. The end result is that many corporations can avoid the capitalizing of leases on the balance sheet.

Investment in and Advances to Subsidiaries. When this item appears on a statement, it is important to know whether the investment is carried at cost or at net asset value; the extent of intercompany relations between the parent and subsidiaries; and the financial condition of the separate subsidiaries. Individual financial statements of the subsidiaries are helpful in evaluating these points.

Miscellaneous Assets. In the simplified statement used for credit analysis, miscellaneous assets include all tangible assets not identified as current or fixed. They include investments; advances to or stock interests in subsidiaries and affiliates; amounts due from officers, directors, and employees; cash surrender value of life insurance; and sometimes prepaid expenses.

Intangibles. These are assets which are not available for payment of debts of a going concern. While they are of importance to an active business, they depreciate greatly or cease to have value in case of liquidation. There is a long list of such items, including goodwill, trademarks, brands, catalogues, designs, contracts, formulas, mailing lists, organization expenses, and treasury stock.

Expenditures for these assets may be incurred in a short period of time or over a number of years. Some firms charge the entire cost to the period in which it was incurred; others, particularly when the cost represents a major outlay of cash, capitalize the amount and show it on the balance sheet. This practice reduces the apparent costs of operation and improves the profit shown for the period. The intangible asset is then amortized; a portion of it is charged as an operating expense annually until the full amount is retired. When these items are included in the statement, they inflate net worth. To get a more useful picture of the business in terms of its financial strength, the credit executive deducts intangibles from the net worth figure. The adjusted value is called tangible net worth and is used in regular financial analysis.

Liabilities

Liabilities are the amounts owed by a company. Current liabilities, by long-accepted definition, are obligations maturing within one year from the date of the statement on which they appear. Also included are demand notes which, although carrying no maturity date, may be presented for payment any time at the option of the holder. Deferred or slow liabilities are represented by mortgages, bonds, debentures, serial notes, purchase-money obligations, and long-term notes which mature more than one year from statement date. Included in this category are demand notes that have been formally subordinated to all other creditors for a period of at least one year from the date of the statement under consideration.

Accounts Payable. These are items owed to suppliers for goods or services and payable within a year. An aging of payables is helpful in analyzing an account, as is a comparison of the balance sheet figure with totals shown on trade clearances.

Notes Payable. These are debts of a business evidenced by notes. It is good accounting practice to show different types of note obligations separately in a balance sheet to indicate the source of the credit, to list unsecured items separately from those secured, and for secured items to indicate the nature of the security or the asset item involved. They may be classified into three categories:

Short-Term Borrowings. Obligations owing to banks or others and payable within a 12-month period are in this category. Analysis is assisted with a knowledge of repayment schedule and details on the security, if any, for the borrowing.

Current Portion of Deferred Debt. Auditors generally segregate current maturities of serial payment mortgages, debenture bonds, and other long-term obligations, or they give sufficient information in the balance sheet to permit such adjustment. For financial analysis purposes, exact information on maturity dates, amount of installments, and interest charges is required.

Unsubordinated Loans. These liabilities, such as loans from officers and stockholders or advances from the parent company, are often described as nonpressing in nature. Since these loans may be repaid at the desire of the management, they should be treated as current obligations in the absence of any formal deferment. A formal subordination of such obligations should be requested in order to lessen the risk involved in extending credit to an account financing operations with borrowings from principals.

Advance Payments. These range from retailers' layaway plan receipts to advance payments from the federal government. They have occasionally been shown as a deduction from inventory. However, careful analysts prefer to increase the reported inventory by the amount of the advance and post the advance as a current liability.

Wages, Taxes, and Accruals. These items represent closing adjustments and are normally payable soon after the statement date. In some instances, special investigation may be necessary to obtain details on liability owing for previous years' taxes or on the presence of an unusually large accrual obligation.

Miscellaneous Obligations. All other indebtedness payable within one year or having an uncertain repayment schedule should be classified as current. Items such as deposits and declared but unpaid dividends fall in this category.

Deferred Debt. This comprises any obligation payable after one year from statement date. Long-term debt includes bond indebtedness, mortgage borrowings, and term loans. Complete details should be obtained regarding security, retirement schedules, interest charges, and possible restrictive clauses which sometimes attach to such borrowings.

Deferred Income. This item, which frequently appears on a balance sheet, represents income that has been received but is not yet fully earned. A typical example is the obligation to provide a service for which payment has already been received. The deferred amount does not pass fully into income until the service has been provided.

Contra Accounts. These items reduce an asset to its net realizable value or book value. Rather than show some financial items as one amount, proper accounting treatment provides for two amounts to be shown in order to furnish additional useful information. These include the allowance for uncollectibles, which is deducted from accounts receivable, and accumulated depreciation, which is deducted from fixed assets. Both were discussed earlier in this chapter.

Contra accounts are sometimes shown as reserves. For example, in the above illustrations they would appear as reserve for bad debts and reserve for depreciation. This would be incorrect, since the term reserve tends to connote something set aside for a particular purpose.

In addition, some items are also incorrectly shown as liability reserves. This is a misnomer, since they are set up to meet actual liabilities; examples are the estimated tax liability and accrued wages.

Some statements show contingent liabilities, either as a footnote to the statement or as a special classification between liabilities and net worth. They are established to reflect situations in which contingent debts may become reality and thereby decrease an asset or create a liability. Notes receivable discounted is one example; another is a likely loss from a lawsuit.

Net Worth

The equity of unincorporated business firms may be called net worth, proprietary interest, partner's capital, or capital. Drawings and withdrawals of capital during the auditing period are reflected in the operating statement and the balance sheet, but some auditors do not specifically cover the contingency of later withdrawals to pay income taxes on each principal's share. On the other hand, some auditors, by statement footnote or general comment, do give an estimate of income taxes based on the partners' distributive shares in the profits when there is a possibility that later withdrawals will be made to meet these personal obligations.

Corporate net worth or stockholders' equity is divided into various classes of outstanding stock and retained earnings. The credit executive is interested in any asset or dividend preferences involved in the classes of stocks as well as in the relationship between owned and borrowed funds. Thus the showing of various classes of stock by order of preference, by dividend requirements, and by indication of preemptive rights, if any, is helpful. The credit executive should pay particular attention to preferred stock and be aware of its rights or covenants. Preferred stock, for example, may have been issued as part of an agreement to defer existing debt. In this instance, it may be preferable to remove such stock from the equity portion of the balance sheet and treat it as long-term debt.

Treasury stock, representing some of its own capital stock that has been bought back or reacquired by a corporation, is shown either as an asset item or as a deduction from outstanding stock. Credit executives prefer the latter treatment. When treasury stock appears as an asset, they place this item among the intangibles which are deducted to determine tangible net worth.

The term surplus is sometimes used in this portion of the balance sheet: earned surplus results from retained earnings; capital that is contributed in excess of par or stated value may be called paid-in surplus; and an increased net worth resulting from an upward appraisal of fixed assets may be termed as appraisal surplus.

IMPORTANCE OF THE STATEMENT OF INCOME AND RETAINED EARNINGS

The statement of income and retained earnings that is issued for credit purposes varies from a complete schedule to a severely condensed version of the audit report, and is sometimes limited to a listing of sales, profits, and dividends.

The relationship of the income statement to the balance sheet is so important that its absence or excessive abbreviation is a severe handicap. The statement provides explanations for changes not only in the equity account but also in assets and liabilities. A balance sheet provides a picture of financial condition at a given date, while a statement of income and retained earnings traces the results of corporate activity over a period of time.

Despite the importance of the income statement to comprehensive analysis of the customer's financial operation, credit executives do not insist uniformly on having this schedule furnished. While it is common practice to include the income schedule on statement request forms, compliance by customers often depends on the size of the order and the custom in the trade. Income statements are furnished as a matter of course in markets where credit groups frankly exchange information, in industries that are subject to sharp seasonal influences, and where the credit sought is large compared with the customer's working funds.

An income statement should contain information on sales, cost of goods sold, expenses, net operating profit, information on other income and expenses, and profit before and after taxes. In short, the income statement provides a summary of income and expenses for a specific period of time.

Sales

This item refers to the dollar volume of transactions involving company products and services. It is valued at selling price rather than at cost of merchandise. Gross sales should be separated into cash sales and credit sales whenever a substantial amount of cash business is done. The net sales figure is used in credit analysis. It is obtained by deducting returns, allowances, and any applicable discounts from the gross sales figure.

Other information can be determined from this part of the income statement. By comparing sales discounts with selling terms and gross sales, the credit executive can learn about the competitive strength and collection experience of the customer. Returns and allowances are clues to the quality of output and customer satisfaction with the product. It is important to determine if sales returns are put back into inventory and counted again.

The figure shown as sales should represent actual transactions during which title changes hands. Goods placed on consignment, for example, are not sold, though a credit executive will see unaudited statements in which no distinction is made between the two. Further, customers' commitments are sometimes incorrectly shown as sales. Or sales may occasionally be held off beyond the closing date of a period in order to reduce the reported income. Intercompany sales between affiliates can also be manipulated to show a higher or lower sales volume. These practices are all misleading and can be overcome by careful reading of the financial statement figures and footnotes.

Cost of Goods Sold

This item represents the cost of materials, labor, and factory overhead needed to bring to a marketable state the goods that have been sold. The figure can be affected by the way that purchases are listed in this part of the operating statement. Agency forms usually require purchases to be listed net after purchase discounts on the theory that final cost of the goods should be set after trade and cash discounts. Often, however, the gross purchases are used in calculating the cost of goods sold, while purchase discounts are treated as other income. An operating statement presented in this way gives the credit executive an opportunity to discover how much of the final profit was earned by taking purchase discounts and how much by operations.

Manufacturing expenses should be separated into direct labor costs and factory overhead. The latter consists of indirect labor, supervisory costs, maintenance, supplies, factory or plant proportionment of depreciation, taxes, insurance, and other expenses.

Opening and closing inventories are major items in determining the cost of goods sold and gross and net profits. If inventory is incorrectly stated, profits can be materially distorted. Claims to hidden cushions in inventory (the undervaluing of inventory to reduce tax obligations) should be carefully investigated, as this practice can be used equally well to cover up losses in an unprofitable period.

Gross Profit

Cost of goods sold is deducted from net sales to arrive at the gross profit. The relationship of gross profit to net sales is a very valuable analytical tool for internal analysis and for comparing the financial affairs of a concern with others in the same line. This percentage is stable within an industry because competitive factors tend to keep the price of purchases and selling prices in fairly close alignment. Consequently, gross profit is a major determinant of a firm's ability to stay in business. A return considerably below that of the industry may be due to insufficient volume, poor purchasing habits, or high labor costs. An explanation of any major deviation is essential for understanding the account.

Year-to-year variations in a company's gross profit would be caused by changes in selling prices or cost of goods sold, variations in product mix between high- and low-priced items, or a combination of these factors.

Expenses

A breakdown of operating expenses and their separate relationships to net sales are extremely helpful when appraising operations and comparing them with those of other companies. These include administrative and general expenses, distribution costs (sales, shipping, and sales advertising expenses), and changes in the allowance for uncollectibles.

Certain expenses, like rent and administrative costs, tend to remain constant while others vary considerably, most often in relation to sharp increases or declines in sales. For instance, it would be normal for advertising and sales commissions to increase with expanding volume.

Each expense item should be considered and its contribution to results weighed wherever possible. Depreciation, taxes, telephone costs, and rent may be apportioned among the various departments. Selling expenses are directly attributable to the sales effort and would include such items as sales department salaries, freight out, and advertising. Administrative and general expenses are often combined and include clerical salaries, directors' fees, legal and auditing expense, and the like.

Net Operating Income

After the cost of goods sold and expenses are deducted from net sales, a firm has either an operating profit or loss. This is a good measure of ability to operate successfully. It represents income derived from normal business operations but does not take into account cash discounts given or received, interest on borrowed funds, and all extraordinary charges and income that are not separate adjustments of retained earnings.

Other Income and Expenses

Income from incidental ventures, such as rentals or interest, would be classed as other than operating income, while items such as loss on foreign exchange would be classed as nonoperating expense. Such items have a definite bearing on overall company results but should be examined separately because of their special nature; the key analysis should be directed to the customer's day-by-day operations, its line of business.

Extraordinary Items

Nonrecurring events such as fire damage, storm losses, or gains or losses on sales of plant and property would distort the income statement if credited to income or charged as expense on a direct basis. It is preferable to set up a separate section for them on the income statement.

Federal Income Taxes

The tax requirements shown in the statement of income represent those estimated by management for the period covered. As the firm has made scheduled payments during the year, this figure does not represent the amount owing.

Net Income

After the provision for federal income taxes has been made, the final net income remains. This may be retained or partially paid out to stockholders and owners. Rapid-growth companies normally retain earnings in order to increase their working assets, while slow-growth companies distribute earnings. For closely held corporations, dividend payout constitutes additional compensation to the principals. Moreover, when dividends are paid and loaned back by the principals, the creditor must be aware that the loans may be payable on demand.

Retained Earnings

This information links the statement of income and retained earnings to the opening and closing balance sheets. This reconciliation may appear in the continuation of the statement of income, in a supporting schedule as shown in the financial statement forms of agencies, or in the net worth section of the balance sheet. It reflects profits or losses, dividends, and lists accounting transactions which were not included in the regular income statement because of their technical or extraordinary character.

STATEMENT OF CHANGES IN FINANCIAL POSITION

The statement of changes in financial position can be most useful for analyzing financial strength. In two separate parts, it reports the flow of funds during the period among the various asset, liability, and net worth accounts; and analyzes changes in net working capital.

The concepts presented here depend upon the idea of cash flow. That is defined as net profit after adding back items which have been charged to production costs or expenses but do not currently involve a cash outlay, and after deducting items which do not represent cash inflows. Here are some examples:

1. Depreciation does not involve a current cash outlay but it is a cost of doing business and is recovered in the selling price of goods.

2. Amortization of deferred income does not involve a current inflow of cash but does represent a credit to income.

3. Timing differences between financial reporting and income tax reporting can result in deferred tax liabilities which may be a source of funds.

Since the principal components of cash flow are net profit and depreciation, it follows that the way in which they are calculated will largely determine the reported cash flow in the firm. Thus accounting policy can affect the financial reporting. Specifically, a conservative accounting policy tends to understate earnings and thus could give a poorer-than-actual picture of the firm's operations. This would be reflected in its cash flow. On the other hand, a liberal accounting policy which tends to overstate earnings could give a cash flow picture which is better than the firm's actual operations might warrant.

Source and Application of Funds

This analysis gives a different financial view of the firm. It addresses itself to how it will obtain resources and how it will apportion them among cash, accounts receivable, inventory, plant and equipment, and other assets in a manner that fulfills the company's financial requirements; or the resources may be used to liquidate indebtedness. Changes in assets, liabilities, and net worth segments may be regarded as sources or applications of funds, and may be summarized as follows:

Source	*Application*
Decrease in any asset	Increase in any asset
Increase in any liability	Decrease in any liability
Increase in net worth	Decrease in net worth

While individual changes may be classed as either a source or an application, they do not stand alone. Thus a source may be reflected in one or more applications, and an application may be supported by one or more sources of funds. Year-to-year changes in components reflect net differences from one statement to the next, though in fact these changes are continuous during the course of business. The impact of funds flow through financial statements may be illustrated by several situations:

1. Earnings retained in a business increase net worth and are a source of funds. In turn, those funds may be used to purchase plant and equipment, thereby increasing assets.

2. The payment of accounts payable is an application of funds, since it reduces liabilities. The accompanying reduction of cash serves as the source of funds for this payment.

3. Declining levels of inventory are a source of funds that may be used to increase accounts receivable, increase cash balances, acquire additional assets, or reduce liabilities.

4. Depreciation charges tend to reduce the book value of plant and equipment, thus acting as a source of funds.

Changes in Net Working Capital

A further refinement in the examination of the flow of funds may be made by measuring the changes taking place in the net working capital position during the period under review. Net working capital is defined as current assets minus current liabilities (items included in these groupings are considered above-the-line items) and represents uncommitted current assets available for the conduct of business operations. A high net working capital position with items properly proportioned is a sign of an efficient financial operation, flexible enough to take advantage of opportunities.

In the case of a business that plans to expand, changes in net working capital play an important part in funds flow. In addition to net profit, depreciation, and deferred tax liabilities, external funds are an important factor. By taking on long-term debt or additional investment by stockholders, the company establishes future charges against net income or earned surplus, be they interest or stockholder dividends.

Any transaction affecting only above-the-line items or only below-the-line items does not affect net working capital. However, changes in net working capital do occur when a transaction involves a current item and one that is not current. Here are some examples:

1. The purchase of inventory on a 30-day basis causes inventory and accounts payable to increase in equal amounts but does not change the net working capital.

2. Inventory purchased for cash increases the inventory and decreases cash but does not affect the total of current assets or net working capital.

3. Payment of accounts payable reduces the current assets and current liabilities but does not change net working capital.

4. The acquisition of equipment for 20 per cent cash down payment and 80 per cent by mortgage payable after one year reduces net working capital by the amount of the down payment.

5. As net profit is retained, both current assets and net working capital generally increase unless the net profit is diverted for noncurrent use.

Each noncurrent item in the balance sheet should be examined separately to determine those changes tending to increase net working capital and those tending to decrease it. The transactions that affect net working capital can be summarized as follows:

Increase	*Decrease*
Decrease in noncurrent assets	Increase in noncurrent assets
Increase in long-term debt	Decrease in long-term debt
Increase in net worth	Decrease in net worth

Once this has been completed, changes in the composition of the net working capital should be examined by noting variations in the items that comprise the current assets and current liabilities.

CONSOLIDATED FINANCIAL STATEMENTS

The parent company of interrelated companies will occasionally issue only consolidated financial figures of the parent company and one or more subsidiary concerns, with all intercompany accounts regarding investment, advances, revenues, expenses, and distribution of income cancelled out. Only statements of subsidiary concerns may properly be consolidated with that of the parent company. A concern is designated as a subsidiary when over 50 per cent of its controlling capital stock is owned by the parent concern. When 50 per cent or less of its stock is held by the parent company, the related concern is called an affiliate. The interest in the affiliate is shown as an investment item in the noncurrent assets, and amounts owed between the two concerns are indicated as receivable or payable items.

The consolidated statement is recognized as synthetic or amalgamated, relating to no one corporate entity but reflecting the pooling of accounts of two or more legal entities for the purpose of presenting a composite picture. It should be kept in mind that each underlying unit still retains a separate legal corporate status, with control over its own assets and distribution of dividends, and no general liability for the debts of the other units or the parent. A consolidated statement inadequately discloses the immediate position of the parent concern because of the mixture of other corporate assets and liabilities. By itself, it gives no indication of the status of assets and liabilities of each subsidiary, nor does it indicate which ones are operating at a profit and which at a loss. Varying degrees of control are exercised in consolidations. In some cases, purchasing, borrowing, and lending functions of the combine are centralized in the parent company or a designated subsidiary; in others, the separate corporations have more or less autonomy in this respect.

The following points should be checked when reviewing consolidated statements:

1. That the consolidated units are over 50 per cent owned and controlled.
2. That each of the individual statements included in the consolidated statement is of approximately the same date.
3. That the method of consolidating has been followed consistently or any departures have been noted.
4. That changes in the subsidiaries making up the consolidated companies have been noted.
5. That the accounting methods of the companies consolidated are uniform and their business policies are substantially the same.
6. That the valuation bases of the assets are the same.

These assurances are usually given or implied in the certificate of a responsible auditor. Where the consolidated statement does not include all subsidiaries, the creditor should know which have been included and which have been excluded, since the choice is a prerogative of the parent concern. A complete analysis of a consolidated financial statement requires working papers showing the individual statements of the consolidated companies along with the intercompany items that are canceled in the consolidation.

Sometimes credit is checked on the consolidated statement of a parent company when analysis discloses no reason to go behind the overall figures. The credit executive is aware, however, that the ratios based on consolidated figures do not relate to an individual concern but are averages obtained by the pooling of assets, liabilities, and income statement items of the several concerns. When the consolidated companies are not wholly owned, that portion of the capital stock and retained earnings attributable to outside interests is shown on the consolidated statement as a noncurrent liability, which is not a part of the consolidated net worth. It should be clearly noted that in the absence of a corporate guaranty, a parent company is not legally responsible for the liabilities of the subsidiary. Furthermore, a subsidiary may be severed from the group under certain conditions—for example, it is common practice to omit captive finance companies from a consolidated statement.

COMBINED FINANCIAL STATEMENTS

There are instances where the shares of two or more companies are owned by the same stockholders, who may submit a statement showing the added assets and liabilities of all the companies so affiliated, even though a parent-subsidiary relationship does not exist. This statement is properly called a combined balance balance sheet rather than a consolidated one. It has no legal standing and should not be used for credit analysis. The statement does not represent the financial picture of a legal entity but only an amalgamation of financial resources owned by the same shareholders. Therefore, it is essential to obtain separate statements on each company.

PRO FORMA FINANCIAL STATEMENTS

A pro forma financial statement shows what the financial condition and operating results of a company would have been if certain events had taken place in the past or will take place in the future. For instance, if a corporation spins off an operating unit to shareholders, pro forma statements could be constructed from historical data that would show what the separate financial conditions and operations of the spun-off unit and its parent would have been at a time before they were actually separated.

A pro forma financial statement may be drawn off to give effect to a significant happening in the future. For a proposed common stock offering to purchase a plant and to provide operating funds to operate the plant, the pro forma statement would show the additional outstanding shares of stock, the new plant, any mortgage on the plant, and added cash. This type of statement is very useful when significant future transactions will cause major changes in the historical statement.

TRIAL BALANCE

The trial balance is a list of the debit and credit balances of the general ledger accounts. It is done monthly in a well-managed business as a test of the posting to these accounts, and is a preliminary step when an annual or interim balance sheet and operating statement are to be prepared.

While the sum total of debits checks with total credits, there is no assurance that the records are correct, since they are not audited. Even when monthly trial balances are prepared by an independent auditor, they usually carry notification that they were prepared from the books without audit or verification and that the auditor assumes no responsibility for their correctness. Other limitations are:

1. The trial balance does not show a closing inventory position and thus prevents an accurate calculation of profit for the period.

2. Accounts receivable represents the general ledger controlling account and may be greater than the receivables shown in the customers' ledger. It may include ledger balances of bankrupt accounts not written off and accounts long overdue, as well as advances to principals, sales representatives' overdrafts, and loans to affiliate interests or relatives. Anticipation or discounts earned by customers would not be reflected in the account.

3. Accounts payable may be understated by showing less than the total amounts that appear on creditors' ledgers. Some concerns forward purchase entries to a following month when the bills have future dating, when the bills have not been approved before the purchase book was closed, or when goods are in transit.

4. Accrued liabilities are not reflected in the trial balance. Omission of the sum of accrued wages, salaries, commissions, rent, and taxes can understate expenses and current liabilities.

5. Loans payable to principals when entered as credits to their salary or drawing accounts can understate liabilities and expenses.

6. Productive labor may incorrectly include indirect costs such as factory supervision because factory prime cost and expense have not been separated.

Despite these limitations, and because many firms do not prepare quarterly or semiannual financial statements, the trial balance is often viewed as the means to obtain the latest interim financial information. It is helpful especially with customers in volatile lines where seasonal conditions affect operations drastically and competition is severe. It also has certain advantages as a source of credit information and as an analytical tool:

1. It is easy to prepare and can be very current. Interim financial details required for close following of marginal accounts will be up to date and can be quickly supplied. Credit decisions are more apt to be correct when based on facts as they exist at the time of the decision.

2. With due allowance for analytical adjustments that may be required, the trial balance shows the current cash, accounts receivable, and debt position of a concern—in short, its liquid position.

3. The trial balance shows seasonal influences on balance sheet items and on operating costs. A succession of monthly trial balances discloses much more information than is possible by comparison of semiannual financial statements.

4. The trial balance supplies information useful in setting up cash budgets and in comparing actual operations against these guides.

SPREADING THE STATEMENTS

Analysis is much easier when the customer's statements are recast into a standard format that is familiar to the credit executive. Therefore, exact classification and proper grouping of the balance sheet and profit and loss items should be an early step in financial statement analysis.

Balance Sheet Spread Sheet

The spread sheet (also called the posting sheet) shown in Figure 20–4 is used for balance sheet items. This is a ruled form on which a financial statement can be posted under a few primary groupings. For example, machinery and office equipment can be grouped under fixed assets. Appropriate headings are also provided for important income statement items, supplementary details, and computed ratios.

The order in which these segments are posted and the headings used for individual lines are established by company procedure, the preference of the credit executive, and the need for quick reference. For instance, a

NAME						ACCOUNT OPENED				D & B RATING
ADDRESS										
RISK CLASS		CUST. #	HQ. #							
DATE	LINE	TERMS	PRODUCT	BY		SIC #				

ASSETS		%		%		%		%	BANKS			
Assets												
Cash												
Marketable Securities												
Notes Receivable												
Accounts Receivable												
Inventory												
Raw Materials												
Goods in Process												
Finished Goods												
Other									A/P CONTACT & TELEPHONE NO.			
Current Assets												
Fixed Assets												
Other Assets												
Total Assets		100.0		100.0		100.0		100.0				
Liabilities									REVIEWED			
Accounts Payable									DATE	HIGH	L/SALE	RECORD
Due Banks												
Term Debt-Current												
Taxes												
Other												
Current Liabilities												
Term Debt-Deferred												
Capital Stock												
Retained Earnings												
Net Working Capital												
Current Ratio												
Quick Ratio												
Inventory/Net Working Capital												
Fixed Assets/Tang. Net Worth												
Current Debt/Tang. Net Worth												
Total Debt/Tang. Net Worth												
Funded Debt/Net Working Capital												

FIG. 20–4. Balance Sheet Spread Sheet.

spread sheet used to tabulate balance sheet items and operational highlights of a utilities concern or a sales finance company would emphasize different figures than a mercantile operation, and would require special nomenclature to describe some items. The spread sheet condenses the number of balance sheet items and lists them in the groupings. This group sequence follows the standard arrangement in auditors' reports: current items first among the assets, followed by fixed assets and other resources; current obligations heading the liabilities, followed by the slow or deferred debts and equity capital. Most comparison forms provide blank spaces for writing in items peculiar to an individual concern, or items normally combined with others but requiring segregation because of their special analytical significance in a particular case.

Income Statement Spread Sheet

This spread sheet is based on the operating statement and provides the means for studying the causes that underlie the financial condition. Income and expense items are set up in the manner described for balance sheet posting, paralleling the same item on the preceding income statement.

Major items are also shown as ratios or percentages to the net sales of the statement period, since consideration of these relationships is necessary for comprehensive analysis. Figure 20–5 illustrates an income statement spread sheet.

NAME ADDRESS RISK CLASS			CUST.#		HQ.#			ACCOUNT OPENED			D & B RATING
DATE		LINE	TERMS		PRODUCT	BY		SIC #			
			%		%		%		%	BANKS	
Net Sales											
Cost of Goods Sold											
Materials											
Labor											
Manufacturing											
Gross Profit											
Selling Expenses										A/P CONTACT & TELEPHONE NO.	
Administrative & General											
Research & Development											
Depreciation											
Total Expenses											
Operating Profit										REVIEWED	
Other Income										DATE HIGH L/SALE RECORD	
Other Expenses											
Net Income Before Taxes											
Federal Income Taxes											
Net Income After Taxes											
Extraordinary Income											
Extraordinary Expenses											
Final Net Income			100.0		100.0		100.0		100.0		
Retained Earnings, 1/1											
Dividends											
Retained Earnings, 12/31											

FIG. 20–5.   Income Statement Spread Sheet.

Condensed Forms

Many credit departments and agencies prefer condensed forms (see Figure 20–6). If serious trends or disproportions are indicated on this form, a more detailed spread sheet can be set up for an exhaustive analysis. The condensed form saves laborous posting and exhaustive detail for a majority of statements. Short comparisons of income and expenses are also posted on the form, directly below the balance sheet items, and room is provided for calculated ratios.

Adjustment of Items

In the transfer of the items from the original financial statement to the spread sheet, two types of adjustment may be required. The first is made when the credit executive does not agree with the auditor's classification of an item as current or noncurrent (see Figure 20–7). Such adjustment does not affect the totals of assets, liabilities, or net worth but may change the current and other ratios.

NAME					ACCOUNT OPENED		D & B RATING
ADDRESS							
RISK CLASS		CUST.#	HQ.#				
DATE	LINE	TERMS	PRODUCT	BY	SIC #		

ASSETS		%		%		%		%	BANKS			
Cash												
Marketable Securities												
Notes Receivable												
Accounts Receivable												
Inventory												
Other									A/P CONTACT & TELEPHONE NO.			
Current Assets												
Fixed Assets												
Other Assets												
Total Assets		100.0		100.0		100.0		100.0				
Liabilities									REVIEWED			
Accounts Payable									DATE	HIGH	L/SALE	RECORD
Due Banks												
Term Debt-Current												
Taxes												
Other												
Current Liabilities												
Term Deferred												
Net Worth												
Net Sales												
Net Income												
Dividends												
Net Working Capital												
Current Ratio												
Quick Ratio												
Inventory/Net Working Capital												
Current Debt/Tangible Net Worth												
Total Debt/Tangible Net Worth												
Net Sales/Total Assets												
Net Income/Net Sales												

FIG. 20–6.   Condensed Spread Sheet.

The other is a scaling down of assets judged to be inflated and elimination of intangible items in the posting. This is done to remove slow or uncollectible receivables for which no allowance was made, and to allow for a probable loss in inventory value because of dead stock or unrealistic pricing. Assets are also scaled when stated book values of investments are in excess of reasonable market value and when questionable accounting procedure is used. When items are scaled, figures are usually posted in two columns side by side. The original posting serves as a check on the accuracy of the transfer, and the adjustment column highlights the changes made.

Assets	Current	Noncurrent	Intangible	Liabilities	Current	Noncurrent	Net Worth
Accounts Receivable				Accounts Payable			
Customers (Less Reserves)..	✓			For Merchandise..........	✓		
From Affiliate, if concern is in healthy shape and accounts are being paid on regular terms...........	✓			For Services..............	✓		
				To Directors..............	✓		
				To Employees............	✓		
				To Officers...............	✓		
From Affiliate, if concern is in unhealthy shape, or accounts are not being paid on regular terms........		✓		To Partners...............	✓		
				To Related Concerns.......	✓		
				Sundry...................	✓		
From Directors...........		✓		Accruals			
From Employees..........		✓		Commission..............	✓		
From Officers............		✓		Interest..................	✓		
From Partners............		✓		Other Expenses...........	✓		
From Subsidiary, if concern is in healthy shape, and receivables are being paid on regular terms........	✓			Pay Rolls.................	✓		
				Rent.....................	✓		
				Salaries..................	✓		
				Taxes....................	✓		
From Subsidiary, if concern is in unhealthy shape, or accounts are not being paid on regular terms........		✓		Wages...................	✓		
				Advances from Customers....	✓		
Miscellaneous............		✓					
Other...................		✓		Bills Payable (*Same as* Notes Payable)................			
Advances				Bonds			
For Merchandise..........	✓			Amount Maturing within One Year..............	✓		
For Mining Royalties.......		✓		Amount Maturing after One Year...................		✓	
For Traveling.............		✓		No Definite Maturity Date..	✓		
To Affiliate..............		✓					
To Employees.............		✓					
To Subsidiary.............		✓					
Advertising................			✓	Capital (If Partnership or Proprietorship)..........			✓
Assets, Miscellaneous........		✓		Capital Stock			
Automobiles................		✓		A, B, or C Stock..........			✓
Bills Receivable (*Same as* Accounts Receivable).......				Common Stock............			✓
Blending Rights..............			✓	Minority Interest..........		✓	
Bond Discount..............			✓	Preferred or Preference Stock...................			✓
Bonds.....................	✓						
Bookplates				Capital Surplus.............			✓
At Cost..................			✓	Chattel Mortgage..........	✓		
Metal Value..............		✓		Common Stock.............			✓
Bottling Rights..............			✓	Conditional Bill of Sale.......	✓		
Brands, Trade..............			✓	Contingencies, Reserve for....			
Building and Loan Shares......	✓			Contracts Payable...........	✓		
Buildings...................		✓		Credit Balance..............	✓		
Canadian Government Securities...................	✓			Customers' Deposits.........	✓		

FIG. 20–7. Guide to Classification of Balance Sheet Items.

Assets	Current	Noncurrent	Intangible	Liabilities	Current	Noncurrent	Net Worth
Cash				Debentures			
In Bank	✓			Amount Maturing within			
In Closed Bank		✓		One Year	✓		
In Sinking Fund		✓		Amount Maturing after One			
On Hand	✓			Year		✓	
Restricted		✓		Deferred Credits or Income		✓	
Cash Value of Life Insurance		✓		Deferred Income		✓	
Catalogues			✓	Deposits			
Claims for Refunds under				From Customers	✓		
Carry-back Provisions of				From Employees	✓		
Tax Law	✓			From Officers	✓		
Coal Lands		✓		From Salesmen	✓		
Contracts			✓	Depreciation (Deduct from			
Copyrights			✓	Related Asset)			
Debenture Discount			✓	Dividends Payable	✓		
Debtors, Sundry		✓		Donated Surplus			✓
Deferred Charges (See also		✓		Due Factor	✓		
Prepaid Items)							
Deficit (Profit and Loss)			✓	Earned Surplus			✓
Delivery Equipment		✓		Earnings			
Deposits				Employed in Business			✓
With Factor	✓			Reinvested			✓
With Mutual Insurance Com-		✓		Retained			✓
pany				Employees' Deposits	✓		
With Workmen's Compen-							
sation Commission		✓		Federal Income Taxes	✓		
Designs			✓	Funded Debt			
Development Expense			✓	Amount Maturing within			
Dies			✓	One Year	✓		
Docks		✓		Amount Maturing after One			
Drawings			✓	Year		✓	
Emergency Plant Facilities		✓					
Equipment		✓		Income Deferred		✓	
Experimental Expense			✓	Income Taxes	✓		
Exploration Expense			✓	Loan from Factor	✓		
Federal Government Securities				Loans Payable (Same as Notes			
(see United States Govern-				Payable)			
ment Securities)							
Financing Expense			✓	Minority Interest		✓	
Fixed Assets		✓		Mortgages			
Fixtures		✓		Amount Maturing within			
Foreign Assets—Restricted		✓		One Year	✓		
Formulas			✓	Amount Maturing after One			
Franchises			✓	Year		✓	
Furniture		✓		No Definite Maturity			
Goodwill			✓	Date	✓		
Government Securities (see							
United States Government				Net Worth (If Partnership			
Securities)				or Proprietorship)			✓

FIG. 20–7 (cont'd.).

Assets	Current	Noncurrent	Intangible	Liabilities	Current	Noncurrent	Net Worth
Improvements		✓		Notes Payable			
Insurance Deposits		✓		For Merchandise	✓		
Insurance Premium, Prepaid	✓			To Banks	✓		
Interest, Accrued	✓			To Individuals	✓		
Inventory				To Others	✓		
Advances on Merchandise	✓			To Partners	✓		
Finished Goods	✓			To Stockholders	✓		
In Transit	✓			Term Loans (Same as			
On Consignment	✓			Bonds)			
Raw Materials	✓						
Supplies	✓			Officers' Deposits	✓		
Work in Process	✓						
Investments		✓		Paid-in Surplus			✓
Investments in and Advances				Preferred or Preference Stock			✓
to Subsidiaries and Affili-				Provision for Income Taxes	✓		
ates		✓					
Land		✓		Reinvested Earnings			✓
Lasts			✓	Rent, Unpaid	✓		
Leasehold Improvements		✓		Retained Earnings			✓
Leaseholds			✓	Reserves			
Licenses			✓	Bad Debts (Deduct from			
Life Insurance Cash Surrender				Accounts Receivable)			
Value		✓		Contingencies			
Listed Securities	✓			Depletion (Deduct from			
Loan to Affiliate		✓		Related Assets)			
Loan to Subsidiary		✓		Depreciation (Deduct from			
Machinery		✓		Related Assets)			
Magazine Titles			✓	Discounts (Deduct from			
Mailing Lists			✓	Accounts Receivable)			
Maintenance Materials and				Inventory Adjustments (De-			
Parts		✓		duct from Related As-			
Marketable Securities	✓			sets)			
Merchandise (see Inventory)				Obsolescence (Deduct from			
Mineral Land		✓		Related Asset)			
Mines		✓		Retirement Capital Stock	✓		
Miscellaneous Assets		✓		Self-insurance		✓	
Miscellaneous Receivables		✓		Taxes	✓	✓	
Models			✓	Unexpired Subscriptions		✓	
Mortgages Receivable		✓		Unrealized Profit		✓	
Municipal Bonds	✓						
Municipal Bonds in Default		✓		Salaries	✓		
Notes Receivable (Same as Ac-							
counts Receivable)							
Organization Expense			✓				
Packaging and Shipping Items	✓						
Patents			✓				
Patterns			✓				
Pension Funds		✓					

FIG. 20–7 (cont'd.).

Assets	Current	Noncurrent	Intangible	Liabilities	Current	Noncurrent	Net Worth
Plant	✓			Salesmen's Deposits	✓		
Prepaid Items				Sales Lien	✓		
Insurance	✓			Separation Allowances	✓		
Rent	✓			Social Security Taxes	✓		
Royalties	✓			Stock			✓
Supplies	✓			Stock Subscriptions	✓		
Taxes	✓			Subordinated Debentures			
Processes			✓	(*Same as* Debentures)			
Profit and Loss (Deficit)			✓	Sundry Accounts Payable	✓		
Property		✓		Surplus Account			
Quarries		✓		Capital Surplus			✓
Real Estate		✓		Deficit (*Deduct*)			✓
Refundable Federal Taxes on				Donated			✓
Income	✓			Earned			✓
Research Expense			✓	Paid-In			✓
Revenue Stamps	✓			Profit and Loss—If Red			
Rights, Publishing			✓	(*Deduct*)			✓
Royalty, Prepaid		✓		Surplus			✓
Savings and Loan Shares	✓			Surplus from Appreciation			✓
Securities		✓		Undivided Profits			✓
Ships		✓					
Sight Drafts Outstanding	✓			Taxes, Unpaid	✓		
Sinking Fund		✓		Withheld at Source	✓		
State Bonds	✓			Term Loans (*Same as* Bonds)			
Stocks and Bonds		✓		Trade Acceptances Payable	✓		
Stock Subscriptions			✓				
Subscription Lists			✓	Unearned Income		✓	
Sundry Debtors			✓				
Surplus (Deficit)			✓	Wages, Unpaid	✓		
Timber (Standing or Uncut)		✓					
Tools		✓					
Tracings			✓				
Trade Acceptances	✓						
Trade Brand			✓				
Trademarks			✓				
Trade Name			✓				
Treasury Bonds		✓					
Treasury Stock			✓				
Trucks		✓					
Unamortized Mortgage or							
Bond Expense			✓				
United States Government							
Securities	✓						
Agencies of the Federal Gov-							
ernment	✓						
Unlisted Securities		✓					
Vessels		✓					

Source: Roy A. Foulke, *Practical Financial Statement Analysis*

FIG. 20–7   (cont'd).

CHAPTER **21**

ACCOUNTING CONVENTION IN RELATION TO CREDIT ANALYSIS

Credit executives must understand the terminology and conventions employed by the accounting profession. These have been fairly well standardized by regulations and pronouncements of the national, state, and local accounting societies.

ROLE OF THE AUDITOR

The terms of an auditor's engagement determine the extent of the audit, the number and detail of the schedules produced, and the amount of verification work done. The adequacy of the audit and the experience and reputation of the auditor are weighed by the credit executive against the size and financial condition of the customer. This should be the initial step in financial analysis.

Types of Audit

The report of an independent auditor engaged solely to prepare or verify the financial report may be a complete, detailed audit with verification of all items and transactions. At the other end of the scale, it may be simply a book audit, concerned only with arithmetic accuracy in transferring ledger figures and other records into the balance sheet, statement of income and retained earnings, and other schedules. Between these extremes, limited audits include some items with insufficient verification because of restrictive circumstances or because of management's insistence that certain figures be accepted without complete checking; the auditor notes these limitations in order to avoid misleading others as to the the extent of the verification.

Unaudited Statements

When a report indicates that the auditor has *reviewed* the financial data, this means that the statement has not been audited. The auditor makes inquiries concerning the internal procedures of the client but does not make any external inquiries, observe physical inventories, review internal control, or perform other mandatory auditing procedures. Moreover, the auditor's statement attached to the review represents a disclaimer of opinion. While a review offers limited assurance, a *compilation* is even less assuring. Its financial information is the representation of management without any attempt by the auditor to verify figures or to provide any assurance on the statements.

Among the figures seldom audited are interim statements; at most, they are subjected to a limited audit, even when it is issued on the stationery of the auditor. In large concerns, these figures are usually prepared and released by the controller.

Small firms frequently engage auditors to personally take off monthly trial balances or prepare interim statements. Usually, however, the scope of the work is limited and is done by the bookkeeper with only casual supervision or direction by the auditors. The publishing of such data on an auditor's stationery is frowned upon, as is the practice of distributing statements that omit the auditor's full certificate, which might contain significant qualifications.

The Auditor's Certificate

The letter of transmittal in which the auditor reports the results of the audit to the client is termed the certificate. The letter may be in a short form or in the more comprehensive long form. The short form certificate describes the scope of the work in general terms, noting exceptions to usual practice or procedure. It also expresses the opinion which may or may not be qualified. An unqualified opinion is one that states the schedules are prepared accurately, fairly present the results of operations for the period reported, and show the actual financial condition of the concern on the date of the statement. A qualified opinion is one that explains the qualifications detailed in the footnotes, usually referenced by the footnote number, which may have a material effect on a company's operating results and financial condition. The long form certificate usually details the computation processes and verification tests made in connection with all material assets and liabilities, besides including standard phrases used in the short certificate. It is prepared primarily for management purposes, while the short certificate usually goes to creditors. When an opinion is qualified, a credit executive should compare successive statements to uncover material changes in phrasing or omissions that could prove significant on further inquiry.

The short certificate covering a detailed audit usually assures the client and the creditors that:

1. The accounting records of the client were actually audited for the period indicated.

2. The examination was made in accordance with generally accepted auditing standards.

3. Such tests of the accounting records and other auditing procedures were made as were deemed necessary under the circumstances.

4. The major assets and liabilities were confirmed or checked, with exceptions noted.

5. In the opinion of the auditor, the facts and figures reported fairly present the affairs of the client and were arrived at in conformity with generally accepted accounting principles, *which were applied in a manner consistent with that of the preceding year.*

The importance of the last statement is such that its absence should be questioned. This phrase gives assurance that, in the absence of notice to the contrary, no changes have been made from one year to another in methods of evaluation or in determining depreciation charges and allowances, and that income statement items have not been shifted from one category to another.

Customary Schedules in Audit Reports

Primary exhibits or schedules are the balance sheet, statement of income and retained earnings, and statement of changes in financial position. The report may also include various supporting and analytical schedules. Their scope and character depend on the size of the concern, the complexity of organization and operations, and on the client's instructions.

It is customary for comprehensive audit reports to present these exhibits and schedules for at least two successive years. Comparisons stated in dollars and on a percentage basis facilitate analysis by management and creditors. Special-purpose schedules are occasionally included for managerial use or because of special interest on the part of the suppliers and bankers. The first appearance of unusual schedules should suggest that special study is needed.

Notes to the Financial Statements

These are items that do not lend themselves readily to the financial statement form of presentation but which are significant to the statement as a whole. Examples are contingencies such as leases, merchandise in transit, pending purchase contracts, commitments for plant expansion, liability for dividends in arrears, events occurring subsequent to the balance sheet date, and pending litigation. The auditor may also deem it appropriate to comment upon pending tax examinations and the last tax year examined by the various authorities.

With regard to any notes referring to a firm's pension plan, it is particularly important to determine whether the actuarially computed value of vested benefits exceed the plan assets. If so, the Pension Benefit Guarantee Corporation would have a preferred claim of up to 30 per cent of the net worth if the company were to liquidate.

As a first step in analyzing the figures, the credit executive should adjust all balance sheet and income accounts for the transactions reflected in the footnotes. The auditor is telling a story that can be only partly presented in statement form. The footnotes are as important to the story as the classified items.

Responsibility for Financial Reporting

While the auditing firm is liable for its opinion of the financial statement, company management is responsible for the statement's integrity and objectivity. In a note to shareholders and directors, the management of a large company will acknowledge its responsibility for maintaining internal accounting control systems that provide reasonable assurance as to the reliability of the financial records. Moreover, an audit committee of the board of directors, comprised solely of members who are not employees of the company, oversee the financial reporting. This committee usually meets jointly and separately with the independent auditors and management to review their activities.

APPRAISAL OF AUDIT RELIABILITY

The audit and certification is generally accepted as adequate endorsement of the correctness of a financial statement, but seasoned credit executives take two additional factors into consideration: the experience of the auditor with the type of business and how often the client's books are examined. They keep a close working relationship with the auditor and client, and become wary when the auditor is changed.

Specialization by Auditors

Practically every trade and industry has a group of auditors who concentrate their practice in that field. Often this specialization is along functional lines. In the textile industry, some auditors specialize in mill operations, others in wholesaling or jobbing, and still others in segments of the cutting-up industry—manufacturers of shirts, coats and suits, or dresses. By cooperating with the credit executives of suppliers and with their close knowledge of specific products, processes, and market conditions, these auditors become authorities in particular lines. Consequently, their audits are preferred by some credit executives over those of less specialized auditors.

Frequency of Audit

Continuity of engagement and continuous audit are not the same type of service. In the first, an independent auditor is regularly employed to prepare annual and other statements, and does so for successive years. Under continuous audit, the auditor makes periodic inspections of the books and records between annual statement periods, but not necessarily an audit, and may supervise or prepare monthly trial balances and quarterly or semiannual statements. Continuous audit enables the auditor to follow the client's affairs more closely than is possible during a single annual visit. As a consequence, credit executives can place greater credence on financial figures prepared under this type of arrangement.

Change in Auditor

When the regular auditor quits an engagement, it is important to unearth the underlying reason. A desire to lower auditing costs is often given as the motive, but the move may also have credit implications. A substantial cut in auditing fees may foreshadow looser auditing work and less verification effort. The change in auditors may have been occasioned by a difference of opinion between auditor and management regarding the treatment and certification of material items in the statement.

Some auditors announce they are no longer "on the books" of a former client but, understandably, do not give the reason. Credit executives should carefully compare the certificate of the new auditor with that of the former one.

Auditor-Client-Creditor Relationships

Auditors prepare financial statements and supporting schedules for clients, and not to meet the special needs of creditors. Their work is governed by their intensive training, strict regulation of auditing procedures and conventions, and their accountability to professional societies. They do, however, have a responsibility to clarify items in their audits when questions are raised, and usually give such explanations readily.

The creditor should have the customer's permission before asking the auditor for additional schedules, exhibits, or other information ordinarily withheld from publication. Auditors differ as to the degree of their cooperation with small- or medium-sized clients. Some believe their audit report meets the terms of their engagement; others give additional information which may benefit their clients. In some lines of business, notably segments of the textile industry, auditors accompany their clients on credit interviews and supply additional information to creditors. Many credit executives and bank lending officers welcome an opportunity to become acquainted with an auditor on whom they expect to rely.

USE OF FINANCIAL STATEMENT FORMS

Financial statement forms supplied by creditors, credit reporting agencies, or credit associations are frequently used to submit financial reports. They are convenient, and indicate the kind of information desired and the order in which it should be given. Many credit departments prefer to receive statements on their own forms to be certain that needed information has been furnished and to allow for uniform analysis. A copy of the complete audit is requested only when additional information or verification is considered necessary. Credit agencies, concerned with speedy duplication of the statement for distribution to clients, prefer to have the significant facts in a voluminous audit report condensed to the one or two pages of their standard forms.

Financial Statement Design

Financial statement forms must be carefully designed to ensure that their information is adequate and valid. They should have:

1. Item headings and write-in spaces for all balance sheet items customarily listed by auditors. Valuation basis should be required on major asset items.

2. Space and headings (outside of the balance sheet form, if necessary) for posting the information given by supporting schedules of the audit. These include balance sheet item breakdowns, agings, allowance and depreciation schedules, insurance coverage, contingencies, and all other details.

3. Space and headings for posting complete condensed operating statement and net worth or retained earnings reconciliation schedule. If the complete statement of income and retained earnings is not required, there should be room to list sales, profits, dividends, and other details.

4. Provisions for establishing the validity and responsibility for the financial statement: name, address, and professional status of the auditor; scope of audit; assurance that statements and data submitted on the forms agree with auditor's examination and client's books; specific permission to refer to the auditor for additional information or for verification; and responsibility and valid use clauses signed in the name of the concern by an authorized person or principal. It should be stated that the information given is true and accurate to the best knowledge of the signer, and that the statement is submitted as a basis for credit with a company or with subscribers in the case of a credit agency.

False Financial Statements

Though normal credit analysis is based on the assumption that the facts submitted by the customer are true, there is always the possibility that a false and misleading financial statement may be intentionally submitted.

Statements should be signed by a principal of the business. Besides the psychological effect on the business executive, the principal's signature to a financial report has legal implications. The title of the principal should also be included, as well as the date of the signing. When unsigned balance sheets or operating statements are received, some credit executives will send them back for signature. Although this may seem time-consuming, it protects the creditor's interest in case of litigation.

Continuing and Acceleration Clauses. Most statement forms contain a continuing clause. This is a declaration signed by the principals, attesting that there has been no unfavorable change in the financial condition of the business from the date of the figures to the date of the signing. Further, it is declared that the firm receiving the statement will be notified of any such change. Until notice is given, the statement may be regarded as continuing to reflect the firm's financial condition.

The acceleration clause is ordinarily used in connection with bank loans. It gives the bank the option to call a loan ahead of time if the financial condition of the borrower changes so much that it increases the bank's risk.

Fraud. Blackstone defines fraud as "An intentional perversion of truth for the purpose of inducing another in reliance upon it to part with some valuable thing belonging to him or to surrender a legal right."

The essential characteristic of fraud is the intent to deceive. If this element is lacking in any act or series of acts or representations, it is wrong to call such acts or representations fraudulent, even though they have caused loss to a creditor. A principal may be incompetent or negligent in managing the business or may be even willfully wasteful of the firm's assets, by gambling for instance. But unless creditors were at some point intentionally deceived on a material fact, the principal cannot properly be charged with fraud.

Investigation concerning false financial statements is an important part of the work of the NACM Fraud Prevention Department. Particularly where fraud is suspected but, for one reason or another, the case does not go to the bankruptcy courts or state courts, this department is often the only practical recourse of defrauded creditors. The information developed during these investigations if it warrants prosecution is turned over to the state or federal authorities, who then proceed with the action.

If a prosecution for mail fraud based on a financial statement is to be successful, the prosecutor will expect that one (and preferably more than one) creditor will provide (1) proof of reliance on (2) a detailed statement, not estimated or in round numbers, in which (3) provable material falsity exists, as of (4) a certain date, which was (5) signed by the person to be charged, and to which (6) proof of mailing is attached. The detail required in successful prosecution makes it extremely important for the credit executive to observe the points outlined earlier here when asking for and receiving a customer's financial statement.

Federal Law. False financial statements sent through the mails have been the basis for a great number of prosecutions, thereby giving rise to the idea that there is a specific federal law covering this offense. Actually the mail fraud statute nowhere mentions financial statements as such, and in early cases it was argued that the sending of a false financial statement through the mails was not covered by the statute. In 1916 the U.S. Supreme Court decided that such an act was a "scheme or artifice" within Section 1341 of the Criminal Code. This decision of the Supreme Court remains the law today.

United States Code Title 18, Section 1341
Whoever, having devised or intending to devise any scheme or artifice to defraud, or for obtaining money or property by means of false or fraudulent pretenses, representations, or promises, or to sell, dispose of, loan, exchange, alter, give away, distribute, supply, or furnish or procure for unlawful use any counterfeit or spurious coin, obligation, security, or other article or anything represented to be or intimated or held out to be such counterfeit or spurious article, for the purpose of executing such scheme or artifice or attempting so to do, places in any post office or authorized depository for mail matter, any matter or thing whatever to be sent or delivered by the Post Office Department, or takes or receives therefrom, any such matter or thing, or knowingly causes to be delivered by mail according to the direction thereon, or at the place at which it is directed to be delivered by the person to whom it is addressed, any such matter or thing, shall be fined not more than $1,000 or imprisoned not more than five years, or both.

Certain essential elements, aside from use of the mails, must be proved before there can be a conviction for mail fraud by false financial statement. The statement must be false, it must be known to the maker to be false, and it must be made with the intent that it be relied upon by the prospective creditor. Also, for all practical purposes, the creditor must sustain a loss through reliance upon it for granting credit.

The falsity of the statement is proved either by an audit of the debtor's books and records following bankruptcy or an assignment for the benefit of creditors, or by a reconstruction of the debtor's records if the books are unavailable. This is a job for an auditor, retained either by the trustee or assignee under court order or by creditors acting independently.

State Laws.   Many states have laws which make it criminal to obtain goods on credit by a false financial statement. Unlike the federal mail fraud statute, these laws usually denominate the offense a misdemeanor. The New York statute, which is typical, states the following:

New York Penal Law, Section 1293-B
Obtaining property or credit by use of false statement.
Any person
1. Who shall knowingly make or cause to be made, either directly or indirectly, or through any agency whatsoever, any false statement in writing, with intent that it shall be relied upon, respecting the financial condition, or means or ability to pay, of himself, or any other person, firm or corporation, in whom he is interested, or for whom he is acting, for the purpose of procuring in any form whatsoever, either the delivery of personal property, the payment of cash, the making of a loan or credit, the extension of a credit, the discount of an account receivable, the execution, making or delivery by any person, firm or corporation of any bond or undertaking, or the making, acceptance, discount, sale or indorsement of a bill of exchange, or promissory note, for the benefit of either himself or of such person, firm or corporation; or
2. Who, knowing that a false statement in writing has been made, respecting the financial condition or means or ability to pay, of himself, or such person, firm or corporation in which he is interested, or for whom he is acting procures,

upon the faith thereof, for the benefit either of himself, or of such person, firm or corporation, either or any of the things of benefit mentioned in subdivision one of this section; or

3. Who knowing that a statement in writing has been made, respecting the financial condition or means or ability to pay of himself or such person, firm or corporation in which he is interested, or for whom he is acting, represents on a later day, either orally or in writing, that such statement theretofore made, if then again made on said day, would be then true, when in fact, said statement if then made would be false, and procures upon the faith thereof, for the benefit either of himself or of such person, firm or corporation, either or any of the things of benefit mentioned in subdivision one of this section.

Shall be guilty of a misdemeanor and punishable by imprisonment for not more than one year or by a fine of not more than one thousand dollars, or both fine and imprisonment. Added L. 1912, c. 340; amended L. 1921, c. 306, eff. July 1, 1921.

Even if a false statement is received through the mail, it may be advisable to proceed under the state law if the proof of mailing is weak or absent entirely, since provable use of the mails is essential under the federal law.

Points To Be Observed. Certain precautions will reduce the likelihood of loss because of fraudulent statements.

1. *Avoid estimated statements.* Rounded figures and statements bearing the word "estimated" on their face cannot be regarded as reflecting the true financial condition of the debtor. On the other hand, a detailed financial statement is not estimated. It is either true or false.

2. *Make sure of date.* Every credit executive has at some time received an undated financial statement. Perhaps the date the statement was prepared or the date that the figures were supposed to reflect was omitted. Statements should not be accepted unless both dates are set forth and are consistent with each other. Omission of date or the insertion of a date obviously incorrect is not always an oversight. Under certain circumstances it can defeat prosecution.

3. *Be certain of the signature.* The statement should be signed by the debtor and preferably bear the name of a witness. If more than one document is submitted, the customer should sign each paper. In one case the debtor had mailed a balance sheet and a profit and loss statement in the same envelope. The profit and loss statement was signed but the balance sheet was not. Although investigation established that the balance sheet was materially false, prosecution was declined because the balance sheet was unsigned.

4. *Do not assist the customer to prepare a statement.* The debtor should make up its own statements. There have been cases in which the representative of the creditor firm wrote in figures and the customer then signed the statement. In such cases it is difficult to prove knowledge of falsity on the part of the debtor.

5. *Insist on mailed statements where possible.* In the light of experience, it is advisable to be wary of the customer that obviously goes out of the

way to deliver a statement by hand rather than mail it. Mail fraud is a felony, while the usual state statute covering false statements makes the offense only a misdemeanor. Also, if the statement is secured in the field by a representative of the supplier company, the customer should mail it. The credit representative of the supplier should not do this, even if asked to do so.

6. *Retain proof of mailing.*   It is standard procedure to have the financial statement and the envelope in which it is received both dated and initialed by the person receiving them. In other instances, standard forms may be printed so the statement is folded and addressed directly, eliminating the need for an envelope. This method is accepted as proof that a statement was received through the mails.

Other correspondence from a fraudulent debtor may be valid evidence in proving a scheme to defraud. It is thus advisable to retain with envelopes letters from a debtor asking for extension of time on a past-due account, correspondence dealing with "N.S.F." checks, and similar material.

7. *Look for omissions and unanswered questions.*   A financial statement which is materially false may nevertheless not support a successful prosecution if significant information is left off the statement or material questions are left unanswered.

For example, a debtor that had assigned all its receivables to a finance company issued a statement showing such receivables to be free assets. This was clearly a material misrepresentation. However, the debtor left unanswered on the statement form the question, "Are any of your assets pledged?" It was argued at the trial that the failure to answer this question should have put prospective creditors on notice that the statement was defective for credit purposes, and that creditors had no right to assume that the answer was "No." Apparently the jury in this instance agreed with this argument, because it acquitted the defendant.

CHAPTER 22

FUNDAMENTALS OF FINANCIAL ANALYSIS

Methods of analysis may be divided into two general categories: internal and comparative. Internal analysis uses figures from the financial statements of any one date or period to gain an understanding of the company. Comparative analysis may be used to determine trends when two or more successive sets of figures are reviewed, or may be used to evaluate a given company's financial statement against industry standards. These methods may be used separately or in combination. They enable experienced credit executives to reach a credit decision.

INTERNAL ANALYSIS

As an important first step in internal analysis, the financial statement should be examined for validity and general correctness. Estimates have sometimes been mistaken for accurate figures, vague terminology has been overlooked, unauthorized signatures have been accepted, and the mere notation of an auditor's name has at times been taken as evidence of a proper audit. In some instances, neglect of this phase of the examination has proved costly to creditors.

After the statement has been accepted as valid and reasonably accurate, ratios should be calculated and the figures analyzed in the sequence suggested by these questions:

1. Do the statement proportions or turnovers indicate low, average, or active rates of net working capital and inventory turnovers? Were operations profitable? If an operating statement is not available, a current income tax liability on the balance sheet indicates profits have been earned; but because of carry-forward provision of the tax law, the absence of such provision does not necessarily mean there were no earnings in the current period. Also, retained earnings may be indications of past earnings but are not positive assurance of current profits.

2. In keeping with sales, are current assets in proper relationship to each other and to current debts? Does the concern use bank accommodation? If so, on what basis? Does it use other types of current financing? If current assets are being hypothecated (pledged), that may affect ratios and make it necessary to have the full operating statement.

3. Are funds being diverted into miscellaneous accounts, such as loans to principals or outside investment? If so, they may have a significant impact on finances.

4. Is net working capital sufficient for indicated scope of operations? Is it being reinforced by a heavy funded debt or by subordinated loans?

5. Are fixed assets disproportionate to tangible net worth or net working capital?

6. Does net worth show a reasonable margin over total debts?

7. Can the company be classified as a good risk or at least not below industry averages? If not, the decision should be held up until additional information is obtained.

Internal analysis calls for an examination of items within a single financial statement for the purpose of judging their significance in relation to the capital of the company, its method of operation, and conditions prevailing within the industry. When sales, profits, or other operating details are not available, emphasis must be placed on internal analysis of the balance sheet. The major tools for internal analysis are balance sheet ratios and a working knowledge of the line of business, including the method of operation and seasonal influences.

Ratios are mathematical aids for appraisal and comparison of financial statements. They are used to supplement dollar amount inspection, to examine inter-item relationships, and to compare a specific company's performance against its industry standard.

The use of ratios reduces the influence of dollar size on analysis, since these comparisons are expressed as percentages, fractions, decimals, or rates of turnover. The number of ratios that can be developed from the balance sheet and income statement is limited only by the combinations that could be made of the items appearing in both schedules. The type of operation represented by the account and the nature of the risk have an important bearing on what ratios are to be computed and studied.

Caution is necessary in the interpretation of ratios. For instance, under profitable operating conditions and high sales activity, proportions that would ordinarily be criticized might be quite acceptable. Consequently, the credit executive must look for evidence which will indicate the results of operations and the volume of business. Evidence may be difficult to obtain when only a single balance sheet is available, but many credit executives approach the problem in innovative ways.

Balance Sheet Ratios

With ratios it is possible to determine if asset and liability relationships are reasonably aligned. While ratios are not an end in themselves, they should be considered in conjunction with accompanying information. Used in the proper fashion, they are useful tools in determining the creditworthiness of an account.

Current Ratio. This is the relationship between current assets and current liabilities and is determined by dividing the current assets by the current liabilities. Current assets are basically the sum of cash, short-term marketable securities, notes and accounts receivable, and merchandise inventories. Current debt is the total of all liabilities falling due within one year. Usually the higher the ratio, the greater is the protection to the short-term creditor. However, it is generally conceded that cash and receivables have higher liquidating values than merchandise. Consequently, if cash and receivables are high in relation to inventory, a lower current ratio could be satisfactory from a credit standpoint.

The size of the current ratio should be considered in relation to the seasonal influences at statement date. Current assets and current liabilities normally expand with an increase in activity and decrease when business levels off or reaches the end of a season. Therefore, it is normal for a concern engaged in highly seasonal activities to show wide fluctuations in its current ratio at different stages of the seasonal cycle. Thus a heavy credit purchase of merchandise would lower the current ratio despite the fact that both current assets and current liabilities are increased by identical amounts in the transaction. This is demonstrated by the following example:

	Before	*Transaction*	*After*
Current Assets	$50,000	plus $5,000 merchandise purchased	$55,000
Current debts	$25,000	plus $5,000 increase in trade debt	$30,000
Current ratio	2.0 to 1		1.83 to 1

Conversely, at the end of the season merchandise inventory should be low, and the funds released by inventory liquidation and collection of receivables should cause a sharp reduction in current debt. This is the time of year when a concern should show its highest current ratio. If its fiscal year coincides with the seasonal lull, the firm will show its best condition to creditors. In many lines of business, however, the calendar yearend does not coincide with the natural seasonal lull; further, a stepup or slowdown in seasonal activity will affect the ratio of businesses which normally reach a liquidated position at yearend.

Quick Ratio. Also called the liquid ratio and acid test, this is the ratio of the sum of cash, marketable securities, and receivables to current liabilities. It should provide at least a small margin over current debts, and a high liquid ratio can often support a low current ratio. If the ratio is too low, the firm must rely on quick marketing of merchandise for funds to meet maturing debts. A slow turnover of receivables worsens the quality of the liquid ratio. Within this ratio, many credit executives like to see the cash item equal to one month's expenses of the business.

Inventory to Net Working Capital.   This ratio expresses the relationship between merchandise inventory and net working capital. Net working capital represents the excess of current assets over current liabilities and constitutes a cushion for carrying accounts receivable and inventories, and for financing day-to-day operations. A high ratio for the type of operation may indicate overbuying, falling sales, or excessive carryover of old stock; a low ratio indicates liquidity in the current assets. With a manufacturer, the proportions of inventory in raw materials, goods in process, and finished merchandise may be very significant. Inventory should be related to annual sales and the basis on which it is valued is extremely important when the ratio is poor.

Fixed Assets to Tangible Net Worth.   This ratio relates the investment in fixed assets to the ownership interest. When this ratio is higher than average, a low net working capital is indicated and, in all likelihood, an overworking of net working capital. A high ratio could also mean that net working capital needed for operations is being diverted to plant and equipment; this restricts operating funds and leaves a business vulnerable to business downturns.

Total Noncurrent Assets to Total Capitalization.   Total capitalization is defined here as the total deferred debt and tangible net worth. This ratio may have more significance to short-term creditors than the one above since it relates funds invested in noncurrent assets to the total capitalization. A low ratio indicates that cash inflows from current assets are not used to support the investment in noncurrent assets. As the ratio approaches 1.0, it becomes more likely that some of the cash inflows from current assets are being used in that capacity; this weakens the position of the short-term credit grantor.

Current Debt to Tangible Net Worth.   This ratio measures the relationship between all current debt and the tangible net worth of a company. A ratio greater than 1.0 means that short-term creditors have more at risk in the business than the owners do. In this situation, a firm is highly vulnerable to changes in business conditions and increasingly dependent on the good will of creditors. Any interruption of cash inflow, such as a period of difficult collection or falling prices or sales, may make it impossible for the debtor to meet obligations on schedule.

Total Debt to Tangible Net Worth.   In this computation the liabilities include all funded debt (long-term liabilities) as well as current debts. The ratio is broader than current debt to tangible net worth, since it includes the risk of long-term creditors. It is an indicator of the firm's ability to leverage, and of the relative investments made in the firm by stockholders and by all creditors. A high ratio indicates high leveraging and potential danger to creditors.

Funded Debt to Net Working Capital. This important measure relates long-term obligations to net working capital. When this ratio is high, funded debt often places a strain on the business, necessitating a heavier or more frequent turnover of net working capital in order to meet interest charges on the indebtedness.

It is important to study the nature of the funded debt. Certain forms of deferred debt carry convertible features and may at the option of the holder be exchanged for capital stock. Such transactions will improve this ratio and total debt to tangible net worth. Care should be taken, however, to fully understand the terms of the conversion from deferred debt to preferred stock. The conversion to preferred stock may actually be a move to improve the position of the deferred creditor at the expense of other creditors—that is, the preferred stock agreement may actually be more restrictive than the original loan agreement.

Turnover Rates

Turnover rates have the sales figure as the numerator and generally measure the number of times per period that an asset is used.

Net Sales to Tangible Net Worth. This ratio describes the rate at which tangible net worth is turned in the business and is a measure of management ability. It is desirable to utilize investor capital as actively as possible while maintaining a sound financial position.

Net Sales to Total Assets. This ratio measures the productive use of business assets. Usually only tangible assets are considered. The higher the turnover, the greater is the productivity. A low turnover infers that a portion of the assets is unproductive, while a very high rate may indicate that the firm is overtrading.

Net Sales to Net Working Capital. This ratio examines the turnover of net working capital. It measures the tendency of a business to depend upon its suppliers, short-term borrowings, and funded debt to meet its financing needs. A high turnover would indicate active trading, while a low figure would reflect undertrading or ineffective use of net working capital.

Net Sales to Inventory. This relationship is a guide to the condition of inventories in that it shows the number of times they are turned in the course of a year. Some credit executives use an average inventory figure for this calculation; they add beginning and ending inventories and divide by two. Others use ending inventory only. Still others relate inventory to the cost of goods sold. Regardless of which method is used, it is important to apply it consistently when analyzing the figures of successive years for any company.

Net Sales to Accounts Receivable. This turnover rate of accounts receivable measures the efficiency with which company resources are employed in accounts receivable. A high number indicates rapid turnover of funds, while a low one might reflect slow collections, granting of special terms, seasonal variations in selling patterns, or an unexpected sharp rise in the volume of business.

Overtrading. When a company's sales volume seems too great for financial resources, the question arises as to whether it is overtrading. This phenomenon is signaled by unusual values of net sales to tangible net worth, net sales to total assets, or net sales to net working capital; and can be confirmed by a low ratio of current assets to current debt and a high ratio of total debt to tangible net worth.

The large amount of inventory needed to meet the heavy sales volume in this circumstance is financed primarily by trade suppliers. As long as there is close coordination among sales, credit, purchases, and payables, a company with good management can prosper. However, the delicate balance between cash inflows and cash outflows can be easily upset. A decline in sales could cause a serious imbalance in inventory and jeopardize a firm's ability to pay its obligations. Using its capital and credit to the limit, the company that is overtrading has no reserve operating funds to carry it through a period of adversity. This is a dangerous situation for its creditors.

Profit Ratios

These calculations divide particular assets into net sales in order to show their yield to the business.

Gross Profit on Net Sales. This relationship, sometimes called gross margin, measures a firm's ability to stay in business. It tends to vary little from firm to firm within an industry because competitive factors tend to keep the price of purchases and selling prices in fairly close alignment. A return considerably below that of the industry suggests a number of possibilities, including insufficient volume and excessive purchasing or labor costs. An explanation should be sought of any major deviation in gross profit from that which is standard for an industry.

Net Income on Net Sales. This ratio measures the return on volume and is useful for gauging the effectiveness of management. If the figure is small in comparison to industry standards, the credit executive should examine the income statement for the cause of the modest return. Maybe the salary scale for management is too liberal or selling expenses are too high or a nonrecurring item such as a bad-debt writeoff was responsible for the low rate of return.

Net Operating Income on Net Sales. Many credit executives prefer to analyze net operating income rather than net income. The former does not include extraordinary charges and income that may be included in the final net income figure. Moreover, the net operating income is not affected by the income tax provision which could vary considerably from one firm to another.

Net Income on Net Working Capital. This ratio is particularly useful in measuring the profitability of concerns that have their net working capital derived in large part from long-term borrowings, and their invested capital is small in relation to sales.

Net Income on Tangible Net Worth. This relationship measures the rate of return on equity. It complements the net income on net sales as a tool for gauging the effectiveness of management, since it reflects the efficiency with which owner's interest is used in the business.

Appraising the Use of Ratios

Ratios have to be used with great care. Because of the way in which they are calculated, they may mislead the unsuspecting user. For example, a company can improve its current position by substituting long-term debt for short-term debt. This would improve the current ratio, inventory to net working capital, and current debt to tangible net worth. However, its improved current position would be gained through the use of long-term debt. By calculating funded debt to net working capital, a credit executive would determine the reason for the improved current position.

A ratio is obtained by dividing one number by another; therefore, a change in either the numerator or denominator will change the end figure. When identical ratios of different dates are being compared, the full significance of the change cannot be apparent unless the fluctuations of the components are kept in mind. For example, if the ratio of net income on net sales has increased, it is well to note whether the change resulted from unchanged net income and decreased net sales, increased net income and static sales, net income that increased more quickly than net sales, or net income that decreased more slowly than sales decreased.

Ratios are affected by a company's line of business and its method of operation; furthermore, some vary from year to year with changes in the economic climate. As a basis for comparison, specific figures are compiled each year on numerous lines of business by credit agencies, banking groups, and trade associations. If it is not possible to obtain a set of standard ratios or a pattern statement for a particular line, the credit executive may wish to compile a typical line statement by using the data from combining and averaging financial statements of other firms in the same industry.

For credit purposes, the financial affairs of an account are usually mirrored by four to eight ratios, carefully selected as indexes to the soundness of the current position and profitableness of the operation. When disproportions are evident, additional ratio comparisons can usually clarify or confirm the situation and point to problem areas. Ratio selection should be based upon the type of credit being considered. To the short-term credit grantor, for example, net income on net sales could be misleading if this ratio improves at the expense of liquidity. As a rule of thumb, the short-term credit grantor, relying upon cash inflows generated by current assets, should look to liquidity and turnover ratios. Conversely, the long-term credit grantor, relying on cash flow created by profits, should be more concerned with the profit margin and return on investment type ratios.

TREND ANALYSIS

The technique described here enables the credit executive to determine the trend of operations by comparing a current financial statement with two or more prior statements of the same concern. Trend analysis can mix interim statements with annual figures, but comparing successive annual financial statements of the same calendar date eliminates seasonal variations in the figures. The same auditing technique and presentation should be employed on all statements, or changes in valuation basis and treatment of individual items should be explained.

Balance Sheet Trends

Item-by-item comparison of two or more successive statements of the same concern will give definite information on the trend of the business and the direction and velocity of change. Individual balance sheet items and ratios will vary considerably with the season, volume changes, collection and payments, and the ordinary daily activities of a business.

Cash. This item should be examined, as reasonable amounts must be maintained to meet internal expenses as well as customer obligations. An unusually small cash balance might suggest that trade payments are running slow.

Accounts Receivable. When volume decreases, it would be normal to expect a smaller receivables position, but this is not always the case. Sales might actually increase from year to year, while the receivables position in the year of the higher volume might be smaller than that of the lower year. This may be attributable to improved collections or a change in seasons or a variation in the method of operation.

Inventory. This also tends to rise and decline with increases and decreases in volume, though not always. A disproportionately large or small inventory position requires a satisfactory explanation.

Noncurrent Assets. Changes in these items should be examined in detail. If fixed assets are expanded sharply, at least a moderate sales increase might be expected during the current year with a further gain anticipated in the future. Steady declines in the fixed asset position might suggest that depreciation is being applied but that no new equipment is being purchased. Disproportionate changes in other noncurrent assets should be reviewed for whatever significance they may have.

Current Liabilities. These tend to expand with volume increases. Where this pattern is not evident, the credit executive should explore further. For instance, sales might increase and payables actually decline because long-term borrowings are being used to finance operations. Such financing might actually permit a better handling of payables than when volume was lower.

Funded Debt. Again, the manner in which operations are financed can affect the firm's financial posture. Long-term debt allows greater flexibility to management but also involves a steady drain on earnings for debt-service charges.

Tangible Net Worth. A steady increase in equity is generally regarded as a sign of good corporate health. It is significant to note that a net worth increase does not necessarily indicate profitable operations; nor does a decline mean that operations resulted in a loss. For example, an operating loss could be more than offset by the sale of additional stock. Similarly, dividends paid in excess of net earnings could produce a decline in equity.

Net Working Capital. The trend of this figure measures the organization's continuing ability to finance operations. It should trend upward, particularly in the case of a progessive organization interested in widening its sales base. When net working capital is turned too actively in relation to volume, overtrading may result. This could endanger the firm's future. Situations may arise when net working capital needs may decline as, for instance, when volume decreases through the sale of a certain segment of the business or through slack industry conditions. Even here, a prudent management would normally conserve net working capital in anticipation of possible future needs.

Ratios. It is wise to examine ratios in pairs or sets, and to evaluate the trend of all complimentary ratios rather than to be misled by the trend of any single one. For example, both the current and quick ratios measure a firm's ability to handle its obligations, particularly current debts, in an orderly manner. Yet the current ratio might reflect a year-to-year increase while the liquid ratio was actually declining. This could occur through a shifting of current assets into inventory rather than into receivables from one year to the next, while current liabilities remained unchanged. Worsening ratios should be examined in detail. Trends of a retrogressive nature often forewarn of a slowing down in trade payments and should be followed closely.

Similarly, the ratios of current debt to tangible net worth and total debt to tangible net worth give related views of creditor to ownership interest in a company. The most favorable trend is toward a greater interest on the part of owners. Changes in debt structure, from current debt to funded debt or in the other direction, should serve as signals for more careful analysis. Dangers are always present when indebtedness is excessive in relation to equity. Temporary increases in the relationship of debt to equity may be needed during business expansion, as when borrowed funds are utilized to finance plant or inventory, but excess debt is never desirable.

In yet another illustration, rising values in the ratio of inventory to net working capital would spotlight increasing concentration in inventories or reduced liquidity in the firm's net current assets. Conversely, a year-to-year decline in this ratio would point either to lower inventory requirements or greater ability for the firm to make alternative uses of its current assets.

Turnover Rates. These are valuable measures of the efficiency with which the company uses its resources. For instance, a slowdown in collection of outstanding receivables might impair financing ability and cause a company to start running slow in the trade. It might also suggest that its credit policy is being relaxed because of competitive pressures or poor supervision of the credit function. Seriously delinquent accounts pose major collection problems and often result in writeoffs.

Another example is the trend of inventory turnover. Generally a high turnover is desirable as this indicates a movement of goods and suggests the presence of little or no obsolete material in the final inventory. Turnover rates vary according to the method of operation and industry, and credit executives should be aware of the normal rates for the industries with which they deal. If any slowing down in the turnover rate is detected, the merchandising ability and techniques of management should be investigated.

Income Statement Trends

The component items of the statement of income and retained earnings can also be compared year to year for clues as to the financial operations.

Net Sales. The trend of a firm's sales is of vital importance. Normally a steady volume increase is desirable as it is an indication of growth and progress. As with most other factors, sales must be considered in light of both economic and industry conditions. Where a particular industry is expanding, a firm with declining volume might be cause for alarm. The decline should be investigated to determine the cause and to better decide whether the situation is temporary in nature or a sign of deterioration. A sales increase, while usually a favorable sign, need not necessarily indicate progress. It may be that unit sales have actually declined and price increases have resulted in slightly higher sales. Or prices may have been cut to a break even or lower scale, resulting in an increased but undesirable larger volume.

Cost of Goods Sold and Gross Profit. The trends of these items should be closely watched. Variations up or down are considered a measure of management's ability to compete. For a manufacturing organization, the cost of goods sold consists of material costs, labor costs, and factory overhead. If a firm can obtain these items at competitive rates, its gross profit should be high enough for the firm to show a net profit. Should costs exceed those typical for the industry, a loss is likely unless expenses are controlled. It is important to determine why a firm's gross margin is better or worse than that normal for an industry and use this information in making an evaluation of the account.

Expenses. These indicate management's ability to control costs. Selling expenses will normally climb when volume is increasing and decline when sales drop. Office help might have to be increased during busy periods or be cut back when activities slacken. Variations from normal expense trends should be explored.

Net Income. A favorable sign is to see net earnings increase from year to year. Even if earnings remain constant, the creditor will probably be protected. When the trend of earnings is downward or losses are being sustained, the debtor may become financially distressed. Earnings normally relate to sales, and in most cases increasing volume brings greater profits. If volume is reduced drastically, however, losses will probably result.

Statement of Changes in Financial Position

As described in Chapter 20, this statement consists of two parts: source and application of funds, and changes in net working capital. They are based upon a detailed comparison of the information presented in the balance sheets of two consecutive periods.

The principle that decreases in assets represent a source of funds is readily understood when the operating cycle of a business is called to mind. Merchandise is reduced by sales to provide receivables; receivables are collected to reinforce cash; and cash is used to retire indebtedness. A liquidation or reduction of noncurrent assets has the same effect of releasing funds. Increases in assets tie up additional funds in these items and accordingly are an application of funds.

Increases in liability accounts are associated with similar changes in assets, whether they represent purchases of goods, borrowed money, or expense accruals, and are a source of funds. Decreases in liabilities are a direct application of funds.

An increase in net worth or retained earnings may reflect contributions, sale of additional stock, or the retention of earnings, and thus represents a source of new funds available to the company during the period. On the other hand, when net worth is reduced by an operating loss, retirement of capital funds, or dividends, the change represents an application of funds.

Careful study of the schedule will point up any disproportionate buildup of asset items, and how they were financed. It will also show the extent to which liabilities were liquidated and the sources of funds used to reduce those liabilities.

Changes in net working capital are similarly examined by reviewing the variations that have taken place in assets, liabilities, and equity. In this phase, the objective is to determine shifts in the magnitudes of current and noncurrent assets, short-term and long-term debt, and equity components. Later, when dollar amounts have been established, the individual items can be reviewed to note their separate impacts on composition of net working capital.

INDUSTRY STANDARDS

Inherent in any analysis is an expressed or implied concept of the normal or proper size and proportions of the items being examined. This concept of the normal (not necessarily the ideal) is the premise on which financial statement analysis is based. The normality of the showing, or the degree of variation of an individual statement from the norm, may be established by comparison with the statements of other representative concerns in the trade doing business under similar conditions. For example, a normal current ratio for a paint manufacturer would differ from that of a textile dyer, yet both would be considered acceptable in their respective industries.

Percentage Statements

Credit executives have found that percentage statements are a helpful analytical tool. It is a device which strives to eliminate complete reliance on organizational size by reducing balance sheet and income statement components to percentages. Every asset item in the balance sheet is shown as a percentage of total assets, while every liability and stockholders' equity item is shown as a percentage of the total of liabilities and stockholders' equity. In the income statement, every income and expense item is shown as a percentage of total sales.

There are two types of percentage statements: composite and pattern statements. Composite statements, also called common size, are merely averages arrived at by combining financial statements of many organizations within an industry with no regard to size or condition of individual firms. For example, two firms having tangible net worths of $100,000 and $102,000 could be combined and averaged, and show a composite tangible net worth of $101,000. In like fashion, the composite tangible net worth of two other firms, one having a worth of $2,000 and the other of $200,000, would also be $101,000.

Pattern statements are also comprised of average figures but they are compiled on a more selective and refined basis than composite statements. In some pattern statements, items are related to total assets and total liabilities and stockholders' equity, while in others the items may be related to other bases, such as tangible net worth or net working capital. Net sales is usually the base for operating data in both composite and pattern statements.

The real application of percentage statements lies in the ability to measure the relative condition of the firm being studied against that typical for its industry. This is helpful when the credit executive does not know a particular industry. Such statements are also good indicators of general industry conditions.

The wise use of percentage statements avoids overemphasis on absolute changes in account items. Special consideration is placed on relationships or ratios, and an increase or decrease in a particular item will be considered only when the change is disproportionate to the base. Thus an absolute increase of $100,000 in inventory position from one year to the next might be considered normal if its percentage to total assets remained fairly constant. However, a major increase in inventory accompanied by an important deviation from its normal relationship to total assets would be cause for further investigation.

A major limitation to percentage statements is that they do not provide trend information of a useful nature. They do not measure trends of individual items but only trends of relationships to total assets, total liabilities and stockholders' equity, or sales. Much of the information they provide is also available from straight ratio analysis, which is often more usable since it permits weighing relationships between assets and liabilities as well as between certain assets and income items.

The credit executive should seek an explanation of a wide variance from typical industry figures. Peculiarities in the operation or marketing endeavors of a particular firm may justify a condition that deviates from the industry norm. Variations should not in themselves be considered in a favorable or unfavorable light but should signal the need for further investigation.

Sources of Financial Statement Standards

A number of sources provide statement norms for almost every field of business in which credit is extended. Credit agencies, bankers, and industry associations, in particular, are in a position to assemble sufficient statements for this purpose. Credit departments of large companies can provide comparable data on their own customers by careful selection and combining of customers' statements; these figures would have the advantage of reflecting the seller company's policy because they would be made up of customers that have been approved.

The Robert Morris Associates publishes composite financial data on over 300 lines of business—manufacturers, wholesalers, retailers, services, and contractors. Industry data are presented according to company size, with the exception of the contractor industries where revenues are used to differentiate different size classes. The statements of each industry or trade are tabulated into four groups, according to size of assets; in addition, there is a composite for all sizes. The Robert Morris Associates is very careful to point out that its statement studies, which are copyrighted, should be regarded only as general guidelines and not as absolute industry norms.

Dun & Bradstreet compiles 14 key business ratios for most major industries. Developed by Roy A. Foulke, these ratios cover manufacturing, wholesaling, retailing, mining, construction, and other lines of business.

For each, the values of upper quartile, median, and lower quartile are given as a basis of direct comparison in credit analysis. Unlike the studies by Robert Morris Associates, however, the Dun & Bradstreet figures do not present ratios according to common size classification.

CHAPTER 23

CASE ANALYSIS

The methods of financial analysis described in the previous chapter have been applied in a sample case shown here. No specific line of business has been given to the sample company, although it may be assumed that it has operated for a number of years in an industry of moderate growth and no particularly hazardous economic influences. In an actual situation, of course, the analysis would be influenced by the debtor's method of operation and the prevalent economic conditions in that industry.

INTERNAL ANALYSIS

This analysis will depend upon figures shown in several financial exhibits, posted or calculated from three successive fiscal statements submitted by the debtor firm. The statements have been audited and were accompanied by unqualified opinions of a certified public accountant.

Ratio calculations have already been made for year one and year two. Using Figures 23–1 and 23–2, the credit executive can now obtain ratios for year three and enter them on the Financial Ratios comparison shown in Figure 23–3.

Current Ratio

The relationship between current assets and current liabilities is determined by dividing the current assets by the current liabilities:

$$\frac{\text{Current Assets}}{\text{Current Liabilities}} \quad \frac{139{,}915}{46{,}267} = 3.0 \text{ times}$$

Sometimes this ratio is spelled out in full as 3.0 to 1. The current ratio reveals that the short-term creditor has excellent coverage. However, a further test, the quick ratio, is required to determine the extent to which current assets are made up of cash or items that can quickly be converted to cash. The quality of receivables and the turnover of inventory are vital factors to consider.

Assets	Year One	Percent	Year Two	Percent	Year Three	Percent
Cash	$ 13,766	9.2	$ 13,168	8.5	$ 13,040	8.2
Accounts Receivable	30,933	20.7	33,567	21.6	36,564	23.0
Inventory	87,386	58.6	89,662	57.8	90,311	56.7
Current Assets	132,085	88.5	136,397	87.9	139,915	87.9
Fixed Assets	12,214	8.2	13,350	8.6	13,660	8.6
Miscellaneous Assets	1,501	1.0	1,628	1.1	1,532	0.9
Intangibles	100	0.1	100	0.1	100	0.1
Miscellaneous Receivables	1,307	0.9	1,427	0.9	1,360	0.8
Other Assets	2,019	1.3	2,181	1.4	2,678	1.7
Total Assets	$149,226	100.0	$155,083	100.0	$159,245	100.0
Liabilities and Stockholders' Equity						
Accounts Payable	$ 15,071	10.1	$ 21,387	13.8	$ 26,583	16.7
Due Banks	16,000	10.7	16,000	10.3	2,400	1.5
Federal Income Tax Payable	11,108	7.5	10,670	6.9	8,416	5.3
Accruals	5,242	3.5	5,468	3.5	5,868	3.7
Term Debt-Current	3,000	2.0	3,000	2.0	3,000	1.9
Current Liabilities	50,421	33.8	56,525	36.5	46,267	29.1
Term Debt-Deferred	24,000	16.1	21,000	13.5	33,000	20.7
Common Stock	33,200	22.2	33,200	21.4	33,200	20.8
Paid-In Surplus	7,943	5.3	7,940	5.1	7,940	5.0
Retained Earnings	33,662	22.6	36,418	23.5	38,838	24.4
Total Liabilities and Stockholders' Equity	$149,226	100.0	$155,083	100.0	$159,245	100.0
Quick Assets	$ 44,699		$ 46,735		$ 49,604	
Net Working Capital	81,644		79,872		93,648	
Tangible Net Worth	74,705		77,458		79,878	

FIG. 23–1. Comparative Balance Sheets.

Quick Ratio

By excluding inventory from the current assets, the credit executive is in a better position to evaluate the liquidity of the company. The quick ratio for this company is:

$$\frac{\text{Quick Assets}}{\text{Current Liabilities}} \quad \frac{49{,}604}{46{,}267} = 1.1 \text{ times}$$

This ratio reveals that the company has sufficient liquid assets to pay off short-term creditors without regard to the inventory turnover. Before a definite conclusion can be made, however, an evaluation of the accounts receivable is in order.

Inventory to Net Working Capital

This ratio offers an additional way to evaluate the balance of the current ratio position. It is obtained by dividing the inventory by the difference between the current assets and current liabilities:

	Year One	Percent	Year Two	Percent	Year Three	Percent
Net Sales	$433,074	100.0	$436,933	100.0	$460,997	100.0
Cost of Goods Sold	359,921	83.1	365,554	83.7	385,288	83.6
Gross Profit	73,153	16.9	71,379	16.3	75,709	16.4
Selling, General, and Administrative Expense	52,231	12.1	56,304	12.9	58,697	12.7
Depreciation and Amortization	788	0.2	923	0.2	1,009	0.2
Net Operating Income	20,134	4.6	14,152	3.2	16,003	3.5
Other Income	525	0.1	520	0.1	407	0.1
Other Expenses	1,100	0.2	1,426	0.3	1,479	0.3
Net Income Before Taxes	19,559	4.5	13,246	3.0	14,931	3.3
Federal Income Taxes	10,834	2.5	6,612	1.5	7,902	1.8
Net Income	8,725	2.0	6,634	1.5	7,029	1.5
Adjustments:						
Add Excess Allowance for Uncollectibles			955	0.2		
Deduct Prior Years' Income Taxes			225	0.0		
Net Income as Adjusted	8,725	2.0	7,364	1.7	7,029	1.5
Retained Earnings at Start	35,759		33,662		36,418	
Cash Dividends	4,635		4,608		4,609	
Stock Dividends	6,037					
Stock Redemption Premium	150					
Retained Earnings at End	$ 33,662		$ 36,418		$ 38,838	

FIG. 23–2.   Comparative Statements of Income and Retained Earnings.

	Year One	Year Two	Year Three
Current Ratio	2.6x	2.4x	3.0x
Quick Ratio	0.9x	0.8x	1.1x
Inventory to Net Working Capital	107.0%	112.3%	96.4%
Fixed Assets to Tangible Net Worth	16.3%	17.2%	17.1%
Total Noncurrent Assets to Total Capitalization	17.3%	19.0%	17.1%
Current Debt to Tangible Net Worth	67.5%	73.0%	57.9%
Total Debt to Tangible Net Worth	99.6%	100.1%	99.2%
Funded Debt to Net Working Capital	29.4%	26.3%	35.2%
Net Sales to Tangible Net Worth	5.8x	5.6x	5.8x
Net Sales to Total Assets	2.9x	2.8x	2.9x
Net Sales to Net Working Capital	5.3x	5.5x	4.9x
Net Sales to Inventory	5.0x	4.9x	5.1x
Net Sales to Accounts Receivable	14.0x	13.0x	12.6x
Gross Profit on Net Sales	16.9%	16.3%	16.4%
Net Income on Net Sales	2.0%	1.5%	1.5%
Net Operating Income on Net Sales	4.6%	3.2%	3.5%
Net Income on Net Working Capital	10.7%	8.3%	7.5%
Net Income on Tangible Net Worth	11.7%	8.6%	8.8%

FIG. 23–3.   Financial Ratios.

$$\frac{\text{Inventory}}{\text{Net Working Capital}} \quad \frac{90,311}{93,648} = .9644 \text{ or } 96.4\%$$

Since this ratio is less than 100 per cent, it shows that the company is able to finance its unsold inventory requirements out of net working capital. An overtrading situation or the presence of slow-moving inventory may keep the ratio high. Conversely, a low figure and a disproportionately large net working capital might indicate that the company is not carrying enough merchandise to meet its customer requirements.

Fixed Assets to Tangible Net Worth

This ratio relates the investment in plant and equipment to the stockholders' equity:

$$\frac{\text{Fixed Assets}}{\text{Tangible Net Worth}} \quad \frac{13,660}{79,878} = .1710 \text{ or } 17.1\%$$

The company has only a small percentage of its invested capital tied up in "bricks and mortar." This releases the funds for its daily cash needs. A small percentage might also mean that the company is not expanding its plant and equipment investment to meet the demands of new markets.

Total Noncurrent Assets to Total Capitalization

This ratio is significant to short-term credit grantors. It relates noncurrent assets to the total deferred debt and tangible net worth:

$$\frac{\text{Total Noncurrent Assets}}{\text{Total Capitalization}} \quad \frac{19,330}{112,878} = .1712 \text{ or } 17.1\%$$

This low ratio indicates that cash inflows from current assets are not being used to support the investment in noncurrent assets; this enhances the position of short-term creditors.

Current Debt to Tangible Net Worth

This ratio spotlights the interest of short-term creditors as against that of the owners:

$$\frac{\text{Current Debt}}{\text{Tangible Net Worth}} \quad \frac{46,267}{79,878} = .5792 \text{ or } 57.9\%$$

Short-term creditors are supporting the operations in reasonable alignment with the owners. If the ratio were disproportionately large, the organization might be overtrading or conducting a volume not easily supported by invested capital.

Total Debt to Tangible Net Worth

The figure is obtained by dividing total debt by tangible net worth:

$$\frac{\text{Total Debt}}{\text{Tangible Net Worth}} \quad \frac{79,267}{79,898} = .9921 \text{ or } 99.2\%$$

While the current debt to tangible net worth showed a reasonable alignment, the interest of creditors comes very close to that of stockholders. Creditors are supporting this operation to a greater extent than was first evident. It is usually better for long-term creditors if the debtor's ownership interest exceeds that of creditors. This facet is not as important to the short-term creditor, provided that a substantial part of the debt is long term and profits are sufficient to service and retire the long-term debt within the terms of the loan agreement. This generalization applies to most industrials; there are exceptions, notably utilities, which in large measure rely upon long-term borrowings.

Funded Debt to Net Working Capital

This measure reveals the extent to which liquidity is supported by long-term debt. The funds to pay long-term debt are usually derived from net profits, although the debt may be rolled over (new debt used to replace the old).

$$\frac{\text{Funded Debt}}{\text{Net Working Capital}} = \frac{33,000}{93,648} = .3524 \text{ or } 35.2\%$$

In this case, funded debt is a significant factor in financing the day-to-day operations. More than one-third of the net working capital is attributable to this source.

Net Sales to Tangible Net Worth

This figure reflects a company's success at turning over its capital investment:

$$\frac{\text{Net Sales}}{\text{Tangible Net Worth}} = \frac{460,997}{79,878} = 5.8 \text{ times}$$

This company turns its equity investment very actively and profitably by leveraging with funded debt.

Net Sales to Total Assets

This shows the turnover rate of total assets, indicating the efficiency with which all tangible assets are utilized in the business (intangibles of $100 are excluded):

$$\frac{\text{Net Sales}}{\text{Total Assets}} = \frac{460,997}{159,145} = 2.9 \text{ times}$$

Total tangible assets of this firm turn quite actively, since only a small portion of its assets are fixed and the others are in reasonable proportions.

Net Sales to Net Working Capital

This ratio indicates how effectively a company turns its operating funds:

$$\frac{\text{Net Sales}}{\text{Net Working Capital}} \quad \frac{460,997}{93,648} = 4.9 \text{ times}$$

Net working capital is turned at a good rate, with support given to it by funded debt.

Net Sales to Inventory

This relationship provides a guide to the condition of inventories by showing the number of times they are turned in the course of a year:

$$\frac{\text{Net Sales}}{\text{Inventory}} \quad \frac{460,997}{90,311} = 5.1 \text{ times}$$

If cost of goods sold is used instead of net sales, the calculation is:

$$\frac{\text{Cost of Goods Sold}}{\text{Inventory}} \quad \frac{385,288}{90,311} = 4.3 \text{ times}$$

In either case, the figures indicate a satisfactory turnover. Comparison with industry standards would give a clearer picture of how efficiently inventory is being turned.

Net Sales to Accounts Receivable

This ratio shows the firm's turnover of its accounts receivable investment. Its calculation is as follows:

$$\frac{\text{Net Sales}}{\text{Accounts Receivable}} \quad \frac{460,997}{36,564} = 12.6 \text{ times}$$

The rate of turnover can be converted to number of days sales carried in receivables by dividing it into 360 days:

$$\frac{360}{12.6} = 28.6 \text{ days}$$

This rate is very favorable, since it is in line with the 2/10, net 30 day terms offered by the company. This confirms that the company has a liquid financial condition.

Gross Profit on Net Sales

This ratio reflects the ability of the firm to compete, and it gauges how well the firm controls its material and labor costs.

$$\frac{\text{Gross Profit}}{\text{Net Sales}} \quad \frac{75,709}{460,997} = .1642 \text{ or } 16.4\%$$

The gross profit appears below acceptable standards. However, this can only be confirmed by examining the ratios prevailing in the industry.

Net Income on Net Sales

This ratio is important in determining profitability, since it reflects the extent to which all costs and expenses are controlled.

$$\frac{\text{Net Income}}{\text{Net Sales}} \quad \frac{7{,}029}{460{,}997} = .0152 \text{ or } 1.5\%$$

The net profit margin appears quite small. However, the industry in which a company operates determines its acceptability.

Net Operating Income on Net Sales

Many credit executives consider this ratio of great significance:

$$\frac{\text{Net Operating Income}}{\text{Net Sales}} \quad \frac{16{,}003}{460{,}997} = .0347 \text{ or } 3.5\%$$

It excludes factors over which operating management has no control and is said by many to give a more realistic figure for evaluating management.

Net Income on Net Working Capital

This measure is particularly useful when a company's operating funds are provided in large part by funded debt:

$$\frac{\text{Net Income}}{\text{Net Working Capital}} \quad \frac{7{,}029}{93{,}648} = .0751 \text{ or } 7.5\%$$

The company's return on net working capital is nearly as high as its return on tangible net worth. This is true of many companies that leverage their finances.

Net Income on Tangible Net Worth

This ratio measures the return that shareholders receive on their investment:

$$\frac{\text{Net Income}}{\text{Tangible Net Worth}} \quad \frac{7{,}029}{79{,}878} = .0880 \text{ or } 8.8\%$$

Despite the fact that the company has a low profit margin, its return on equity is good. This is due to the fact that the firm uses funded debt to leverage its equity position.

TREND ANALYSIS

A thorough trend analysis would require every item on the spread sheets to be scrutinized for its value over the three year period. In that way, significant changes may be highlighted and marked for additional inquiry. Figures 23–1, 23–2, and 23–3 are used for this analysis.

The initial step is a visual inspection of the spread sheets. This identifies the items requiring extra investigation. In the sample company, most items show no significant change. However, a few do stand out.

Accounts Receivable

These show a steady rise of close to 10 per cent each year. If the sales increase justifies this rise, there is no problem. Neither during year two nor year three, however, did sales increase at a 10 per cent rate; so the increased receivables must be due to slower turnover. This hypothesis can be confirmed by noting the decline in the turnover rate of receivables, from 14.0 for year one to 12.6 in year three.

Accounts Payable

There is a steady rise in accounts payable, which indicates increasing reliance on trade creditor financing.

Due Banks

This short-term liability decreased sharply, from $16,000 to $2,400, probably because of the greater emphasis on trade credit financing. Both accounts payable and bank loans are current liabilities; yet the ratio of current debt to tangible net worth decreased in year three, after a rise in year two. This would prompt the credit executive to look elsewhere for the reasons that the ratio decreased.

Term Debt-Deferred

If last year's schedule of retirement had been continued, this item would have been $18,000 in year three. Instead, it rose to $33,000, indicating new long-term financing had been used to pay short-term debt and provide operating capital.

Retained Earnings

Figure 23–2 shows net earnings for each year were partly retained in the business, while cash dividends were paid. Briefly, the components of Figure 23–2 showed rises in year three that followed the increased sales volume. It is questionable, however, whether these increases were as favorable as they might have been. A clearer view of the operating figures is given by the analysis of turnover rates and profit ratios given below.

Balance Sheet Ratios

Figure 23–3 shows that the balance sheet ratios had been moving unfavorably from year one to year two, but turned around significantly during year three. This is evident in the current ratio, which now stands at 3.0; in the quick ratio, which moved up to 1.1; and inventory to net working capital, which shows greater liquidity.

Two other ratios are particularly useful in explaining this marked improvement. Current debt to tangible net worth moved sharply downward from 73.0 per cent to 57.9 per cent. Meanwhile, funded debt to net working capital rose from 26.3 per cent to 35.2 per cent. These movements substantiate the earlier finding that the company has restructured its finances, substituting long-term debt for current liabilities.

Turnover Rates

Most of the turnover rates remained fairly level during the three years. One notable exception is net sales to net working capital. During year two, net working capital was inadequate and had to turn actively to support sales. In year three, however, bolstered by the added net working capital generated by the restructuring, this ratio showed a marked improvement.

Profit Ratios

The profit ratios give more detail on the finances. The key finding is that, despite the restructuring, net income on net sales did not improve in year three. Further, net operating income on net sales has declined sharply over the three-year period. This can be attributable to a decline in the gross profit on net sales and an increase in operating expenses.

Net income on tangible net worth dropped sharply in year two and has

Assets	Year Two	Year Three	Change	Source	Application
Cash	$ 13,168	$ 13,040	−128	$128	
Accounts Receivable	33,567	36,564	2,997		$ 2,997
Inventory	89,662	90,311	649		649
Current Assests	136,397	139,915			
Fixed Assets	13,350	13,660	310		310
Miscellaneous Assets	1,628	1,532	−96	96	
Intangibles	100	100	—		
Miscellaneous Receivables	1,427	1,360	−67	67	
Other Assets	2,181	2,678	497		497
Total Assets	$155,083	$159,245			
Liabilities and Stockholders' Equity					
Accounts Payable	$ 21,387	$ 26,583	5,196	5,196	
Due Banks	16,000	2,400	−13,600		13,600
Federal Income Tax Payable	10,670	8,416	−2,254		2,254
Accruals	5,468	5,868	400	400	
Term Debt-Current	3,000	3,000	—		
Current Liabilities	56,525	46,267			
Term Debt-Deferred	21,000	33,000	12,000	12,000	
Common Stock	33,200	33,200	—		
Paid-In Surplus	7,940	7,940	—		
Retained Earnings	36,418	38,838	2,420	2,420	
Total Liabilities and Stockholders' Equity	$155,083	$159,245		$20,307	$20,307

FIG. 23-4. Source and Application of Funds.

recovered minimally in year three. Meanwhile, net income on net working capital dropped in year two; with the infusion of net working capital in year three, it decreased even more.

Source and Application of Funds

The next step in the analysis calls for an examination of the source and application of funds, shown in Figure 23–4. This exhibit helps to trace the effects of profits retained or losses sustained by the firm.

Sources and applications of funds are collected under the appropriate columns in Figure 23–4. Thus the main applications are accounts receivable, due banks, and federal income tax payable. As sources, the main items are accounts payable, term debt-deferred, and retained earnings. The net effect of all transactions was to reduce cash slightly.

Changes in Net Working Capital

The difference between current assets and current liabilities was improved by $13,776 during year three (see Figure 23–5). The funds obtained from term debt were used to bolster the net working capital position. The schedule reveals that accounts receivable were increased by nearly $3,000

Source of Funds:	
Net Profit Retained	$ 2,420
Term Debt-Deferred	12,000
Miscellaneous Assets	96
Miscellaneous Receivables	67
	14,583
Application of Funds:	
Fixed Assets	310
Other Assets	497
	807
Increase in Net Working Capital	$13,776
Changes in Composition of Net Working Capital:	
Increase (Decrease) in Current Assets:	
Cash	$ (128)
Accounts Receivable	2,997
Inventory	649
	3,518
Decrease (Increase) in Current Liabilities:	
Accounts Payable	5,196
Due Banks	(13,600)
Federal Income Tax Payable	(2,254)
Accruals	400
	10,258
Increase in Net Working Capital	$13,776

FIG. 23–5. Changes in Net Working Capital.

and accounts payable were reduced by $5,196. But the greatest impact on the composition of net working capital was the $13,600 decrease in the current liability called due banks. Thus the overall effect was that long-term debt was substituted for short-term borrowing to improve the net working capital position of the firm.

OVERALL APPRAISAL

The current position of the sample company was good each year, with liquid assets approximating the current debt. The current ratio, quick ratio, and inventory to net working capital all showed improvement. In addition, cash is more than adequate to cover one month's operating expenses. The turnover of accounts receivable is good, since the firm sells on 2/10, n/30 day terms. Thus the company is not dependent upon the turnover of inventory to meet maturing obligations.

One area of weakness lies in the inventory position. It approximates net working capital and is turning an average of five times a year. Another is that total debt is almost equal to the tangible net worth.

Since fixed assets are relatively small, the firm relies upon funded debt to support day-to-day operations. This was attributable to the substitution of long-term debt for short-term borrowings. This is further supported by the sizable decrease in the ratio of current debt to tangible net worth and the large increase in the funded debt to net working capital.

With the improved net working capital position, the net income as a percentage of this item showed a decline, along with a decline in the net sales to net working capital. Both these ratios moved as expected, considering the larger base that is supporting the net income and net sales.

While sales have been increasing, the net income has not kept pace. This was caused in part by a decline in the gross profit percentage and an increase in the operating expenses. Both of these figures improved slightly in year three.

The overall appraisal shows that the sample company has improved its current financial position by converting a significant portion of the short-term borrowings into long-term debt. Future developments should be closely followed to determine if the company could improve its profitability and permit it to reduce its debt by retained profits rather than to improve its financial position by restructuring the debt.

CHAPTER 24

ADDITIONAL FINANCIAL ANALYSIS TECHNIQUES

The financial analysis may be held to a minimum for the strong, well-known, and obviously profitable customer. The need for additional techniques arises in analyzing marginal customers. Such firms may have tight net working capital, weak cash, low sales, poor profit records, and so forth. Their difficulties may be due to inadequate management analysis or planning, high costs, tough competition, very rapid or unbalanced growth, or any number of other factors. In situations of this kind, trial balance analysis and analysis by sales can be very helpful.

TRIAL BALANCE ANALYSIS

The transcending value of a trial balance lies in the fact that it supplies the interim financial details required for close following of marginal accounts. Decisions are more apt to be correct when based on facts as they exist at the time of the decision.

A trial balance is a listing of all the debit and credit balances in a firm's general ledger. Well-managed firms prepare trial balances on a quarterly or monthly basis. The chief benefit of the trial balance is its timeliness. Normally it takes two to four months to prepare audited financial statements. Inventories must be counted, accounts receivable and debts must be verified, and other adjustments and closings must be made. In the meanwhile, the trial balance figures for the year can give a close approximation of the financial condition and operating statement. During the year, when financial statements are not to be prepared, the trial balance enables the credit executive to inspect all accounts, except inventory. This item is carried over from the last balance sheet unless the firm utilizes a perpetual inventory system. Nor is the net worth figure current on a trial balance. It usually reflects the position at the date of the latest balance sheet. However, inventory can be estimated by methods described later in the chapter, and profits can thereby also be estimated.

Trial Balance Worksheet

Interpretation of the trial balance figures is facilitated when the data are set up in balance sheet and operating statement form. Since trial balances are an abstract of the general ledgers, they vary in the order and designation of items. Figure 24–1 shows a work sheet that is useful to classify the items before setting up the figures in balance sheet and operating statement form for analysis.

	Debit	Credit
Cash	$ 16,250	
Accounts Receivable	39,495	
Fixed Assets	13,660	
Miscellaneous Assets	1,630	
Intangibles	100	
Miscellaneous Receivables	1,390	
Other Assets	2,535	
Accounts Payable		$ 25,030
Due Banks		1,800
Accruals		5,373
Term Debt-Current		2,800
Term Debt-Deferred		32,570
Common Stock		33,200
Paid-In Surplus		7,940
Retained Earnings		38,838
Net Sales		124,672
Inventory (beginning)	90,311	
Purchases	46,732	
Labor	32,520	
Factory Overhead	11,548	
Selling Expenses	4,495	
General Expenses	5,475	
Administrative Expenses	6,082	
	$272,223	$272,223

FIG. 24–1.   Trial Balance as of End of 1st Quarter, Year Four.

The debit column shows the assets from the balance sheet and the expense items from the operating statement. The credit column lists the liabilities and capital account from the balance sheet, as well as the income items of the profit and loss schedule. Balance sheet items are shown at their status as of the trial balance date—except inventory and equity, which relate to the beginning of the trial balance period. The trial balance figures might not, however, reflect complete accruals, depreciation, and auditing adjustments that are usually made when the final fiscal statements are prepared.

Interpretation of Trial Balance Figures

Accounts normally shown on the balance sheet and operating statement (except inventory and net worth) can be compared directly with the last fiscal closing and with the trial balance for the corresponding period of the prior year. (For instance, March 31 of year two would be compared with December 31 of year one, and March 31 of year one.) In addition, certain relationships between the figures can be calculated and compared. The following examples show typical uses of trial balance figures.

1. Cash position can be compared directly against the fiscal closing to learn the net change in cash, and against the prior interim figure to offset seasonal factors in the changed cash position.

2. Accounts receivable can be compared with those of twelve months ago, and with sales for the current period. For instance, an increase in accounts receivable should be accompanied by an increase in sales. An increase in receivables while sales declined or remained steady would indicate a slowdown in the rate of collections, which could result from increased delinquency, a lengthening of sales terms, or a combination of both.

3. Fixed assets are best compared with the last fiscal closing. A normal amount of depreciation and asset replacement should be expected. If the net increase or decrease in fixed assets were out of line with expectations, it might indicate a major change in the company's use of financial resources. The evidence would be found in the balance sheet or the operating statement.

With rising fixed assets, higher depreciation charges would result. If the assets were purchased to meet additional production needs, sales might have increased. On the other hand, if sales had been declining because the company had been unable to meet production demands, new fixed assets may have been necessarily purchased. This would tend to reduce current assets and increase equipment obligations.

If fixed assets showed a marked decline, it may mean the company has sold some equipment and machinery. Production facilities may have exceeded normal demands and the management may have decided to sell its unused equipment. This would improve the company's liquidity and ability to carry receivables.

Or fixed assets may have been sold and leased back. A sale and leaseback is generally negotiated with a financing institution. Assets are sold, then immediately leased back. The topic is discussed in more detail in Chapter 27. The firm would show an improved financial condition, since fixed assets are removed from the balance sheet and replaced by current assets. In doing this, however, the firm contracts to make future rental payments for the duration of the lease; this may either increase or decrease profits, depending upon whether lease payments are greater or smaller than depreciation would have been. It will also affect cash flow, since it removes depreciation from the finances.

4. Accounts payable are compared with the fiscal close to learn the net change, and with the corresponding trial balance of last year to determine the change free of seasonal influences. A year-to-year increase in payables may indicate increased sales volume or slower retirement of trade debt. Conversely, a lower accounts payable balance may reflect lower inventory purchases or better trade payments.

Before a conclusion can be drawn as to the favorable or unfavorable nature of reduced payables, it is necessary to examine loans payable. The loans may be due to banks, relatives, or principals. An increase in these loans may offset a reduction in accounts payable. In that case there has been no major change in the liability position of the firm, since the loans were made to retire accounts payable and one type of liability was substituted for another. However, if the new debt is long term, the result is an increase in liquidity.

5. Current liabilities and total liabilities likewise can be compared with previous amounts to uncover changes in the financial condition. Seasonal trial balances can be expected to show current liability increases over fiscal closings, since the company would normally be at an interim stage of its production cycle. But large increases from the corresponding year-ago period should prompt an inquiry to find out if they are justified by increased sales.

Cash and accounts receivable are often compared with current obligations in the quick ratio. A relationship of about 1:1 indicates that cash and accounts receivable are sufficient to pay maturing bills.

6. Sales are examined for trend. Yearly figures are compared directly. Interim figures are compared with last year's fiscal results and with sales for the corresponding period of last year. This helps establish seasonal sales performance. In addition, trial balance sales figures can be compared with the earlier sales estimates of management to determine if those projections had been met, and if they were realistic.

7. Purchases are compared with those of the previous period. Fluctuations may be due to increasing or decreasing needs because of sales variations, early commitments which had to be honored, changes in purchasing policy requiring larger (or smaller) materials requirements to be kept on hand, and stricter (or more liberal) control over suppliers' delivery and invoice dates.

8. Selling, general, and administrative expenses are examined and compared with previous figures in order to identify major variations in expenditure patterns.

These are only some of the comparisons that can be made. The extent of trial balance questions depends on the credit executive's familiarity with the line of business, awareness of relative operating costs, and knowledge of trade conditions.

A succession of figures for comparable periods of previous years is helpful to the credit executive who is asked to help a customer establish an operating budget. Trial balances can also be used to check reports of the customer's income, expenses, and purchasing, and to confirm any other reports on operations that are being periodically submitted in connection with budgeted operations.

Break-Even Inventory Analysis

Another common use of trial balance figures is called break-even inventory analysis. This technique enables the credit executive to estimate the profit earned over the period by comparing a theoretical inventory which would have been on hand if operations had been at break even with an estimate of the inventory actually on hand at trial balance date. This may be explained by a series of statements.

1. Break-even operation implies that neither a profit was earned nor a loss incurred during the period. Consequently, there is no change in net worth. Thus the beginning net worth may be substituted for the net worth at trial balance date to prepare a break-even balance sheet. In the event that additional capital was invested or that capital was withdrawn from the business, appropriate adjustments would be made in the net worth shown in the trial balance.

2. The total of liabilities and net worth in the break-even balance sheet usually exceeds assets, since inventory is not included. The difference between the two figures is the amount of inventory which would bring the two sides of the statement into balance, assuming that operations were conducted without profit or loss. This figure is called inventory required to break even, or break-even inventory.

3. The break-even inventory may then be compared with an estimate of the inventory on hand to determine the profit or loss during the period. If the estimate is greater (lower) than the break-even inventory; the difference is equal to the probable profit (loss).

Figure 24–2 shows how the trial balance worksheet may be used to calculate the break-even inventory. The first set of figures is the trial balance. Asset, liability, and net worth items are posted to the balance sheet, while income and expense items are posted to the operating statement.

Since the inventory shown in the trial balance was on hand at the beginning of the period, it is charged to production and is posted to the operating statement. The inventory required to break even would be shown as a debit on the balance sheet and as a credit on the operating statement to balance the figures.

	Trial Balance		Balance Sheet		Operating Statement	
	Debit	Credit	Debit	Credit	Debit	Credit
Cash	$ 16,250		$ 16,250			
Accounts Receivable	39,495		39,495			
Fixed Assets	13,660		13,660			
Miscellaneous Assets	1,630		1,630			
Intangibles	100		100			
Miscellaneous Re- ceivables	1,390		1,390			
Other Assets	2,535		2,535			
Accounts Payable		$ 25,030		$ 25,030		
Due Banks		1,800		1,800		
Accruals		5,373		5,373		
Term Debt-Current		2,800		2,800		
Term Debt-Deferred		32,570		32,570		
Common Stock		33,200		33,200		
Paid-In Surplus		7,940		7,940		
Retained Earnings		38,838		38,838		
Net Sales		124,672				$124,672
Inventory (beginning)	90,311				$ 90,311	
Purchases	46,732				46,732	
Labor	32,520				32,520	
Factory Overhead	11,548				11,548	
Selling Expenses	4,495				4,495	
General Expenses	5,475				5,475	
Administrative Expenses	6,082				6,082	
	$272,223	$272,223	$ 75,060	$147,551	$197,163	$124,672
Inventory Re- quired to Break Even			72,491			72,491
			$147,551	$147,551	$197,163	$197,163

FIG. 24–2.   Break-Even Inventory Schedule.

Methods of Estimating Inventory

Once a break-even inventory figure has been established, the next task is to determine whether the inventory on hand exceeds, equals, or is less than that required to break even. The most accurate method is to make a physical count of raw materials, work in process, and finished goods. Good accounting practice requires this to be done at least once a year. In addition, though several methods are used to estimate the value of inventory. While every method has some shortcomings, they are used because they provide quick and convenient means to obtain a figure.

Perpetual Inventory Records.   Many companies maintain a perpetual inventory control as part of their cost accounting systems. A record is kept of all materials coming into a plant and of all merchandise leaving it. The net balance is therefore always current. By referring to inventory control records, the accountant or manager can obtain a close estimate of inventory actually on hand at any time. That figure can easily be added to the trial balance figures.

Perpetual records provide much additional information about the inventory. An exact physical amount is recorded at all times and can be converted to dollar figures for financial analysis. Together with detailed work tickets and job orders, the records provide a precise breakdown by stage of production of all inventories on hand. In addition, they help determine the profitability of specific products.

Despite the apparent precision of perpetual inventory records, a physical count should be taken at least once each year as a check against discrepancies:

1. The clerk making the entries (either in or out) may have made a mistake.
2. An original error in a supplier's invoice may have been carried over to the inventory records.
3. Changes in the price or cost of inventory may have been overlooked.
4. Inventory may have been charged out by mistake.
5. Actual inventory may shrink because of theft, pilferage, spoilage, and other causes.

Visible Estimates. This is a much cruder method. The manager makes a visual examination of inventory and places a dollar value on it, or estimates the physical amount of each class of inventory and converts them to dollar equivalents. The method is subject to large errors of estimation. In addition, the credit executive should question the objectivity of the estimate made by the firm's manager.

Gross Profit Percentage. A third method extends known operating statement information to estimate the missing figure, inventory. In this method, it is assumed that gross profit percentage has not changed since the last audited figures. That percentage is applied to the known net sales for the trial balance period and a gross profit is estimated. The difference between net sales and gross profit is the cost of goods sold.

Now that cost of goods sold is known, the next step is to fill in the trial balance figures for beginning inventory, purchases, labor, and factory overhead. The difference between that sum and cost of goods sold is equal to the estimated inventory on hand.

Selling, general, and administrative expenses are then deducted from the gross profit, and operating profit is estimated. The value is, of course, subject to taxes and accruals.

The calculations for the sample company are shown in Figure 24–3. Gross profit on net sales for year three was 16.4 per cent. That figure is

Net Sales		$124,672	100.0%
Inventory at Beginning Period	$ 90,311		
Purchases	46,732		
Labor	32,520		
Factory Overhead	11,548		
	181,111		
Estimated Inventory on Hand	76,885		
Cost of Goods Sold		104,226	83.6
Gross Profit		20,446	16.4
Selling, General, and Administrative Expenses		16,052	12.9
Estimated Operating Profit		$ 4,394	3.5%

FIG. 24–3.   Estimating Inventory by Gross Profit Percentage Method.

applied to net sales of $124,672 transacted during the trial balance period, and gross profit is calculated. From there, the procedure is a straight forward transfer of figures from the trial balance.

Evaluation of Trial Balance Analysis

A caution is in order regarding the use of trial balance figures in credit analysis. Usually they omit certain liabilities. For instance, withholding taxes and estimated income tax for the trial balance period may not be indicated. In an organization operating very profitably, the tax liability could assume considerable proportions. Also, a trial balance may not contain a liability covering inventory in transit; this could be a sizable amount.

Accounts payable are not normally confirmed with creditors when a trial balance is prepared and certain inaccuracies may arise in this item. The company may have taken deductions which will not be allowed by the creditor. The reverse situation could exist in accounts receivable. A debtor might have taken a deduction which is not reflected in the company's accounts receivable; this would overstate the receivables.

Despite these limitations, a trial balance that is properly adjusted puts the user in a position to make more valid judgments. The skillful credit executive may determine the following facts by a careful review of a trial balance:

1. Liquidity—the coverage afforded current indebtedness by the total of cash, receivables, and government securities.
2. Amount of inventory necessary to break even.
3. Purchases as contrasted with payables.
4. Percentages of expenses to sales.
5. Percentage of return on gross volume.

Trial balance analysis is a useful credit management tool in all industries but has particular application in lines with high volatility. Drastic changes in condition can occur in very brief periods and this danger makes trial balance analysis a necessity.

ANALYSIS BY SALES

In undertaking analysis by sales, the place that sales have in the internal cycle of a business should be continually kept in mind. Business income flows from merchandise into receivables, from receivables into cash, and from cash back into merchandise. Merchandise is accumulated in keeping with an expected sales demand, receivables rise and fall with the flow of sales, and cash fluctuates with the income from sales and the disbursements made to create or replenish the merchandise.

It is important to note that analysis by sales assumes that sales remain relatively constant from one period to the next, and that expenditures during the period under review are made in the same proportion as they were in the previous period. The influence of sales on plant, machinery, fixtures, and other noncurrent assets can also be traced, but this discussion will concentrate on the quick, or trading assets, and current liabilities.

The direct objective in analysis by sales is to transpose the monetary value of statement items into periods representing the length of trading time of each item:

1. The period of time represented by accounts receivable, also called turnover period, will indicate whether customers are paying promptly; the probability that old, or unusual accounts, have been included in receivables; whether receivables are being hypothecated; or if selling terms have been lengthened.

2. The period of time required to move the merchandise on hand will indicate whether the inventory represents a normal supply, or is disproportionately large or small.

3. The period of time required to liquidate the indebtedness for merchandise.

Elements of Sales

The income of a concern is distributed in many directions. It is used to pay for merchandise, meet payrolls, pay rent and taxes, and take care of the many other debts. For analysis by sales, these disbursements are placed into three groups called elements of sales: materials costs, manufacturing costs, and expenses and profits. While technically profit is an element distinct from others, its percentage to net sales is usually small (2 to 5 per cent); consequently, it is grouped with expenses to simplify the analysis.

These elements of sales vary in themselves and in their respective size, depending on the method of operation and activity of a concern. There are elements in the sales of a manufacturer that are not present in the sales of a wholesaler. In the former case, cost of material might take up about half of the sales income; in the latter, it might be all but a minor fraction of the sales. Overall, the cost of material in each dollar of sales is least in manufacturing, greater in retailing, and largest in wholesaling. Conversely, the wholesaler can use the greatest part of sales income to pay merchandise bills or bank debt incurred to finance this purchasing; the retailer has a lesser part available for this purpose; while the manufacturer has an even smaller share of income available to pay these external debts.

It should be kept in mind that labor costs and other expenses have first call on sales income and that trade bills and bank debts are paid only after such internal charges have been met. For this reason it is extremely important to break down sales into elements of expenses and other charges when analyzing the ability of a concern to pay obligations.

Procedure for Manufacturers

Each current asset contains some or all of the elements for sale. The analysis is made easier when inventory is divided into raw materials, goods in process, and finished goods.

Raw Materials. The cost of raw materials charged to production is equal to purchases for the period, plus inventory on hand at the beginning, less inventory on hand at the close. A basic assumption is made that manufacturing costs, or direct labor and factory overhead, included in the beginning inventory are offset by those contained in the ending inventory.

Once the cost of raw materials charged to production has been determined, it is divided by the number of months in the period to calculate one month's consumption of raw materials. The balance sheet figure for raw materials is then divided by the figure for one month's consumption to indicate how long the raw materials will last. Usually the figures are calculated on an annual basis.

Goods in Process. Since there is no way to examine a balance sheet and determine the stage of completion of goods in process, all such inventories are arbitrarily assumed to be half-finished. Thus one month's supply of goods in process consists of one month's raw materials plus one-half month's manufacturing costs. The annual manufacturing costs are shown in the operating statement.

When one month's supply of goods in process is obtained, it is divided into the inventory of goods in process to determine how many months of goods in process are on hand.

Finished Goods. Finished merchandise is usually valued on the basis of cost of material plus direct labor and factory overhead, exclusive of selling costs and profits. Administrative and general expenses are disregarded. One month's supply of finished goods will consist of one month's cost of raw materials plus manufacturing costs. When finished merchandise is divided by this figure, the number of months supply is determined.

Total Inventory. Adding the number of months supply in raw materials, goods in process, and finished goods will give the number of months' sales represented in inventory if average monthly sales continue at the same rate.

Receivables for Merchandise. As a first step, all receivables sold with recourse must be added back to the receivables listed on the balance sheet. One month's average sales are then divided into total receivables to establish the number of months receivables on the books.

Current Liabilities. These include accounts and notes payable for merchandise, bank debts, and all other obligations maturing within one year. All must be paid out of current income, and the procedure for aging any of them is identical.

As stated before, sales income is used to pay manufacturing costs and other internal charges before external liabilities such as trade bills and bank debt. Only the portion of income equal to materials costs can be used to pay these external debts. Thus materials cost elements of sales reduced to a monthly average and then divided into accounts payable will give the number of months needed to liquidate that liability. An adjustment should be made for size of cash position; excess cash over normal requirements (one month's manufacturing costs and expenses combined) should be deducted before current debt is analyzed.

Procedure for Wholesalers and Retailers

The elements of sales of the wholesaler and the retailer are also used to reduce their respective statement items into terms of trading time. Although the procedure is the same as for the manufacturer, certain qualifications are important. These concerns do no manufacturing, so the elements of their sales do not include manufacturing costs. Accordingly, the entire inventory in the statement is in finished goods and includes no manufacturing or conversion cost. Therefore, the process employed for raw materials of manufacturers is used to age the entire inventory of wholesalers and retailers.

The combination of cash and credit sales is peculiar to the retailer. Consequently, the retailer's receivables cannot be properly aged unless the amount of cash business has first been deducted from total sales. The residue, the sales on credit, can then be reduced to a monthly average and the usual procedure followed to determine the number of months receivables on the books.

Application of Analysis by Sales

This technique will be illustrated using fiscal data of year three for the sample company. They are taken from Figures 23–1 and 23–2 to prepare Figure 24–4. It is assumed that the breakdown of inventory and cost of goods sold was obtained from a footnote to the statements of year three.

Calculating Elements of Sales. The first step is to break down net sales of $460,997 into its elements and calculate monthly averages.

Current Assets:			Net Sales	$460,997
Cash		$ 13,040	Inventory-beginning	89,662
Accounts Receivable		-36,564	Purchases	194,412
Inventory:			Direct Labor	136,243
Raw Materials	$31,308		Factory Overhead	55,282
Goods in Process	13,847			475,599
Finished Goods	45,156	90,311	Inventory-ending	90,311
Total Current Assets		$139,915	Cost of Goods Sold	385,288
Current Liabilities:			Gross Profit	75,709
Accounts Payable		$ 26,583	Total Expenses	59,706
Due Banks		2,400	Net Operating Profit	16,003
Taxes Payable		8,416	Other Expenses & Taxes	8,974
Accruals		5,868	Net Income	$ 7,029
Term Debt-Current		3,000		
		$ 46,267		

FIG. 24–4.   Selected Figures for Analysis by Sales.

Aging of Items. Monthly averages in the right-hand column are used to age the balance sheet items:

Elements of Sales	12-Month Basis	Monthly Average
Materials Costs*	$193,763	$16,147
Manufacturing Costs**	191,525	15,960
Expenses and Profit***	75,709	6,309
Net Sales	$460,997	$38,416

* Materials costs equal inventory at the start of $89,662, plus purchases of $194,412, less inventory at the end of $90,311.

** Manufacturing costs represent the sum of direct labor and factory overhead.

*** Expenses and profit are equivalent of the total expenses and net operating profit.

Cash. This should normally be sufficient for one month's internal expenses. Average monthly outlay for manufacturing costs is $15,960 and for expenses $6,309. Cash of $13,040 is almost 60 per cent of the sum of these figures. Consequently, there is no excess cash to be deducted from accounts payable in determining if trade creditors will be paid on time.

Receivables. One month's average sales amount to $38,416. When outstanding receivables of $36,564 are divided by this figure, the result indicates that .95 months average sales are on the books.

Inventory of Merchandise. Inventory is aged according to completion stage.

Raw Materials. This item is $31,308 on the balance sheet. To obtain the average month's supply on hand, it is divided by the $16,147 monthly average of materials costs to equal 1.94 months supply.

Goods in Process. One month's supply of goods in process is equal to

$16,147 raw materials plus one-half month's supply of manufacturing costs for a total of $24,127. Divided into $13,847, this gives 0.57 months supply of goods in process on hand.

Finished Goods. This balance sheet item of $45,156 is divided by $32,107, the sum of the average materials costs and the average manufacturing costs, to show 1.41 months supply of finished goods.

Total Inventory. This is the sum of the above calculations:

	Average Month's Supply
Raw Materials	1.94
Goods in Process	0.57
Finished Goods	1.41
Total	3.92

Accounts Payable. Since manufacturing costs and expenses and profit have first call on sales income, they have to be deducted:

Average Income from Monthly Sales		$38,416
Less Manufacturing Costs	$15,960	
Expenses and Profit	6,309	22,269
Left to Pay Accounts Payable		$16,147

The balance sheet shows that accounts payable total $26,583; divided by the $16,147 left to pay accounts payable, it shows that 1.65 months must pass before trade bills are paid. Other current liabilities would be worked the same way. For instance, the item due banks $2,400, divided by the $16,147, gives .15 as the number of months that must pass before the bank loan can be paid by the residual cash. For taxes payable, it is .52 months; for accruals, .36; and for term debt-current, .19. When all have been calculated, they are summed to understand how current liabilities compare against income from sales. In this example, current liabilities represent 2.87 months of cash generation after making provision for paying manufacturing costs and expenses and profits.

Analysis by Sales Without Operating Statement Details

When actual figures cannot be obtained from an operating statement of the concern, average percentages established for that type of activity can be used as the ratios for the elements of sales. Tables of these average percentages are published or can be computed from surveys which show the costs of doing business in various lines. The technique is illustrated below—the yearend statement is that of a jobber with sales of $600,000 for the year covered by the figures.

Cash	$ 20,000	Trade Debt	$130,000
Receivables	100,000	Bank Debt	15,000
Merchandise	200,000		
Current Assets	$320,000	Current Debts	$145,000

Through experience or by consulting surveys, the credit executive knows that expenses in this type of operation usually are 15 per cent of sales. A jobber has no manufacturing costs. The elements of sales can then be readily computed as follows:

		Annual	Monthly Average
Merchandise Costs (computed)..	85%	$510,000	$42,500
Manufacturing Costs	0	0	0.
Expenses and Profits	15	90,000	7,500
Net Sales	100%	$600,000	$50,000

On the basis of the monthly averages, it is apparent that cash covers monthly expenses better than 2.5 times ($20,000 ÷ 7,500), but probably is being accumulated to pay off the bank debt. The size of the trade debt indicates a pressing need to use some of this cash. About 3.1 months of average income are needed to pay the suppliers ($130,000 ÷ $42,500). Receivables average two months sales ($100,000 ÷ $50,000), and inventory represents a 4.7 months supply ($200,000 ÷ $42,500).

Evaluation of Analysis by Sales

While analysis by sales is a useful tool which the credit executive may employ in reaching a decision, it is subject to definite shortcomings. Before a valid conclusion can be drawn, the following factors must be taken into consideration:

1. Seasonal factors are not taken into account. This would be more significant in some industries than in others.
2. Sales are seldom the same from one year to the next. Contemplated increases or decreases would have to be viewed in line with the conditions in the industry.
3. Expenditures for possible capital imporvements have to be evaluated for their impact on cash balances.
4. Available borrowing and unused bank lines should be factored in when paying ability is being analyzed.

PART VI

TRADE AND
NONTRADE FINANCING

CHAPTER 25

TERMS OF SALE

Arrangements between buyer and seller that specify the conditions required in payment for goods or services are known as terms of sale. They indicate if credit is to be part of the sales transaction, the length of time for which credit is to be extended, and other features such as discounts. Since most business transactions in the United States involve a title transfer prior to the requirements of payment from the purchaser, terms of sale play an important role in financing the growth of a business enterprise.

ROLE OF TERMS OF SALE

Terms of sale, also referred to as credit terms, selling terms, or payment terms, are concerned solely with the payment aspects of the sale. It is important to distinguish them from other provisions of sales contracts, such as warranties, delivery guaranties, and cancellation privileges. These provisions, more commonly described as conditions of sale, are not within the scope of business credit.

Terms of sale are an integral part of each sales contract and, like the price, require agreement by both buyer and seller. It is the seller's prerogative to set terms for its products. If the buyer's purchase order stipulates different payment arrangements, the seller can refuse the order or the matter can be negotiated. If any departure from the terms regularly employed for the sale of a product is contemplated, the seller should be fully aware of the provisions of the Robinson-Patman Act regarding discrimination in terms of sales. The particular facts of unusual situations should be carefully studied and the advice of counsel obtained. Special terms should be offered only in unusual circumstances, and the supplier should insist that the customer meet regular terms as soon as possible.

In order to avoid misunderstanding between buyer and seller, it is desirable for companies to include credit terms on important documents relating to the transaction, such as price lists, purchase orders, sales contracts, and the invoice itself.

It is important to stress that the terms of sale must be individually arrived at without collusion or conspiracy or else a violation of the antitrust laws can occur.

FACTORS INFLUENCING TERMS OF SALE

Once terms of sale are established, they are quite slow to change. Since terms of sale have both marketing and cost aspects, it is important that decisions related to establishing or changing terms for an individual company be made jointly by the company's sales and financial management. Terms also vary widely according to products and marketing situations within the same industry. These dissimilarities are in the broadest sense a reflection of competition and market and product characteristics.

Competition

A company that contemplates offering terms to all of its customers that differ significantly from standard terms for its product line or from terms of competitors must weigh the competitive aspects and the ultimate influence on profits. Unless the product holds a large share of the market or is priced much lower than competing items, short terms can divert business to competitors that offer less stringent arrangements. Conversely, while unusually long terms may help build sales, they produce higher costs, greater capital investment and cost of carrying accounts receivable, higher collection expenses, heavier losses from bad debts, and reduced margins of profit. Any competitive advantage may be only temporary, since it can lead competitors to offer other inducements to the same customers.

Longer terms place the burden of financing the transaction upon the seller. For the same reason, buyers seek longer credit terms or larger cash discounts. Payment arrangements balance these opposing interests. Basically, therefore, terms of sale are an element much like prices in the overall competitive scene. Uniformity of terms within an industry minimizes their competitive aspects, but even under these circumstances a change in competitive conditions is likely to produce changes in terms. For instance, during a buyer's market there is a tendency to offer longer terms as an inducement to buy. Conversely, terms may be expected to shorten when demand for materials exceeds their availability.

Market and Product Characteristics

These range widely in impact and complexity, from production time to physical characteristics of raw materials. Principal factors are discussed briefly below.

Operations Cycle. It is commonly believed that terms should coincide with the length of time it takes a customer to process the material, sell it, and collect the funds. In practice, however, a portion of the customer's operations cycle is usually funded by its own capital. If selling terms are shorter than the customer's cycle, the supplier is said to have a favorable spread; if longer, then the buyer is said to have the advantage. In the latter case, for instance, suppliers could be furnishing a disproportionate share of the funding for a customer that buys on long terms and sells on short terms.

Raw Materials. Basic materials are sold to manufacturers on shorter terms than intermediate or finished goods, apparently because of the short period of time raw materials retain their original form in the hands of the manufacturer. Terms rarely exceed the normal manufacturing cycle and storage time. Chemical products, such as agricultural oils and minerals, are normally sold on longer terms than their raw components. Likewise, in the textile industry, cotton greige goods frequently call for shorter terms than the finished fabrics and garments.

Perishability. Perishable items have a short shelf life, rapid turnover rate, and short selling terms. Meats, fresh vegetables, and dairy products fit this category. Less perishable foods, such as canned goods and manufactured or processed foods products, have a longer turnover period, since they can be stocked in larger quantities by the retailer. They are sold on longer terms.

Seasonal Demand. Merchandise having a seasonal demand often carries longer terms during the off season than during the active period. For instance, accounts receivable generated from the sale of toys build up during the year in contemplation of the Christmas season. The supplier finances a great portion of the buyer's needs, but maintains steadier production levels during the year and reduces storage problems that would have been created by large preseason stocks.

Consumer Acceptance. Goods protected by trademarks enjoy widespread consumer acceptance and frequently turn more rapidly than unknown brands. This difference is often reflected in shorter terms for the more popular product.

Cost. Relatively inexpensive items tend to be sold on shorter terms than more costly products. Thus terms for drug items are shorter than terms for floor coverings and many furniture items. Diamonds and expensive jewelry, which generally have a longer operations cycle than any of the above products, are purchased by retailers on terms that range from four to six months.

Type of Customer. For a given product, companies often employ different terms for different types of customers. Retailers may receive one set of terms, jobbers another, and institutional buyers still another. Paint manufacturers, for example, grant longer terms to retailers than to industrial accounts purchasing for use rather than resale.

Profitability. Higher profit margins can support longer terms than low margins, and selling terms may take this factor into consideration. In practice, however, competition may nullify this principle by forcing a seller to offer longer terms in lines where depressed prices yield little or no profit.

ELEMENTS OF SELLING TERMS

Terms of sale are the basis of which the buyer and the seller come together. They are made up of many factors, some of which are similar from industry to industry and some of which are different. In application they represent a commitment of funds by the seller. They should therefore be carefully understood.

Maturity

This is the length of time allowed for payment of the face amount of the invoice. Also called the credit period, or net credit period, it is usually computed from the date of the invoice, although in a few industries it is computed from the date the goods are received by the customer. In the common sales terms which call for payment in 30 days with a 1% discount offered for payment in 10 days (abbreviated 1% 10, net 30), the net credit period is 30 days.

Cash Discount

The cash discount is an inducement for the purchaser to pay ahead of maturity. It is a deduction allowed from the invoice amount if the customer pays within a specified period of time. It is usually expressed as a percentage but can also be stated as a dollar amount. In the example above, terms of 1% 10, net 30 allow the customer to deduct 1 per cent from the face amount if the invoice is paid within 10 days. The discount rate is 1 per cent and the discount period, 10 days.

Credit executives disagree on the economic justification of cash discounts. The practice is staunchly defended by some, but regarded by others as an economic anachronism. The fact that the question arises so frequently indicates doubt that the cash discount accomplishes its purpose, to speed cash inflows to the seller. Nevertheless, the use of cash discount terms is firmly established.

Turnover of Funds. Assuming that a majority of customers pay on discount terms, the seller may expect a quicker turn of funds, with reduced net working capital requirements, reduced credit and collection expenses, and reduced delinquencies and credit losses.

Some disclaim these advantages, asserting that prompt payments are at least partly a matter of habit or fulfillment of agreement on terms. This presumes that collections would be as prompt on terms of net 10 days as on 1% 10, net 30 days. This assumption may be valid if the seller's customers are all strong financially and if competitors sell on similar terms. As a practical matter, however, most credit executives would agree that the offering of cash discounts does shorten the average collection period. This can be a very real advantage to the concern that has exhausted most of its possible sources of financing and has a strong need for faster turnover of its accounts.

Administration.   Once discount terms are established, customers will try to take unearned discounts by deducting them from payments made beyond the prescribed discount period. Administration of discount terms thus presents a major problem in customer relationships. If cash discounts are to serve their purpose, the seller must not allow unearned discounts; they can be an important influence on seller's costs, and therefore on profits.

Strict administration of discount terms may cause customers to charge that they are being penalized if there is no allowance for mail time, transportation time, and other delays. Correspondence between buyer and seller over these matters is costly and often impairs good sales relationships.

Practices in regard to enforcing discount terms vary widely, but most allow only a few days' grace beyond the discount period and do not allow unearned discount. Many companies charge back unearned discounts, although some actually return the customer's check as not acceptable.

Cost of Capital.   In every firm, all assets are allocated in the expectation that they will yield a return. Unless this return is at least equal to the cost of capital of the invested assets, that particular allocation will have a negative effect on overall yield. A seller firm should be aware of the relationship between what it is giving up and what it is gaining when it offers a cash discount. On the one hand, it gives up the dollar amount of the discount. On the other hand, it gains a number of days use of the funds collected early; if, for example, the discount period is 10 days and the invoice matures in 30, the seller gains 20 days use of funds collected during the discount period.

Most firms will show a difference between the funds given up and those gained. This is so because of the discrepancy between the cost of capital rate and the rate of the discount offered. At some point, however, the cost of capital can be high enough so the dollars lost by giving a discount will be recovered because of early collections. The rate at which this will occur may be called the indifference rate—it will literally make no difference whether customers take the discount or pay at maturity.

The indifference rate of cost of capital is equivalent to the rate of the discount offered. For terms of 2% 10, net 30 it may be calculated as follows:

$$\text{Indifference Rate or Equivalent Rate of Discount Offered} = \frac{\text{Discount Rate} \times 360}{\text{Number of Days Saved}}$$

$$= \frac{.02 \times 360}{20}$$

$$= .36 \text{ or } 36\% \text{ per annum}$$

What this calculation points out is that the seller firm's cost of capital would have to reach 36 per cent before the seller became indifferent as to whether customers pay at discount or at maturity. Only then should the seller be willing to accept a 2 per cent reduction in the face amount of billings as a tradeoff for the extra 20 days use of funds.

This may be further illustrated by using Figure 25–1 which shows equivalent rates of various cash discount terms. This figure enables a seller to determine the indifference rate for specified cash discount terms.

Cash Discount Percent (X%)	Cash Discount Terms					
	X% 15 Net 30 Days	X% 10 Net 30 Days	X% 30 Net 60 Days	X% 15 Net 60 Days	X% 10 Net 60 Days	X% 30 Net 90 Days
½	12%	9%	6%	4%	3.6%	3%
1	24	18	12	8	7.2	6
1½	36	27	18	12	10.8	9
2	48	36	24	16	14.4	12
2½	60	45	30	20	18.0	15
3	72	54	36	24	21.6	18
3½	84	63	42	28	25.2	21
4	96	72	48	32	28.8	24
4½	108	81	54	36	32.4	27
5	120	90	60	40	36.0	30

FIG. 25–1.　Table of Equivalent Rates of Various Cash Discount Terms.

The first column lists the various cash discount percentages, ranging from ½ per cent to 5 per cent. Various terms are shown in the remaining six column headings. Below each is the cash discount equivalent annualized rate for that set of terms. For example, under terms of ½% 15, net 30 days the equivalent annualized rate is 12 per cent; with 1% 15, net 30, the rate is annualized at 24 per cent; and so on. The same procedure is used for the other columns.

The table may be used to locate those cash discount rates which equal the cost of capital. A seller with a cost of capital of 18 per cent per annum can note the following corresponding term equivalents: under terms of X% 15, net 30 days, the equivalent rate falls between ½ and 1 per cent, or ¾ per cent; under X% 10, net 30 days the equivalent rate is 1 per cent; under X% 30, net 60 days it is 1½ per cent; under X% 15, net 60 days the rate falls between 2 and 2½ per cent, or 2¼ per cent; under terms of X% 10, net 60 days it is 2½ per cent; and under X% 30, net 90 days the rate is 3 per cent.

Trade Discount

Allowances to purchasers because of the line of business and for quantity purchases are known as trade discounts. They should not be confused with the cash discount, since trade discounts bear no relationship to time of payment and may be deducted regardless of when the bill is paid.

Two separate trade discounts are sometimes offered, one for being in the trade and another for quantity purchases. Thus trade discounts of 20 per cent and 10 per cent might be offered by a manufacturer to a dealer (20 per cent) that buys in large quantities (10 per cent).

Trade discounts may be given in addition to regular cash discounts. If the selling terms are so arranged, the above dealer, for example, might take three discounts: 20 per cent and 10 per cent in trade discounts, and 2 per cent cash discount.

The Robinson-Patman Act prohibits quantity discounts unless such discounts can be justified by cost differences to the manufacturer. In addition, trade discounts are allowed only to purchasers at a different distribution level. That is, manufacturers may offer trade discounts to wholesalers or retailers; wholesalers to retailers; and so on.

Chain discounts, or successive discounts from the original price, are a form of trade discount. Manually, the calculation is made by successively applying the discounts to the quoted price. Thus terms of 10 per cent and 5 per cent on a $100 invoice would allow a 10 per cent reduction of $100, then a 5 per cent reduction of the remaining $90, for a net due of $85.50. The computation of these discounts can be simplified by the use of the table in Figure 25–2. It shows the single discount equivalents of a number of chain discounts.

To use the table, first find the combination of discounts quoted. The order in which discounts are to be taken is immaterial, as noted in the tables. To find the total discount, multiply the gross invoice amount by the figure shown under "decimal equivalent." To find the net amount, multiply the gross amount by the figure under "multiplier." For example, a $10,000 order is offered with a discount of 5-2½ per cent. The decimal equivalent is .074 while the multiplier is .926. The total discount is $10,000 multiplied by .074, or $740; the net amount is $10,000 multiplied by .926, or $9,260.

Anticipation

In some industries it is customary to allow anticipation, a deduction from the amount due, for payment before the final due date. Anticipation is figured in the same way as interest, usually geared to the prime rate, for the number of days from the date of payment to the due date.

Computation. Anticipation is based on either a 360- or 365-day year, depending on general industry practice and the terms of sale. With net terms, such as net 60 days, anticipation is allowed for payment at any time before the due date. When terms include a cash discount period and a longer net period, such as 2% 10, net 60, anticipation applies only to payments made after the cash discount period and before the final due date. In both cases anticipation is computed on the gross amount of the invoice. For example, an invoice for $1,470 dated May 2 is paid on June 20. Terms of sale are 2% 10, net 60. The cash discount period has expired, but antici-

Discount	Decimal Equivalent	1.—Decimal Equivalent or the Multiplier	Discount	Decimal Equivalent	1.—Decimal Equivalent or the Multiplier	Discount	Decimal Equivalent	1.—Decimal Equivalent or the Multiplier
2½	.025	.975	40-10-6	.493	.507	50-15-10-5	.637	.363
5-2½	.074	.926	40-10-7½	.501	.499	50-15-10-5-5	.655	.345
5-5	.098	.902	40-10-7½-5	.525	.475	50-16⅔	.583	.417
10-2½	.123	.877	40-10-10	.514	.486	50-16⅔-5	.604	.396
10-5	.145	.855	40-10-10-5	.538	.462	50-20-5	.62	.38
10-5-2½	.167	.833	40-10-10-10	.563	.437	50-20-10	.64	.36
10-10	.19	.81	40-10-10-10-5	.584	.416	50-25	.625	.375
10-10-2½	.211	.789	40-10-12½	.528	.472	52½	.525	.475
10-10-5	.231	.769	40-10-16⅔	.55	.45	52½-10	.573	.427
10-10-5½	.2345	.7655	40-10-16⅔-5	.573	.427	52½-10-16⅔	.644	.356
10-10-7	.247	.753	40-12½	.475	.525	55-5	.573	.427
10-10-10	.271	.729	40-15	.49	.51	55-10	.595	.405
10-10-10-5	.308	.692	40-15-5	.515	.485	55-10-10	.636	.364
10-10-10-5-2½	.325	.675	40-16⅔	.50	.50	60-5	.62	.38
10-10-7-15	.359	.641	40-16⅔-5	.525	.475	60-5-5	.639	.361
10-10-10-10	.344	.656	42½	.425	.575	60-5-10	.658	.342
10-10-10-10-5	.377	.623	42½-10	.483	.517	60-10	.64	.36
10-10-10-10-10	.41	.59	42½-10-16⅔	.569	.431	60-10-5	.658	.342
12½	.125	.875	45-5	.478	.522	60-10-5-5	.675	.325
12½-2½	.147	.853	45-10	.505	.495	60-10-10	.676	.324
12½-5	.169	.831	45-10-5	.529	.471	60-10-10-5	.692	.308
12½-10	.213	787	45-10-10	.555	.445	60-10-15-5	.71	.29
15-2½	.172	.828	45-10-10-5	.577	.423	60-15-5	.677	.323
15-5	.193	.807	45-10-10-10	.599	.401	60-20-5	.696	.304
15-10	.235	.765	45-10-10-10-5	.619	.381	60-20-15	.728	.272
15-10-5	.273	.727	45-10-12½	.567	.433	62½	.625	.375
15-10-10-5-5	.379	.621	45-10-16⅔	.588	.412	62½-5	.644	.356
16⅔	.1666	.8333	45-12½	.519	.481	62½-7	.651	.349
16⅔-5	.209	.791	45-15	.533	.467	62½-10	.663	.337
16⅔-5-2½	.229	.771	45-15-5	.556	.444	62½-10-5	.679	.321
16⅔-5-5	.248	.752	45-16⅔	.542	.458	62½-10-7	.687	.313
16⅔-10-2½	.269	.731	50-5	.525	.475	65-5	.668	.332
16⅔-10-5-2½	.306	.694	50-10	.55	.45	65-10	.685	.315
16⅔-10-5-5	.323	.677	50-10-5	.572	.428	66⅔	.6667	.3333
20-5	.24	.76	50-10-5-5	.594	.406	66⅔-5	.684	.316
20-10	.28	.72	50-10-10	.595	.405	66⅔-10	.701	.299
20-10-5	.316	.684	50-10-10-5	.615	.385	66⅔-10-5	.716	.284
25	.25	.75	50-10-10-5-5	.634	.366	67½	.675	.325
25-5	.288	.712	50-10-10-5-5-5	.653	.347	67½-10	.708	.292
25-10	.325	.675	50-10-10-7	.624	.376	70-5	.715	.285
25-10-5	.359	.641	50-10-10-7-15	.68	.32	70-10	.73	.27
30-5	.335	.665	50-10-10-10	.635	.365	70-10-5	.744	.256
30-10	.37	.63	50-10-10-10-5	.653	.347	70-10-10	.757	.243
30-10-5	.402	.598	50—4-10's	.672	.328	70-10-10-5	.769	.231
30-10-5-5	.432	.568	50—4-10's—5	.689	.311	70-10-10-10	.781	.219
30-10-5-5-5	.46	.54	50—5-10's	.705	.295	70-10-10-10-5	.792	.208
30-10-12½	.449	.551	50—5-10's—5	.72	.28	70—4-10's	.803	.197
30-10-12½-5	.477	.523	50—6-10's	.735	.265	70—4-10's—5	.812	.188
30-12½	.388	.612	50—6-10's—5	.748	.252	70—5-10's	.822	.178
30-16⅔	.4167	.5833	50—6-10's-5-5	.76	.24	70—5-10's—5	.831	.169
30-16⅔-5	.446	.554	50—7-10's	.759	.241	70—6-10's	.84	.16
30-16⅔-10	.475	.525	50—7-10's—5	.772	.228	70—6-10's—5	.848	.152
30-16⅔-10-5	.502	.498	50—7-10's-5-5	.783	.217	80-5	.81	.19
32½	.325	.675	50—8-16's	.784	.216	80-10	.82	.18
32½-10	.393	.607	50-10-12½	.606	.394	80-10-5	.829	.171
32½-10-16⅔	.494	.506	50-10-15-5-5	.657	.343	80-10-10	.838	.162
33⅓	.3333	.6667	50-10-16⅔	.625	.375	80-10-10-5	.846	.154
33⅓-5	.367	.633	50-10-16⅔-5	.644	.356	85-5	.857	.143
33⅓-10	.401	.599	50-10-25	.663	.337	85-5-10-5-5	.883	.117
33⅓-10-5	.43	.57	50-10-25-5	.68	.32	85-10	.865	.135
35-5	.383	.617	50-10-25-10	.696	.304	87½	.875	.125
40-5	.43	.57	50-12½	.563	.437	87½-5	.882	.118
40-6	.436	.564	50-15	.575	.425	87½-5-10	.894	.106
40-10	.46	.54	50-15-5	.596	.404	87½-5-10-5	.899	.101
40-10-5	.487	.513	50-15-10	.618	.382	87½-5-10-5-5	.904	.096

Given discount reduced to its decimal equivalent and also the remainder after subtracting the decimal equivalent from unity 1.

Regardless of the rotation of discounts the net results are the same. Example: 50-10-20% is the same as 10-20-50%.

FIG. 25-2.   Table of Equivalents of Chain Discounts.

pation at 6 per cent is allowed for the 11 days from June 20 until July 1, the due date. The amount due June 20 is computed as follows:

Amount of Invoice	$1,470.00
Anticipation: $1,470 × .06 × 11	−2.70
Amount Due 360	$1,467.30

With terms under which the discount period and the net period coincide, such as 2% 10 days, 60 extra, both cash discount and anticipation are allowed for payment before the due date. Anticipation in this case is figured on the net amount after deduction of cash discount.

For example, an invoice for $2,300, dated March 18, is paid May 12. Terms of sale were 2% 10 days, 60 extra; payment is due May 27. Cash discount is allowed, plus anticipation at 6 per cent for the 15 days from May 12 to May 27.

Amount of Invoice	$2,300.00
Cash Discount: $2,300 × .02	−46.00
Net Amount	$2,254.00
Anticipation: $2,254 × .06 × 15	−5.64
Amount Due May 12 360	$2,248.36

Use of Tables.   Tables are available to speed the computation of anticipation. For instance, Figure 25–3 can be used to find anticipation at 6 per cent on the basis of a 360-day year. The first column shows anticipation based on a gross amount of $1,000; the other columns show anticipation on the net amount after various cash discounts are deducted. The table is used by multiplying the gross invoice amount by the factor under the given cash discount and opposite the number of days. The result is divided by 1,000, since the anticipation is based on $1,000. The procedure is illustrated below:

Anticipation on $1,470 at 6% for 11 Days.   No cash discount is allowed, so the first column of the table is used. Multiply the factor opposite 11 days, or 1.83333, by the gross amount and divide by 1,000:

$$\frac{\$1,470 \times 1.83333}{1,000} = \$2.70 \text{ anticipation}$$

Anticipation of $2,300 at 6% for 15 Days, After 2% Cash Discount Is Allowed.   Under the column for 2% discount, the factor opposite 15 days is 2.45. Multiply this by the gross amount and divide by 1,000:

$$\frac{\$2,300 \times 2.45}{1,000} = \$5.64 \text{ anticipation}$$

Anticipation discounts most often occur when extra dating is granted but are sometimes allowed under proximo terms. They may be specifically stated in the terms of sale or may be a matter of industry custom.

Int. on $1000	Days	Interest on $1000 less Cash Discount								
		1%	2%	3%	4%	5%	6%	7%	8%	9%
.166 67	1	.17	.16	.16	.16	.16	.16	.16	.15	.15
.333 33	2	.33	.33	.32	.32	.32	.31	.31	.31	.30
.500 00	3	.50	.49	.49	.48	.48	.47	.47	.46	.46
.666 67	4	.66	.85	.65	.64	.63	.63	.62	.61	.61
.833 33	5	.83	.82	.81	.80	.79	.78	.78	.77	.76
1.000 00	6	.99	.98	.97	.96	.95	.94	.93	.92	.91
1.166 67	7	1.16	1.14	1.13	1.12	1.11	1.10	1.09	1.07	1.06
1.333 33	8	1.32	1.31	1.29	1.28	1.27	1.25	1.24	1.23	1.21
1.500 00	9	1.49	1.47	1.46	1.44	1.43	1.41	1.40	1.38	1.37
1.666 67	10	1.65	1.63	1.62	1.60	1.58	1.57	1.55	1.53	1.52
1.833 33	11	1.82	1.80	1.78	1.76	1.74	1.72	1.71	1.69	1.67
2.000 00	12	1.98	1.96	1.94	1.92	1.90	1.88	1.86	1.84	1.82
2.166 67	13	2.15	2.12	2.10	2.08	2.06	2.04	2.02	1.99	1.97
2.333 33	14	2.31	2.29	2.26	2.24	2.22	2.19	2.17	2.15	2.12
2.500 00	15	2.48	2.45	2.43	2.40	2.38	2.35	2.33	2.30	2.28
2.666 67	16	2.64	2.61	2.59	2.56	2.53	2.51	2.48	2.45	2.43
2.833 33	17	2.81	2.78	2.75	2.72	2.69	2.66	2.64	2.61	2.58
3.000 00	18	2.97	2.94	2.91	2.88	2.85	2.82	2.79	2.76	2.73
3.166 67	19	3.14	3.10	3.07	3.04	3.01	2.98	2.95	2.91	2.88
3.333 33	20	3.30	3.27	3.23	3.20	3.17	3.13	3.10	3.07	3.03
3.500 00	21	3.47	3.43	3.40	3.36	3.33	3.29	3.26	3.22	3.19
3.666 67	22	3.63	3.59	3.56	3.52	3.48	3.45	3.41	3.37	3.34
3.833 33	23	3.80	3.76	3.72	3.68	3.64	3.60	3.57	3.53	3.49
4.000 00	24	3.96	3.92	3.88	3.84	3.80	3.76	3.72	3.68	3.64
4.166 67	25	4.13	4.08	4.04	4.00	3.96	3.92	3.88	3.83	3.79
4.333 33	26	4.29	4.25	4.20	4.16	4.12	4.07	4.03	3.99	3.94
4.500 00	27	4.46	4.41	4.37	4.32	4.28	4.23	4.19	4.14	4.10
4.666 67	28	4.62	4.57	4.53	4.48	4.43	4.39	4.34	4.29	4.25
4.833 33	29	4.79	4.74	4.69	4.64	4.59	4.54	4.50	4.45	4.40
5.000 00	30	4.95	4.90	4.85	4.80	4.75	4.70	4.65	4.60	4.55
5.166 67	31	5.12	5.06	5.01	4.96	4.91	4.86	4.81	4.75	4.70
5.333 33	32	5.28	5.23	5.17	5.12	5.07	5.01	4.96	4.91	4.85
5.500 00	33	5.45	5.39	5.34	5.28	5.23	5.17	5.12	5.06	5.01
5.666 67	34	5.61	5.55	5.50	5.44	5.38	5.33	5.27	5.21	5.16
5.833 33	35	5.78	5.72	5.66	5.60	5.54	5.48	5.43	5.37	5.31
6.000 00	36	5.94	5.88	5.82	5.76	5.70	5.64	5.58	5.52	5.46
6.166 67	37	6.11	6.04	5.98	5.92	5.86	5.80	5.74	5.67	5.61
6.333 33	38	6.27	6.21	6.14	6.08	6.02	5.95	5.89	5.83	5.76
6.500 00	39	6.44	6.37	6.31	6.24	6.18	6.11	6.05	5.98	5.92
6.666 67	40	6.60	6.53	6.47	6.40	6.33	6.27	6.20	6.13	6.07

FIG. 25–3.   Anticipation Factors at 6 Per Cent for a 360-Day Year.

Late-Payment Service Charges

When goods are purchased on credit, the supplier finances the purchase during the credit term period. This financing is regarded as a necessary cost of business and is included in the selling price. However, unless the bill is promptly collected at maturity, the cost for carrying the account thereafter falls upon the supplier alone. Without late-payment service charges, overdue accounts receivable represent capital advanced to the customer without compensation for the supplier.

Late-payment service charges should be clearly distinguished from interest payments. The latter are charges made by financial institutions for money loans. They have no place in a discussion of service charges that seek to recover the added costs of carrying the collecting slow-paid receivables.

Important Considerations. Many suppliers do not use late-payment service charges. They claim a wish to accommodate the customer and preserve good will. They fear losing good will; doubt their ability to collect these charges and will not institute such a program; or fear that sales will be lost if such charges are applied, especially if their competitors do not use them. Moreover, many suppliers consider the costs of carrying overdue accounts as comparatively small, so they decide to absorb them.

In favor of service charges, other considerations should be evaluated. Payment made beyond invoice terms uses the supplier's capital without consent. With no charge for the use of this capital, the customer has an unfair advantage over competitors that pay promptly. This may be construed as a price concession on the purchase of merchandise, determined solely by the slow payer. From the viewpoint of the seller too, the costs of carrying overdue accounts receivable are not confined to the cost of money but are increased by added collection expenses and more likely bad-debt losses.

Legal Aspect of Late-Payment Service Charges. The Robinson-Patman Act is designed to prevent unfair trade discrimination and can be briefly described as an act which outlaws discriminatory pricing or selling practices in sales of products for use or resale within the United States, if these may result in an injurious effect on competition or a tendency toward monopoly in a particular product or line of commerce. Prohibited discriminatory pricing may result from furnishing or paying for services of facilities, discounts, rebates, allowances, or other forms of direct or indirect price concessions.

Corporate attorneys emphasize that late-payment service charge programs should be applied equally to all like customers or to like groups of customers, or they may be interpreted as a form of price discrimination. Each corporation must seek legal counsel before instituting a service charge program to make sure they are applied properly under the law. The main concern centers around treating all like customers fairly, utilizing a clear definition of like customers. The issue is not the validity of using late-payment service charges but how to implement them under the law.

Further, under some state laws late-payment service charges can constitute a violation of the usury laws if the amount is in excess of the maximum permitted by state law.

CLASSIFICATION OF TERMS OF SALE

All selling terms do not include every element given earlier in this chapter. Some do not offer a cash discount or trade discount, others offer no anticipation, and many industries do not impose a service charge for late payment. In any stated terms, the cash discount is shown first; trade discount follows; and then net maturity is indicated, together with penalties if they are charged. The most common terms are discussed in this chapter. Names used to designate various types of terms are not completely standard; common alternative designations are given, but those less frequently used are omitted.

Terms Based on Invoice Date

This category includes the most commonly used terms of sale. The time periods for discount and maturity begin with the date of the invoice. Thus, on 30 day terms, the bill would be due 30 days after invoice date. If the terms offered a 10-day discount period, that would also commence on the invoice date.

Selling terms that specify a discount also specify the discount period. In every case they establish the maturity or net due date of the invoice. Typical terms of this type include the following:

Net 30 Days. The invoice is due in full 30 days after the invoice date. No discount period is offered.

2% 10, Net 30. The buyer may deduct 2% of the face amount of the invoice if payment is made within 10 days of the invoice date. The full amount is due 30 days after the invoice date.

Single Payment or Lumped Order Terms

In a number of industries customers buy over a period of time, usually two weeks or one month, and make one payment after the end of each period. These arrangements reduce paper work and bookkeeping. On the other hand, they limit the seller's cash receipts to one or two peaks a month. Single payment terms include several variations.

End-of-Month (E.O.M.) Terms. Shipments during a month are invoiced in a single statement dated as of the last day of that month or the first day of the following month. The credit period is computed from this date and is usually 10 days. For example, terms of 10 days E.O.M. require payment for all purchases of one month on the 10th of the following month. Where a cash discount is offered, as is usually the case, the discount period is usually identical with the net period. Thus a customer buying under terms of 2% 10 days E.O.M. and paying by the 10th of the following month is entitled to the discount; beyond this date the full price is owed and the account is past due.

In some industries leeway is permitted. An invoice dated after the 25th of the month is considered dated the first day of the following month. Under these circumstances the credit period may range between 15 and 45 days. If the invoice is dated September 25, for example, it must be paid by October 10. Dated September 26, however, the invoice is not due until November 10. Customers wanting the maximum credit period naturally concentrate their purchases immediately after the 25th.

Middle-of-Month (M.O.M.) Terms.   These are a variation of E.O.M. Shipments made between the 1st and the 15th of any month are invoiced or billed as of the 15th of that month. Shipments between the 16th and the end of the month are invoiced as of the end of the month or the 1st of the next month. The credit and discount period is usually 10 days and dates from the 15th and the 1st, respectively. M.O.M. terms allow shorter credit periods than E.O.M.; the maximum is 25 days for a shipment made on the 1st and due on the 25th or made on the 16th and due on the 10th of the following month.

Proximo Terms.   This is another type of term that specifies payment in the month following shipment. (Proximo, abbreviated prox., is Latin for "next" or "next following.") Net 10th prox. terms require payment of all the previous month's invoices on the 10th of the following month. Such an arrangement is identical to terms of 10 days E.O.M., although under proximo terms billings are usually made at the time of shipment rather than once monthly. Like E.O.M. terms, proximo arrangements may give identical discount and net credit periods, for example, 2% 10th prox. However, proximo terms often contain a discount period shorter than the net period. Thus terms of 2% 10th prox., net 30th permit a discount for payment on the 10th of the following month, with the full amount due on the 30th, or 20 days later.

Special Dating Terms

Some industries offer lengthened terms through various dating arrangements such as seasonal dating, receipt of goods, and extra dating.

Seasonal Dating.   Where demand for a product is seasonal, sellers encourage off-season purchases by granting terms which postpone payments to coincide with buyers' selling seasons. The customer benefits from having the goods on hand without any immediate investment of funds. The seller gains the advantages of more constant sales, level production, and reduced storage problems.

The seller usually dates the invoice as of the beginning of the production season; regular terms are computed from that date. Additional incentives may be offered to the buyer in the form of extra discounts for early purchase.

Receipt of Goods (R.O.G.).   These terms permit the buyer to compute the cash discount period from the date on which the merchandise is received rather than from the invoice date. Thus a distant buyer wanting the cash discount is not pressed to remit before examining the shipment, as may happen when the discount period commences from the invoice date. The net credit period, however, is always calculated from the invoice date and not from the date of arrival. R.O.G. terms are common in the importing of raw sugar and are used by firms in other lines for water shipments between the coasts of the United States.

Extra Dating. Extra dating arrangements, found primarily in the textile industry, extend the discount period. Terms of 2% 10, 60 extra extend both the discount period and the net credit period to 70 days from the date of the invoice. Since extra terms have identical discount and net credit periods, there is no inducement for the buyer to pay prior to maturity. To overcome this, extra terms are sometimes expressed as 3% 10, 2% 10, 60 extra. This indicates that 3% may be deducted if payment is made within 10 days, but only 2% is deductible if payment is made by the end of 70 days. The extra 1% is in effect an anticipation discount.

Cash Terms

Cash terms, as the expression is usually employed, do not require immediate payment but involve a nominal credit period, commonly ten to fourteen days. This interval allows the buyer sufficient time to examine and accept the merchandise. Cash terms do not ordinarily offer any discount. Some cash terms require payment before the merchandise is delivered. Their use implies unwillingness on the part of the seller to extend credit.

Net Cash. Under this arrangement, the customer is traditionally allowed ten days to inspect the merchandise before being required to pay for it. The terms often are used for the sale of raw materials. The supplier takes some risk with cash terms. On seasonal items, particularly, the time elapsed in shipping goods to the purchaser, then having them rejected and returned, makes the vendor less able to sell the goods to someone else. Further, the seller has assets tied up in inventory being transported around the country when it should be returning a profit.

Bill-to-Bill. These are also called drop delivery, or load-to-load terms, and are often found in lines involving weekly deliveries. The invoice covering the previous shipment is paid when a new delivery is made. Perishable foods sold to retail stores and gasoline sold to retail service stations are this type of modification to cash terms.

Cash on Delivery (C.O.D.). Under C.O.D. terms, merchandise is shipped but is not released to the customer until the transportation company has received payment for the full invoice amount. Should a C.O.D. shipment not be accepted by the buyer, the seller risks the loss of freight charges in both directions, preparation and packaging costs, and possible deterioration of the product. Sellers are often willing to assume these risks in the interest of sales volume, and C.O.D. terms are used extensively where credit has not been established and where the merchandise is standard.

Cash With Order (C.W.O.) or Cash in Advance (C.I.A.). These terms are the most severe from the buyer's standpoint since the seller assumes little or no risk. Their use is largely on customers with no credit standing. Where goods are not standard in nature, orders from customers in this group are not processed until the advance payment has been received and cleared.

Cash Before Delivery (C.B.D.). C.B.D. terms are only slightly less severe than cash with order. The seller may prepare and package merchandise but will not ship until payment is received.

Sight Draft/Bill of Lading (SD/BL). Under these very secure terms, a negotiable bill of lading together with the invoice and a sight draft drawn on the buyer is forwarded by the seller to the customer's banking connection. The merchandise cannot be obtained from the carrier without the bill of lading. In turn, the bill of lading will not be released by the bank until the customer honors, or agrees to pay, the draft. As with C.O.D. shipments, the seller's risk is confined to packaging and two-way transportation costs in the event the buyer does not pay the draft. These arrangements are employed fairly frequently in sales of carload quantities of meats, grains, and flour. This instrument is discussed in more detail in Chapter 26.

Terms Other Than Open Account

Some terms provide more security than the straight, open-account terms described above. They may be traditional in an industry or may be established because a customer is not a strong credit risk. Detailed descriptions of these terms are given in Chapter 28, but some brief comments are given here to show how they are used in business.

Guaranties. If the financial position of the debtor is not strong enough to warrant open-account credit, a creditor may ask that the obligation be guaranteed by someone else. The guarantor may be a natural person, a corporation, or both. From the creditor's point of view, it is important to know how much of the customer's debt has been guaranteed or secured in any way. It is also important to know that the guarantor has sufficient assets to back all the claims in the event the debtor defaults on obligations.

Secured Transactions. Some sales are secured by a pledge of an asset or by a lien on the business property. This enables the creditor to salvage a default situation. It is useful when a sale is made to a high-risk account, when terms of sale are long, when a large amount is involved, or when material is at a customer's place of business for a long time.

Trust Receipts. These instruments are commonly used in floor planning high-priced durable goods such as automobiles and household equipment. As with any other inventory loan, the manufacturer and the customer can execute a single security agreement. The manufacturer, as the secured party, can protect its interest by filing a financing statement covering the goods and proceeds without having to execute new agreements as more items are sold.

Letters of Credit. While used primarily to finance purchases from abroad, letters of credit are also used for some domestic transactions. A formal letter is issued by a bank that authorizes its customer to write drafts on the bank up to the limit specified in the letter. The bank thus substitutes its credit for that of the customer in the eyes of the creditor.

Advances

When work is done to the customer's specification, it is customary to ask for a partial payment with the order. This provides the creditor with some working funds for the job and offers some protection in case the customer cancels the order. Where advances are not usual, they may nevertheless be used for partial protection when a customer is not in a strong financial condition.

Progress Payments

Partial payments are sometimes made on a contract as it progresses. This holds true especially when manufacturing or construction time is long and the creditor cannot afford to finance production.

The construction industry is typical of those using progress payment terms. In the erection of a building, the prime contractor submits monthly billings to the owner for work done during that month. The bill includes a proportionate share of the total profit. For example, a $750,000 job is expected to run for three months and to yield a $100,000 profit to the general contractor. If one-third of the job were completed in the first month, the contractor would bill the client for $250,000.

The client normally holds back between 10 and 15 per cent of the progress payment to assure proper completion of the contract. This is called a retainage. It is paid after the job has been substantially completed and approved by the architect.

Contra Accounts

Some companies find that they are reciprocal suppliers. When that is so, a company may both owe money to a supplier and be its creditor. The company may consider paying its trade obligations by reducing its accounts receivable from the supplier.

This technique of contra-account settlement may be perfectly natural between two strong companies. It is also useful, however, in case a strong supplier wants to protect itself against a customer that is financially weak. Then the supplier may insist on a contra-account arrangement. When the right of offset is to be exercised, the selling terms should be specific in stating that a contra-account arrangement has been made.

It is important for a creditor to know if a customer has made such arrangements with other suppliers, since the supplier with the contra-account arrangement has a potentially stronger call on the customer's assets.

Commitments

A commitment is an agreement to deliver or accept merchandise of definite specifications at a fixed price some time in the future. It is mostly used in buying and selling commodities and raw materials. In the commodities markets, such as the Chicago Board of Trade, this is known as dealing in futures. Manufacturers use this type of arrangement to assure adequate supply of raw materials when needed. The creditor of a customer making advance commitments should be sure the purchaser has taken adequate precautions against losses arising from fluctuations in commodity prices.

Consignment

These terms are not strictly selling terms. There is no requirement that title to the goods shall ever pass to the consignee (receiver of the goods). While there is no binding obligation on the consignee to buy or pay for the goods, there is an obligation to account for the proceeds when the goods are sold or to return the goods if they are not sold.

Consignment sales may stimulate volume, since they enable a company to place goods on the premises of concerns which might not be able to pay for them within normal open-account credit terms. By the same token, they increase the financing burden on the supplier, since payment cannot be expected until the goods have been sold.

Selling on consignment is popular in several industries and characteristic where merchandise is high-priced. The jewelry industry in particular is well known for selling "on memorandum," a specialized terminology meaning the same thing.

Technically, the consignor (shipper of the goods) does not have to comply with the provisions of the Uniform Commercial Code. However, the consignor wishing to protect its interest against other creditors of the consignee is well advised to follow the filing and notice requirements under Section 9–114 of the Code.

CHAPTER 26

NEGOTIABLE INSTRUMENTS

Commercial paper, consisting of notes and drafts, has for centuries played an important role in business and commerce. Although the time when it first came into use is somewhat obscure, the 14th century probably comes closest to the mark. Even today, it reflects the needs of merchants, traders, and importers. These were the groups responsible for the development of the negotiable instrument and the eventual establishment of a set of rules for the settlement of disputes between themselves in courts they established for that purpose. Their rules became known as the law of negotiable instruments, or the "law merchant."

These merchants' courts were ultimately recognized by the legislatures and became official courts for the settlement of merchant disagreements. In order to avoid confusion and overlapping decisions, a codification of all the rules gradually took place. California was the first state to codify in 1877, and eventually every state followed suit and enacted some statute on the subject. Finally, a uniform negotiable instruments act was passed by every legislature, although judicial interpretation did not always conform to a uniform pattern.

When the Uniform Commercial Code (UCC) was promulgated by the National Conference of Commissioners and the American Law Institute with the endorsement of the American Bar Association, its Article 3 contained the statutory law that governs commercial paper. That statute as enacted in the different states now varies in minor details, but the principal provisions are practically identical in all the states.

This chapter gives a discussion of specific points of particular interest to credit executives working with negotiable instruments.

ESSENTIAL ELEMENTS OF A NEGOTIABLE INSTRUMENT

Article 3 of the Uniform Commercial Code states that in order to qualify as negotiable instrument a document must be in writing and signed by the maker or drawer, contain an unconditional promise or order to pay a sum certain in money, be payable on demand or at a specified time, and be payable to order or to bearer.

Negotiability

Commercial paper may be divided into two types of instruments: negotiable and nonnegotiable. Both types are valid contractual agreements. The distinction between them, however, lies in the effect each instrument has on parties beyond the two original contracting parties. Both instruments may be transferred or assigned, but the nonnegotiable instrument is transferred under the same infirmities as any ordinary contract. It can only be assigned or transferred with the same rights and disabilities that the original holder possessed in it. The negotiable instrument, on the other hand, can be transferred with greater rights than the original holder possessed; its impact on commerce can be easily seen when a subsequent holder may come into possession of it unshackled by any defenses of the maker.

Number of Parties

Each type of instrument may further be divided into two classifications, according to the number of parties included in the transaction. There are two parties to a promissory note: the maker and the payee. The maker promises to pay a certain sum of money directly to the payee or to any subsequent holder. In a draft (bill of exchange), there are three parties: the drawer, the payee, and the drawee. The drawer of the draft promises to pay the payee or a subsequent holder through a third party, the drawee.

In Writing

The negotiable instrument must be in writing. It may be typed or handwritten and in any language known and understood.

Promise or Order To Pay

Every negotiable instrument must include a promise to pay. This promise is an undertaking to pay and must be more than an acknowledgement of an obligation. It is intended to make clear that a mere I.O.U. is not a negotiable instrument. For example, a statement that says "This is to certify that I have borrowed $100 from John Doe" is nothing more than an acknowledgement of indebtedness. However, in a statement that reads "I have borrowed $100 from John Doe, to be repaid 30 days from date" is a clear indication on the maker's part to pay a certain sum of money. This definite intention to pay implies the promise to pay.

An order is a direction to pay and must be more than an authorization or request. The dividing line between a direction to pay and an authorization or request may not be clear cut. The use of the words "please pay" or "kindly pay" should not be considered a mere request. On the other hand,

"I wish you would pay" would not qualify as an order and such an instrument would not be negotiable.

The promise or order to pay must be unconditional. There can be condition attached to the promise or order to pay. When the words "on the condition that," "provided that," "if," or similar phrases are employed, the order obviously is conditional. However, there are occasions when the instrument may contain conditions which are not so clearly discernible. Occasionally notes refer to a particular fund out of which payment is to be made. For example, an instrument that reads "Pay to the order of John Doe out of the treasurer's surplus" includes a condition that the treasurer must have a surplus fund. Since there can be no guarantee that the surplus fund will remain in existence or that it will continue to have sufficient funds to meet the note, the order to pay is conditioned on the solvency of the fund. Thus, at the time the note is written, it cannot be determined from its face that it will be paid.

The UCC makes an exception to this general rule in the case of instruments issued by a governmental agency. A provision that such an instrument is limited to payment out of a particular fund or the proceeds of a particular source does not render the instrument nonnegotiable.

It is not considered a condition when the instrument merely refers to the consideration or transaction upon which it is based. For example, "Pay to the order of John Doe $10,000 for the purchase of two panel trucks" does not introduce a condition but merely describes the transaction. Thus the instrument would be negotiable.

The same rule applies to executory contracts, or contracts to be performed in the future. A note reading "Pay to the XYZ Corporation or order $5,000 for three carloads of widgets to be delivered six months from date" is negotiable. The distinction between this type of instrument and one that requires payment to be made out of a particular fund is not readily apparent. However, the UCC specifically provides that a reference to a mere executory consideration does not destroy negotiability.

There is another class of notes where this problem may appear. Some instruments refer to specific agreements which form the basis of the consideration of the note. For example, a note may read "Pay to the order of John Jones $5,000 as per Royal Mining Contract." In accordance with the rule that allows a reference to the consideration, such a note would be negotiable. However, if the same note were to read "subject to Royal Mining contract," it would no longer be negotiable. Obviously, if the payment of the note is contingent upon the performance of a particular contract, the promise to pay cannot be unconditional. There is only one seeming exception to this, and that is really no exception at all. The same note may read "subject to the conditions of the contract attached hereto." If the attached contract contained no conditions whatever, the note would be negotiable. The reason for this is that it can be seen from the face of the note (the contract being a part of the note) that payment is really not conditioned upon anything.

Sum Certain

The sum of money to be paid must be ascertainable from the instrument itself. When a specific amount is stated, there is no problem. In some cases, however, allowances may be offered, penalties may be charged, or additional charges may be made. In these instances, it is sufficient that the holder is able to determine through computation the amount payable in the note. Thus a stated discount or addition for early or late payment does not affect the certainty so long as the computation can be made from the instrument itself without reference to any outside source.

A $1,000 note which provided for a 6 per cent discount if paid on or before the due date would meet this requirement. Similarly, a note which permitted a 6 per cent discount if paid on its due date would be negotiable. However, on a note which reads "Pay to John Doe or order $1,000 for the purchase of two dozen widgets plus any freight or shipping charges thereon," the amount of the full payment cannot be determined from the instrument. Hence it is not negotiable.

Maturity Should Be Specified

Drafts or notes should be payable either on demand or at a definite time in the future. If a time is not specified, the note is automatically payable on demand. Here are some examples:

1. A note which is due on February 15, 1982 specifies the date of payment.

2. A note that is due one year after the death of the payee does not comply with this requirement. While the event is certain to happen it is uncertain as to time.

3. A note payable one month after a particular product has been developed does not meet this requirement, either. Since it is not certain that the product will ever be developed, this type of maturity is uncertain and not determinable. Therefore, the note is not negotiable.

4. An undated note payable "30 days after date" is not payable at a definite time, since the time of payment cannot be determined on its face. However, the holder may insert the true date; this makes the note negotiable, since it is now payable at a definite time.

5. Payment of a note may be accelerated for specific conditions and the note remains negotiable. The certainty of time of payment is not affected by any acceleration clause, whether it is at the option of the maker or holder, or is automatic upon the occurrence of some conditional or unrestricted event. For example, the maker of a note may pay ahead of time; the note remains negotiable so long as the maker does not receive a discount for accelerated payments that cannot be determined through computation.

In another instance, the entire outstanding amount may become due upon default of a scheduled payment. Those circumstances are outside the control of the holder and qualify the note for negotiability.

6. An instrument will occasionally provide the extension of the maturity date at the option of the holder. This clause, even without a time limit, does not affect negotiability, since the holder is given a right already possessed without the clause. If the extension is at the option of the maker or acceptor or is automatic, a definite time limit must be stated; otherwise the time of payment is uncertain and the instrument is not negotiable.

Payment in Money

The promise must be made to pay in money rather than a commodity. Any recognized form of currency is sufficient. The promise may be in U.S. dollars, English pounds, French francs, and so on.

An instrument payable in "currency" or "current funds" means that it is payable in money. Commodities, such as gold dust or beaver pelts, are not deemed money because of uncertain and fluctuating value.

Consideration

Consideration may be defined as doing some act that one would not otherwise be legally required to do as an inducement for the act or promise of the other contracting party. For example, paying money or performing a service or refraining from doing some act or making an equivalent promise therefore would be deemed consideration. In terms of commercial credit, consideration is generally the sale of merchandise or the lending of money.

Since a negotiable instrument requires a signature, it has an advantage over the open account in that a valuable consideration is presumed. If it is necessary to sue on a negotiable instrument, the creditor need not introduce evidence that there was consideration.

Antecedent debt constitutes good consideration in a negotiable instrument. If a $500 open account is past due, the debtor may make a promissory note to the creditor. There is generally regarded to be consideration in this instance.

Signature

A signature must appear on the face of the instrument before any party may become liable on it. The signature may be at any place on the face of the document and includes any mark that the maker, drawer, or endorser intends as a signature. For example, a rubber stamp with the person's name is perfectly proper provided that the stamp is intended to represent the person's signature. The same would apply to an "X" mark, a seal, a symbol, or any mark intended to represent the party's signature.

An instrument may also be signed by a party using a trade name. For example, John Doe is the owner of a firm doing business as Doe Fuel Company. All notes or checks of the firm may be signed with a rubber stamp bearing the words, Doe Fuel Company. John Doe would be personally liable, however, since the trade name is used on the note as the owner's signature.

Quite often negotiable instruments are signed by agents on behalf of their principals. If an agent signs an instrument but does not indicate the name of the principal any place on the face thereof, the principal cannot be liable on that instrument. The agent will be liable under these circumstances, even though the note was signed in a manner indicating merely an agency relationship.

If the agent signing a negotiable instrument also places the principal's name on the face of the document, the principal will be liable but the agent will not be. This is true, however, only if the agent was authorized to make such an instrument. If the agent acted without authority, the principal will not be liable but the agent will be.

Payee

The payee of an instrument must be indicated with reasonable certainty. The most common type of negotiable instrument is the one made payable to the order of a specific payee. However, the instrument may be made payable to the drawer. An example of this is the check made out to "cash." An instrument may also be made payable to the drawee. For example, an individual who maintains a checking account with the ABC Bank may also have taken a loan with that bank. In meeting loan payments, the individual can make a check drawn on the ABC Bank payable to the ABC Bank.

A document may also be made payable to two or more payees, in which case all named payees must endorse to further negotiate the instrument. Or it may be made payable to alternative payees, in which case any one of those named may endorse it.

An instrument may also be payable to the order of the representative of an estate, trust, or fund. For example, "Pay to the order of the Treasurer, Heart Fund." In this case, the instrument is payable to the order of the appropriate representative or successor.

The UCC also provides that when instruments are made payable to the order of a nonexistent person or when the payee of such instrument does not purport to be the name of any individual, they are bearer instruments. Examples of the foregoing would be "Pay to the order of Abraham Lincoln," or "Pay to the order of Moby Dick."

Drawee

The drawee is the third party on a draft, through whom payment is to be made. However, the drawee must accept the instrument for payment before becoming liable. That means that the drawee must agree to make the payment. The drawee who fails to accept may be liable to the drawer or to the holder for breach of the terms of a letter of credit or any other agreement in which an obligation to accept exists.

The drawee must be indicated with a fair amount of certainty on the face of the document. Joint or alternative drawees are acceptable. In the case of joint drawees, both have to sign; where payable in the alternative, either may sign.

FORMS OF NEGOTIABLE INSTRUMENTS

As already noted, negotiable instruments generally can be classified as to the number of parties included in the transaction. However, these two major classifications may be divided into several categories.

Promissory Note

A negotiable promissory note is "an unconditional promise in writing made by one person to another, signed by the maker, engaging to pay on demand or at a fixed or determinable future time, a sum certain in money to order or bearer." There are two general classifications of promissory notes: straight or serial.

Straight Note. This is the more common instrument, used merely as evidence of indebtedness. Figure 26–1 illustrates a straight note. In order to make certain that the note is negotiable, the word "order" in one form or the other must be used.

Serial Note. In this form, the amount to be paid is covered by a series of notes usually of equal amounts and with maturity dates equally spaced. There usually is added a provision that in the event of a default in payment, all subsequent notes become due and payable. Thus notes with stated maturities are converted into demand instrument under this provision.

Promissory notes come in the following forms:

1. *Single-name paper.* This is a note signed by the maker only. The maker's creditworthiness is the only assurance that the note will be paid.

FIG. 26–1.   Straight Note.

2. *Double-name paper.* This is a promissory note signed by two or more makers or signed by the maker and endorsed by others. With additional people standing behind the note, the likelihood of payment is increased.

Promissory notes are commonly used for bank loans. They are not frequently used for merchandise transactions. However, some credit executives will ask their customers to sign a note for past-due accounts, believing that it will stimulate payment. This practice provides written acknowledgement of the past-due debt, but also postpones the due date of the account until the date stated on the note.

Collateral Note. This is a note that is secured by certain collateral, such as stocks, bonds, personal property, or mortgages. Its outstanding feature is that the collateral is held by the creditor while the note is outstanding. Such a note may be negotiated in the same manner as any negotiable note, whether the collateral be assigned or not.

Judgment Note. Judgment notes, also known as confessions of judgment, are matters controlled by state law and have many technical requirements associated with them. This type of note is generally given in connection with a separate agreement by the maker who consents to have a judgment entered should payment not be made on the note when due. A separate agreement consenting to the judgment is known as a confession of judgment, which in turn is based on the judgment note.

Upon a default of payment, this confession of judgment authorizes the seller (the payee) to enter judgment in a court of law against the debtor (the maker), who thereby surrenders the opportunity to defend the case. The attorney for the debtor appears in court, admits that the obligation is owing, and the judgment is then automatically recorded. As a result, the creditor is in a position to enforce collection immediately.

The note may be endorsed and negotiated by the payee in the same manner as any other negotiable instrument. The confession of judgment is not negotiable but may be assigned by the payee to an endorsee along with the note. However, in certain consumer transactions this practice has become subject to criticism as violating constitutional rights of due process.

Bonds. Bonds are a more formal type of promise to pay, and many states have adopted restrictive legislation. In essence, the maker of the bond promises to pay someone else a certain sum of money by a specified time. The features of every bond can be determined by reading the indenture.

Check

A check is a written order by a depositor (drawer) to the depositor's bank to pay a specified sum on demand to a payee. A check does present a credit risk because there is no guarantee that the drawer has sufficient funds to cover the check, or that the drawer will have sufficient funds when the payer presents it for payment. Figure 26–2 illustrates a check.

March 5, 19** 1-23/210

Pay to the order of Scott C. Robertson $58,230.50

Fifty-Eight Thousand Two Hundred Thirty and 50/100 Dollars

Morgan Guaranty Trust Company
OF NEW YORK MADISON AVENUE OFFICE

Memo

SPECIMEN

John Doe

BURROUGHS- EW/IW

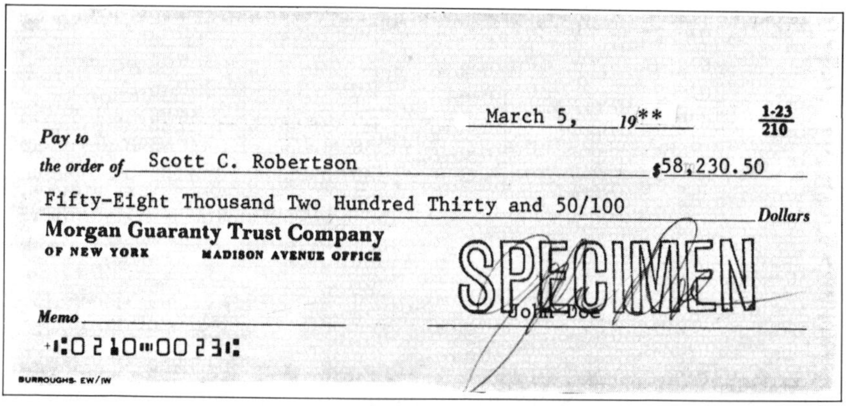

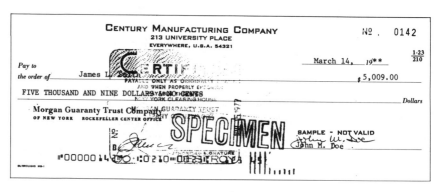

FIG. 26–2. Check.

Certified Check

When a drawer has a check certified by a bank, the bank guarantees the funds on deposit for payment. On some occasions, the drawer of a check has it certified before delivery is made to the payee. On many occasions, however, the holder has the check certified after it has been delivered. This technique is used when there is reason to question the creditworthiness of a customer. A certified check is shown in Figure 26–3.

CENTURY MANUFACTURING COMPANY
213 UNIVERSITY PLACE
EVERYWHERE, U.S.A. 54321

No. 0142

March 14, 19** 1-23/210

Pay to the order of James L. Smith $5,009.00

FIVE THOUSAND AND NINE DOLLARS AND NO CENTS Dollars

Morgan Guaranty Trust Company
OF NEW YORK ROCKEFELLER CENTER OFFICE

SPECIMEN

SAMPLE - NOT VALID

John M. Doe

FIG. 26–3. Certified Check.

Cashier's or Treasurer's Check

This type of check is drawn by the cashier of a bank on the cashier's own bank. Since the bank accepts the check as drawee, it makes itself absolutely liable for payment. The holder need look only to the bank for payment (Figure 26–4). This ranks with the certified check as a means of guaranteeing payment from customers of questionable creditworthiness.

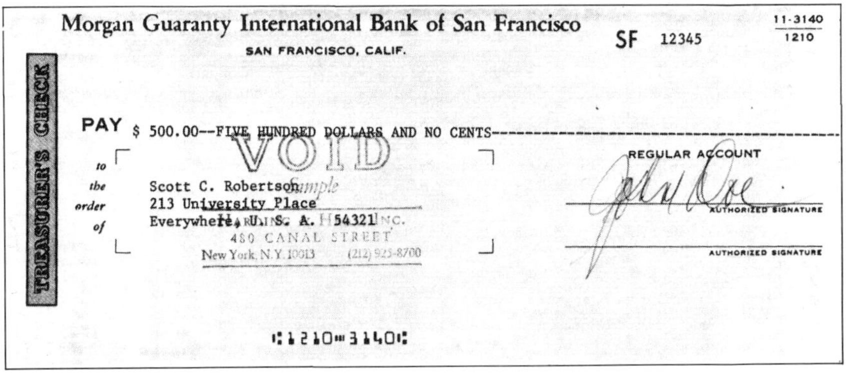
TREASURER'S CHECK

Morgan Guaranty International Bank of San Francisco
SAN FRANCISCO, CALIF.

SF 12345

11-3140
1210

PAY $ 500.00--FIVE HUNDRED DOLLARS AND NO CENTS-----

VOID

to the order of
Scott C. Robertson
213 University Place
Everywhere, U. S. A. 54321

REGULAR ACCOUNT

AUTHORIZED SIGNATURE

AUTHORIZED SIGNATURE

⑆1210⑈3140⑆

FIG. 26–4. Cashier's Check or Treasurer's Check.

Postdated Check

Rather than wait for payment of a past-due account, a creditor may sometimes accept a check dated ahead and hold it for deposit until that future date. A postdated check is not usually covered in the bad-check laws of the states.

Draft (Bill of Exchange)

A draft is an unconditional order in writing by one person upon another, signed by the person giving it, and ordering the person to whom it is directed to pay on demand or at a definite time a sum certain in money to order or to bearer. There are two types, the sight draft and the time draft. The sight draft is payable upon acceptance (Figure 26–5), while a time draft is made payable a specified number of days after the instrument has been accepted, or "30 days after sight," "60 days after sight," and so on (Figure 26–6).

A draft differs from other instruments of credit in that the drawer makes

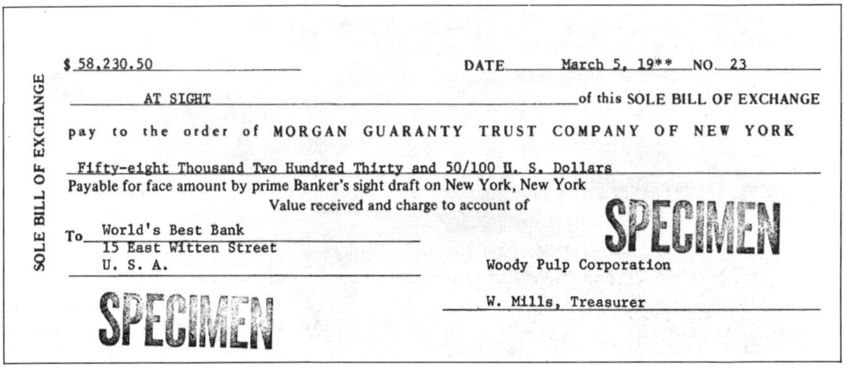
SOLE BILL OF EXCHANGE

$ 58,230.50 DATE March 5, 19** NO. 23

AT SIGHT of this SOLE BILL OF EXCHANGE

pay to the order of MORGAN GUARANTY TRUST COMPANY OF NEW YORK

Fifty-eight Thousand Two Hundred Thirty and 50/100 U. S. Dollars

Payable for face amount by prime Banker's sight draft on New York, New York

Value received and charge to account of

To World's Best Bank
15 East Witten Street
U. S. A.

SPECIMEN

Woody Pulp Corporation

W. Mills, Treasurer

SPECIMEN

FIG. 26–5. Sight Draft.

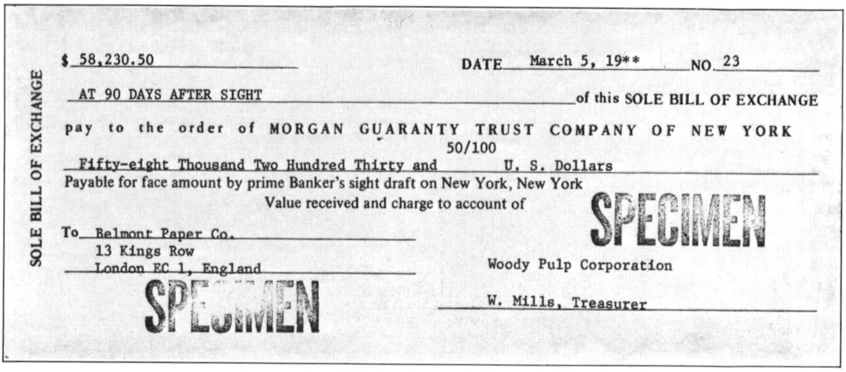

FIG. 26–6. Time Draft.

the instrument to the drawer's order, drawn on the drawee. The drawee then accepts the instrument by writing the word "accepted" across its face and signing it. Once that is done, the obligation to pay is absolute, and only then does the draft become a negotiable instrument.

Trade Acceptance

This form of draft is used by merchants and manufacturers in some industries. It should be used for specific transactions rather than to confirm past-due accounts, as the promissory note is sometimes used. In a typical business transaction, the drawee would be the buyer and the drawer would be the seller. This type of instrument may be discounted at the seller's bank, may be negotiated, or may be held until maturity. Figure 26–7 shows a trade acceptance.

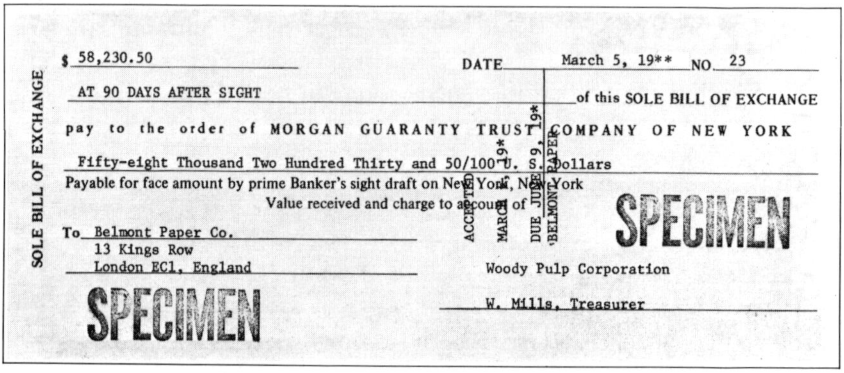

FIG. 26–7. Trade Acceptance.

Banker's Acceptance

Though based upon the same transaction as the trade acceptance, a banker's acceptance applies more psychological pressure upon the debtor.

Rather than being drawn upon the buyer, the banker's acceptance is drawn upon the buyer's bank. It must be accepted by that bank in order to be negotiable (Figure 26–8).

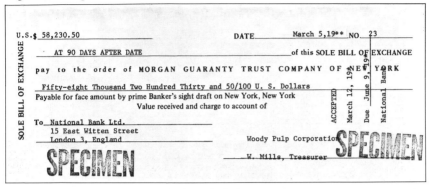

FIG. 26–8. Banker's Acceptance.

When the buyer's bank receives the draft and accepts it, the bank becomes liable for payment. Before it does so, however, the bank will undoubtedly advise its customer that the draft has been received. Customarily the buyer advises the bank beforehand that it plans to purchase merchandise from a particular seller and requests the bank to accept a draft covering the amount of the sale. If it agrees to accept such a draft, the bank may require the buyer to deposit certain collateral, such as the shipping documents that carry the title to the goods to be purchased. Or the bank may require the buyer to keep a certain amount on deposit. Obviously the seller will prefer the banker's acceptance to the simple trade acceptance, since a draft drawn upon a bank is much more easily negotiable than one drawn upon an individual buyer.

Sight Draft/Bill of Lading (SD/BL)

The sight draft may be combined with an order bill of lading in a procedure which ensures collection before merchandise is relinquished. This is referred to as "Sight Draft Accompanied by Order Bill of Lading" (Figure 26–9).

The order bill of lading represents title to the shipment. When properly endorsed by the seller and attached to a sight draft and shipping documents covering the transaction, it is sent, either directly or through the seller's bank, to the purchaser's bank for collection. After acceptance and payment of the sight draft, the purchaser receives the order bill of lading. The purchaser may then obtain possession of the merchandise by presenting the order bill of lading properly endorsed to the carrier.

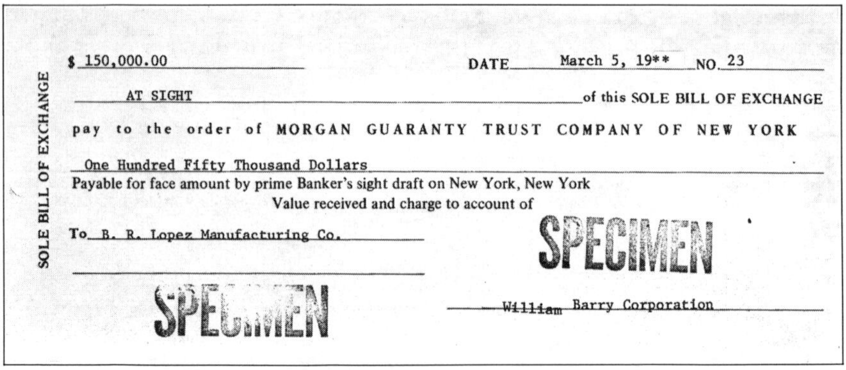

SOLE BILL OF EXCHANGE

$ 150,000.00 DATE March 5, 19** NO. 23

AT SIGHT of this SOLE BILL OF EXCHANGE

pay to the order of MORGAN GUARANTY TRUST COMPANY OF NEW YORK

One Hundred Fifty Thousand Dollars

Payable for face amount by prime Banker's sight draft on New York, New York

Value received and charge to account of

To B. R. Lopez Manufacturing Co.

SPECIMEN

SPECIMEN

William Barry Corporation

FIG. 26–9. Sight Draft/Bill of Lading.

TRANSFER

An instrument may be transferred by negotiation or by assignment. Negotiation requires an endorsement (bearer instruments excepted), whereas an assignment is accomplished by an agreement in writing.

Negotiation

Negotiation of an instrument begins only upon its leaving the hands of the original payee. It may be negotiated to a subsequent holder, by that holder to another, and so on. The instrument is negotiated by delivery of a bearer instrument or by delivery and endorsement of an order instrument.

The endorser is one who signs an instrument after obtaining possession of it in order to negotiate it further. The payee, for example, becomes an endorser when negotiating a document.

Ordinary endorsers are those who sign a particular document in the normal course of business. They are distinguished from accommodation endorsers, who may or may not receive consideration from the maker for applying their signatures to the instrument. Each type has a different liability, which will be described in detail later in the chapter.

If there is no room left on the original document for additional endorsements, these may be made on a separate piece of paper. This must be firmly affixed to the instrument so that it becomes an extension or part of it. Such a paper is referred to as an allonge.

Blank Endorsement. Of the broad types of endorsement, this is the more common. The payee or subsequent holder signs the instrument and delivers it to the next holder. When that happens the instrument automatically becomes a bearer instrument, regardless of its original classification (as a bearer or order instrument). It can remain a bearer instrument from then on if subsequent holders do no more than deliver it. Although most subsequent holders will ask for endorsements before they will accept it, those

UNITED STATES LINES CO.

(SPACES IMMEDIATELY BELOW FOR SHIPPERS MEMORANDA—NOT PART OF BILL OF LADING)

FORWARDING AGENT—REFERENCES		EXPORT DEC. NO.
① ALL TRANSPORT, INC. 17 BATTERY PLACE, N. Y. C.		

DELIVERING CARRIER TO STEAMER:	CAR NUMBER — REFERENCE
MOORE MAC	

SHORT FORM BILL OF LADING
NORTH ATLANTIC SERVICES — OUTWARD
(NOT NEGOTIABLE UNLESS CONSIGNED "TO ORDER")

SHIP MORMACSAGA　10/24	FLAG	PIER 23 ST. BROOKLYN	PORT OF LOADING
PORT OF DISCHARGE FROM SHIP	AM	THROUGH BILL OF LADING	NEW YORK
(Where goods are to be delivered to consignee or On-carrier)	VALENCIA	MADRID	
If goods to be transshipped beyond Port of Discharge, from ship show destination Here ➡ To			

SHIPPER ②　　THE WILLIAM BARRY COMPANY

CONSIGNED TO: ORDER OF　ORDER OF SHIPPER

③　B. R. LOPEZ MANUFACTURING COMPANY

ADDRESS ARRIVAL NOTICE TO　RUA GENERAL ARGOLO NO. 15 MADRID, SPAIN

PARTICULARS FURNISHED BY SHIPPER OF GOODS

MARKS AND NUMBERS	NO. OF PKGS.	DESCRIPTION OF PACKAGES AND GOODS	MEASUREMENT	GROSS WEIGHT IN POUNDS
B. R. LOPEZ	9	ON BOARD		30#
# 1/9		TEXTILES		
# 10	1/10	50 YDS. PER ROLL RED TWEED		3#/33

SPECIMEN

FREIGHT AND CHARGES PAYABLE IN	NEW YORK

_____ @_____ PER 2240 LBS..$_____		
_____ @_____ PER 100 LBS..$_____		
_____ FT. @_____ PER 40 CU. FT.$_____		
_____ FT. @_____ PER CU. FT... $_____		
	_____ $_____		
	_____ $_____		
	_____ $_____		
	TOTAL .$_____		

RECEIVED from the shipper, the goods or packages said to contain goods herein mentioned, in apparent good order and condition, except as otherwise indicated herein, to be transported to the port of discharge named herein and/or
(TERMS OF THIS BILL OF LADING CONTINUED ON REVERSE SIDE HEREOF)
IN WITNESS WHEREOF,
THE MASTER OR AGENT OF SAID VESSEL HAS SIGNED　3
BILLS OF LADING, ALL OF THE SAME TENOR AND DATE, ONE OF WHICH BEING ACCOMPLISHED, THE OTHERS TO STAND VOID,

UNITED STATES LINES COMPANY

By

I _____

B/L No.　ISSUED AT NEW YORK, N. Y.　FOR THE MASTER

REVISED 3-15-60

OCTOBER　23　19**
MO.　DAY　YEAR

FIG. 26–9 (cont'd.).

endorsements are not legally necessary for negotiation. With the endorsement, however, the takers assure themselves of the endorser's identity and gain the benefit of the endorsement contract.

Special Endorsement.　This type of endorsement signifies the person to whom or to whose order it makes the instrument payable. An instrument specially endorsed becomes payable to the order of the special endorsee and may be further negotiated only by endorsement. A holder may convert a blank endorsement by writing, over the signature of the endorser in blank, any contract consistent with the character of the endorsement. The special endorsee may of course make it payable to bearer by endorsing it in blank.

Restrictive Endorsement. A blank or a special endorsement may also be a restrictive endorsement. This applies to an endorsement which is either conditional or purports to prohibit further transfer of the instrument; includes the words "for collection," "for deposit," "pay any bank," or like terms; or otherwise states that it is for the benefit or use of the endorser or of another person. As such, these endorsements do not prevent further transfer or negotiation of the instrument.

Assignment

In addition to the methods of negotiation described, an instrument may be transferred by an assignment, in which the rights of a holder may be assigned in writing to a third party.

The obligations of a holder may not be assigned. For example, John Doe, the payee of an order instrument, states, "I hereby assign all my right, title, and interest in the written note to John Smith." In this instance, John Smith acquires title to the note and is entitled to sue the maker for the full amount. When John Smith, the assignee, accepts the note, he is subject to all defenses that the maker may have against the original payee. He is, however, given the right to require the original payee to endorse the note to him, in which case he becomes a holder in due course, provided the instrument has not yet matured.

HOLDER IN DUE COURSE

The holder of a negotiable instrument is one who acquires it after negotiation. The holder can claim against the original maker or drawer and against other endorsers.

Conditions

A holder becomes a holder in due course if the following conditions are met:

1. The instrument was acquired in good faith and for value. The holder may be the bearer of a bearer instrument or the endorsee of an order instrument.
2. The document must be complete as to the payee's name, the maker's or drawer's name, and (in the case of a draft) the drawee's name.
3. The face of the instrument must have no apparent and obvious alterations.
4. Possession of the instrument must have been gained without notice that it is overdue.
5. Possession of the instrument must have been taken without notice that it has been dishonored or that there is any defense against or claim to it on the part of any person.

Defenses

A holder in due course benefits chiefly in that the negotiable instrument is taken free from all claims to it on the part of any person (e.g., any claim of legal title, liens, equities, etc.) and free from all defenses of any party to the instrument with whom the holder has not dealt (e.g., failure or lack of consideration, fraud in the inducement, etc.). However, a party with whom the holder in due course has not dealt retains the following defenses:

1. Infancy to the extent that it is a defense to a simple contract. Protection is afforded the infant against any undue course of actions by others, even at the expense of an occasional loss to an innocent purchaser.
2. Such other incapacity of duress or illegality of the transaction that renders the obligation of the party a nullity.
3. Incompetence, meaning mental incompetence, guardianship, ultra vires acts or lack of corporate capacity to do business, or any other incapacity apart from infancy.
4. Duress, in that the maker of a note may claim that an action was not taken freely because of undue pressure or influence, usually the result of misconduct on the part of the other party.
5. Illegality, which is most frequently a matter of gambling or usury but may arise in many other forms under a variety of statutes.
6. Misrepresentation that has induced a party to sign the instrument who has neither knowledge nor reasonable opportunity to gain knowledge of its character or essential terms. This exists where a maker intends to give a negotiable instrument, but the purpose for which it was to be given was fraudulent. For example, a promissory note may be given to pay for an asset which is fraudulently misrepresented. In that case, the maker intended to make the instrument but discovered later that it was for a fraudulently induced purchase. The maker would not be liable on the instrument to the original payee or to endorsers but would be liable to the holder in due course.
7. Discharge in bankruptcy, in that a holder in due course is subject to the defense of the debtor's discharge in bankruptcy.
8. Any other discharge of which the holder has notice when taking the instrument. A notice of discharge leaving other parties liable in the instrument does not prevent the purchaser from becoming a holder in due course. For example, the cancellation of an endorsement which leaves the maker and prior endorsers liable. As to these parties, the purchaser may be a holder in due course but takes the instrument subject to discharge of which the purchaser has notice.

Consumer Credit Limitations

In those states that have adopted the Uniform Consumer Credit Code, the use of negotiable notes in consumer transactions is prohibited, other than a check as evidence of the obligation of the buyer or lessee. Consequently, legislative limitations have been placed on the holder in due course doctrine.

Further, the Federal Trade Commission's "Holder in Due Course" trade regulation rule became effective in 1976. This rule, entitled "Preservation of Consumers' Claims and Defenses," is designed to end the practice in consumer credit transactions of the seller separating the customer's duty to pay from the seller's reciprocal duty to keep its promises. The holder in due course doctrine was used to require a customer to make full payment for a purchase despite nondelivery, failure of consideration, breach of warranty, misrepresentations, or even fraud on the part of the seller.

In adopting its holder in due course rule, the Commission determined that it constitutes an unfair and deceptive practice within the meaning of the Federal Trade Commission Act for a seller to take or receive a consumer credit contract or to accept the proceeds of a purchase money loan that it helped arrange, unless the underlying contract contains a notice provision. This notice declares that any holder of the contract, such as a subsequent purchaser, is subject to all claims and defenses which the debtor could assert against the seller. The notice further indicates that any recovery by the debtor against the holder of the contract under this clause shall not exceed the amounts paid by the debtor.

LIABILITIES OF THE PARTIES

The question of liability of the parties is legal and technical but some general information can be given. The persons liable on a negotiable instrument are the maker and endorser of a promissory note; the drawer, drawee (when the drawee accepts), and endorser of a draft. A payee only becomes liable on an instrument upon endorsement.

Liability of the Maker

The liability of the maker on a promissory note is unconditional and absolute. The maker is obliged to pay a time instrument on the day after maturity and a demand instrument upon its date, or if no date is stated, on the date of issuance. The maker also warrants the existence of the payee and the payee's capacity to endorse the instrument.

Liability of the Drawer

The drawer of a draft is secondarily liable, promising to pay only if the drawee bank does not first pay. The drawer does, however, admit the existence of the payee and the payee's capacity to endorse. Moreover, the drawer also acknowledges the debt and agrees that payment will be made to the holder or any subsequent endorser. The drawer is given the right to limit liability, though, by express stipulation in the instrument.

The drawer of an instrument becomes liable if the drawee does not pay or accept it, but only after receiving notice that the draft has been dishonored, unless this provision has been waived.

In most cases, the holder merely has to present the draft for payment. If the drawee refuses payment, the holder may then proceed directly against the drawer. This would not follow if there had been a previous stipulation to the effect that the instrument had to be presented for acceptance first.

This would occur when the draft is payable after sight; when presentment for acceptance is necessary to fix the maturity of the instrument (e.g., when the draft is made payable "in 60 days"); or when the draft is drawn payable elsewhere than at the residence or place of business of the drawee.

When a draft is made payable 60 days after sight, presentment for acceptance must be made before the drawer can be sued. However, should the drawee specifically refuse acceptance before the time period expires, then the holder need not wait until the end of that period to look to the drawer.

Even though the instrument is neither paid nor accepted, as the case may require, the drawer is still not liable until the notice of dishonor has been received. The procedure for giving this notice is discussed later in this chapter.

Liability of the Drawee

Upon accepting a draft, the drawee becomes the acceptor and is primarily liable. The drawee also warrants the existence of the drawer, the genuineness of the drawer's signature, the drawer's capacity and authority to draft the instrument, and the existence of the payee and the payee's capacity to endorse the instrument.

The drawee's acceptance must be in writing and signed. Customarily, the drawee's signature is written vertically across the face of the instrument, but the signature in any other place, even on the back of the instrument, is sufficient. It need not be accompanied by such words as "Accepted," "Certified," or "Good." It must not, however, bear any words indicating an attempt to dishonor the draft.

A draft may be accepted even though it has not been signed by the drawee or is otherwise incomplete, is overdue, or has been dishonored.

Where a draft is payable at a fixed period after sight and the acceptor fails to date the acceptance, the holder may complete it by supplying a date in good faith.

An acceptance may also be partial (where only a portion of the draft is accepted) or conditional. However, when the acceptance is either partial or conditional, the holder may treat it as a complete dishonor and then take the necessary proceedings against the drawer. If the holder accepts the partial or conditional acceptance, the drawer and all endorsers are discharged from liability unless they expressly or by implication authorize such acceptance by the holder. To avoid an implied authorization, the holder and endorsers must expressly indicate their opposition to the partial or conditional acceptance within a reasonable time after learning of it.

Liability of the Endorser

Any person signing an instrument other than as a maker, drawer, or acceptor is deemed to be an endorser, unless the person clearly indicates an intention to be bound in some other capacity. An endorser warrants that:

1. Good title to the instrument is possessed.
2. All signatures are genuine.
3. The instrument has not been materially altered.
4. There is no defense of any party good against the endorser.
5. Knowledge is not held of any insolvency proceeding initiated with respect to the maker or acceptor or the drawer of an unaccepted instrument.

An endorser engages that the paper will be honored; or if dishonored and the proper steps taken, the endorser will pay the amount of the instrument to the holder or to any subsequent endorser.

By endorsing the instrument "without recourse" the endorser disclaims liability for payment of the note. However, the words "without recourse" do not disclaim the endorser's liability for breach of the above five warranties. In lieu of the warranty that there is not a good defense against the endorser, an endorsement "with recourse" warrants that the endorser has no knowledge of such a defense.

Thus, even if any endorser's signature were obtained by fraud, the endorser would still be liable on the instrument if it had passed into the hands of one who had no knowledge of a defect and who had accepted the instrument in good faith and before maturity.

The last holder may sue any of the endorsers if the primary or secondary parties should fail to pay. Moreover, the last holder has the right to sue the endorsers in any order selected. In turn, endorsers usually have the right to sue previous endorsers to recover any losses sustained on the instrument.

Liability of the Accommodation Party

An accommodation party signs an instrument with or without receiving consideration for the purpose of enhancing the credit of another person who is to pay the paper when it falls due. The accommodation party's signature may appear on the instrument as a maker, acceptor, drawer, or endorser. The usual situation arises when an endorser signs for the accommodation of the payee. Other significant characteristics are:

1. When the instrument is taken for value before it is due, the accommodation party is liable to the holder.
2. Except as against a holder in due course, oral evidence is admissible to prove that the party has signed for accommodation.
3. An endorsement which shows that it is not in the chain of title (an irregular endorsement) is notice to all subsequent takers of its accommodation character.
4. An accommodation party is not liable to the accommodated party. If the accommodation party pays the instrument, however, a right of recourse is retained against the accommodated party.

Finality of Payment or Acceptance

Section 3-418 of the UCC follows the rule of *Price* v. *Neal*, an English case decided in 1762, which holds that a drawee who accepts or pays an instrument on which the signature is forged is bound by the action and cannot recover the payment. The rule is not limited to drawees but applies equally to the maker of a note or to any party who pays an instrument.

In *Price* v. *Neal,* two forged drafts were drawn on a certain drawee. Before the first draft was presented to the drawee, it was endorsed to a third party who paid value for the draft and was innocent of the forgery. The second draft was presented to the drawee who accepted it. It was then endorsed to the same third party. Subsequently, the drawee paid the entire amount to the third party then holding both instruments. After discovering the forgery, the drawee sought to recover the amounts paid out to the innocent holder. On each instrument recovery was denied. As to the second instrument, once the draft had been accepted the warranty as to the genuineness of the signature operated to prevent a recovery. In the case of the first instrument, the court reached its decision on the theory that the holder was innocent of the forgery and had paid value.

There are certain limitations to this section, however. One is that the person obtaining the payment or acceptance does not disclaim the five warranties of presentment and transfer noted above. Further, there is a bank collection provision that permits a payer bank to recover a payment improperly paid if it returns the item or sends notice of dishonor within the limited time provided in Section 4-301 of the Uniform Commercial Code— Bank Deposits and Collections.

NOTICE OF DISHONOR

The holder of a negotiable instrument must give notice to the drawer or endorser if the instrument should not be honored, except where the provision is waived. The notice indicating that acceptance or payment has been refused may be either written or oral, and delivered personally or by mail. The notice must be given within three days after dishonor or receipt of notice of dishonor.

PROTEST

Protest is a certificate of dishonor made under the seal of a U.S. consul or vice consul or a notary public or other persons authorized to certify dishonor by the law of the place where dishonor occurs. It is not necessary except on drafts drawn or payable outside the United States.

The protest must identify the instrument and need not be in any particular form. It need not be annexed to the instrument and may be forwarded separately, but annexation may help to identify the instrument. The protest is normally followed with the notice of dishonor.

CHAPTER 27

OUTSIDE FINANCING

Every successful business needs outside financial support and obtains it from its principals, trade creditors, and a variety of nontrade sources. Most business loans are short term in nature, either time or demand. A maturity date is specified in the time loan, usually 30, 60, 90, or 120 days; while a demand loan may be repaid by the borrower or called by the bank at any time. The lender may ask for collateral or may simply make an unsecured or signature loan.

Short-term loans are used to meet a temporary need for funds. The reason for the cash shortage may be that the borrower had a poor year and must meet some major expenses in the near future, or extra funds may be needed for the seasonal requirements of the business. In all short-term loans, the borrower is expected to repay once the need for the loan ceases. This means a sound company will clean up its borrowings at least once a year.

If the need for supplemental funds is consistent and if the credit position of the borrower is sound, it may be possible to satisfy these long-term needs by one of the methods discussed in this chapter. The customer can thereby meet the financial requirements to finance expansion or add to the physical facilities of the organization.

Because many companies use factors and financing companies as regular sources of outside financing, a knowledge of these techniques is a necessity for the credit executive, essential for proper analysis of a customer's financial situation. The receivables concerned in both factoring and financing are open account, not installment account sales.

A business firm may make use of outside financing for a large number of reasons: to avoid dilution of ownership equity and control which would result from raising funds through issuing more common stock or taking in partners; to obtain large amounts of operating cash expeditiously and simply; to secure operating cash on a flexible basis; to improve net working capital position; to take advantage of cash discounts and other profit opportunities; to protect and improve its financial position and credit rating; and to benefit from the technical assistance provided by the specialized financing institutions.

FACTORS

Factoring grew out of the specific need for working funds in some industries, such as the textile and fur trades. It provides the means for business executives to convert receivables to cash before they are due without retaining liability for their payment. It had its inception in early American history, when factors acted as commission merchants handling goods on consignment. During the latter years of the 19th century and the early years of the present century, factors began to stop acting as sales agents for their clients. The general factor thus gradually evolved into the modern factor. The great growth of factoring, the entrance of a variety of financing institutions into this field, and the widespread use of such financing in many different lines of business are all quite recent phenomena, developing since the beginning of the present century.

Among the principal reasons that modern-day companies use a factor are to limit credit and collection expense, including credit losses, to a definite percentage of credit sales; to reduce credit and collection expense ratio (including credit losses) or obtain a more efficient performance of credit and collection; to increase sales through the credit granting and collection services provided by the factor; and to increase its profits by concentrating on product development, production, and sales.

Factoring Procedure

In factoring, the accounts receivable are purchased by the factoring concern, which assumes the credit risk without recourse to the seller. The seller's customers are notified to make payment directly to the factor.

The business firm entering into a factoring agreement not only contracts to sell its receivables to the factor but also relieves itself of the credit and collection function, including the cost and risk of decisionmaking with regard to credit and collections. This role is assumed by the factor for a fee. Under no other method of short-term financing do business firms shift the credit and collection job to the financing institution. When a business firm is being factored, it shows on its invoices a notice that payment for the goods is to be made to its factor.

The factor approves credits for the business firm, termed the client. As the latter makes shipments, it sends copies of the invoices and the shipping documents to the factor. It may obtain immediate cash for the full net face value of the invoices (i.e., the gross amount of the invoices less any discounts and allowances granted to the firm's customers) from the factor, minus only the commission for services rendered and a reserve to offset returned goods, merchandise claims, and the like. The remainder due the client is made available at the average due date of the invoices; any credit losses are borne by the factor.

The above is a brief description of the factoring procedure and it may be summed up in the following definition of an old-line factor.

A factor checks credits, purchases resultant accounts receivable, and cashes sales on an advance basis or at maturity, on a notification basis, without recourse. The balance of this discussion is oriented towards this type of factoring, and each of the elements in the definition will now be discussed in detail.

Checks Credits.   When a factor checks credits, it takes over the credit and collection functions of its clients. The clients no longer need to conduct credit investigations and analysis, make credit decisions, keep records of accounts receivable, collect accounts receivable, and sustain bad-debt losses.

When an order is received from a customer, the client calls the factor for a recommendation. The factor usually has a credit file on the account or will set one up when the request is received. The file contains agency reports, memoranda of the factor's interviews with the principals and the accountant, trade reports, bank investigations, and other information normally contained in a credit folder. In addition, there is a record of inquiries on the account, the factor's current exposure, and the recommendation. If the recommendation is favorable, the factor approves the client's order.

Purchases Resultant Accounts Receivable.   When the factor approves a client's order, there is a concurrent agreement that the receivables resulting from the order will be purchased by the factor. This distinguishes factoring from pledged borrowing: in factoring, title to the claim passes from the client to the factor; in pledged borrowing, title remains with the client. In this way the client is assured of a stated amount of money each time the factor approves an order. There is no need for accounts receivable followup or for collection procedures. The likelihood of bad-debt losses is completely eliminated on approved accounts.

The only exception to this procedure occurs when a client ships an order which has not been approved. In that case the factor is not obligated to participate in the transaction. The order is shipped at client's risk. There the factor reserves the right to turn down the receivable arising from that particular transaction or may advance money against it with recourse, which makes the client contingently liable on the account.

Cashes Sales.   At any time after the receivable is created, the client may turn it over to the factor. This function of the factor is called cashing receivables, or cashing sales, on an advance basis (prior to maturity) or at maturity.

On an Advance Basis.   Upon the request of the client, the factor advances funds against the receivables that have been checked or approved. This client forwards the invoices and usually receives 85 to 90 percent of the face amount purchased before maturity; the factor holds back the balance for such contingencies as returns and discounts, disputed receivables, and client's risk receivables. This provides funds to the client before the due date of the invoice.

A company that is trading actively on its invested capital and does not want to tie up its assets in receivables will find this feature useful. Much of the need for borrowing is eliminated, ownership of the business can remain undiluted, the liquidity of the firm is strengthened, and net working capital is turned actively.

At Maturity. The factor does not advance any funds but remits monthly on the average due date of the invoices purchased in any given month. Banks will often make unsecured loans with greater confidence to a client factored under a maturity agreement.

Notification. This means the factor's clients notify their customers that their invoices are being sold to the factor. Each invoice is stamped to that effect. The client's customers pay directly to the factor which now owns the receivable. Thus the factor acts as a middleman in the regular creditor-debtor relationship.

In industries such as textiles and furs, where factoring is common, factors keep extensive files on companies. Their clients are constantly asking for recommendations on their customers. By the same token, the customers recognize the role of the factor and are willing to submit complete credit information so their account can be analyzed.

Without Recourse. Under an old-line factoring agreement, the factor purchases accounts receivable without recourse and bears the entire burden of collection and risk of bad-debt losses. The client that has sold the account receivable is immediately relieved of any responsibility concerning its payment. This feature is especially attractive to a company which must plan cash requirements very carefully and cannot afford extraordinary bad-debt losses.

Loans on Inventory. In addition to purchasing clients' accounts receivable without recourse, factors offer a number of other services. Chief among these is the lending of money against inventory. This method of secured borrowing is often used by customers to finance temporary needs for working funds. When the client sells inventory, it turns over the resultant receivable to the factor and liquidates the loan.

Other Types of Loans. The factor will sometimes make loans or advances for other purposes in the same way as any other financial institution. The client may wish to purchase equipment and machinery, build additions to the physical facilities, purchase the interest of retiring or deceased principals, expand operations by purchasing other companies, or reorganize the financial structure of the firm by retiring bonds or preferred stock.

Cost of Factoring

The factor charges a commission or fee for performing the credit and collection function and for purchasing the firm's receivables without recourse for credit losses. In addition, the factor charges interest on funds provided when it cashes receivables. This interest charge is usually two to three percentage points above the bank prime rate.

The factor's commission for service ranges between 2 per cent and 3 per cent of sales, or the net face value of receivables purchased over one year. It is determined beforehand by negotiations between the client and the factor, and depends upon a number of conditions:

1. The nature of the client's industry, including style considerations, seasonal aspects, stability of items, and whether customers are manufacturers, wholesalers, or retailers.
2. Annual sales volume of the client. As volume mounts, the percentage charged will usually tend to decline.
3. Average size of the orders processed. Large orders are no more time-consuming to process than small orders and produce more revenue for the factor. Therefore, the factor's commission rate may be expected to decline as the size of the individual orders rises.
4. Average annual sales volume per customer. As this figure rises, there is less work and followup for the factor, since the client's business is becoming concentrated in few accounts. The commission rate will therefore tend to decline.
5. Credit position of the client's customers. Where the client sells only to high-quality accounts and the risk is relatively small, the factor's commission may be lower. On the other hand, a company that concentrates its sales on accounts of questionable credit desirability should expect to pay a higher commission if the factor is willing to go along with those accounts.
6. Client's selling terms. If they are long, the factor must wait to collect its receivable. This would necessitate a higher fee.
7. Other services such as billing, which may be provided by the factor, will increase costs and therefore raise the charge to the client.

Evidence of a Factoring Agreement

Credit executives should develop an understanding of the reasons why companies need additional cash, what methods they may choose to obtain it, and what to look for on the financial statement of their customers that would indicate the presence of such outside financing.

The balance sheet of a company that uses a factor on an advance basis may list a small amount of money Due from Factor, since most of the proceeds from the sold receivables have already been realized. By the same token, the balance sheet will not list accounts receivable, since they will have been sold to the factor.

When analyzing a balance sheet of a company on an advance arrangement, the credit executive should be alert to the fact that the customer is not only obtaining a credit service but an increase in the availability of cash. This calls for a searching analysis of how that cash has been applied.

Where the arrangement is on a maturity basis, the amount listed Due from Factor will usually reflect the total amount of proceeds from the sale of receivables. The balance sheet will show little or no accounts receivable.

Questions to Ask

Due to the confidential, contractual relationship between the customer and its factor, it may be difficult to obtain frank answers to all of the questions posed below. It may be necessary to have the customer authorize the factor to disclose whatever information may be sought.

On an Advance Basis.   Initially, it is important to determine whether the factoring arrangement is on an advance basis. If so, the balance sheet of the customer may hide more meaningful data than it reveals. For example, a statement of $22,750 Due from Factor cannot be taken at face value. If the arrangement calls for advances on accounts receivable, the factor should be asked the following:

1. What is the contractual advance percentage? Is it fully used?
2. Are there any arrangements for unsecured overdrafts? If so, what are they? An overdraft is a verbal agreement by the factor to provide funds in excess of the contractual advance percentage on receivables, usually to a stated limit for a specific period of time.
3. Are there any overdrafts outstanding? If so, how much? When an arrangement calls for overdrafts in addition to advances, the reason should be determined. It could indicate that the customer is financially strained, since inordinately high sales would necessitate increased purchases of merchandise. Therefore, it is essential to obtain profit and loss figures to ascertain whether this increased activity yields commensurate profits and does not weaken the firm. In addition, interim trial balance figures are an aid in determining the current profitability of operations.
4. Are the overdrafts stated as an amount over 100 per cent of the purchased receivables or over the contractual advance percentage?
5. Have overdrafts been requested but refused or restricted?

Maturity Arrangement.   If the arrangement calls for payment on the average due date, it is essential to determine the following:

1. Is the item Due from Factor pledged to a third party, such as a bank, to secure a loan.
2. Is there any intercompany offset situation? Does the factor have other affiliates or subsidiaries that are suppliers of credit to the customer?

General.   Under either an advance or maturity basis, it is important to determine if the item Due from Factor has been diluted by such contingencies as returns and advances, disputed receivables or receivables taken at the client's risk; or through advances on overdrafts where additional collateral may be taken.

Upon inquiry, a factor will usually state, in either an advance or maturity arrangement, the customer's range of credit balances, or the gross differences between the accounts receivable purchased and the advances that the factor has already made. It should also be determined whether the factor will apply a reserve against that amount for returns and discounts, disputed receivables, or accounts receivable not guaranteed by the factor and therefore at client's risk.

If the customer has credit balances under either an advance or maturity arrangement, it should be ascertained to what extent these credit balances can be diluted as outlined above. Moreover, even when the customer has a credit balance, the factor may have additional collateral to cover contingencies. If overdrafts are granted, the factor may have taken additional collateral.

The profit and loss statement should be examined carefully to note the added costs of using a factor. They may offset the decreased credit and collection costs of using the factor.

FINANCE COMPANIES

Finance companies make loans against pledged or assigned collateral such as accounts receivable, inventory, or fixed assets. Their services differ from those of factors in that the finance companies do not buy accounts receivable or other assets; they look to their client for the repayment of these loans.

Finance companies are different from commercial banks in that they do not create checkbook money. A commercial bank makes a loan by establishing a credit in favor of the borrower's account. The borrower may write checks on that amount to pay other creditors. A finance company lends funds directly to the borrower.

Accounts receivable financing, as a method to advance operating cash to business, was pioneered in the decade preceding World War I. For more than a quarter of a century its growth was relatively slow, and it was not until 1941 that receivables financing became a significant source of funds. Now practically all of the major banks in America have financing operations and many finance companies are subsidiaries of bank holding companies. Also, many commercial finance companies specialize in accounts receivable financing, and many factors have accounts receivable financing departments. Moreover, some finance companies are owned by manufacturers, while some of the larger finance companies own their own commercial banks.

One important result of the development is that accounts receivable financing has become increasingly important in the world of finance. The necessity for the use of receivables as collateral arises because the borrower is trading actively on invested capital and needs funds to finance its current operations. With the variety of institutional sources available, small business firms as well as medium-sized and large companies are able to obtain funds through receivables financing.

Proportionally, more of the small and medium-sized companies make use of receivables financing, although many users are among the larger firms in their field. Business firms making use of receivables financing find it more advantageous than other methods in achieving the largest possible profits in view of their particular situations and opportunities for growth. Some firms finance receivables infrequently, perhaps to take advantage of an exceptional business opportunity. Some pledge their receivables only at certain seasons during the year, or for only a few years; others use the technique as an established financial procedure.

Financing Procedure

In financing, a loan is secured by accounts receivable which are assigned to the finance company or purchased by it with full recourse to the borrower in the event of a default by the debtor. Under this type of arrangement, banks and most finance companies use the nonnotification form of assignment, which means that the borrower's customer is not notified that the account has been assigned. For this reason financing is sometimes called nonnotification financing. However, there are instances when notification is part of the agreement, in which case the debtor makes payment directly to the financing agency.

A company entering into an accounts receivable financing agreement continues to operate its own credit department as before. It makes credit decisions, maintains its customary detailed accounts receivable records, and handles its own collections, dealing directly with debtors. Meanwhile, the company signs a formal covering agreement with the finance company. This is known as an underlying agreement or working plan and is a continuing arrangement for funds to be advanced by the finance company.

Banks frequently use a collateral loan form of agreement, since they do not have statutory authority to purchase open accounts receivables outright. Commercial finance companies use the purchase form of agreement; accounts are purchased for 100 per cent of their value but a reserve is retained to secure the collection of the accounts. The effect of both procedures is the same. The agreement specifies what percentage of the value of the assigned accounts will be available to the borrower. The percentage varies depending upon industry, current economic conditions, the standing of the borrower, and so on. The agreement also outlines the overall conditions, such as maximum limit, interest rate, service fee, if any, and the rights and liabilities of each party.

The procedure for obtaining funds varies according to the agreement. In some instances, the borrower signs a note and submits it with a schedule of specific accounts to be assigned, duplicate invoices, and evidence of shipment or delivery. In other cases, invoices and shipping documents are not required and the borrower continuously assigns its total accounts receivable which are certified by an outside accountant.

The method used to collect pledged accounts depends upon whether the arrangement is on a notification or nonnotification basis. For the most part, banks and finance companies use the nonnotification method and the borrower's customer is not aware that the account has been pledged. Consequently, payment is made by the customer to the borrower in the normal manner, and in turn by the borrower to the lender.

If the notification plan is used, the original invoice sent to the customer carries a notation to the effect that the invoice has been assigned and that payment is to be made directly to the financing agency.

If an account is not paid at maturity, it is carried 30 to 60 days following which the amount advanced is charged back to the borrower. In the event the account was purchased outright, other accounts are substituted as collateral or the borrowed amount is repaid.

Loans Against Accounts Receivable. The steps in accounts receivable financing are:

1. The borrowing firm makes its own sales, conducts its own credit investigations, makes its own credit decisions, passes on its own orders, makes its own collections, and absorbs its own bad-debt losses.

2. As it makes deliveries, the concern notifies the financing company how much money it wants to borrow against receivables. The amount which can be borrowed is a predetermined percentage of the face amount of the invoices presented. Usually the finance company will require some evidence that the borrower has shipped or delivered the goods covered in the arrangement.

The percentage advanced against invoices is determined separately from the per diem rate. The finance company and the client agree upon the percentage to be advanced based upon the borrower's number and quality (credit ratings) of customers, volume of business, selling terms, line of business, type of merchandise, collection efficiency, bad-debt experience, average size of orders, number of returns, and other specific details of the business.

3. The advance is paid back from the proceeds of the pledged receivables. The borrower generally endorses and delivers the customers' checks direct to the finance company.

4. After waiting a stated number of days (three to five normally) for checks to be collected funds, the finance company credits the client's account for sums collected on the individual pledged accounts. It then deducts the amounts already loaned and sends the balance to the client or makes the funds available to the client upon request.

Loans Against Inventory. A finance company will make inventory loans in much the same way as a factor. These loans are generally made to meet short-term capital requirements of the client, but occasionally a client will borrow this way on a fairly steady basis.

The method is quite satisfactory from the viewpoint of the finance company. As inventory is used in manufacturing or is sold, chances are it will be or has been replaced through additional purchasing. When the periodic reports show a reduction, then a loan reduction may be in order.

Loans Against Other Assets. The finance company sometimes engages in other types of lending.

Unsecured.   In this instance, the finance company's analysis of the borrower is based on the four "Cs", in much the same way that a commercial bank would consider a request for an unsecured loan. Usually these loans cover temporary capital needs of the client.

Mortgage Loans.   These are usually made on the client's plant and equipment. They are long-term in nature and are repaid on a regular schedule.

Loans Secured by Miscellaneous Assets.   These are negotiated to meet the particular needs of the client and may be secured by life insurance policies, bank books, stocks and bonds, or any other valuable assets owned by the borrower company, its endorsers, or its guarantors.

Equipment Financing and Leasing.   Equipment financing enables a company to acquire fixed assets, such as industrial equipment and machinery, and pay for them on an installment basis.

The plans are arranged by finance companies and instituted through dealers that are their clients. Terms are arranged at the convenience of the borrower and include such considerations as the financial strength and cash requirements of the borrower, useful life of the equipment to be purchased, and the seasonal characteristics of the borrower's line of business.

The borrower makes a down payment at the time the equipment is purchased, then pays the balance, including installation, delivery and carrying charges, in a series of installments. These may be paid monthly or arranged to correspond to the seasonal periods when the borrower has large amounts of cash on hand. Sometimes payment schedules and amounts are geared to the depreciation charges to be taken on the purchased equipment. The length of the contract does not exceed the useful life of the equipment. If the borrower prefers, however, it may accelerate payments to reduce the carrying charges on the installment loan. This method permits the borrower to have use of the asset while it is being paid for. At the same time, it releases funds which would otherwise have gone to retire the debt created when the equipment was purchased.

In circumstances where the user of the equipment may prefer to lease rather than own it outright, finance companies can offer complete programs to meet those needs. As title is held by the finance company, a monthly leasing charge is paid by the client for the use of the equipment. This arrangement has been extended to include all types of fixed assets used in industry, such as plant and equipment, automobiles and trucks, and conveyors and other materials handling facilities.

Cost of Financing

There is only one charge incurred by a business firm in making use of accounts receivable financing at any major finance company. Throughout the period of the financing agreement, the borrower firm is billed at the end of each month in accordance with the extent of its borrowing activity during that month. Every business firm does not pay the same rate. In fact, the rate usually runs from two to eight percentage points above the bank prime rate. These differences in rates tend to reflect the differences in the size of accounts accepted, in the degree of risk assumed, and in other services rendered by the financing institutions.

Evidence of a Financing Arrangement

The balance sheet of a company borrowing against receivables should show evidence of this fact, either on the statement or in the accompanying footnotes. Often receivables and corresponding short-term loans are linked together by an explanatory note. If that is not done, the credit executive should look for signs that a financing arrangement does exist.

Questions To Ask

An understanding of a customer's arrangement with its finance company may be properly resolved by obtaining answers to the following questions:

1. Is the arrangement normal? With a normal financing arrangement there is no notification to the client's customer that receivables are being pledged to secure a loan. If the agreement differs from the normal arrangement in that it provides for notification, this should act as a warning that the finance company considers the client a higher than ordinary risk.
2. What is the contract percentage advanced by the finance company against pledged receivables?
3. What is the customer's overall line with the finance company? A finance company will advance a contract percentage against pledged assets, although there is an overall dollar limit to the loan.
4. Does the customer draw the full amount available? Are there any arrangements for overadvances above the contractual percentage? If the customer does not draw the full loan amount available, this is probably a favorable sign. If it is doing so, it either signals full dependency on the finance company or possibly indicates that finances are in a strained position. On the other hand, overadvances may indicate a great deal of confidence by the finance company. A conclusion as to which way the scale is balanced can only be drawn after all the facts and circumstances are weighed.
5. What is the customer's gross receivables amount and its current loan balance with the finance company? The difference between these two items is the customer's equity. Equity can be diluted by discounts and reserves, contras and concentrations, or delinquent accounts receivable. Discounts and reserves are direct reductions of face amount. Contras are potential reductions, in that the client's customer may offset an amount owed by the client to the customer. Concentration of receivables from few large companies poses a danger to those receivables and the market position of the seller. Finally, delinquent accounts are potential bad debts.
6. What is the usual delinquency percentage? The quality of the account's receivables gains in importance because the company is contingently liable on them.
7. What is the accounts receivable turnover experience?
8. Is there any pledge of the accounts receivable equity to the finance company, the finance company's affiliates or subsidiaries, or to any other third party?

IMPACT OF LIENS UNDER UCC

It is important to note that both factoring and financing require a security agreement between the parties, a filing under the Uniform Commercial Code (UCC) in the state capital, and in some states, filing in the county, instead or as well.

It is equally important to note that there may be additional hidden liens against the collateral held by the factor or finance company. Factors and finance companies sometimes take inventory as collateral and do not record this lien under the UCC. This can be done through the use of field warehouse, a third-party public warehouse, or through direct possession of the physical asset. In all of these instances, a valid lien can exist under the Uniform Commercial Code.

In addition, the assets that are pledged may extend to a lien on every tangible asset on the customer's balance sheet. Furthermore, while guaranties or letters of credit issued by the factor or finance company are only a contingent liability, they can become real, thereby increasing the customer's indebtedness to the factor or financing company and possibly diminishing the availability of funds.

TERM LOANS

During a period of expanding business growth, many firms cannot fill their financial needs solely through additional investment and retained profits. Consequently, they are forced to look for long-term outside funds. Some texts distinguish between intermediate and long-term financing, but for this discussion no distinction is made.

Although long-term borrowing cannot be considered part of the owner's investment in a business, the company does have the opportunity to use those funds over a relatively long period of time. Generally they are used to purchase machinery, fixtures, equipment, real estate, and other assets of a durable nature. This procedure frees the invested capital to carry accounts receivable, pay for inventories, and meet the daily cash needs of the business.

This type of financing has a usual maturity date of between three and five years. When interest rates are low and banks have funds available for lending, the terms tend to be longer; they tend to shorten when interest rates rise and the supply of money declines.

Each loan is a separate agreement between the borrower and the lender, so the terms of the transaction may be specified in the contract. Installment payments are common and may be made quarterly, semiannually, or annually. Payments may also be made at irregular intervals, depending on the capital needs of the business. Prepayment of the loan is usually allowed, though sometimes a penalty clause may be part of the agreement.

Interest rates on terms loans generally run slightly higher than for short-term loans. Administration costs are higher. There may be an escalator clause, which is a provision in the loan agreement for the interest rate to change over the period of the loan.

Restrictive Covenants

The lender may make an unsecured term loan, require a pledge of collateral, or secure a lien against the property as an additional margin of safety. Any kind of personal property may be pledged, while a lien on tangible property is created by a mortgage. The arrangements are quite similar to those made in short-term financing. In addition to a promissory note, however, the borrower signs a term loan agreement which specifies how the business may be conducted while the loan is outstanding. Some of the points usually covered in the agreement are:

1. The borrower may not pay excessive dividends, borrow from other sources, sell business assets, guarantee the debts of other companies, merge or consolidate with other companies, or buy back any outstanding shares of stock.

2. The borrower generally is required to maintain a certain relationship between current assets and current liabilities, maintain the physical and real assets of the company in good condition, employ the proceeds of the loan in the way prescribed, provide adequate insurance coverage on the business, maintain accounting records and have them available for review, or submit periodic balance sheet and operating statements to the lender.

3. Property acquired by the borrower after the agreement is signed may become subject to the terms of the loan agreement by the after-acquired clause. This means that the property is automatically pledged, although the borrower did not own it at the time the loan was made.

4. The interest rate may change during the life of the agreement through the use of the escalator clause.

5. The entire loan may become due immediately if the borrower fails to live up to the agreement. This is called an acceleration clause. Where the borrower cannot meet the terms of the note, the lender may institute foreclosure proceedings. The court renders a judgment and orders the property sold to satisfy the claim. If the proceeds of the sale satisfy the amount owed to the creditor, any excess is returned to the debtor. Should the proceeds be insufficient to pay the claim, the creditor may seek a deficiency judgment against the personal assets of the debtor for the difference.

Public and Private Placements

Many of the institutions making long-term loans are not required to keep a major portion of their resources in liquid assets and can therefore provide money for buildings, machinery, and equipment. Their loans are usually evidenced by collateral bonds, mortgages, or debentures of high-quality credit risks. This enables a borrower to obtain funds without having to repay the loan in one year. It enlarges the financial resources available to a business and releases other funds for day-to-day operation.

When a public offering is to be made, the borrower decides what terms will attract the investor at minimum cost to the borrower. The distribution and administrative details of the bond issue are usually turned over to an investment banker specializing in this field. The banker usually guarantees a minimum price for the bonds.

When a private placement of a bond issue is to be made, the buyer can exert somewhat more influence on the terms of the issue. The indenture, deed of trust or contract, will specify the terms of the loan and repayment. Some features may be included which are particularly desirable to the borrower or to the lender. Since the contract is only between two parties, these points can be readily determined.

LEASING

Leasing is a long-established practice. It dates as far back as ancient Egypt, when the Pharaohs arranged the sale and leaseback of land between subjects. However, it was not until the period of rapid industrial expansion and inadequate depreciation allowances that followed World War II that leasing became widely accepted as a method of acquiring the use of assets other than real estate.

Lease contracts allow use of equipment by lessees in return for periodic rental payments to lessors over a specified time period. They stipulate the number, size, and time sequence of lease payments, and include clauses covering cancellation rights, conditions for renewal or a purchase option, the treatment of tax benefits and obligations, and the servicing responsibilities of lessor and lessee. Where no purchase option is provided in a lease contract, residual value reverts to lessor, which may recoup costs by selling or releasing the asset.

The Financial Accounting Standards Board set forth comprehensive guidelines for classifying leases into two broad categories: operating leases and capital leases. Since leases are designed to transfer substantially all of the benefits and risks incident to ownership of property from one contracting party (the lessor) to another (the lessee), these leases are tantamount to completed exchanges and the accounting for them should mirror that reality. Further, if a lessor can effect such a full transfer of benefits and risks through a lease, the lessee has assumed those very same benefits and risks through the lease; thus a form of proportion should exist in the accounting by lessees and lessors. The lessor by transfer through the lease has converted its ownership of property into an investment in a lease contract (a receivable in accounting terms); the lessee has acquired an asset (an intangible) and incurred an obligation (a liability in accounting terms). Leases of this full transfer variety are called capital leases by accountants and finance leases by other finance people. All other leases are called operating leases.

With either form of lease, additional charges may be added for services which the lessor is providing, but which the lessee could provide either itself or through an outside contract. These might include administration, insurance, maintenance, and property taxes. In both types of contracts legal title is retained by the lessor. Entering into a finance lease does have many of the characteristics of an investment decision in that once the contract is signed the stream of payments to be made cannot be changed by management's subsequent decisions.

Operating Leases

These leases are typically short-term or spot rentals of equipment and property, and are cancellable on short notice. They usually provide such nonfinancial services as insurance, delivery, maintenance, and repair by the lessor. The most important feature is that the sum of the rental payments bears no direct relationship to the total cost of the assets being leased. Therefore, a user can acquire use of an asset for a fraction of its useful life, and count its cost as a straight operating expense.

Lessors include manufacturing companies, independent leasing companies, lease brokers, commercial finance companies, and most of the nation's largest commercial banks. Many equipment manufacturers use leasing as a marketing tool, offering equipment either for sale or on operating leases.

Finance Leases

These leases are completely net leases and are noncancellable over the basic lease term. The lessee is required to make a series of rental payments, which sum is equal to the initial cost of the asset being leased plus interest. Thus the lessee has a definite fixed commitment as in any other form of term financing. Conversely, lessors with excess earnings obtain ownership benefits, which include depreciation allowances, interest tax deductions, and investment tax credits—often passed on to lessees in the form of lower rental rates.

There are basic requirements inherent in any lease before it is considered a true lease. As owner, the lessor must bear the risk of ownership, which includes the possible decline in the economic value of the equipment. In addition, the lessee cannot build equity interest in the leased equipment with lease payments nor can the lessee assume title after making a specified number of lease payments. The lease terms must be less than the economic life of the equipment so that it has a residual value of at least 15 per cent of its original value and an economic life of at least 2 years or 10 per cent, whichever is greater, of the lease term.

A common practice in the past was to disclose the pertinent details of a lease agreement in the footnotes to a balance sheet. Now, however, the balance sheet of the lessor under a finance lease shows the receivable from the lease as an asset, classified into current and noncurrent portions. As for the lessee, the lease rights are shown as an asset and the lease obligations as a liability, classified into current and noncurrent portions. Consequently, the balance sheets of business enterprises transacting finance leases now show significantly larger investment in property and larger liabilities. These larger liabilities mean larger debt-to-equity ratio. The number of times interest charges are covered by earnings also is affected. Since the lessee's obligation is declining over the term of the lease, interest charges in the early years are higher than in the later years. For a company with growing commitment to finance leasing, the effect would be to decrease net income.

An innovative feature of a finance lease is that it may be leveraged. Variously called leveraged leases, leveraged tax leases, and tax shelter leases, they have been especially popular with financial institutions and with individuals in high tax brackets who act as the lessors. The leveraged lease is a segmented financing arrangement whereby up to 80 per cent of the purchase price of equipment is supplied by long-term lenders, with the lessor of the equipment, typically a financial institution, providing the remainder amount as equity. The debt in these arrangements is secured by a security interest in the equipment, a pledge of the lease payments, and an assignment of the rights of the owner under the lease document. It is serviced from lease payments during the life of the lease.

The leveraged lease is also tax-oriented, in that the equity investor receives tax benefits based upon the total costs of the equipment. These benefits consist of investment tax credits and tax deferrals arising because the accelerated depreciation and interest expense exceeds rental income in the early years of the lease. The lessor also receives nontax-oriented benefits to the extent of lease payments in excess of debt service requirements and whatever residual value of the equipment is realized following the end of the lease. A portion of the lessor's tax benefits is transferred to the lessee in the form of reduced rental payments, thus making the structure attractive to lessees, especially those users that are not in a tax situation whereby they could efficiently utilize the tax benefits through direct ownership of the equipment.

Sale-Leaseback Arrangement

In a sale-leaseback arrangement, a company sells property or equipment to an insurance company or other institutional investor and arranges for a long-term lease. The rental consists of a predetermined rate of return plus amortization of the purchase price over the life of the lease, which generally runs from 25 to 30 years. The company as lessee continues to assume all of the risks, taxes, insurance, maintenance, and other costs of ownership. Moreover, the company sometimes can obtain an option to make an offer to buy the property for the remaining unamortized balance of the investment plus a penalty payment. If the offer is rejected, the company has the right to either continue in possession or vacate.

The institutional buyer's decision to enter into the sale-leaseback arrangement depends heavily on the lessee's credit standing, earnings record, and management ability. The location and quality of the property or equipment in question is also an important factor. In addition, commercial buildings such as apartment houses and office buildings have greater appeal than industrial property to institutional investors.

The sale-leaseback device is used by many cash-poor companies to raise cash. While raising cash under this method alleviates the debtor's short-term cash inflow crunch, credit executives must be alert to the distortion it makes in their debtor's financial position despite the relief of knowing that current bills can now be paid. The balance sheet appears more liquid since cash has been built up, but short- and long-term obligations have been increased, the profit and loss statement will show increased rental payments, and the overall capital strength has been weakened. This does not mean that sale-leaseback arrangements should not be used as well as all types of leasing arrangements. But rather, that their use must be taken into account when reviewing the credit decision

GOVERNMENT PROGRAMS

The U.S. Government has set up various agencies to assist small business in meeting their capital needs. The principal agency for accomplishing this goal is the Small Business Administration, which was given the authority under the Small Business Act of 1953 to make direct loans and to guarantee portions of loans made by commercial banks and other lenders.

Small Business Administration

Designed to assist small businesses to finance capital needs for growth and expansion, the Small Business Administration (SBA) participates in loans made by private lenders or may lend directly when the private institutions do not consider the prospect a satisfactory credit risk.

For business loan purposes, the SBA defines a small business as one that is independently owned and operated, not dominant in its field, and meets sales standards developed by the agency. Its clients comprise businesses that may be undercapitalized, lack sufficient collateral, and have not established an operating history. Consequently, the SBA establishes loan ceilings and provides its clients with free management assistance.

By law, the SBA cannot make a loan if a business can obtain funds from a bank or other private source on reasonable terms. The prospective borrower must first seek financing from at least one bank—two in a city with a population greater than 200,000—before applying for an SBA loan. The prospective borrower is also not eligible for an SBA loan if funds can be secured through the sale of assets which the business does not need in order to grow.

Types of Loans. Of the loans participated in by the SBA, the guaranteed loan is the more common. Under this program all funds come from the commercial lender. The SBA guarantees 90 per cent of the loan while the bank's risk is limited to 10 per cent. A borrower that has been in business for a number of years may be required to supply 5 per cent of the loan, thus limiting the bank's liability to 5 per cent.

On a direct placement loan, however, the borrower must supply 10 per cent while the SBA guarantees the remaining 90 per cent of the funds provided by the bank. Since the funds are guaranteed by the SBA under this type of loan, the bank has no risk.

If the bank will not participate in an SBA guaranteed loan, then the agency will consider making an immediate participation loan. The agency's share in this type of loan is restricted to a certain amount; however, funds may not be available for the agency to lend because of federal fiscal restraints.

Small firms that cannot get a line of credit from a bank may apply to the SBA for regular and seasonal lines of credit. However, the firms must supply proof of their ability to perform on contracts and show repayment capabilities. Regular business loans are also available for those firms that have a reasonable amount of capital invested. Where the firms have principals of minority origin, the application procedure is simplified and the loan processing is expedited. However, the term, interest rate, and loan limit are the same.

Economic Opportunity Loans also are available to aid the low-income or disadvantaged persons who lack the opportunity to start or strengthen a small business and cannot obtain necessary financing from other sources on reasonable terms. Small firms that must make changes in their equipment, facilities, or operations because of new federal, state, or local laws and regulations may apply for Regulatory Economic Inquiry Loans. Firms that have deviations from the normal safety code standards established by the Administration may receive Coal Mine Health & Safety Loans or Occupational Safety and Health Administration Loans. Concerns that suffer injury because of additions to or alterations in their plant, facilities, or methods of operation to meet the requirements of the Pollution Control Acts are eligible for Air Pollution, Water Pollution, and Vapor Recovery Loans. Small firms are also eligible for loans from the SBA if they have suffered economic injury because of displacement by federally aided contruction projects, disease or toxicity of products, closing of or severe reduction in the scope and size of a major federal military installation, significant reduction in the scope or amount of federal support in connection with strategic arms and facilities, shortages of fuels and energy resources, and physical damage to property resulting from a natural disaster.

Restrictions. In addition to the usual commercial loan restrictions and covenants, government lenders may require an assignment of insurance concerning net proceeds, cash surrender value, loans, distributions, and other benefits. The loan agreement also restricts the use of the proceeds; places limits on fixed asset acquisitions, distributions and compensation, and so on.

Small Business Investment Corporations

Given its power through the Small Business Investment Company Act of 1958, the SBA makes private capital and long-term credit more readily available to small business concerns. It grants licenses to small business investment corporations (SBICs) and provides them with financial assistance. In turn, these SBICs provide funds and managerial assistance to businesses in their area. This type of investment company has grown considerably since its inception and now plays a significant role in the small enterprise sector of the economy.

The Act provides tax breaks not only for the investor but also to the SBIC itself. The earnings of the SBIC are not subject to the holding company surtax or penalty on accumulation of retained earnings, assuming the accumulation is properly invested. Most of the funds invested in SBIC represent the private capital of individuals, commercial banks, and investing public; the balance comprises money borrowed from the federal government. An SBIC may be eligible for a government loan up to twice its paid-in capital and retained earnings, thus providing significant leverage. There is no limit to the private capital that may be used to establish an SBIC.

EVALUATION OF CUSTOMERS

The credit executive's interest in the customer's outside financing stems from the influence it exerts on the liquidity of the account; the liability of the account for debts; the creditor's position of preference in claiming the assets of the account; and the account's dependence on outside financing for funds to operate the business.

Liquidity of the Account

It is reasonable to state that a company with cash available to pay trade debt is in a better financial position than one which has its assets tied up in inventory and slow-moving accounts receivable. It is therefore necessary to determine how much of the liquidity requirements of an account can be met from invested funds and how much must be borrowed.

Leveraging is of particular concern with a customer whose sales and profits are vulnerable to business downturns. Borrowing long-term enables the customer to leverage operations but, in doing so, the customer shifts the risk of loss to creditors. With high fixed costs, a sharp reduction in sales could pave the way for losses by that customer.

On the other hand, long-term debt may not be burdensome if sales and profits are steady or on the rise, and if total debt to tangible net worth is reasonable. The customer can then service the debt without affecting the creditors' position. If the customer has bonds outstanding, their indenture provisions may require sinking fund payments to liquidate the indebtedness. Moreover, these provisions may also restrict actions by the customer.

The answers to the five questions below are helpful in evaluating a factored or financed customer:

1. Has the customer accelerated payments and at the same time increased profits?
2. Has the customer, starting out with an undercapitalized business, been tempted to overtrade so that it becomes an increased risk?
3. Has the customer's increased borrowing power brought about an overexpansion of its inventory or created a condition that has brought about the retention of slow-moving merchandise?
4. Has the customer used the funds gained through pledge of current assets to expand investment in fixed assets? If that is the case, to what extent? Any diversion of current assets can affect a customer's ability to pay trade bills.
5. Has the customer used the funds gained from the factor or finance company for a nonbusiness purpose? If so, the customer may be "milking" the business.

Liability

When an account borrows short term, the financial operation of the company must be productive enough to generate the funds for repayment within the terms of the loan.

When a company borrows long term to finance plant expansion, this could be construed as a favorable sign. But often the debt may be incurred to improve a company's net working capital position by simply replacing short-term debt with long-term obligations. This is a distinct warning sign to the credit executive and should be tracked carefully.

Preference

The credit executive must be sure that a customer's assets are readily accessible. Certain obligations may be incurred by a company with the understanding that a particular creditor may have first claim on the firm's assets. All other creditors are then in a less favorable position.

Some bank loans, for example, may be made with the understanding that the officers of the borrower company will subordinate to the bank any loans they have made to the firm. In most instances, this type of subordination agreement will also include an assignment clause whereby the officers, as creditors, assign their rights to the bank. This could place the bank in a preferred position. Other creditors, having approved orders on the strength of these officers' loans to the company, may find their positions weakened by the assignment clause in the bank subordination.

Dependence on Outside Financing

Although it is not likely that any company will operate solely with its own funds, there is a point beyond which additional creditor financing becomes dangerous. A sound financial condition generally shows a one-to-one proportion of total debt to tangible net worth. This means that the owners of the company have as much invested in it as do the creditors.

Moreover, there is a limit to the extent to which funds can be raised through long-term debt. When certain standards of total debt to tangible net worth are exceeded, financial prudence dictates that this type of financing would no longer be available should a future need arise.

CHAPTER 28

SECURITY DEVICES

Parties to commercial transactions need not rely exclusively on the ability of the party with whom they contract to pay or perform. They may demand some sort of security as collateral should the other party breach the contract. This security may stem from some other person or from some thing. The means by which a company extending credit may secure its position include the following devices: guaranty, whereby some other person guarantees the performance of a party's obligation; subordination, whereby one creditor agrees to defer a claim until another claim is paid; real estate mortgage, whereby property may be used to secure transactions; and personal property, whereby liens, pledges, and assignments may be used to secure performance under a contract.

The following paragraphs provide an introduction to the elements of different security devices, and some of the distinctions between them. The credit executive is cautioned that the forms illustrated should never be used unless reviewed by local counsel. This is a highly technical field and one in which many claims may be competing for priority. Consequently, each step in dealing with a security device should be accompanied by proper legal advice.

GUARANTIES

Guaranties assure the performance of the principal. The company to which credit is advanced, known as the debtor, is called the principal; the corporation advancing credit is known as the creditor; and the corporation guaranteeing the credit is known as the guarantor or surety. In any contract of guaranty, it is important to properly set forth the rights and duties which the three parties assume.

There are two types of guaranties that are generally recognized: the guaranty of payment and the guaranty of collection. It is preferable to obtain the guaranty of payment rather than of collection. When a guaranty of payment is obtained from a third party, the creditor may present the obligation for payment to the guarantor immediately after it becomes due if it is not paid by the original debtor. With a guaranty of collection, the creditor will eventually collect the amount owed but only after having tried to collect from the original debtor.

Credit guaranties are normally used with customers having substantial credit requirements. Personal and corporate guaranties are essentially the same guaranties except for the different parties involved and there can be a guaranty for a partnership. All forms recommended to be used by a firm should have the approval of legal counsel. In addition, each situation could present a different legal problem and should be reviewed by counsel.

It is appropriate to point out that credit guaranties, particularly from individuals, should be used with restraint. These documents along with other legal documents, no matter how well prepared or secured, depend to a great extent on the honesty and integrity of the guarantor. The best of intentions often melt away when it becomes obvious to the guarantor that personal assets have to be given up to cover debts the company cannot pay.

An example of a personal guaranty is present in Figure 28–1. In order for the guaranty to be effective, it must be supported by due consideration. It is essential that each individual signing the guaranty supply a personal financial statement of assets and liabilities (both real and contingent). The statement, which must be signed and dated, is important because it shows the assets of the guarantor upon which the supplier is relying to back up the customer's credit.

Figure 28–2 illustrates a corporate credit guaranty and Figure 28–3 is a certificate showing the resolution of the guarantor's board of directors which must accompany the guaranty. This resolution authorizes the company officers to execute the guaranty agreement in behalf of the corporation. The guaranteeing corporation must supply a recent statement of financial condition, if such information is not available through regular credit channels. This type of third-party guaranty is often used when the parent company guarantees the obligations of a financially weak subsidiary. Another form of this type of guaranty is found when an officer or major stockholder of a financially weak corporation accepts responsibility for its debts. Third-party guaranties also arise when promissory notes of a financially weak customer are endorsed by a third party and then given to the creditor. If the customer fails to pay the note at maturity, the seller may protest a nonpayment and proceed against the endorsing third party upon the latter's endorsement.

While contract of guaranty is a three-party contract, the primary duty rests on the debtor. But if the debtor does not perform, the guarantor will. If the guarantor performs and satisfies the debtor's duty to the creditor, then the guarantor is entitled to whatever rights the creditor had against the debtor. In that case the guarantor is said to be subrogated to the rights of the creditor—that is, the guarantor is required to pay a debt which right-

INDIVIDUAL CREDIT GUARANTY

GUARANTY, given by the undersigned to _____ , an _____ corporation, of City, State, hereinafter called "_____," in order to induce _____ to extend credit in hereinafter called the "Customer."

The undersigned hereby guarantees to _____ the prompt payment, when due, of any and all obligations or indebtedness to _____ from the Customer, without deduction for any setoff or counterclaim of the Customer. The obligation of the undersigned under this guaranty is a primary and unconditional obligation, and covers all existing and future indebtedness of the Customer to _____ .

This is a continuing guaranty and shall remain in force until written notice of revocation sent by the undersigned by registered mail is received by _____ , which revocation shall be effective only as to obligations or indebtedness of the Customer to _____ arising out of transactions entered into after receipt of such notice.

The undersigned waives notice of acceptance hereof, and notice of orders, sales, and deliveries to the Customer, and of the amounts and terms thereof, and of all defaults or disputes with the Customer, and of the settlement or adjustment of such defaults or disputes. The undersigned, without affecting liability hereunder in any respect, consents to and waives notice of all changes of terms, the withdrawal or extension of credit or time to pay, the release of the whole or any part of any indebtedness, the settlement or compromise of differences, the acceptance or release of security, the acceptance of notes, trade acceptances, or any other form of obligation for the Customer's indebtedness, and the demand, protest, and notice of protest of such instruments of their indorsements. The undersigned also consents to and waives notice of any arrangements or settlements made in or out of court in the event of receivership, liquidation, readjustment, bankruptcy, reorganization, arrangement, or assignment for the benefit of creditors of the Customer, and anything whatsoever, whether or not herein specified, which may be done or waived by or between _____ and the Customer, or the Customer and any other person whose claims against the Customer have been or shall be assigned or transferred to _____ .

This guaranty shall be binding upon the undersigned and his legal representatives and assigns, and shall insure to the benefit of _____ and its successors and assigns.

The undersigned warrants that there is attached hereto and made apart hereof, a statement of net worth (disclosing all assets and liabilities) of the undersigned and that said statement of net worth is true and accurate and fairly represents the net worth of the undersigned as of the date hereof.

The undersigned warrants that he has no guaranties outstanding as of this date, other than those disclosed in the statement of net worth attached hereto as provided above.

The undersigned covenants that he shall not, during the life of this guaranty, guarantee the obligations of others, including the customer, without first notifying _____ and obtaining written approval thereof in advance.

IN WITNESS WHEREOF, the undersigned has executed this guaranty on the _____ day of _____ , 19__ .

_____

STATE OF _____)
) SS.:
COUNTY OF _____)

Before me, a notary public, in and for said county, personally appeared the above named _____ , who acknowledged that he did sign the foregoing instrument and that the same is his free act and deed.

IN TESTIMONY WHEREOF, I have hereunto subscribed my name and affixed my official seal at _____ , _____ , this _____ day of _____ , 19__ .

_____
                                        Notary Public

FIG. 28–1.   Individual Credit Guaranty.

CORPORATE CREDIT GUARANTY

GUARANTY, given by the undersigned to _____ , an _____ corporation, of City, State, hereinafter called "_____," in order to induce _____ to extend credit in hereinafter called the "Customer."

The undersigned hereby guarantees to _____ the prompt payment, when due, of any and all obligations or indebtedness to _____ from the Customer, without deduction for any setoff or counterclaim of the Customer. The obligation of the undersigned under this guaranty is a primary and unconditional obligation, and covers all existing and future indebtedness of the Customer to _____.

This is a continuing guaranty and shall remain in force until written notice of revocation sent by the undersigned by registered mail is received by _____, which revocation shall be effective only as to obligations or indebtedness of the Customer to _____ arising out of transactions entered into after receipt of such notice.

The undersigned waives notice of acceptance hereof, and notice of orders, sales, and deliveries to the Customer, and of the amounts and terms thereof, and of all defaults or disputes with the Customer, and of the settlement or adjustment of such defaults or disputes. The undersigned, without affecting liability hereunder in any respect, consents to and waives notice of all changes of terms, the withdrawal or extension of credit or time to pay, the release of the whole or any part of any indebtedness, the settlement or compromise of differences, the acceptance or release of security, the acceptance of notes, trade acceptances, or any other form of obligation for the Customer's indebtedness, and the demand, protest, and notice of protest of such instruments of their indorsements. The undersigned also consents to and waives notice of any arrangements or settlements made in or out of court in the event of receivership, liquidation, readjustment, bankruptcy, reorganization, arrangement, or assignment for the benefit of creditors of the Customer, and anything whatsoever, whether or not herein specified, which may be done or waived by or between _____ and the Customer, or the Customer and any other person whose claims against the Customer have been or shall be assigned or transferred to _____ .

The undersigned warrants that there is attached hereto and made a part hereof financial statements prepared by the accountants for the undersigned and that said statements are true and accurate and fairly represent the financial condition of the undersigned as of the date hereof.

The undersigned warrants that it has no guaranties outstanding as of this date, other than those disclosed in the financial statements attached hereto as provided above.

The undersigned warrants that it shall not, during the life of this guaranty, guarantee the obligations of others, including the customer, without first notifying _____ and obtaining written approval thereof in advance.

The undersigned states that this guaranty is given pursuant to authority of its Board of Directors at a meeting duly convened for such purpose and that the giving of this guaranty does not contravene any law of the State of incorporation of the undersigned and that the same is fully binding upon the corporation and not inconsistent with its Articles of Incorporation.

This guaranty shall be binding upon the undersigned and its successors and assigns, and shall insure to the benefit of _____ and its successors and assigns.

IN WITNESS WHEREOF, the undersigned has executed this guaranty on the _____ day of _____ 19__ .

JOHN DOE COMPANY

By _____
    Its _____

And _____
     Its _____

STATE OF _____)
) SS.:
COUNTY OF _____)

Before me, a notary public, in and for said county, personally appeared _____ , and _____ , _____ , of _____ , the corporation when executed the foregoing instrument, who acknowledged that the seal affixed to

FIG. 28–2. Corporate Credit Guaranty.

said instrument is the corporate seal of said corporation; that they did sign and seal said instrument as such _____ and _____ in behalf of said corporation and by authority of its Board of Directors; and that said instrument is their free act and deed individually and as such _____ and _____
and the free and corporate act and deed of said _____ .
    IN TESTIMONY WHEREOF, I have hereunto subscribed my name and affixed my official seal at _____ , _____ this _____
day of _____ , 19__ .

_____
                                        Notary Public

FIG. 28–2   (cont'd.).

CERTIFICATE

    I, _____ , hereby CERTIFY that I am the duly elected, qualified and acting Secretary of _____ , a _____ corporation and that a meeting of the Board of Directors of said corporation was duly called and held on _____ , 1970 and the following resolution was unanimously adopted:

> RESOLVED, that the corporation be, and it hereby is, authorized to enter into a certain Guaranty agreement in the form attached, and marked "Exhibit A" and the President or any Vice President or the Treasurer of the corporation and the Secretary thereof be and they hereby are authorized to execute said Guaranty agreement in behalf of the corporation.

    I FURTHER CERTIFY that the foregoing resolution has not been superseded or rescinded and is now in full force and effect.

_____
                                        Secretary

Dated at _____

_____ , 19__ .

FIG. 28–3.   Corporate Resolution.

fully should be paid by the debtor. Throughout the performance of the contract of guaranty, certain duties are imposed on the creditor to make certain that the rights of the guarantor are preserved.

The creditor must recognize that the laws of suretyship apply when it has knowledge that it is dealing with others in a suretyship situation. If the creditor wishes to hold the guarantor, it must then observe the rules applicable and not do anything which would discharge the guarantor, such as extending the time for performance of the debtor's contract without reserving its rights against the guarantor. The creditor must not modify the contract with the debtor in a manner which is not beneficial to the guarantor or which materially increases a compensated guarantor's risk. The creditor must be careful not to release the debtor unless the creditor reserves its rights against the guarantor in the release, or unless it obtains the consent of the guarantor to remain liable. If the creditor alters the instrument expressing the debtor's obligation and thereby discharges the debtor, the guarantor is also discharged.

SUBORDINATIONS

Subordinations are a matter for agreement between parties to a transaction. There may be sound business reasons for an individual having prior secured position to defer to someone who would otherwise be junior to the claim.

The subordination of debt by a customer is usually obtained when a supplier firm is unwilling to grant credit unless it will be in a preferred position relative to other creditors. Figure 28–4 illustrates an agreement in which the debtor is a corporation. Usually no alterations or amendments are made to a creditor's subordination form without express approval of its legal counsel.

Another common example of a subordination comes in connection with bank loans to a corporation. Principal officers and stockholders of a corporation may hold notes of the corporation for money advanced by them to the corporation. If the corporation goes to a bank for unsecured borrowing, the bank may require the officers to execute a subordination agreement stating that if the corporation fails, they will not collect on their notes from the corporation until the bank has collected on its notes. Thus the officers subordinate their position to that of the bank but they still remain general creditors of the corporation.

REAL ESTATE MORTGAGES AND DEEDS OF TRUST

A real estate mortgage or deed of trust loan is a transaction in which the title to a parcel of land is given as security for the performance of the transaction. The transaction is usually a loan of a sum of money to the borrower, known as the mortgagor or trustor, from the lender, known as the mortgagee or beneficiary. In a deed of trust loan, a trustee is named to hold the title to the land and take action in the event of a default. In a mortgage loan, the title or a lien on the land is held by the mortgagee. In a large corporate bond issue secured by a number of parcels of real estate, a trustee is named in the bond indenture to hold title to the land and to perform the administrative acts required to pay the interest and principal on the bonds.

A mortgage loan transaction has two phases. The first is the business phase, in which the borrower and lender get together to establish the amount of the loan, as well as the interest rate, payment schedule, and maturity date. As a rule, the loan will be payable in equal installments over the life of the loan. These installments will pay the loan in full at the end

SUBORDINATION AGREEMENT

SUBORDINATION AGREEMENT, given by the undersigned to THE MEAD CORPO-
RATION, an Ohio corporation, of Dayton, Ohio, and/or each of its present or future subsidiary
or affiliated companies, hereinafter called "Mead", in order to induce Mead in its sole discretion to
extend credit in respect of sale of goods from time to time to _____ ,
hereinafter called the "Customer".

The Undersigned hereby subordinates any and all indebtedness of Customer to the Undersigned to
any and all indebtedness of Customer to Mead. The undersigned hereby agrees that it will not
demand or receive from the Customer payment in whole or part of any indebtedness now or hereafter owing by the Customer to it or any security given therefore until this agreement is revoked
and unless and until all of the indebtedness of the Customer to Mead, whether now existing or at
any time hereafter incurred, shall have been fully paid to Mead.

Should any payment, distribution or security or proceeds thereof be received by the Undersigned upon or with respect to any indebtedness of Customer to the Undersigned prior to the
satisfaction of all indebtedness of Customer to Mead, the Undersigned shall immediately deliver the
same to Mead in the form received (except for endorsement or assignment by the Undersigned
where required by Mead), for application on any indebtedness of Customer to Mead, and, until so
delivered, the same shall be held in trust by the Undersigned as the property of Mead.

This is a continuing agreement of subordination and shall remain in force until written notice
of revocation sent by registered mail is received by Mead, which revocation shall not affect any
obligations or liabilities of the Customer to Mead incurred prior to Mead's receipt of such notice
and, as to such obligations and liabilities, such revocation shall not become effective until such
obligations and liabilities are fully paid to Mead.

The undersigned hereby expressly waives notice of acceptance by Mead and the Customer of
this subordination agreement. It is agreed that Mead may enter into any agreement or agreements,
and amendments thereof, with the Customer as it may deem proper and extend the time for payment of and/or renew any or all of the present and future obligations of the Customer to it, in
whole or in part, and may surrender any security underlying all or any of such obligations, all
without notice to the undersigned and without in any way impairing or affecting this subordination
agreement.

As security for the indebtedness of the Customer to Mead, whether now existing or at any time
hereafter incurred, the undersigned hereby assigns, transfers and sets over unto Mead all its right,
title and interest in and to any and all amounts now or hereafter owing by the Customer and any
and all claims of every kind and description which the undersigned may now or hereafter have
against the Customer. Should the Customer become insolvent or should an insolvency proceeding
be instituted by or against it, or should the Customer call a meeting of its creditors, or should any
event happen whereby it becomes desirable to present claims against the Customer for payment,
the undersigned authorizes and empowers Mead to file a proof of claim for any amounts then owing
to the undersigned, in Mead's name, as the true and lawful owner of said claim, entitled to receipt
of all payments thereon and to apply such payments to any matured or unmatured indebtedness
owing to Mead, and the undersigned agrees to provide Mead with all information and documents
necessary to file said proof of claim. The undersigned hereby empowers Mead for and in its stead
to vote for or against any proposal or resolution that may then be submitted under the Act of
Congress relating to bankruptcy, to vote for a trustee or for a Committee of creditors, to accept or
reject any arrangement proposed by the Customer, to receive payments or dividends or other consideration, and to otherwise exercise such rights and privileges which, except for this assignment,
could be exercised by the undersigned in connection with any such arrangement or other proceedings. The undersigned shall have no right of subrogation, reimbursement or indemnity whatsoever
and no right of recourse to or with respect to any assets or property of the Customer or to any
collateral for the Customer's indebtedness or obligations.

Notwithstanding any other provision hereof, as further security and inducement to Mead to
extend credit as aforesaid, the undersigned hereby assigns to Mead any and all rights and security
interests it may have under certain Security Agreements between it and the Customer, copies of
which Security Agreements, together with all documents reflecting the same, are attached hereto
and made a part hereof, and further agrees to execute any and all documents necessary to effectively
assign the said interests to Mead and to assist Mead in perfecting such security interests; and Mead
agrees to reassign the said security interests to the undersigned upon the satisfactory completion
and termination of the terms and conditions of this subordination agreement. The undersigned
further agrees to similarly assign any security interests which it may obtain hereafter in the Customer's assets.

FIG. 28–4. Subordination Agreement.

As of the date of this Agreement, the Customer is indebted to the Undersigned in the amount of $_____ . The Undersigned shall not assign, transfer, hypothecate or dispose of any claim it has or may have against Customer while any indebtedness of Customer to Mead remains unpaid, without the prior written consent of Mead.

The undersigned understands that there are no conditions or limitations to this subordination agreement except those written herein and that no alterations or modifications shall be made to this agreement except by a writing signed by both the undersigned and Mead. Mead's delay in or failure to exercise any right or remedy shall not be deemed a waiver of any obligation of the Undersigned to Mead.

This subordination agreement shall be construed in accordance with the laws of the State of Ohio and shall inure to the benefit of Mead and its successors and assigns and shall be binding upon the undersigned and its successors and assigns.

The undersigned states that this subordination agreement is given pursuant to authority of its Board of Directors at a meeting duly convened for such purpose and that the giving of this subordination agreement does not contravene any law of the State of incorporation of the undersigned and that the same is fully binding upon the corporation and not inconsistent with its Articles of Incorporation.

IN WITNESS WHEREOF, the undersigned has executed this subordination agreement on the _____ day of _____ , 19__ .

(CORPORATE SEAL)   JOHN DOE CORPORATION
ATTEST:

_____   By _____
                        Secretary   Its _____

STATE OF _____)
) SS:
COUNTY OF _____)

On the _____ day of _____ , 19__, before me personally came _____ ,
_____ and _____ ,
Secretary of _____ , the corporation which executed the foregoing instrument, who acknowledged that the seal affixed to said instrument is the corporate seal of said corporation; that they did sign and seal said instrument as such _____ and Secretary in behalf of said corporation and by authority of its Board of Directors; and that said instrument is their free act and deed individually and as such _____ and Secretary and the free and corporate act and deed of said _____ .

_____
                                                   NOTARY PUBLIC

The above Subordination Agreement is received this date.

THE MEAD CORPORATION
_____ Division
By _____
Date: _____

FIG. 28–4   (cont'd.).

of the term, together with payments of interest on the outstanding balance of the loan. There will be other provisions: to keep the property insured, to pay the real property taxes, and to cover assessments for betterments. There may be provisions for paying off the loan before its final maturity, known as a prepayment clause. In this event, the lender may charge a premium or penalty for prepayment. There may also be provision for the advancement of additional amounts to the borrower.

The second phase of the mortgage loan is the legal one. Instructions are sent to a law firm or title company to examine the title to the land and buildings to make sure that, when the mortgage transaction is complete the lender will be secured by a first claim upon the mortgaged land if the borrower defaults. Obviously the lawyers must know what parcel of land they are examining. Usually a survey is made by civil engineers showing the boundaries of the land the borrower owns, the location of the buildings, and other identifying features on the land. Also shown are building setback lines; common walls between buildings on the property and buildings on adjoining land, known as party or partition walls; rights of others to pass over the property, known as easements; and encroachments on the property by buildings or fences erected on adjoining land, or encroachments onto adjoining land by structure on the property. In addition, the attorneys receive a title search or abstract of title directing them to the deed or other instrument by which the borrower obtained title, and obtain an abstract of titles of the preceding owners of the property to confirm title and to determine whether the parties in possession of the property are consistent with the record owners or are claiming adversely through some other right. It is also necessary to go beyond the record title to find out what municipal regulations, such as zoning and building bylaws, affect the property. After all the questions raised have been resolved to the satisfaction of the lender's attorneys, the note, mortgage, and other necessary papers are signed. The mortgage is then recorded and the borrower is given the money.

The lender can rest secure as long as the monthly or quarterly mortgage payments and real estate taxes are being made, the property is kept insured and in good repair, all other duties of the borrower are being performed, and the title remains with the borrower. This tranquility may be interrupted, however. Assume the borrower sells the property to someone else and the lender acquires knowledge of the sale. If the sale has been made to a grantee who assumes and agrees to pay the mortgage, the grantee now becomes the principal debtor and the original debtor becomes a surety. If the grantee does not assume the mortgage but takes subject to it, the original borrower, the mortgagor, is regarded as a surety to the extent of the value of the land. Now the lender must be careful not to discharge the original borrower, who has become a surety, since the laws of suretyship apply.

Another complex set of rules enters the picture when the borrower defaults on the obligations under the mortgage. This raises the question of whether or not to accelerate the balance due on the mortgage and proceed to foreclose. At this point the credit executive should seek legal counsel and follow instructions that are consistent with good business sense.

PERSONAL PROPERTY SECURITY DEVICES

The use of personal property is still another means of securing performance of the duties undertaken by a party to a commercial transaction.

Personal property may be many things. It is not real estate; it is not land or the buildings, machinery, and equipment affixed thereto. But whether property is real or personal may be difficult to determine. Although it is attached to the land or to a building on the land, it still may not be so permanently affixed as to constitute part of the real estate.

Personal property may be tangible, such as machinery, or intangible, such as accounts receivable. It may be subject to prior claims of others who assert a right of ownership or a right to hold the property in payment for a debt. Therefore, if personal property is taken to secure performance of a contract, the party taking it should make every reasonable effort to ascertain that it is in fact personal property and is not subject to any prior claims. In all fairness, it must be admitted that these prior claims cannot be discovered in every case.

Where the use of the property may be the means of producing the money to repay the debt, it is obvious that some way must be found to preserve the creditor's security interest in the property and at the same time give the property to the debtor so that it may be put to its intended use. One way is to mortgage property, in much the same manner as one would mortgage real estate. Another way is for the seller to retain title to the property, but to let the buyer use it provided required payments are made. Or the seller may place control of the property in the hands of a third person, as in the case of financing on warehouse receipts. In each case, the buyer-debtor has the use of the property and the creditor has a security interest. This is satisfactory as long as only two parties, the creditor and the debtor, have any claim to the property. But there may be others asserting claims to the property. An innocent person may pay money to buy a piece of property, only to find that someone has a prior security interest in it. Or someone may lend money on the security offered by a piece of personal property, only to find the security interest is impugned by someone claiming a prior security interest. To prevent such confusion, the states have adopted the Uniform Commercial Code (UCC). The UCC now governs personal property security devices and consolidates all the various devices previously used to create a security interest into a single form known as a secured transaction. The rules for creating and perfecting the security interest under Article 9 of the UCC are discussed in Chapter 29.

Liens

A lien may be described as the right of someone to retain possession of another's personal property until paid for materials and services expended on it. A lien does not constitute an ownership interest in the property; it is merely a right to detain the property. The common law lien, as it is called, constitutes only a right to hold the property, not to sell it. Two exceptions are factor's liens and vendor's liens; in these instances, at common law, the goods upon which the lien is given could be sold to pay the amounts due the factor or the unpaid seller.

Most liens arise out of agreement between the parties, although some liens arise as a matter of law. Liens provided by Article 9 of the UCC are an example of consensual liens. The most significant statutory liens on personal property which would be of interest to commercial credit grantors are summarized in the *Credit Manual of Commercial Laws*.

Pledges

A pledge is a security device by which property is delivered to a pledgee for the purpose of securing some debt. The person delivering the pledge is known as the pledgor. A pledge may also be created by identifying bulky goods over which the pledgee assumes control.

The principal difference between a lien and a pledge is that a pledge is delivered especially for the purpose of securing an obligation, whereas with a lien the property is delivered for some other purpose and the lienor's right to hold the property subject to the lien arises only when payment or performance is not received.

The interest of the person claiming the pledge is lost if possession of the property is given up. The pledge may be delivered to secure the performance of a duty by someone other than the pledgor, to secure an antecedent debt, or to secure future advances. Unless the pledgee is bound to make future advances, intervening creditors and lienors or bona fide purchasers from the pledgor may diminish the pledgee's interest.

When a pledge is created, the pledgee is obligated to take reasonable care of the pledged property; if an instrument representing a claim against a third person is pledged, the pledgee has a duty to preserve and collect the claim. The pledgee ordinarily has no right to use the property pledged, and such use without authority amounts to a conversion of the property, for which the pledgee is liable. The pledgee is under a duty to return the pledged property when performance is fulfilled or tender of performance of the obligation owed to the pledgee is given.

A pledge is made to assure performance of an obligation. If the obligation is not performed or if the performance is not tendered, the pledgee has a right to sell the pledged property after giving reasonable notice of the sale to the pledgor. If the property is owned by someone other than the pledgor, notice must be given to the owner. If bills or notes are pledged, the pledgee may collect them. The pledgee may also maintain a bill in equity to foreclose the interest of the owner in the pledged property and to obtain a deficiency judgment against the pledgor. The pledgee must then account to the pledgor for the proceeds of the sale, taking only that which is due for the obligation plus expenses incurred in keeping the pledged property and in making the sale.

Only property capable of being delivered can be pledged, such as inventory and equipment. Other collateral pledged to secure a loan include:

Bank Book. Under this procedure, the borrower agrees to pledge his bank book to secure a loan and assigns his rights to the lending bank, which retains possession of the book until the loan is repaid. The owner (borrower) continues to have title to the book and to the deposits carried in the bank account but cannot withdraw from the book without the express permission of the lender.

Stocks and Bonds. A similar procedure is followed when loans are secured by stocks and bonds. The bonds may be in the name of the borrower or owned by a third party whose securities are pledged as collateral to the borrower. The lender obtains physical possession of the securities and the right to own them upon default of the loan. Thus the original owner of the security keeps title unless the loan is not repaid on time.

Because of the fluctuating values of stocks and bonds, the lender may require that a certain ratio be maintained between the amount borrowed and the value of the pledged securities. If the market price drops, for instance, the value of the pledged securities will also drop. The lender may then require the pledge of additional securities or the partial repayment of the loan.

Life Insurance Policies. There is little fluctuation in the cash surrender value of life insurance policies. They may be readily pledged to secure loans. The owner's rights in the policy are assigned to the lender until the loan is repaid. In the event the borrower dies before repaying the loan, the lender may claim against the policy for the amount of the loan. In that way the lender is assured of payment.

Accounts Receivable Financing

Accounts receivable financing is an important security device that has recently broadened in its application. As outlined in Chapter 27, many companies use factors and finance companies as a regular source of outside financing. Collateral such as accounts receivable, inventory, or fixed assets are pledged or assigned to secure the loans.

Chattel Mortgages and Conditional Sales Contracts

The Uniform Commercial Code has superseded the Uniform Conditional Sales Act and the laws relating to chattel mortgages, and is now in effect. Under the UCC, no distinction is made between chattel mortgages and conditional sales, both being secured transactions to which Article 9 of the UCC is applicable.

Consignments

Consignment terms add a warehousing feature to payment provisions. Merchandise is shipped to the buyer's premises under an agreement that title remains with the seller. The buyer (consignee) is authorized to withdraw goods from stock when they are sold by the consignee and reimburse the seller (consignor) either at the time of withdrawal or at a specified time thereafter. Consignees are generally retailers, distributors, or commission houses rather than manufacturers. Consignment terms are particularly suited to the introduction of new product lines in which the customer is reluctant to invest funds. They are also used in the distribution of goods through a buyer with a credit standing that does not justify regular terms for the amounts involved and that lacks the resources to purchase under C.O.D. or sight draft/bill of lading arrangement.

Except where delivery is made to a person who is known to be selling the merchandise of others (such as an auctioneer) or where there is compliance with a sign-posting law, a consignment is treated as a secured transaction. Without a perfected security agreement, the consigned merchandise can be levied upon by the creditors of the buyer and is subject to the superior rights of the buyer's trustee in the event of bankruptcy.

A pertinent illustration is a purchase order signed by the buyer. It is a security agreement if it provides that title to the merchandise is retained by the seller until payment is made. Between the parties, this provision is valid for all purposes. If the seller desires to protect its lien on the merchandise against the other creditors of the buyer, it must comply with the filing requirements of the UCC. However, one filing may be sufficient for an entire course of dealings or a series of transactions.

In those businesses in which consignment selling has been prevalent, the UCC creates a real problem. If the buyer wants the right to return the merchandise and the seller the right to reclaim it, the agreement between them is valid and enforceable under the UCC. But if the buyer's credit is poor and the buyer should go bankrupt before the merchandise is returned, the seller cannot reclaim its merchandise unless the filing requirements of Article 9 were complied with.

Trust Receipts

Trust receipt financing is used where a large number of similar units are given as security and provision is made for selling or withdrawing the units from time to time. The financing institution pays for and gets security title in the property. It then, as entruster, entrusts the goods to the dealer, called the trustee, either for storage under a warehouse receipt or for sale. If the trustee sells the property for new value, the buyer is protected. But the entruster is protected against the claims of the trustee's creditors by complying with Article 9 of the Uniform Commercial Code governing trust receipts.

A trust receipt is used domestically principally in connection with the purchase of household equipment and automobiles by dealers from their manufacturers. The manufacturer receives an order from the buyer, ships the goods, and forwards the bill of lading or other documents to the bank or other lending institutions for payment—at which time the seller ceases its part in the transaction. The buyer then issues a trust receipt to the bank, which permits it to release the documents that a buyer needs to claim the goods. The buyer receives the goods as trustee for the bank—which retains title—and agrees to hold them, or the proceeds if they are sold, in a separate account clearly marked.

Warehouse Receipts and Bills of Lading

A warehouse receipt is a receipt issued by a firm engaged in the business of storing goods for hire, while a bill of lading is a document evidencing the receipt of goods for shipment by a firm engaged in the business of transporting or forwarding goods. These documents of title may be negotiable of nonnegotiable, the distinction being that the negotiable form permits the goods to be delivered to the bearer or to the order of a named firm while the goods are to be delivered only to a named firm under the nonnegotiable form. The laws governing documents of title are found under Article 7 of the Uniform Commercial Code.

Warehouse Receipts. In warehouse receipt financing, the buyer delivers the goods to an independent warehouseman and obtains a warehouse receipt stating the quality and quantity of goods stored. This receipt identifies the specific items placed in the warehouse by serial number or other distinguishing characteristics. The only time this does not hold true is when units of the merchandise are fungible—that is, completely interchangeable. Commodities such as wheat or rye, for example, need not be identified specifically so long as they are of comparable quality.

The buyer then can use the warehouse receipt as security for borrowing (the loan proceeds go to the seller as payment for the goods), and the lender obtains a perfected security interest in the goods merely by holding the receipt as assurance either that the borrower will pay or that the lender can obtain the goods. When the borrower wishes to obtain the warehoused merchandise, it must pay the bank and receive authorization for the release of the goods.

Where firms have storage facilities convenient to their manufacturing facilities and wish to eliminate some of the inconvenience and cost of storing merchandise in a public warehouse, they use a modified method known as field warehousing. Under these circumstances, merchandise is stored on the premises of the business concern (the borrower) while the bank secures its loan with a warehouse receipt. It is segregated from other merchandise, however, and physically controlled by independent warehouse employees. When the firm needs merchandise, it must pay the bank in full or in part. Then an official of the bank authorizes the release of the appropriate amount of inventory from the field warehouse.

The lender, in accepting warehouse receipts as collateral for loans, must take certain steps to minimize risk:

1. Protect the physically stored merchandise against spoilage, rust, dampness, fire, and wind damage. The lender must be certain that ade-

quate safeguards and insurance coverage are maintained at the warehouse location. The borrower is usually required to provide this.

2. Protect the owners of stored merchandise against theft. Bonded warehouses may provide maximum protection for the lender because they must post bonds. The dollar requirements of the bond are not always fixed, however, and some warehouses may store hundreds of thousands of dollars of merchandise and carry a small bond. In any case, the warehouseman should have a good reputation for honesty and the ability to store merchandise in good condition.

3. Shield the owners against merchandise price levels that may fluctuate while it is being stored. This is called the commodity risk and is offset in one of two ways. First, the bank will lend only a partial dollar amount of the collateral pledged. This may run from 50 per cent to 80 per cent, depending on the type of material and current market conditions. The bank will also look more favorable on warehouse receipt loans on inventories which have a ready and wide market.

Second, if a hedging contract can be obtained, price level fluctuations are minimized. For instance, if a firm has $10,000 raw materials that will not be sold for six months, it can offset the risk of changing market prices in the commodity by contracting to sell an identical physical amount for $10,000 six months from date. This is called "selling futures." It stabilizes raw materials costs. Should the commodity price decline by 10 per cent in that six-month period, the value of the warehoused raw materials would become $9,000 and the firm would have a potential $1,000 loss when the merchandise is sold. However, the firm offsets that loss and protects its profit through the sale of the futures contract. If, on the other hand, the price of the commodity should rise to $11,000, the firm would realize $1,000 greater profit on the sale of the material, but this would be offset by the loss in the futures contract. By hedging, the firm can concentrate on earning a normal gross profit from operations and not by speculating in the basic raw materials market.

Bills of Lading. Since bills of lading represent the right of the holder or the person therein named to receive goods from a carrier, they too may be used in a security transaction. For example, a seller has an order (negotiable) bill of lading issued in its favor, attaches to it a sight draft or a time draft drawn on the buyer, and discounts it at its bank. The bank has the draft presented through its correspondent to the buyer for acceptance if a time draft, or for payment if a sight draft. In this transaction, the bill of lading is pledged to the discounting bank as security for the payment or acceptance of the draft.

In another example, a borrower may deliver a straight (nonnegotiable) bill of lading or a nonnegotiable warehouse receipt to a lender, which in turn notifies the carrier or independent warehouseman that the pledge has been made. Or the borrower may cause a nonnegotiable warehouse receipt to be issued in the name of the lender, so that the lender may authorize the warehouseman to withdraw the goods in odd lots.

LETTERS OF CREDIT

While not a personal property security device, letters of credit have been known and used for many years in international transactions. Despite their wide usage, there is no uniform legislation dealing with this type of financing mechanism. Article 5, known as Uniform Commercial Code—Letters of Credit, deals primarily with the rules and concepts covering documentary credits issued by banks—that is, letters of credit which require the drawer's draft to be accompanied by one or more documents. Others are covered by the Uniform Customs and Practice for Commercial Documentary Credits, adopted by the International Chamber of Commerce. Both compilations of rules are useful, although neither is a complete statement of all the rules that may apply to letters of credit.

Letters of Credit Defined

A letter of credit is an instrument issued by a bank establishing an arrangement whereby the bank acting in accordance with the instructions of its customer (the buyer) is to make payment to a third party (the seller). Additionally, the issuing bank may accept drafts drawn by the seller, or negotiated by another bank against stipulated documents, assuming compliance with the seller's terms and conditions. Expressed simply, the letter of credit substitutes the bank's credit for the credit of the buyer because the bank agrees to honor drafts presented to it by the seller for payment of merchandise shipped.

Letters of credit, by their very nature, are distinct and separate transactions from the sales or other contracts on which they may be based. Consequently, all parties deal in documents and not in goods. Thus the issuing bank's obligation to the buyer is to examine all documents with reasonable care to ascertain that they appear on their face to be in accordance with the terms and conditions of the credit. If they are, fulfillment of the terms and conditions of the contract between seller and buyer is not a factor. If the letter of credit conforms, the seller must be paid by the bank under the letter of credit, and any disputes about the terms of the contract will have to be settled between the seller and buyer.

The most secure form of letter of credit is one that is confirmed and irrevocable. When the buyer's bank requests its correspondent bank in the seller's locale to honor the credit, such confirmation binds the correspondent bank as well. Where the letter of credit is irrevocable, it is a definite undertaking by the issuing bank and cannot be cancelled or modified except by agreement of all parties—that is, the seller, the buyer, and the issuing bank.

Domestic Letters of Credit

While the use of letters of credit is more common in international trade (see Chapter 37), some domestic trade is conducted by this means. When the terms of sale provide that payment is to be made by letter of credit, the following steps generally take place:

1. The buyer arranges with its bank to open a letter of credit. This is a private transaction between the buyer and the bank; the seller is not a party in the transaction. The letter specifies the amount that has been made available to the buyer and the conditions under which claims against the letter will be honored.
2. The letter of credit is sent to a bank in the locale of the seller. That bank is authorized to accept drafts against the letter of credit within the conditions stipulated.
3. The seller is notified by the local bank that a letter of credit has been opened in its favor.
4. As merchandise is shipped, the seller prepares a draft against the letter of credit and presents it, with pertinent shipping documents, to the bank which holds the letter in its favor.
5. The bank satisfies itself that the conditions of the letter have been met, then pays the draft. The amount of the draft is charged against the issuing bank.
6. The papers are mailed to the issuing bank, which in turn charges its customer. The customer obtains the necessary papers from its bank and claims the merchandise.

Under a sight draft letter of credit, the seller presents its drafts and necessary documents to the bank and receives its money; whereas under a banker's acceptance letter of credit, payment is not made until some specified period after presentation (when accepted, bankers' drafts can be discounted readily at the prevailing rate for eligible prime bankers' acceptances).

Standby Letter of Credit

When a supplier is not certain that a particular customer can pay on time, it may be possible to use a standby letter of credit as an added measure of security. Generally this type of letter provides that drafts can be drawn only for invoices that are 30 days past due, or that have matured. The seller must first look for payment directly from the buyer when the money is due and owing. Should the buyer be unwilling or unable to pay its bill according to the terms and conditions as set forth in the standby letter of credit, the seller then presents the drafts and necessary documents to the bank and receives its money. Figure 28–5 illustrates a form letter that is given by a bank covering an irrevocable revolving letter of credit that is used for domestic orders.

In essence, the standby letter of credit is a revolving credit between the buyer and seller, and can remain so until the buyer fails to pay its due bill. For example, Doe Company asks Smith Company for a $50,000 line of

---

(date)_____

Gentlemen:

We hereby establish our Irrevocable Revolving Letter of Credit in your favor, for account of _____ (customer's name) _____ ,

_____ (customer's full address) _____ for a sum (or sums) not exceeding $_____ . (Amount outstanding at any one time.)

This credit is issued for a period of ____ (length of time) ____ and will expire on ____ (expiration date) ____ , unless extended by us in writing. Shipments made by you on or before ____ (expiration date) ____ will be considered within the terms of this agreement although the final invoice due date may not be within the ____ (length of time) ____ period.

It is understood that no drafts will be drawn upon us under this credit or any invoice unless such invoice is not paid by ____ (customer's name) ____ on or before the due date of such invoice, in which event you may make a draft or drafts upon us for payment of all invoices to said ____ (customer's name) ____ which are then past due. Each such draft shall be accompanied by a copy of the invoice or invoices, together with a statement by you that such invoice or invoices have not been paid by their due dates.

Yours very truly,

(NAME OF BANK)

FIG. 28–5.   Letter Given by Bank Covering Irrevocable Revolving Letter of Credit on Domestic Orders.

credit for merchandise purchases. The seller does not consider Doe Company strong enough to warrant a $50,000 line on open account, and requests that the customer obtain a standby letter of credit from its bank. Doe Company is able to do this, and Smith Company can now sell its merchandise on the strength of the standby letter.

When payment for the first shipment becomes due, Doe Company pays promptly. The firm then orders five additional $50,000 shipments from Smith Company and in each instance the bills are paid promptly. In this example, the supplier has been able to sell $300,000 worth of merchandise to a marginal customer with absolute security. The seller always had a $50,000 guaranty of payment for each and every sale. Should the buyer have failed to pay the seller for any single sale, the seller would have received $50,000 under the standby letter of credit. It is conceivable that in time the buyer could improve its financial condition to a point where it could buy merchandise without the aid of the credit.

CHAPTER 29

CREDIT RISK UNDER UCC

Credit executives sometimes will find themselves in a troubled position when they seek to protect themselves in secured transactions under Article 9 of the Uniform Commercial Code (UCC). One reason is that in enacting the UCC, a number of states made local amendments to some provisions. Consequently, variations must be checked when dealing with the UCC in more than one state.

The UCC is divided into nine articles and extends over the law of sales, negotiable instruments, bank deposits and collections, letters of credit, bulk sales, documents of title, investments securities, and secured transactions. Many of the provisions of the UCC are not especially relevant to the daily work of the credit executive, but some are of particular interest:

1. Article 9 defines a security interest and discusses types of security agreements that may be encountered by a credit executive. It also discusses how a creditor may gain protection against the claims of third parties; and the rights and claims of a creditor in case of a default.

2. Remedies available to the seller under Article 2 of the sales law, especially where a buyer rejects a shipment of goods and where the seller may recover goods shipped to an insolvent buyer.

3. Article 6 covers notice and disclosure rules that prevail under the bulk transfer law.

SECURED TRANSACTIONS UNDER ARTICLE 9

According to Article 9 of the UCC, a secured transaction includes any transaction that is intended to create an interest or right in personal property, to secure either the payment of a debt or the performance of some other kind of obligation. Generally speaking, personal property includes everything except real estate.

Security Agreement

The security interest is a lien created by an agreement between the secured party and the debtor called a security agreement. The significant factor is that all security devices are brought into the one law and this provides the unified concept of a single lien. The form of the transaction is no longer controlling; the differences that do exist for various kinds of transactions are related solely to their function and purpose.

The language in the agreement may be very simple. It need only say that the secured party is given a security interest in certain described property of the debtor. If the old forms, such as chattel mortgage or trust receipt, are used, they are treated as security agreements. The agreement must contain a description of the collateral; should specify the obligation that the collateral secures; and must be signed by the debtor, although it is advisable for both the debtor and the creditor to sign.

Article 9 abolishes many of the old distinctions between security devices that existed under the old law. Instead of having conditional sales contracts, chattel mortgages, assignments of accounts receivable, trust receipts, factor's liens, and the like, there is a single type of device known as security interest. Further, the role of the security device on the personal property has been clarified. Until now, the secured party was subject to the many intricacies of the various statutes that might apply. If a chattel mortgage was used when it should have been a conditional sales contract, the lien was generally voided. If a filing was made in the wrong place, the creditor's security was declared invalid. To make a multiple-purpose loan on equipment, inventory, and accounts receivable, the creditor had to draft several different documents and comply with separate filing requirements for each.

The distinctions between the different types of security interest under the UCC are now more functional than formal. A purchase money security interest is different from a security interest that secures an old debt in that the collateral secures the purchase price of itself. Likewise, a security interest in which the collateral is accounts receivable is different from a security interest in which the collateral is inventory. Both of these differ from a security interest in which the collateral is fixtures or equipment. But again, the differences between these security interests exist only because the nature of their collateral is different.

Under Article 9, the security agreement may contain many other provisions in other than the simplest transaction. Future advances may be secured and the security interest may include after-acquired property. Future advances refer to a provision in a lending agreement by which a lender agrees to make loans from time to time, with the future loans secured by the same collateral as the original advance. After-acquired property clauses provide that all subsequently acquired property of the debtor shall constitute additional collateral for the secured party. This means that the merchandise sold by an unsecured creditor to a customer that has a security agreement with another creditor may serve as collateral for the secured creditor under an after-acquired property clause contained in that security agreement.

Floating Lien.   Perhaps the greatest feature of Article 9 is that it permits the parties in one transaction and even in one document to create a security interest in inventory, equipment, accounts receivable, and to provide for future advances on after-acquired property. The so-called floating lien is an integral feature of this approach. However, the floating lien used to extreme could tie up a debtor's entire inventory. For example, one creditor and the debtor may agree between themselves that the creditor is to have a security interest in every item of merchandise coming into the debtor's shop, from the moment it crosses the threshold or from the moment it arrives at the train station or from the moment the seller puts the goods on the train. Even before the goods have arrived at the buyer's place of business, that creditor, possibly a financing company or bank, may have a lien on the goods. Understandably, this weakens the position of other creditors.

Secret Security Agreements.   A change brought about by the UCC is that where the debtor is a business enterprise, secret security interests are invalid against creditors of the business enterprise. In some states, for example, before the UCC, a business could assign its accounts receivable to a finance company or bank, and no one would be obligated to record the assignment or otherwise give notice to the general public that a substantial asset of the business had been assigned as security. Under the UCC, however, if the assignment of accounts receivable alone or in conjunction with other assignments to the same assignee constitutes a significant part of outstanding accounts or contract rights of the business, a financing statement must be filed with the Secretary of State.

Choice of Collateral.   A creditor that wants security or collateral is allowed a virtually unlimited choice. The creditor may conceivably have an interest in the business machinery and equipment, inventory, accounts receivable, bank accounts, and may also provide for a security interest in every item of inventory or equipment or other asset that is acquired by the debtor after the date of the execution of the security agreement. In sum, a creditor may acquire by contract a security interest on every asset, present or future, of a debtor's business.

In the past, a seller of merchandise that sold on credit relied on the inventory and bank account of a customer as assets which could not be readily tied up by a bank or finance company. Under the UCC, however, any asset of a business may be used as collateral.

Accountability.   Section 9-205 repeals the rules of law that required strict accounting for the segregation of collateral in order for a secured party's interest to be valid against creditors. Under the Section, a security interest is valid against creditors even though the debtor has the right:

1. To use or dispose of all or part of the collateral, including what has been returned or repossessed.
2. To collect or compromise accounts or contract rights.

3. To accept the return of goods or make repossessions.
4. To use or dispose of proceeds.

Prior to the UCC, the law in many states was derived from the old Supreme Court case of Benedict v. Ratner. The rule of this case was that a debtor that had created a lien on inventory or accounts receivable, collateral which was constantly changing or shifting, could not be permitted to exercise dominion over the proceeds or to commingle them with other funds. The debtor had to account to the secured party for such proceeds immediately; failure to do so and failure by the secured creditor to enforce this requirement were grounds for the entire lien to be declared invalid by the court. Policing is no longer legally required to validate a security interest. However, those engaged in secured financing know that policing is still essential as a practical consideration, to make certain that collateral is not being dissipated. A lien, even though valid, has little value if the collateral is gone.

Classification of Goods

Before discussing the perfection of a security agreement, which is the very essence of Article 9, it will be instructive to define selectively the classification of goods under the various categories in the UCC, since the provisions for various classes of goods vary from state to state.

Inventory. Goods are inventory if they are held by a person for sale or lease, whether they be raw materials, work in process, or materials used and consumed in a business. The principal test for inventory is whether the goods are held for immediate or ultimate sale. The acid test, in addition to the immediate or ultimate sale, is whether the sale is made in the ordinary course of business.

Farm Products. These products are defined as crops, livestock, or supplies used or produced in farm operations. However, these products lose their status as farm products if they are subjected to a manufacturing process. For example, extensive canning operation causes products to lose this classification; on the other hand, pasteurization of milk or boiling sap to produce maple syrup or maple sugar do not.

Consumer Goods. These are goods used or bought basically for personal, family, or household use.

Equipment. These are goods used or bought for use in business, or goods which are not included in the definitions of inventory, farm products, or consumer goods. For example, machinery used by manufacturers is considered equipment, not inventory.

Fixtures. These are negatively described in the UCC, in that they do not become part of a structure as do lumber, steel, tile, or bricks. Thus it is other laws, not the UCC, which determine when chattels are so affixed to realty that they become part of it and lose their identity as chattels.

Upon ascertaining which classification fits the collateral covered by the security agreement, the financing statement should be filed in the proper offices. The filing requirements adopted by each state for each classification of goods are outlined in the *Credit Manual of Commercial Laws*. It is important that the filing be done as soon as possible after the security interest is created.

Perfecting the Security Agreement

In a few situations the security agreement alone will give the secured party the needed protection. But in the usual commercial transaction some form of filing is required for complete protection. The contract itself may be filed if it is signed by both parties, but this is generally too cumbersome.

Instead, the UCC provides for the filing of a financing statement. Its purpose is to give notice of the existence of a secured transaction and the nature of the collateral. Many states have given the Secretary of State or other filing officer the power to prescribe an official or approved form. When a secured transaction is first contemplated, the prospective secured party should write to the Secretary of State of the state in which the financing statement has to be filed, and request copies of the official financing statement for that state or the address of an office from which a financing statement can be purchased.

Instead of arbitrarily deciding on one proper place for filing the financing statement, the authors of the UCC presented three options from which each state could make a choice. As a result, there is no uniformity in this requirement, except for financing statements that cover fixtures. The filings for fixtures are made in the office where a mortgage on real estate would be filed or recorded.

Option 1. Filing security documents for all goods except fixtures are made in a central location, the office of the Secretary of State.

Option 2. Filing security documents for consumer goods are made in the country or town in which the debtor resides; if not a resident, then in the county or town where the goods are kept. Security documents for all other goods besides fixtures are filed in the office of the Secretary of State.

Option 3. Security documents for consumer goods are filed in the county or town where the debtor lives; if not a resident, then where the goods are kept. For all other goods besides fixtures, documents are filed in the office of the Secretary of State *and* in the county or town where the debtor has a place of business. If the debtor does not have a place of business in the particular state but lives in that state, the filing is made in the county or town of residence.

Thus filing may be in either the county or the state capital, or in both places, depending upon the option of the UCC that has been adopted by the state. Among other significant points, no affidavit or witnesses are required; a filing is good for five years, but then must be renewed; and a filing may be made at any time, even before the agreement is entered into, and should certainly be made before an advance is given or before merchandise is shipped if it is a purchase money security interest.

Default

In case of default, secured creditors must be aware of both their rights and obligations. By doing so, they will either realize the greatest recovery possible or not lose part of their recovery through failure to conform to the legal rights of the debtor and subordinate secured parties.

When a debtor is in default under a security agreement, secured creditors may reduce their claims to judgment, foreclose, or otherwise enforce the security interest by any available judicial procedure. Unless otherwise agreed, secured creditors have the right to take possession of their collateral. This may be done without judicial process, providing it can be conducted without breach of peace.

A secured creditor may sell, lease, or otherwise dispose of the collateral through public or private sale. Any sale of goods is subject to Article 2 of the UCC—Sales. The secured creditor must give the debtor reasonable notice of the time and place of a public sale or a private sale, unless the debtor has signed after default a statement renouncing or modifying the right to notification of sale. In cases other than consumer goods, the secured creditor must also give notice of the sale to any other creditor that has filed a security interest or is known by the secured party to have a security interest in the same collateral.

It is important that a creditor that forecloses on property subject to a security interest conduct the sale in a commercially reasonable manner or else the creditor may be subject to damages and not be able to obtain a deficiency judgment.

If the proceeds from the sale exceed the amount owed to the secured creditor, plus allowable expenses, the excess monies must be given to subordinate creditors, providing they ask for the excess sum in writing. If there are no subordinate creditors, then any excess proceeds are returnable to the debtor. When the proceeds fall short of the debt, the debtor is liable for the deficiency.

At any time before the secured creditor has disposed of the repossessed collateral or contracted for its disposition, the debtor may redeem the collateral by making payment in full satisfaction of the debt, plus reasonable and allowable expenses incurred.

Credit Analysis of Secured Debtors

Since Article 9 has made the use of secured credit more uniform, there is a greater trend to use this type of transaction in sales to marginal accounts. The decision to sell to a buyer that is involved with a secured creditor will depend upon the merits of each case. The credit executive cannot readily ascertain the amount of debt that is being secured where there is a security interest in inventory and the proceeds of inventory. Every asset of the business except machinery and equipment not specifically identified may be subject to the lien of the secured creditor. This type of problem did not exist prior to the UCC because the earlier law in most states did not afford a secured creditor a method of obtaining a lien on all inventory whenever acquired and all proceeds of such inventory. Under the circumstances, extreme caution should be exercised in extending credit to any business against which a financing statement covering inventory and proceeds has been filed.

On the other side of this question, the UCC includes a specific provision requiring the exercise of good faith in all transactions covered by the act. A secured lender that has obtained a complete package—namely, a lien on equipment, inventory, and accounts receivable, including provisions for future advances and after-acquired property—is still required to exercise good faith with regard to the debtor's business. It is the task of the unsecured creditors to aggressively preserve their rights in situations where undue emphasis may be placed upon security agreements rather than upon straightforward credit analysis.

REMEDIES UNDER LAW OF SALES

Article 2 of the UCC is a complete revision and modernization of the Uniform Sales Act. The present Article is much more extensive than the old one and covers all aspects of transactions in goods. However, of particular interest to the credit executive are the remedies under Article 2 that pertain to rejected merchandise and recovery of merchandise.

Rejected Merchandise

A change in Article 2—Sales deals with suing for the price of the merchandise if the buyer fails to pay. Before the UCC, title to the goods generally passed to the buyer once merchandise was shipped. Whether the buyer retained the merchandise or rejected it, the seller could sue for the full purchase price. Of course, whether the seller recovered a judgment depended upon the buyer's right to refuse the shipment because it was defective, or for some other reason.

Under the UCC this has been modified. If the buyer rejects a shipment, rightly or wrongly, the seller must first resell the goods at the best price obtainable; then sue for the difference between the proceeds and that which was due, plus any incidental damages. The only exception is where the merchandise is of a special nature and not readily salable at a reasonable price; in that case the old rule still applies and the seller can sue for the full purchase price. Of course, if the buyer retains the shipment and then tries to return it much later, the seller is not obligated to accept the return and can sue for the full amount.

There are many variations of this kind of problem, and the UCC provides all sorts of rules to deal with them. The above rule covers the simplest and most common situation. Consequently, a seller can no longer hold rejected merchandise for a buyer and then sue for the purchase price, but has to sell the goods first and then sue only for any loss. If the seller has no loss on the resale, then only the profit on the original sale can be recovered.

Reclamation Clause

This is an important innovation in the law of Sales. Under the old law, if merchandise were shipped to a buyer that was insolvent and about to go out of business or into bankruptcy, the seller could rescind the sale and recover the merchandise only by proving a misrepresentation of solvency, a clear intention not to pay, or fraud. The old law varied widely from state to state; whether the seller was successful in reclaiming such merchandise usually depended on the state in which the sale took place.

Section 2-702 of the UCC has a different rule. The seller may recover merchandise under either of the following two situations:

1. If a seller demands the return of merchandise from an insolvent buyer within 10 days of the receipt of the shipment and the buyer fails to comply, the seller may recover the goods without proving any misrepresentation of solvency or fraud. Insolvency under the UCC is defined to include the so-called equity rule (inability to pay debts as they mature) as well as the bankruptcy definition (liabilities exceeding assets.)
2. If a misrepresentation of solvency is made in writing within 3 months before delivery, the 10-day limitation does not apply and the demand may be made at any time.

Except in these two situations, the seller may not recover merchandise on the basis of any misrepresentation of solvency. For example, if the seller fails to demand the return of merchandise within 10 days of its receipt, it cannot be reclaimed from any insolvent buyer even though the buyer had made all kinds of misrepresentations of solvency, unless they were in writing and made within 3 months of delivery.

APPLICABILITY OF BULK TRANSFER LAW

Since the creation of a security for the performance of an obligation is a legitimate financing transaction, it is not a bulk transfer under Article 6. This Article of the Uniform Commercial Code was enacted to supplement the fraudulent conveyance legislation that states had adopted to protect unsecured creditors. Nevertheless, some differences exist because a number of states have enacted their own versions of particular sections in the UCC.

Any transfer of a major part of inventory not in the ordinary course of business is subject to this Article. A transfer of a substantial part of equipment is also a bulk transfer if it is made in conjunction with a bulk transfer of inventory, but not otherwise. Creditor protection under this Article is designed to prevent two types of fraud:

1. To stop the conveyance type of sale where both parties, the debtor and the buyer, may have conspired to defraud creditors by transferring goods at less than their true value; so the debtor may then reestablish the business.
2. To prevent a debtor from selling the bulk of stock in trade, even for full value, to a buyer that may not be in collusion with the debtor; and then either dissipating the proceeds or disappearing with them, leaving creditors unpaid.

Notice and Disclosure

The underlying idea of Article 6 is to protect unsecured creditors that rely only on the general security offered by the debtor's stock of goods. The law does not cover a service business or a manufacturer that only fills orders and does not stock merchandise. The principal protection is brought about by the provision for notice and disclosure of the transfer. This is accomplished as follows:

1. The buyer of a major part of the inventory of a company that is subject to Article 6 must obtain and file a sworn list of that company's creditors and a schedule of the property to be transferred.
2. The buyer also must maintain the list and schedule for inspection by the debtor's creditors or, in some cases as an alternative, file them in a specified public office.
3. The buyer is required further to give at least 10 days notice to the creditors before taking possession of the goods.

This procedure enables creditors to investigate proposed bulk sales in advance; contact the debtor, the buyer, or both; and arrange to be paid from the proceeds or otherwise effect a claim against the goods being sold.

There is one provision of this article that is set forth as optional. It requires the transferee to hold the proceeds and see to it that the funds are applied directly to the claims of the seller instead of making payment to the seller. If the consideration or purchase price is not enough to pay all those debts in full, pro rata distribution is made. A forced settlement is in effect concluded between the debtor and the creditors. There has been much criticism of the use of bulk transfer laws in such situations. The transaction amounts to an assignment for the benefit of creditors without the usual safeguards.

Creditor's Action

A creditor receiving notice that a customer is selling under a bulk sale must immediately contact both the debtor and buyer to ascertain how much time will elapse before the sale; obtain a description of the property to be sold, its value, and the names of other creditors and the amounts due them; determine whether the debtor's debts are to be paid in full or in part from the proceeds; and find out where claims should be sent.

A creditor that did not receive any such notice but learns that a sale of the debtor's goods has been made which may be subject to Article 6 should find out whether the debtor, the sale, or both are exempt from the UCC; if either or both are subject to the UCC, whether a claim can be filed; or if a claim cannot be filed, what rights creditors have against the buyer if either the debtor or buyer has failed to comply with the UCC. The creditor must move quickly in order not to be barred from relief under the law.

PART VII

MANAGING THE ACCOUNTS RECEIVABLE PORTFOLIO

CHAPTER 30

RECEIVABLES PORTFOLIO EVALUATION

An essential function of any management is the determination of the creditworthiness of its customers. In this context, the credit function should be concerned with maximizing revenues and profits rather than with minimizing risks of credit losses. To best contribute to a credit grantor's financial growth, a credit executive should adopt a broad approach in implementing company policies and in solving problems; possess the proper tools of analysis for the appraisal of present or potential customers' profit possibilities; and concentrate on judging a customer's value to a portfolio of accounts and on offering help to a customer where feasible.

Ideally, every firm would like to sell all of its output at best price to only high-grade credit risks, while sustaining no bad-debt losses. In a more practical sense, the seller accepts all the business it can from its best customers but looks to less desirable credit risks as customers to meet its marketing and profit goals. In other words, the seller is ready to accept some risk in return for the opportunity to earn more profit.

Two risk factors, well understood by credit executives, are usually taken into account when investment in receivables is being evaluated: added cost of collection from accounts that will pay slow and bad-debt losses on accounts that will never pay. Another factor, however, is not so well understood—namely, the cost of carrying accounts receivable and the financial implications of that cost on the firm's profitability.

The financial concepts of cost of capital and time value of funds introduced here are applied to develop a method for analyzing the profitability of receivables. They are used to provide a clearer understanding of how profitability is affected by the cost of carrying receivables. The technique is not intended to be used for determining the profitability of any individual transaction or account but is suggested as an approach when the overall composition of a receivables portfolio is being considered. To be used for analyzing the entire receivables portfolio, it must be possible to collect historical information concerning the classes of account that make up the portfolio.

A method for calculating cost of capital is given in this chapter. It may not be necessary to make this calculation if the firm has already determined its cost of capital. The technique of calculation may be useful, however, when cost of capital is being discussed with the firm's customers.

To make the presentation easier to follow, a hypothetical company has been set up, with appropriate sales, operating figures, and financial statements used for all of the illustrations.

Throughout the chapter, emphasis is on the usefulness and practicality of the techniques. Only enough theory is given to enable the receivables manager to follow the presentation. Formulas are kept to absolute minimum, and mathematical derivations of those formulas are deliberately omitted. In addition, some of the calculations are simplified, where such simplification does not materially affect the result. This approach makes the techniques easier to apply and keeps the mathematics simple. Those who wish an expanded theoretical treatment of the concepts presented here are referred to a standard text on corporation finance and to the journals of the various professional association and societies.

COST OF CAPITAL

Since "time is money," the dollar amount invested in receivables and the length of time it is invested represent a cost of capital to the firm. This is because resources invested in receivables cannot be used in any other corporate activity, and because the longer any particular receivable is held (i.e., the longer the days sales outstanding) the more expensive that investment becomes.

Technically, the cost of capital (K) is a factor by which any future value of investment must be discounted back over time to determine its present value. For any company, the cost of capital may be considered as the sum of the weighted average costs of attracting and holding each type of capital component (trade payables, short-term debt, long-term debt, preferred stock, and common stock and retained earnings).

Formulas

Methods of determining the cost of capital for each component are now shown; for simplicity the abbreviations shown in Figure 30–1 are used in the formula presentations.

Accounts Payable. K_a will be zero if the firm takes its discounts or buys only on net terms. If it passes an offered discount, however, the cost is high:

On terms of 1/10 n/30, the passed discount comes to 18 per cent of the payable.
On terms of 2/10 n/30, the passed discount comes to 36 per cent of the payable.
On terms of 3/10 n/30, the passed discount comes to 54 per cent of the payable.

K	overall cost of capital of the firm
k	monthly equivalent of K
K_a	cost of capital—accounts payable
K_{std}	after-tax cost of capital—short-term debt
K_{ltd}	after-tax cost of capital—long-term debt
K_{pfd}	cost of capital—preferred stock
K_e	cost of capital—common stock and surplus
i	interest rate on notes and loans payable
TR	income tax rate of the borrower (48 per cent)
P_o	original selling price
P_{ar}	face amount of long-term debt
n	term (number of years) of debt
P	current price (or book value) of common share
D_{pfd}	stated dividend per share of preferred stock
E	net earnings per share of common stock (after taxes and dividends)
g	growth rate of earnings

FIG. 30–1. Abbreviations for Cost of Capital Calculations.

The risk of the passed discount for other terms may be obtained by appropriate substitution in the formula:

$$\frac{360}{\text{Days to Maturity—Days for Discount}} \times \text{Discount Term Rate} = \text{Passed Discount}$$

Short-Term Debt. For short-term notes and loans payable, where there are no premiums or discounts involved, K_{std} is the interest rate adjusted by the tax rate of the borrower:

$$K_{std} = i \times (1 - TR)$$

Long-Term Debt. K_{ltd} is calculated after taxes by this formula, which relates the face amount of the debt, the original selling price, the interest rate, the term (years) of the debt, and the tax rate of the firm:

$$K_{ltd} = \frac{2 \times \left[(P_{ar} \times i) + \frac{(P_{ar} - P_o)}{n} \right]}{(P_{ar} + P_o)} \times (1 - TR)$$

If the long-term debt is originally sold at par, or full face value, the calculation may be made with a simplified formula identical to that used for short-term debt, so that:

$$K_{ltd} \text{ sold at par} = i \times (1 - TR)$$

Preferred Stock. K_{pfd} is obtained by dividing the contract rate, or stated dividend per share, by the net proceeds from the original sale of each preferred share:

$$K_{pfd} = \frac{Dpfd}{P_o}$$

Common Stock and Retained Earnings. While the cost of capital for common stock and for retained earnings may be determined separately, it is convenient and accurate to combine the two items for this calculation.

A number of methods are used to find this particular cost of capital. Some divide price into dividends, while others use the earnings-to-price ratio; all of them increase the value thus obtained by adding a growth factor based on recent performance.

From a managerial view, the cost of capital is a measure of the cost related to attracting and keeping the necessary financial resources in the firm. In this chapter, dividends on common stock are considered part of that cost. Therefore, the numerator for the cost of capital calculation is established as "net earnings per share after taxes and dividends."

The technique is to find the rate, K_e, that will equate the present value of all future net earnings per share after taxes and dividends to the current market price (or book value in a company that is not traded on the stock exchanges), and to add a growth rate for those earnings. This is done by dividing price into net earnings, and adding the growth factor:

$$K_e = \frac{E}{P} + g$$

Component Costs of Capital

To illustrate the application of the formulas to a particular situation, it is assumed that a company has the financial statement summary shown in Figure 30–2. The calculations for component costs of capital are given below.

Accounts Payable. Since all discounts are taken, the cost of capital is 0.

Notes Payable. The formula for short-term debt is used here:

$$\begin{aligned} K_{std} &= i \times (1 - TR) \\ &= (.0925) \times (1 - .48) \\ &= .0481 = 4.81\% \end{aligned}$$

Debenture Bond. The formula for long-term debt, with the company in the 48 per cent tax bracket, gives:

$$K_{ltd} = \frac{2 \times \left[(P_{ar} \times i) + \frac{(P_{ar} - P_o)}{n} \right]}{(P_{ar} + P_o)} \times (1 - TR)$$

$$= \frac{2 \times \left[(1000 \times .0825) + \frac{(1000 - 960)}{10} \right]}{(1000 + 960)} \times (1 - .48)$$

$$= \frac{2 \times [82.50 + 4.]}{1960} \times (.52)$$

$$= .0459 = 4.59\%$$

Balance Sheet

Assets		Liabilities and Stockholders' Equity	
Cash	$ 160,000	Accounts Payable	$ 250,000
Accounts Receivable	242,000	Notes Payables	150,000
Inventory	280,000	Current Liabilities	400,000
Current Assets	682,000		
		Debenture Bond	180,000
Fixed Assets (Net)	238,000		
		Preferred Stock	50,000
Other Assets	80,000	Common Stock	100,000
		Retained Earnings	270,000
		Total Liabilities and	
Total Assets	$1,000,000	Stockholders' Equity	$1,000,000

Notes to Balance Sheet:
Accounts Payable: all discounts are taken.
Notes Payable: mature in three months, interest at 9¼% per annum.
Debenture Bond: 10-year term, initially sold at 96 (per cent of face value), bears
  interest at 8¼% per annum.
Preferred Stock: nonparticipating, pays $6 on $100 face value, initially sold at $92.
Common Stock: $100 par, fully paid.

Record of Net Earnings

Year	Net Profit After Taxes	Preferred Dividend	Common Dividend	Net Earnings After Taxes and Dividends	Net Earnings Per Common Share	Growth Rate
1	$117,000	$3,000	$51,000	$63,000	$63	—
2	126,000	3,000	55,000	68,000	68	.0794
3	136,000	3,000	59,000	74,000	74	.0882
4 (now)	147,000	3,000	64,000	80,000	80	.0811

FIG. 30–2.   Financial Statement Summary.

Preferred Stock. For this category the formula is:

$$K_{pfd} = \frac{D_{pfd}}{P_0}$$

$$= \frac{6}{92}$$

$$= .0652 = 6.52\%$$

Common Stock Capitalization. Common stock and retained earnings are combined to determine the cost of capital for common stock capitalization. Where the stock is publicly traded, some prefer to use the market value of the shares; however, in smaller companies closely held by the principals, there is a very small market for the shares. In that case the book value of the shares may be used. With those figures, the calculated cost of capital is higher than it would be for a successful company, publicly traded. This is because the book value of shares is normally lower than the market value, if in fact a market does exist for the shares. Since cost of capital is determined by dividing the price into net earnings, a higher price would give a lower value for $\frac{E}{P}$.

In this example the formula for K_e is used, except that P is the book value rather than the current market value of each share of common stock. The price is equal to $100 par, plus the $270 proportionate share of surplus; and the growth rate for the past year is .0811.

$$K_e = \frac{E}{P} + g$$
$$= \frac{80}{370} + .0811$$
$$= .2973 = 29.73\%$$

Overall Weighted Average Cost of Capital

Once the methods have been learned to calculate the cost of capital of debt and equity, the individual steps may be combined to obtain an overall cost of capital of the firm. For this, the technique of weighted average is useful. This method assigns a cost to each source of capital, that cost being in direct proportion to the weight of that particular type of liability or equity in the balance sheet.

In applying this method, it is necessary to take certain specific steps: (1) determine the proportion of financing that each source (liability or equity) contributes to the total resources of the firm, (2) multiply the individual cost rates by the proportions obtained in (1) to calculate individual weighted average costs, and (3) add together the individual weighted average costs to establish the overall cost of capital of the firm.

Thus, if a company's balance sheet shows notes payable as 15 per cent of all liabilities and net worth (total capitalization), the cost of capital rate for short-term debt (K_{std}) is multiplied by the proportion of that short-term debt (.15) to obtain the component cost factor. The calculation is carried out for each component. Then the components are totaled to determine the overall weighted average cost of capital.

This procedure has been used on the sample company to construct the table shown in Figure 30–3. The proportions are derived from the balance sheet and the component capital costs from the previous calculations. Figure 30–3 shows that the firm has an overall cost of capital of .1288, or nearly 13 per cent. That value will be used for further calculations in this chapter.

Source	Amount	Proportion		K		Weight Average K
Accounts Payable	$ 250,000	.25	×	0	=	0
Notes Payable	150,000	.15	×	.0481	=	.0072
Debenture Bond	180,000	.18	×	.0459	=	.0083
Preferred Stock	50,000	.05	×	.0652	=	.0033
Common Stock and Retained Earnings	370,000	.37	×	.2973	=	.1100
	$1,000,000	1.00				
		Overall K for the Firm			=	.1288 = 13%

FIG. 30–3.   Weighted Average Cost of Capital.

Importance of Taking Offered Discounts

The table used to determine overall cost of capital is useful in showing how a firm's cost of capital increases dramatically when offered vendor discounts are not taken. For instance, a company may seek to finance expansion with "free" trade creditors' money and therefore hold off paying accounts payable until maturity.

If it is assumed that payments go from 10 days to 30 days on terms of 2/10 n/30, the dollar amount of payables would triple, to $750,000. The corresponding rise in assets could be reflected in any of a number of items on the left-hand side of the balance sheet. Aside from hurting the financial condition of the company in terms of traditional ratio analysis, the decision would have a marked effect on the firm's cost of capital.

To illustrate this point, Figure 30–3 has been recast, but now it is assumed that the firm has not taken the 2/10 discount offered by all of its suppliers. Accounts payable have consequently increased threefold, to $750,000; total sources of capital have increased to $1,500,000; and the pro-

Source	Amount	Proportion		K		Weighted Average K
Accounts Payable	$ 750,000	.50	×	.3600	=	.1800
Notes Payable	150,000	.10	×	.0481	=	.0048
Debenture Bond	180,000	.12	×	.0459	=	.0055
Preferred Stock	50,000	.03	×	.0652	=	.0020
Common Stock & Surplus	370,000	.25	×	.2973	=	.0743
	$1,500,000	1.00				
		Overall K for the Firm			=	.2666 = 27%

portion of capital provided by each source has changed. This strategy costs the firm 36 per cent on its payables portion, and the overall cost of capital increases 14 percentage points to 27 per cent. The calculations are tabulated in Figure 30–4.

TIME VALUE OF FUNDS

Traditionally, an open-account transaction is made on the basis that the buyer will pay at some maturity date in the future for goods or services delivered today, or in a short time. The selling price, quoted in the present, is the dollar amount that will be received in the future. Therefore, if the seller is to realize its required earnings on the sale, a price should be quoted that takes into account the required or ordinary profit, the risk premium, and the cost of carrying the receivable until maturity date.

In most instances, the first two factors are included in the pricing mechanism. The cost of carrying receivables, however, is usually ignored. This oversight acts as a price cut and forces the seller to absorb a cost not considered when the price is being set.

Present Value

The concept of present value, which may be applied to calculate this loss of profit, states that the future value of any investment must be discounted backwards in time to determine the present value of that investment. In the illustrated case, the discount factor (the rate by which the future value must be reduced in order to obtain the present value) is .1288 per annum, the overall weighted average cost of capital for the firm. Thus the present value of a $100 receivable due in one month is the $100 less one month's cost of capital for the $100. The formula for this calculation is:

$$PV = \frac{FV}{(1+k)^n}$$

PV is the present value of the receivable; FV, its future value; k is the monthly compound equivalent of the annual cost of capital; and n is the time period, one month.

Strictly speaking, the value for k in this formula should be the monthly compound equivalent of .1288 per annum. This is equal to .01015 compounded monthly for 12 months and may be obtained from financial tables prepared for such calculations. Further, the n in the denominator is the power to which $(1+k)$ must be raised for the calculation to be precise.

A simpler method may be used, however, to give a close approximation:

$$PV = FV - FV\ (k \times n)$$

Here the value for k is obtained by dividing the annual cost of capital into 12 equal monthly segments $(.1288 \div 12 = .01073)$. That figure multiplied by n, the number of monthly periods that the receivable is outstanding, and then by the amount of the invoice, gives the cost of carrying that receivable. Finally, the cost is subtracted from the future value, or face amount of the receivable, to calculate the present value. Calculations under the two methods are shown below.

Under the strict method, the present value of a $100 receivable due in one month is:

$$PV = \frac{\$100}{(1 + .01015)^1} = \$99.00$$

If the simple method is used, instead of the monthly compound equivalent method, the present value is:

$$PV = \$100 - \$100\ (.01073 \times 1) = \$98.93$$

By using the monthly compound interest equivalent of K and the more exact formula for a $100 sale made on 60-day terms, the present value is:

$$PV = \frac{\$100}{(1 + .01015)^2} = \$98.00$$

If the simpler calculation, using the straight two-month deduction for the $100 sale on 60-day terms, the present value is:

$$PV = \$100 - \$100\ (.01073 \times 2) = \$97.85$$

Future Value

To recover the profit erosion caused by the time value of funds, it is possible to determine the required profit, then project it forward to maturity date by applying the cost of capital factor to it. In this instance, the formula is rearranged so that:

$$FV = PV\ (1 + k)^n$$

Assuming that the seller wishes to establish a price equal to $100 plus the cost of carrying the receivable for 30 days, the calculation is:

$$FV = \$100\ (1 + .01015)^1 = \$101.02$$

For 60 days, the future value (or full selling price) would need to be set at:

$$FV = \$100\ (1 + .01015)^2 = \$102.04$$

Again, though, a simpler method may be used by which the cost of capital is added directly to the amount of the receivable:

$$FV = PV + PV\ (k \times n)$$

With the simpler calculation, the selling price for 30-day maturity is:

$$FV = \$100 + \$100\ (.01073 \times 1) = \$101.07$$

and for 60 days, it is:

$$FV = \$100 + \$100\ (.01073 \times 2) = \$102.15$$

The value figures obtained by either the compound monthly equivalent or the simple monthly equivalent are close enough to permit, for receivables management, the use of the simple monthly equivalent method. For periods of time that are longer, and stretch into years, the variances between the two methods become wider. When the time span is measured in months, however, the difference is negligible. Consequently, the simpler method will be used.

CAPITAL COST OF INVESTMENT IN RECEIVABLES

As previously brought out, investment in receivables entails a cost to the company, just as any other commitment does. Furthermore, the longer is the term of this investment the greater is its cost. In other words, receivables lose value as time goes on, and a sales dollar collected immediately is worth more to the firm than a sales dollar collected some time in the future.

Present Value of Future Receipts

The factor by which future receipts are to be discounted is the cost of capital. If, for further simplification, net selling terms are assumed with no discount offered, it is possible to establish the present value of future receipts according to when they are received. To do this, it is necessary to adjust (discount) the receivable amount by the appropriate factor that equalizes the future receipt to its present value. For this illustration, the discount factor is the annual cost of capital, .1288, divided into monthly equivalents. For ease in calculation, the simple monthly equivalent basis (.01073) is used. Though less precise than the compound monthly equivalent, its simplicity makes it more useful at little loss of accuracy.

On a $1.00 net sale, with the monthly cost of capital at .01073 and collections made in the periods as shown, the present value of future receipts will be those indicated in Figure 30–5. This cost applies equally to all receiva-

Receipts	Days	Cost of Capital	Present Value
$1.00	0	0	$1.00
1.00	30	.0107	.99
1.00	60	.0215	.98
1.00	90	.0322	.97
1.00	120	.0429	.96
1.00	150	.0537	.95
1.00	180	.0644	.94
1.00	210	.0751	.92
1.00	240	.0859	.91
1.00	270	.0966	.90
1.00	300	.1073	.89
1.00	330	.1181	.88
1.00	360	.1288	.87

FIG. 30–5.   Present Value of Future Receipts.

bles, regardless of class, and is directly related to days sales outstanding (DSO).

Cost of Carrying Receivables

The average receivables balance, multiplied by the annual cost of capital, will give the annual cost of carrying receivables. In the example company, if receivables average $242,000 and the cost of capital is .1288 per year, the annual cost of carrying the $242,000 investment in receivables is $31,170.

If the company could keep its investment in receivables at a lower figure and turn it more actively to achieve the same volume of sales, the cost of carrying receivables would be lower. Thus, with average receivables at $180,000, the cost of carrying the portfolio would be $23,184.

Conversely, if the company found it necessary to increase its receivables portfolio to $265,000, the annual cost of carrying it would be $34,132.

For another view of this idea, it is assumed that the sales volume of the company amounts to $2,000,000 per year. Then the $242,000 accounts receivable on the balance sheet represent 43.6 days sales outstanding. To determine the cost of carrying the $242,000 for 43.6 days, it is necessary to multiply the portfolio size by the DSO and by the daily cost of capital:

$$\$242,000 \times 43.6 \times (.1288 \div 360) = \$3,775$$

If, for the same annual volume, the portfolio could be kept at $195,000, this would represent 35.1 days sales outstanding. The cost of carrying the $195,000 for the 35.1 days would be:

$$\$195,000 \times 35.1 \times (.1288 \div 360) = \$2,449$$

But if the portfolio were allowed to stretch out to $275,000, or 49.5 days, the cost of carrying the portfolio for one full turnover would be:

$$\$275,000 \times 49.5 \times (.1288 \div 360) = \$4,870$$

Effect of Discount Terms on Profit

The concept of time value of funds is useful for understanding how cash discount terms offered by the firm affect its receivables cost of capital and profit. For instance, if regular selling terms are 2/10 n/30 and K is .1288, then the firm's profit on any particular receivable will vary, according to when the customer pays the invoice.

This may be shown by a series of comparable sales situations. In all instances that follow, selling price is $100, terms are 2/10 n/30, and usual operating statement costs (except K) are $86. However, since the time for payment is varied, the cost of carrying each particular receivable is also varied.

Immediate Payment. When a customer pays cash and takes the discount, the present value of the receivable is immediately reduced by the discount amount. All other figures require no time value adjustment, since they are in the present. Costs of $86 are subtracted from the $98 received and the profit is $12. In this instance, there is no receivable and therefore no capital cost of carrying it.

Sale (Receivable)	$100.00
Cash Discount	2.00
Cash or Present Value	98.00
Cost at Present Value	86.00
Profit at Present Value	$ 12.00

Payment on 10th Day. When payment is received on the 10th day, or the last day of the discount period, the firm sustains two types of profit reduction: the customer is entitled to deduct the discount, and the seller firm has incurred the capital cost of carrying the receivable for ten days. Thus receipts are $98; but because it has cost 36 cents to carry the $100 receivable for the ten days, the cash or present value of the receipt is $97.64. With the deduction of $86 costs, the profit becomes $11.64.

Sale (Receivable)	$100.00	
Cash Discount	2.00	
	98.00	
Cost of Carrying Receivable	.36	$100 × 10 days × (.1288 ÷ 360)
Cash or Present Value	97.64	
Cost at Present Value	86.00	
Profit at Present Value	$ 11.64	

Payment on the 11th Day. If the customer pays on the 11th day but does not take the discount (admittedly, an unlikely situation), the seller firm gains the cash discount at the expense of one more day's capital cost of carrying the receivable. This sets the cash or present value of the receivable at $99.61 and the profit at $13.61.

Sale (Receivable)	$100.00	
Cash Discount	0	
	100.00	
Cost of Carrying Receivable	.39	$100 × 11 days × (.1288 ÷ 360)
Cash or Present Value	99.61	
Cost at Present Value	86.00	
Profit at Present Value	$ 13.61	

Payment on 30th Day. When payment is received on the maturity date of the receivable, the seller has carried the receivable for one month and incurred the corresponding cost of capital, $1.07. However, the payment is for the full amount of the invoice, or $100, and profit is $12.93.

Sale (Receivable)	$100.00	
Cash Discount	0	
	100.00	
Cost of Carrying Receivable	1.07	$100 × 30 days × (.1288 ÷ 360)
Cash or Present Value	98.93	
Cost at Present Value	86.00	
Profit at Present Value	$ 12.93	

Payment on 60th Day. For the last illustration, it is assumed that payment is received on the 60th day, or 30 days past due. No discount is lost by the seller, but it has been necessary to carry the receivable for 60 days at a cost of capital of $2.15. This reduces the cash value of profit to $11.85.

Sale (Receivable)	$100.00	
Cash Discount	0	
	100.00	
Cost of Carrying Receivable	2.15	$100 × 60 days × (.1288 ÷ 360)
Cash or Present Value	97.85	
Cost at Present Value	86.00	
Profit at Present Value	$ 11.85	

The different situations are tabulated in Figure 30-6. The table shows the 11th day after invoice date as yielding the greatest profit to the firm. Next most profitable is the maturity date, and cash payment is the third most profitable. Under the circumstances stipulated (i.e., terms are 2/10 n/30 and K is .1288), however, it also shows that the firm loses less on payments received 30 days slow than it does on payments received on the last day of the discount period, with that discount taken by the customer.

It is a straightforward exercise to repeat these calculations for different terms of sale and different costs of capital. By this means, the firm will be able to understand the cost/profitability tradeoff when it is studying its discount terms or the possible imposition of late-payment charges.

Payment Date	0	10	11	30	60
Sale	$100.00	$100.00	$100.00	$100.00	$100.00
Cash Discount	2.00	2.00	0	0	0
	98.00	98.00	100.00	100.00	100.00
Cost of Carrying Receivable	0	.36	.39	1.07	2.15
Cash or Present Value	98.00	97.64	99.61	98.93	97.85
Cost at Present Value	86.00	86.00	86.00	86.00	86.00
Profit at Present Value	$ 12.00	$ 11.64	$ 13.61	$ 12.93	$ 11.85

Note: Terms are 2/10 n/30
      Cost of Capital is .1288

FIG. 30–6.   PV of Profit at Different Payment Dates, When Discount Is Offered.

DATA COLLECTION

To understand the composition of the firm's portfolio, the receivables manager must go to company records and compile certain data about the company's accounts. In addition to the usual operating figures, the data should identify the percentage of total sales made to each class of account, the typical or average accounts receivable balance for each class of account, and the days sales outstanding (DSO) measure for each class of account.

Initially, this may be done monthly for a period of one year; as the system becomes installed, it will be a simple matter to refine the data by such statistical techniques as moving averages.

If the company already has a classification system, the data can be collected in a routine manner, either from the past year's records or by tracking sales for the next twelve months. If not, the manager should first classify the accounts, then either go back into 12 months' records for those accounts or keep track of them for the next year.

Class Sales

To illustrate how this is done, it is assumed that the accounts of the seller firm are separated into four classes, according to desirability:

Class A: most desirable, no added cost of collection, no bad debts.
Class B: •
Class C: •
Class D: least desirable, greatest cost of collection, highest bad debts.

Further, it is assumed that records show the firm's annual sales volume of $2,000,000 was made as follows: 21.4 per cent ($428,000) to Class A accounts, 34.0 per cent ($680,000) to Class B accounts, 35.4 per cent ($708,000) to Class C accounts, and 9.2 per cent ($184,000) to Class D accounts.

Average Receivables

Average accounts receivable balances may be obtained directly from company records. In the example, average receivables portfolio is found (assumed) to be $242,000, made up as follows: Class A, $42,000; B, $72,000; C, $88,000; and D, $40,000.

Days Sales Outstanding

These balances are used to calculate DSO for each class of account, by the following formula:

$$\frac{\text{Average A/R Balance}}{\text{Class Annual Sales}} \times 360 = \text{Class DSO}$$

Class A: $\dfrac{42,000}{428,000} \times 360 = 35.3 \text{ days}$

Class B: $\dfrac{72,000}{680,000} \times 360 = 38.1$ days

Class C: $\dfrac{88,000}{708,000} \times 360 = 44.7$ days

Class D: $\dfrac{40,000}{184,000} \times 360 = 78.3$ days

Class Proportions of Receivables Portfolio

To find the proportion of each class that is represented in the total receivables balance, it is necessary to divide the individual balances by $242,000:

Class A: $\dfrac{42,000}{242,000} = .174 = 17.4\%$

Class B: $\dfrac{72,000}{242,000} = .297 = 29.7\%$

Class C: $\dfrac{88,000}{242,000} = .364 = 36.4\%$

Class D: $\dfrac{40,000}{242,000} = .165 = 16.5\%$

The data and calculations are tabulated in Figure 30-7. They show some interesting features about the company's receivables portfolio. Most important is the fact that receivables due from "best" and "poorest" accounts are about equal, even though sales to best accounts are more than double those made to poorest customers. The explanation lies in the DSO figures, which show that it takes 35 days to turn Class A accounts, and 78 days to collect Class D accounts.

Class	Decimal of Sales	Class Annual Sales	Average Receivables	Class DSO	Decimal of Portfolio
A	.214	$ 428,000	$ 42,000	35.3	.174
B	.340	680,000	72,000	38.1	.297
C	.354	708,000	88,000	44.7	.364
D	.092	184,000	40,000	78.3	.165
Total	1.000	$2,000,000	$242,000	43.6	1.000

FIG. 30–7.   Summary Receivables Information by Class of Accounts.

Clearly, the firm is selling to as many Class A accounts as it can find. They do not provide enough volume, however, to support production, so the firm then looks to its B and C customers. When those are used up, it takes on the marginal or D customers.

Credit and Collection Expense and Bad-Debt Loss

Company records show that some credit and collection costs are the same for all classes of account, while others vary according to the class or risk involved. Similarly, bad-debt losses increase greatly with risk. The hypothetical findings are tabulated in Figure 30-8.

| Class | Annual Class Sales | Credit and Collection Expense | | Bad-Debt Loss |
		Fixed	Variable	All Variable
A	$ 428,000	$12,412	$ 0	0
B	680,000	19,720	7,480	1,292
C	708,000	20,532	16,284	2,832
D	184,000	5,336	9,568	3,349
Total	$2,000,000	$58,000	$33,332	7,473
Decimal Proportion	1.0000	.0290	.0167	.0037

FIG. 30–8.   Credit and Collection Expense and Bad-Debt Loss.

The distinctions between classes of accounts are especially evident in variable credit and collection expense. With comparable sales volume, Class C accounts require more than twice as much variable credit and collection expense as do Class B customers; and Class D accounts, with 9 per cent of the volume, use up nearly 29 per cent of the variable credit and collection expense.

As might be expected, the greatest portion (almost 45 per cent) of the company's bad-debt losses arises from sales to Class D customers. Also, there is a sharp distinction in loss experience between B accounts and C accounts, while A customers show no bad-debt losses.

Annual Cost of Capital for Receivables by Class

The cost of carrying receivables described earlier may now be examined in greater detail by segregating the different classes of account and calculating the applicable cost for each class. To do this, it is necessary to identify the dollar amount in each class, then to multiply those amounts by the cost factor. The results are tabulated in Figure 30-9.

Approximately two-thirds of the cost of capital goes for the B and C customers that account for nearly 70 per cent of sales. The notably sharp difference, however, is seen between A and D customers. With comparable investments in receivables and with comparable annual costs of capital, the company can sell over twice as much to A customers as it does to D cus-

Class	Average A/R Balance	Cost of Capital Factor	Annual Cost of Capital
A	$ 42,000	.1288	$ 5,410
B	72,000	.1288	9,274
C	88,000	.1288	11,334
D	40,000	.1288	5,152
Total	$242,000	.1288	$31,170

FIG. 30–9. Annual Cost of Capital for Receivables by Class.

tomers. This is reflected by the direct relation of DSO to cost of investment in receivables. The DSO for D accounts is more than double the DSO for A customers. Consequently, the slower collections from D customers makes that portion of the receivables portfolio sluggish and expensive.

Allocation of Costs

Decimal proportions of fixed and variable costs are next calculated, keeping in mind that all fixed costs are spread evenly among all classes of account. In a conventional analysis of receivables, these and the bad-debt losses would be the total costs considered. However, since this analysis also includes the cost of capital for investment in receivables, it is necessary to add the data from Figure 30-9. Arranged in tabular form, the allocations and costs are shown in Figure 30-10.

	All Accounts	A Accounts	B Accounts	C Accounts	D Accounts
Annual Class Sales	$2,000,000	$428,000	$680,000	$708,000	$184,000
Credit and Collection					
Fixed—dollars	58,000	12,412	19,720	20,532	5,336
—decimal	.0290	.0290	.0290	.0290	.0290
Variable—dollars	33,332	0	7,480	16,284	9,568
—decimal	.0167	.0000	.0110	.0230	.0520
Bad-Debt Loss					
Variable—dollars	7,473	0	1,292	2,832	3,349
—decimal	.0037	.0000	.0019	.0040	.0182
Average Receivables Balance	242,000	42,000	72,000	88,000	40,000
Cost of Capital	.1288	.1288	.1288	.1288	.1288
Cost of Carrying Receivables	31,170	5,410	9,274	11,334	5,152

FIG. 30–10. Allocation of Credit and Collection Expense, Bad-Debt Loss, and Cost of Carrying Receivables.

Other Operating Data

Now that receivables costs have been identified, all that is needed for the profitability analysis are certain relevant data available from the operating statement. Cost of goods sold; gross profit; and warehousing, selling, and administration expenses are extracted, identified as either fixed or variable costs, and presented as decimal proportions of sales in Figure 30-11.

| | Decimal Proportions of Sales | | |
	Total	Fixed	Variable
Cost of Goods Sold	.7015	0	.7015
Gross Profit	.2985	0	.2985
Warehousing	.0430	.0310	.0120
Selling	.0520	.0185	.0335
Administration	.0126	.0111	.0015

FIG. 30–11.   Selected Operating Data.

PROFITABILITY ANALYSIS

Conventional profitability analysis considers only those real costs that are reflected in the company's financial statements. Credit and collection expense are a real cash outlay, while bad-debt losses are a direct reduction of profit. Although giving some insight into the financial impact of receivables, this type of analysis ignores the imputed cost of carrying the firm's investment in accounts receivable. A more precise evaluation requires that it be included. Only then can informed strategic decisions be made regarding the portfolio.

To demonstrate the technique, appropriate data are now arranged into a method that gives weight to the cost of carrying receivables while analyzing the profitability of receivables investment. While quite similar to a conventional profitability analysis based on accounting statements, the analysis discussed here also makes allowance for the cost of carrying receivables. Although that cost cannot be readily identified and assigned under ordinary accounting procedures, the method described here allows the receivables manager to do so. It can be used for the entire portfolio and for each class of account.

Before proceeding, however, it is important to point out that the analysis results may differ considerably, depending upon what assumptions are made about the output of the firm. Specifically, two interpretations will be illustrated. One is based on the assumption that Class D customers are needed to absorb the production output of the firm and share all costs equally. In this case, all fixed costs are distributed evenly among all sales. In the second analysis, it is assumed that customers in Classes A, B, and C absorb the fixed costs of the firm, and Class D customers contribute incremental income against which only variable costs are charged.

To begin the first analysis, the data are spread onto an analysis sheet that shows sales, costs, and profit for all accounts and for each class of account. This format allows each class of account to be examined for component income, cost, and profitability.

		Decimal of Sales	All Accounts	A Accounts	B Accounts	C Accounts	D Accounts
Sales		1.0000	$2,000,000	$428,000	$680,000	$708,000	$184,000
Cost of Goods Sold		.7015	1,403,000	300,242	477,020	496,662	129,076
Gross Profit		.2985	597,000	127,758	202,980	211,338	54,924
Warehousing	—Fixed	.0310	62,000	13,268	21,080	21,948	5,704
	—Variable	.0120	24,000	5,136	8,160	8,496	2,208
Selling	—Fixed	.0185	37,000	7,918	12,580	13,098	3,404
	—Variable	.0335	67,000	14,338	22,780	23,718	6,164
Administration	—Fixed	.0111	22,200	4,751	7,548	7,859	2,042
	—Variable	.0015	3,000	642	1,020	1,062	276
Credit and Collection							
	—Fixed	.0290	58,000	12,412	19,720	20,532	5,336
	—Variable	.0167	33,332	—	—	—	—
		.0000	—	0	—	—	—
		.0110	—	—	7,480	—	—
		.0230	—	—	—	16,284	—
		.0520	—	—	—	—	9,568
Bad Debts—All Variable		.0037	7,473	—	—	—	—
		.0000	—	0	—	—	—
		.0019	—	—	1,292	—	—
		.0040	—	—	—	2,832	—
		.0182	—	—	—	—	3,349
Operating Expenses Before K			314,005	58,465	101,660	115,829	38,051
Cost of Capital for Receivables			31,170	5,410	9,274	11,334	5,152
Operating Expenses After K			345,175	63,875	110,934	127,163	43,203
Operating Profit After K			$ 251,825	$ 63,883	$ 92,046	$ 84,175	$ 11,721
Average Receivables Balance			242,000	42,000	72,000	88,000	40,000
Total Cost of Receivables			129,975	17,822	37,766	50,982	23,405
Annual Service Cost Per Dollar of Receivables Carried			.5371	.4243	.5245	.5793	.5851
Operating Profit Margin$_K$			.1259	.1493	.1354	.1189	.0637
Return on Receivables			1.0406	1.5210	1.2784	.9565	.2930

FIG. 30–12. Analysis Sheet.

Inclusion of the imputed cost of capital for receivables causes some changes in the final operating statement figures. Those changes are not customarily included in published reports of the company. They are, however, essential from the viewpoint of managerial analysis for planning and control, since they provide a clearer understanding of the financial implications of a firm's investment in receivables. For this reason, operating expenses are shown both before and after cost of capital. The analysis sheet is given in Figure 30-12.

Total Cost of Receivables

Credit and collection expense, bad-debt losses, and cost of carrying receivables are next isolated for further study, and are tabulated in Figure 30-13.

The financial implications of considering cost of capital for receivables investment are pointed out in Figure 30-13. Costs associated with receivables would conventionally be shown as the total of credit and collection expense and bad-debt loss, or $98,805. With the imputed cost K included, however, the total receivables costs increase to $129,975.

The corresponding costs for each class of account are shown in the appropriate columns. It is seen more clearly than before that the cost of carrying receivables causes major adjustments in the conventional analysis of the receivables portfolio. For instance, without giving weight to the cost of capital, a conventional analysis would identify the relation of receivables costs to Class A accounts as $12,412 \div $428,000$, or .0290. Similarly, the figure for B accounts would be .0419; for C accounts, .0560; and for D accounts, .0992.

When K is included in the receivables costs, however, the corresponding figures are: A accounts, .0416; B accounts, .0555; C accounts, .0720; and D accounts, .1272.

	All Accounts	A Accounts	B Accounts	C Accounts	D Accounts
Annual Sales	$2,000,000	$428,000	$680,000	$708,000	$184,000
Average Receivables Balance	242,000	42,000	72,000	88,000	40,000
Credit & Collection —Fixed	58,000	12,412	19,720	20,532	5,336
—Variable	33,332	0	7,480	16,284	9,568
Bad Debts	7,473	0	1,292	2,832	3,349
Cost of Capital	31,170	5,410	9,274	11,334	5,152
Total Cost	$ 129,975	$ 17,822	$ 37,766	$ 50,982	$ 23,405

FIG. 30–13.   Total Cost of Receivables.

Annual Service Cost Per Dollar of Receivables Carried

Overall, the relation of total cost of receivables to average receivables balance is $129,975 ÷ $242,000, or .5371. It costs about 54 cents per year to service one dollar of receivables as it turns over on the company's books. In other words, the return on receivables investment is reduced by 54 cents. For the different classes of account, the component figures are shown below. Clearly, Class D accounts are most expensive to service.

All Accounts	$129,975 ÷ $242,000 = .5371
Class A	17,822 ÷ 42,000 = .4243
Class B	37,766 ÷ 72,000 = .5245
Class C	50,982 ÷ 88,000 = .5793
Class D	23,405 ÷ 40,000 = .5851

Operating Profit Margin$_K$

The operating profit margin on sales (after including the cost of carrying receivables) is determined by dividing sales into operating profit after K. For the example company, the results are shown below.

All Accounts	$251,825 ÷ $2,000,000 = .1259
Class A	63,883 ÷ 428,000 = .1493
Class B	92,046 ÷ 680,000 = .1354
Class C	84,175 ÷ 708,000 = .1189
Class D	11,721 ÷ 184,000 = .0637

The operating profit margin$_K$ for all accounts is .1259, or 13 per cent. That calculation, however, ignores the fact that each class of account has a different level of expenses for credit, collection, and bad debts. When the individual classes are examined, it becomes evident that Class A accounts are most profitable, while Class D accounts are least profitable.

Return on Receivables

The return on receivables (ROR) is obtained by dividing operating profit after K by the average accounts receivable balance for the entire portfolio and for each class of account:

$$\text{Return on Receivables} = \frac{\text{Operating Profit After K}}{\text{Average Accounts Receivable}}$$

This measure is an adaptation of the return on investment (ROI) concept. While other measures may be used that seek to allocate profit among receivables, inventory, and capital equipment, they would be no more precise than the one used here. For ease, therefore, this treatment assumes that all operating profit is lodged in accounts receivable.

Earlier, it was determined that average accounts receivable balances for the company are: All accounts, $242,000; Class A, $42,000; Class B, $72,000; Class C, $88,000; and Class D, $40,000. Applying these amounts in the formula gives the yields shown below.

All Accounts	ROR	$251,825 ÷ $242,000 = 1.0406
Class A		63,883 ÷ 42,000 = 1.5210
Class B		92,046 ÷ 72,000 = 1.2784
Class C		84,175 ÷ 88,000 = .9565
Class D		11,721 ÷ 40,000 = .2930

These figures give a clear picture of the yield realized on receivables investment, segregated by class of account. Here return on receivables is highest in A and lowest in D. The calculation is helpful in clarifying the level of risk a firm is taking, and relating that risk to the potential gain from it. If there is a threshold yield below which management does not wish to accept a risk, comparison of these figures against that standard will aid the receivables manager to set a cutoff point for the types of accounts to be accepted as customers.

PV Analysis of Receivables Contribution to Profit

The concept of time value of funds may be used to obtain another view of the receivables portfolio contribution to profit. It is an established principle of finance that no investment should be made unless it improves the investor's net worth. Applying that principle to sales and receivables, it is possible to evaluate each class of customer in the portfolio and determine the extent to which it does increase the firm's net worth.

This is best done separately for each class of account. Briefly the procedure is to establish the present value of sales over the course of a year by deducting the cost of capital for receivables from the face amount. A further reduction by all other costs gives the present value of the annual profit contribution of the entire portfolio and of each class of account.

Using the data from Figure 30–12, the receivables cost of capital is subtracted from the annual sales to calculate the present value of sales. Next, all costs except K are obtained by adding cost of goods sold and operating expenses before K. That total is subtracted from the PV of sales to obtain the present value of annual profit contribution. The method is illustrated in Figure 30–14.

On Class A accounts, for example, the data show that the annual profit contribution is $63,883, earned on $428,000 of sales. This is merely another way of presenting the operating results of the firm, but it does have the feature of placing emphasis on the important role that time value of funds plays in the company's profitability evaluation.

INCREMENTAL PROFITABILITY ANALYSIS

The difference between incremental profitability analysis and that illustrated earlier lies in one principal assumption—namely, that sales to A, B, and C customers are sufficient to cover all fixed costs, so that only variable costs need be charged against sales to D customers. This reporting conven-

	All Accounts	A Accounts	B Accounts	C Accounts	D Accounts
Sales	$2,000,000	$428,000	$680,000	$708,000	$184,000
Cost of Capital for Receivables (K)	31,170	5,410	9,274	11,334	5,152
PV of Sales	1,968,830	422,590	670,726	696,666	178,848
Cost of Goods Sold	1,403,000	300,242	477,020	496,662	129,076
Operating Expenses Before K	314,005	58,465	101,660	115,829	38,051
All Costs Except K	1,717,005	358,707	578,680	612,491	167,127
Annual Profit Contribution (PV)	$ 251,825	$ 63,883	$ 92,046	$ 84,175	$ 11,721

FIG. 30–14.   Receivables PV Contribution to Profit.

tion reduces the profitability showings of the top three classes of customers and improves the reported yield on D accounts. It is a useful technique for supplementary analysis of receivables, particularly when fixed costs can be allocated to A, B, and C customers.

Adjusted Receivables Costs

As in the previous method, this analysis begins with the gathering of data on credit and collection expense and bad-debt losses, then an allocation of fixed and variable expenses among the different classes of account.

The totals for each of the items remain the same, but the concentration of fixed credit and collection expense into Class A, B, and C accounts causes a difference in the two lines related to that item. Dollar figures for the top three classes are adjusted upward to absorb the $5,336 previously charged to Class D accounts. This brings their decimal calculation upwards, to .0319 of class sales, while the D accounts carry no fixed charges.

After this has been done, bad-debt losses and the cost of capital for receivables are introduced to give the table shown in Figure 30–15.

Other Operating Data

Recasting the fixed warehousing, selling, and administration expenses in the same way transfers the overhead burden to the first three classes of account, and gives the table in Figure 30–16. Again the totals remain the same.

The data are now ready to be spread onto the analysis sheet in Figure 30–17. Variable costs have not been altered from those in Figure 30–12; the changes all reflect the assumption that no fixed costs are borne by Class D accounts.

	All Accounts	A Accounts	B Accounts	C Accounts	D Accounts
Annual Class Sales	$2,000,000	$428,000	$680,000	$708,000	$184,000
Credit and Collection					
Fixed—dollars	58,000	13,670	21,718	22,612	0
—decimal	.0290	.0319	.0319	.0319	.0000
Variable—dollars	33,332	0	7,480	16,284	9,568
—decimal	.0167	.0000	.0110	.0230	.0520
Bad-Debt Loss					
Variable—dollars	7,473	0	1,292	2,832	3,349
—decimal	.0037	.0000	.0019	.0040	.0182
Average Receivables Balance	242,000	42,000	72,000	88,000	40,000
Cost of Capital	.1288	.1288	.1288	.1288	.1288
Cost of Carrying Receivables	31,170	5,410	9,274	11,334	5,152

FIG. 30–15. Adjusted Allocations of Credit and Collection Expense, Bad-Debt Loss, and Cost of Carrying Receivables.

	Warehousing	Selling	Administration
Class A	$14,612	$ 8,720	$ 5,232
Class B	23,216	13,855	8,313
Class C	24,172	14,425	8,655
Class D	0	0	0
Total	$62,000	$37,000	$22,200

FIG. 30–16. Adjusted Allocations of Warehousing, Selling, and Administration Expenses.

Total Cost of Receivables

Credit and collection expense, bad-debt losses, and cost of carrying receivables are again extracted from the analysis sheet to prepare Figure 30–18.

Whereas, under the full-costing analysis (Figure 30–13), total cost of carrying receivables from A accounts is $17,822, the corresponding figure under incremental analysis is $19,080. For B accounts and C accounts, total cost has likewise gone up. However, for D accounts, total cost of carrying receivables has decreased from $23,405 to $18,069. This will show as a direct profit to D accounts and will improve their calculated profitability.

	Decimal of Sales	All Accounts	A Accounts	B Accounts	C Accounts	D Accounts
Sales	1.0000	$2,000,000	$428,000	$680,000	$708,000	$184,000
Cost of Goods Sold	.7015	1,403,000	300,242	477,020	496,662	129,076
Gross Profit	.2985	597,000	127,758	202,980	211,338	54,924
Warehousing —Fixed	.0341*	62,000	14,612	23,216	24,172	0
—Variable	.0120	24,000	5,136	8,160	8,496	2,208
Selling —Fixed	.0204*	37,000	8,720	13,855	14,425	0
—Variable	.0335	67,000	14,338	22,780	23,718	6,164
Administration —Fixed	.0122*	22,200	5,232	8,313	8,655	0
—Variable	.0015	3,000	642	1,020	1,062	276
Credit and Collection						
—Fixed	.0319*	58,000	13,670	21,718	22,612	0
—Variable	.0167	33,332	—	—	—	—
	.0000	—	0	—	—	→
	.0110	—	—	7,480	—	—
	.0230	—	—	—	16,284	—
	.0520	—	—	—	—	9,568
Bad Debts—All Variable	.0037	7,473	—	—	—	—
	.0000	—	0	—	—	—
	.0019	—	—	1,292	—	—
	.0040	—	—	—	2,832	—
	.0182	—	—	—	—	3,349
Operating Expenses Before K		314,005	62,350	107,834	122,256	21,565
Cost of Capital for Receivables		31,170	5,410	9,274	11,334	5,152
Operating Expenses After K		345,175	67,760	117,108	133,590	26,717
Operating Profit After K		$ 251,825	$ 59,998	$ 85,872	$ 77,748	$ 28,207
Average Receivables Balance		242,000	42,000	72,000	88,000	40,000
Total Cost of Receivables		129,975	19,080	39,764	53,062	18,069
Annual Service Cost Per Dollar of Receivables Carried		.5371	.4543	.5523	.6030	.4517
Operating Profit Margin$_K$		.1259	.1402	.1263	.1098	.1533
Return on Receivables		1.0406	1.4285	1.1927	.8835	.7052

*In this sheet, fixed cost decimal proportions are higher than in Figure 30–12 because they are allocated only among A, B and, C accounts. Consequently, the decimals do not apply to All accounts and D accounts.

FIG. 30–17.   Adjusted Analysis Sheet.

Annual Service Cost Per Dollar of Receivables Carried

As expected, this calculation shows service cost increases for the first three classes of account. For D accounts, however, there is an important reduction, from .5851 to .4517.

All Accounts	$129,975 ÷ $242,000 = .5371
Class A	19,080 ÷ 42,000 = .4543
Class B	39,764 ÷ 72,000 = .5523
Class C	53,062 ÷ 88,000 = .6030
Class D	18,069 ÷ 40,000 = .4517

	All Accounts	A Accounts	B Accounts	C Accounts	D Accounts
Annual Sales	$2,000,000	$428,000	$680,000	$708,000	$184,000
Average Receivables Balance	242,000	42,000	72,000	88,000	40,000
Credit & Collection —Fixed	58,000	13,670	21,718	22,612	0
—Variable	33,332	0	7,480	16,284	9,568
Bad Debts	7,473	0	1,292	2,832	3,349
Cost of Capital	31,170	5,410	9,274	11,334	5,152
Total Cost	$ 129,975	$ 19,080	$ 39,764	$ 53,062	$ 18,069

FIG. 30–18.   Total Cost of Receivables.

Operating Profit Margin$_K$

Similarly, operating profit margin$_K$ on sales is reduced for Class A, B, and C, while it is improved dramatically for D accounts.

$$
\begin{array}{llll}
\text{All Accounts} & \$251,825 \div \$2,000,000 = .1259 \\
\text{Class A} & 59,998 \div & 428,000 = .1402 \\
\text{Class B} & 85,872 \div & 680,000 = .1263 \\
\text{Class C} & 77,748 \div & 708,000 = .1098 \\
\text{Class D} & 28,207 \div & 184,000 = .1533 \\
\end{array}
$$

Return on Receivables

Finally, the calculation of return on receivables follows the same pattern, lowering the reported yield on the first three classes of account, but oftentimes pushing the ROR on D accounts above the threshold receivables yield requirement. In this example, the D ROR is more than doubled.

$$
\begin{array}{llll}
\text{All Accounts} & \text{ROR} & \$251,825 \div \$242,000 = 1.0406 \\
\text{Class A} & & 59,998 \div & 42,000 = 1.4285 \\
\text{Class B} & & 85,872 \div & 72,000 = 1.1927 \\
\text{Class C} & & 77,748 \div & 88,000 = .8835 \\
\text{Class D} & & 28,207 \div & 40,000 = .7052 \\
\end{array}
$$

Comparison of the Two Methods

The differences between full-costing profitability analysis and incremental profitability analysis are summarized in Figure 30–19. Again it is pointed out that totals for All accounts do not change, but component calculations create a bias in favor of D accounts when incremental analysis is used.

This situation, typical when a firm is able to meet fixed expenses with regular sales, allows the manager to view D accounts as sources of incremental income. On this basis, the total cost of receivables is borne to a greater extent by the top three classes of account. Annual service cost per dollar of receivables carried also appears to be higher for A, B, and C accounts, and lower for the marginal customers. Operating profit margin$_K$,

	Full Costing	Incremental
Total Cost of Receivables		
All Accounts	$129,975	$129,975
Class A	17,822	19,080
Class B	37,766	39,764
Class C	50,982	53,062
Class D	23,405	18,069
Annual Service Cost Per Dollar of Receivables Carried		
All Accounts	.5371	.5371
Class A	.4243	.4543
Class B	.5245	.5523
Class C	.5793	.6030
Class D	.5851	.4517
Operating Profit Margin$_K$		
All Accounts	.1259	.1259
Class A	.1493	.1402
Class B	.1354	.1263
Class C	.1189	.1098
Class D	.0637	.1533
Return on Receivables		
All Acounts	1.0406	1.0406
Class A	1.5210	1.4285
Class B	1.2784	1.1927
Class C	.9565	.8835
Class D	.2930	.7052

FIG. 30–19.   Data Comparison—Full-Costing and Incremental Profitability Analysis.

somewhat lower for the top three classes, is sharply up for D accounts; and the same type of changes are seen for return on receivables.

EXPANDING SALES TO MARGINAL ACCOUNTS

A simpler analysis may be made if primary interest is on expanding sales to marginal accounts. For instance, the prospect of additional business from D accounts may cause management to examine existing marginal accounts and project the financial implications of taking on more marginals. The purpose of the analysis would be to determine their contribution to overall operating profit margin; the cost of carrying the additional receivables; whether they are worth the risk; and whether they should be taken on.

Simplified Analysis of Current Sales

To start this analysis, pertinent data for the first three classes of account are combined, and only Class D accounts are isolated. As in the previous illustrations, the data are obtained from the firm's financial statements and

		Decimal of Sales	All Accounts	A, B, C Accounts	D Accounts
Sales		1.0000	$2,000,000	$1,816,000	$184,000
Cost of Goods Sold		.7015	1,403,000	1,273,924	129,076
Gross Profit		.2985	597,000	542,076	54,924
Warehousing	—Fixed	.0341*	62,000	62,000	0
	—Variable	.0120	24,000	21,792	2,208
Selling	—Fixed	.0204*	37,000	37,000	0
	—Variable	.0335	67,000	60,836	6,164
Administration	—Fixed	.0122*	22,200	22,200	0
	—Variable	.0015	3,000	2,724	276
Credit and Collection	—Fixed	.0319*	58,000	58,000	0
	—Variable	.0167	33,332	—	—
		.0131	—	23,764	—
		.0520	—	—	9,568
Bad Debts—All Variable		.0037	7,473	—	—
		.0023	—	4,124	—
		.0182	—	—	3,349
Operating Expenses Before K			314,005	292,440	21,565
Cost of Capital for Receivables			31,170	26,018	5,152
Operating Expenses After K			345,175	318,458	26,717
Operating Profit After K			$ 251,825	$ 223,618	$ 28,207
Average Receivables Balance			242,000	202,000	40,000
Total Cost of Receivables			129,975	111,906	18,069
Annual Service Cost Per Dollar of Receivables Carried			.5371	.5540	.4517
Operating Profit Margin$_K$			.1259	.1231	.1533
Return on Receivables			1.0406	1.1070	.7052

*In this sheet, fixed cost decimal proportions are higher than in Figure 30–12 because they are allocated only among A, B, and C accounts. Consequently, the decimals do not apply to All accounts and D accounts.

FIG. 30–20. Simplified Analysis Sheet.

from the cost of capital calculation. They are spread onto the simplified analysis sheet, as in Figure 30–20

With this recasting of the data, the simplified analysis shows that marginal customers (9 per cent of total sales) account for $40,000, or nearly 17 per cent of the firm's accounts receivable. Meanwhile, they provide $28,207, or nearly 11 per cent of the total profit. However, since it is stipulated that A, B, and C accounts cover all of the fixed costs, the operating profit margin$_K$ on D accounts is higher (15 per cent) than the overall average margin.

Annual service cost per dollar of receivables carried from Class A, B, and C customers is $111,906 ÷ $202,000, or .5540; for Class D customers it is $18,069 ÷ $40,000 or .4517. Operating profit margin$_K$ is .1231 for A, B, and C accounts and .1533 for D accounts. Return on receivables investment is 1.1070 for the top three classes and .7052 for Class D.

Analyzing Projected Additional Marginal Sales

In Figure 30–21, the data have been modified to show the effect of taking on an additional $100,000 in sales to D accounts. Most of the figures do not change, but total sales increase to $2,100,000 and D sales increase to $284,000. Fixed expenses remain the same, but variable expenses increase because of the added sales volume. Generally, these changes affect cost of goods sold and the variable portions of warehousing, selling, and administration expenses. With regard to receivables costs, the additional sales increase credit and collection expense, bad-debt losses, and the cost of carrying receivables.

Operating Costs. The extra costs are determined by applying the appropriate decimal cost proportions to the additional sales. Thus D accounts incur a variable administration expense equal to .0015 of sales; the extra $100,000 will require an additional $150 in variable administration expense, so the total for all D accounts will be the previous $276 plus the new $150, or $426.

Credit and Collection Expense. Similarly, the extra $100,000 in sales will cost an additional $5,200 in variable credit and collection expense. This will bring the total variable credit and collection expense to $14,768 for all D accounts; and for the proposed expanded volume of $2,100,000 the variable credit and collection expenses for All accounts will amount to $38,532.

Allowing for Uncertain Collections. On the present volume of $2,000,000, the proportion of bad-debt losses for this company is .0037 of sales. This means that on an overall basis, there is a .0037 likelihood that any particular amount receivable will not be paid by customers. As determined earlier, company records show that for each class of account, bad-debt loss experience has been: A accounts, 0; B accounts, .0019; C accounts, .0040; and D accounts, .0182 of sales.

These findings, incorporated into the analysis, may be used to gauge the uncertainty of collection associated with each particular class of account. Further, when projections are being made, they serve as beginning points for estimates of potential bad-debt losses from future sales. For instance, if additional sales are being contemplated to marginal accounts, bad-debt experience with D accounts will help the company make adequate provision for such losses on the expanded sales.

This approach is more straightforward than one that requires "certainty-

		Decimal of Sales	All Accounts	A,B,C Accounts	D Accounts	Additional D Accounts	All D Accounts
		1.0000					
Sales			$2,100,000	$1,816,000	$184,000	$100,000	$284,000
Cost of Goods Sold		.7015	1,473,150	1,273,924	129,076	70,150	199,226
Gross Profit		.2985	626,850	542,076	54,924	29,850	84,774
Warehousing	—Fixed	.0341*	62,000	62,000	0	0	0
	—Variable	.0120	25,200	21,792	2,208	1,200	3,408
Selling	—Fixed	.0204*	37,000	37,000	0	0	0
	—Variable	.0335	70,350	60,836	6,164	3,350	9,514
Administration	—Fixed	.0122*	22,200	22,200	0	0	0
	—Variable	.0015	3,150	2,724	276	150	426
Credit and Collection	—Fixed	.0319*	58,000	58,000	0	0	0
	—Variable	.0183	38,532	—	—	—	—
		.0131	—	23,764	—	—	—
		.0520	—	—	9,568	5,200	14,768
Bad Debts—All Variable		.0044	9,293	—	—	—	—
		.0023	—	4,124	—	—	—
		.0182	—	—	3,349	1,820	5,169
Operating Expenses Before K			325,725	292,440	21,565	11,720	33,285
Cost of Capital for Receivables			33,974	26,018	5,152	2,804	7,956
Operating Expenses After K			359,699	318,458	26,717	14,524	41,241
Operating Profit After K			$ 267,151	$ 223,618	$ 28,207	$ 15,326	$ 43,533
Average Receivables Balance			263,770	202,000	40,000	21,770	61,770
Total Cost of Receivables			139,799	111,906	18,069	9,824	27,893
Annual Service Cost Per Dollar of Receivables Carried			.5300	.5540	.4517	.4513	.4516
Operating Profit Margin$_K$			.1272	.1231	.1533	.1533	.1533
Return on Receivables			1.0128	1.1070	.7052	.7040	.7048

*In this sheet, fixed cost decimal proportions are higher than in Figure 30–12 because they are allocated only among A, B, and C accounts. Consequently, the decimals do not apply to All accounts and D accounts.

FIG. 30–21. Pro Forma Analysis Sheet for Expanded Marginal Accounts.

equivalent coefficients" to establish the likelihood or probability rates at which class receivables will be collected. It achieves the same result, however, by charging off bad-debt losses directly in the pro forma analysis sheet.

At the .0182 rate that now exists for bad debts from D accounts, the additional $100,000 will cause an extra $1,820 in losses. Adding that to the $3,349 already being lost will give a projected total bad-debt loss of $5,169

from the D accounts. The additional losses will move the bad-debt proportion upward, to .0044 on total sales of $2,100,000.

Cost of Carrying Receivables.   It is a simple matter to calculate the cost
of carrying the extra receivables when marginal sales are expanded to
$284,000 per year. It was determined earlier that D accounts have a DSO
of 78.3 days. On the assumption that the new D accounts will pay at the
same rate, the larger D portfolio will hold $61,770 of receivables, an in-
crease of $21,770. Multiplying the $21,770 by the cost of capital, .1288,
will give $2,804, the added cost of capital for the extra receivables.

Analyzing the Impact.   After these changes have been incorporated into
Figure 30–21, it is possible to analyze the additional marginal accounts, all
D accounts, and the total operation of the company at the expanded vol-
ume.

The new $100,000 in marginal sales will yield $15,326 in additional
profit, at a .1533 operating profit margin$_K$ that is consistent with sales to
the other D accounts and considerably higher than the overall profit margin. It will require an additional $21,770 in the receivables portfolio, at a
cost of capital of $2,804 and total receivables cost of $9,824. The ROR on
these added receivables will be .7040.

For all D accounts, the company's receivables portfolio will include
$61,770 from this category, at a $7,956 annual cost of capital and a .7048
return on receivables. Operating profit margin$_K$ on D accounts will be
.1533, to produce $43,533 operating profit.

A present value analysis of receivables contribution to profit is shown in
Figure 30–22, which is prepared with data from Figure 30–21. Essentially,
it gives a condensed version of the findings, with emphasis on the time
value of receivables and their effect on profitability. It also highlights infor-

	All Accounts	A,B,C Accounts	D Accounts	Additional D Accounts	All D Accounts
Sales	$2,100,000	$1,816,000	$184,000	$100,000	$284,000
Cost of Capital for Receivables (K)	33,974	26,018	5,152	2,804	7,956
PV of Sales	2,066,026	1,789,982	178,848	97,196	276,044
Cost of Goods Sold	1,473,150	1,273,924	129,076	70,150	199,226
Operating Expenses Before K	325,725	292,440	21,565	11,720	33,285
All Costs Except K	1,798,875	1,566,364	150,641	81,870	232,511
Annual Profit Contribution	$ 267,151	$ 223,618	$ 28,207	$ 15,326	$ 43,533

FIG. 30–22.   Receivables PV Contribution to Profit—Expanded Marginal Accounts.

mation about the desirability of taking on marginal customers after fixed costs have been met by sales to A, B, and C accounts. If additional D sales are taken on, total marginal sales will account for $284,000, which constitute .1352, or nearly 14 percent of annual volume; and for $43,533 in operating profit, which is .1630, or 16 per cent of the year's total. At the same time, receivables will make up .2342, or 23 per cent of the firm's portfolio.

The financial impact of the proposed expanded volume on company receivables is summarized in Figure 30–23. It will take a longer-than-average time to collect the receivables from the added marginal accounts. This will increase overall receivables investment, so ROR will decrease. However, since the added receivables will incur only variable expenses, there will be a drop in the annual service cost per dollar of receivables carried.

An extra investment of $21,770 will be needed in the receivables portfolio, and this will be maintained at a $2,804 annual cost of capital. In addition, all variable costs will increase, but the additional operating profit earned will exceed all those costs by $15,326. As a result, operating profit margin$_K$ will increase.

	Volume of Sales		Change
	$2,000,000	$2,100,000	$100,000
Credit and Collection —Fixed	58,000	58,000	0
—Variable	33,332	38,532	5,200
Bad Debts	7,473	9,293	1,820
Cost of Capital for Receivables	31,170	33,974	2,804
Total Cost of Receivables	129,975	139,799	9,824
Operating Profit After K	251,825	267,151	15,326
Average Receivables Balance	242,000	263,770	21,770
Annual Service Cost per Dollar of Receivables Carried	.5371	.5300	−.0071
Operating Profit Margin$_K$	.1259	.1272	.0013
Return on Receivables	1.0406	1.0128	−.0278

FIG. 30–23.   Receivables Impact of Expanded Marginal Accounts.

CHAPTER 31

CASH BUDGETS AND OTHER FINANCIAL PROJECTIONS

◆

Oftentimes the difference between a marginal customer that succeeds and one that fails is that the latter does not have access to sophisticated financial management techniques that have been well-established and are quite commonly used by large companies. These include the use of financial forecasts and an understanding of the interdependence among the sales forecast, the production and purchase budgets, the cash budget, the projected statement of income and retained earnings, and the projected balance sheet.

The procedures described in this chapter can be used by credit and financial executives to counsel their customers on the techniques of cash budgeting and the use of other projections in their financial planning. Such consultations should help their customers improve their decisionmaking capabilities.

At the same time, the use of these techniques allows a creditor to make a clearer judgment of the credit risk involved in any account. They supplement the information provided by historical data and provide a better means to determine whether a customer is adequately financed to meet further obligations promptly.

ROLE OF THE CASH BUDGET

The flow of cash is a basic part of every business operation. It is used to pay for materials which in turn become receivables and again become cash. Cash is used to pay for the labor and factory overhead that transforms raw materials into finished goods which may be sold as part of the business cycle. The operating efficiency of a business is determined to a large extent by the manner and timing within which this business cycle is completed.

As with any business forecast, the major advantage of the cash budget is that it allows management to plan. It takes much of the guesswork out of cash programming by showing the amount of cash needed or available month by month, week by week, or day by day. It also establishes norms against which adjustments can be made as conditions change and provides a measure for determining the effectiveness of the plan.

The cash budget assists management by pointing out periods when cash balances will be in excess of requirements and periods when borrowing will be needed. The business manager can thereby plan loan requirements and take advantage of the least costly source of funds; furthermore, a definite schedule can be set up for the repayment of loans in light of the cash expected to be available each month.

In analyzing a marginal risk or in considering a substantial line of credit to a rapidly expanding business, a credit executive should find the customer's cash budget an effective way to determine the amount of credit required by an account. The budget enables the credit executive to judge whether net working capital and available financing will be sufficient to carry the customer through the projected operating period and to estimate whether the debt will be retired within an acceptable period of time.

The cash budget is largely a projection of past experiences, but it also must take into account changing business influences, general economic environment, internal plans for growth and expansion, sales expectations, and spending habits of customers. Consequently, the budget should be revised when the needs arise or the underlying assumptions to the original budget change.

Estimate of Cash Receipts

The primary source of cash for a business is the collection of accounts receivable. Estimated collections are therefore the key component of the cash forecast. Cash receipts generated directly by sales will depend on the amount and regularity of total sales, the percentage of sales made for cash, the terms for credit sales, and collection effectiveness.

All of this points directly to the sales forecast as a critical prerequisite to a useful cash budget. A realistic determination of future sales possibilities is best made by analyzing past sales experience to establish a sales trend. Economic conditions, the financial prospects for the industry, a study of each product being sold, an analysis of their geographic and territorial potentials, and the extent of sales promotional effort all bear an important influence on the sales forecast.

Two methods are commonly used to estimate cash receipts: monthly collection ratio and aging of sales.

Monthly Collection Ratio. Past experience is used to compute the collection ratio for each month of the budget year. This is done by calculating monthly collection ratios for a number of successive years, say five, and using the average of those figures to estimate the percentage of receivables that will be collected during each month of the budgeted year. Thus, to determine the expected collection ratio for January, use the January average for the past five years; for the coming February, the average for the past five Februaries; and so on. The formula for calculating the monthly collection ratio is:

$$\frac{\text{Collections Made During Month}}{\text{Receivables Outstanding at Beginning of Month}} = \text{Monthly Collection Ratio (\%)}$$

It is possible to estimate future collections by rearranging the factors and applying the average monthly collection ratio to expected receivables at the beginning of that month, as follows:

$$\begin{array}{c}\text{Expected Receivables}\\\text{Outstanding at the}\\\text{Beginning of the Month}\end{array} \times \begin{array}{c}\text{Average Collection Ratio}\\\text{for the Month (\%)}\end{array} = \begin{array}{c}\text{Expected Collections}\\\text{During the Month}\end{array}$$

Assuming that the collection ratio for September is 72.9 per cent, the following example will demonstrate a simple collection forecast.

Accounts Receivable, September 1	$39,551
Estimated Collections for September (72.9%)	28,833
Past-Due Receivables Carried Through September	10,718
Estimated Sales for September	30,000
Accounts Receivable, October 1	$40,718

Naturally, some adjustments may be required before these figures take their final form, to reflect any pending unusual economic or industry events.

Collection Ratio Applied Against Receivables Aging.   An adaptation of the collection ratio method applies it against an aging of accounts receivable to estimate future collections. In preparing to use this method, it is first necessary to determine by examining past records the percentage of collections that have been made against current receivables, those 30 days past due, 60 days past due, and so on.

This is done by noting that, in an aging, receivables not collected when due move to the next column. Thus, if a previous February aging showed $740 receivables past due 1–30 days, it would mean that $740 of January's current receivables had not been collected. If those current receivables had been $7,400, it would mean that 10 per cent had not been collected; hence 90 per cent had. The collection ratio for current receivables would therefore be 90 per cent.

Continuing with the example, if in March the receivables past due 31–60 days totalled $185, this would indicate that $555 of the receivables shown past due 1–30 days in the February aging had been collected ($740–555), for a collection ratio of 75 per cent.

The collection ratios thus obtained are then used against projected receivables for the budget year in order to construct a table similar to that shown below:

	Not Due	Current	Past Due				Total
			1–30	31–60	61–90	90+	
Collection Ratio for Category		90%	75%	40%	20%	10%	
Estimated A/R January 1	3,000	8,000	2,000	1,000	700	300	15,000
Collections Estimate		7,200	1,500	400	140	30	9,270
							5,730
Estimated Sales, January	4,000	16,000	—	—	—	—	20,000
Estimated A/R February 1	4,000	19,000	800	500	600	830	25,730
Collections Estimate		17,100	600	200	120	83	18,103
							7,627
Estimated Sales, February	5,000	20,000	—	—	—	—	25,000
Estimated A/R March 1	5,000	24,000	1,900	200	300	1,227	32,627

In the table, the January 1 accounts receivable are the same as those for the December 31 balance sheet and aging. Figures for other months are estimated from the sales forecast.

Collections estimates are made by applying collection ratios to the different categories of aged receivables. Thus, if past experience shows that 90 per cent of current receivables are collected on time, the collections estimate for January will be 90 per cent of the $8,000 current receivables, or $7,200. In the same way, 75 per cent of the $2,000 past due 1–30 days will be collected during January; 40 per cent of the $1,000 past due 31–60 days; and so on.

Collections for the month will total $9,270, leaving uncollected receivables of $5,730. To that figure, sales made during January are added to obtain total receivables of $25,730.

In the aging for February 1, the sales estimate is used to determine the receivables that are current and not due. Then: since $7,200 of January's receivables are expected to be collected, $800 will not be collected and are shown in the past due 1–30 column; since $1,500 of January's past due 1–30 is expected to be collected, $500 will not be collected and are shown in the February past due 31–60 column; since $400 of January's past due 31–60 is expected to be collected, $600 will not be collected and are shown in February's past due 61–90 column. This procedure is followed methodically for each month until the collection estimates have been calculated for the entire budget period. The buildup in receivables past due over 90 days is constrained by periodic writeoffs to bad debts from that column.

In a more precise application of the method described above, it is possible to obtain monthly collection ratios for each aging category and apply them to calculate expected collections. By examining past agings and collections histories, a table can be constructed showing those monthly collection ratios for each aging category, thus:

	Current	Past Due			
		1–30	31–60	61–90	90+
January	90%	75%	40%	20%	10%
February	88	77	42	21	12
March	85	78	41	19	13
•	•	•	•	•	•
•	•	•	•	•	•
•	•	•	•	•	•

Collection Ratio Applied Against Sales Aging. A conventional method of projecting cash receipts requires an aging of sales and a more detailed forecast of collections. This is achieved through an analysis of past collections experience, ultimately to obtain an estimate of collectibility that is related to time.

This method is used later to illustrate the preparation of a cash budget. Basically such an analysis might show that 5 per cent of sales are collected in the same month as they are made, 65 per cent during the next month, 20 per cent in 60 days, 5 per cent in 90 days, 4 per cent in 120 days, and 1 per cent is written off as bad debts. The corresponding percentages are applied to sales for successive months in order to estimate cash receipts for any given month. This can be demonstrated for the month of January by the following table that makes use of the percentages shown above, and assumes monthly sales as shown:

	Sales	Per Cent Collected	Cash Inflow
September	$28,000	4	$1,120
October	24,000	5	1,200
November	16,000	20	3,200
December	12,000	65	7,800
January (this month)	14,000	5	700
Total Collected in January			$14,020

In addition to the receipts generated by collection of accounts receivable, the receipts from cash sales, interest, and miscellaneous earnings can usually be estimated from an analysis of those activities. Collections from notes receivable can be scheduled according to stated maturity dates with some allowance for possible bad debts.

Estimate of Cash Disbursements

A realistic forecast of purchases and expenses anticipated over the period of the budget can usually be derived from other budgets and schedules prepared by the company. Materials purchases will be reflected as trade accounts payable and are usually tied closely to production schedules which in turn are based upon the sales forecast. Long-term obligations ordinarily are in the form of notes payable and usually require periodic installment payments that can be included under disbursements for the months in which they are due.

Other disbursements are direct labor, factory overhead, selling expense, general and administrative expenses, commissions, and taxes. The calculation of cash outflows for these items is based upon the level of operations indicated by other budgets and schedules, and upon allocations predetermined by the company.

The method of applying these principles to the actual preparation of a cash budget is now illustrated.

PREPARING A CASH BUDGET

The annual budget is prepared by methodical calculation of each month's cash inflows and outflows. The accountant or controller of a small business would ordinarily draw up the cash budget, since this person would have a detailed knowledge of the business. In a larger company, the budget department usually performs this function.

Data for Preparation of Cash Budget

The cash budget takes into account all historical data, and adds to that the effects of economic conditions on collections, projected expenditures for new plant and equipment, and other plans for volume expansion. The basic elements for preparing a cash budget include monthly estimates of:

1. Sales volume.
2. Collection of receivables.
3. Raw materials purchases.
4. Fixed and variable expenses (direct labor, factory overhead, general and administrative expenses, and selling expense).
5. Short-term capital needs.
6. Payments of long-term debt.
7. Proposed financing of fixed asset acquisitions.

Figure 31–1 sets forth a one-year budget for a sample company using the aging of sales method. In this example, it is assumed that selling terms are net 30 days, and the heaviest season occurs during the late summer and early fall months.

To simplify the example, it also is assumed that the company manufactures only one product line, with factory overhead being charged by units produced. In companies where many products are manufactured, other methods may be used to diffuse factory overhead: direct labor hours, machine hours, or a combination of both, depending upon which method best allocates these costs.

Cash Receipts

The top line of the exhibit shows the expected monthly sales. This is followed by a subheading for cash receipts based upon the following aging:

	1st Quarter			2nd Quarter			3rd Quarter			4th Quarter			Total
	Jan.	Feb.	Mar.	Apr.	May	June	July	Aug.	Sept.	Oct.	Nov.	Dec.	Total
Net Sales	14,000	16,000	14,000	16,000	18,000	20,000	24,000	32,000	30,000	26,000	18,000	16,000	244,000
Cash Receipts:													
5% of Sales—this month	700	800	700	800	900	1,000	1,200	1,600	1,500	1,300	900	800	12,200
65% of Sales—last month	7,800	9,100	10,400	9,100	10,400	11,700	13,000	15,600	20,800	19,500	16,900	11,700	156,000
20% of Sales—2 mos. ago	3,200	2,400	2,800	3,200	2,800	3,200	3,600	4,000	4,800	6,400	6,000	5,200	47,600
5% of Sales—3 mos. ago	1,200	800	600	700	800	700	800	900	1,000	1,200	1,600	1,500	11,800
4% of Sales—4 mos. ago	1,120	960	640	480	560	640	560	640	720	800	960	1,280	9,360
Total Cash Receipts	14,020	14,060	15,140	14,280	15,460	17,240	19,160	22,740	28,820	29,200	26,360	20,480	236,960
Cash Disbursements:													
Raw Materials Paid	4,800	4,200	4,800	5,400	6,000	7,200	9,600	9,000	7,800	5,400	4,800	5,400	74,400
Direct Labor	2,400	2,100	2,400	2,700	3,000	3,600	4,800	4,500	3,900	2,700	2,400	2,700	37,200
Fixed Factory Overhead	2,500	2,500	2,500	2,500	2,500	2,500	2,500	2,500	2,500	2,500	2,500	2,500	30,000
Variable Factory Overhead	1,600	1,400	1,600	1,800	2,000	2,400	3,200	3,000	2,600	1,800	1,600	1,800	24,800
Selling Expense	2,700	2,800	2,700	2,800	2,900	3,000	3,200	3,600	3,500	3,300	2,900	2,800	36,200
Administrative Expense	2,000	2,000	2,000	2,000	2,000	2,000	2,000	2,000	2,000	2,000	2,000	2,000	24,000
Income Tax Payments				600		600			600			600	2,400
Dividend Disbursement												2,000	2,000
Fixed Assets Purchased						6,000							6,000
Bank Loan Payments									6,000	12,000	8,000		26,000
Total Cash Disbursements	16,000	15,000	16,000	17,800	18,400	27,300	25,300	24,600	28,900	29,700	24,200	19,800	263,000
Net Cash Gain or (Loss)	(1,980)	(940)	(860)	(3,520)	(2,940)	(10,060)	(6,140)	(1,860)	(80)	(500)	2,160	680	
Cash Recapitulation:													
Cash, beginning of month	5,000	3,020	2,080	2,220	2,700	2,760	2,700	2,560	2,700	2,620	2,120	4,280	
Net Cash Gain or (Loss)	(1,980)	(940)	(860)	(3,520)	(2,940)	(10,060)	(6,140)	(1,860)	(80)	(500)	2,160	680	
Indicated Cash or (Shortage)	3,020	2,080	1,220	(1,300)	(240)	(7,300)	(3,440)	700	2,620	2,120	4,280	4,960	
Bank Loans Required			1,000	4,000	3,000	10,000	6,000	2,000					
Cash, end of month	3,020	2,080	2,220	2,700	2,760	2,700	2,560	2,700	2,620	2,120	4,280	4,960	

FIG. 31–1.   Cash Budget (Aging of Sales Method).

5 per cent of sales are collected in the same month they are made,
65 per cent of sales are collected in 30 days (within terms),
20 per cent of sales are collected in 60 days (30 days slow),
5 per cent of sales are collected in 90 days (60 days slow),
4 per cent of sales are collected in 120 days (90 days slow), and
1 per cent of sales are not collected (bad-debt writeoffs).

To make the cash receipts complete for the early months of the year, it was necessary to use collections from sales made before the start of the budget year. In subsequent months, the collections are based upon the projected monthly sales. As the company has borrowing capacity readily available at its bank, a minimum cash balance of $2,000 was established.

Cash receipts for January are arrived at as follows: 5 per cent of January sales totalling $14,000 are to be collected, or $700; 65 per cent of assumed December sales in the prior year totalling $12,000 are to be collected, or $7,800; 20 per cent of assumed November sales of $16,000, or $3,200; 5 per cent of assumed October sales of $24,000, or $1,200; and 4 per cent of September sales of $28,000, or $1,120.

This procedure is followed for each month, so that monthly cash receipts may be determined for planning purposes.

In this example, bad debts are assumed to be equal to 1 per cent of sales. They are reflected as a direct reduction of collections and are written off in the same month as the sales are made. Thus the collection of the $14,000 January sales is made as follows: $700 collected in January, $9,100 in February, $2,800 in March, $700 in April, and $560 in May. Collections will total $13,860 on projected sales of $14,000, with the $140 difference being considered the bad-debt writeoff.

Cash Disbursements

The figures in the disbursement section of the cash budget are drawn from the production budget and other schedules of the company, all dependent upon an accurate breakdown of the sales forecast. While at first the procedure may seem complicated, once understood it is largely a mechanical process of inserting the appropriate figures in the correct spaces.

The following rules will apply for the sample company in the preparation of the cash disbursements projections:

1. Materials for the next month's sales are purchased last month, produced this month, and paid this month. The cost is $3.00 per unit.

2. Direct labor is charged against the month of production at the rate of $1.50 per unit, as shown on the production schedule for that month.

3. Fixed factory overhead is $30,000 per year, allocated in twelve equal monthly charges of $2,500.

4. Variable factory overhead is based upon the production schedule for the month and is charged at the rate of $1.00 per unit produced.

5. Selling expense consists of two parts: a fixed $24,000 allocated at

$2,000 per month, and a variable expense equivalent to 5 per cent of the sales made during the month.

6. Administrative expense is fixed at $24,000 and charged in 12 equal monthly amounts of $2,000.

7. This budget makes no provision for compensating balances at the bank or bank service fees.

9. In line with forthcoming requirements of the Internal Revenue Code, the company has provided for estimated income tax payments to be made in April, June, September, and December.

9. The company will declare and pay a cash dividend in December.

In a simplified form, here are some of the schedules that will be helpful in preparing the cash disbursements section:

Month	Next Month's Sales	This Month's Production	Last Month's Purchases Due This Month
January	$16,000	1,600 Units	$4,800
February	14,000	1,400	4,200
March	16,000	1,600	4,800
April	18,000	1,800	5,400
May	20,000	2,000	6,000
June	24,000	2,400	7,200
July	32,000	3,200	9,600
August	30,000	3,000	9,000
September	26,000	2,600	7,800
October	18,000	1,800	5,400
November	16,000	1,600	4,800
December	18,000	1,800	5,400

With the preparations thus made, it is a relatively simple matter to proceed with the budget preparation. The appropriate entries are made in the various columns and spaces of the budget sheet. The statement shows the projected cash position of the company and points out its main sources of income and expenses.

Specifically, for January the company's income will be from collection of receivables, as shown in the January column. Its expenses are for last month's purchases and for January labor, overhead, and selling and administrative expenses.

Cash, which will be $5,000 at the beginning of the month, will be increased by collections totalling $14,020. It will be diminished by disbursements of $16,000, and the closing cash balance will be $3,020.

Bank Loans

While preparing the budget, management will note that during the course of the year the company will need bank support to carry on its business. The budget pinpoints the amounts and specific months when that will be necessary. For instance, $26,000 will be required to support the peak production period during the late spring and early summer.

There is early warning at this stage that outside funds will be needed and time enough for loan arrangements to be made. Repayment of the bank loan can be scheduled from September through November, since the firm's cash balances will be high enough at that time to support the business.

Budget Using Collection Ratio Method

Figure 31–2 shows the company's budget prepared using the collection ratio method. As previously noted, a separate ratio is computed for each month. If this ratio is accurately determined, it should give substantially the same results as those arrived at through the aging of sales method, as shown in Figure 31–1.

Since this method relies on monthly accounts receivable balances, it is necessary to provide a reconciliation of accounts receivable as a supplement to this budget. In Figure 31–2, this reconciliation is shown immediately below the cash budget.

USING THE BUDGET FOR CONTROL

Budgeting plays a dual role because it is both a planning and a control device. By establishing an operating and financial program for a future period, a manager can identify problems in advance. This is accomplished by using standards, or the proper relationship of one set of factors to another. Comparing the performance with the plans, a manager can make necessary adjustments to minimize discrepancies from the projected goal. In this way, the firm not only controls operations but also can delegate authority without the loss of control.

After one or two months have gone by into the budget year, the firm's actual operations may be compared with the budget to determine whether operations are on course. If the budget is being met, there is no need for corrective action. If certain items seem out of line with budget, however, it is time for adjustments that will bring the budget back into line.

Figure 31–3 shows a comparison between budget and actual for the month of March and for the three months ended March. In this statement, an income variance is favorable when actual income exceeds projected income, and unfavorable when actual income is lower than budgeted. When actual expenditures are less than the budget, a favorable variance exists; when more, the variance is unfavorable.

The month had an unfavorable variance of $550, or 3.6 per cent; for the 3-month period, the unfavorable variance totalled $600, but on a percentage basis the variance was only 1.4 per cent.

Because volume exceeded the budget for March and for the three months ended March, actual cash disbursements exceeded those budgeted. The time delay between expenditures and receipts caused projected cash to fall short of the budgeted figure. This necessitated an early drawing down of the company's line of credit to maintain minimum balances.

	1st Quarter			2nd Quarter			3rd Quarter			4th Quarter			Total
	Jan.	Feb.	Mar.	Apr.	May	June	July	Aug.	Sept.	Oct.	Nov.	Dec.	
Cash Receipts:													
Accounts Receivable, beginning of month	19,200	19,044	20,830	19,547	21,098	23,453	26,015	30,628	39,551	40,418	36,976	28,469	325,229
Collection Ratio—per cent	73.0	73.8	72.7	73.1	73.3	73.5	73.6	74.3	72.9	72.2	71.2	72.0	72.9
Total Cash Receipts	14,016	14,054	15,143	14,289	15,465	17,238	19,147	22,757	28,833	29,182	26,327	20,498	236,949
Cash Disbursements:													
Raw Materials Paid	4,800	4,200	4,800	5,400	6,000	7,200	9,600	9,000	7,800	5,400	4,800	5,400	74,400
Direct Labor	2,400	2,100	2,400	2,700	3,000	3,600	4,800	4,500	3,900	2,700	2,400	2,700	37,200
Fixed Factory Overhead	2,500	2,500	2,500	2,500	2,500	2,500	2,500	2,500	2,500	2,500	2,500	2,500	30,000
Variable Factory Overhead	1,600	1,400	1,600	1,800	2,000	2,400	3,200	3,000	2,600	1,800	1,600	1,800	24,800
Selling Expense	2,700	2,800	2,700	2,800	2,900	3,000	3,200	3,600	3,500	3,300	2,900	2,800	36,200
Administrative Expense	2,000	2,000	2,000	2,000	2,000	2,000	2,000	2,000	2,000	2,000	2,000	2,000	24,000
Income Tax Payments				600		600			600			600	2,400
Dividend Disbursement												2,000	2,000
Fixed Assets Purchased						6,000				12,000			6,000
Bank Loan Payments											8,000		26,000
Total Cash Disbursements	16,000	15,000	16,000	17,800	18,400	27,300	25,300	24,600	28,900	29,700	24,200	19,800	263,000
Net Cash Gain or (Loss)	(1,984)	(946)	(857)	(3,511)	(2,935)	(10,062)	(6,153)	(1,843)	(67)	(518)	2,127	698	
Cash Recapitulation:													
Cash, beginning of month	5,000	3,016	2,070	2,213	2,702	2,767	2,705	2,552	2,709	2,642	2,124	4,251	
Net Cash Gain or (Loss)	(1,984)	(946)	(857)	(3,511)	(935)	(10,062)	(6,153)	(1,843)	(67)	(518)	2,127	698	
Indicated Cash or (Shortage)	3,016	2,070	1,213	(1,298)	(233)	(7,295)	(3,448)	709	2,642	2,124	4,251	4,949	
Bank Loans Required			1,000	4,000	3,000	10,000	6,000	2,000					
Cash, end of month	3,016	2,070	2,213	2,702	2,767	2,705	2,552	2,709	2,642	2,124	4,251	4,949	
Accounts Receivable Reconciliation:													
Beginning of Month Balance	19,200	19,044	20,830	19,547	21,098	23,453	26,015	30,628	39,551	40,418	36,976	28,469	
Sales	14,000	16,000	14,000	16,000	18,000	20,000	24,000	32,000	30,000	26,000	18,000	16,000	
	33,200	35,044	34,830	35,547	39,098	43,453	50,015	62,628	69,551	66,418	54,976	44,469	
Cash Receipts	14,016	14,054	15,143	14,289	15,465	17,238	19,147	22,757	28,833	29,182	26,327	20,498	
Bad-Debt Writeoffs	140	160	140	160	180	200	240	320	300	260	180	160	
	14,156	14,214	15,283	14,449	15,645	17,438	19,387	23,077	29,133	29,442	26,507	20,658	
End of Month Balance	19,044	20,830	19,547	21,098	23,453	26,015	30,628	39,551	40,418	36,976	28,469	23,811	

FIG. 31–2.   Cash Budget (Collection Ratio Method).

	March				Three Months Ended March 31				Remarks
	Budget	Actual	Variance	Per Cent	Budget	Actual	Variance	Per Cent	
Net Sales	14,000	16,000	2,000	14.3	44,000	45,000	1,000	2.3	Since the variance is not substantial and is expected to be remedied in the next month, no change is contemplated in the budget for the remaining 9 months.
Cash Receipts:									
5% of Sales—this month	700	800	100	14.3	2,200	2,250	50	2.3	
65% of Sales—last month	10,400	9,750	(650)	(6.3)	27,300	26,650	(650)	(2.4)	
20% of Sales—2 mos. ago	2,800	2,800	—	—	8,400	8,400	—	—	
5% of Sales—3 mos. ago	600	600	—	—	2,600	2,600	—	—	
4% of Sales—4 mos. ago	640	640	—	—	2,720	2,720	—	—	
Total Cash Receipts	15,140	14,590	(550)	(3.6)	43,220	42,620	(600)	(1.4)	
Cash Disbursements:									
Raw Materials Paid	4,800	5,100	(300)	(6.3)	13,800	14,400	(600)	(4.3)	
Direct Labor	2,400	2,550	(150)	(6.3)	6,900	7,200	(300)	(4.3)	
Fixed Factory Overhead	2,500	2,500	—	—	7,500	7,500	—	—	
Variable Factory Overhead	1,600	1,700	(100)	(6.3)	4,600	4,800	(200)	(4.3)	
Selling Expense	2,700	2,800	(100)	(3.7)	8,200	8,250	(50)	(0.6)	
Administrative Expense	2,000	2,000	—	—	6,000	6,000	—	—	
Total Disbursements	16,000	16,650	(650)	(4.1)	47,000	48,150	(1,150)	(2.4)	
Net Cash Gain or (Loss)	(860)	(2,060)	(1,200)		(3,780)	(5,530)	(1,750)		
Cash Recapitulation:									
Cash, beginning of period	2,080	2,530			5,000	5,000			
Net Cash Gain or (Loss)	(860)	(2,060)			(3,780)	(5,530)			
Indicated Cash or (Shortage)	1,220	470			1,220	(530)			
Bank Loans Required	1,000	2,000			1,000	3,000			
Cash, end of period	2,220	2,470			2,220	2,470			

FIG. 31–3.   Comparison of Budget and Actual.

The distorted first-quarter sales picture did not increase anticipated total sales for the year; it represented early sales that would have otherwise been made in later months. Consequently, no change was made in the budget for the remaining nine months. If it had indeed represented a greater annual volume, budget adjustments upward in income and expense would have been required.

PROJECTED STATEMENT OF INCOME AND RETAINED EARNINGS

The purpose of the projected statement of income and retained earnings is to give a preview of operations if all budgets are met for a given period. The statement accounts for all sources of income to be realized and all classes of expenses to be incurred, and is prepared on an accrual rather than cash basis. This is different from the cash budget, which accounts for all expected inflows of cash, whether from income from operations or from nonincome items, such as bank loans; and for all cash outflows, whether attributable to current operations, prior periods, subsequent periods, or to payments not related to expenses, such as the purchase of fixed assets.

Some transactions that affect cash budgets and the statement of income and retained earnings in different ways are:

1. Collections of accounts receivable from prior fiscal or calendar period would be included in the cash budget but excluded from the statement of income and retained earnings.

2. Current sales to be collected in subsequent periods would be excluded from the cash budget but included in the statement of income and retained earnings.

3. Depreciation charges would be excluded from the cash budget but included in the statement of income and retained earnings.

4. Borrowings from banks and their subsequent repayment are included in the cash budget but excluded from the statement of income and retained earnings.

Preparing the Statement

The projected statement of income and retained earnings can be prepared by using figures from the previous balance sheet and from the various budgets representing the current period (see Figure 31–4).

To start, the estimated sales figure for the coming period is obtained from the sales forecast. Next, the components of cost of goods sold are obtained.

Raw Materials, Beginning of Year.   This figure is the same as the ending raw materials from the previous balance sheet.

Purchases.   This may be obtained from a purchasing budget or from the cash budget. Figures from the cash budget must be adjusted, however, as purchases of raw materials are made one month prior to being used or paid. Thus raw materials of $4,800 used and paid in January of this year

Net Sales		$244,000
Cost of Goods Sold:		
Raw Materials, beginning of year	$ 4,800	
Purchases	75,000	
Total	79,800	
Raw Materials, end of year	5,400	
Raw Materials Used		74,400
Direct Labor		37,200
Fixed Factory Overhead*		36,300
Variable Factory Overhead		24,800
Total Materials, Labor, and Over- head		172,700
Finished Goods Inventory:		
Beginning of year	10,700	
End of year	12,950	2,250
Cost of Goods Sold		170,450
Gross Profit		73,550
Selling Expenses	36,200	
Administrative Expense	24,000	
Bad-Debt Writeoffs	2,440	62,640
Net Operating Profit		10,910
Provision for Taxes		2,400
Net Profit		8,510
Retained Earnings, beginning of year		14,900
		23,410
Dividend Disbursement		2,000
Retained Earnings, end of year		$21,410

*Depreciation of $6,300 was charged to production costs, allowing for normal depreciation plus an additional $300 for 6 months use of equipment to be purchased in June.

FIG. 31–4. Projected Statement of Income and Retained Earnings.

were purchased in December of last year and would be eliminated from this projection. Conversely, raw materials of $5,400 to be used in next January's scheduled production are to be purchased in December of this year and will be added to this projection. Thus total purchases for the year will be $75,000.

Direct Labor and Factory Overhead.   These items are obtained from the cash budget.

Finished Goods Inventory.   The figure for the beginning of the year is the same as the previous balance sheet's ending inventory (here assumed to be $10,700). For purposes of illustration it has already been assumed that the following January's sales would require $5,400 in materials, to this would be added direct labor $2,700, fixed factory overhead $2,500, depreciation $550, and variable factory overhead $1,800. The total for finished goods at projected yearend thus would be $12,950.

In the example, it has been assumed that all goods put into production in any month are completed the same month, so no goods in process are shown in the statement. In practice most budgets likewise make no provision for goods in process. It is assumed that goods in process at the beginning of the period represent a normal inventory, and it is expected that a like amount of goods will remain in process at the end of the period. If such were not the case, it would be necessary to determine the value of materials, direct labor, and factory overhead contained in goods in process, and include that item in the budget calculations.

Selling and Administrative Expenses. After the gross profit is determined, the selling expense and administrative expenses are entered from the cash budget. Provision is made for bad-debt writeoffs, here shown as one per cent of sales. The company is in the 22 per cent tax bracket, so that adjustment is made. Finally, dividends are paid and retained earnings reconciled.

Evaluation

This technique enables the management, as well as the creditor, to foresee the operations of a business and to spot troublesome financial areas. It allows time for necessary operating modifications to be made. If, for example, the profit picture were not satisfactory, there would still be time for some phases of the operation to be changed, so a more satisfactory result could be obtained.

PROJECTED BALANCE SHEET

The budget system also enables management to construct a projected balance sheet by using the previous actual balance sheet, and adding to it figures from the cash budget and the projected statement of income and retained earnings.

Preparing the Balance Sheet

The projected balance sheet shows the expected future financial position of a company, based upon the transactions that will take place during a given period (see Figure 31–5). In the illustration, the projected balance sheet would be prepared as shown below.

Cash. This figure, $4,960 for December, is obtained from the cash budget (Figure 31–1).

Accounts Receivable. This is the sum of uncollected receivables arising from the sales made during September, October, November, and December, after those receivables have been reduced by the 1 per cent bad-debt writeoff:

Month	Sales	Bad-Debt Per Cent	Per Cent Collected	Per Cent Uncollected	Accounts Receivable
December	$16,000	1	5	94	$15,040
November	18,000	1	5 + 65	29	5,220
October	26,000	1	5 + 65 + 20	9	2,340
September	30,000	1	5 + 65 + 20 + 5	4	1,200
					$23,800

Inventory. This consists of finished goods $12,950 and raw materials $5,400, obtained from the projected statement of income and retained earnings (Figure 31–4).

Plant and Equipment. The contemplated purchase of $6,000 additional plant and equipment in June is recorded in this item.

Accumulated Depreciation. Normal depreciation plus an extra $300 representing six months depreciation on the new equipment purchased in June.

Common Stock. The figure is unchanged from the previous year's statement. Additional issues or retirement of stock would cause a change in this item.

Retained Earnings. The projected new figure is obtained from the projected statement of income and retained earnings.

Current Liabilities. The only current liability for projected yearend is Accounts Payable $5,400 for raw materials to be used in January production. The firm has cleaned up its bank loan.

		Fiscal Year		Projected Year
Cash		$ 5,000		$ 4,960
Accounts Receivable		19,200		23,800
Inventory		15,500		18,350
Current Assets		39,700		47,110
Plant and Equipment	60,000		66,000	
Accumulated Depreciation	30,000	30,000	36,300	29,700
Total		$69,700		$76,810
Accounts Payable		$ 4,800		$ 5,400
Common Stock		50,000		50,000
Retained Earnings		14,900		21,410
Total		$69,700		$76,810
Net Working Capital		$34,900		$41,710

FIG. 31–5. Projected Balance Sheet.

Evaluation

The preparation of a projected balance sheet allows a look at the future condition of the company and can put the management (or its creditors) on guard regarding specific financial strengths or weaknesses that may develop during the business year.

PROJECTED STATEMENT OF CHANGES IN FINANCIAL POSITION

In addition to the statements already described, the business manager can prepare a projected statement of changes in financial position. This can be most rewarding in analyzing future financial strength, since it reports source and application of funds among the various asset, liability, and net worth accounts during the forecast period, and analyzes changes in net working capital.

Source and Application of Funds

In Figure 31–6, comparative statements have been set up for the fiscal year and the projected year. The changes in the individual items are used to prepare a projected statement showing source and application of funds.

Careful study of this statement will point up any disproportionate buildup of asset items, and how they were financed. It will also show the extent to which liabilities were liquidated and the source of funds used to reduce those liabilities.

	Fiscal Year		Projected Year		Increase/ (Decrease)	Source	Appli- cation
Cash		$ 5,000		$ 4,960	(40)	40	
Accounts Receivable		19,200		23,800	4,600		4,600
Inventory		15,500		18,350	2,850		2,850
Current Assets		39,700		47,110			
Plant and Equipment	60,000		66,000		6,000		6,000
Accumulated Depreciation	30,000	30,000	36,300	29,700	6,300	6,300	
Total		$69,700		$76,810			
Accounts Payable		$ 4,800		$ 5,400	600	600	
Common Stock		50,000		50,000			
Earned Surplus		14,900		21,410	6,510	6,510	
Total		$69,700		$76,810		13,450	13,450
Net Working Capital		$34,900		$41,710			

FIG. 31–6.   Projected Source and Application of Funds.

Changes in Net Working Capital

After the transactions affecting net working capital have been examined, changes in its composition should be analyzed. This can be accomplished by noting variations in the items that comprise the current assets and current liabilities. The variations can then be summarized in a format shown in Figure 31–7.

Source of Funds:	
Operations:	
Net Profit Retained	$ 6,510
Depreciation	6,300
Funds Derived from Operations	12,810
Application of Funds:	
Addition to Plant and Equipment	6,000
Increase in Net Working Capital	$ 6,810
Changes in Composition of Net Working Capital:	
Increase (Decrease) in Current Assets:	
Cash	$ (40)
Accounts Receivable	4,600
Inventory	2,850
	7,410
Increase in Current Liabilities:	
Accounts Payable	600
Increase in Net Working Capital	$ 6,810

FIG. 31–7.   Projected Changes in Net Working Capital.

The credit executive concerned with extending a line of credit to a marginal-risk account and wanting an accurate appraisal of future net working capital will find this technique a particularly effective way to project such an estimate. It highlights the source and application of funds that make up an increase or decrease in net working capital and points out the changes in its component parts.

RECAPITULATION

The forecasting techniques shown in this chapter are designed to give the manager and the credit executive a clearer understanding of how financial plans may be developed. Customarily the reports shown here have been used to present historical data. They have served the purpose of managerial control, so corrective action could be taken to adjust an unfavorable trend. By applying the techniques to projected operations, however, it is possible to foresee troublesome areas and amend the plans before they materialize.

In the sample company, the cash budget was used as the starting point of a series of statements that projected into the following year its income and retained earnings, financial condition, source and application of funds, and changes in composition of net working capital.

To summarize our example, the plans of its management are as follows:

What It Plans to Do		How It Plans the Financing	
Purchase Plant & Equipment	$ 6,000	Funds from Operations:	
Increase Accounts Receivable	4,600	Net Profit Retained	$ 6,510
Expand Inventories	2,850	Depreciation	6,300
		Increase Accounts Payable	600
		Decrease Cash	40
	$13,450		$13,450

Basically the company's plans call for the acquisition of new plant and equipment amounting to $6,000 to be financed by cash flow of $12,810. To cope with a greater volume, the financial plan will increase net working capital so it can support an additional $4,600 in accounts receivable and an inventory buildup of $2,850. These increases will be offset by a rise of $600 in accounts payable. As a result of these transactions, the cash position will be drawn down by $40 to $4,960.

The prepared reports have helped the management of the company to plan the next year's operations. They can also clarify many questions that may be in the minds of its creditors.

CHAPTER 32

CREDIT DEPARTMENT REPORTING SYSTEM

Effective management requires informative and timely reports that describe the condition of the operation and allow for adequate control and realistic planning. They should highlight the department's operations and be presented in a clear and concise manner.

These reports keep corporate management informed of credit department activities and are an effective medium to improve liaison between credit and other company functions. In decentralized firms, they inform divisional management and corporate staff, and build liaison with other divisions and major underlying units. They provide top management with feedback from the operating divisions to determine if policy is in line with corporate requirements. Moreover, an effective credit reporting system enables the credit executive to:

1. Obtain facts easily and quickly.

2. Obtain comparative data for the purpose of determining trends.

3. Plan, organize, coordinate, and control the activities of the credit department.

4. Keep credit department personnel informed on matters related to the credit department, other departments, and the company as a whole.

5. Coordinate the credit function with other functions in the company.

6. Inform top corporate management of credit department objectives, and how well these objectives are being attained.

ELEMENTS OF AN EFFICIENT REPORTING SYSTEM

Thoughtful planning of credit management reports makes it easier for the chief credit executive to take part in the formulation of credit policy and to implement it through smooth operation of the department. This planning involves careful thought as to the reasons for the reports, their content and distribution, and the personnel responsible for preparing them.

544

Responsibility for Preparing Reports

While overall planning of the credit department reporting system must be the responsibility of the chief credit executive, the actual preparation of reports should in most cases be delegated to subordinates. The chief credit executive should be relieved of the details of day-to-day operations and concentrate on the effective administration of the department. This delegation must be clearly defined to avoid misunderstanding as to who will collect or provide the information, who will classify and analyze it, and who will draft the report.

Steps in Planning and Preparation

The first step is to determine what information is needed by each of the various groups to whom reports will be distributed. Reports already prepared should be examined to minimize duplication of information in reports received by the same people. In some cases, exsiting reports may be combined or their distribution broadened. In others, new reports may be introduced.

After the need has been evaluated, the sources of the required information must be determined. Much of the material will come from credit department records or other sources within the company, such as the accounting department. Additional data can be secured from periodicals concerned with various aspects of credit and finance, government publications, and other published material. Interviews with people who have special knowledge of particular topics are another source of information.

Next the information must be gathered, studied, analyzed, and classified. The needs of the persons or departments that will receive the information must be kept in mind, as well as the frequency with which the information is required and can be collected. If a report is expected to be very long, it will be helpful to accumulate the data on cards, which can be reanalyzed as the plan of the report is developed, or revised for other reports.

Reports should be kept as short as they can be without losing effectiveness. Unless the subject is exceptionally large or complex, lengthy reports should be discouraged because they take too much time to prepare and read. If a report has to be long, it is good procedure to make the first page a summary of conclusions and recommendations from which the reader can proceed to the supporting data.

Forms of Presentation

A report's form of presentation can increase or decrease its effectiveness. A simple and orderly format is always appropriate. It should be noted, however, that strict adherence to any set form restricts the possibility of imaginative presentation and may weaken the impact of the report. The three basic forms of presentation are narrative, graphic, and tabular.

Narrative reports should be clear and concise. Since this form of report is entirely verbal, there should be a careful choice of words so that the exact meaning is conveyed. It is permissible to use technical terms only if the readers of the report are familiar with them. Otherwise the language should be easily understood by all prospective readers. In every case the language should be matter of fact, and no opinions should be expressed unless they are clearly labeled. The report should be complete in itself without any reference to other reports or information.

Reports that utilize graphs are very effective in establishing statistical relationships quickly and clearly. In many cases, such reports are used to compare current performance with that of prior periods. It is important that the graphs be neat, accurate, and not too complicated.

Many reports issued by the credit department contain statistical data which are best presented in tabular or columnar form. Many variations are possible in response to special needs, but most tabular presentations used by the credit department follow a basic form that includes accounts receivable, amount past due, sales and collections for a given period, and comparative figures for one or more past periods.

The tabular form of report is the backbone of statistical reporting. Tables condense large volumes of information into a minimum of space. In the process, however, significant relationships and observations may become submerged. Excessive use of tables in credit department reports should be avoided in order to spare the recipient the burden of analyzing and interpreting too much of the data. Narrative and graphic presentations often will increase the value of tabular material. To choose the best combination of forms in a particular case, one must bear in mind not only the purpose of the report but also the needs of those who will receive the data.

Report Format and Content

The type and format of reports will differ depending upon the level of reporting. Reports submitted by credit analysts to the credit manager should be precise and detailed, and concentrate on the status of accounts. The credit manager then will summarize them for the top-level or middle-level chief credit executive. This report will be less specific but will enable the chief credit executive to evaluate the receivables portfolios without being bogged down by detail.

Achieving Control. Reports submitted to the chief credit executive should be standard as to the kind of information required, and how and when they must be submitted. The credit executive should invite credit personnel to submit reports, and even opinions, on how credit policy is working out in practice. These can help maintain a more flexible and up-to-date policy. By the same token, regular written reports should be issued to department personnel, giving management's interpretation of credit policy and advising them of current policy.

Progress Reports.   Progress reports usually contain information about important developments in the credit department, such as special projects, personnel changes, news about large customers, indications of trends, and other facts not included in the regular statistics. These reports help direct attention and effort to special problems, communicate activity, and instill a sense of group participation and accomplishment.

Special Reports.   Special reports grow out of the specific needs of an individual business and usually cover nonrecurring subjects. They may deal with important news items or studies from outside sources. They may also cover such diverse matters as personnel training and legal opinions.

General Reports.   Credit executives keep up to date through membership in credit associations and nonspecialized business associations, acquaintance with other business people, and continued formal and informal education. A variety of published materials, such as credit association publications, credit journals, finance and accounting periodicals, government publications, and trade journals help them stay abreast of changes in the business world. One useful technique is to have a newsletter for credit personnel, containing information on developments in the field of credit management and on the professional activities of credit personnel. Another is to report the information to the company's research department, which would then incorporate it into reports on business conditions for circulation throughout the organization.

Business Conditions.   Some reports contain information on general economic conditions and trends which may affect the performance of the credit department, and which may require action. They analyze economic conditions in various parts of the country and show which customer accounts need reexamination. Actions by the Federal Reserve Board, strikes in basic industries, and changes in government stockpiling policies can affect the buying potential of customers. The credit executive must be alert and sensitive to the environment in which the business functions, and must evaluate the effect of changing conditions on departmental operations and policy.

Distribution of Reports

Credit management reports sent to corporate management describe the status of accounts receivable, analyze credit department expenses, forecast cash inflows, and discuss other important information. They enable corporate management to appraise the company investment in accounts receivable and to evaluate the overall performance of the credit operations.

Most reports are distributed to the vice presidents-finance and treasurers, but other senior management people also receive them, including members of the board, presidents, and executive vice presidents. Since credit has a close relationship with accounting and sales, copies of these reports should go to the comptrollers and vice presidents-marketing.

Reports from the chief credit executive also are sent to credit department personnel. They are an effective tool for implementing credit policy and coordinating activities with the department. They also give the department personnel an opportunity to view the credit department's performance as a whole and to note the significance of their personal contribution.

Role of Feedback

A key ingredient to any reporting system is the provision for feedback that is the basis for finding out how the system is working, and what adjustments need to be made in it. It gives the people in the credit department an opportunity to see themselves through management's eyes. This should be continuous and active, acknowledging good circumstances and poor alike. Many companies comment only when negative situations arise, claiming that good performance should be expected but not acknowledged. Others, at little additional effort, acknowledge good performance and use those opportunities to cement relationships with employees and supervisors. At the same time, they can comment on required minor adjustments that would not warrant a full review.

Periodic Review and Appraisal of Reports

It is good management practice to review the list of reports periodically, and to discontinue those that no longer serve a purpose. Without such review, the files of the credit department could soon overflow with unwanted, unread, and expensive documents. The questions to ask when deciding whether to continue a report include:

1. Why was it first issued?
2. Does this need still exist?
3. Is it being met by the present report?
4. Would other reports presently being issued serve this purpose better?
5. Are superfluous data included? Are important data missing?
6. Is the chosen form of presentation the most readable, the most easily prepared? Would a different type of presentation serve the need better, more economically?
7. If this report is one of a series, has an analysis been made of its relationship to the others in the series to determine whether there is any overlapping?
8. Who is assembling the data for the report? Is this the most efficient way to obtain this information?
9. Would shorter or more concisely organized reports accomplish the same purpose?

10. Is the overall time spent in preparing the report proportionate to its value?

11. Are the present recipients of the report actually making use of it?

12. Could this report serve others who are not at present receiving it?

13. What is the frequency of need for the material covered by the report?

14. Does this differ from department to department?

15. Are some departments receiving this report too often? Not often enough?

STATISTICAL PRESENTATION OF FINANCIAL DATA

Credit executives are frequently called upon to analyze and present figures which describe certain aspects of credit department operations. Agings of accounts, past-due percentages, and bad-debt losses are only a few of the reports which regularly command attention. In many cases, simple statistical measures are helpful in summarizing and comparing data.

A wealth of published statistical data also comes to credit executives in such forms as government reports and industry bulletins. The same statistical measures are used in them, and the credit executive must be able to understand and use them effectively.

A few approaches to analysis of quantitative data are described briefly here to suggest ways of presenting credit department operating data. Anyone who expects to make extensive use of these methods should consult a text in business statistics.

Statistical analysis starts with a number of comparable figures. It develops one or a few figures which will represent or describe all of the individual data, then makes systematic comparisons among such summary figures or among figures representing different time periods. To use this type of analysis, the credit executive should first look critically at the individual figures on which analysis will be based. What information is needed? Do these figures provide it? Are they all derived in the same way; are they really comparable? If they do not include all the relevent sources of information, are they representative?

The point of these questions is to ascertain that statistical analysis of the data will yield information that is reasonably reliable and that will actually bear on the problem at hand. No analysis can be useful if the data are irrelevant to begin with. If the data are not comparable or representative, an analysis based on them may be actually misleading.

Arithmetic Mean

When working with a number of comparable individual measures, analysts often try to find a central value about which all the measures tend to cluster. The most commonly used value is the arithmetic mean. This is the measure usually meant by the term "the average." The arithmetic mean may be explained as the value each measure would have if all measures were equal and their total remained the same. It is computed by adding the values of the individual measures and dividing that sum by the number of measures. For example, the arithmetic mean of the values 2, 4, and 6 is:

$$\frac{2+4+6}{3}=4$$

The chief disadvantage of the mean is that its value is substantially affected by extremely large or extremely small component measures. For instance, if the distribution of the values to be used is lopsided, containing many small and moderate values and a few very high values, the mean may not be an appropriate summary. This kind of distribution is very often found in business and economic data. For example, personal incomes, sales volumes, and bad-debt losses are very likely to be overbalanced on either the high or the low side.

When averaging values, it is sometimes logical to assign more importance to some than to others in order to obtain a weighted average. The weights used by most credit executives reflect dollars as opposed to frequencies. This system is particularly useful in determining how a customer is paying. For example, the table below shows two sets of calculations of a customer's payment record on five invoices. The straight arithmetic mean gives too much weight to the past-due status of the small invoices. A more realistic approach is the days per average invoice dollar; this gives more weight to the larger invoices.

Invoice Amount	Days Past Due	Weighted Total
$100,000	-0-	-0-
10,000	15	$150,000
1,000	30	30,000
100	60	6,000
10	90	900
$111,110		$186,900

Arithmetic Mean $=\dfrac{0+15+30+60+90}{5}=$ 39.0 days past due. Days Per

Average Invoice Dollar $=\dfrac{186,900}{111,110}=1.7$ days past due.

Median and Quartiles

In dealing with figures, the median is often a more appropriate measure. It is the middle value, which divides the number of values in half; as many are higher than the median as are lower. The following values are arrayed in decending order to illustrate the procedure:

27, 25, 23, 20, 17, *15*, 13, 11, 10, 8, 6

In this group of 11 figures, the median is 15, the sixth or middle value. If the group contained an even number of values, the median would be an average of the two middle measures. The median value is affected only by the number of measures. Thus, in a distribution concentrated at one end of the scale with a scattering of extreme figures at the other end, the median can more reasonably be considered representative of the group as a whole.

In an expansion of this approach, data will often be shown in quartiles. Thus the upper or third quartile figure would be one in the array that had 75 per cent of the values lower than it and 25 per cent higher; the median or second quartile would have half higher and half lower; and the lower or first quartile value would have 75 per cent higher and 25 per cent lower than itself.

Mode

The mode is the value that appears most frequently in a series of readings. It is the most probable value of the thing being measured. If, for example, a series of readings were 27, 25, 25, 20, 17, 15, 15, 15, 13, 12, 8, 6, and 6, the mode would be 15, the most frequent number.

Because many sets of data have no clear-cut mode, the measure is less commonly used. Where data can be reported in ranges rather than as exact values, it may be useful to set up modal intervals, ranges within which the measures fall. This can be done particularly with confidential information, where exact figures are not given.

Range

Any average gives some notion of the central value of a group of measures, but it does not indicate how widely the figures vary. There are precise statistical measures for this characteristic.

One, the range, simply indicates the total spread of the values reported. Thus bad-debt losses would range from .35% to .05% in an array of net bad-debt losses percentages that read .35%, .30%, .29%, .25%, .22%, .20%, .17%, .15%, .10%, .09%, .05%.

Where the range is too wide to be useful, and has a few extreme values at either end, it may be more informative to show the values that span the middle half of the measures. This is also called the interquartile range. In the above illustration, the upper quartile is .29% and the lower quartile is .10%. The interquartile range extends from .29% to .10%.

Time Series

The most common comparison required of the credit executive involves information gathered from the same sources at different points in time. Following changes in gross national product, comparing the condition of accounts receivable from one month to the next, and analyzing trends in a customer's financial condition all require this sort of comparison. In all of them, the credit executive should take care not to interpret as a significant trend a difference which may be coincidental.

Ratios and Percentages

It may be appropriate to separate the categories and determine the relationship of each category to the whole or to some other base. This is done through ratios or percentages. It is a standard procedure in financial analysis but can also be used for other purposes.

Figure 32–1 is a simple report that tabulates monthly sales and collections, overdue amounts at month end, and the difference between sales and collections on both a monthly and cumulative basis.

Upon casual inspection of the raw data in Figure 32–1, the average reader will not be able to draw meaningful or accurate conclusions. On more thorough examination, the reader should observe a tendency toward seasonal sales, with increases in December through February, and a three-month seasonal peak in collections which falls a month later than the peak for sales. The amount outstanding shows a steady increase, whereas the amount overdue is reasonably constant. Monthly collections are below monthly sales in eight months out of thirteen, with December collections falling significantly below December sales. These conclusions will be reached only by the careful reader because of the manner in which the data are presented. Many will not study the table closely enough and may actually draw false conclusions.

Figure 32–2 shows another tabular report based on the same data. In this case, however, the raw material has been converted into percentages indicating relationships between the figures. The calculation of the percentages makes the data easier to interpret and also permits more accurate appraisal. For example, the relation of collections to sales shows that collections are increasing relative to sales, and that the amount outstanding as a percentage of sales is decreasing. This conclusion is not clearly indicated by the raw data in Figure 32–1, where only a constant increase in the amount outstanding is evident.

Comparing Summary Figures

Summary figures representing the same information about two or more comparable groups must often be presented. For example, a company might wish to evaluate its collection experience for different regions by comparing the percentage of accounts past due in each region; or to compare its own collection experience to a summary figure for the industry.

Two questions might be asked in making such comparisons. First, are the two figures comparable? For data on different segments of one company, this will seldom be a serious problem. When the figures are from two or more different sources, however, such as company figures and industry figures, the data should be carefully checked for comparability.

	Monthly Sales	Sales to Date*	Monthly Collections	Collections to Date*	Overdue Amount†	Collections	
						Above or Below Sales to Date	Above or Below Sales This Month
Year Ago							
June	$ 895,000	$ 4,680,000	$1,320,000	$ 3,430,000	$360,000	−1,250,000	+425,000
July	768,000	5,448,000	869,000	4,299,000	345,000	−1,149,000	+101,000
August	657,000	6,105,000	747,000	5,046,000	387,000	−1,059,000	+ 90,000
September	723,000	6,828,000	625,000	5,671,000	412,000	−1,157,000	− 98,000
October	869,000	7,697,000	794,000	6,465,000	406,000	−1,232,000	− 75,000
November	912,000	8,609,000	901,000	7,366,000	418,000	−1,243,000	− 11,000
December	1,684,000	10,293,000	879,000	8,245,000	397,000	−2,048,000	−805,000
This Year							
January	1,458,000	11,751,000	1,246,000	9,491,000	402,000	−2,260,000	−212,000
February	1,372,000	13,123,000	1,293,000	10,784,000	418,000	−2,339,000	− 79,000
March	1,086,000	14,209,000	1,168,000	11,952,000	435,000	−2,257,000	+ 82,000
April	984,000	15,193,000	994,000	12,946,000	387,000	−2,247,000	+ 10,000
May	989,000	16,182,000	858,000	13,804,000	412,000	−2,378,000	−131,000
June	897,000	17,079,000	787,000	14,591,000	394,000	−2,488,000	−110,000

* Amounts reflect totals since founding of company.
† These amounts were extracted from accounts receivable.

FIG. 32–1. Tabular Report Using Raw Data.

Collections to Date as Per Cent of Sales to Date	Collections Per Month as Per Cent of Previous Month's Sales (Above or Below Last Month's Sales)		Per Cent of Outstanding Overdue
Year Ago			
June 73.3			28.8
July 78.9	− 26,000	97.1	30.0
August 82.7	− 21,000	97.3	36.5
September 83.0	− 32,000	95.1	35.6
October 84.0	+ 71,000	109.8	33.0
November 85.6	+ 32,000	103.7	33.6
December 80.1	− 33,000	96.4	19.4
This Year			
January 80.8	−438,000	74.0	17.8
February 82.2	−165,000	88.7	17.9
March 84.1	−204,000	85.1	19.3
April 85.2	− 92,000	91.5	17.2
May 85.3	−126,000	87.2	18.1
June 85.4	−202,000	79.6	15.8
Increase			*Decrease*
June *Year Ago* 85.4			28.8
over June *This Year* 73.3			15.8
12.1			13.0

FIG. 32–2.   Tabular Report Using Calculated Data.

Second, do the differences which appear in the figures represent actual differences (for example, in effectiveness of collection efforts) or are they simply an incidental result of the processes which produced the figures? What appears to be a difference may be only a coincidence. The methods of answering this question in complex situations are presented in statistics textbooks, though a common-sense evaluation will suffice in most instances.

Index Numbers

In dealing with changes over time, it is often convenient to express the data in terms of some base period which is taken as equal to 100. Measures for any other period are then expressed as a percentage of the measure for the base period. Series of data treated in this way are said to consist of index numbers. They are calculated by dividing a particular item of a given year by the item in the base period, and multiplying the resulting ratio by 100.

Composite Indexes

Sometimes it is desirable to use a summary measure of one characteristic as an index or indicator of a characteristic not directly measurable. When measures of two or more characteristics are combined into a single figure for this purpose, the figure is called a composite index. Composite indexes are widely used in describing economic conditions; the index of leading indicators, the index of industrial production, producer price index, and many others are familiar to most business executives. Individual measures are combined into a single number by some system of assigning weights to the component parts, usually according to an independent indication of their importance. The composite index is not stated in terms of any unit such as dollars or tons, and thus it can combine figures which must be expressed in different units, as in the industrial production index.

The use of the same base period for various series of index numbers facilitates comparison of changes among the different series. Moreover, in looking at changes in composite indexes, different measures within the composite index may change at different rates. Because it has several components that may be changing independently of each other, moves in the composite index must be further examined for changes in the components.

Moving Averages

Time series changes may be of several kinds. They may be minor random or episodic movements. In some series there are distinct seasonal variations. Over a longer period of time there may be changes related to the business cycle. Finally, there are long-term trends which may be regarded as basic changes.

Where it is known that there is regular variation in a given series of data, allowance should be made for this fact in making comparisons. One method of taking account of seasonal variation, for example, is to compare points in time which represent the same phase of the seasonal movement.

To eliminate the effect of seasonal variation and in other situations where it is desirable to smooth out short-term variation, a moving average can be used. The measure for each time period is determined by taking the mean of values for a number of successive periods, including the latest. When a new period is added, the earliest is dropped, so the total number of periods used remains the same. The measure should cover the complete seasonal or other cycle. For example, if seasonal variation covers a year, a 12-month moving average could be computed each month. The separate values for each month would be added, and the sum divided by 12. On the 13th month, that would be added while the 1st month would be eliminated.

GRAPHIC ANALYSIS

Putting a series of data in graphic form is often a help in comprehending their meaning. Many types of charts may be drawn for different kinds of data and different purposes. Provided that an appropriate kind of chart is chosen and it is accurately constructed, visual presentation often provides the quickest, most direct means of analyzing a series of numbers, and may point out facts which are not immediately obvious in examination of the figures. These changes may be expressed in absolute numbers, percentages, or index numbers.

Use of Graphs in Analysis

Graphs depicting financial events may be prepared on arithmetic scales as well as on semilogarithmic scales. An arithmetic graph is one in which the horizontal and vertical spacing of lines is equal throughout. The semilogarithmic graph, or rate of change graph, is arithmetically scaled along the horizontal axis and logarithmically scaled along the vertical axis. The physical difference is obvious from a visual review of the two papers.

The narrowing spaces in the semilogarithmic graph permit the plotting of the absolute changes in the financial items and also reveal relative changes. An arithmetic chart is adequate for comparing fluctuations in series of data if there is not too much variance in the absolute size of the quantities; semilogarithmic graphs, on the other hand, permit comparisons of series of data varying widely in absolute size. Moreover, semilogarithmic graphs are preferred, because in addition to reflecting absolute changes shown by arithmetic graphs they reflect rates of change in the items being compared.

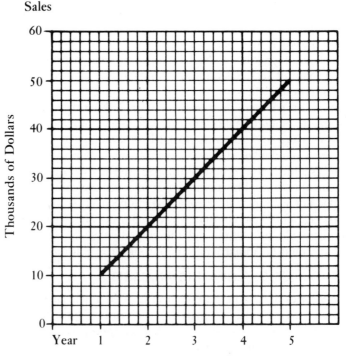

FIG. 32–3.   Sales Over Time on an Arithmetic Graph.

Rate of Change.   A comparison of sales growth as represented on arithmetic and semilogarithmic graphs serves to emphasize the difference between them. Sales plotted on the arithmetic chart in Figure 32–3 suggests a constant rate of growth, while the same data on the semilogarithmic scale of Figure 32–4 show a declining rate of growth, the true picture.

Year	Sales	Growth Rate
1	$10,000	—
2	20,000	100%
3	30,000	50
4	40,000	33
5	50,000	25

The use of a semilogarithmic graph avoids placing too much emphasis on percentage changes of financial data. In straight ratio analysis, for example, a decline of 25 percentage points in the quick ratio from one year to the next would be noted, but this observation could overlook the sizable changes in the absolute figures that constitute the numerator and the denominator. Since the rate of change is indicated by the slope of the line in

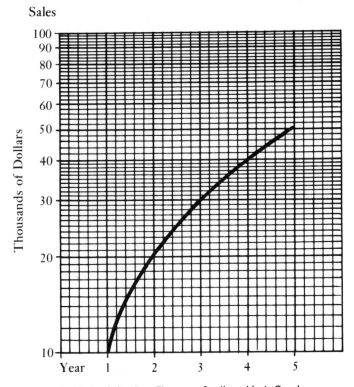

FIG. 32–4.   Sales Over Time on a Semilogarithmic Graph.

a semilogarithmic graph, both the percentage change and the absolute change in the item are reflected from one period to another. When two or more items are being compared, the item with the greater rate of change shows a steeper slope. This is best demonstrated by showing the following trend details over a five-year period:

	Year				
	1	2	3	4	5
Quick Assets	$125,000	$250,000	$150,000	$200,000	$225,000
Current Liabilities	$100,000	$250,000	$200,000	$200,000	$150,000

Figure 32–5 shows that the current liabilities, starting from a lower base, rose more sharply than quick assets between years one and two. Between years two and three both variables declined, although quick assets declined more sharply than current liabilities. Quick assets rose between years three and four, but current liabilities remained constant. Quick assets rose between years four and five, while current liabilities declined.

Comparing Related Information. When plotting absolute values and ratios on the same chart, care must be taken that the variables are related to each other. For instance, the same chart may be used to show the movements over time of quick assets, current liabilities, and quick ratio; the two absolute values are components of the ratio calculation. It would be inap-

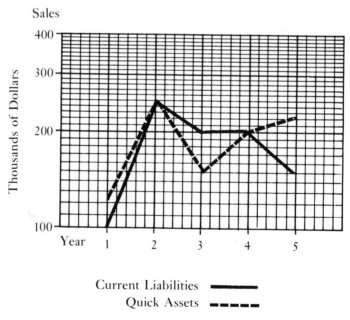

FIG. 32–5.   Charting Two Variables on a Semilogarithmic Graph.

propriate, on the other hand, to seek a relationship between tangible net worth and quick ratio by plotting them both on the same set of axes. One is an absolute value, while the ratio consists of two other values not related to tangible net worth.

In fact, when one of the variables is expressed as a ratio, it is not enough to observe the direction of that ratio. A ratio can follow changes in either or both of its components, so it is important to look for the underlying movements of those components. Using the quick assets and current liabilities of the previous example and adding the corresponding quick ratio would give the following data, which are then plotted on Figure 32–6.

	Year				
	1	2	3	4	5
Quick Assets	$125,000	$250,000	$150,000	$200,000	$225,000
Current Liabilities	$100,000	$250,000	$200,000	$200,000	$150,000
Quick Ratio	125%	100%	75%	100%	150%

The quick ratio declined between years one and two because current liabilities rose faster than quick assets. A further decline occurred between

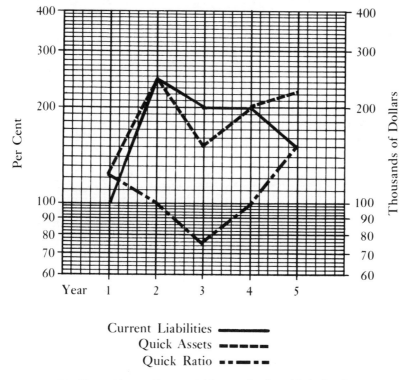

FIG. 32–6.   Charting Three Variables on a Semilogarithmic Graph.

years two and three because quick assets decline faster than current liabilities. The next year the quick ratio improved because quick assets increased while current liabilities remained constant. Further quick ratio progress was recorded during the last year, as quick assets increased while current liabilities were declining.

In this example two-cycle paper is used. Each cycle of values is expressed in powers of ten—that is, 1 to 10, 10 to 100, 100 to 1,000, and so on. This is needed because the quick ratio dips below 100 per cent. When only the quick assets and current liabilities were plotted, one cycle was sufficient. It is not essential to show all the numbers for a given cycle; in the above chart, only the percentages from 60 to 400 are shown, and the lines are centered on the graph. This gives the graph a sense of balance and overall attractiveness.

Since the cycles in the semilogarithmic chart are plotted in powers of 10, the starting point is never 0. In the arithmetic chart, however, it always begins with 0; otherwise intermediate values would be removed from the

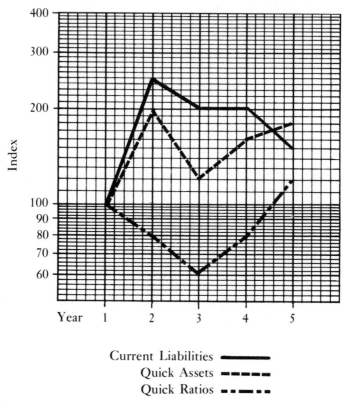

FIG. 32–7. Charting Three Variables on a Semilogarithmic Graph Using Index Numbers.

scale and this would cause a distorted presentation. However, where there is a large difference between the 0 and the numbers being plotted on an arithmetic chart, a broken scale can be used at a point between the 0 and the lowest number plotted.

Use of Index Numbers

In Figure 32–6, it was necessary to use two different scales, per cent and dollars. One way to simplify the presentation of different scales is to reduce the figures to index numbers and present them as percentages of a base year. Care should be used in selecting the base year to avoid distortion. Its values should not be extremes, such as at the peak or trough of a business cycle.

The values of the previous example have been converted to index numbers and plotted in Figure 32–7. Year one is chosen as the base year. Each of the numbers shown in the subsequent years is divided by the number listed in year one. That is, the quick assets of $250,000 for year two are divided by $125,000 to get an index of 200 per cent; $150,000 for year three are divided by $125,000 for an index of 120 per cent; and so on. The same procedure is followed for current liabilities, using $100,000 as the base; and for quick ratio, using 125% as the base. The tabulation for the five-year period shows:

	Year				
	1	2	3	4	5
Quick Assets	$125,000	$250,000	$150,000	$200,000	$225,000
Index Number	100	200	120	160	180
Current Liabilities	$100,000	$250,000	$200,000	$200,000	$150,000
Index Number	100	250	200	200	150
Quick Ratio	125%	100%	75%	100%	150%
Index Number	100	80	60	80	120

The use of index numbers is also warranted when there is a wide range of values and a more concise presentation is desired. Total liabilities and tangible net worth for five years are shown as absolute values in Figure 32–8, and then as index numbers in Figure 32–9. The data are:

	Year				
	1	2	3	4	5
Total Liabilities	$200,000	$250,000	$240,000	$250,000	$200,000
Index Number	100	125	120	125	100
Tangible Net Worth	$2,000,000	$2,000,000	$1,800,000	$1,500,000	$1,700,000
Index Number	100	100	90	75	85

The slopes of the lines in both charts are identical, but Figure 32–9 presents them close together and makes it easier to view them. Both charts

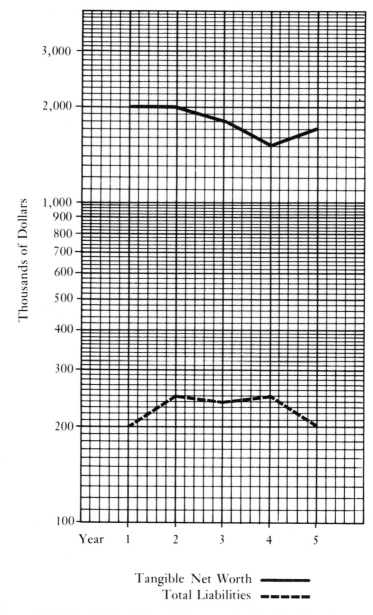

Tangible Net Worth ━━━━━
Total Liabilities ▬ ▬ ▬ ▬

FIG. 32–8. Charting Absolute Numbers on a Semilogarithmic Graph.

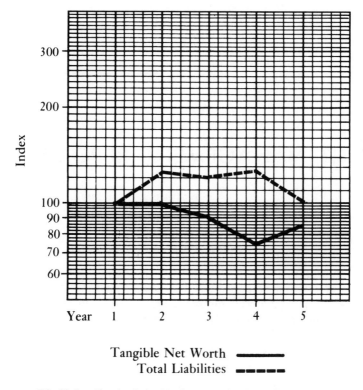

Tangible Net Worth ▬▬▬

Total Liabilities ▬ ▬ ▬ ▬

FIG. 32–9.   Charting Index Numbers on a Semilogarithmic Graph.

show that total liabilities rose sharply between years one and two while tangible net worth remained constant. Both variables declined the next year, with tangible net worth declining at a sharper rate. The tangible net worth continued its decline in the following year while the total liabilities rose. In the final year, total liabilities declined sharply while tangible net worth improved sharply.

CHAPTER 33

CREDIT MANAGEMENT REPORTS

Top management must be kept informed as to the status of the accounts receivable investment. Periodically, usually monthly, the chief credit executive should report the condition of the accounts receivable investment to corporate or division management. It is not enough for these reports to emphasize the favorable and minimize the negative; in fact, they should identify the potential problems as early as possible, state whether the problems are under control, and what is being done to resolve them.

Reports tend to vary according to the size and scope of each credit department organization and the operating style of each company. Regardless of these variations, credit executives should give careful consideration to the type and quality of information contained in the reports and to the frequency of their compilation and distribution.

AGING OF ACCOUNTS RECEIVABLE

An aging of accounts receivable is a distribution of outstanding accounts, arranged according to the time periods they have been outstanding. The most common classification system is current, overdue 1 to 30 days, 31 to 60, 61 to 90, and over 90. This keeps a clear-cut record of accounts that have remained open beyond their regular terms of sale. It helps to assure good collections and proper control of accounts.

These breakdowns are generally drawn from a monthly trial balance and are available at regular monthly intervals. Companies differ greatly in this practice, however, depending upon the extent of their automation. Accounts are aged continuously by some companies, with a different alphabetical group processed each day. At the other extreme, some companies age their receivables only in conjunction with annual or semiannual audits.

Conventional Aging of Accounts

In completing an aging of accounts, it is general practice to determine the percentage of the total receivables that are current and then the portions

Customer	Total Owing	Current	1–30 Days Past Due	31–60 Days Past Due	61–90 Days Past Due	Over 90 Days Past Due
All American Co.	$ 3,629.15	$2,110.00	$1,519.15			
Best, R.U. Inc.	739.20				$739.20	
Cord & Bord	629.00	629.00				
Donald Corp.	2,769.25	2,717.50	48.15	$ 3.60		
Ever Sales	592.00					$592.00
Fashion Center	417.80	417.80				
Garner, Geo. C.	1,140.61	745.30	175.50	219.81		
Hamilton Co.	329.00	329.00				
Total	$10,246.01	$6,948.60	$1,742.80	$223.41	$739.20	$592.00
Per Cent of Total	100	68	17	2	7	6

FIG. 33–1.   Aging of Accounts Receivable.

of the total that fall into the several aging categories. This provides additional points of comparison for collection people or may be worked into reports to top management. Figure 33–1 illustrates a typical aging form.

Another method of presenting an aging of receivables is by charting. Figure 33–2 shows receivables balances current and over 30 days past due. The data for the previous year and the current year-to-date are charted by months. Absolute figures are not shown in this type of presentation, but the charts present a comparative picture of the current month with that of one year ago, and of the current year-to-date with that of the previous year.

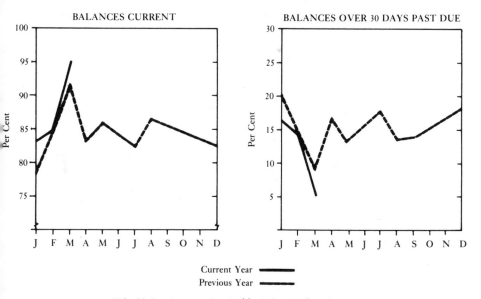

FIG. 33–2.   Accounts Receivable Aging in Chart Form.

Date	Trade Receivables (000)	Total Dollars				Per Cent to Total Dollars			
			Past Due				Past Due		
		Current	1–30	31–60	61 and Older	Current	1–30	31–60	61 and Older
		Industrial Division							
Current	$5,740	$4,520	$1,040	$160	$20	78.8	18.1	2.8	0.3
Prior Month	5,640	4,640	920	45	35	82.3	16.3	0.8	0.6
One Year Ago	5,940	4,425	1,320	180	15	74.5	22.2	3.0	0.3
		Packaging Division							
•	•	•	•	•	•	•	•	•	•
•	•	•	•	•	•	•	•	•	•
•	•	•	•	•	•	•	•	•	•

FIG. 33-3.　Accounts Receivable Aging by Divisions.

An aging of all accounts receivable can also be prepared by product line, by divisions, by regions, or by type of customer. Figure 33–3 shows a complete accounts receivable aging by divisions. For each aging category, the report shows the dollar investment and its percentage in relation to total dollars for the current month, the prior month, and the corresponding month one year ago. This report gives corporate management an opportunity to view the condition of the total receivables portfolio and to evaluate the significance of each corporate division to the total picture.

Figure 33–4 shows a summary by customers sold on regular terms and those sold on special terms. Claims are not aged although they are included in the accounts receivable.

Analysis by Risk Classification

A detailed analysis of the receivables portfolio may be made if all of the company's accounts have been classified as to risk category. This type of breakdown may be carried out within the broader framework of an industry or product line classification of accounts. Usually these categories are:

1. Prime—large, well-established firms involving no real credit risk.

2. Good—companies that can be expected to discount but lack the stature of prime accounts.

3. Limited—companies that are suspect enough to be held within close limits.

4. Marginal—high-risk accounts that bear constant watching.

The utility of measures derived from this approach depends upon the care taken in rating individual accounts. All information available to the credit department should be used in rating the accounts, including agency reports, interchange reports, bank letters, financial statements, sales repre-

	Current Month		Previous Month		Year Ago Month	
	Amount	Per Cent	Amount	Per Cent	Amount	Per Cent
Regular terms:						
Not yet due	$ 6,000	49.6	$ 6,306	53.6	$3,822	39.1
Past due:						
1–30 days	1,208	10.0	916	7.8	752	7.7
Over 30 days	348	2.9	408	3.5	486	5.0
Special-term accounts:						
Not yet due	3,554	29.4	3,341	28.4	3,798	38.9
Past due:						
1–30 days	501	4.2	280	2.4	412	4.2
Over 30 days	258	2.1	273	2.3	384	3.9
Claims	220	1.8	242	2.0	112	1.2
		100.0		100.0		100.0
Gross receivables	12,089		11,766		9,766	
Less allowance................	(321)		(320)		(278)	
Net receivables	$11,768		$11,446		$9,488	

FIG. 33–4.   Aging of Customer Receivables by Terms.

sentatives' reports, and the like. Provision should also be made for a systematic review of all ratings.

Two types of measures are commonly developed from a basic risk classification of accounts. One is a breakdown showing the distribution of outstanding accounts by risk categories as of a given date; normally this breakdown will show both the dollar volume of accounts in each category and their percentage to the total. The second type of measure is a dollar or percentage breakdown of cumulative sales to different classes of accounts for a given period.

Aging reports prepared according to risk classifications should validate the risk class assigned to the accounts; those having the greatest risk will normally have the highest proportion of delinquent accounts. In viewing this measurement, emphasis should be placed on the percentages, not on the dollars. Figure 33–5 illustrates an aging by risk classification.

Distributions of this kind can be used to advantage in assigning accounts responsibility, for they permit the experience and ability of personnel to be matched with the risk and difficulty of handling accounts. This approach makes more sense in many situations than the usual procedure of assigning alphabetical or geographical blocs of accounts to individual credit executives.

They also can be used to detect significant changes in the pattern of

Risk Class	Total Receivable	Current	Per Cent	Past Due							
				1–30	Per Cent	31–60	Per Cent	61–90	Per Cent	Over 90	Per Cent
Good	$ 1,075	$ 860	80.0	$ 200	18.6			$ 15	1.4		
Fair	2,700	2,025	75.0	415	15.4	$170	6.3	40	1.5	$ 50	1.9
Limited	4,980	3,400	68.3	667	13.4	315	6.3	310	6.2	288	5.8
Marginal	1,745	1,150	65.9	206	11.8	145	8.3	113	6.5	131	7.5
	$10,500	$7,435	70.8	$1,488	14.2	$630	6.0	$478	4.6	$469	4.5

FIG. 33–5. Aging by Risk Classification.

credit decisions from one period to another, and consequent changes in a company's exposure to loss and the expected value of its receivables. Moreover, they also can contribute to a better analysis of the probable timing of future collections and thus to the preparation of better short-range cash budgets.

The second type of measure derived from a risk classification of accounts is a running breakdown of sales by established classes. These figures are particularly useful, for they highlight the additional sales volume obtained from customers judged to be marginal or submarginal risks. Sales of this type are apt to appear insignificant as a fraction of total sales but very important as a fraction of sales above a company's break-even point.

This type of analysis has proved extremely useful to those responsible for the formulation and periodic reevaluation of credit policy. However, it is very difficult for companies that have not built some form of risk classification into their regular credit systems to compile the data. Except for companies that have automated their credit and receivables functions, comprehensive breakdowns are rarely prepared. On the other hand, partial breakdowns for key groups of accounts may supply most of the desired information, and they can be managed in many situations where a comprehensive distribution would be impractical. A month-to-month analysis of amounts of risk, for example, may well be confined to sizable accounts if they represent a substantial part of a company's total exposure.

Past-Due Accounts Receivable

These summaries reveal the past-due segment of the accounts receivable portfolio. They may list all past-due accounts or may include only those past due more than a specified number of days, according to the instructions of the chief credit executive. The reports also may note what action is being taken with regard to the collection of these accounts.

Figure 33–6, the conventional form of analysis, lists all past-due accounts, the dollar amounts for the current month according to aging categories, and the amounts in each category are expressed as a percentage of the total past dues. The procedure is repeated for the prior month. The

Days Past Due	Current Month	Per Cent	Prior Month	Per Cent	Increase or (Decrease)	Year Ago Month	Per Cent
1–30	$3,169,573	75.1	$2,474,675	72.4	$694,898	$3,072,507	68.0
31–60	493,795	11.7	355,711	10.4	138,084	908,743	20.1
61–90	430,488	10.2	497,566	14.5	(67,078)	425,673	9.4
Over 90	126,614	3.0	92,348	2.7	34,266	113,477	2.5
	$4,220,470	100.0	$3,420,300	100.0	$800,170	$4,520,400	100.0

FIG. 33–6.   Comparative Analysis of Past-Due Accounts.

dollar change of the current month over the previous month is then shown by the same aging categories. The procedure for preparing the data for the corresponding month one year ago is identical to that shown for the current and prior months. These figures enable corporate management to view the past-due receivables in both an absolute and relative sense and determine changes in the components of the aging categories.

Figure 33–7 presents an analysis of delinquent accounts by product line. End-of-month figures and a twelve-month moving average for the current month are shown in dollars for delinquent accounts; then the percentage delinquent is reported. The procedure is repeated for the previous month of the current year and the corresponding month one year ago. This method not only shows the actual end-of-month figure but also adjusts the data for seasonal variations.

	Paper-board	Corrugated Containers	Kraft Paper	Pulp	Total
Current Month					
Delinquent Accounts (000):					
End of Month	$632.4	$649.6	$348.6	$664.2	$2,575.0
12-Month Moving Average	624.0	618.8	304.2	621.0	2,540.5
Per Cent Delinquent:					
End of Month	12.5%	16.8%	6.1%	12.8%	11.6%
12-Month Moving Average	14.0	17.3	7.9	14.0	13.5
Previous Month					
•	•	•	•	•	•
•	•	•	•	•	•
•	•	•	•	•	•

FIG. 33–7.   Delinquent Accounts Receivable and Percentage Delinquent.

High cost of capital and borrowings focuses attention on large problem accounts with past-due balances. Accounts that exceed an assigned credit line or that have past-due balances greater than established amounts are listed for special action. Some explanation should be given as to what actions have been taken on these accounts or what recent events have taken place that would bring these accounts into proper perspective. For example, management should know if payment has been requested, if there was a price discrepancy, if a portion has been returned for credit, if future orders are being withheld, or if any cash has been recently collected from those firms.

One method of presenting a detailed analysis of the top 10 accounts is shown in Figure 33–8. It excludes accounts having a high credit appraisal with an estimated financial strength of $300,000 or more.

Name of Account	Terms of Sale	Credit Line	Highest Credit	Amount Owing	Total Past Due	Over 90 Days Past Due	Comments
ABC Co.	Net 30	$ 50,000	$ 62,400	$ 55,400	$15,000	$ 100	—
XYZ Co.	"	125,000	146,700	136,700	82,700		April Cash Rec'd 36,700
RFC Co.	"	125,000	250,000	220,400	37,425	3,940	April Cash Rec'd 31,450
•	•	•	•	•	•	•	•
•	•	•	•	•	•	•	•
•	•	•	•	•	•	•	•

FIG. 33–8. Monthly Report of the Top 10 Accounts in Dollars Owing.

Other Variations

There are many other ways that agings presentations are made. The most frequent additional method shows the number of accounts, as well as the dollar totals, under each aging category. In some simpler systems, only the accounts that are overdue more than 90 days are identified. This provides less detail but may be useful for interim presentations. Another familiar measure is the delinquency ratio. This makes no distinction among degrees of delinquency and expresses the total of overdue receivables as a percentage of all receivables.

Usefulness

Aging presentations are a help in developing a list or file of customers requiring statements, collection letters, or vigorous collection. Agings are equally important for any thoroughgoing analysis of the condition of a company's receivables. In many companies, particularly small ones, they may well be the only statistical information used in appraising collection operations.

An aging of accounts is a good measure of collection performance since it provides a direct statement of the importance of past-due accounts. While customers can be encouraged to discount or pay bills promptly, the department's main function is to prevent a tie-up of funds in overdue or uncollectible accounts.

Agings do have shortcomings. Nevertheless, they can serve a useful control purpose. An increase in the relative importance of overdue accounts may point to lax collection procedures. True, it also may reflect a deliberate change in credit policy or general business conditions, or a drop in sales with no change in the dollar amount of delinquent accounts. No matter what the reason, the aging highlights the variation and signals the need for deeper inquiry.

Limitations

Despite its directness, an aging of accounts does have limitations as a measure of collection performance. Agings are best thought of as weighted averages in which the weights are the dollar amounts of outstanding accounts. If there are wide differences in the size of the individual accounts, and large accounts make up a considerable part of the total, the ratio will be dominated by these accounts. Size of account and the practice of discounting or automatically paying within terms are often highly correlated. For this reason, the number of overdue accounts may be regarded as a better measure of collection performance than the dollar amount of such accounts. Whether this point of view is justified will depend upon the facts of the situation and the collection objectives of the company concerned. This aspect of the figures explains why some companies prepare agings both in terms of numbers and size of accounts.

Agings are sometimes criticized as performance measures because they are held to be too transitory, too much the product of accidental factors which affect the timing of cash receipts. This type of objection can be raised against most balance sheet ratios and also against any collection measures which incorporate the accounts receivable figure. While there is undoubtedly some merit to this objection, it should be regarded as an argument for aging accounts at frequent intervals, not abandoning them altogether. Random factors tend to average out over time, and serious situations can be noticed if agings are made available at regular monthly intervals.

Some object that agings are too costly to compute and too broad to be useful. The analysis may be limited to certain types of accounts or additional classification criteria may be introduced. If a company has only small accounts, it could dispense with regular agings and rely on aggregate turnover figures for information on collection results. On the other hand, if large and small accounts are intermixed, it may be desirable to age accounts but confine the breakdown to the large accounts. For similar reasons, some companies confine their aging to accounts within specified risk categories or industry distributions.

If accounts are sold on deferred payment terms or special terms and are not segregated from ordinary trade accounts, an aging report could mislead officials who have no direct knowledge of the department's operations. Month-to-month comparisons and comparisons with performance standards are distorted by them. One solution is to tabulate the deferred and unusual items separately, and omit them from the usual aging and all similar measures of collection performance.

COLLECTIONS

All credit departments should compile some measure of collection experience, for collections have a bearing on the financial and sales aspects of a business. There are two basic methods used for evaluating collections. One is to show the cash collected as a percentage of accounts receivable or sales of the prior month. Another is to compare collections against a cash forecast.

Collections as a Percentage of Accounts Receivable

The most common percentage measure compares cash collected during a month against the receivables outstanding at the beginning of the month. Since collection activities are directed not only at the sales of the preceding period but also at the uncollected sales of earlier periods, most companies use receivables rather than sales as the denominator for the calculation.

Figure 33–9 shows this method. Collections are divided by receivables outstanding to calculate a collection ratio. The ratio is then multiplied by 12.0, representing an ideal twelve turns per year to obtain the actual turnover rate for the receivables. Thus for August, 90.9 per cent times 12.0 gives a turnover rate of 10.9.

Month	Receivables Outstanding	Month	Cash Collections	Collection Ratio	Turn-over
Aug.	$2,200	Sept.	$2,000	90.9%	10.9×
Sept.	2,600	Oct.	2,500	96.2	11.5
Oct.	2,500	Nov.	2,600	104.0	12.5

FIG. 33–9.   Collection Ratio Method.

The major limitation of this measure is its tendency to hide the growth of delinquent accounts when there is an increase in accounts paying promptly. The only sure way of preventing misinterpretation is to provide specific data on overdue accounts. Also, since the collection ratio is an average or summary figure, it conceals the peculiarities of individual cases. Many credit executives believe that the department's collections effectiveness should be judged by its success in dealing with the most difficult collection problems. The latter includes situations where it is necessary to arrange extended payment schedules or participate in creditors' committees.

Despite these shortcomings, the development of historical figures enables a company to determine when collections are best, and how much money it can expect from collections during a given period. As a result, the collection ratio is commonly used to estimate cash receipts when a cash budget is being prepared. This procedure is described in more detail in Chapter 31.

Collections Compared to a Cash Forecast

This method requires a cash forecast and actual records of collections. The cash forecast is based upon an analysis of collections during a comparable past period. Most of the credit departments that prepare this report forecast cash on a monthly basis, although it may be done more or less frequently. Some companies that prepare monthly and weekly forecasts also break down the data day by day to better gauge cash inflows. Figure 33–10 shows a forecast in which cash receipts are projected three months ahead, with the first month shown by weeks.

	Month 1				Month 2	Month 3
	Week 1	Week 2	Week 3	Week 4		
Cash Receipts:						
Domestic Customers	$10,000	$12,000	$11,000	$14,000	$46,000	$50,000
Export Customers	1,000	1,500	1,300	1,500	6,000	7,000
Other Receipts	200	210	220	210	850	900
Total	$11,200	$13,710	$12,520	$15,710	$52,850	$57,900

FIG. 33–10.   Cash Forecast.

Actual cash receipts may deviate from the forecast, so comparisons between estimated and actual performance should be made regularly. Some firms make these comparisons weekly or even daily. The forecast should be adjusted to reflect known changes, as well as any new conditions that can be foreseen.

Figure 33–11 shows a method of computing collections with the cash forecast, with total receivables, and with the total collectible balance, which is defined as the beginning accounts receivable balance plus sales for the current month. It also shows the percentage of collections over or under the prior month's sales.

Region	Cash Collections	Per Cent Over (Under) Cash Forecast	Per Cent Collected Total Receivables	Per Cent Collected Collectible Balance	Per Cent Over (Under) Prior Month's Sales
1	$ 13,900	(4.2%)	72.4%	41.9%	6.9%
2	17,500	1.7	74.5	40.2	(2.8)
3	30,000	3.4	75.0	45.5	3.4
•	•	•	•	•	•
•	•	•	•	•	•
•	•	•	•	•	•
Total	$180,000	1.1%	74.4%	43.5%	2.9%

FIG. 33–11.   Collections Compared to Cash Forecast.

DAYS SALES OUTSTANDING

The average days sales outstanding provides a convenient summary of a company's investment in receivables. It can readily be compared with a company's credit terms or similar standard. Theoretically, companies selling on 30-day terms, for example, may expect a complete turnover of receivables within 30 days and may act to stiffen collection procedures when the turnover period exceeds 30 days. As with other overall figures, this measure covers up the behavior of delinquent accounts when other accounts are discounting their bills. In addition, marketing considerations such as datings could have an adverse impact on the measure. For these reasons, it is generally supplemented with information helpful in evaluating individual or classes of accounts.

There are three basic formula methods for calculating the relationship of accounts receivable to sales and expressing the resulting figure in days: the Credit Research Foundation's Days Sales Outstanding, or DSO; Last-In, First-Out; and the Optimum Method.

DSO

The Credit Research Foundation uses this index of investment in receivables in its National Summary of Domestic Trade Receivables to track the movement of business receivables on a national scale as well as by industry and by product line. As a measure of macroeconomic investment in receivables, this index is obtained from a sample of companies that are polled quarterly. It expresses in one number the relation between accounts receivable and sales. In order for the number to have meaning from a comparative standpoint, each variable in the calculation should be clearly defined. Both the accounts receivable in the numerator and the sales in the denominator should include comparable financial data.

The CRF formula for calculating DSO is as follows:

$$\frac{\text{Average Trade Receivables Balance Last 3 Monthends} \times 90}{\text{Credit Sales for Last 3 Months}}$$

The three monthends average accounts receivable balance is used in the formula in order to smooth the data. If the balance at the end of the quarter were used, the DSO would be prone to move sharply up or down, particularly if the accounts receivable were abnormally high or low at the quarter's end. This would tend to create a sawtooth effect on any DSO trend line being developed.

This formula, used by respondents in submitting data to the National Summary of Domestic Trade Receivables, may be adapted for single company use. Even if the DSO is developed by formula other than that recommended by the Foundation, it may still be compared to industry standards. While the DSO will differ from the published figure, its trend would be comparable and thus usable for analysis.

The DSO also may be calculated according to risk classes. By dividing the accounts into quality groups, a credit department is able to provide a review schedule keyed to the degree of risk and can devote more time and effort to the problem accounts. This increases the efficiency of the department and provides a more effective gauge for judging the department's effectiveness in optimizing the company's investment.

Last-In, First-Out Method

This method measures the equivalent of the number of prior days sales that remain on the books. Receivables are reduced by subtracting the current month's sales, then the sales of successive preceding months, until the receivables balance is zero. Actual days sales are counted while this is being done. The technique is particularly helpful where company sales have wide seasonal variations. The following example illustrates the procedure:

Assume that at December 31 a company's accounts receivable balance is $20,800,000, and sales for the last three months are: October $6,000,000, November $8,800,000, and December $10,000,000.

DSO calculation is computed as follows:

December 31 Balance	$20,800,000	
Deduct December Sales	10,000,000	30 Days
Balance	10,800,000	
Deduct November Sales	8,800,000	30
Balance	2,000,000	
Deduct October Sales*	2,000,000	10
	-0-	70 Days

*Only ⅓ of the October sales (10 days worth) are needed to reduce the outstanding receivables to zero.

This method for calculating DSO allows analysis based on facts that can be related to specific monthly sales or accounts receivable rather than on averages.

Optimum DSO

As its name implies, the Optimum DSO measure seeks to establish the most efficient investment in receivables after taking into account the various factors that affect it. Two basic methods are used to develop the measure. One extracts the financial variables that affect DSO unfavorably, such as datings, deductions, and sales to marginal accounts. The other develops the best possible days sales outstanding by using current accounts receivable in lieu of total accounts receivable.

Extracting Variables. In calculating an Optimum DSO under the first method, the items that cause temporary dislocations in the DSO are excluded from both the accounts receivable and sales. This is usually done as a secondary calculation, and the impact of these items can be determined by calculating the actual DSO based upon total dollars and then subtracting the Optimum DSO.

For example, a company's sales for the last 3 months totaled $60,000,000 and the average accounts receivable balance was $32,000,000. Included in these figures are $5,000,000 in postdated sales.

Under the full calculation DSO is:

$$\frac{32,000,000 \times 90}{60,000,000} = 48.0 \text{ days}$$

After the postdated sales are excluded the Optimum DSO is:

$$\frac{(32,000,000 - 5,000,000) \times 90}{(60,000,000 - 5,000,000)} = 44.2 \text{ days}$$

The impact of postdated sales is 48.0 less 44.2, or 3.8 days.

This method underscores the impact that datings have upon accounts receivable turnover and provides a better measure for evaluating the receivables investment.

Best Possible DSO.   This method assists the credit executive to distinguish between length of selling terms and delinquency as causes for shifts in DSO. If all customers paid on the due date, all receivables would be in the current column of an aging report. Hence, if the current receivables is used in the CRF formula for DSO, the Best Possible DSO would result. Its formula is expressed as follows:

$$\frac{\text{Average CURRENT Receivables Balance Last 3 Monthends} \times 90}{\text{Credit Sales for Last 3 Months}}$$

Average Days Delinquent.   The calculation for the Average Days Delinquent (ADD) is arrived at by subtracting the Best Possible DSO from the actual DSO. The following example illustrates the procedure:

Month	(000) Sales	(000) Total Receivables	(000) Current Receivables
July	$ 9,324	$14,935	$ 9,519
August	10,960	17,078	11,713
September	9,371	15,936	9,458
Total	$29,655	$47,949	$30,690
Average	—	15,983	10,230

$$\text{DSO} = \frac{15,983,000 \times 90}{29,655,000} = 48.5$$

$$\text{Best Possible DSO} = \frac{10,230,000 \times 90}{29,655,000} = 31.1$$

Average Days Delinquent = 48.5 − 31.1 = 17.4 days

To prevent misinterpretation of results, ADD must be expressed in days rather than in dollars. A company that has steadily increasing sales with a declining ADD should show a decline in ADD. Because of increasing sales, however, it might also show successively higher dollar amounts in ADD. It would be misleading to concentrate on the dollars interpretation without recognizing that the receivables condition was improving, as evidenced by the declining number of days ADD.

The ADD measure is also a better tool for evaluating delinquent accounts than the ordinary aging. In those cases where sales fluctuate considerably, for example, the percentage of delinquent accounts could move widely while the absolute dollar value remains fairly static.

The ADD may be expressed in dollars as a measure of the average funds tied up in delinquent accounts. On those occasions where delinquency has driven up a company's DSO, it is possible to calculate what average receivables should be at a desired level of DSO; then subtract that figure from actual average receivables to determine monies that would be freed for other use at the desired level of DSO. As an example, assume that the company desires to determine the impact on its portfolio of a DSO reduction from 48.5 days to 45.0. The calculation is as follows:

$$\frac{\text{Actual 3-Month Sales} \times \text{Desired DSO}}{90} = \text{Calculated Average Receivables}$$

$$\frac{29,655,000 \times 45}{90} = 14,827,500$$

Actual 3-Month Average Receivables	$15,983,000
Calculated Average Receivables	14,827,500
Monies Freed for Other Use	$ 1,155,500

Thus, if DSO were reduced 3.5 days, the accounts receivable investment would decrease from $15,983,000 to $14,827,000 and there would be $1,155,500 freed up for other corporate use.

Figure 33–12 shows one method of presenting this information. Actual

Division		Billings	Trade Receivables			Measurements			
			Total	Current	Over 90 Days Past Due	DSO	Best Possible DSO	ADD	ADD$
A	This Month	$11,450	$14,565	$10,800	$437	42.5	30.6	11.9	$3,832
	Last Month	9,418	14,020	10,374	420	44.7	31.7	13.0	3,344
	Last Year	9,420	14,130	10,100	424	43.5	30.9	12.6	3,271
•	•	•	•	•	•	•	•	•	•
	•	•	•	•	•	•	•	•	•
	•	•	•	•	•	•	•	•	•

FIG. 33–12.   Monthly Credit Report.

DSO is determined to be 42.5 and Best Possible DSO, 30.6. This gives 11.9 as the Average Days Delinquent.

Next it is assumed that sales for the three months ended this month are $28,980. This figure is divided by 90 to obtain average daily sales of $322, which is then multiplied by the ADD of 11.9 to show $3,832 tied up by delinquent receivables. Wide monthly variations in sales will affect the calculations of Best Possible DSO and ADD. However, the swings may be minimized by using 12-month moving averages in the calculations.

UNCOLLECTIBLE ACCOUNTS

An important consideration usually associated with the collection responsibility is the maintenance of an allowance for uncollectibles. It is necessary to anticipate accounts that may prove uncollectible and then establish a reserve of profits to which such uncollectible accounts will ultimately be charged. It should be feasible to review an organization's collection experience as a start in determining how much of an allowance is needed. This involves a review of previous bad-debt writeoffs and special problem accounts of substantial size that may be currently owing, as well as the general trend of business conditions.

Allowance for Uncollectibles

Conservative management generally likes to establish an allowance for uncollectibles on the high side, so that any portion of the allowance not needed at the end of the accounting period can be released into the profit column after a reasonable balance has been retained for the new accounting period. This approach has distinct advantages if a serious number of insolvencies are encountered. On the other hand, it is sometimes criticized by other schools of accounting for being unrealistic and leading to understatement of profits in the course of the business year as the large allowance is accumulated.

The individual charged with the collection responsibility is likely to be most familiar with the customer accounts and should make the initial calculations and recommendations for the allowance for uncollectibles. A practical approach is to consider the allowance as consisting of two parts. A new accounting period is entered with a certain total of outstanding accounts receivable on the books actually representing sales made in the previous fiscal period. A sum considered adequate to cover any bad-debt contingencies in that group becomes the beginning balance in the allowance for uncollectibles for the new fiscal period. Then the budget of sales for the new fiscal period is studied and made the basis for an additional amount of allowance, accrued usually on a predetermined monthly basis. When combined with the starting sum, this gives the total allowance for uncollectibles for the next fiscal period.

Accounts are commonly charged against the allowance for uncollectibles when it appears doubtful that collection can be made, or when it is certain that only a portion of the total account outstanding can be recovered. Such recoveries as may ultimately be obtained from diligent followup or litigation can be taken as a credit to the allowance for uncollectibles account when they are received, whether in the current accounting period or at some later time.

Writeoffs

Ultimate collection and the charging off of an account to bad debts are the two ways in which a customer may be liquidated from the company's books. The percentage of sales ultimately charged off to bad debts has been a misunderstood and often misused measure of the effectiveness of credit and collections. A record of bad-debt losses should be maintained by every business, but it is dangerous to let this become the sole criterion of how good a job has been done. Management must review the record of bad-debt losses in the light of the profit margin, the goal of full production, and company plans to enter new markets or expand operations with new products.

The simplest measure of bad-debt writeoffs is a statement of their amount and number. Where losses are very small, there may be no reason to record loss results in any other form. Even in this simple form, however, figures for different companies usually lack comparability because of differences in the timing of realization and content. In some companies, losses may be written off when accounts reach a predetermined age; in others they may not be written off until they are placed for collection or the final outcome has been settled. Measurement procedures also differ with respect to the treatment of bad-debt recoveries. In some cases recoveries are deducted from the gross amount of concurrent losses, while in other companies the gross amount of loss is regarded as the most relevant figure for purposes of appraising credit decisions.

To facilitate their use in industry and in product line comparisons, losses are generally shown net of the recoveries of prior years and expressed as a percentage of all sales. Technically, writeoffs should be related only to credit sales in order to avoid the distorting effect of variations in the proportion of cash and credit sales, but this refinement may not be considered important or convenient if cash sales are a small or constant percentage of total sales.

The bad-debt writeoff ratio has limitations for interperiod comparisons which may not be generally recognized. The ratio typically pairs bad-debt losses originating in one period with sales of the following period. If there is a considerable delay in the recognition of losses, as frequently happens, any number of developments may impair the value of the ratio as a measure of effectiveness. An increase in sales, a change in credit policy, or a change in business conditions may alter successive figures to such an extent that they give no indication of the credit department's selectivity in extending credit during the period under consideration. This weakness of the ratio may be overcome to some extent by using a comparatively short writeoff period and an appropriate moving average for sales, but this is a little-used adjustment. Needless to say, these same considerations must be taken into account in judging the performance of one credit department against others on the basis of their respective bad-debt ratios.

To give another dimension to writeoffs, the customary bad-debt writeoff ratio can be accompanied by a comparison of these same losses with the company's sales to the accounts that produced the losses. Real differences of opinion are possible on the most appropriate period to be used in tabulating sales for such a comparison, but irrespective of this, the measure has the virtue of relating bad-debt losses to the specific decisions which gave rise to them. The comparison helps management determine whether the original decisions were profitable. Too often the volume of past collections from an account is forgotten, and an eventual bad-debt loss is taken as unequivocal evidence of poor judgment in extending credit to the account.

Bad-Debt Analysis

An important consideration in receivables management is the proper determination of uncollectible accounts and the establishment of an allowance for uncollectibles to which such uncollectible accounts will ultimately be charged. Figure 33–13 shows a statement of allowance for uncollectibles that is prepared following the close of the period. It reflects the allowance balance at the beginning of each year, adjustments prior to current year writeoffs, minus the current year writeoffs, plus the current year adjustments, leaving the allowance balance at the end of the year.

To determine the trend in net writeoffs and to serve as a guide for estimating future bad-debt losses, an examination of prior years' net writeoffs

	Wholesale Accounts	Total
Allowance at Beginning of Year	$1,052,600	$3,032,850
Allowance Adjustment Prior to Current Year Writeoffs	(6,850)	(6,850)
Less Current Year Net Writeoffs	113,610	975,300
Per Cent to Credit Sales	.05%	.31%
Plus Current Year Allowance Adjustments	235,860	808,650
Per Cent to Credit Sales	.11%	.26%
Allowances at End of Year	1,168,000	2,859,350
Per Cent to Yearend Accounts Receivable Balance	3.64%	5.35%
Increase (Decrease) Versus Year Ago	115,400	(173,500)

FIG. 33–13.   Statement of Allowance for Uncollectibles.

	Wholesale Accounts		Total	
	Total Amount	Per Cent To Credit Sales	Total Amount	Per Cent To Credit Sales
Current Year	$113,610	.05%	$ 975,300	.31%
One Year Ago	204,709	.12	1,616,809	.64
Two Years Ago	202,518	.13	1,428,875	.60
Three Years Ago	237,835	.18	842,297	.40
Four Years Ago	177,138	.14	685,025	.49
Average	$187,162	.12%	$1,109,661	.40%

FIG. 33–14.   Statement of Net Writeoffs.

can be made. Figure 33–14 analyzes the experiences for the current year and four prior years.

ACCOUNTS RECEIVABLE MANAGEMENT REPORTS

Rather than prepare separate reports for aging of accounts receivable, collections, days sales outstanding, and uncollectible accounts, these activities may be incorporated into one management report. The variables chosen would be those that best determine a company's commitment to its accounts receivable investment.

Status Report

The status of the accounts receivable investment and other information of particular interest to top management may be designed so that these data can be included in the financial report that is reviewed by the directors at their monthly meeting.

In Figure 33–15, the three column data under DSO can be presented in this way. It shows that Division C's DSO is considerably under budget, and that the total company DSO is on target for the current year, although 0.3 days higher than one year ago. The same table also shows information the chief credit executive may use for control purposes: sales and average receivables balances, and the net loss rate per $1,000 by divisions and total company.

Activity Report

Another type of management report could include an evaluation of key credit activities for corporate management. These could include the comparison of the growth in credit sales and accounts receivable by various product lines for the current year and several prior years, and the status of accounts.

In Figure 33–16, the growth of accounts receivable exceeded that of sales for wholesale accounts, while the growth of sales in the chemical product

Division	Sales This Period	Sales This Year To Date	Average Receivables Outstanding	Net Loss Rate Per $1,000	DSO This Year	DSO Plan	DSO Last Year
		—(000,000)—					
A	$ 70.5	$ 871.0	$33.6	.15	13.3	13.1	13.0
B	8.9	105.7	7.3	.43	23.0	22.5	22.6
C	15.5	166.0	9.5	.19	17.1	17.9	17.5
•	•	•	•	•	•	•	•
•	•	•	•	•	•	•	•
•	•	•	•	•	•	•	•
Current Year	153.4	1,781.9	80.5	.15	14.7	14.7	
Prior Year	121.9	1,450.3	62.5	.21			14.4
Increase (Decrease)	31.5	331.6	18.0	(0.6)	0.3		
Average Daily Sales	5.5						
Actual Receivables Outstanding			76.6				

FIG. 33–15.   Status Report.

(Dollars in Millions; Accounts in Thousands)	Current Year	Year Ago	Two Years Ago	Per Cent Increase or (Decrease) Over Previous Year Current Year	Year Ago
Wholesale Accounts					
Credit Sales-Year to Date	$274.3	$220.8	$196.6	24%	12%
Balance Outstanding	$ 31.4	$ 22.7	$ 20.1	38	13
Days Sales Outstanding	44.3	45.2	42.4		
Balance Outstanding—Mtges	$ 5.6	$ 6.5	$ 7.5	(13)	(14)
No. Active Whlse & Mtge Accounts	28.6	26.8	23.4	5	15
•	•	•	•	•	•
•	•	•	•	•	•
•	•	•	•	•	•
Chemicals					
Credit Sales-Year to Date	$ 28.0	$ 27.3	$ 34.2	3	(20)
Balance Outstanding	$ 3.2	$ 3.4	$ 5.3	(5)	(36)
No. Active Accounts	0.2	0.4	0.5	(50)	(11)
Condition of Accounts:					
Current	82.5%	72.3%	72.5%		
Past Due	17.5	27.7	27.5		
Days Sales Outstanding	32.7	40.1	38.5		

FIG. 33–16.   Credit Department Activities.

line was small and accounts receivable balance declined. Moreover, the number of accounts for chemicals also declined by 50 per cent for the current year as compared to the prior year, while collections and accounts receivable turnover improved.

OTHER MANAGEMENT REPORTS

While most reports from the credit department are concerned with the status of accounts receivable, some cover a wide variety of data such as accounts in litigation or under court jurisdiction, customer visits, business refused and gained due to credit and collection reasons, new business leads to sales, and annual review of operations.

Accounts in Litigation or Under Court Jurisdiction

This report covers financially distressed debtors with lawsuits instituted, and accounts operating under court jurisdiction, such as corporation reorganizations or arrangement proceedings. It is generally prepared monthly to report current status.

Customer Visits

Many managements know that personal visits to customers are an important way to establish relationships of mutual trust and to learn as much as possible about the customers' operations. Typically they include credit and collection calls, good will calls, and sales office and plant visits. These reports are prepared as the visits are made, but may be submitted to senior officers on a scheduled basis, generally monthly.

Business Refused and Gained Due to Credit and Collection Reasons

This report could typically indicate the customer name and location, the division or product line, the amount of the order, and the reason for accepting or rejecting it. It can range from monthly to quarterly to annually, or as required.

New Business Leads to Sales

A report on this subject typically includes the customer name and location, division or product line, and pertinent remarks on the lead. Departments that prepare these reports for corporate management generally do so as the leads develop, although others prepare them monthly, quarterly, or annually.

Annual Review of Operations

Chief credit executives should prepare an annual review of the department operations and plans for the coming year. This report should highlight and analyze the company's investment in the accounts receivable and its bad-debt experience. Other topics could include the operating budget, controllable costs, development of department personnel, credit and money-market conditions, and sales appraisals of credit and collection policies.

OPERATING CRITERIA FOR CREDIT DEPARTMENTS

While pursuing the profitability goals of the receivables investment, the credit executive must also consider the quality of the credit department's daily performance. This requires the development of guidelines to evaluate the staffing requirements, determine the efficiency of the credit department, appraise the types of credit and accounts receivable systems being used, and evaluate selected expense ratios. The most effective way to measure performance in this respect is to compare the department operation against operating criteria compiled periodically by the Credit Research Foundation.

The staffing requirements of each department obviously differ. Credit approval and collection followup require a staff of credit and collection managers, clerks, typists, and other office workers. When payment application and claims and adjustments are included in the credit executive's duties, these extra functions may call for cash control clerks, adjusters, cash appliers or processors, and the like.

The extent to which computers are being used in credit and accounts receivable administration has a direct impact on the staffing requirements and duty responsibilities in the credit department. Credit approval, collections, payment application, handling of claims and disputes, and other accounting functions are costly and time-consuming. While not designated to replace people, computers contribute to the overall effectiveness of the department by optimizing the workload and increasing productivity. At the same time, they bring added equipment costs to credit administration. Thus the systems used in the administration of credit and accounts receivable will influence the type and amount of departmental costs.

Further, the scope and extent of activities under the jurisdiction of the chief credit executive will determine the cost of department operation. One, for example, may be charged with expenses for office services while another may not. One may be charged for computer services while another may not. A clearer picture is obtained when total costs are segregated into separate categories or criteria. They may then be compared against data compiled by the Credit Research Foundation or against goals set for the department. Discrepancies may be noted and adjusted, or goals may be revised if it becomes clear they cannot be achieved or are unrealistic.

Standard Measures

The operating criteria for credit departments compiled by the Credit Research Foundation are prepared from periodic surveys of its members. The studies describe the sample according to annual sales, active customer accounts, annual number of invoices, and extent of automation in the credit and accounts receivable system, and then present key data for different sizes of receivables portfolios.

Staffing. This section of the studies shows the staffing requirements for implementing credit lines, handling credit extensions and collections, and facilitating payment application and claims and adjustments.

1. Number of credit and collection employees.
2. Number of clerks, typists, and other office workers.
3. Additional employees handling accounts receivable function.
4. Additional employees handling claims and adjustments.

Employee Performance. In this section are shown three measures that relate to employee performance.

1. Annual dollar sales per credit and collection employee.
2. Active customer accounts per credit and collection employee.
3. Annual number of invoices per credit and collection employee.

Selected Expense Ratios. Here one set of exhibits shows selected expense ratios. Greater detail is given in additional sets that reflect the extent to which payment applications and claims and adjustments are part of the credit function. The figures are expressed as dollars per $10,000 sales.

1. Salaries, other compensation, and payroll taxes.
2. Communications expense.
3. Outside information services.
4. Collection agency, credit insurance, and lawyers' fees.
5. Supplies, forms, and printing.
6. Conferences, meetings, and travel and entertainment.
7. Office services.
8. Computer charges.
9. Office machines rental.
10. Miscellaneous expenses.

Budgetary Control

In addition to straight comparisons of company criteria against those compiled by outside sources, budgetary control should be a regular procedure in every credit department. The budget is custom-fitted to the needs of the department and can be its most effective performance measure.

Figure 33–17 is a monthly administrative expense analysis which shows the budget for the current month, expenditures for the current month, and the variance of the current month to the budget. In addition to expressing the variance in dollars, the report may show the variance by percentage changes. When the actual expenditures are less than the budget, a favorable variance exists; when more, the variance is unfavorable. The procedure is repeated on a year-to-date basis.

Expense	Budget Current Month	Expenditures Current Month	Variance Current Month	Year-To-Date		
				Budget	Actual	Variance
Regular Salaries	$ 8,000	$ 8,250	$(250)	$40,000	$39,800	$200
Temporary Employees	500	450	50	2,500	2,550	(50)
Overtime	—	—	—	—	—	—
Subtotal Salaries	8,500	8,700	(200)	42,500	42,350	150
Rent	1,000	1,000	—	5,000	5,000	—
Supper Money	250	200	50	1,250	1,000	250
Printing & Postage	200	220	(20)	1,000	1,100	(100)
•	•	•	•	•	•	•
•	•	•	•	•	•	•
•	•	•	•	•	•	•
Subtotal Expenses	3,500	3,550	(50)	17,500	17,700	(200)
Total Salaries & Expenses	$12,000	$12,250	$(250)	$60,000	$60,050	$ (50)

Remarks: Since the variance is not substantial and is expected to be remedied within the next month, no change in the budget is contemplated.

FIG. 33–17. Monthly Administrative Expense Analysis.

PART VIII

HANDLING DISTRESSED DEBTORS

CHAPTER 34

OUT-OF-COURT SETTLEMENTS

The ways of handling the affairs of insolvent or financially distressed business debtors may be divided into two classes: those designed to keep the debtor in business and restore the business to profitability; and those designed to put the debtor out of business, realize the assets, and distribute the proceeds among creditors.

Creditors usually prefer to rehabilitate a distressed debtor by voluntary out-of-court settlement. When rehabilitation is not possible, however, they may liquidate assets outside of bankruptcy proceedings through a general assignment for the benefit of creditors. The credit executive, who is familiar with both of these methods, their requirements, advantages, and disadvantages, will be able to participate effectively and intelligently in whatever action is taken when a customer becomes insolvent.

SYMPTOMS OF THE DISTRESSED DEBTOR

Prompt action must be taken if a distressed debtor is to be salvaged, restored to solvency, and maintained as a customer. The astute credit executive learns to recognize symptoms of approaching business difficulties. There are several warning signs:

1. The debtor stopped discounting bills.
2. The debtor's credit payments are lagging.
3. Lawsuits are being instituted against the debtor.
4. Tax liens are being filed against the debtor.
5. The debtor constantly is shifting from one source of supply to another.
6. The debtor is in default with its lending institutions.
7. The financial condition of the company is deteriorating.

In most metropolitan centers, daily legal newspapers list new actions brought and liens filed. Credit executives may subscribe to such newspapers or instruct their counsel to check these listings daily, to ascertain whether lawsuits are being instituted or tax liens are being filed against the debtor. Reports of credit agencies and trade associations should also be consulted regularly.

A debtor with liabilities exceeding assets is deemed insolvent. One that cannot pay debts as they mature is not liquid. In business, a debtor may be insolvent or may be solvent but not liquid. Credit executives should distinguish between a business that can be salvaged and rehabilitated financially and one in which liquidation for the benefit of creditors, in or out of bankruptcy, is necessary. They should also learn to recognize the dishonest debtor that could be rehabilitated, but should instead be liquidated and prosecuted.

VOLUNTARY SETTLEMENTS

Voluntary settlements between debtors and creditors are the preferred answer to a financial problem. They are generally known as general compositions and extension agreements. Composition agreements are usually those by which the debtor pays less than is due, and an extension agreement is one by which the amount due is not paid at the due date. Usually an agreement includes both a composition and an extension, and provides for rehabilitation of the debtor and for its continuance in business. Moreover, the general composition requires agreement of approximately 90 per cent of the creditors.

Expressed in another way, a voluntary settlement is simply a contract between the debtor and creditors that settles their claims for the most the debtor can pay and the most the creditors can get. It keeps the debtor in business and avoids court costs. The creditors may take a temporary loss but expect the debtor to emerge stable and solvent, a prospective future customer.

The principal advantage of voluntary settlements is their simplicity. There are no cumbersome court proceedings. They are essentially informal, around-the-table transactions that are legally binding on the debtor with specific penalties for nonperformance. Because of this, voluntary settlements are economical. Apart from the absence of court costs, the general costs of administration are lower than for court proceedings. Dividends are therefore usually larger. This is an important consideration.

Voluntary settlements are difficult to arrange when there are secured or priority claims on the debtor. Secured claims may consist of mortgages on the debtor's real property or perfected security interests in property subject to the Uniform Commercial Code. Priority claims may consist of taxes, wages, unpaid rent, and the like entitled under federal or state law to priority of payment over unsecured claims. If there are secured and priority claims, creditors will not generally accept voluntary settlements or extensions unless they are given absolute assurance that the secured and priority claims have been adequately disposed of by the debtor. The validity of such claims should be reviewed by counsel for the creditors.

Initiation of the Voluntary Settlement

Voluntary settlements may be initiated by either the debtor or the creditors. Most frequently, a debtor that is in financial difficulty goes to an attorney for advice. The attorney may consult with a few of the largest creditors and may arrange a meeting attended by the debtor, a limited number of the largest creditors, and representatives of both sides. Such a meeting may also be called by a few of the most interested or largest creditors that have reason to be suspicious of the debtor's financial condition. In the latter case, the creditors usually work closely together through a local NACM affiliate or adjustment bureau.

Creditors' Committee

The first meeting of the creditors' committee can be a confused affair or it can be well organized; much depends on the debtor and the creditors. Occasionally a debtor will come well-prepared, accompanied by both counsel and accountant. The debtor will have current financial statements, be prepared to give the entire financial history of the business as well as the reasons for its distressed condition, and be able to answer most questions.

At the first meeting, a creditors' committee should be selected. This committee generally consists of five or seven of the largest unsecured creditors and perhaps one or two representatives of the larger body of smaller creditors. Even though the proceedings are out of court, the committee should be limited in number, with other creditors serving as alternates or ex-officio members. As a practical matter, the size of the creditor companies can have some bearing on who is selected to work on the committee. Moreover, some company names can lend prestige to the proceedings. Sometimes only the larger companies will go to the expense of sending a representative to the creditors' meetings, particularly if they are held at some distance away. The people serving on the committee must be knowledgeable in this type of work and have the time to serve and work in the best interest of all creditors. The committee should select a chairman, secretary, and counsel. The creditors should also ask that an auditor be retained to make an independent audit of the debtor's books and records at the expense of the debtor or its estate.

The chairman is often from the largest creditor, but it is more important to have a chairman who is knowledgeable. The secretary is usually a representative of a local adjustment bureau and has facilities for communicating with all creditors. Counsel is usually a lawyer experienced in this work and may be recommended by the local adjustment bureau, represent one or more of the larger creditors, or be independent of all creditors.

Creditors' Investigation

Only in rare cases will a satisfactory plan of settlement evolve at this first meeting. Frequently a debtor needs time to interest new capital, or creditors will want to know all the facts. The creditors should obtain an up-to-date inventory count and evaluation. One or more members of the creditors' committee who are experts in the type of business may evaluate the inventory, or an appraiser may be retained, again at the expense of the debtor or its estate. It is important to ascertain what the assets would realize at forced sale; this would be an indication of what the dividend might be in bankruptcy proceedings, and set the floor for a voluntary settlement.

Creditors should also compare the debtor's present and former status. In addition to seeking information about income tax payments over a period of years, they should seek reasons for the financial distress: excessive rent and overhead, exhorbitant withdrawals from the business, declining sales volume, or inadequate markup on goods. Questioning the debtor about all these matters can help determine the size of the settlement, and whether the offer is the best possible under the circumstances.

During its investigation, the creditors' committee may uncover indications of possible dishonesty. These include sudden increases in purchases without corresponding increases in sales, materially false financial statements, an unaccountable or unexplained reduction in inventory or cash, recent repayment of loans, hypothecation of assets, missing books and records, evasiveness by the debtor in answering questions or supplying information, and exhorbitant salaries or expense accounts.

In such instances, the reaction of the creditors' committee to the debtor must be unfavorable. The committee may decide that court proceedings are preferable, with opportunities for investigating fully, for denying the debtor a discharge from its obligations, and even for imposing criminal sanctions. The committee may decide to retain a fraud prevention bureau to investigate the debtor or turn the case over to the Federal Bureau of Investigation.

If, on the other hand, the committee finds that the debtor has been honest and a worthwhile customer in the past and that the business can be salvaged, they should ask the debtor to present a plan.

The Settlement Plan

Working out a settlement plan is largely a matter of bargaining. Armed with the information it has acquired, the committee is in a position to bargain for a settlement that will ensure maximum return to creditors but which will still enable the debtor to emerge solvent. If the committee encounters difficulties in persuading the debtor to accept its position, it may be useful to remind the debtor that in its present distressed condition the business belongs to the creditors. The debtor could also be informed that the alternative to this voluntary settlement is a court proceeding.

During the negotiation period, objecting creditors are free to institute suit or to levy against or attach the debtor's assets in satisfaction of their claims, landlords are likewise free to distrain, and taxing authorities are free to levy. Thus one creditor or landlord or a taxing authority may prevent the settlement from being consummated. The debtor can prevent this only by executing a statutory assignment for the benefit of creditors or by filing a petition under Chapter 11 of the Bankruptcy Reform Act. Thus the success of a voluntary settlement depends upon the full cooperation of all creditors as well as the debtor. For example, a secret preferential arrangement between the debtor and even one creditor, giving this creditor a larger settlement than others will receive, is a valid basis for any creditor to rescind the settlement for fraud.

Voluntary settlements usually take one of three forms: extension, pro rata cash settlements, or combination settlements. Which plan evolves depends in large part upon the negotiating ability of the creditors' committee. Occasionally the committee may arrive at a plan in which an extension is accepted by some of the creditors, while a pro rata cash payment is made to other creditors preferring that kind of settlement.

Extension. Under an extension plan, the debtor proposes to pay creditors in full over a period of time. It is a moratorium. The debtor continues to operate the business and buys on a cash basis temporarily. The creditors' committee acts in an advisory capacity only. Obviously an extension requires a rather optimistic prospect of future operations.

Establishing Adequate Controls. Creditors' acceptance of an extension plan is predicated on considerable faith in the debtor. Creditors should make sure that adequate controls are instituted for the operation of the business and, in the event rehabilitation is not possible, over the liquidation of assets and disposition of the proceeds. This is to provide reasonable assurance that assets are protected from improper use and to produce records from which reliable reports can be prepared. Various devices used for exercising this control are described below.

One technique assumes that the business in effect belongs to the creditors. The committee may request or insist that the debtor execute an assignment for the benefit of creditors, to be held in escrow by the committee. If the debtor defaults in performance of extension payments, the assignment becomes effective. The assignee may then liquidate the assets for the benefit of all creditors.

Another device is effective where the debtor is a corporation. In addition to the assignment, or as a substitute, the committee may have the stockholders transfer their stock certificates to the committee or to an adjustment bureau, to be held in escrow. If the extension plan is fully performed, the shares are returned. If not, the transfer becomes effective and the entire corporation becomes the property of the committee, to be liquidated for the benefit of creditors. The committee may also receive and hold in escrow the written resignation of all officers and directors of the debtor corporation. The committee will thus be in a position to assume complete ownership and control if the debtor defaults under the plan. During the extension period, the committee may designate its accountant to supervise operations or have a representative countersign all checks and control expenditures.

It is important to stress that throughout this entire process the committee serves in an advisory role only and should not assume active control of the business. The debtor continues to remain in possession.

Security. Under the extension plan, the debtor presumably will execute extension notes to the creditors, payable in installments. In addition, the committee may request or demand some form of security for payment. The form of security may be a mortgage on the debtor's real estate, which is frequently owned by the debtor and spouse; a mortgage on the inventory and fixtures, to give existing creditors priority over new ones created during the period of extension; an assignment of accounts receivable; or endorsement of the extension notes by a responsible third party acceptable to the committee. Mortgages on inventory and fixtures and the assignment of accounts receivable must be perfected under the Uniform Commercial Code (UCC).

While a security agreement taken under the UCC gives old creditors some security, the position of new trade creditors should also be given some attention. In order to obtain their cooperation, a security interest under the UCC could be given to the creditors with the old debt; and they in turn could subordinate that debt to the new trade creditors to give them a priority and thus encourage shipments to the debtor.

This type of arrangement has to be fully documented and comply with the UCC with respect to the lien and the subordination. It is widely used in rehabilitation cases and does give a good measure of flexibility in workout problems.

Composition Agreement. With this type of pro rata settlement, the debtor proposes to settle with creditors for less than the full amounts owed. This is the quickest of all voluntary settlements. The debtor pays in cash to its creditors a uniform percentage of its obligations to be accepted in full settlement. The percentage depends upon what the debtor's assets are, what the debtor is able to pay, and what the creditors are able to procure in the bargaining proceedings. Possibly, also, the debtor may obtain third party funding in loans or equity capital to make a settlement with creditors.

The most important criterion in determining the rate of settlement is what the dividend would be in bankruptcy proceedings. A pro rata voluntary settlement should provide at least a slightly larger dividend than would result from bankruptcy proceedings. Other advantages are that the costs of administration are less and the debtor avoids the stigma of bankruptcy.

On the other hand, bargaining for a pro rata cash settlement is sometimes difficult. Some creditors will, as a matter of policy, accept extensions of time but not pro rata cash settlements. If they cannot be persuaded to accept the pro rata cash settlement, it may be necessary to proceed to liquidate under Chapter 7 of the Bankruptcy Reform Act, and creditors may realize a smaller percentage of their claims.

Creditors with small claims frequently hold out for payment in full. It is often advisable to provide that creditors with claims of $100 or less, or some other specified small amount, shall be paid in full, to reduce the number of creditors and eliminate the nuisance value of those claims. Further, it may be wise to provide that creditors agreeing to reduce their claims to the specified amount will receive 100 per cent of their claims. Thus, if a plan provided for payment in full to creditors with claims of $100 or less and payment of 25 per cent to larger creditors, a creditor with a claim of $104 would receive only $26; but if the claim were reduced to $100, it would be paid in full. This approach eliminates another source of difficulty in getting creditor agreement to a voluntary settlement.

Combination Settlement. The usual settlement calls for a pro rata cash payment combined with an extension of time. For example, the settlement may provide a cash payment of 20 per cent and three future installments of 5 per cent each, or a total of 35 per cent in full settlement. The installment payments, usually evidenced by notes, may be payable at 3-, 6-, 9-, or 12-month intervals. The disbursements are usually made by an adjustment bureau rather than by the debtor company. Since this method involves a time settlement, control over the debtor's business and security for creditors during the extension period should be carefully provided.

Administration Costs

Over and above the settlement amount to creditors, the plan must provide for payment of all administration costs. These include any expenses incurred by the committee, such as cost of counsel and auditor, court costs, and out-of-pocket expenses of committee members. The costs of administration for voluntary settlements are usually modest.

Execution of the Settlement

When the committee has approved a plan, it should, with the aid of counsel, prepare a letter to all creditors explaining what has happened and recommending that creditors accept the settlement plan. A form of acceptance should accompany the letter for signature by creditors and return to the committee. If the transaction is complicated, the letter should include a form of agreement drafted by the committee's counsel.

Funds necessary for immediate payment to creditors are usually deposited by the debtor with the secretary of the creditors' committee. The secretary may also hold the outstanding notes on behalf of creditors.

ASSIGNMENT FOR THE BENEFIT OF CREDITORS

While creditors' efforts are ordinarily directed toward rehabilitating the distressed debtor, some debtors are so hopelessly insolvent and lacking in prospects that they cannot be rehabilitated. In those cases, the debtor may be asked to execute a general assignment for the benefit of creditors, a liquidation technique by which the debtor goes out of business. Though assignments are less frequently utilized now than in the past, the credit executive should be familiar with them. There are two types of assignments: common law assignment and statutory assignment.

Common Law Assignment

The common law assignment is a device whereby a debtor transfers title to all assets to a third party, designated as assignee or trustee, with instructions to liquidate the assets and distribute the proceeds among creditors on a pro rata basis. The assignment may be made by a debtor without prior consultation with the creditors, or it may be executed after meetings with creditors or a creditors' committee when it becomes obvious that a voluntary settlement cannot be made. In the latter instance, an adjustment bureau if frequently appointed assignee.

Sale of Assets. The assignee proceeds to liquidate the assets, most frequently by public sale through a recognized auctioneer with adequate advertising to ensure competitive bidding. In rare instances, the assignee may sell at a private sale when a better price can be gotten that way. The assignee also takes steps to collect or sell accounts receivable.

Distribution. After deducting administration costs, the assignee distributes the proceeds from the sale of assets pro rata among all unsecured creditors. Because a common law assignment is not under the supervision or control of a court, administration costs are low; dividends to creditors may be correspondingly higher than in proceedings under court control.

No creditor is obliged to accept a pro rata settlement. The creditor may refuse it and claim in full. As a practical matter, however, creditors usually accept, since the dividends are apt to be larger than those obtainable in bankruptcy, and their old claim may have little or no value unless the debtor subsequently acquires new assets.

Discharge. In a common law assignment, the debtor does not receive a discharge from obligations. The debtor merely has its assets sold and the proceeds distributed among creditors. If, for example, the pro rata distribution is 35 per cent, creditors retain their claims against the debtor for the balance of 65 per cent. The principal users of this device are corporations that are going out of business; a claim for the balance is immaterial since the corporation will be dissolved. Individual debtors seeking discharge from their obligations will couple the assignment with a proposal for settlement in full.

The credit executive should also bear in mind that if dividend checks issued under a common law assignment are not accompanied by an agreement for discharge, no discharge is granted. The creditors may therefore cash the checks and receive their dividends without agreeing to discharge the debtor. Claims for the balance are retained. The creditor must read the wording on the check to determine whether it can be cashed only by creditors accepting it in full settlement.

The common law assignment, with or without provision for settlement in full, generally offers a greater dividend to creditors than does a filing under the Bankruptcy Reform Act. This is its principal advantage to creditors.

Statutory Assignment

Most states regulate assignment for the benefit of creditors. Some statutes are simple; others provide machinery for administration as complicated as that found in the Bankruptcy Reform Act. In some, a common law assignment may be completely invalid. In others, a debtor may execute either a common law or a statutory assignment. While assignment statutes vary greatly from state to state, the following generalizations may be helpful:

1. If the state statute on assignments provides for involuntary petitions against the debtor and for compulsory discharge from obligations, it is considered by the courts as a bankruptcy law and is superseded by provisions of the Bankruptcy Reform Act.

2. If the state statute provides merely that the debtor upon executing an assignment may offer the dividends in full settlement with an option to the creditors to accept or reject (thereby retaining their claims in full), the statute remains in force.

A statutory assignment accomplishes much the same results as a common law assignment but requires more formalities. The debtor executes an instrument of assignment, which is recorded, thus giving notice to all third parties. The court appoints an assignee and supervises the proceedings, including sale of the assets and distribution of the proceeds. The debtor does not receive a discharge from remaining obligations. If a dividend check is not accompanied by a statement or endorsement indicating that payment is made in full settlement, creditors retain their claims for the balance. In order for a debtor to get a discharge under an assignment for the benefit of creditors, it must be a voluntary discharge agreed to by the creditors so as not to conflict with the federal supremacy of bankruptcy. For example, in New York under its assignment for the benefit of creditors statute, a discharge can be granted if two-thirds of the creditors agree to grant the debtor a discharge.

By placing the assignment under control of a court, the state statute often provides a means to examine the debtor's affairs. Creditors can uncover facts to guide them in determining whether to accept or reject the debtor's proposal. However, since statutory assignment involves extensive court proceedings, it is apt to be as expensive as bankruptcy without clear-cut discharge provisions or the same opportunity to uncover voidable transactions of the debtor.

EVALUATING SETTLEMENT OFFERS

The voluntary settlement of accounts receivable is an everyday problem for the credit executive. As noted earlier, the debtor sometimes offers immediate proportionate payment and asks the creditor to forgive the balance. Other times, the debtor may propose a series of partial payments that over a stated period constitute what is generally considered 100 cents on the dollar.

Traditionally, these offers are made and considered with little attention given to the time value of funds involved. Thus 100 per cent settlement over two years, or even over five years, is usually deemed full recovery of a claim. Furthermore, in tax accounting, writeoffs and recoveries are always depicted at face value, regardless of when they are made. In order to choose effectively, the credit executive should be familiar with certain finance concepts.

The analysis departs from the traditional view in that it takes into account the time value of funds under consideration, and treats final losses and recoveries from the viewpoint of managerial accounting and decision-making. It examines a typical situation in which a creditor, or group of creditors, is offered a number of repayment alternatives by the debtor. Each offer is probed to learn its tax implications to the creditor and its present value. Finally, the overall proceeds of each offer are calculated and compared, so the creditor may have a basis for deciding which provides the greatest financial yield.

To establish the analysis, it is assumed that a creditor has been approached by a debtor in financial difficulty, wanting to make an out-of-court settlement on a claim of $100,000 that is now owing and past due. The regular series of collection efforts has been exhausted, and it does not appear likely that the debtor can pay all of the outstanding debt at this time. However, the creditor is satisfied that the customer proposing the settlement is an honest debtor. The analysis then seeks the choice which yields the greatest financial recovery to the creditor.

One-Time Partial Payment

The simplest offer would be for the debtor to pay a percentage of the outstanding debt and have the creditor agree to forgive the rest. For instance, the agreement may be for 20 per cent payment and the balance to be written off.

The creditor would receive 20 per cent of the total receivable, or $20,000. At the same time, $80,000 would be charged as a bad debt. When the tax implications of this offer are considered, however, the creditor benefits more than the $20,000 settlement would indicate. Assuming that the creditor pays income taxes at the 50 per cent rate, the creditor is able to recover half of the bad-debt writeoff in the form of lower income taxes to pay. Thus the total funds recovered by accepting the 20 per cent settlement offer are shown as follows:

20 Per Cent Settlement		$20,000
Writeoff	$80,000	
Tax Reduction @ 50 Per Cent		40,000
Total Funds Recovered		$60,000

Figure 34–1 shows total funds recovered under different one-time settlement percentages:

Settlement Per Cent	Writeoff	Tax Reduction	Total Funds Recovered
10	$90,000	$45,000	$55,000
20	80,000	40,000	60,000
30	70,000	35,000	65,000
40	60,000	30,000	70,000
50	50,000	25,000	75,000

FIG. 34–1.   Recoveries Under One-Time Settlement Percentages.

Present Value of Serial Payments

In the previous example, all of the actions take place in the immediate present. Consequently, there is no need to consider the time value or the present value (PV) of funds when deciding whether to accept or decline the debtor's offer.

When, however, a schedule of serial payments is offered, a new set of variables must be considered. Since a dollar collected today is worth more than a dollar collected some time in the future, the creditor should consider more than just the face amount of any extended offer. Instead, the offer should be regarded as a stream of future payments to be discounted back to the immediate present. The full offer would then be equal to the sum of the present values of all the payments.

In the examples that follow, the factor used for discounting future payments is the equivalent of 15 per cent per annum—the assumed cost of capital of the creditor firm. Most financial textbooks and reference sources contain tables useful for such discounting. The time periods in these tables are given in years, while those in the examples that follow will be given in half-years. To determine the mid-year equivalents of the discount factor, the mid-point values can be interpolated. Thus for 6 months, at 15 per cent per annum, the factor would be $(1,000 + .870) \div 2 = .935$; for 18 months it would be $(.870 + .756) \div 2 = .813$; and so on.

With these calculations it is possible to construct the table shown in Figure 34–2. There the left column shows the number of the payment; the second column, the number of 6-month periods elapsed since the first payment; and the right column, the discount factor, calculated for 6-month periods at the equivalent of 15 per cent per annum.

Payment No.	Periods Elapsed	Discount Factor
1	0	1,000
2	1	.935
3	2	.870
4	3	.813
5	4	.756
6	5	.707
7	6	.658
8	7	.615
9	8	.572
10	9	.535

FIG. 34–2.   Discounting Half-Year Future Payments at 15 Per Cent.

Two-Year Payout.   When the debtor offers five equal semiannual payments of $20,000 each, the first to be made immediately, the creditor can determine the potential total recovery at each time period by setting up a table similar to that shown in Figure 34–3.

On the left are shown the individual payments made under this schedule. Next the dollar amount of each payment is shown: first at face amount, then after application of the PV factors for each period at present value. Total collected is tabulated next, first at face and then at present value; the PV amount for each period is a simple sum of previous PV amounts ($20,000 + $18,700 + . . . + $15,120). These figures allow the creditor to estimate the present value of the total collected after any particular payment has been made. Thus after one payment the PV of the total collected would be $20,000. After 6 months, when the second payment is made, the PV of the total collected would be $38,700. Finally, after all five payments, the total collected would have a present value of $87,480, or 87.5 per cent of the face amount. The difference between that figure and the present value of the original debt would have been eaten up by the passage of time.

The right half of Figure 34–3 is useful in another way. It shows additional information for "what if" alternative evaluations—specifically, what if after the plan has been approved the debtor makes some payments and defaults on the rest. Present value factors are applied against potential tax reductions at each payment stage, so the creditor may estimate potential recovery if the debtor were to discontinue paying at any time. The number

No. Payments Made	Payment			Total Collected		Default Payment No.	Potential Writeoff	Tax Reduction			PV Total Funds Recovered
	Face Amount	PV Factor	PV Amount	Face Amount	PV Amount			Face Amount	PV Factor	PV Amount	
1	20,000	1.000	20,000	20,000	20,000	2	80,000	40,000	.935	37,400	57,400
2	20,000	.935	18,700	40,000	38,700	3	60,000	30,000	.870	26,100	64,800
3	20,000	.870	17,400	60,000	56,100	4	40,000	20,000	.813	16,260	72,360
4	20,000	.813	16,260	80,000	72,360	5	20,000	10,000	.756	7,560	79,920
5	20,000	.756	15,120	100,000	87,480	—	0	0	—	—	87,480

FIG. 34–3. Recoveries Under Two-Year Payout.

of the defaulted payment is shown, then the potential writeoff at that particular time. Tax reduction is shown next: first at face amount, then after application of the appropriate PV factor at present value. The last column shows the present value of total funds recovered at any period, by adding the PV amounts for the total collected and the tax reduction.

Suppose, for example, that after the plan had been accepted, the debtor made only one payment and then defaulted on the second. The creditor could write off the balance as a bad debt and gain the tax reduction of $40,000. That would be a future writeoff, however, and to bring it back to the present, it is necessary to multiply it by .935, the PV factor applicable to that period. Thus the present value of the tax reduction is $37,400. Added to the funds of the first payment of $20,000, it gives a present value of $57,400 for total funds recovered.

Similarly, if the debtor made the first two payments without incident and then defaulted when the third was due, the creditor would have a potential writeoff of $60,000, for a tax reduction of $30,000 at face amount. The PV factor applicable to that period is .870. Thus the present value of the tax reduction would be $26,100. Meanwhile, the creditor would have collected two installments, having a total present value of $38,700. Here the PV of total funds recovered would be $38,700 + $26,100 = $64,800.

With each payment the present value of the total collected would increase, while the PV of potential writeoff and tax reduction would decrease. Finally, with the fifth payment the face amount of the debt would be discharged and the potential writeoff would become zero. Total funds recovered would reach $87,480, the highest possible figure under this plan taking into account the time value of funds.

Ten Equal Payments.   When the debtor's plan offers a longer term for full repayment of the debt, the creditor can proceed, as before, to construct a table of present values for the particular schedule. Figure 34–4, for example, shows a plan for ten equal semiannual payments, to begin at once.

In this case, the maximum present value recovery is 74.6 per cent. It is evident that the ten-payment plan yields roughly the same present value as does a 50 per cent one-time payment. Further, if the debtor cannot meet all payments, the one-time plan yields a higher total recovery.

Increasing Payments.   For this final illustration, it is assumed that the debtor's plan offers smaller payments in the beginning, then increases the amount of later payments so that 100 per cent is paid at the end of the four and one-half years. The creditor's table would look like Figure 34–5.

This type of 100 per cent repayment plan provides the greatest relief to the debtor. At the same time it is the most expensive for the creditor, as maximum present value recovery is only 69.4 per cent. It takes four payments before the creditor's recovery equals what it would be for an immediate total writeoff, and the total funds recovered at any stage are less than they would be under a plan that calls for an equivalent number of equal payments.

No. Payments Made	Payment			Total Collected		Default Payment No.	Potential Writeoff	Tax Reduction			PV Total Funds Recovered
	Face Amount	PV Factor	PV Amount	Face Amount	PV Amount			Face Amount	PV Factor	PV Amount	
1	10,000	1.000	10,000	10,000	10,000	2	90,000	45,000	.935	42,075	52,075
2	10,000	.935	9,350	20,000	19,350	3	80,000	40,000	.870	34,800	54,150
3	10,000	.870	8,700	30,000	28,050	4	70,000	35,000	.813	28,455	56,505
4	10,000	.813	8,130	40,000	36,180	5	60,000	30,000	.756	22,680	58,860
5	10,000	.756	7,560	50,000	43,740	6	50,000	25,000	.707	17,675	61,415
6	10,000	.707	7,070	60,000	50,810	7	40,000	20,000	.658	13,160	63,970
7	10,000	.658	6,580	70,000	57,390	8	30,000	15,000	.615	9,225	66,615
8	10,000	.615	6,150	80,000	63,540	9	20,000	10,000	.572	5,720	69,260
9	10,000	.572	5,720	90,000	69,260	10	10,000	5,000	.535	2,675	71,935
10	10,000	.535	5,350	100,000	74,610	—	0	0	—	—	74,610

FIG. 34–4. Recoveries Under Ten Equal Semiannual Payments.

No. Payments Made	Payment			Total Collected		Default Payment No.	Potential Writeoff	Tax Reduction			PV Total Funds Recovered
	Face Amount	PV Factor	PV Amount	Face Amount	PV Amount			Face Amount	PV Factor	PV Amount	
1	5,000	1.000	5,000	5,000	5,000	2	95,000	47,500	.935	44,413	49,413
2	5,000	.935	4,675	10,000	9,675	3	90,000	45,000	.870	39,150	48,825
3	7,500	.870	6,525	17,500	16,200	4	82,500	41,250	.813	33,536	49,736
4	7,500	.813	6,098	25,000	22,298	5	75,000	37,500	.756	28,350	50,648
5	10,000	.756	7,560	35,000	29,858	6	65,000	32,500	.707	22,978	52,836
6	10,000	.707	7,070	45,000	36,928	7	55,000	27,500	.658	18,095	55,023
7	12,500	.658	8,225	57,500	45,153	8	42,500	21,250	.615	13,069	58,222
8	12,500	.615	7,688	70,000	52,841	9	30,000	15,000	.572	8,580	61,421
9	15,000	.572	8,580	85,000	61,421	10	15,000	7,500	.535	4,013	65,434
10	15,000	.535	8,025	100,000	69,446	—	0	0	—	—	69,446

FIG. 34-5.   Recoveries Under Increasing Payments.

Overall Evaluation

The conclusions reached here are based purely on an application of present value concepts to repayment schedules offered to a creditor. They seek to identify the financial implications of alternative plans. They do not take into account nonfinancial factors, such as the desire to rehabilitate a particular customer or the need to make a vital penetration into a desirable market area. The consideration of nonfinancial factors may outweigh the potential financial recovery in any given instance. Even then, however, the creditor should develop the tables shown here so as to clarify the tradeoffs being considered.

The illustrations point to a general finding that creditors benefit most, or lose least, when a settlement plan calls for large payments made soon after the plan begins. Stretched out repayment schedules cause large losses in the present value of total recovery, even if the debtor adheres to the schedule. Schedules that provide for small early payments and large payments made later in the plan also erode the present value of total funds recovered. The worst possible plan from the creditor's point of view is one that provides for a long period of repayment and also proposes installments that are small in the beginning and increase as time goes on.

As a side comment, it is noted that potential losses in the present value of total funds recovered are directly related to the cost of capital of the creditor firm: they are lowest when cost of capital is low, and increase directly as the cost of capital increases. Furthermore, if the cost of capital tended to rise while a plan was in effect, the creditor would doubtless realize a lower maximum present value recovery than had been projected by the earlier calculations.

CHAPTER 35

BANKRUPTCY CODE PROCEEDINGS

The Bankruptcy Act of 1898 and its amendments governed financial embarrassments during most of the 20th century. In 1938, the Chandler Act amendment provided for Chapter XI and other reorganization proceedings for distressed debtors. The adoption of the Uniform Commercial Code (UCC) and the growing importance of consumer credit pointed to a need for reform which led to the enactment by Congress of the Bankruptcy Reform Act of 1978. This was a complete revision of the bankruptcy system and was signed into law November 6, 1978. In general, the substantive law under Title I took effect on October 1, 1979. The pilot program of U.S. trustees and various powers entrusted to the court became effective October 1, 1979; other features relating to the judiciary and the courts, not until April 1, 1984.

GENERAL PROVISIONS, ADMINISTRATION, AND THE ESTATE

The first three chapters of the Bankruptcy Code contain general provisions; administration of a case; and treatment of creditors and their claims, debtor's duties and benefits, and the estate. Except where noted, the provisions are applicable to all cases regarding liquidation (Chapter 7), reorganization (Chapter 11), and adjustment of debts of an individual with regular income (Chapter 13).

Commencement of a Case

A case may be commenced as a voluntary case by the debtor, as a joint case by a debtor and his or her spouse, and as an involuntary petition brought about by creditors.

Voluntary Petition. A voluntary case commences when a debtor files a petition with the bankruptcy court and results in the automatic entry of an order for relief, formerly an adjudication in bankruptcy.

Joint Petition. A joint case commences when a single petition is filed by an individual debtor and his or her spouse. This constitutes an order for relief. The court then determines the extent, if any, to which the debtors' estates are to be consolidated.

Involuntary Petition. An involuntary petition may be filed only against debtors actively engaged in business. They may be proprietorships, partnerships, or corporations; excluded are farmers and not-for-profit businesses.

The action may be commenced by three or more creditors provided their claims aggregate at least $5,000. If a claim is secured by a lien, the value in excess of the lien is used to arrive at the $5,000 aggregate claim. If there are fewer than 12 creditors, one or more holders with aggregate claims of at least $5,000 may commence the action. Where a petition has been filed but before the case is dismissed or relief is ordered, a creditor holding an unsecured claim may join in the petition as if it were one of the petitioning creditors.

After a notice and hearing, the court may require the petitioners to file a bond to indemnify the debtor for any costs and property damages should the court dismiss the petition other than on consent of all petitioners and the debtor.

It is no longer necessary for petitioners to establish that the debtor has committed an act of bankruptcy. Any three creditors may allege that the debtor is unable to pay debts as they become due. However, it is not automatic that an involuntary petition for liquidation or reorganization will be granted by the court. It will conduct a hearing and may dismiss the petition if it is in the best interests of the parties. Unless the court orders otherwise and until the order of relief, a debtor may remain in possession of the business and continue to operate it; and may use, acquire, or dispose of property as if an involuntary case had not been commenced.

At any time after the commencement of an involuntary case under Chapter 7 but before an order for relief, the court may appoint an interim trustee to take possession of a debtor's business and operate it. However, the debtor may regain possession of the business after filing a bond that the court may require.

Officers

The Bankruptcy Reform Act of 1978 created the office of United States trustee to administer the Bankruptcy Act, assisted by a panel of private trustees and an examiner.

United States Trustee. On a five-year pilot program, U. S. trustees have been appointed in 10 districts by the Attorney General. Each trustee is appointed for a term of seven years but continues to perform the duties of trustee until a successor is appointed. The Attorney General may appoint one or more assistant U.S. trustees in any district when the public interest so requires.

The U.S. trustee's primary function is to create and maintain the panel of private trustees eligible to serve in Chapter 7 cases. In addition, under the Bankruptcy Code the U.S. trustee must serve as trustee and perform the duties of trustee when required and supervise the administration of cases and elected trustees.

Examiner. If a trustee is not appointed in a Chapter 11 case, the court must appoint an examiner upon request of a party in interest and after notice and hearing if such appointment is in the interest of creditors.

An examiner must also be appointed upon the request of a party at interest and after notice and hearing in those cases where the debtor's debts, other than debts for goods and services or taxes or owing to an insider, exceed $5,000,000.

The examiner's role is to investigate the conduct and financial condition of the debtor and report to the court.

Administration Powers

The U.S. trustee has broad administration powers in reorganization or liquidation proceedings, particularly with respect to the use, sale, or lease of property; the obtaining of credit; and the treatment of executory contracts.

The filing of a petition acts as an automatic stay against litigation and creditor action with certain exceptions. Some of the actions that are stayed include existing actions or those that could have been commenced, such as judicial proceedings; attempts to obtain possession of the estate's property; lien actions against the property; tax proceedings before the U.S. Tax Court; and any claim against the debtor that arose before the commencement of the case.

Actions that are not stayed include criminal actions or proceedings against the debtor; alimony, maintenance, or support from property that is not part of the estate; enforcement of policies and regulatory powers of governmental agencies; foreclosure proceedings by the Housing and Urban Development of insured mortgages; and tax deficiencies.

An important aspect of the Bankruptcy Code is the concept of adequate protection. This is designed to protect creditors from any decrease in the value of their security interest in the property. It requires that a stay be vacated if adequate protection cannot be afforded to the objecting party. This protection may be provided by requiring the trustee to make periodic cash payments, give additional or replacement security, or grant other relief (except an administrative priority) that will give the objecting party a value equivalent to its interest in the property.

Except where relief is granted by the court, the stay of an act against property of the estate continues until the property is no longer part of the estate. Moreover, the stay of any other act continues until the case is closed or dismissed; or if it concerns an individual under Chapter 7 or a case under Chapter 11, until a discharge is granted or denied.

Use, Sale, or Lease of Property.   This section of the Bankruptcy Code controls when property of the estate may be used, sold, or leased notwithstanding the claims of secured creditors.

In other than the ordinary course of business, the trustee may use, sell, or lease property or collateral of the estate only after a notice and hearing. In the ordinary course of business, the trustee may use, sell, or lease property without notice and hearing. However, these actions are subject to restrictions where cash collateral is involved, such as cash, negotiable instruments, documents of title, securities, deposits, or other cash equivalents. The trustee may not use, sell, or lease such collateral unless consent is obtained from each creditor having an interest in the cash collateral or the court authorizes the use, sale, or lease.

The court is required to prohibit or condition the use, sale, or lease of property as is necessary to provide adequate protection to a creditor having an interest in the property. In any hearing brought by an objecting creditor before the court, the trustee has the burden of proof on the issue of adequate protection.

Obtaining Credit.   In the ordinary course of operating a business, the trustee may obtain unsecured credit or incur unsecured debt for allowable administrative expenses such as costs and expenses of preserving the estate, taxes, and fines and penalties.

If unable to obtain unsecured credit, the trustee may be authorized after notice and hearing to obtain credit or incur debt that has a priority over administration expenses, is secured by a lien on property not otherwise subject to lien, or is secured by a junior lien on property that is subject to a lien. Moreover, the trustee may also be authorized to obtain credit or incur debt secured by a senior or equal lien on property providing there is adequate protection afforded the existing secured creditors.

The Bankruptcy Code does not address itself to the perfecting requirements on secured transactions under the UCC. While the exclusive jurisdiction of the court over property of the estate should prevent the need for such filing, a creditor should handle a secured transaction as though a bankruptcy proceeding has not been filed.

Executory Contracts.   An executory contract is one in which both parties have something remaining to be done under a contract in order to fulfill all of its terms and conditions. An unexpired lease is also an executory contract in that both parties have rights and obligations under the terms of the unexpired lease.

A trustee has the power to either assume or reject any executory contract or unexpired lease. If there has been a prior default under an executory contract or unexpired lease, the trustee must cure the default or provide adequate assurance that the default will be promptly cured; the trustee will also be required to provide adequate assurance of future performance. In addition, the trustee must compensate or provide adequate assurance of compensation to any party to the contract or lease for the compensation of any actual pecuniary loss to such party resulting from the debtor's prior default.

In a liquidation case under Chapter 7, if the trustee does not assume or reject the executory contract or unexpired lease within 60 days after the order for relief, then the contract or lease is deemed to have been rejected by the trustee. Any lease that automatically terminates a lease upon the bankruptcy of the tenant is invalid.

Creditors and Claims

The Bankruptcy Code permits the broadest possible array of claims to participate in reorganization or liquidation proceedings.

Filing Proof of Claims. A proof of claim is a statement that a claim is justly due and owing. It shows the amount of the claim, the consideration therefore (e.g. for merchandise sold), and what payments have been made. It must be in writing and signed by the creditor or his authorized agent, but it need not be under oath.

A proof of claim is filed by a creditor or indentured trustee. In the event that the creditor does not file a proof of claim, then the debtor or the trustee may file one. In fact, anyone who is liable with the debtor to such unfiled creditor may file a proof of claim. The time of filing proofs of claims is set by the bankruptcy court rules; it is generally six months.

A proof of claim is deemed filed under Chapter 11 proceedings when the debtor furnishes a list of creditors to the court. This is a duty of the debtor; but if the debtor has not done so, it then becomes the duty of the trustee. The filing of a proof of claim is not required if a creditor's claim is properly listed by the debtor. In addition, a proof of claim need not be filed in a no-asset case. As a matter of practice, however, creditors should not rely upon the debtor's list but should file appropriate proofs of claim.

Allowance of Claims. A creditor's proof of claim is allowed unless an objection is filed. The claim, even though once allowed, may be reconsidered for cause and reallowed or disallowed based upon the merits of the case at any time before the case is closed.

Grounds for disallowance are spelled out in the Bankruptcy Code. They include claims that are unenforceable under any agreement or under applicable law for a reason other than the claim is contingent or unmatured, claims that are for unmatured interest, claims that offset a mutual debt owing by such creditor to the debtor, claims for tax assessments that exceed the value of the interest of the estate in the property, claims for services of an insider or attorney of the debtor that exceed reasonable value for services, and claims by a lessor for damages resulting from the termination of a lease of real property.

Determination of Secured Status. The proof of a secured claim sets forth the existence and the amount of the security. If the property value is less than the creditor's lien, the claim is secured to the value of the property and the balance of the claim is unsecured.

The same principle applies to claims subject to setoff. This is the right of a creditor to offset a mutual debt owing by such creditor to the debtor that arose before the filing of the petition. The amount subject to setoff is secured to the extent of the creditor's claim subject to offset, and is unsecured to the extent that the amount subject to setoff is less than the amount of the allowed claim.

Priorities. Certain claims have priority over unsecured claims. They are ranked in the following order:

1. Administrative expenses, such as the necessary costs and expenses of preserving the estate, including reasonable compensation for the trustee and professional persons, and other necessary expenditures.

2. Unsecured claims arising in the ordinary course of business after the filing of an involuntary petition but before the appointment of a trustee.

3. Wage, salary, and compensation claims earned within 90 days but not to exceed $2,000 for each individual.

4. Claims for contributions to employee benefit plans within 180 days before the filing of the petition or the date of the cessation of the debtor's business, whichever occurs first; for each plan, this is limited by an arithmetical computation set forth in the Bankruptcy Code.

5. Claims by individuals, not to exceed $900, arising from deposits of money in connection with property or services for personal, family, and household use; this priority is available only to consumers.

6. Claims of governmental units for taxes, including income or gross receipts, property assessments, employment, excise, and customs.

Debtor's Duties and Benefits

The Bankruptcy Code imposes certain duties on the debtor seeking its benefits. It is essential that the debtor be honest in negotiations with the court and creditors, thus avoiding the expenditure of needless time, effort, and money.

Debtor's Duties. There are four statutory duties of the debtor:

1. File a list of creditors, a schedule of assets and liabilities, and a statement of affairs.

2. Cooperate with the trustee, if one is serving, so the trustee may perform the required duties.

3. Surrender all property, books, and records to the trustee, if one is serving.

4. Appear at the discharge hearing.

Exemptions. The Bankruptcy Code outlines specific exemptions for property of the debtor. Moreover, it gives the debtor some avoiding powers over liens and involuntary transfers of exempt property.

An individual debtor may choose between two alternatives: the exemptions granted in the Bankruptcy Code; or the exemptions provided for under state laws. A state, however, may by statutory enactment determine that the federal exemption shall not apply, and that only the state law shall govern.

The debtor must file a list of the property claimed to be exempt. A dependent may file the list if the debtor does not. A creditor may object to the claim of exemption; if successful, a complete appraisal of all the debtor's property is normally required.

There are basically two types of exemptions: those for specific property of the kind needed for an ordinary life in modern society, and those of a dollar amount with few, if any, strings attached. The former applies to specific property that is exempt regardless of value and that which is exempt to a limited value or to the extent reasonably necessary for support of the debtor and dependents. The latter applies to the debtor's aggregate interest not to exceed $400 in value in any property specified under the Bankruptcy Code, plus any unused amount of homestead exemption.

The first type of exemption also needs further explanation. These exemptions are either unlimited or limited in value. Unlimited exemptions include virtually all conceivable public and governmental benefits, such as Social Security benefits, unemployment compensation, public assistance, veteran's benefits, alimony and support payments, as well as stock bonuses, pensions, profit sharing, and annuities. Other exemptions are limited in value. For example, the exemption of a debtor's interest in residential property cannot exceed $7,500, exemption in one motor vehicle cannot exceed $1,200, exemption in any particular household item cannot exceed $200, and exemption in professional books and tools of the trade cannot exceed $750.

A life insurance policy owned by the debtor under which the insured is the debtor or a person whom the debtor is a dependent enjoys two exemptions: the policy itself is exempt, and any loan value of the policy is exempt up to $4,000. A life insurance contract is only exempt to the extent reasonably necessary for the support of the debtor and any dependents of the debtor.

Avoiding Powers. To the extent that a lien impairs an exemption to which the debtor would have been entitled, the Bankruptcy Code grants a debtor the right to avoid credit judicial liens and certain nonpossessory, nonpurchase money security interests in household furnishings, goods, wearing apparel, appliances, jewelry, and the like that are held primarily for personal, family, or household use; professional books or tools of the trade of the debtor; or professionally prescribed health aides for the debtor or his dependents. The debtor may also exempt property that a trustee recovers under certain sections of the Bankruptcy Code to the extent that the debtor could have exempted such property if it had not been transferred under specified conditions.

Debts Not Affected by Discharge. In liquidation and reorganization cases, the Bankruptcy Code does not discharge the following debts:

1. Certain taxes levied by the United States, any state, or any political subdivision as specifically defined in the Bankruptcy Code.

2. Money, property, or services obtained under false pretenses, fraud, or the use of a false financial statement which was relied on.

3. Unscheduled claims unless the creditor has notice or actual knowledge of bankruptcy in time to file or claim.

4. Liabilities created by fraud, defalcation while acting in a fiduciary capacity, and for embezzlement or larceny.

5. Support obligations to a spouse, former spouse, or child of the debtor for alimony to, maintenance for, or support of both spouse or child in connection with a separation agreement, divorce decree, or property settlement agreement.

6. Willful and malicious injury by the debtor to another entity or to the property of another entity.

7. Governmental fines, penalties, and forfeitures to the extent that they do not represent compensation for actual pecuniary loss.

8. Student loans if owed to a governmental unit or a nonprofit institution of higher learning, unless such loan first became due more than five years before the filing of the petition or if excepting such debt from discharge will impose undue hardship on the debtor.

In cases involving the adjustment of debts of an individual, the exceptions to discharge are more limited in scope. A debtor who completes payments under the plan will be discharged from *all* debts provided for by the plan or disallowed by the court, except those to be paid after the plan has been consummated or for obligations of support. On the other hand, a debtor who does not complete the payments under the plan will be discharged from all *unsecured* debts provided for by the plan or disallowed by the court, except those to be paid after the plan has been consummated or for obligations of support.

Benefits of Discharge. In addition to the intermediate benefits afforded the debtor by statute, the actual discharge voids any judgment on discharged debts and enjoins any future action to enforce personal liability of such debt or upon the property of the debtor, including community property.

Reaffirmation agreements (an agreement to revalidate a claim which is based upon a debt that is dischargeable under the Bankruptcy Code) are unenforceable in most instances. To be enforceable, the agreement must be made after bankruptcy but before discharge. In addition, the debtor must appear at a hearing, be advised of his rights, and be told of the consequences of reaffirmation. A creditor's request for reaffirmation may violate the provision of the Bankruptcy Code that operates as an automatic stay of litigation and creditor action. Moreover, court approval is required for reaffirmation of consumer debts and the Bankruptcy Code sets forth the requirements which must be met before the court will grant such approval.

The Estate

The property of the estate is very broadly defined and includes, wherever located, tangible and intangible property, rights of action, and essentially all of the types of property not held to be exempt. It includes:

1. All legal or equitable interests of the debtor in property as of the commencement of the case.

2. All interests of the debtor and the debtor's spouse in community property as of the commencement of the case.

3. Any interest that the trustee recovers through a turnover of property by a custodian, recovery from avoided transfer, or recovery from general partners in partnership.

4. Any interest in property preserved for the benefit of or ordered transferred to the estate.

5. Property that the debtor acquires within 180 days after filing by bequest, devise, or inheritance; as a result of a property settlement with debtor's spouse or of interlocutory or final divorce decree; or as beneficiary of a life insurance policy.

6. Interest of the debtor in property becomes property of the estate, notwithstanding any provision that restricts or conditions transfer of such interest by the debtor, or that is conditioned on the insolvency of the debtor on the commencement of a case or on the appointment of or taking possession by a trustee or a custodian; and effects or gives an option to effect a forfeiture, modification, or termination of a debtor's interest.

7. Rights of the debtor to legal title even with no equitable interest such as a mortgage secured by real property.

8. Benefits or defenses available to a debtor as against other entities.

The property of the estate does not include any power that the debtor may exercise solely for the benefit of an entity other than the debtor. There is also a restriction on the transfer to the estate of a beneficial interest of a debtor in a trust that is enforceable under applicable nonbankruptcy law.

Turnover of Property to the Estate. Any entity other than a custodian that is in possession of property of the estate must deliver to the trustee and account for such property or its value, unless the property is of inconsequential value or benefit to the estate.

Any entity owing a debt that is property of the estate and has matured, is payable on demand or payable on order, must pay such debt to the trustee unless such entity has a setoff.

Any entity that transfers property of the estate, or pays a debt owing to a debtor in good fatih to an entity other than the trustee, is protected if it has neither actual notice nor knowledge of the commencement of a case. This provision does not permit a bank setoff in violation of the automatic stay, even if the bank is unaware of the case.

A custodian appointed prior to a bankruptcy case is required to turn over property to the trustee and account for such property. Upon learning of the commencement of a case, the custodian must stop all administration with regard to the property of the debtor, except such action necessary to preserve the estate; deliver the property or the proceeds of property to the trustee at the commencement of the case; and file an accounting. The court must then protect the entity to which the custodian is obligated, provide the custodian for payment of reasonable compensation, and impose a surcharge on the custodian for any improper or excessive disbursement. The court is given the discretion to permit the custodian to continue in possession when it is the best interests of the creditors.

Trustee as a Lien Creditor.   Under a "strong arm" clause, the trustee has the right and power to avoid any transfer of property of the debtor or any obligations incurred by the debtor that is avoidable by:

1. A creditor with a judicial lien as at the date of the petition on all property on which a creditor on a simple contract could have obtained a judicial lien, whether or not such creditor exists.

2. A creditor with an execution at the date of filing against property of the debtor that is returned unsatisfied, whether or not such a creditor exists.

3. A bona fide purchaser of real property from the debtor, against whom applicable law permits such transfer to be perfected, whether or not such a purchaser exists.

Under the action of the Bankruptcy Code, the trusteee also may avoid a transfer of an interest of the debtor in property or any obligation incurred by the debtor voidable under applicable law by a creditor holding an unsecured claim.

Statutory Liens.   The trustee may avoid the fixing of a statutory lien on property of the debtor to the extent that the lien first becomes effective against the debtor when a case under this title concerning the debtor is commenced, when an insolvency proceeding other than under this title concerning the debtor is commenced, when a custodian is appointed or takes possession, when the debtor becomes insolvent, when the debtor's financial condition fails to meet a specified standard, or at the time of an execution against property of the debtor levied at the instance of an entity other than the holder of such statutory lien.

The trusteee may also avoid the fixing of a statutory lien to the extent that such lien is not perfected or enforceable on the date of the filing of the petition against a bona fide purchaser that purchases such property on the date of the filing of the petition, whether or not such a purchaser exists; is for rent; or is a lien of distress for rent.

Limitations on Avoiding Powers.   This is a statute of limitations sections of the Bankruptcy Code which serves to limit certain of the trustee's rights and avoiding powers. It provides that an action or proceeding dealing with the trustee as a lien creditor on statutory lien avoidances, on fraudulent transfers, or on setoffs may not be commenced two years after the appointment of a trustee or after the case is closed or dismissed, whichever is earlier.

Reclamation.   The trustee's rights and powers in his dealings as a lien creditor, with statutory liens, with preferences, and transactions commencing after the filing of the petition are subject to any statutory right or common law right of a seller that in the ordinary course of business sells goods to the debtor, to reclaim such goods if the debtor has received them while insolvent. In order to meet this requirement, the seller must demand in writing reclamation of the goods before 10 days after receipt of the goods by the debtor; and the court may deny reclamation to a seller that has a reclamation right and has made demand, only if the court grants the claim of such seller priority as an administrative expense or secures such claim by a lien. Therefore, the purpose of this provision is to recognize in part the validity of Section 2-702 of the Uniform Commercial Code, while permitting the court to grant relief other than reclamation and still protect the seller. In addition, reclamation is a procedure by which a person can recover property to which he is entitled that is in possession of the trustee in bankruptcy.

Under Section 2-702, creditors can reclaim goods if they notify their customer that it should pay or return the shipment within 10 days after delivery. Unless the merchandise or equipment is essential for the operation of the debtor, in which case provisions for the protection, return, or payment of the merchandise will be made. If creditors are dealing with an order of relief, the actual claim may be considered as an administrative expense in liquidation.

Preferences.   The Bankruptcy Code gives expanded powers to the trustee in bankruptcy with regard to voidable preferences. Preferences are payments within 90 days prior to the filing of a petition for an antecedent debt when the creditor was insolvent. Insolvency is defined as that condition when the sum of the entity's debt is greater than its property at a fair valuation exclusive of exempt property and property transferred with intent to hinder, delay, or defraud creditors.

The debtor is presumed to be insolvent during the 90-day period, and it is not necessary to prove that the creditor had reasonable cause to believe the debtor was insolvent. Because of the presumption of insolvency and the elimination of the need to prove reasonable cause to believe, payments of all antecedent unsecured debts within three months with limited exceptions are vulnerable to the trustee's attack.

Payment of an old unsecured debt is recoverable upon proof of only three facts: the payment or transfer was to or for the benefit of a creditor in full or partial payment of an antecedent debt, which payment occurred within 90 days prior to the filing of the bankruptcy case; the transfer occurred when the debtor was insolvent; and the creditor received more than it would receive in a liquidation case under Chapter 7.

Once the trustee establishes that a creditor received funds or property within the 90 day period on an antecedent obligation, the case is complete. Unless a defense is presented, the bankruptcy court will grant the trustee judgment against the preferred creditor. Therefore, the expense of long distance litigation in terms of defense and prosecution is shifted to the creditor. Consequently, creditors may forego an available defense in lieu of the expense involved in defending the action.

The Bankruptcy Code distinguishes between transfers made to an insider and to those made to creditors that are not considered as such. An insider includes a relative, partner, director, officer, or affiliate of the debtor. Under these circumstances, the Bankruptcy Code enables the trustee to recover upon proof of any payment or transfer to an insider within one year of payment; of insolvency of the debtor on the date of the transfer; and that the insider had reasonable cause to believe the debtor was insolvent if the transfer occurred more than three months before bankruptcy. However, the presumption of insolvency does not apply with respect to transfers occurring more than 90 days before bankruptcy.

Transfers Excluded as Preferences. Since almost every transfer made within 90 days is a preference, the Bankruptcy Code gives the preferred creditor an opportunity to exclude certain transfers from recovery by the trustee.

Certain transfers of property are excluded to the extent that they are a substantially contemporaneous exchange for new value. For example, transactions intended to be cash sales but which unavoidably involved a short extension of credit are excluded from attack.

Transfers that a trustee may not avoid contain certain key features. They must be made in payment of a debt incurred in the ordinary course of business of the debtor and the creditor, made not later than 45 days after the debt was incurred, and made according to ordinary business terms.

A security interest in property acquired by a debtor which permits it to acquire new value with the proceeds of the loan—technically known as enabling loans—is free from attack under this section of the Bankruptcy Code. The additional credit must not be secured by an otherwise unavoidable transfer to or for the benefit of the creditor.

A secured creditor is able to obtain the benefit of the debtor's subsequent acquisition of new collateral or the increased value arising from the conversion of goods to a finished status. This is known as the after-acquired clause. While the Bankruptcy Code frees from attack the floating lien concept under this clause, the benefits accruing to the secured creditor are reduced. For example, where a secured party's collateral consists of inventory or receivables or their proceeds and they increase in value during the preference period to the detriment of the estate and unsecured creditors, this increase is preferential and recoverable by the trustee.

This section exempts statutory liens from attack as preferences provided that the liens are not voidable.

Fraudulent Transfers and Obligations. The trustee may avoid any transfer of property by the debtor or any obligation incurred by the debtor that was made or incurred within one year prior to the commencement of the case with actual intent to hinder, delay, or defraud any existing or future creditors, or which was made for less than a reasonably equivalent value if the debtor was insolvent or became insolvent on the date of the transfer; was engaged in business or was about to engage in business or in a transaction for which any property remaining with the debtor was unreasonably small capital; or intended to incur or believed that it would incur debts beyond its ability to pay as they mature.

LIQUIDATION

From the creditors' point of view, Chapter 7 is generally the last resort for insolvent or distressed debtors. Many no-asset cases are filed, in which there are no dividends for anyone, even priority creditors. There are also debtors that have priority obligations so large that they consume the estate. Tax claims are frequently inordinately large; in fact, debtors, instead of paying withholding taxes, may have been surviving on tax money or on general creditors. In such cases, there is little or nothing left for dividends to creditors.

Accordingly, when creditors are primarily interested in the best possible return, they decide to utilize liquidation proceedings only after voluntary settlements or assignments for the benefit of creditors have proved unavailing or unsuccessful. The exception is the case of the debtor suspected of being dishonest; of having wasted, concealed, or fraudulently transferred assets; or of having committed criminal offenses. The Bankruptcy Code affords the most adequate machinery for uncovering such acts or ommissions.

Since a debtor is to be liquidated rather than rehabilitated, the part of the credit executive is less critical than in rehabilitation proceedings. It is important, however, and credit executives are strongly urged to attend creditors' meetings and to participate actively.

Trustee

Promptly after a petition is filed, the court appoints an interim trustee to serve until the initial meeting of creditors. At this meeting, creditors holding an allowable claim may elect one person to serve as trustee. To be elected, a candidate is required to receive the votes of at least 20 per cent of the claims and more than half in the amount of the total claims held by creditors. If a trustee is not elected, the interim trustee continues to serve in the case. The duties of the trustee comprise the following:

1. Collect and reduce to money the property of the estate for which such trustee serves and close up such estate an expeditiously as is compatible with the best interests of parties in interest.

2. Account for all property received.

3. Investigate the financial affairs of the debtor.

4. If a purpose is served, examine proofs of claims and object to the allowance of any claim that is improper.

5. If advisable, oppose the discharge of the debtor.

6. Unless the court orders otherwise, furnish such information concerning the estate and the estate's administration as is requested by a party in interest.

7. If the business of the debtor is authorized to be operated, file with the court and with any governmental unit charged with responsibility for collection or determination of any tax arising out of such operation periodic reports and summaries of the operation of the business, including a statement of receipts and disbursements, and such other information as the court requires.

8. Make a final report and file a final account of the administration of the estate with the court.

Creditors' Committee

At the meeting of creditors, those eligible to vote may elect a creditors' committee of not fewer than three, and not more than eleven. The elected committee may consult with the trustee in connection with the administration of the estate, make recommendations to the trustee respecting the performance of the trustee's duties, and submit to the court any question affecting the administration of the estate.

Handling the Estate

When a debtor is to be liquidated, the trustee is required to collect the property, liquidate the assets, and distribute the proceeds to the creditors. During this time, the court may authorize the trustee to operate the debtor's business for a limited period of time if it is the best interests of the estate and consistent with its orderly liquidation.

The debtor may convert a case under this chapter to a case under reorganization proceedings at any time, providing it has not been originally converted from a Chapter 11 proceeding. Any waiver of the right to convert is unenforceable. Moreover, the court may dismiss a case under this chapter for unreasonable delay by the debtor that is prejudicial to creditors and for nonpayment of any required fees and charges.

Redemption of Property. An individual debtor may redeem tangible personal property subject to a lien by paying the creditor for the amount of the secured claim. The lien must secure a dischargeable consumer debt and property must be primarily for personal, family, or household use; be exempt from the estate; or have been abandoned by the trustee as burdensome and of inconsequential value to the estate.

Treatment of Certain Liens. The trustee may avoid a lien that secured a claim for fines, penalties, forfeitures, or damages arising before the earlier of either the order of relief or the appointment of a trustee, to the extent that such claims are not compensation to the creditor for actual pecuniary loss. Priority is given to property that is not avoidable and that secures an allowed claim for taxes. However, any creditor with a lien on property that is senior to the tax lien receives first priority.

Disposition of Certain Property. After the commencement of a case under this chapter but before the final distribution, the trustee shall dispose of any property in which an entity other than the estate has an interest, such as a lien, and that has not been disposed of under another section of this title.

Distribution of Property of the Estate. Some actions are subordinated for the purposes of distribution, such as an action by the court to subordinate certain allowed claims under the principles of equitable subordination. With respect to a subordination agreement, it is enforceable to the same extent that this agreement is under applicable nonbankruptcy law. Except for provisions of this nature, property of an estate in liquidation is distributed in the following order:

1. Payment of secured claims.

2. Payment of claims subject to priority treatment.

3. Payment of any allowed unsecured claim if timely filed. A tardily filed claim is allowed if the creditor that holds the claim did not have actual knowledge of the case for timely filing.

4. Payment of any allowed claim filed tardily other than the late-filed claim specified above.

5. Payment of any allowed claim, whether secured or unsecured, for fines, penalties, forfeiture, or damages to the extent they are not compensation for actual pecuniary loss suffered by the creditor. The payment must have arose before the earlier of the filing of the petition or the appointment of a trustee.

6. Payment of interest at the legal rate from the date of filing of the petition of any claim cited above.

7. Payment of any residual to the debtor.

Payment among claims of the kind specified in a particular class is made pro rata. On cases converted from Chapter 11, administrative expenses incurred after conversion have priority of those administrative expenses incurred before such conversion.

If the debtor has interests in community property, this property or the proceeds of such property are segregated from the estate.

Discharge

Only individuals are entitled to discharge from all allowable claims under liquidation proceedings; corporations and partnerships are not. With certain exceptions, these include all obligations incurred before the filing of the petition. The individual debtor is entitled to discharge unless:

1. The debtor, with intent to hinder, delay, or defraud a creditor or an officer of the estate, has (or permitted to be) transferred, removed, destroyed, or mutilated property of the estate within one year before the filing of the petition; or property of the estate after filing of the petition.

2. The debtor has failed unjustifiably to keep proper financial records and books.

3. The debtor has knowingly and fraudulently made a false oath, presented a false claim, improperly obtained money or property, or withheld information from an officer of the estate.

4. The debtor has failed to explain satisfactorily any deficiency in assets.

5. The debtor has refused to obey a lawful order of the court or to testify on the ground of self-incrimination in response to a material question.

6. The debtor has been granted a discharge within six years before the filing of the petition. One exception is where the debtor makes a 100 per cent settlement on claims or a 70 per cent settlement proposed by a debtor in good faith and represented best efforts.

7. The court approves a written waiver of discharge executed by the debtor after the order for relief.

The actions noted above must have taken place within one year before the filing of the petition.

The trustee or creditor may object to a discharge. In this event, the court may order the trustee to examine the acts and conduct of the debtor to determine whether a ground exists for denial of discharge. Moreover, the court may revoke a discharge granted if it were obtained through the fraud of the debtor ascertained after the granting of a discharge, the debtor acquired property that was rightfully part of the estate, or if the debtor refused to obey a lawful order of the court.

The trustee or creditor may request a revocation of a discharge within one year after the discharge was granted, or before the later of one year after the granting of the discharge and the date the case was closed, or both, depending upon the violation.

REORGANIZATION

The rehabilitation proceedings set forth in the previous law as Chapter X, XI, and XII are now consolidated into one new reorganization, Chapter 11. The three chapters of the old law were rarely alternative courses. Each had a special purpose: Chapter XII was only available to individuals and partnerships; Chapter X was available only to corporations, and then only if Chapter XI would not provide adequate relief.

By utilizing reorganization proceedings under Chapter 11 of the Bankruptcy Reform Act, a debtor can frequently surmount many of the obstacles encountered in voluntary settlements. Chapter 11 proceedings can be initiated voluntarily by the debtor or commenced by a creditor on an involuntary basis; both actions begin with the filing of a petition with the bankruptcy court.

These actions may arise under one of three sets of circumstances, all involving a debtor that is financially distressed but hopeful of being rehabilitated rather than liquidated.

1. If negotiations for an out-of-court settlement break down because of inability to secure the consent of important creditors, perhaps the next best step is for the debtor to file a voluntary petition under this chapter.

2. If the creditors are not receiving the best possible return, perhaps the alternative is for the creditors to file a petition under this chapter.

3. The debtor may decide not to undertake an out-of-court settlement and proceed at once to file under this chapter.

Creditors' Committee

As soon as practical after the order for relief, the court appoints a committee of creditors holding unsecured claims. It generally comprises creditors that hold the seven largest claims against the debtor. It may comprise members of a committee organized by the creditors before the order of relief, if such committee was chosen fairly and is representative of different kinds of claims.

If requested, the court may appoint additional committees of creditors if they are necessary to ensure adequate representation of creditors. Moreover, the court may change the membership or size of a committee if the membership is not representative of the different kinds of claims.

At a scheduled meeting of the committee at which a majority of the members are present, the committee may employ one or more attorneys, accountants, or other agents to represent or perform services for the committee. While employed by the committee, the designated persons may not represent any other entity in connection with the case. In the performance of its duties, the committee may:

1. Consult with the debtor in possession or the trustee concerning the administration of the case.

2. Investigate the acts, conduct, and financial affairs of the debtor; the operation of the debtor's business; the desirability of continuing the business; and other relevant matters.

3. Participate in the formulation of the plan, advise other creditors of the plan's recommendations, and collect and file the acceptance of the plan with the court.

4. Request the appointment of a trustee or examiner if one had not been previously appointed.

5. Perform other services that are of interest to the other creditors.

As soon as practical after the appointment of the committee, the trustee meets with the committee to transact any necessary and proper business.

Trustee or Examiner

At any time after the commencement of a case but before confirmation of the plan, the court upon request and after a notice of hearing may order the appointment of a trustee for cause, including fraud, dishonesty, incompetence, or gross mismanagement of the affairs of the debtor; or make such appointment if in the interests of creditors, any security holders, and other interests of the debtor. This action may be taken without regard to the amount of assets and liabilities of the debtor or the number of holders of the debtor's securities.

A trustee performs the following duties:

1. Accounts for all the property received.

2. If a purpose is served, examines proofs of claim and objects to the allowance of any claim that is improper.

3. Unless that court orders otherwise, furnishes such information concerning the debtor's estate and its administration if requested.

4. If the debtor's business is to be operated, files with the court and the governmental tax authorities periodic financial reports on the operation as required.

5. Makes a final accounting of the administration of the debtor's estate with the court.

If the debtor has not already done so, the trustee must file a list of the creditors. In addition, unless the court orders otherwise, the trustee must file a schedule of assets and liabilities and a statement of the debtor's financial affairs; investigate the acts, conduct, and financial status of the debtor's business; determine the desirability of the continuance of the business; and pursue any other matter of importance.

A statement of this investigation, including any fact pertaining to fraud, mismanagement, or incompetance, is filed with the court, and a copy or a summary is furnished to the creditors' committee, equity security holders, any indentured trustee, and any other entity that the court designates.

As soon as practical, the trustee must file the plan of reorganization; file a report of why a plan will not be filed; or recommend conversion of the case to a case under Chapter 7 (liquidation), Chapter 13 (adjustment of debts), or dismissal of the case.

After confirmation of the plan the trustee must file such reports as are necessary or as the court orders.

At any time before the confirmation of the plan and after notice and a hearing, the court upon request may terminate the trustee's appointment and restore the debtor to possession and management of the property and the operation of the business.

If the court does not appoint a trustee, the court may appoint an examiner to handle the debtor's affairs at any time before confirmation of the plan. The examiner will conduct such investigation of the debtor as deemed appropriate, including investigations of allegations of fraud, dishonesty, incompetence, misconduct, mismanagement, or irregularity in the management of the debtor's affairs by current and former management. This is providing that the appointment is of interest to the creditors, equity security holders, and other interests of the debtor's estate; or that the debtor's fixed, liquidated, unsecured debts (other than debts for goods, services, taxes, or debts owing to an insider) exceed $5,000,000.

A debtor that filed under this chapter on a voluntary basis and is operating in possession of the business may request that the business be liquidated under chapter 7. On the other hand, the court may convert a case under this chapter to Chapter 7 if it is in the best interests of the creditors. Some reasons for such an action include: small likelihood that the business will be rehabilitated, inability to effect a plan, inability to obtain confirmation of a plan, and a material default by the debtor with regard to a confirmed plan.

The Plan

The debtor may file a reorganization plan in a voluntary or involuntary case until after 120 days after the date of the order for relief, although the plan may be filed by the debtor with the petition commencing a voluntary case. However, any party at interest, including the debtor, trustee, creditors' committee, equity security holders' committee, a creditor, an equity security holder, or any indentured trustee, may file a plan only if a trustee has not been appointed, if the debtor has not filed a plan before 120 days after the date of the order for relief, or if the debtor has not filed a plan that has been accepted before 180 days after the date of the order for relief. Upon request of a party at interest and before notice and a hearing, the court may increase or reduce the 120 day or 180 day period.

The effect of the plan is to provide that the debtor will normally have 120 days to come up with a reorganization plan regardless of the number of creditors or shareholders. This represents a decided change for the large public corporations typically reorganized under the old Chapter X. There the trustee was usually appointed immediately and from that time forward the debtor has little role in the reorganization process.

Moreover, the plan is no longer limited to the debtor's ability to finance a proposed reorganization but is now open to obtaining funds in the marketplace. Any party in interest may come in after 180 days and offer creditors a better plan, thereby maximizing creditors' recovery or eventual recovery in a proposed payout plan of arrangement.

Classification of Claims. A plan may provide for a classification of claims into particular classes if they are essentially similar. The apparent goal is to divide claims into two basic types: secured and unsecured. Essentially, the rights of secured creditors at the time of confirmation are based upon their entire claims, not simply the secured segment. In addition to the two basic types, there is generally a separate classification for small claims.

Contents of a Plan. The contents of a plan contain both mandatory requirements and those where individual judgment is required. Among the mandatory requirements, a plan shall:

1. Classify certain kinds of priority claims. Excluded are administrative expenses, claims arising in the ordinary course of business that occurred after the filing of an involuntary petition but before the earlier of the appointment of a trustee or the order for relief, or certain tax claims.

2. Specify any class of claims or interests that is not impaired under the plan.

3. Specify the treatment of any class of claims or interests that is impaired under the plan.

4. Provide the same treatment for each claim or interest of a particular class, unless the holder of a particular claim or interest agrees to a less favorable treatment.

5. Provide adequate means for the plan's execution, such as the retention by the debtor of any property, transfer of property to the estate, sale or distribution of property, curing of any default, satisfaction or modification of any lien, extension of maturity date or change in the interest rate of outstanding securities, amendment of debtor's charter, issuance of securities, or the merger or consolidation of the debtor into one or more firms.

6. Provide that a corporate debtor include in its charter a provision prohibiting the issuance of nonvoting securities, adequate voting powers where more than one class of securities is issued, and adequate provisions for the election of directors for those securities with dividend preferences in the event of default in dividend payment.

7. Contain only those provisions that are consistent with the interest of creditors and equity security holders and with public policy with respect to the section of officers for administering the plan.

In addition to the mandatory requirements listed above, a plan may have several discretionary matters whereby it may:

1. Impair or leave unimpaired any class of claims, secured or unsecured.

2. Provide for the assumption or rejection of any executory contract or unexpired lien of the debtor.

3. Settle or adjust any claim or interest belonging to the debtor or to the estate, or retain or enforce any such claim or interest.

4. Provide for the sale of the property in the estate and for the distribution of the proceeds of the sale to the creditors.

5. Include any other appropriate provision not inconsistent with the applicable provisions of the Bankruptcy Code.

In the event that the debtor is an individual, a plan proposed by an entity other than the debtor may not use, sell, or lease exempt properties without the debtor's approval.

Postpetition Disclosure and Solicitation.   After a case has commenced, an acceptance or rejection may not be solicited from the holder of a claim unless that holder is provided adequate information on which to make an informed judgment. The same disclosure statement is required to be given to each holder, but there may be distributed different information as between classes of creditors.

While the court is required to approve a disclosure statement that describes the plan before its transmittal to the creditors, this may be done without an appraisal or valuation of the debtor's assets.

Acceptance of the Plan.   A creditor may accept or reject a plan. This may be obtained before the filing of the petition, providing the acceptance or rejection was in compliance with applicable nonbankruptcy law, or as long as adequate information has been given if there is no such law.

A class of claims is accepted by creditors if those holding two-thirds in amount and more than one-half in number of the allowed claims vote to accept the plan. A class of claims that is not impaired (creditors' rights are unaltered) is not required to vote; that class is deemed to have accepted the plan. If a class of claims is not entitled to any payment, that class is deemed to have rejected the plan.

After a notice and hearing, the court is permitted to eliminate any claim from the plan that is not made in good faith.

Confirmation Hearing.   After notice, the court holds a hearing on confirmation of a plan at which time a creditor may object to confirmation of a plan. The Securities and Exchange Commission may appear at the hearing, be heard, but may not appeal from the court's decision.

Confirmation of Plan.   The court confirms a plan only if all of the following requirements are met:

1. The plan must comply with the applicable provisions of the Bankruptcy Code.

2. The proponent of the plan must comply with the applicable provisions of the Bankruptcy Code.

3. The plan must be proposed in good faith and not by any means forbidden by law.

4. Payments made in connection with the plan must be disclosed and be reasonable.

5. Proponent of the plan must disclose the identity and affiliation of those proposed to serve in an official capacity and to the best interests of the creditors after the plan has been confirmed.

6. Rate changes received the approval of the appropriate regulatory agencies.

7. With respect to each class of claims, it is required that each creditor

or interest has either accepted the plan or will receive property of a value not less than such holder would receive in a liquidation; or if allowed as a secured claim, receive property of a value not less than the value of such creditor's interest in the property that secures such claims.

8. Each class is required to accept the plan or such class is not impaired by the plan. The significance of this statement is that if a class of creditors accepts a plan or is unimpaired, there is no need of the "fair and equitable" test which would require a valuation of the business.

9. Deferred cash payment with interest for certain priority claims (e.g. wages, salaries, employee benefit plans, etc.) are permitted as long as a class approves. With regard to tax claims, deferred payments with interest not exceeding six years are permitted without the consent of the holder. Since these claims may not be properly classifiable into one class, class consent is not relevant.

10. At least one class of claims has accepted the plan, determined without including the claims of insiders in the computation of the acceptance.

11. Confirmation of the plan is not likely to be followed by liquidation or the need for further reorganization of the debtor, unless such liquidation or reorganization is proposed in the plan.

Despite the fact that each class may not accept the plan as required above, the court is still required to confirm the plan if it does not discriminate unfairly, and is fair and equitable with respect to each class of claim that is impaired and has not accepted the plan. This is referred to as the cram down provision.

With respect to a class of secured claims, the plan must provide that the holders retain their liens securing such claim and receive deferred cash payments totalling at least the value of the holder's interest in the estate's interest in such property.

If the property is to be sold free and clear of encumbrances, any existing liens will attach to the proceeds of the sale and the lien on the proceeds as above or the holders will receive unquestionable equivalent of such claims. This covers those situations where the collateral is abandoned and a lien on collateral of equal value is given. The holder of such claim that purchases the property, however, may offset the claim against the purchase price.

With respect to a class of unsecured creditors, the plan must provide that each class of dissenting creditors receive property of value equal to the amount it claims, or any creditor with a junior claim will receive no payment.

Effects of Confirmation. The provisions of a confirmed plan bind the debtor and any creditor, whether or not the claim is impaired or the creditor has accepted the plan. Except as provided in the plan, the confirmation vests all property of the estate in the debtor, provides that all property dealt with by the plan is free and clear of all claims, and discharges the debtor from any debt that arose before the date of confirmation; certain claims that were not assumed or did not arise until after the commencement of the case, such as unassumed executory contracts and taxes entitled to priority, are treated as if they had arisen before the filing of the petition.

The confirmation of a plan does not discharge a debtor if the plan calls for a liquidation of all or substantially all of the property of the estate, if the debtor does not engage in business after consummation of the plan, and if the debtor would be denied a discharge if the case were tried under Chapter 7 of the Bankruptcy Code. Moreover, the confirmation of a plan does not discharge an individual debtor from any debt outlined earlier in this chapter as exceptions to discharge.

The court may approve a written waiver of discharge executed by the debtor after a petition has been filed.

Revocation of an Order of Confirmation. On request of a party in interest at any time before 180 days after the date of the entry of the order of confirmation and after notice and a hearing, the court may revoke an order procured by fraud. This revocation shall contain such provisions as are necessary to protect any entity acquiring rights in good faith relying on the order of confirmation and shall revoke the discharge of the debts.

Execution of a Plan

Despite any otherwise applicable nonbankruptcy law, rule, or regulation relating to its financial condition, the debtor and any entity organized for the purpose of carrying out the plan shall carry out the plan and comply with any orders of the court. The court also may direct the debtor and any other necessary party to execute or deliver any instrument required to effect a transfer of property and to perform any other act, including the satisfaction of any lien, that is necessary for the consummation of the plan.

If a plan requires presentment or surrender of a security or the performance of any other act as a condition to participation in distribution under the plan, such action shall be taken not later than five years after the date of the entry of the order of confirmation. Any entity that does not abide by these requirements may not participate in distribution under the plan.

ADJUSTMENT OF DEBTS

Instead of undergoing reorganization proceedings under Chapter 11, certain business debtors may choose to file under Chapter 13, "Adjustment of Debts of an Individual." Under this chapter, Congress provides the wage earner and the small noncorporate business with a means of paying off debts with future earnings. The principal requirements are that the debtor has income sufficiently regular to enable payment under a plan, and that unsecured debts are less than $100,000 and secured debts are less than $350,000.

Trustee

The principal duty of the trustee is the disbursement to creditors of payments under the plan. The trustee also is accountable for all property received, must investigate the financial plans of the debtor, and advise and assist the debtor in performance of the plan. The trustee is not granted the power to operate a business as may be done under Chapter 11.

The Plan

Chapter 13 is a completely voluntary action. Thus a debtor has the exclusive right to propose a repayment plan. It can be in the form of an extension, where creditors are paid in full, or a composition where creditors are paid some portion of their account. It generally is payable over a three-year period but can be expanded up to five years for cause.

The basic provisions are that a plan shall:

1. Provide for the submission of all or such portion of future earnings or other future income of the debtor to the supervision and control of the trustee as is necessary for the execution of the plan.

2. Provide for the full payment in deferred cash payments of all claims entitled to priority unless the holder of a particular claim agrees to a different treatment of such claim.

3. Provide for identical treatment of each claim within a particular class.

Once a plan is filed, all of the debtor's property including future income is under the jurisdiction of the court. Moreover, the debtor is protected by an automatic stay order issued against litigation and collection efforts.

A debtor who is in business is permitted to remain in business unless the court orders otherwise. The debtor may retain property and protect assets while agreeing to pay creditors over a period of time. The creditor may gain added benefits if the plan provides for payment to creditors out of property other than future income or earnings of the debtor.

While the secured creditor is prevented from repossession by the stay, sections of the Bankruptcy Code provide for numerous kinds of full or partial relief from the stay. If the collateral is used in business, the creditors may successfully claim priority rights. However, the flexibility provided by and the protection given under the sections create numerous methods to satisfy the court that the secured claim will receive fair treatment without necessity of reclamation.

Confirmation of Plan

There are six separate requirements for plan confirmation:

1. The plan complies with the provisions of Chapter 13 and any other applicable provisions of the Bankruptcy Code.

2. All required fees have been paid.

3. The plan has been proposed in good faith.

4. The value of property distributed under the plan for allowed unsecured claims is not less than the amount that would have been paid under a liquidation plan.

5. With respect to each allowed unsecured claim: the holder of the claim has accepted the plan, the holder of the claim is retaining a lien or recovering the value of the claim, or the debtor is surrendering the property securing such claim to the claimholder.

6. The debtor is able to make all payments and otherwise comply with the plan.

Claims and Creditors

Unsecured creditors have no voice in the confirmation process. However, they are protected by the requirement that they receive no less than they would receive in a liquidation proceeding. The only other remedies available to them are the possible lack of good faith on the debtor's part or the possibility that a composition plan is not the debtor's best effort.

Secured creditors must either accept the plan, receive their collateral back, or receive value that is not less than the value of the allowed secured amount and still retain their lien. In addition, secured creditors do not benefit from any increase in the value of their collateral during the life of the plan. Moreover, there is no provision for postconfirmation reevaluation of the collateral. This could be significant in composition cases where payments on unsecured claims are minimal.

Discharge

The court must grant the debtor a discharge as soon as practicable after completion of payments under the plan. Waiver of the discharge with court approval is permitted. The court may also grant a hardship discharge when the debtor has not completed payment if the debtor could not be held accountable for the circumstances precluding payment; the debtor must have paid at least liquidation value; and modification of the plan is not practicable.

It is important to point out that under Chapter 13 there is no six-year bar to obtaining a succeeding discharge as there is in liquidation proceedings.

PART IX

EXPORT TRANSACTIONS

CHAPTER 36

EXPORT CREDIT

Sales to customers in other countries account for a large portion of U.S. business. The procedure that a credit executive follows in making an export credit decision differs little from that used in making a domestic credit decision. In both, the credit executive amasses information on every aspect of the credit risk, and uses the traditional "Cs" of credit to guide the search for information. The credit decision is made only after careful analysis and evaluation of the information. The techniques used for evaluating both foreign and domestic credit information are similar, and success depends primarily upon experience gained in daily administration.

EXPORT CREDIT RISKS

Although the decisionmaking procedure is the same, the nature of the risk in export trade is greater and more difficult to evaluate than a domestic risk. Accepting the buyer means accepting the risk of the buyer's country as well. Not only must the character, capacity, and capital of the buyer be evaluated but also the other risk conditions of the buyer's country. For instance, a buyer's credit rating may be satisfactory, but payment may be delayed because of exchange restrictions, arbitrary changes in export-import regulations, or adverse economic conditions.

Government

The economy and business climate of any nation is directly influenced by the attitudes and policies of its government. The degree of promotion or regulation often makes the difference between dynamic business activity and economic stagnation. The political orientation of the government also affects its economic policy and the degree to which it regulates internal commerce and external trade. In underdeveloped countries marked by rising nationalism or political unrest, the credit executive must consider the dangers of currency inconvertibility, confiscation, expropriation, war, civil commotions, and restriction or cancellation of import licenses. According to the existing or anticipated political situation, shipments should not be undertaken on normal terms and conditions but on special arrangements that will ensure delivery and payment.

Economic Stability

In all countries, the general economic picture, business cycle, crop failures, and many other factors will cause a fluctuation in the standard of living and in the demand for imports or the supply of goods for export.

External actions or conditions can also have considerable impact upon a specific country's trade. For example, a reduction in the U.S. sugar consumption quota for one country can seriously affect its economy. At the same time, it can exert a favorable effect on the economies of other sugar producing countries if their quotas were increased. In another way, a rise or fall of two or three cents a pound in the price of coffee, bananas, or tin may have a strong impact on the trade of certain countries that base their economies on exports of these products.

Laws

Commercial laws vary greatly from country to country, particularly as regards protesting of drafts, laws of contract and passing of title to goods, bankruptcy, registration of trademarks and patents, and commercial arbitration. An attorney familiar with international law must be consulted if specific compliance with the law is required to protect the exporter's interest.

Import regulations vary widely from country to country, are highly technical, and may be subject to frequent change. A great many countries require their importers to obtain import licenses either for all goods or for some types of shipments. It is important for the credit executive to check these requirements because goods arriving without proper license are sometimes subject to confiscation or fines by the foreign government. Where import licenses and/or exchange licenses are required, importers cannot buy U.S. dollars to pay for the goods unless they hold a current valid license.

Sellers unfamiliar with the customs or consular regulations of a foreign country are better off dispatching shipments through an export freight forwarder rather than through their own traffic departments. A freight forwarder must be able to handle details, arrange for freight space and trucking services, provide for marine and war risk insurance, and must know how to secure required documentation such as ocean bills of lading, consular invoices, and dock receipts. The same type of service is provided an importer by the customs broker, who is particularly useful for managing the arrival of shipments in ports where the importer has no office. The customs broker arranges for clearance of goods through customs and for delivery of goods to their ultimate seaboard or inland destination.

Language

Costly misunderstandings can arise from language differences between the seller's and the buyer's country, and can be reflected in the foreign sales contract, shipping documents, and all followup correspondence with the customer. Abbreviations, idioms, and other expressions not directly translatable must be avoided. Exact translations of trade names or of terms of weights and measures, for example, are often misleading. The word, ton, cannot be translated accurately without understanding whether it applies to the gross or long ton, metric ton, or short ton. Price must refer to the currency and unit of goods to which it applies. Language differences in the shipping documents can make the goods appear not to conform to the buyer's specifications.

To eliminate disputes arising from inconsistent and ambiguous price and term quotations in sales contracts, various trade groups have issued definitions of common abbreviations. These cover not only price and credit terms but also such important issues as passing of title to the goods, place and time of delivery, buyer's right of inspection, and bearing of transportation and other risks. At present there are two widely used sets. One is the Revised American Foreign Trade Definitions—1941, prepared by a joint committee representing the Chamber of Commerce of the United States of America, the National Council of American Importers Inc., and the National Foreign Trade Council Inc. The other is Incoterms 1953, drafted by the International Chamber of Commerce. They vary on several points of substance, but either set may be given the force of law in the buyer's country by including within the sales contract a clause stipulating their application.

Geography

The time lapse between the purchase of goods and their receipt by the foreign buyer has been a major factor in determining foreign credit terms. Obviously, if a term of credit begins with the arrival of the goods abroad, shipping distance becomes important, and the foreign account receivable will be outstanding for a longer period than a comparable domestic account would be. To extend credit abroad, therefore, requires greater financing capacity than extending credit in the domestic market. This time lapse also compounds the difficulty in judging other risks which change from day to day, such as exchange risks and shifts in import regulations.

Exporters must take into consideration not only the climate of the country of destination but also the various zones through which the shipment will pass. Obviously the climate of the buyer's country and its seasonal cycle will affect the sale of certain types of products and the seasonal dating of invoices, and may cause losses and damages that are not included in insurance coverage.

Methods of transportation are another important factor. The delivery of goods in a few days by air transportation requires different credit terms than goods that will travel by ship.

Marine Risk

Goods being shipped overseas are naturally exposed to marine risk through which they can be damaged or lost. Fortunately, the shipping hazards of export trade to most countries have long been covered by some form of marine insurance. Today almost every exporter operates under a form of marine insurance commonly referred to as the "Open Policy," which automatically protects the exporter against transportation risks on all shipments within specified geographic areas. Merchants not holding open policies may insure individual shipments.

In arranging for marine insurance, the selling firm should work closely with the insurance broker to make certain that no hazard is overlooked, and that every shipment is covered from origin of shipment to final destination. Overland hazards must not be overlooked.

The exporter may also want to protect against the risk of the buyer's refusal to accept the goods, or of the goods being damaged or lost while title remains with the seller. As a matter of fact, regulations in some countries specify that insurance must be placed by the buyer with an insurance company in that country. Because such a policy would call for insurance payment in local currency of the buyer, a loss or long delay may result if the exchange authorities of that country fail to provide for the transfer of the equivalent in U.S. dollars. In such instances, U.S. exporters can protect themselves by arranging contingency insurance with their own insurance company; this carries a lower premium rate than regular insurance.

War risk insurance generally covers while merchandise is on the high seas but does not protect the shipment after its arrival at destination. Special insurance which gives added protection to consignment stocks in certain countries may be obtained by those who have credit insurance with Foreign Credit Insurance Association.

Convertibility Risk

Many American firms invoice their export sales in U.S. dollars and receive payment in U.S. dollars without any intervening conversion of foreign currencies. Others make sales to foreign customers and accept payment in the currency of the buyers' countries. This receipt of payment in foreign currencies introduces several additional risks.

The first of these is convertibility risk, which pertains to the possibility that dollars will not be available when the payer seeks to settle the account. This is particularly true in the case of less-developed nations, and may occur when a country runs into serious national trade and balance of payment deficits. Even if the seller has denominated the sale in dollars, the importer may not be able to convert currency to dollars, no matter how good the currency may be. Moreover, if the seller has denominated the sale in local currency, U.S. banks might be unable to make the exchange.

One way to solve the problem of convertibility is to arrange the financing and collection in advance. On smaller sales, bank letters of credit can provide the certainty of dollar receipt. On big ticket items, bank financing can often be arranged. In this case, a bank lends to the purchaser but the funds actually flow to the exporter; the bank stands the risk of convertibility as well as the credit risk.

Exchange Restrictions. Because of economic disequilibrium, many governments have found it necessary to intervene over the rights of their citizens to convert local currency into the currency of a foreign country. These controls seriously affect the payment performance of foreign importers of our goods. The importers must sell U.S. goods in their own countries for native currencies and then convert those currencies into U.S. dollars with which to pay their suppliers.

In general, exchange restrictions follow the same basic pattern in all countries. Foreign monies can be obtained only from the local exchange authority which generally operates in conjunction with the central or national bank of the particular country. Further, any receipts of foreign money must be deposited with the agency for conversion into local currency. Exchange controls fluctuate in rigidity with the political and financial condition of the country, and are generally coordinated with export-import regulations and needs.

Exchange restrictions are of as much concern to the export credit executive as the credit risk, and strongly influence the terms extended to foreign buyers. U.S. exporters generally invoice their goods in dollars and are very concerned about the importer's ability to transfer local currency into the required dollars. The foreign buyer may be totally prevented by exchange controls from remitting dollars to the U.S. supplier.

In determining the exchange risk of the buyer's country, the export credit executive will check that country's past performance in regard to its dollar obligations. A country with an unfavorable trade balance is more likely to have used up its dollar and gold reserves than one showing a favorable trade balance. The export credit executive will want to note the sufficiency of that deficit-trading country's dollar reserves before allowing shipment.

International Monetary Fund. The IMF had its origin in Bretton Woods in July 1944 and began operations March 1, 1947. Each member of the IMF has a quota expressed in U.S. dollars and this is determined prior to membership. Quotas determine the voting power, subscription of each member, and the normal quantitative limitations on the use of the IMF's resources by each member.

The general purpose of the IMF is to promote exchange stability and to provide resources to assist members in solving their payment problems. This assistance is granted on a short-term and revolving basis. The IMF imposes restrictions on the purchase of currencies in any 12-month period beyond the first 25 per cent of quota to ensure that steps are being taken to correct the borrower's currency problem.

A member is obligated to repurchase its currency from the IMF under two conditions: when its monetary reserves improve, and in any year in which it purchases foreign exchange from the IMF and does not draw equally on its own reserve.

Although the ultimate purpose of the IMF is the elimination of exchange restrictions, the IMF recognizes the existence of exchange restrictions in many countries and in effect condones their retention for limited periods.

Exchange Rate Risk

Another risk is that the foreign currency will be devalued while the receivable is outstanding. A country that seriously devalues its currency hampers the ability of its importers to pay obligations incurred prior to the devaluation; importers will then have to pay more of their native currency per dollar of outstanding debt. Most exchange rates are established by market forces and therefore move in an unpredictable pattern. However, an exporter can minimize the risk of loss due to a devaluation by invoicing in dollars, indexing the sales price, and using the foreign exchange market.

Invoicing in Dollars. The simplest solution is to invoice in dollars. The purchaser may be retailing the product in local currency at a markup. If, however, the local currency can be readily converted to U.S. dollars, there should be no problem in meeting trade obligations when due.

The market is itself often a dollar market and worldwide sales prices are always quoted in dollars, no matter what the souce of the product. This is the case in most commodity and raw material markets.

Usually the matter of the invoicing currency is determined by competition. The buyer compares the cost in local currency against that in U.S. dollars or other currency, and presses for the most advantageous circumstance. Often the foreign exchange market is used for multicurrency conversions to achieve the best price. Similarly, an exporter that is in an extremely strong position can choose the currency of billing.

Indexing Sales Price. Where the competition permits and where there has been an established pattern of devaluation, as in some Latin American countries, it has been a practice to index the local curency sales price to the official exchange rate. Therefore, if the U.S. dollar is revalued upward 20 per cent against the local currency, the price would be increased 20 per cent, restoring the dollar equivalent of the original sales price. A less direct method yielding much the same result would be to link the price to a measure of the local inflation rate.

Foreign Exchange Market. The foreign exchange market may be used by the U.S. exporter to protect profits from swings in exchange rates of other currencies. This can be done either by spot or by forward transactions.

By using the spot market, a U.S. seller can receive funds in dollars usually within two days. To illustrate, a foreign firm would arrange for the immediate transfer of $1,000 to the account of the U.S. corporation to pay for a purchase of goods. Assuming an exchange rate of $.40, the foreign firm would request its bank to charge its account for 2,500 foreign currency. The bank would do so, and cable instructions to a U.S. bank to credit the seller's account for $1,000.

The forward exchange market stabilizes prices by enabling a seller expecting payment in a foreign currency to contract to sell those receipts for U.S. dollars at a specified rate, established at the inception of the contract. Foreign currency rates are normally quoted for fixed period of one, three, or six months; but actual contracts in major currencies usually can be arranged for a specific date up to one year, and on occasion up to three years. Use of this medium enables the importer to stabilize the dollar value of receivables.

TRADING IN FOREIGN CURRENCIES

The basic trading intermediaries in the foreign exchange markets are commercial banks, money brokers, and central and reserve banks if they choose to intervene in the open commercial market. The major U.S. banks normally deal with each other through brokers but deal directly with the major foreign banks in Canada and Europe. In overseas markets, however, foreign branches of U.S. banks deal directly with their head offices, foreign banks, and with brokers, and may even trade directly with foreign branches of other U.S. banks.

Smaller U.S. banks which do not make a market or maintain a position in foreign currencies may deal either with the major U.S. banks, with money brokers, or with their most important correspondent banks abroad.

Handling foreign exchange is a complicated task that requires expertise, experience, and a keen sense of timing. The credit executive should rely upon the services of trading intermediaries when involved in this market. No direct fee is charged to corporations for these services, as the banks cover their costs by buying and selling foreign currencies.

Forward Rate

The forward rate of the currency is often misunderstood to be the market's perception of the expected spot rate on that future date. Actually the cost of the forward contract, which may be either positive or negative, depends on the difference in interest rates between the two currencies. This means that while the major determinant of the spot rate is the economic condition of the foreign country relative to the rest of the world, the forward rate is affected primarily by relative interest rates in the given country and other nations. Theoretically, it is set so as to equalize yields on comparable investments. The following example shows how to calculate a forward rate:

Interest Rate on U.S. Dollars: 14% per annum
Interest Rate on Foreign Currency (FC): 6% per annum
Foreign Currency = $.40 U.S. (spot rate)
Time Period: 6 Months

In six months, $1.00 invested at 14 per cent per annum would be worth $1.07.

Meanwhile, $1.00 invested in FC at the 6 per cent annual foreign rate would be equal to $1.03.

If R is the forward exchange rate which will equalize the two investments, then the following equation holds:

$$1.03 \div .40 = 1.07 \div R$$
$$1.03R = .4280$$
$$R = .4155$$

In practice, the equivalent or forward rate serves as the starting point of negotiations between buyers and sellers of currencies, and the end result is the "bid and asked" quotations that are used in the market.

Since strong currencies typically have lower interest rates, reflecting low inflation, and weak currencies typically have higher interest rates, it is easy to misinterpret the forward rate as an indicator of where the rate is expected to be.

Swap

On a long-term sale, where the exact date of funds receipt is unknown, a device known as a swap can be employed. In this case, the foreign currency is sold forward to the earliest expected date. On that date, the exporter would purchase the foreign currency spot and again sell it forward to the exact date, which is more likely to be known then. The spot purchase and forward sale is the swap.

Discount and Premium

Both the spot and forward rates are subject to discounts and premiums. Spot rates are based on market factors, while forward rates are calculated by applying either discount or premium factors to the spot rate that prevails at the time the contract is negotiated. A forward discount represents an interest cost to the holder, while a forward premium is a return.

If one currency sells at a premium to another currency in the forward market, the holder will receive more than the present spot rate when the contract expires. On the other hand, if one currency sells at a discount relative to another currency in the forward market, the holder will receive less than the present spot rate at maturity.

Hedging

Sophisticated companies hedge, or think in forward values, when they set up sales which are to be paid in a foreign currency sometime in the future. Moreover, in setting the price of the foreign currency which they will sell for U.S. dollars, they assume the worst possible situation. What that might be depends on the strength or weakness of a particular country's economy, but a 10 per cent estimated change in value is usually considered prudent, especially in countries with strong currencies.

If a company is working on a high profit margin, the rate of foreign currency is relatively unimportant. On the other hand, if a company is working on a slim profit margin, the rate of foreign currency becomes extremely important. Thus a U.S. company selling in a country with a weak currency might find the cost for buying forward to be 20 per cent of the selling price. With a profit margin below 20 per cent, the exporter would be losing on every sale. Moreover, the cost of a forward contract should never exceed the net profit margin except for a strong competitive or marketing reason; and then only if there will be a long-range benefit in exchange for this temporary loss.

Unhedged Position

When a U.S. company is willing to accept future payment in foreign currency and does not commit itself to a forward contract, there is no way of making certain that the future value of the currency will be equal to or greater than the spot rate. In fact, there is always the possibility that the future rate will sink below the spot rate. This additional risk is illustrated in the following example of a U.S. company in an unhedged position.

The U.S. company agreed to sell goods to a foreign buyer with payment due in six months in the foreign currency. The agreed price is 40,000 FCs (foreign currency), and is based upon the fact that the spot value of the FC is $.40 to the U.S. dollar. The FC is considered a strong currency in the international market and for some time its rate has neither risen nor fallen by more than 10 per cent. Consequently, it is expected that the price will swing no lower than $.36 nor higher than $.44 until the time for payment in six months.

Several things could happen. If the price of the FC should fall below

$.40, the U.S. corporation would realize a lower profit on its sale by absorbing the drop in value of the FC. It is very likely that there would still be some profit, since gross profit was set at a higher rate than the shrinking value of the FC. On the other hand, the U.S. corporation would realize a greater profit if the price of the FC rose above $.40 in six months.

Contracts Dealing in Strong Currencies

Using the same illustration above, the U.S. exporter could enter into a forward contract to sell 40,000 FCs at $.41, the going six-month rate in the forward market. The contract would be timed to coincide with the receipt of payment from the foreign customer.

The U.S. firm would be committed to sell the 40,000 FC payment at $.41 in six months, regardless of the exchange rate at that time. In this way, it fixed the rate of exchange and the cost of the transaction. Since it contracted to sell at $.41 when the FC was currently valued at $.40, the cost to the exporter was equal to $1 \div 40$, or 2.5 per cent.

If the foreign customer does not pay on time, the U.S. firm would be obliged to buy FCs in the spot market to deliver on its forward contract. This situation is the exception, however, rather than the rule.

Contracts Dealing in Weak Currencies

In another situation, the sale may have been made to a buyer that insisted on paying in a weak foreign currency. The price is again 40,000 FCs. During the past year, the rate of the FC fell from $.20 to $.15, a decline of 25 per cent. Because of this dramatic drop, large banks are quoting a six-months forward rate of $.14. This amounts to an annualized forward drop of 13.3 per cent. In this instance, three options are available to the U.S. company:

1. It may enter into a forward contract to sell 40,000 FCs at $.14 if it wants to fix its cost, and providing it regards the discount rate as less than the anticipated devaluation.

2. It may go into the sale on an unhedged basis. The current value of the sale is 40,000 FCs at $.15, or $6,000. If in six months the FC is valued at $.14, the receivable would be worth $5,600 and the exporter will lose $400. Similarly, if the FC drops to $.13, the exporter will lose $800. On the other hand, if the FC rises to $.16, the exporter will gain an additional $400 on the transaction.

3. If it cannot obtain a contract with a discount no greater than the anticipated devaluation, it can either ride out the future, hoping the FC will go no lower than $.14, or it can forego the sale.

FOREIGN CREDIT INFORMATION

Credit information is readily available on foreign customers and their countries. Financial statements are not as easy to obtain. Furthermore, they are difficult to evaluate because accounting practices and tax regulations differ widely from country to country. Because the time required to gather information is greater than in domestic operations, many export credit executives build a comprehensive file of information on prospective foreign customers so they may make quick decisions when necessary.

Credit information sources range from the customer to the comprehensive economic and business data compiled in the United States by governmental agencies, by the foreign departments of banks, by private trade promotion organizations, and by publishers and organizations that foster foreign commerce.

Customer

The best starting point for credit information is the customer. The prospect will be most cooperative if the U.S. manufacturer solicits the information at an opportune time. It is easier to soothe a customer's objections and fears during prosperous times than it is during recession. By establishing a rapport with the foreign customer, a supplier can develop a sound basis for granting continued credit. A tactful way of soliciting this information is for the U.S. manufacturer to initiate an exchange of antecedent and financial information between the seller and the buyer.

The information supplied by the customer may range from excellent to worthless. At best, the buyer may volunteer valuable data including financial reports, a detailed biography of the principals, and a history of the business going back over several generations. At worst, the buyer will provide no information at all, feeling that such a request reflects upon the integrity of the principals. Due to differences in accounting methods, financial statements cannot generally be analyzed in the same way as domestic statements.

Bank

An excellent source of valuable credit information is the exporter's bank. An inquiry directed through this source stands a better chance of obtaining useful information than one directed to the foreign customer's bank. Foreign banks vary widely in their cooperation with American requests for information, and like information received from the customer, the credit information secured directly from the foreign customer's bank varies in value. It may consist merely of a report that the foreign buyer is a respected member of the community. Only occasionally is complete information reported.

The domestic bank, on the other hand, usually has extensive credit information on many foreign houses. This information may be issued free of charge to clients upon request. Credit executives wanting this information should address a letter to the bank's credit department, giving the full name and address of the foreign customer, its local bank if known, and the nature of the sale including terms and amount. These facts can be of great assistance in obtaining a complete reply. In many cases, credit information on a buyer may already be in the bank's file or may be obtainable from other domestic sources, and a reply will be received very quickly. In other cases, it will be necessary for the bank to get the information from its foreign offices or correspondents abroad. This is usually done by airmail. If the information is urgently required, arrangements may be made with the bank to obtain the information by cable.

Bank information generally includes a history of the foreign firm, antecedents of the principals, and some financial data. A fairly complete picture of a firm's credit standing often may be obtained, but where large credit risks are undertaken by the seller, bank reports should be supplemented by information from other sources.

Exporter's Foreign Sales Representative

The exporter's sales representative abroad can also be a valuable source of information. In all probability the sales agent has known the customer for a long period and has had the opportunity to study its business practices firsthand. The agent is known in the customer's trade circle and has access to credit information from local banks and commercial sources. The representative can therefore offer a fair picture of a customer's financial condition, as well as confidential data which would be difficult to obtain from any other source. The information may comment on the foreign customer's aggressiveness or personal problems that may affect business dealings, on the buyer's standing in the trade and the community, and on past record and future prospects.

Commercial Credit Reporting Agencies

Dun & Bradstreet International writes business information reports on foreign companies which are similar in content and format to domestic reports. These reports may be purchased individually or contracted for in advance. In general, the international reports provide the following information:

1. A history of the firm, including the background of the business and identification of the principals and their commercial experience, allowing the user to evaluate management capabilities and degree of success.

2. A brief description of the present operation of the business, allowing for better interpretation of the financial information.

3. An estimate of net worth and financial condition in local currency, based on information from an authorized representative of the business and/or outside sources. When available, financial statements are included. This helps the decisionmaker to better estimate the firm's ability to meet its business commitments.

4. Trade investigations regarding the terms of sale and record of payment, which provide a meaningful guideline for predicting how a company might pay their bills, and also for establishing terms.

Reference books with ratings for individual businesses, similar to those offered in the United States, are available for Latin American, Continental Europe, and other foreign markets.

Inquiries are routed by telegraphic communications to the country in which the subject of inquiry is located. Priority service is available upon request.

FCIB-NACM Corporation (FCIB)

This function of the National Association of Credit Management provides services to firms doing business internationally. It was organized in 1919 and is an increasingly important source of information for international transactions. Some of the services provided to FCIB members are credit reports, free reciprocal reports, biweekly economic and market bulletins, roundtable conferences in the U.S. and Europe, worldwide collection service, and semiannual survey of terms and conditions in overseas markets.

The operations of the FCIB are conducted from offices located in New York City and Brussels. Contacts are maintained in all countries of the free world.

Credit Reports. Credit and ledger information on over 400,000 foreign firms is available to exporters that are members of the FCIB. These reports emphasize ledger experiences with the foreign customer and their purchases and payment patterns with other exporters, and include historical and financial information. Each member reports the account's rating, how long the account has been sold, the highest recent credit, terms of sale, and how the buyer pays on those terms. A careful coding system protects the confidential nature of the information.

Procedure. In seeking credit information on a particular account, a member completes a subscriber's inquiry ticket and forwards it to FCIB. Through its system of trade clearance, FCIB obtains the latest ledger information from all known suppliers and bank references, and publishes the results together with general information about the account.

Figure 36–1 shows a sample report. The information format is similar to that in the domestic credit interchange report. Two notable differences are the method of reporting terms of sale and manner of payment, and the references are asked to assign ratings to the account. Since the terms of sale may vary so widely, space is provided for the reference to indicate its own terms using the code shown at the top of the report.

In Figure 36–1, for example, the first reference reports having sold the account for 5 years on Draft at 120 Days Sight D/A. The key for sight draft is "11" and the number 120 is shown in the column headed "days."

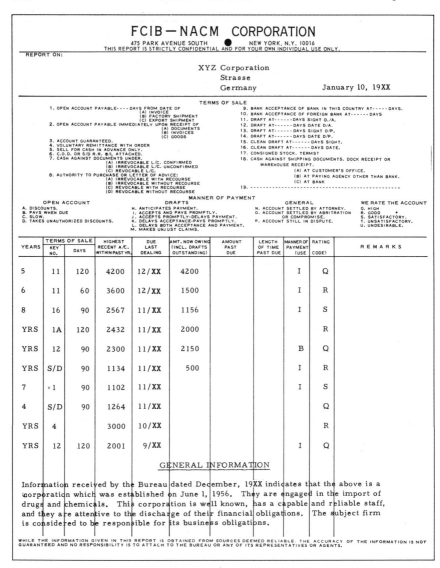

FIG. 36–1. Foreign Credit Information Report.

Manner of payment "I" means the customer accepts and pays promptly and the supplier rates the account "Q," or high.

Free Reciprocal Reports.   As an inducement to respond, the references and members that contribute their ledger experience on an account receive a free reciprocal copy of the report on that firm if they request one when they reply.

Additional Services.   Additional services are offered by the FCIB to broaden the executive's knowledge of foreign economic conditions and markets. Bulletins on significant and timely topics are issued biweekly. Regular and frequent roundtable conferences in the United States and Europe are attended by executives who discuss common problems and industry conditions, and who receive verbatim minutes of these discussions. Industry credit groups meet to keep abreast of developments in their special fields of interest and to discuss problem accounts. A special international collection division, which is part of a worldwide network of professional collection agencies, offers a facility for collecting overdue overseas accounts. The FCIB is the sole agent for the network in the United States.

U.S. Department of Commerce

United States foreign service offices, such as embassies and consulates, provide reports on foreign markets, industries, and importers. The information in these reports is relayed by the Department of State to the Department of Commerce, where it is compiled into individual country or industry bulletins and trade lists.

Information on individual buyers is compiled into World Traders Data Reports. These reports may be helpful in evaluating a foreign firm's financial standing by offering a brief history of the firm and its antecedents, and perhaps the number of its sales outlets and sales employees; estimates as to its capital and annual sales volume; and similar information. However, World Traders Data Reports are not credit reports and are generally used only as supplementary material.

TERMS OF SALE

The selling arrangements in foreign trade vary according to the buyers' creditworthiness and the countries in which they are located. A number of terms and arrangements are discussed in this chapter, while a full discussion of documentary credits is left for Chapter 37.

Export Agencies

Foreign credit administration poses no new problems for the company which markets its product abroad indirectly through export marketing agencies such as export commission houses, manufacturers' export agents, export merchants, buyers for export, export and import brokers, and combination export managers that handle a number of noncompetitive products for different manufacturers. The export agency not only assumes many of the sales expenses but sometimes assumes all credit and exhange risks. The U.S. manufacturer is thus permitted to engage in export business on almost a riskless basis. Naturally, though, this security has a cost attached to it, for the export agent charges a service fee or commission.

Cash with Order

An exporter may choose to request payment in cash, in part or in whole, before shipping merchandise. This payment arrangement could arise when any of the following conditions exist:

1. The customer's credit standing is not satisfactory.
2. Exchange conditions within the customer's country are such that the return of funds from abroad may be delayed for an unreasonable period.
3. A letter of credit is not obtainable.
4. The goods are manufactured to special order and would have little resale value elsewhere.

In some countries, because of local exhange restrictions, importers are not permitted to make payment in advance of shipment. Further, foreign buyers may be unwilling to tie up capital for the length of time involved in a foreign transaction, and may hesitate to bear the risk of the shipper's possible default or bankruptcy. As a result, the volume of business handled on cash terms is negligible.

Consignment

Merchandise may be shipped on consignment to a foreign branch or subsidiary of the exporter, to a resident agent or representative abroad, to an import house, or to a foreign bank. Because the credit risks are similar to those on open-account sales, consignment shipments to other than branches or subsidiaries are infrequent in export trade. The foreign agent sells the goods in the local currency, then has to buy U.S. dollars to pay the exporter. Thus consignment selling is feasible only when dollar exhange is readily available, when exchange restrictions are not burdensome, when the character of the goods and the market is stable, and when the exporter can finance the inventories abroad until they are sold.

The credit reputation of the agent is also a serious consideration because foreign laws on passing of title to goods may differ from those in the United States. In some countries, repossession and conditional sales laws give the consignment sale dubious legal status; the importing agent's physical receipt of the goods may mean automatic passing of title. Furthermore, should legal action be necessary, the exporter would have no useful, tangible evidence of obligation. On another score, consignment accounts subject the exporter to taxation in some countries.

As a means of some security in countries with free ports or free trade zones, consigned merchandise may be placed under bonded warehouse control in the name of a foreign bank. Arrangements can then be made to release partial lots of the consigned merchandise against payments on specified terms. Merchandise would be cleared through customs after the sale has been completed. This type of consignment arrangement should not be made until regulations and conditions are verified, and storage facilities are assured. Many foreign banks will not accept merchandise consigned directly to them; consequently, goods should not be consigned until prior arrangements have been made. It is also advisable to verify that goods not sold may be readily returned to the country of origin.

Authority to Purchase

This is an instrument used primarily by banks in the Far East as a way for their clients to make payment for goods bought abroad. It authorizes the exporter to draw documentary drafts on the customer or on the customer's bank. It specifies a bank in the exporter's country where the exporter may negotiate a draft with documents attached, and thus obtain funds immediately.

However, the U.S. bank is under no obligation to pay unless it adds its confirmation to the authority to purchase. Unless stated otherwise, the exporter's draft will be negotiated with recourse. The exporter remains liable to the bank until the draft is paid by the customer or drawee abroad. This liability may be eliminated by obtaining authority from the foreign bank to negotiate the draft without recourse; the words "without recourse" should then appear on the draft above the drawer's signature. An authority to purchase may be revocable or irrevocable. The bank designated to negotiate drafts may confirm an authority issued irrevocably.

Occasionally an authority to pay may be issued. This instrument differs from the authority to purchase in that the drafts under it are drawn on a bank in the United States. Once the drafts have been paid, the exporter is no longer liable as drawer.

Open Account

Exporters often use open-account credit terms, sometimes as a competitive tool to break into a new market; and at others, to meet competitive pressures. More and more, open-account terms are used because they are convenient for both the buyer and the seller. The advantages of these transactions are simplicity and avoidance of additional charges connected with other payment arrangements.

In many cases, the seller prefers to assume the credit risk and to use an export agency only as a sales resource. In others, the exporter may market directly through its own sales department. Direct exporting gives a manufacturer full control of sales promotion and distribution, and permits close cooperation with foreign outlets. It allows for a greater degree of coordination with domestic operations and gives first-hand experience with the requirements of the market.

Manufacturers that assume the risks of foreign credit must develop a foreign credit policy to control the risks. The costs of foreign credit administration and the technical details of shipping, financing, and insurance should be offset by the savings in not having to share profits with an export marketing agency. Other factors are the financial resources of the company, the availability of personnel trained in foreign trade, the sales price for the products, and arrangements required for servicing the products.

The economic and legal atmosphere of the buyer's country should be stable for an exporter to sell on open account. Additionally, this type of credit is confined to customers of good credit standing in established markets. One of the reasons is that bank financing is not as readily available on open-account transactions as it is on more secure terms.

In countries with dollar exchange shortages, buyers on open account are sometimes unable to obtain U.S. dollars readily. This problem becomes magnified in countries where applications for exchange to settle dollar drafts take precedence over applications for exchange to settle open-account transactions. Further, if a customer does not pay, the open-account sale offers no tangible evidence of obligation that may be used in litigation. Finally, the maturity date on an invoice does not have the same coercive effect as the maturity date on a draft or other instrument of credit presented to a customer by its bank.

EXPORT COLLECTIONS

Collection procedures for open-account export credit must be clearly defined so the underlying reasons for improper payment can be identified. It is much easier to trace letter of credit discrepancies, for they provide a record of conditions that must be met before payment can be made. Equally, though, if those conditions are met, the payment is made as a matter of course.

Open-account transactions offer more variety and more opportunity for buyers to pay slow. Among the chief reasons are their paying habits and policies, the billing practices of the exporter, and the payment instructions issued by the exporter. Other conditions may include late shipments, unsatisfactory quality of goods, or sudden changes in import restrictions of the customer's country.

Customer Paying Habits and Policies

The buyer will sometimes try to impose different arrangements on a sale than those quoted by the seller. The customer may pay only at fixed dates, say once or twice a month; may interpret payment terms in a biased way to gain more time; or may unilaterally stipulate longer terms as a matter of buying policy. Diplomacy and perseverance must be judiciously mixed by the credit executive to speed collections, yet hold the customer.

Billing Practices

The efficiency of the collection process is often hampered by the selling company's billing practices. Many of the errors encountered in domestic sales occur in export sales, such as arithmetic errors in price computation and extension and late billings.

The exporter should take great care to invoice the customer at the proper location. Material is often shipped to one location, while the original documents are sent to a centralized purchasing department for payment approval. The invoice should identify the exact content of the shipment, be accompanied by a complete set of requested documents, and contain the purchase order reference number. Very often the order entry point is the source of errors and omissions.

Payment Instructions

Companies generally invoice their shipments in U.S. dollars. This ensures that the amounts collected will be the same as the amounts billed. In the event that some customers insist on being invoiced in their local currency, care should be taken to compensate for both convertibility and exchange rate risks.

Each invoice should indicate the manner in which payment is to be transmitted. Payment instructions prepared in the debtor's language would be a great help.

Many of the methods used domestically can be adapted for overseas customers. Instructions may direct that payments be mailed to a lockbox in the United States or to a specified country. Payments may be made by the customer's bank through its correspondent to the seller's bank in the United States. Commercial banks are continually developing programs that will help their customers speed the flow of cash and minimize float, the time lag between the moment a customer initiates a payment and the moment the money becomes available for the seller's use.

Past-Due Accounts

Collections of past-due foreign accounts is difficult and expensive. The great variance in commercial laws from country to country makes unpaid and disputed claims costly to litigate, and the bankruptcy laws of some countries do not protect the rights of the creditor as well as they do in the United States. Export credit executives must use extra care to screen prospects that do not have a good payment record.

As far as possible, it also is important to avoid customers that may become delinquent because of exchange or export-import regulations. In most countries, a legal obligation is considered discharged when the customer has deposited local currency in the bank to pay for an invoice or draft of a foreign supplier. However, exchange restrictions may prevent the transfer of these funds to the seller and make this customer actually, if not technically, delinquent.

Collection efforts on past-due foreign accounts follow much the same pattern as for domestic past-due accounts. Letters could be in the debtor's language to avoid any misunderstandings arising from translation. The initial letter should always be sent airmail. If it is not successful, two or three followup letters should be sent. After that, it is wise to telex, cable, or make a telephone call to the foreign customer.

Where a company has a subsidiary or affiliate located in the debtor's country, it is preferable for the underlying unit to handle the collection procedure. As an alternative, the collection effort should be reinforced by the exporter's foreign sales representative and the collecting bank. If the sale is on draft terms, the creditor may wish to authorize protest, although drafts are protested only in extreme cases; such action quite often disrupts normal business relations between buyer and seller.

Delinquent accounts failing to yield to these methods may be turned over to commercial credit agencies with special experience in foreign collections. Finally, placing the account for collection with an attorney is costly and complicated. The exporter undertaking such action may obtain the names of lawyers specializing in international law from the bank or from law lists such as *Martindale-Hubbell Law Directory*.

Commercial Arbitration

Delays in meeting delivery dates, differences over contract specifications, losses and damages in transit, and scores of other daily occurrences give rise to business controversy. Many such disputes with foreign buyers, which hitherto would have resulted in costly litigation and loss of customer good will, are now being speedily and inexpensively settled by commercial arbitration. The process is free of the jurisdictional problems of legal action. Because of the composition of the arbitration tribunals, arbitration decisions have the added advantage of being reached by the exercise of mercantile judgment rather than by legal considerations alone.

Parties to a dispute define the issue between them, select the arbitrators themselves or agree upon a method of selection, determine the place of arbitration to suit their mutual convenience, and agree in advance to accept the arbitrator's decision as final and binding. Rules of procedure of an agency administering arbitrations protect the voluntary agreement of the parties from being short-circuited by delays or deadlocks.

A worldwide system of arbitration, organized by the American Arbitration Association (AAA) and cooperating trade associations and chambers of commerce, has been in operation for many years. Panels of arbitrators have been established which include experts in every branch of international commerce and all the professions.

Arbitration Clause. The most practical way of providing for arbitration is to incorporate in the sales contract an agreement to settle by arbitration any future dispute that might arise under such contract. The arbitration clause should, if possible, contain not only agreement of the contractual parties to submit their disputes to arbitration but also agreement as to the place of arbitration and the rules to be used.

The parties can agree at the time they write their contracts that they will arbitrate in the United States, regardless of their nationality or residence. In some instances, parties cannot know at the time that they sign a contract where they would prefer to have an arbitration. Goods in dispute or certain evidence, for example, might be available for examination in one country and not in another. Under the circumstances, it might not be convenient to designate in advance in the contract either the place of arbitration, the administering agency, or the rules to be applied.

Special arbitration clauses may be required for particular contracts. Before inserting an arbitration clause in the contract, the credit executive should be familiar with the laws for enforcement of arbitration agreements and awards in the buyer's country. Arbitration awards are generally enforceable by law in leading trade countries of the world; where this is not yet so, they are often enforceable by trade practice.

When a dispute arises under any contract which includes an AAA arbitration clause, the claimant may initiate arbitration by giving notice to the other party setting forth the date of the contract, the text of the arbitration clause, a brief statement of the controversy, the amount of money involved, and the relief sought. Such a notice is called a Demand for Arbitration. Two copies of the Demand for Arbitration should be sent to the AAA, together with the appropriate fees established under the rules. The AAA will then arrange for filing of answering statements, for the selection of arbitrators, and for time and place of hearings, in accordance with the agreement of the parties and AAA Rules.

Initiating Arbitration in Absence of Arbitration Clause. If there is no arbitration clause in a contract, arbitration may be initiated through the execution by both parties of an agreement to arbitrate the particular dispute. This submission agreement should set forth the nature of the dispute, the amount of money involved, and the relief sought.

U.S. GOVERNMENT PROGRAMS

A number of programs established by the U.S. government also affect the national economies of nations that may be good prospects for U.S. export trade. These include the Export-Import Bank of the United States, the Agency for International Development, and the International Bank for Reconstruction and Development.

The Export-Import Bank (Eximbank)

The Export-Import Bank of the United States was established in 1934 and presently operates under the Export-Import Bank Act of 1945, as amended. Its paid in capital is $1-billion subscribed by the U.S. Treasury and it has authority to borrow an additional $6-billion from that source. It also can, and does, borrow in the open market with the backing of the full faith and credit of the U.S. government.

Eximbank functions primarily to promote the exchange of goods between the United States and foreign countries through direct loans for the purchase of U.S. goods and services, and through guaranties and insurance on export transactions. The agency's loans are made and payable in U.S. dollars. They are granted only when a reasonable assurance of repayment is offered, and are designed to supplement and encourage private capital rather than compete with it.

Eximbank's principal activity since its establishment has been to make loans to foreign governments and to a lesser extent foreign corporations. However, in recent years the bank has been stressing its guaranty and insurance functions.

Guaranties. Eximbank issues guaranties to commercial banks for the payment of receivables that banks purchase from exporters without recourse. The receivables may have maturities from 181 days to 5 years and sometimes longer, and the amount of receivables purchased by banks without recourse to the exporter normally cannot exceed 90 per cent of the financed portion of the sale.

The covered risks are of two types, political and commercial. If the lender is not concerned about the commercial risk, Eximbank can guarantee against political risk only; this includes convertibility of foreign currency into dollars, cancellation of export and import licenses, or other foreign government activities harmful to trade. If, on the other hand, a commercial or credit risk is involved, Eximbank will guarantee appropriate portions of loans against receivables that have run for 18 months.

The guaranty applies to repayment of principal and to payment of interest up to the rate charged by Eximbank on long-term project loans at the time the guaranty was issued.

Under certain conditions, Eximbank will issue a comprehensive guaranty, called a financial guaranty, to cover a loan made by a U.S. commercial bank to a foreign borrower for the purpose of financing the export of large quantities of U.S. goods or services. A financial guaranty generally gives political and commercial risk coverage on 100 per cent of the principal of the loan and on the interest up to 1 per cent per annum above the rate being paid by the U.S. Treasury on borrowings of similar maturity. The rate is determined at the time of Eximbank's formal and final commitment. If a financial guaranty is issued to a non-U.S. bank that is lending to a buyer outside the United States to finance a purchase from a U.S. supplier, the extent of the interest-rate guaranty is subject to negotiation.

FCIA Insurance Programs. The Foreign Credit Insurance Association, through private insurance companies, issues to American exporters policies covering loss from commercial risks, political risks, or both. It operates in conjunction with the Eximbank, but is not a governmental agency.

The FCIA issues short-term policies involving payment terms up to 180 days and medium-term policies with payment terms from 181 days to 5 years. Coverage up to seven years may be granted to meet government-supported foreign competition in such areas as aircraft and marine sales. In addition, the FCIA issues policies that provide coverage under a single comprehensive policy for all of an exporter's sales to foreign buyers on terms of up to five years. Shipments covered by irrevocable letters of credit and shipments to buyers in Canada normally may be excluded on short-term comprehensive risk policies.

Other Programs. Eximbank has a number of other programs. In one, it considers a direct application from an exporter that is unable to arrange financing from commercial banks or insurance from FCIA. In another, it participates in large projects in foreign countries utilizing U.S. exports. It combines direct lending by Eximbank to a foreign borrower with loans from the private sector. In still another, Eximbank extends a line of credit directly to a non-U.S. financial institution, which in turn relends the funds to small or medium-sized importers of U.S. goods and services.

Agency for International Development (AID)

This agency was founded in 1961 to centralize the administration of the U.S. government's foreign economic aid activities. One aspect of the AID's operations comprises development loans that may be made to promote the economic development of the less-developed countries. These loans are made in dollars, although it is possible for the borrower to repay the loan in local currency to friendly governments or qualifying private businesses. The proceeds in most cases must be spent for U.S. goods and services. Before granting a development loan, AID considers the availability of funds at reasonable rates from the free-world sources and the debt-bearing capacity of the country or business seeking the funds.

The International Bank for Reconstruction and Development

The International Bank of Reconstruction and Development, generally known as the World Bank, had its origin in Bretton Woods in July 1944 and formally opened for business on June 25, 1946. The Bank is one of three related international financial institutions, known as the World Bank Group, whose purpose is to help member countries develop their economies. The other institutions are the International Development Association (IDA) and the International Finance Corporation (IFC).

The World Bank is owned by the member countries, and each member has subscribed to its capital stock in an amount determined prior to membership. In general, the amounts of the subscriptions are based on the economic resources of the member countries. In addition to the capital subscriptions, the Bank obtains funds from bonds sold in world markets, sales of loans, repayment of principal, and income from operations.

The World Bank's chief objective is to provide long-term loans to member countries for reconstruction and development of production facilities and resources. Immediately after World War II, most loans were made to European countries to aid in the reconstruction of those countries. In recent years, most of the Bank's activities have been in making loans to aid the less-developed countries.

The World Bank may guarantee, participate in, or make loans either to member governments, to governmental authorities or agencies, or to private enterprises in the territories of member governments. A loan that is not made directly to the government in whose territories the project being financed is located must be guaranteed as to principal, interest, and other charges by the government or its central bank, or a comparable agency of the government acceptable to the World Bank.

Loans must have productive purposes and must be used only for the purposes for which the loans are granted. Loans which in the Bank's opinion cannot be justified on economic ground are excluded. In making loans, the Bank must act prudently and evaluate the prospects of repayment. The Bank does not make loans that are obtainable in the private market on reasonable terms. Since the Bank is intended to promote private investment, not to compete with it, it does not undertake business that private investors are willing to transact on a reasonable basis.

The objectives of the International Development Association and the International Finance Corporation are similar to those of the World Bank, except that the IDA makes soft loans and the IFC promotes private investment. IDA grants long-term loans on a low-interest or interest-free basis and repayments can be made in local currencies. The loans are granted to the poorest of the developing nations, those that cannot borrow on conventional terms. The IFC invests directly in private enterprise that will benefit the host country and have a reasonable prospect of profitable operation. Profitability is an important factor because the IFC eventually wants to sell its participation to private investors.

CHAPTER 37

DOCUMENTARY CREDITS

The terms of sale in an export transaction are a matter of prior arrangement between the buyer and the seller. Usually the actual collection of payment for goods sold abroad is accomplished through the international facilities of a commercial bank. The choice of payment method, or financial instrument, is dependent on such factors as the credit standing of the foreign buyer; the exchange restrictions, if any, that exist in the country in which the buyer is located; and the competition that the seller faces.

When the credit standing of the buyer is unknown or uncertain, and the risk to the seller is greatest, the cash in advance method is desirable. On the other hand, when little or no risk to the seller is involved, export sales are likely to be made on the open-account basis. Between these two extremes, U.S. exports going through normal channels to buyers abroad are likely to be handled on the basis of either letters of credit or dollar drafts.

EXPORT LETTER OF CREDIT

A letter of credit is essentially a declaration by a bank that it will make certain payments on behalf of a specified party under specified conditions. It is called a letter because it takes the form of a notification to the party or parties likely to be the recipients of the payments. When a letter of credit is used in connection with international transactions, more than one bank normally is involved, usually one in the buyer's country and one in the seller's. One of the fundamentals of the letter of credit system is the fact that banks usually know each other better than do sellers and buyers. Also, established lines of communication are more likely to exist between banks than between industrial or commercial companies.

The letter of credit authorizes the exporter to draw drafts on a bank and to receive the funds by presenting the prescribed supporting documents. The collection of funds from the customer then becomes the work of the banking system. Practically all export letters of credit issued or advised by banks in the United States contain the following stipulation: "This credit is subject to the Uniform Customs and Practice for Documentary Credits (1974 Revision), International Chamber of Commerce, Publication No. 290." It is important that exporters familiarize themselves with these terms and conditions. Reference to them in letters of credit makes them an integral part of the conditions of. such letters of credit and will determine the interpretations of terms therein in the absence of any specific conditions in the credits to the contrary.

Except for cash in advance, export letters of credit give the highest degree of protection to the seller. They may be classified in accordance with the following features of their promises: certainty, time of enforcement, documentary requirements, negotiation, and renewal.

Certainty

The promise in an export letter of credit involves several degrees of certainty. It may be a revocable promise, subject to the issuing bank's unilateral cancellation without notification of any sort. In such a case, the exporter's certainty of enforcing the bank's promise to pay is nonexistent until the moment the customer's bank either accepts or pays.

A revocable letter of credit is rarely used in commercial transactions and commonly serves only as a means of arranging payment. It gives the exporter no protection and may be amended or canceled without the consent of or prior notice to the exporter. Thus a seller may be unable to collect from the buyer's bank under a revoked letter, even though the conditions of the transaction may have been met. As a matter of courtesy, banks generally notify exporters of amendments or cancellations but there is no obligation on their part to do so. Figure 37–1 illustrates a revocable letter of credit.

The promise in an irrevocable credit becomes certain at a given moment after its issuance, usually when the instrument is received. Irrevocable credits may be confirmed or unconfirmed. When confirmed, the irrevocable letter of credit offers maximum assurance to the seller. The promise of the buyer's bank remains unchanged; but, in addition, the irrevocable promise of another bank, usually at the exporter's domicile, is added. Figure 37–2 illustrates the irrevocable letter of credit issued by a foreign bank in favor of a U.S. exporter and confirmed by a U.S. bank.

An irrevocable letter of credit may also be issued so that it is the obligation of only one bank. Figure 37–3 illustrates a credit in favor of a U.S. exporter, issued by a U.S. bank at the request of a foreign bank. In this instance, only the U.S. bank is obliged to honor drafts drawn under the credit.

In an unconfirmed letter of credit, the U.S. bank advises the exporter of the irrevocable credit but does not confirm and has no obligation. Under this arrangement, the U.S. bank acts merely as a notifying and paying agent for the foreign bank. It assumes no obligation to accept or pay any

---

MORGAN GUARANTY TRUST COMPANY
OF NEW YORK
INTERNATIONAL BANKING DIVISION
23 WALL STREET, NEW YORK, N. Y. 10015   April 2, 19*

On all communications please refer to
EXPORT CREDIT NO. R-523744

Raw Cotton Export Co.
Houston
Texas

Dear Sirs:

In accordance with instructions received from

Commercial Bank of London, Ltd., London, England (their No. 79328) . . . .

we have established a REVOCABLE credit in your favor for account of Green & Buckley Textile Co., Ltd., London England

for U.S. $65,000.00 (SIXTY FIVE THOUSAND U.S. DOLLARS) . . . .

available by your drafts at sight on us, accompanied by documents consisting of:

Commercial Invoice in triplicate, describing the merchandise as indicated below

Full set of on board ocean steamer Bills of Lading to order of shipper, blank endorsed, marked "Freight Prepaid",

evidencing shipment of 500 (five hundred) bales of COTTON, middling 7/8 inch, from U.S. to C and F United Kingdom.

Except as otherwise expressly stated herein, this advice is subject to the Uniform Customs and Practice for Documentary Credits (1974 Revision), International Chamber of Commerce Publication No. 290.
THIS CREDIT IS SUBJECT TO REVOCATION OR MODIFICATION AT ANY TIME, EITHER BEFORE OR AFTER PRESENTATION OF DOCUMENTS, AND WITHOUT NOTICE TO YOU.
Drafts and documents must be presented to our Commercial Credits Department, 15 Broad Street, New York, N. Y. 10015, on or before July 15, 19* on which date this credit expires, UNLESS SOONER REVOKED.

Yours very Truly,

Authorized Signature
Immediately upon receipt please examine this credit, and if its terms are not clear to you or if you need any assistance in respect to your availment of it, we would welcome your communicating with us. Documents should be presented promptly and not later than 3 P.M.

FIG. 37–1.   Revocable Letter of Credit.

drafts drawn under the credit. If, upon presentation of proper documents, payment could not be obtained from the U.S. bank for some reason, the exporter would have to look to the foreign bank for payment. Figure 37–4 illustrates an unconfirmed letter of credit.

The certainty of a letter of credit of a foreign bank, or whether it is confirmed or unconfirmed, is most important to the export credit executive. Notification that a letter of credit has been issued must not be construed as confirmation of a domestic bank's responsibility. When a U.S. bank confirms a letter of credit, a statement to this effect is generally placed at the end of the letter.

MORGAN GUARANTY TRUST COMPANY
OF NEW YORK
INTERNATIONAL BANKING DIVISION
23 WALL STREET, NEW YORK, N. Y. 10015   March 5, 19*

Smith Tool Co. Inc.
29 Bleecker Street
New York, N.Y. 10012

On all communications please refer to

NUMBER IC - 152647

Dear Sirs:
            We are instructed to advise you of the establishment by
*Bank of South America, Puerto Cabello, Venezuela . . . .
of their IRREVOCABLE Credit No. 19845 . . . .
in your favor, for the account of John Doe, Puerto Cabello, Venezuela . . . .
for   U. S. $3,000.00 (THREE THOUSAND U.S. DOLLARS) . . . .

available upon presentation to us of your drafts at sight on us, accompanied by:

Commercial Invoice in triplicate, describing the merchandise as indicated below

Consular Invoice in triplicate, all signed and stamped by the Consul of Venezuela

Negotiable Insurance Policy and/or Underwriter's Certificate, endorsed in blank, covering
marine and war risks

Full set of straight ocean steamer Bills of Lading, showing consignment to the Bank of
South America, Puerto Cabello, stamped by Venezuelan Consul and marked "Freight Prepaid",

evidencing shipment of UNA MAQUINA DE SELLAR LATAS, C.I.F. Puerto Cabello, from United
States Port to Puerto Cabello, Venezuela

"This credit is subject to the Uniform Customs and Practice for Documentary Credits (1974 Revision), International Chamber of Commerce, Publication No. 290."
        The above bank engages with you that all drafts drawn under and in compliance with
the terms of this advice will be duly honored if presented to our Commercial Credits
Department, 15 Broad Street, New York, N. Y. 10015, on or before March 31, 19*
on which date this credit expires.
        We confirm the foregoing and undertake that all drafts drawn and presented in
accordance with its terms will be duly honored.
                        Yours very truly,

                        Authorized Signature
Immediately upon receipt, please examine this instrument and if its terms are not clear to
you or if you need any assistance in respect to your availment of it, we would welcome your
communicating with us. Documents should be presented promptly and not later than 3 P.M.

FIG. 37–2. Confirmed Irrevocable Export Letter of Credit Issued by Foreign Bank; Confirmed
Irrevocably by American Bank.

This statement of confirmation should be carefully distinguished from
the waiver of responsibility in the unconfirmed letter of credit. The latter
is simply an advice from the U.S. bank informing the exporter that a letter
of credit has been established by the foreign bank. Before accepting an
unconfirmed credit, the export credit executive should be satisfied with the
reputation and financial standing of the foreign bank. Even if the foreign
bank is acceptable, the exporter may still insist upon a confirmed letter of

MORGAN GUARANTY TRUST COMPANY
OF NEW YORK
INTERNATIONAL BANKING DIVISION
23 WALL STREET, NEW YORK, N.Y. 10015   April 2, 19*

EXPORT CREDIT No. C-974960

Chas. B. Davidson & Co.
50 Broadway
New York, N.Y. 10004

Dear Sirs:
                                    In accordance with instructions received from
Bank of South America, Rio de Janeiro, Brazil (their No. 123456) . . . .
we have established OUR IRREVOCABLE credit in your favor for account of Gomes & Co., Rio
de Janeiro, Brazil

for about U.S. $7,200.00 (SEVEN THOUSAND TWO HUNDRED U.S. DOLLARS)

available by your drafts at sight on us, accompanied by documents consisting of:

Your Receipt in duplicate for amount claimed hereunder, marked: "Drawn under Bank of
South America Credit No. 123456"

Commercial Invoice in five copies of which First, Second, and Third copies visaed by
Chamber of Commerce, describing the merchandise as indicated below, stating "in
accordance with Brazilian Exchange Certificate 55-77/99"

Your Statement to the effect that you will or will not avail of the unused balance (if any)
and in the latter case, your agreement to its cancellation, quoting the respective amount

Full set on board ocean steamer Bills of Lading to order of shipper, blank endorsed
marked "Notify: Gomes & Co., Rio de Janeiro, Brazil" and "Freight Collect"

evidencing shipment of about 25,000 (TWENTY FIVE THOUSAND) kilos of TINPLATE, F.O.B.
Vessel New York, from New York to Rio de Janeiro

This credit is subject to the Uniform Customs and Practice for Documentary Credits
(1974 Revision), International Chamber of Commerce Publication No. 290.
    We hereby agree that drafts drawn in accordance with the terms stipulated herein will
be duly honored upon presentation and delivery of documents as specified if presented to
our Letter of Credit Department, 30 West Broadway, New York, N. Y. 10015, on or before
May 31, 19*   , on which date this credit expires.
                            Yours very truly,

                            Authorized Signature

    Immediately upon receipt please examine this credit, and if its terms are not clear to
you or if you need any assistance in respect to your availment of it, we would welcome your
communicating with us. Documents should be presented promptly and not later than 3 P.M.

FIG. 37–3.   Irrevocable Export Letter of Credit Issued by American Bank.

credit because of adverse exchange or other economic conditions within the
importer's country.

Finally, in honoring a letter of credit, the U.S. paying bank has no authority to deviate from its terms or conditions as established abroad. Therefore, the exporter must check that they agree with those of the sales contract.

MORGAN GUARANTY TRUST COMPANY
OF NEW YORK
INTERNATIONAL BANKING DIVISION
23 WALL STREET, NEW YORK, N. Y. 10015   April 20, 19*

| On all communications please refer to |
| OUR REFERENCE NUMBER |
| A - 890524 |

American Cotton Goods Export Co.
490 Broadway
New York, N.Y. 10012

Dear Sirs:
              We are instructed to advise you of the establishment by
`Imperial Bank, Colombo, Ceylon . . . .
of their Irrevocable Credit No. 45673 . . . .
in your favor, for the account of Ceylon Textiles, Inc., Colombo . . . .
for U.S. $15,000.00 (FIFTEEN THOUSAND U.S. DOLLARS) . . . .

available upon presentation to us of your drafts, drawn at sight D/P on Ceylon Textiles,
Inc., Colombo, without recourse to you, in First and Second of Exchange, payable to the
order of the Imperial Bank, Colombo, Ceylon, accompanied by the following documents:

Commercial Invoice in triplicate - signed, describing the merchandise as indicated below

Negotiable Insurance Policy and/or Underwriter's Certificate, endorsed in blank,
covering marine and war risks

Full set of on board ocean steamer Bills of Lading to order of shipper, blank endorsed,
marked "freight Prepaid",

evidencing shipment of 50,000 (fifty thousand) yards of COTTON PIECE GOODS, C.I.F. Colombo,
from any U.S.A. Port

Except as otherwise expressly stated herein, this advice is subject to the Uniform Customs
and Practice for Documentary Credits (1974 Revision), International Chamber of Commerce
Publication No. 290.
Your drafts must indicate that they are drawn under the aforementioned Irrevocable Credit,
number 45673, dated 4-19-19* of the Imperial Bank, Colombo, Ceylon and must be presented
to our Commercial Credits Department, 15 Broad Street, New York, N. Y. 10015 with
specified documents, not later than June 30, 19* on which date this advice expires.
        THIS LETTER IS SOLELY AN ADVICE AND CONVEYS NO ENGAGEMENT BY US.
                    Yours very truly,

                    Authorized Signature
        Immediately upon receipt please examine this advice, and if its terms are not clear to
you or if you need any assistance in respect to your availment of it, we would welcome your
communicating with us. Documents should be presented promptly and not later than 3 P.M.

FIG. 37-4. Unconfirmed Letter of Credit.

Time of Enforcement

All letters of credit require the seller to present a draft and specified
documents in order to get paid. A sight letter of credit stipulates that the
exporter will receive payment from the issuing or confirming bank immediately upon presentation of a sight draft accompanied by the specified documents. A time draft sets a specified later date for payment.

Under an acceptance credit, also called a usance, the exporter presents a
draft and the required documents to the specified bank. After finding the

documents correct, the drawee bank accepts the draft by writing or stamping the word "accepted" across its face over the date and authorized signature of a bank officer. By so doing, the bank signifies its commitment to pay the face value at maturity.

At this stage the instrument has become a banker's acceptance. The wording of the credit states whether the draft is to be drawn on the issuing bank, the advising bank, or a third bank, and the period for which it must run. If the exporter wishes to cash the draft prior to maturity, it can usually be discounted to put the proceeds at the seller's disposal immediately. Meanwhile, the buyer will be charged with the draft amount only at maturity.

In addition to the above letters of credit, the deferred payment letter of credit deserves mention because of its time-enforcement features. On its face, the deferred payment credit looks like a conventional irrevocable sight credit; it states, however, that payment will be made at a specified time after presentation of the documents. The paying bank sends the documents to the bank which issued the letter of credit, along with an advice showing the date that payment is to be made if all conditions governing the transaction have been met. Letters of credit with time drafts drawn on the paying bank can be readily negotiated or discounted; in contrast, deferred payment credits are not negotiable instruments. Figure 37–5 illustrates an irrevocable deferred payment letter of credit.

When this form of credit is used, it is important that the letter stipulate a latest date for presentation of the shipping documents and an expiration date for the letter, so that the date of deferred payment can be set within the period when the credit is valid.

Documentary Requirements

The most common documents required by export letters of credit are the seller's invoice, a full set of on-board ocean bills of lading or an airway bill, and an insurance policy or certificate. Additional documents that may be required include consular invoice or certification of origin, certificate of weight, quality inspection, and the like.

Instead of requiring shipping documents to be presented at the time of the bank's acceptance or payment, certain commercial letters of credit bear an endorsement in red ink, referred to as a red clause. This allows the confirming or negotiating bank to pay against the exporter's draft alone, provided the draft is accompanied by a promise to furnish shipping documents in the future. As a variation of this, green clause credits allow advances to the exporter before presentation of documents providing shipment to the customer; in contrast to the red clause credits, however, they require storage of the goods in the name of the bank.

Some exporters, particularly those fabricating goods to special order that cannot readily be sold to other than the original purchaser, may require

MORGAN GUARANTY TRUST COMPANY
OF NEW YORK
INTERNATIONAL BANKING DIVISION
23 WALL STREET, NEW YORK, N. Y. 10015   May 2, 19*

General Tool Co.
450 Broadway
New York, N.Y. 10012

| On all communications please refer to |
| Letter of Credit No. DIC-56798 |

Dear Sirs:

We are instructed to advise you of the establishment by Bank of Spain, Madrid, Spain, of their Irrevocable Credit No. 1234, in your favor, for account of Ortega & Co., Madrid Spain

for MAXIMUM U.S. $5,000.00 (FIVE THOUSAND U.S. DOLLARS)

available as follows and after presentation to us not later than June 10, 19* of the following documents:

Signed commercial invoices in seven copies, quoting Spanish License No. 435237, and describing the merchandise as indicated below

Certificate of U.S.A. origin, visaed by the Spanish Chamber of Commerce

Full set of on board ocean steamer bills of lading to order of shipper, blank endorsed and marked "Notify: Ortega & Co., Madrid, Spain" and "Freight Collect"

evidencing shipment of MACHINE TOOLS, F.O.B. Vessel New York, from New York to Bilbao, not later than May 31, 19*

Payment to be effected to you 90 days after the date of the relative bills of lading, at which time you must present your clean drafts at sight on us. Therefore, when presenting documents hereunder please include your letter authorizing us to forward documents to our principals prior to payment.

Except as otherwise expressly stated herein, this credit is subject to the Uniform Customs and Practice for Documentary Credits (1974 Revision), International Chamber of Commerce, Publication No. 290.

The above bank engages with you that all drafts drawn under and in compliance with the terms of this advice will be duly honored if presented to our Commercial Credits Department, 15 Broad Street, New York, N.Y. 10015, on or before August 29, 19* on which date this credit expires, however the documents must be presented not later than June 10, 19*

We confirm the foregoing and undertake that all drafts drawn and presented in accordance with its terms will be duly honored.

Yours very truly,

Authorized Signature

FIG. 37–5.   Irrevocable Deferred Payment Letter of Credit.

that payment under a letter of credit be made against presentation of a certificate of manufacture rather than ocean shipping or other documents. A more common procedure, though, entails the use of letters of credit calling for progress certificates up to 80 per cent of the value of the goods and 20 per cent against shipping documents. Other exporters request letters of credit calling for payment against railroad bills of lading, warehouse or storage receipts, dock receipts, or other domestic documents.

Negotiation

An irrevocable negotiation credit contains a clause that entitles the exporter, as the drawer of the draft, to receive payment from the bank once the exporter has complied with the documentary requirements. Alternatively, the endorsee or bona fide holder may be given that right. The credit may be confirmed or not and, unless stated otherwise in the letter, is subject to the exporter paying the negotiating bank's negotiation fee. The exporter is not authorized to delegate performance of the underlying transaction but only to negotiate the draft subject to the bank's determination that document requirements have been met. Without a negotiation clause, the letter is called a straight credit in favor of only the exporter.

A transferable letter of credit gives the exporter the power to negotiate the draft and also allows a substitute performance of the underlying transaction by another beneficiary.

Renewal

An irrevocable credit may allow the exporter to act upon it only once during a specified period, such as 60 or 90 days from the date of issuance; or it may be used repeatedly by the exporter during the specified period. The latter is a revolving export letter of credit. While there are various types of revolving credits, in most the amount remains constant for a given period of time. Thus, whenever the letter is exhausted by the exporter's drawing, it is automatically available again for the full amount until the end of the period. The letter of credit will always state the conditions upon which it revolves, and the export credit executive should understand and be satisfied with the revolving conditions.

EXPORT DRAFTS

An export draft is an order to pay, drawn by the exporter on the importer. It is less costly than the letter of credit, but should be used only when the exporter feels that a sale represents little commercial or political risk. The terms of the draft are arranged between buyer and seller before the draft is drawn.

Types of Drafts

The draft drawn may be a dollar draft or foreign currency draft, depending on the currency in which it is drawn for payment. It may be a sight draft (Figure 37–6) or a time draft (Figure 37–7). A sight draft is payable upon presentation to the importer while a time draft is payable at a specified later date. If, further, a time draft specifies payment a fixed number of days after date of the draft, rather than after sight, it sets a definite maturity date.

Finally, the draft may be clean or documentary. A clean draft is not

FIG. 37–6. Sight Dollar Draft Covering Export Shipment.

FIG. 37–7. Time Dollar Draft Covering Export Shipment.

accompanied by shipping documents. For instance, the importer may have already received the goods and the draft may be drawn for the purpose of collecting the amount due through usual banking channels. A documentary draft is accompanied by shipping documents, usually consisting of a bill of lading or parcel post receipt, insurance certificate, commercial invoice, consular invoice, and any other documents that may be required in the country of destination. These documents convey title to the goods and are delivered to the importer either against actual payment or against acceptance of the draft.

Most U.S. exporters prefer to route their drafts for collection through a U.S. bank. The bank acts for the exporter in dealing with the foreign collecting bank and the importer. Funds are received and transmitted more quickly, and a systematic followup is possible if need be.

Normally the exporter would initiate the draft through a U.S. bank,

TO: MORGAN GUARANTY TRUST COMPANY OF NEW YORK
23 WALL STREET, NEW YORK, N.Y. 10015

COLLECTION DEPT.

COLLECTING BANK
(IF BLANK, YOUR CORRES-PONDENT)

DATE __July 3, 19--__

WE ENCLOSE THE FOLLOWING ITEM FOR [X] COLLECTION AND [X] CREDIT TO OUR ACCOUNT NUMBER __948 11 579__
[ ] AN ADVANCE [X] REMITTANCE TO US BY CHECK

SUBJECT TO UNIFORM RULES FOR THE COLLECTION OF COMMERCIAL PAPER (1978 REVISION) INTERNATIONAL CHAMBER OF COMMERCE, BROCHURE NO. 322.

DRAWERS REFERENCE NUMBER	DATE OF DRAFT	TENOR	AMOUNT
201	July 3, 19--	120 D/S	$5,321.68

DRAWER	DRAWEE
Coast Textile Machine Supply Inc.	Shoji Merchandise Ltd.
ADDRESS New York, New York	Osaka, Japan

BILLS OF LADING ORIG	PARCEL POST DUP	INSUR. CERT'S. RECEIPTS	INVOICES	CONSULAR INVOICES	PACKING LISTS	WEIGHT CERT'S.	CERT'S. OF ORIGIN	OTHER DOCUMENTS
3		2	2	2				

[X] DELIVER DOCUMENTS AGAINST	[X] ACCEPTANCE	PAYMENT	YOUR CHARGES	$30.00	DRAWEE'S EXPENSE	DRAWER'S EXPENSE
[X] ADVISE BY CABLE	[X] NON-ACCEPTANCE	NON-PAYMENT	MAIL DOCUMENTS		DRAWEE'S EXPENSE	DRAWER'S EXPENSE
REMIT PROCEEDS BY CABLE	DRAWEE'S EXPENSE	DRAWER'S EXPENSE	FOREIGN BANK CHARGES		DRAWEE'S EXPENSE	DRAWER'S EXPENSE
[X] REMIT PROCEEDS BY AIRMAIL			[X] WAIVE CHARGES IF REFUSED			
PROTEST	NON-ACCEPTANCE	NON-PAYMENT	DO NOT WAIVE CHARGES			
[X] DO NOT PROTEST			HOLD FOR ARRIVAL OF MERCHANDISE			

IF DOLLAR EXCHANGE IS NOT IMMEDIATELY AVAILABLE AT MATURITY (OR ON PRESENTATION IF DRAWN AT SIGHT) AND IT IS NECESSARY TO PROVISIONALLY ACCEPT LOCAL CURRENCY PENDING AVAILABILITY OF DOLLAR EXCHANGE, IT MUST BE DISTINCTLY UNDERSTOOD THAT THE DRAWEE SHALL REMAIN LIABLE FOR ALL EXCHANGE DIFFERENCES. AT TIME OF DEPOSIT OF LOCAL CURRENCY OBTAIN FROM DRAWEES THEIR WRITTEN UNDERTAKING TO BE RESPONSIBLE FOR ANY EXCHANGE DIFFERENCES. THE DRAFT MUST NOT BE SURRENDERED TO DRAWEE UNTIL FINAL PAYMENT FOR FACE AMOUNT IN U.S. DOLLAR EXCHANGE.

ALLOW A DISCOUNT OF ___ IF PAID ___

COLLECT INTEREST AT THE RATE OF ___ % FROM ___

IN CASE OF NEED REFER TO		WHO IS EMPOWERED BY US: TO ACT FULLY ON OUR BEHALF I.E. AUTHORIZE REDUCTIONS, EXTENSIONS, FREE DELIVERY, WAIVING OF PROTESTS ETC.	WHO MAY ASSIST IN OBTAINING ACCEPTANCE OR PAYMENT OF DRAFT, AS DRAWN, BUT IS NOT TO ALTER ITS TERMS IN ANY WAY.

OTHER INSTRUCTIONS

1

AUTHORIZED SIGNATURE

$ __5,321.68__

DATE __July 3, 19--__ NO. __201__

__120 DAYS AFTER SIGHT__ of this SOLE BILL OF EXCHANGE

pay to the order of MORGAN GUARANTY TRUST COMPANY OF NEW YORK

__FIVE THOUSAND THREE HUNDRED TWENTY ONE DOLLARS SIXTY EIGHT CENTS************************__
Payable for face amount by prime Banker's sight draft on New York, New York
Value received and charge to account of

To __Shoji Merchandise Ltd.__

__Osaka, Japan__　　　　　　　Coast Textile Machine Supply Inc.

SOLE BILL OF EXCHANGE

FIG. 37-8. Letter of Instructions and Attached Draft.

together with shipping documents such as a bill of lading endorsed in blank, so as to be negotiable, the insurance policy or certificate, commercial invoice, consular invoice, and any other documents that are required in the country of destination; and a remittance letter giving complete and precise instructions to be followed in collecting the draft. For this purpose, banks provide a special combination form for exporters that includes both letter of instructions and draft (see Figure 37-8). This form is initiated by the exporter, completed by the remitting bank, and sent to the collecting bank abroad. A direct sending form, which the exporter can mail direct to the collecting bank, can be used when the port of shipment is so close to the destination that the goods might arrive before the documents if the latter were sent through the remitting bank.

Instructions for the Collecting Bank

The letter of instructions provides spaces for the exporter to answer most questions that may arise in the collection to the draft. The principal points to be covered are release of documents, advice of fate, method of remitting payment, and payment of collection charges.

Release of Documents. In the case of a sight draft, the instructions to the collectiong bank should read D/P, or documents against payment, meaning the documents are to be released to the importer or the importer's bank on payment of the draft. In the case of a time draft, the instructions should read D/A, or documents against acceptance, meaning the documents should be released when the importer accepts the draft.

Technically, a sight draft may be presented for payment, or a time draft for acceptance, as soon as it is received by the collection bank. In practice, however, banks in many countries withhold presentation until the goods arrive in the country. If the exporter wishes specifically to authorize such delay, the letter of instructions should state that the collecting bank may hold for arrival of merchandise. Many overseas banks will do so even without formal instructions.

If a sight draft is drawn in U.S. dollars for payment in a country where dollars may not be available, the exporter can instruct the collecting bank to accept local currency if necessary; but only if the importer assumes the exchange risk. Thus a sight draft and accompanying documents would not be turned over until the collecting bank had obtained such a written commitment from the importer. Similarly, if the sale is on a time draft and the documents had been released on acceptance, the time draft would not be released until a written commitment had been secured by the collecting bank.

Advice of Fate. The collecting bank advises the remittance bank of action taken on drafts presented for payment or acceptance. The letter of instructions should specify the means of communication to be used for this advice. If it is important to receive word without delay, especially in the case of nonpayment or nonacceptance. The instructions should specify that notice is to be given by cable; otherwise airmail is likely to be used.

The exporter receives timely advice of all developments affecting the collection of drafts. If notice of fate is not received within the expected time, the general practice of remitting banks is to send tracers promptly without waiting for client instructions to that effect.

Method of Remittance. If the exporter wishes the proceeds of a collected draft to be remitted by cable, the letter of instructions should so specify. The cable cost will be charged to the exporter unless the buyer has agreed to pay it, in which case the letter of instructions should direct the collecting bank to cable proceeds at drawee's expense.

Exporters normally receive three advices from the bank: acknowledgement that the draft and documents have been received at the bank's office; notice of acceptance of the draft abroad and the maturity date; and notice of payment of the draft, either as an advice of credit to the exporter's account or as a check in favor of the exporter.

Collection Charges. There is no set practice as to whether the buyer or the seller should pay the incidental charges involved in the collection process, such as bank collection fees, draft stamp taxes, and remittance taxes. In order to avoid misunderstanding and delay in payment of drafts, buyer and seller should agree beforehand as to the payment of incidental charges. If the drawee is to pay all collection charges, the instructions should state "All charges for drawee's account." Even with such an instruction, collecting banks abroad sometimes waive charges if the drawee refuses to pay and if collection of the draft itself is jeopardized, or if there is a risk of incurring additional charges on the exported merchandise. When charges are not to be waived under any circumstances, the letter of instructions should state "Do not waive charges." On the other hand, the exporter may have the charges waived rather than risk upsetting the entire deal. In that case the instructions should indicate "Waive charges if refused."

Other Instructions. Certain other points may need to be covered in the letter of instructions. For instance, if interest is to be collected on the draft, this should be specified. The exporter may wish to have a representative or agent contacted in case of nonacceptance, nonpayment, or other problem with the draft. The letter of instructions should indicate this and state the extent of that person's authority to give further instructions.

If the buyer requests that the draft be presented through a particular foreign bank, the exporter should say so in the letter of instructions. In general, it is preferable to let the exporter's U.S. bank select the foreign presenting bank. It can then choose the overseas institution best qualified to serve on behalf of the exporter.

Risks

Exporters selling on a draft basis, particularly on time drafts, must satisfy themselves as to the credit standing of the foreign buyers, for they assume the credit risk until the draft is paid.

With dollar drafts, they also have to weigh the exchange risk. In order to accelerate the return of funds, many exporters confine their sales terms to sight drafts. Under existing exchange conditions in some countries, however, the sight draft has lost some of its effectiveness. Normally documents attached to a sight draft are delivered to the drawee only upon payment in

U.S. dollars. When exchange shortages and restrictions in some countries hold up immediate payment of dollars, documents are delivered against provisional payment in local currency, pending the availability of dollars. This adds another risk for the exporter.

Finally, the U.S. exporter that quotes a selling price in foreign currency must take adequate safeguards against exchange fluctuations. One way to do this is to arrange with its bank for a forward exchange contract that will fix the price of the foreign sale in terms of U.S. dollars.

SELLING TO EXPORTERS

Until now, it has been assumed that the seller has also been the exporter to foreign customers. In this section, however, the export market is viewed from another perspective: the firm seeking to reduce credit risk is selling domestically to a company that will in turn sell those goods abroad on a letter of credit basis. In this case, the original seller can ask for an assignment of proceeds, request a transfer of the letter of credit, or use back-to-back letters of credit.

Assignment of Proceeds

In this procedure, a firm that sells to an exporter that in turn sells overseas on letter of credit can ask the exporter to instruct the bank to pay the original supplier a specified amount of the proceeds of that letter of credit. The amount may be stated in dollars or as a percentage of the covering draft. These instructions must be irrevocable. If the bank accepts the instrument, the original supplier is assured of reimbursement in accordance with the provisions of the assignment; and when the bank honors the draft, the supplier will receive payment. The instrument is shown in Figure 37–9.

An assignment of proceeds can be made regardless of whether the credit is transferable or not. The method is quite straightforward. It does require certain detail, however. The exporter must provide documentary proof that the person requesting the assignment is authorized to execute the instrument; the request for assignment of proceeds must be in a form acceptable to the bank; and the paying or negotiating bank will retain the original credit instrument and all amendments in order to endorse assignments on it, which action prevents assignments from exceeding the face amount of the letter of credit.

This procedure enables the exporter to pay the supplier with customer's funds, and does not affect the exporter's lines of credit either at the bank or with the supplier. It shifts the original supplier's exposure away from the exporter and to the negotiating or paying bank. It does not, however, give the original supplier maximum security and not every supplier is willing to part with merchandise on the strength of an assignment of proceeds. The assignment becomes effective only when and if the bank honors the draft

```
                                                              _____19____

BANK OF AMERICA, N.T. & S.A.
INTERNATIONAL BANKING OFFICE
555 SOUTH FLOWER STREET
LOS ANGELES, CALIFORNIA 90071

                              Re:  Letter of Credit_____issued by
                                   _____
                                   Advice No._____


Gentlemen:

     We hereby authorize and direct you to pay the proceeds of each draft drawn by
us, payable to your order, under and in compliance with the above described Letter of
Credit (herein called the "Credit"), if and when such draft is honored by you, as follows:

     (1)  _____%; not exceeding $_____or

     (2)  at the rate of $_____per_____; not exceeding
          $_____or

     (3)  $_____to:

_____whose address is
_____(herein called the
"Designated Payee"), and to pay the balance, if any, of such proceeds to us.

     This instrument, and your acceptance thereof, is not an assignment of the Credit,
does not give to the Designated Payee any interest therein and does not affect our or
your right to agree to amendments thereto, the cancellation thereof, or any substitution
therefor.

     We warrant to you that we have not, and will not, by negotiation of drafts or
otherwise, assign the right to receive the whole or any part of such proceeds or give any
other authorization or direction to make any payment thereof to any third party.

     Please advise the Designated Payee of your acceptance of this instrument and, in
consideration thereof, we agree that this instrument is irrevocable.

     We transmit to you herewith the Credit (including all amendments, if any) and
request you to note thereon the foregoing authorization and direction, and also enclose
our check for $_____, to cover your charges.

                              Very truly yours,


                              _____
                                   (Signature of Beneficiary)
We accept the foregoing instrument
                                   The above signature with title as stated
Bank of America, N.T. & S.A.       conforms with that on file with us and
International Banking Office        is authorized for the execution of such
Los Angeles, California            instruments.

Los Angeles, California,_____19____   _____BANK

By :_____   By :_____
        Authorized signature                   Authorized signature

662-149
```

FIG. 37–9. Assignment of Proceeds.

of the exporter. If the documents do not conform to the credit and are returned to the exporter, the supplier would receive no payment because no proceeds would be available. Hence, a supplier that takes an assignment of proceeds must have full faith in the expertise of the exporter.

Transferable Letter of Credit

The supplier has a more secure position when the exporter transfers a portion of the original letter of credit to the supplier. In this procedure, the foreign buyer makes the letter of credit transferable and initiates an amendment to that effect. The exporter may then authorize a transfer to the supplier or to various suppliers as long as the original credit permits partial shipments and the sum of the transfers does not exceed the total amount of the credit. Figure 37-10 shows instructions for a partial transfer of credit.

In the eyes of the bank, the name of the exporter can thus be substituted for that of the applicant for the credit; but if the original credit specifically requires that the name of an applicant appear in any document other than the invoice, it must so appear.

A bank that has received an application for a transfer will usually require the request to be executed on a form supplied by the transferring bank; that the transferor be the person authorized for the execution of the instrument; and that no deviation is requested from the original terms and conditions, except for a reduction of the amount and unit price or a curtailment of shipping and expiration dates. The advising or negotiating bank will also ascertain that the credit instrument has been expressly designated as transferable.

Exporter's Rights. The exporter can transfer the credit to the supplier in the same country or in another country unless the credit specifically states otherwise. However, the credit can be transferred only once. Fractions of a transferable credit not exceeding the total amount can be transferred separately, provided partial shipments are not prohibited; and the aggregate of such transfers will be considered as constituting only one transfer.

The exporter has the right to substitute its own invoices at the bank for those of the seller, or second beneficiary, and draw under the credit for the difference, if any, between the two sets of invoices. Since most of the time there will be this type of substitution, the exporter's expertise in preparing documentation in accordance with the original stipulations is an important factor. The exporter has to comply with the letter of credit terms in order for the bank to pay.

The exporter also has the right to request that payment or negotiation be made to the seller at the place to which the credit has been transferred, up to and including the expiry date of the original credit, and without prejudice to the exporter's right subsequently to substitute its own invoices for those of the seller and to claim any difference due. However, when the exporter does not supply its own invoices in exchange for the second beneficiary's invoices, the bank has the right to deliver to the issuing bank the documents received under the credit, including the second beneficiary's invoices, without further responsibility to the exporter.

INSTRUCTIONS FOR PARTIAL TRANSFER OF CREDIT, <u>WITH</u>
SUBSTITUTION OF INVOICES (A) OR <u>WITHOUT</u> SUBSTITUTION
OF INVOICES (B) AS INDICATED BELOW:

BANK OF AMERICA
NATIONAL TRUST AND SAVINGS ASSOCIATION

(Date)
Re: Credit No.:   Issued by:

Your Advice No.:

Gentlemen:

The undersigned acknowledges receipt of your advice of transferable letter of credit No. _____ issued in our favor, the terms of which are satisfactory. We now return to you the original advice of the letter of credit and hereby irrevocably transfer same to the extent of $ _____

to _____
subject to the same terms and conditions as indicated in your original letter of credit advice, with the exception of the following:

1. _____
(Merchandise)

2. _____
(Price)

3. Expiration date: _____ . (This date must be at least five business days before the expiration date of the captioned Credit when substitution of invoices is required.)

By this transfer, all rights of the undersigned beneficiary in such letter of credit are transferred to the second beneficiary (up to the amount aforesaid) and the second beneficiary shall (up to the amount aforesaid) have the sole right as beneficiary thereof, provided, however, that any amendments hereafter made must be approved by the undersigned beneficiary before being advised to the second beneficiary for action.

Please advise the second beneficiary of the terms and conditions of the credit as transferred.

Upon payment by you of the drafts of the second beneficiary under this transfer, or at any time on your demand, we will deliver to you our drafts and commercial invoices drawn in accordance with the terms of the original advice of letter of credit; such drafts and invoices to be attached by you to the shipping documents in substitution of those presented by the second beneficiary. You are then requested to deliver to us the invoices of the second beneficiary, together with your check for the amount by which our draft exceeds the amount of the draft of the second beneficiary provided that our draft and invoices comply with the conditions of the credit. In the event we fail, at your demand, to deliver to you the new drafts and invoices as specified above, you are authorized to dispose of the invoices and other documents accompanying the drafts of the second beneficiary in accordance with instructions from your principals without any responsibility on your part for payment of the difference between the amount of the second beneficiary's draft and the amount authorized to be paid under the original advice of letter of credit.

We enclose our check for $ _____ representing your ¼% transfer commission, (minimum $45.00) and in addition thereto, we agree to pay to you on demand any expenses which may be incurred by you in connection with this transfer.

Please indicate whether A) or B) will apply to this transaction:

A) There will be substitution of invoices.   ☐

B) There will be no substitution of invoices and the paragraph dealing with such substitution is to be disregarded.   ☐

Very truly yours,

_____
(Name of Beneficiary)

_____
(Authorized Signature and Title)

The above signature with title as stated conforms with that on file with us and is authorized for the execution of such instruments.

_____
(Name of Bank)

_____
(Authorized Signature and Title)

FK-166 8-76

FIG. 37–10.   Instructions for Transfer of Credit.

Supplier's Rights.   As noted earlier, the rights and obligations transferred to the second beneficiary, with some exceptions, are identical with those granted by the letter of credit to the original exporter. Consequently, transfers are effective only if the supplier is prepared to abide by the terms and conditions of the letter of credit. This would include furnishing documents for shipment under F.O.B. (free on board), C. & F. (cost and freight) and C.I.F. (cost, insurance, freight).

The exporter requires no line of credit or financial backing in a transfer, since the bank authorized to pay or negotiate merely transfers the promise of the original issuing bank to the second beneficiary, the U.S. supplier. There is no additional credit, so the exporter is not required to furnish financial data to the bank. However, since the supplier's principal risk under a transfer is in the creditworthiness of the issuing or paying bank, the supplier may require that the letter of credit be confirmed by a prime bank in its own locality. The supplier must then be able to produce documents such as certificates of origin, weight certificates, bills of lading, or other third party documents. Also, as the transferee, the supplier should examine the documentary requirements to be sure they do not contain an unusual request of the buyer that might impair or make the letter ineffective.

When the letter of credit is confirmed by a bank in the supplier's locality, some additional expense and delay may be involved. The confirming, paying, or negotiating bank may be reluctant to request the local bank to add its confirmation unless specifically authorized by the issuing bank and may insist on cabling the issuing bank for such authorization; this would cause delay and cable charges usually borne by the exporter. Also, the local bank will charge a confirmation commission, to be paid either by the exporter or the supplier. Furthermore, the supplier assumes certain export risks, such as the possibility of a dock strike, that would prevent or delay procuring the required documentation.

Back-to-Back Letters of Credit

Under a back-to-back letter of credit arrangement, the domestic supplier virtually becomes an exporter and must be prepared to abide by the terms and conditions of the letter of credit. It requires two letters. One is issued from the foreign buyer to the U.S. exporter, while the back-to-back credit is an entirely separate transaction issued on the strength of an underlying letter which the exporter deposits in custody with the bank. The deposited credit is commonly referred to as the backing credit, master credit, or primary credit. The exporter's bank issues its own letter of credit in favor of the supplier. Thus, if the parties of the original credit are unable to comply with the terms of that credit, the back-to-back credit nevertheless would remain valid. The bank issuing the back-to-back credit would still be obligated to fulfill its commitment, even if it were unable to obtain payment under the master credit. Many banks are therefore reluctant to handle back-to-back letter of credit transactions.

In back-to-back transactions, the secondary letter of credit is matched identically to the underlying letter of credit in terms, conditions, and documents. The exception to this rule, as in the transferable letter of credit, is the curtailment of the amount of the credit, unit price, time of shipping, and period of validity; in addition, a bank can eliminate certain documents in the secondary credit, such as insurance policy and import license.

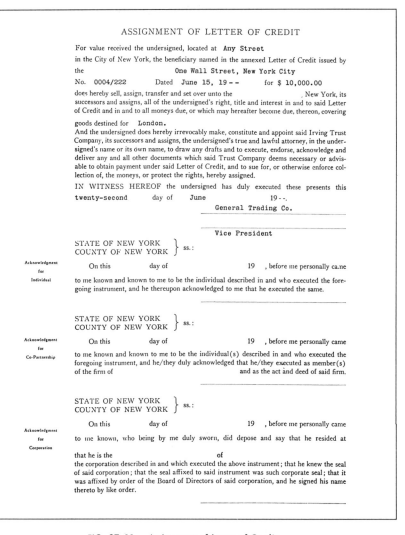

ASSIGNMENT OF LETTER OF CREDIT

For value received the undersigned, located at **Any Street**
in the City of New York, the beneficiary named in the annexed Letter of Credit issued by
the   **One Wall Street, New York City**
No. 0004/222   Dated June 15, 19 - -   for $ 10,000.00
does hereby sell, assign, transfer and set over unto the   . New York, its
successors and assigns, all of the undersigned's right, title and interest in and to said Letter
of Credit and in and to all moneys due, or which may hereafter become due, thereon, covering

goods destined for **London.**
And the undersigned does hereby irrevocably make, constitute and appoint said Irving Trust
Company, its successors and assigns, the undersigned's true and lawful attorney, in the undersigned's name or its own name, to draw any drafts and to execute, endorse, acknowledge and
deliver any and all other documents which said Trust Company deems necessary or advisable to obtain payment under said Letter of Credit, and to sue for, or otherwise enforce collection of, the moneys, or protect the rights, hereby assigned.
IN WITNESS HEREOF the undersigned has duly executed these presents this
twenty-second   day of   June   19 - -.
                                    General Trading Co. ....

                            ....
                            Vice President
STATE OF NEW YORK   ⎫
COUNTY OF NEW YORK   ⎭ ss.:

Acknowledgment
for   On this   day of   19   , before me personally ca.ne
Individual
to me known and known to me to be the individual described in and who executed the foregoing instrument, and he thereupon acknowledged to me that he executed the same.

....

STATE OF NEW YORK   ⎫
COUNTY OF NEW YORK   ⎭ ss.:

Acknowledgment
for   On this   day of   19   , before me personally came
Co-Partnership
to me known and known to me to be the individual(s) described in and who executed the
foregoing instrument, and he/they duly acknowledged that he/they executed as member(s)
of the firm of   and as the act and deed of said firm.

....

STATE OF NEW YORK   ⎫
COUNTY OF NEW YORK   ⎭ ss.:

Acknowledgment   On this   day of   19   , before me personally came
for
Corporation to me known, who being by me duly sworn, did depose and say that he resided at

that he is the   of
the corporation described in and which executed the above instrument; that he knew the seal
of said corporation; that the seal affixed to said instrument was such corporate seal; that it
was affixed by order of the Board of Directors of said corporation, and he signed his name
thereto by like order.

....

FIG. 37–11.   Assignment of Letter of Credit.

The bank issuing the back-to-back or subsidiary credit requires an assignment of the original credit, shown in Figure 37–11, and delivery of the
original letter of credit; and makes certain that it has all the documentation
required under the original credit.

Moreover, the bank supplying the subsidiary credit will usually advise
the issuing bank that its credit was lodged with it for value received. This
is shown in Figure 37-12. Before any commitments concerning the subsidiary credit are made to the exporter, banks usually look to the following
points:

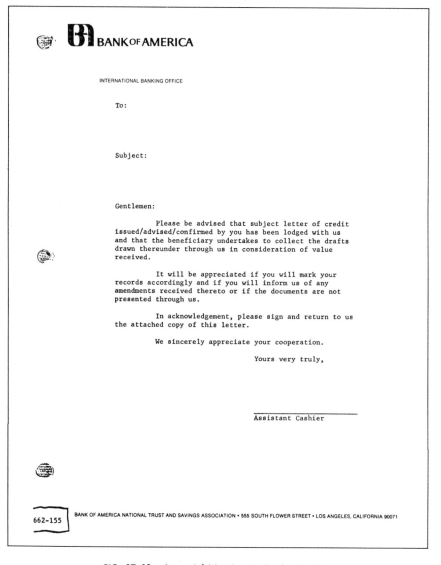

FIG. 37–12. Letter Advising Issuing Bank of Credit.

1. The master credit must be irrevocable and payable with a prime U.S. bank.

2. If any question exists as to the soundness of the issuing bank or country, the master credit must be confirmed by an acceptable U.S. bank.

3. It should require only documents which can be procured under the subsidiary credit. A normal exception allows substitution of the customer's invoice and draft for those received under the master credit.

After determining that the master credit is workable, the terms of the subsidiary credit are reviewed. The subsidiary credit generally differs from the master credit in five points: beneficiary's name, account party's name, amount and prices, expiration date, and insurance on C.I.F. transactions. Other deviations are acceptable if they are more restrictive. In other words, the bank can always tighten the conditions of the subsidiary credit but cannot broaden them without running the risk of losing its ability to draw under the master credit. The subsidiary credit should meet these requirements:

1. Documentation requirements should be identical to those required for the master credit.

2. Merchandise specifications should conform exactly to the master credit.

3. Title documents should be consigned in exactly the same manner as under the master credit.

4. The expiry date should be earlier than the expiry date of the master credit to allow time to negotiate and correct discrepancies. Fifteen days is the usual time.

5. If insurance is required, it must be sufficient to cover the master credit invoice amount.

INDEX

A

Acceleration clause, 357–58, 452
Acceptance letter of credit, 664–65
Accommodation party, liability of, 438
Account establishment, 39
Account referral, 139, 149–51
Accounts payable, 333, 383
Accounts receivable, 44, 326–27, 369, 383
  administration of, 40
  aging reports, 168, 564–72
  bad-debt analysis report, 581–82
  collections as a percentage of, 573
  evaluation of, portfolio, 493–524
  factoring of, 441–46
  financing of, 446–50, 472
  handling, 99–101
  management reports, 582–85
  ratio of net sales to, 366–67, 381
  writeoffs of, 580–81
Accounts receivable department, role in collections, 165–66
Accounts receivable portfolio, evaluation of, 493–524
Accounts receivable systems, automated, 102–11
Accreditation (ABCE), 11
Accumulated depreciation, 331
Acid test; see Quick ratio
Acknowledgement; see Order acknowledgement
Activity report, 582–83
Address, business, 200
Adjustment of debts, 630–32
Adjustments, 10, 40–41
Administration, 63, 136–38
  accounts receivable, 40
  of cash discounts, 407
  in credit training, 79–80
  day-to-day, of credit department, 38–41
Advance basis, factoring on, 445–46
Advance payments, 333, 418
Advice of fate, 670–71
Affiliated interests, 280
After-acquired clause, 452, 481, 619
Aged trial balance; see Trial balance
Agencies
  credit reporting, 220, 224–54
  export, 649
Agency for International Development (AID), 657

Agency ratings
  in calculating credit lines, 150–51
  order limits, 145
Aging of accounts receivable, 168, 564–72
Agricultural credit, 19
Allonge, 432
Allowance for uncollectibles, 327, 579–80
Allowances, 178–79
American Arbitration Association (AAA), 654–55
American Institute of Certified Public Accountants, 223
American Management Association, 88
Analysis; see also Financial analysis
  of bad debts, 581–82
  graphic, 555–63
  incremental profitability, 514–19
  profitability, 510–14
Analysis, nonfinancial, 302–20
Annual financial statements, 324
Annual Statement Studies, 13
Anticipation, 409–12
Appraisal surplus, 335
Arbitration clause, 654–55
Article 2, 480, 486–87
Article 3, 420–39
Article 4, 439
Article 5, 476–79
Article 6, 480, 487–89
Article 7, 474–76
Article 9, 480–86
  personal property security devices, 469–74
Assets, 325–32
  noncurrent, 369
  purchase of, 282–83
Assignment, 434
  for benefit of creditors, 598–600
  of proceeds, 672–73
Associate Award, 87
Attorneys, collection by, 188–89
Audit
  frequency of, 355–56
  types of, 352
Audit reliability, appraisal of, 355–56
Auditors, 201
  change in, 356
  role of, 352–55
  specialization by, 355
Auditor's certificate, 353–54
Authority, delegating, 53–54, 62–63, 80–81, 122–23

Authority to purchase, 651
Automated revision service, 96
Average days delinquent (ADD), 577–79
Averages, law of, 289
Avoiding powers, 614
  limitations on, 617–18

B

Back-to-back letters of credit, 676–79
Bad debts, analysis of, 581–82
Balance forward system, 106
Balance sheet
  guide to classification of items, 348–51
  projected, 539–41
  ratios, 364–66, 383–84
  significance of, 325–35
  spread sheet, 344–45
  trends, 369–71
Bank books as collateral, 471–72
Bank check information; see Bank Information
Bank credit, 18
  vs. business credit, 23
  service, 215
Bank information, 132, 210–18; see also Bank
    investigations and Information
  in export credit, 645–46
Bank investigations, 316–17; see also Bank in-
    formation
  ways to make, 211–15
Bank loans; see Loans
Bank of New York, 302
Bank of North America, 302
Banker's acceptance, 430–31
  in letter of credit transactions, 665
Bankruptcy proceedings, 140, 608–32
Bankruptcy Reform Act of 1978, 6, 10, 608–
    32
Batch mode processing, 103, 106–07, 108
Benedict v. Ratner, 483
Best possible DSO, 577
Bill of exchange; see Drafts
Bill-to-bill terms, 416
Billing, 180
  practices in export trade, 652–53
Bills of lading, 475–76
Blank endorsement, 432
Bonds, 427
  as collateral, 472
Bookkeeping, machine, 100
Break-even inventory, analysis of, 391–92
Bretton Woods Agreement, 7
Bulk Transfers; see also Uniform Commercial
    Code
  applicability of, under Article 6, 487–89
Burglary and theft insurance, 293–94
Business background, 305–10
Business conditions, 161

Business credit, 20–23; see also Credit
  vs. bank credit, 23
Business credit reports; see Reports, agency
    and Reports, credit
Business interruption insurance, 292–93
Business organization, legal forms of, 263–83
Business trust, 276–77

C

Capacity, 304
Capital, cost of; see Cost of capital
Capital, 304–05
  role of, in common law trusts, 277
    corporations, 272
    estates, 275
    joint ventures, 278
    partnerships, 267
    proprietorships, 265
    subchapter S corporations, 274
Capital leases, 454–55
Capital stock, 269–71
Case analysis, 376–86
Cash, 326, 369
Cash in advance (C.I.A.) terms, 417
Cash application, 106–08
Cash before delivery (C.B.D.) terms, 417
Cash budgets, 525–37
Cash on delivery (C.O.D.) terms, 416
Cash disbursements, estimate of, 529–30,
    532–33
Cash discounts, 406–08
  effect on profits, 503–05
  importance of taking, 499
  unearned, 177
Cash forecast; see also Cash budgets
  collections compared to, 573–74
Cash flow, 339
Cash, methods of gathering, 104–05
Cash with order (C.W.O.) terms, 417
  in export transactions, 649–50
Cash receipts, estimate of, 526–29, 530–32
Cash terms, 416–17
Cashier's check, 428
Caveats on requesting bank credit informa-
    tion, 217–18
Centralization and decentralization, 51–55
Certificate of incorporation, 269
Certified check, 428
Chain discounts, 409
Chandler Act, 6
Changes in financial position, statement of; see
    Statement of changes in financial position
Chapter 7, 608, 620–23
  appointment of interim trustee, 609
  handling executory contracts, 612
  panel of private trustees, 609–10
Chapter 11, 140, 608, 623–30
  appointment of examiner, 610
  filing proof of claims, 612

Chapter 13, 608, 630–32
Character, 303–04
Charge accounts, 19
Chattel mortgages, 472
Check, 427
Chicago Board of Trade, 419
Claims, creditors
  classification of, 626–27
  under adjustment of debts, 632
  under bankruptcy proceedings, 612–13
Clean drafts, 667–68
Coding Information, 94
Coinsurance clause, 290, 292, 299
Collateral note, 427
Collection and adjustment bureaus, 184
Collection agencies, 183–88
Collection effort
  degree of, under various credit policies,
    125–27
  special, 181–89
  stages of, 167–75
Collection followup, 96–98, 163
Collection letters, 169–75
  free demand, 185–86
  legal aspects of, 189
Collection problems, common, 176–81
Collection procedures, 162–89
Collection ratio, monthly, 526–29
Collection schedule, 139
Collections, 10, 572–74
  export, 652–55
  followup on, 96–98, 163
  international, 11
  standard procedures in, 40–41, 138–40,
    162–89
Combination settlement, 597
Combined financial statements, 342–43
Commercial arbitration, 654–55
Commitments, 419
Commodity risk, 475
Common law assignment, 598–99
Common law trusts, 276–77
Common size statements, 373
Common stock, 270
Communication, 54, 61
  of credit policy, 121–22
  with customer, 38
Comparative analysis; see Financial analysis
Competition factor in terms of sale, 404
Composite indexes, 554–55
Composite statements, 373
Composition agreement, 592–97
Condensed spread sheet, 346–47
Conditional sales contracts, 472
Conditions of times, 305
Confession of judgment, 427
Consideration, 424
Consignment, 419, 472–73
  in export transactions, 650

Consolidated financial statements, 341–42
Consolidations, 282
Conspiracy, 194–95
Contingent liabilities, 334
Continuing clause, 357–58
Continuing education; see Education
Continuity, role of
  in common law trusts, 276–77
  corporations, 271–72
  estates, 275
  joint ventures, 278
  partnerships, 266–67
  proprietorships, 264
  subchapter S corporations, 273
Consumer credit, 19–20
  use of negotiable notes, 435–36
Consumer goods, classification under UCC,
  483
Consumer loan, 20
Contra accounts, 334, 418
Control; see also Credit department
  expense analysis for budgetary, 586–87
  using budget for, 534–37
Convertibility risk, 638–40
Cooperating committees, 11
Cooperative societies, 279
Corporations, 268–73
Correspondence, collection; see Collection letters
Correspondence, credit, 201–209
Cost of capital, 494–99
  in cash discounts, 407–08
Cost of goods sold, 336–37, 371
Counseling
  customer, 41–45, 208
  within the company, 45–47
Courier pickup system, 105
Covenants, restrictive, 452
Cram down provision, 269
Credit
  components of, 15–16
  definition of, 15
  export, 635–58
  evolution of, 3–7
  flow of, 25–27
  forms of, 17–23
  four "Cs" of, 303–20
  obtaining, under bankruptcy proceedings,
    611
  refusal of, 207–08
Credit and accounts receivable systems, automated, 102–111
Credit administration; see Administration
Credit analysis; see also Financial analysis
  of customers using outside financing, 458–
    60
  early history of, 302–03
  financial statements used in, 323–51
  of secured debtors, 485–86

Credit analyst
  example of job description for, 71
  job qualifications of, 73
Credit approval process, 39, 104, 136–38; see also Credit decisionmaking
Credit cards, 20
Credit conference, 82–83
Credit Congress, 11
Credit decisionmaking, 143–61
  controlling credit exposure, 53
Credit department
  collection responsibility, 164–65
  controls, 31–32, 37–38
  day-to-day administration, 38–41
  operating criteria for, 585–87
  organizational structure, 28–31, 37
  planning, 28
  relationships with other departments, 35–37
  reporting system, 544–63
  setting objectives, 28
  systems and procedures, 90–101
  training in a small, 88–89
  types of, 55–60
Credit Exchange, 225, 248–54
Credit executive; see also Credit executive, top-level chief and Credit executive, middle-level chief
  interest in insurance coverage, 300–01
  job qualifications of, 73–74
Credit executive, chief; see Credit executive, top-level chief and Credit executive, middle-level chief
Credit executive, middle-level chief; see also Chief executive
  authority in decentralized offices, 57–58
  example of job description, 68–69
Credit executive, top-level chief; see also Credit executive
  authority in central office, 55–56
  authority in decentralized offices, 58–59
  authority in staff office, 59–60
  examples of job description, 66–68
Credit exposure, controlling, 53; see also Credit lines
Credit files, 39, 138; see also Filing systems
  construction of, 90–91
  revision of, 96
Credit and Financial Management, 10–11
Credit groups, industry, 10, 219–20
Credit information, 193–223
  considerations in gathering, for automation, 110–11
  decision based on limited, 156–57
  foreign, 644–49
Credit instructions, 90–91, 137
Credit insurance, 298–300
Credit Interchange Bureaus, 219
Credit Interchange Reports; see Reports, credit
Credit interchange with suppliers, 220–21

Credit interdepartmental relationships
  with manufacturing, 36
  marketing or sales, 35
  purchasing, 35–36
  systems and data processing, 36
Credit investigation, 38; see also Credit information and Investigation
Credit library, 84
Credit limits; see Credit lines
Credit lines, 39
  reviewing, 152–56
  revision of, 208–09
  setting, 147–52
Credit management
  generation of, reports, 108–09
  goals of dynamic, 32–33
  reports, 564–87
  responsibilities of, 27–32
  role in financial management, 24
Credit Management Workshops, 12, 87–88
Credit manager
  example of job description, 69–70
  job qualifications of, 73
Credit Manual of Commercial Laws, 10, 129, 263, 273, 471, 484
Credit policy, 34–38, 112–27, 130–31
  and procedural manual, 128–40
Credit policy and procedural manual, 128–40
Credit practices and credit policy, 113
Credit procedures, 123, 131; see also Credit department and Administration
  and credit policy, 113
Credit rating scale, 151
Credit recommendation service, 252–54
Credit recommendations; see Credit approval process
Credit reporting agencies; see Agencies
Credit reports; see Reports, agency and Reports, credit
Credit Research Foundation, 12, 87–88
Credit risks; see Risk classes
Credit sales; see also Net sales
  vs. cash sales, 16–17
Credit and sales relationships, 35, 53
  credit lines for sales department use, 151
  role in credit policy, 122
  sales requests for credit information, 197–99
  use of sales personnel in collections, 166–67
Credit terms; see Terms of sale
Credit training; see Training, credit
Credit women's groups, 11
Creditel of Canda Limited, 13–14
Creditors' claims
  under adjustment of debts, 632
  bankruptcy proceedings, 612–13
Creditors' committee
  in liquidation proceedings, 621
  reorganization proceedings, 624–25
  voluntary settlements, 593

Crime insurance, 295–96
CRT terminal, applying payment using, 107–08
"Cs" of credit, four, 303–05
  application of, 305–20
Current assets, 326–31
Current debt; *see* Current liabilities
Current liabilities, 369–70
  ratio of, to tangible net worth, 365, 379
Current ratio, 364, 376
Customer counseling; *see* Counseling
Customer deductions, 178–80
Customer relations, 35, 38; *see also* Counseling
  in collections, 162–64
  on credit lines, 152
  role in credit policy, 122
Customer service, 52–53; *see also* Communication
Customer-supplied information, 199–210
  in export credit, 645
Customer visits, 132; *see also* Customer relations
  reports of, 584

D

Daily notification lists, 222
Data collection, 506–10
Data processing policy, 294
Database, 101
Days sales outstanding (DSO), 575–79
Debtor's duties and benefits under bankruptcy proceedings, 613–15
Decentralization, 51–54
Deductions, customer, 178–80
Deeds of trust; *see* Mortgages, real estate
Defamation, 195–97
Default under UCC, 485
Defenses, 435
Deferred debt, 334; *see also* Term loans
  current portion of, 333
Deferred income, 334
Deferred payment letter of credit, 665
Delinquent accounts, identifying, 97–98
Demand loan, 440
Deposit arrangements, 136
Depreciation, 331
Difference in conditions policy, 295
Discharge in bankruptcy, 435
  adjustment of debts, 632
  benefits of, 615
  debts not affected by, 614–15
  liquidation proceedings, 622–23
Dishonor, notice of, 439
Disks, 95–96, 100–01
Distressed debtors, symptoms of, 591–92
Distributed processing, 101
Distribution of customers, geographical, 312–13

Divisions, operating, 282
Documentary credits, 659–79
Documentation, 38–39
Documents against acceptance (D/A), 670
Documents against payment (D/P), 670
Dollar drafts, 667
Double-name paper, 427
Drafts, 429–30
  export, 667–72
Drawee, 425–26
  liability of, 437
Drawer, 424–25
  liability of, 436–37
Drop delivery terms, 416
Dun & Bradstreet, 5, 88, 224–25, 226–32
  business ratios, 374–75
  Commercial Collection Division, 184, 226
  International, 646–47
  ratings used for insurance coverage, 299
Duress, 435

E

Earned surplus; *see* Retained earnings
Economic Opportunity Loans, 457
Education, 12, 73; *see also* Training, credit
  continuing, 86–88
Employee enhancement, 85–86
Enabling loans, 619
Encumbrances, 331
End-of-month (E.O.M.) terms, 414–15
Endorsements, types of, 432–34
Endorser, 424–25
  liability of, 437–38
Equal Credit Opportunity Act, 10
  Regulation B, 200
Equifax, 132, 223
Equipment, classification under UCC, 483
Escalator clause, 452
Estate
  in bankruptcy proceedings, 616–20
  handling, in liquidation proceedings, 621–22
Estates, 275–76
Estimated financial statements, 325
Examiner, 610
  in reorganization proceedings, 625–26
Exceptions to credit policy, 114
Exchange of credit information
  legal aspects of, 194–97
  Statement of Principles for, 211
Exchange rate risk, 640–41
Exchange restrictions, 639
Executory contracts under bankruptcy proceedings, 611–12
Exemptions under bankruptcy proceedings, 613–14
Expenses, 337, 372
Export collections, 652–55
Export credit, 635–58

Export drafts, 667–72
Export-Import Bank (Eximbank), 655–57
Expressed powers, 269
Extended terms, 154–56, 183
Extension agreements, creditors', 139–40, 183; *see also* Voluntary settlements
Extortion, 189
Extra dating terms, 416
Extraordinary financial statement items, 338

F

Factors, 441–46, 459
Fair Credit Reporting Act, 10
Fair Debt Collection Practices Act, 10
"Fair and equitable" test, 629
Farm products, classification under UCC, 483
Farm Security Administration, 19
FCIB-NACM Corporation, 11, 647–49
Federal income taxes, 338
Federal Land Banks, 19
Federal Reserve System, 7, 18
Federal Trade Commission, 435–36
Fellow Award, 87
Fidelity bonds, 295–96
Field warehousing, 136, 474
Filing systems; *see also* Credit files
  automated, 95–96
  department, 93–94
  manual, 94–95
Finance companies, 446–50, 459
Finance leases, 454–55
Financial Accounting Standards Board, 453
Financial analysis, 39; *see also* Analysis
  fundamentals of, 362–75
  influence of outside financing on, 458–60
  sample case of, 376–86
  trial balance, 387–95
  by sales, 395–400
Financial information, 201
  graphic analysis of, 555–63
  statistical presentation of, 549–555
Financial reporting, responsibility for, 355
Financial statement forms, 203–06
Financial statements, 43
  combined, 342–43
  consolidated, 341–42
  design of, 357
  false, 357–61
  notes to, 354–55
  pro forma, 343
  request for, 202–07, 208
  spreading, 344–47
  unaudited, 352–53
  used in credit analysis, 323–51
Financing statements; *see* Security agreements
Fire and extended coverage insurance, 291–92
First-in, first-out (FIFO), 328–30

Fixed assets, 331
  classification under UCC, 483
  ratio of, to tangible net worth, 365, 379
Fixtures, classification under UCC, 483
Float, 104–05
Floating lien, 482
Flood insurance, 295
Floor planning, 417
Followup
  systematic, 163
  systems for credit and collection, 96–98
Foreclosure proceedings, 452
Foreign Credit Insurance Association (FCIA), 656–57
Foreign currencies, trading in, 641–44
Foreign currency draft, 667
Foreign exchange market, 641
Foreign sales representative, 646
Forward rate, 641–42
  discount on, 642–43
  premium on, 642–43
Foulke, Roy A., 351, 374
Fraud, 358–61, 488
Fraud Prevention Department, 11, 358
Fraudulent transfers, 620
Free demand letter, 185–86
Funded debt, 370; *see also* Deferred debt
  ratio of, to net working capital, 366, 380
Future value, 501–02

G

General liability insurance, 297
General partnership, 266–68
Good will, preserving, 163–64
Graduate School of Credit and Financial Management, 12, 87
Graphic analysis, 555–63
Green clause endorsement, 665
Gross profit, 337, 371
  method of estimating inventory, 392–94
  ratio of, on net sales, 367, 381
Guaranties, 133, 417, 461–66
  under Eximbank, 656

H

Hamilton, Alexander, 5
Hand-carry method, 105
Hedging contracts, 475, 643–44
Holder in due course, 434–36
Hooper-Holmes Bureau, 223

I

Illegality, 435
Implied powers, 269
Incidental powers, 269

Incremental profitability analysis, 514–19
Income and retained earnings, statement of; *see* Statement of income and retained earnings
Income statement; *see also* Statement of income and retained earnings
  spread sheet, 345–46
  trends, 371–72
Incompetence, 435
Index numbers, 554–55, 561–63
Indexing sales price, 640
Industry characteristics, 310–11
  role in credit policy, 116–18
Industry standards; *see also* Financial analysis
  use in financial analysis, 373–75
Infancy, 435
Information; *see also* Credit Information
  agency sources of, 224–62
In-house training, 82–86
Initial orders, 144–47
Inland marine insurance, 294
Inquiries, 138
  direct, 131
  to other suppliers, 132
  telephone, 138
Insolvency
  under the Bankruptcy Code, 618
  under the UCC Code, 487
Installment credit, 19–20
Insurance, credit and business, 284–301
Insurance, foreign credit, 656–57
Insurance Advisory Council, 11
Intangible assets, 332
Intelligent terminal, 101
Interchange, direct, of trade information, 220–22
Interdepartmental relationships, coordinating, 35–37, 63–64
  in credit policy, 115
Interim financial statements, 324
Internal analysis, 362–69; *see also* Financial analysis
  sample case of, 376–82
International Bank for Reconstruction and Development (World Bank), 657–58
International credit executives (ICE), 11
International Development Association (IDA), 657–58
International Finance Corporation (IFC), 657–58
International Monetary Fund (IMF), 639–40
Interviews
  personal, 209–10
  telephone, 210
Inventory, 369; *see also* Merchandise inventory
  break-even analysis, 391–92
  classification under UCC, 483
  loans against, 448
  methods of estimating, 392–94

Inventory—*Cont.*
  ratio of net sales to, 366, 381
  ratio of, to net working capital, 365, 377–79
Inventory valuation basis, 328
Inventory valuation methods
  first-in, first-out (FIFO), 328–30
  last-in, first-out (LIFO), 328–30
  retail method, 330
Investigation, 131–32; *see also* Bank investigations
  of business background, 305–10
  by creditors in voluntary settlements, 594
  influence of method of operation, 310–16
Investment credit, 18–19
Invoice date, terms based on, 414
Invoices, use of, in collection effort, 170
Invoicing, 180
  in dollars, 640

J

Jewelers' Board of Trade, 225
Job description, 61–65
  examples of, 65–71
  relation of, to job specification, 72
Job evaluation, 63–65
Job rotation program, 84–85
Job specification, 72–74
Joint ventures, 277–79
Judgment note, 427

L

Large numbers, law of, 289
Last-in, first-out (LIFO), 328–30
  method for calculating DSO, 576
Late-payment service charges, 412–13
Leases, 332
  finance, 454–55
  operating, 454
Leasing, 314–15, 453–56
Ledger, loose-leaf, 99
Ledger cards, customer, 97
Legal aspects
  of collection correspondence, 189
  of customer counseling, 41–42
  of exchange of credit information, 194
Legal composition of business, changes in, 280–81
Letter of instructions, 669–71
Letters of credit, 133–34, 418, 476–79
  export, 659–67
Leverage, 310–11, 365–66
Leveraged lease, 455
Liabilities, 332–34
Liability
  of accommodation party, 438
  drawee, 437
  drawer, 436–37

Liability—*Cont.*
   endorser, 437–38
   maker, 436
   reserves, 334
   role in common law trusts, 277
   corporations, 272–73
   estates, 275–76
   joint ventures, 278–79
   partnerships, 267–68
   proprietorships, 265
   subchapter S corporations, 274
Libel, 189, 195–97
Liens, 470–71
   floating, 482
   impact of, under UCC, 451
   statutory, 617
   treatment of certain, under liquidation proceedings, 621–22
Life insurance, 297–98
   policies as collateral, 472
Limited partnerships, 266–68
Liquid assets, 326
Liquid ratio; *see* Quick ratio
Liquidation proceedings under Bankruptcy Code, 620–23
Loading practices, 180
Load-to-Load terms, 416
Loans; *see also* Short-term borrowings
   against accounts receivable, 448
   against inventory, 443, 448
   mortgage, 449
   under SBA programs, 456–57
   unsecured, 449
Location of business, 314–16
Lockbox banks, 40, 105, 140
Long-term debt; *see* Deferred debt
Lumped order terms, 414–15
Lyon Furniture Mercantile Agency, 225, 238–48

M

Maintenance, 180
Maker, 424–25
   liability of, 436
Management; *see also* Credit Management
   role of, in proprietorships, 264
Management reports; *see* Reports, credit management
Management Study Report, 87
Manual, credit policy and procedural, 128–40
Marginal accounts, 157–59
   expanding sales to, 519–20
Marine risk, 638
Marketable securities, 326
Marketing risk, 35
Martindale-Hubbell Law Directory, 654
Massachusetts trust, 276–77
Maturity arrangement, factoring on, 445–46

McCord Company, The, 222
Mean, arithmetic, 549–50
Mechanics' lien, 135
Median, 550–51
Merchandise inventory, 44, 327–30; *see also* Inventory
Mergers, 282
Method of operation, 310–16
MICR information, 105
   applying payment using, 106–07
Microfilm/microfiche, 95
Mid-Career School, 12, 88
Middle-of-month (M.O.M.) terms, 415
Minicomputers, 101
Miscellaneous assets, 332
Miscellaneous obligations, 334
Misrepresentation, 435
Mode, 551
Moody's Industrial Manuals, 132, 222
Moratorium, 595
Mortgages, real estate, 20, 136, 466–69
Moving averages, 555

N

NACM Business Credit Information System, 225, 255–62
   Business Credit Report, 132, 255–60
   Credit Interchange Report, 260–62
Name of business, 200
National Association of Credit Management, 8–12, 211
   collection and adjustment bureaus, 10, 184–88
   credit groups, 10, 219–220
   Credit Interchange Bureaus, 219
   early history of, 6, 8–9
   education, 12, 86–88
   financial statement forms, 203–06
   Fraud Prevention Department, 11, 358
National Banking Act of 1863, 5
National Bankruptcy Law of 1898, 6
National Credit Office, 225, 232–38
   Specialized Credit Report, 131, 234–38
National Institute of Credit, 12, 87
Nature of credit information, confidential, 193–04
Negotiability, 421
Negotiable instruments, 420–39
Negotiation, 432–34
Negotiation clause, 667
Net cash terms, 416
Net income, 338, 372
   ratio of, on net sales, 367, 382
   on net working capital, 368, 382
   on tangible net worth, 368, 382
Net operating income, 338
   ratio of, on net sales, 367, 382

Net sales, 371; *see also* Sales
  ratio of, to accounts receivable, 366–67, 381
    to inventory, 366, 381
    to net working capital, 366, 380–81
    to tangible net worth, 366, 380
    to total assets, 366, 380
  ratio of gross profit on, 367, 381
    net income on, 367, 382
    net operating income on, 367, 382
Net working capital, 370
  changes in, 340–41, 385–86
  projected changes in, 542
  ratio of funded debt to, 366, 380
    inventory to, 365, 377–79
    net income on, 368, 382
    net sales to, 366, 380–81
Net worth, 334–35; *see also* Tangible net worth
Noncurrent assets, 369
  ratio of, to total capitalization, 365, 379
Nonfinancial analysis, 302–20
Not-for-profit organizations, 279
Note arrangements, 139
Notes; *see* Promissory notes
Notes payable, 333; *see also* Loans
Notes receivable, 327
Notice and disclosure, 488
Notice of dishonor, 439
N.S.F. checks, 181

O

Objectives
  in automated systems, 109–10
  in credit policy, 113, 114–15
  in credit training, 78–79
  setting, 28
Observation tours, 83–84
Ocean marine cargo insurance, 294
O'Hanlon Reports, 223
On-the-job training, 81–82
On-line processing, 102–03
Open-account credit, 22–23
  in export credit, 651–52
Open invoice file, 97, 99
Open item system, 106
Opening accounts, 201–08
Operating criteria for credit departments, 585–86
Operating leases, 454
Operating profit margin$_K$, 513
Operations cycle, 404–05
Optimum DSO, 576–79
Order acknowledgement, 201–02, 208
Order entry and billing systems, 103–04
Order entry point, single, 91–92
Order entry points, multiple, 92–93
Order processing, 39–40

Orders
  entry and editing, 179–80
  from established accounts, 208–09
  initial, 144–47
  from overdue accounts, 160, 180–81
Organizational structure, 28–31, 37, 51–60, 63, 130–31
Orientation, 81
Other expense, 338
Other income, 338
Out-of-court settlements, 591–607
Outside borrowing, 44; *see also* Notes payable
Outside financing, 440–60
Overages, 180
Overtrading, 367
Ownership, 201

P

Paid-in surplus, 335
Parent-subsidiary relationships, 281–82
Partnerships, 265–68
Past-due accounts
  in export credit, 653–54
  receivables aging, 569–70
  treatment of, 160
Past-due listing, 97–98
Pattern statements, 373
Pay increases, timing of, 75
Payee, 425
Payment application, 106–08
Payment, guaranty of, 461–62
Payment bonds, 135–36
Payment instructions in export credit, 653
Payment terms; *see* Terms of sale
Pension Benefit Guarantee Corporation, 354
Percentage statements, 373–74
Percentages, 552
Perfecting security agreements, 484–85
Performance
  evaluation of, 74–75
  guaranty of, 461–66
Performance bonds, 135
Perpetual inventory records, 392–93
Personal property as security, 469–76
Personnel
  appraisal of, 74–75
  considerations in automation, 111
  enhancement of, 85–86
  in organizational chart, 130
  role in implementing credit policy, 122
  selection of, 77–78
  special collection, 165
  use of other, in collections, 167
  use of sales, in collections, 166–67
Pickup system, courier, 105
Plan
  under adjustment of debts, 631–32
  under reorganization proceedings, 626–30

Planning, 28, 63–64
Plate glass insurance, 295
Pledges, 471–72
Postbilling, 103
Postdated checks, 176, 429
Postpetition disclosure, 628
Preauthorized debit system, 105
Prebilling, 103
Preemptive rights, 270
Preferences, 459, 618–19
  transfers excluded as, 619
Preferred stock, 270–71, 335
Prepaid expenses, 330–31
Prepayment clause, 468
Present value, 500–01
  of future receipts, 502–03
  of settlement offers, 600–07
Price v. Neal, 438–39
Pricing errors, 179
Principles of collection, 162–64
Private credit; see Credit
Private placement, 452–53
Pro forma financial statements, 343
Production risk, 36
Profitability analysis, 510–14
  incremental, 514–19
Profits, 44–45; see also Net Income
  effect of discount terms on, 503–05
Progress payments, 418
Promissory notes, 176, 426–27
Promotions, timing of, 75
Proof of claims, filing, 612
Property
  distribution of, of the estate, 622
  redemption of, in liquidation proceedings,
    621
  turnover of, to the estate, 616–17
  use, sale, or lease of, under bankruptcy
    proceedings, 611
Property insurance, 291–95
Proprietorships, 264–65
Protest, 439
Proudfoot Reports, 225
Proximo terms, 415
Pseudo corporations, 273–74
Public credit, 17
Public placement, 452–53
Punched card accounting, 100
Purchase order, 473
Purchases, 44

                              Q

Quartile, lower, 550–51
Quartile, upper, 550–51
Quick assets, 326
Quick ratio, 364–65, 377

                              R

Range, 551
Rates, turnover, 366–67, 371, 384
Rating, Dun & Bradstreet, 230–31
Rating keys, Lyon Red Book, 243–45
Ratios, 370–71, 552
  appraising use of, 368–69
  balance sheet, 364–66, 383–84
  profit, 367–68, 384–85
Reaffirmation agreements, 615
Real estate mortgages; see Mortgages, real estate
Real-time processing, 103, 107, 108
Receipt of goods (R.O.G.) terms, 415–16
Receivables portfolio evaluation; see Accounts
    receivable
Reclamation clause, 487, 618
Red Book, Lyon Furniture Mercantile Agency,
    246
Red clause endorsement, 665
Reference Book, Dun & Bradstreet, 232
References, 201
Refusal of credit, 207–08
Regulation B; see Equal Credit Opportunity
    Act
Reinsurance, 289
Rejected merchandise, 486–87
Remedies under law of Sales, 486–87
Reorganization plan, 626–30
Reorganization proceedings under Bankruptcy
    Code, 623–30
Reporting system, credit department, 544–63;
    see also Reports, credit management
Reports, agency, 131–32
  Credit Exchange Report, 248–52
  Dun & Bradstreet Business Information Re-
    port, 227–30
  International business information re-
    ports, 646–47
  Lyon Credit Report, 239–43
  ordering, 225–26
Reports, credit; see also Reports, agency
  Credit Interchange Reports, 260–62
  Foreign Credit Information Report, 647–69
  NACM Business Credit Reports, 255–60
Reports, credit management, 140, 564–87
  generation of, 108–09, 545–48
Reserve for bad debts, 334; see also Allowance
    for uncollectibles
Reserve for depreciation, 334; see also Accumu-
    lated depreciation
Responsibility, collection, 164–67
Responsibility, defining, 37, 62
  in credit policy, 122–23
  in credit training, 80–81
Restrictive endorsement, 434
Retail method, 330
Retainage, 418
Retained earnings, 338–39, 383

Return on receivables (ROR), 513–14
Returned checks, 140, 181
Returns, 179
Revenue Act of 1978, 273
Review
  of credit decisions, 159–61
  of credit lines, 152–56
  of credit management reports, 548–49
  of credit policy, 124–25
Revolving letter of credit, 667
Risk, analysis of, under various credit policies, 125–27
Risk classes, 96, 137–38
  analysis by, 506–24
  aging by, 566–69
Robert Morris Associates, 12–13, 211
  composite financial ratios, 374
Robinson-Patman Act, 116, 403, 409, 413

S

Sale and leaseback, 389–90, 455–56
Sales, 336; see also Net sales
  elements of, 395–96
Sales, analysis by, 395–400; see also Financial analysis
Sales department; see also Credit and sales relationships
  considerations in automation, 110
Seasonal dating, 415
Seasons, 313–14, 405
Secured business credit, 22
Secured debtors, credit analysis of, 485–86
Secured transactions, 132–36, 417
  under UCC, 480–89
Securities and Exchange Commission, 211, 223, 324, 325
  appearance in bankruptcy proceedings, 628
Security agreements, 134–35, 480–83
Security devices, 461–79
Selling terms; see Terms of sale
Semilogarithmic graphs, 556–63
Serial note, 426
Service credit, 20
Setting credit lines, 149–51
Settlement offers, evaluating, 600–07
Settlement plans under voluntary settlements, 594–97
Settlements, 592–97
Sherman Act, 194
Shipping, 180
Short-term borrowings; 333, 383, 440; see also Loans
Short-term debt; see Short-term borrowings
Shortages, 180
Sight draft/bill of lading (SD/BL) terms, 417, 431
Sight drafts, 429–30
  in export credit, 667–72
  in letter of credit transactions, 664

Single-name paper, 426
Single payment terms, 414–15
Slander, 195–97
Small Business Administration (SBA), 17, 456–58
Small Business Investment Corporation (SBIC), 458
Small orders, blanket approval of, 144–45
Social Security, 286
Source and application of funds, 339–40, 385
  projected, 541
Special dating terms, 415–16
Special endorsement, 433–34
Spot market, 641
Spot rate
  discount on, 642–43
  premium on, 642–43
Spreading financial statements, 344–47
Staffing, 30, 37, 61–75
Standard & Poor's, 222
  business and financial data, 256–60
Standby letter of credit, 133–34, 477–79
Statement of changes in financial position, 339–41, 372
  projected, 541–42
Statement of income and retained earnings, 335–39
  projected, 537–39
Statements of account, 168
Statistical presentation of financial data, 549–55
Statistical and probability analysis, 151, 289
Statutory assignment, 599–600
Statutory liens, 617
Stocks as collateral, 472
Storage devices, EDP, 95–96
Straight letter of credit, 667
Straight note, 426
"Strong arm" clause, 617
Subchapter S corporations, 273–74
Subordination agreements, 134, 459, 466
Subsidiaries, investment in and advances to, 332
Subsidiary and parent relationships, 281–82
Surplus; see Retained earnings
Swap, 642

T

Tangible net worth, 332, 370; see also Net worth
  ratio of current debt to, 365, 379
    fixed assets to, 365, 379
    net income on, 368, 382
    net sales to, 366, 380
    total debt to, 365–66, 379–80
Tapes, magnetic, 95, 100–01
Tappan, Lewis, 5, 226
Tax Reform Act of 1976, 273

Taxes and regulations, 54–55
Technical Amendments Act, 273
Telegrams, use in collection effort, 173–74, 187
Telephone, use in collection effort, 170
Term debt; *see* Term Loans
Term loans, 383, 451–53; *see also* Deferred debt
Terminal, intelligent, 101
Terms codes, 137
Terms of sale, 136–37, 207, 318, 403–19
   extended terms, 154–56
   in export trade, 649–52
   in the 19th century, 5–6
   other than open account, 147, 417–18
   spread between buying and selling, 312
Third-party collections, 183–89
Tickler file, 98
Time drafts, 429–30
   used in export credit, 667–72
Time lags, 314
Time loan, 440
Time series, 551–52
Time value of funds, 500–02
Total assets, ratio of net sales to, 366, 380
Total capitalization, ratio of noncurrent assets to, 365, 379
Total debt, ratio of, to tangible net worth, 365–66, 379–80
Trade acceptance, 430
Trade discount, 408–09
Trade information, 218–22; *see also* Trade investigation
   National Weekly Interchange of Trade Experience, 246–48
Trade investigation, 317–20; *see also* Trade information
Traffic claims, 179
Training, credit, 30–31, 54, 76–89
   relation to job specification, 72
   role in credit policy, 120
Transferable letter of credit, 674–76
Treasurer's check, 428
Treasury stock, 335
Trend analysis, 369–72; *see also* Financial analysis
   sample case of, 382–86
Trial balance, 343–44; *see also* Financial analysis
   aged, 97
   analysis, 387–95
Trust receipts, 417, 473–74
Trustee, 609–10
   in adjustment of debts proceedings, 631
   as a lien creditor, 617

Trustee—*Cont.*
   in liquidation proceedings, 620–21
   powers of, 610–12
   in reorganization proceedings, 625–26
TRW Business Profile, 255
Turnaround documents, applying payment using, 107
Turnover rates, 366–67, 371, 384

U

Ultra vires acts, 269
Uncollectible accounts, 579–82
Unearned cash discounts, 177.
Unemployment insurance, 286
Uniform Commercial Code, 22, 134–35, 470
   on bills of lading, 474–76
   on bulk transfers, 283, 487–89
   on consignment terms, 419, 473
   credit risk under, 480–89
   documents issued under letters of credit, 476–79
   early history of, 420
   finality of payment or acceptance, 438–39
   impact of liens under, 451
   reclamation clause, 487, 618
   remedies under law of Sales, 480, 486–87
   trust receipts, 473–74
   in voluntary settlements, 592, 596
   on warehouse receipts, 474–76
Uniform Consumer Credit Code, 435–36
Uniform Customs and Practice for Commercial Documentary Credits, 476, 660
Uniform Partnership Act, 265
U.S. Department of Commerce, 649
University programs, 88
Unrealized capital increment per appraisal, 331
Unsubordinated loans, 333; *see also* Loans
Usance, 664–65

V

Voluntary settlements, 592–97

W

Wages, taxes, and accruals, 333
Wall Street Journal, 222
Warehouse receipts, 474–75
Warehousing, 180
Warranty, 180
Workers' Compensation, 286
Working capital; *see* Net working capital
Writeoffs of uncollectible accounts, 580–81